Design of Experiments
with MINITAB

Also available from ASQ Quality Press:

Introduction to Design of Experiments: A Simplified Approach
Larry B. Barrentine

Glossary and Tables for Statistical Quality Control, Fourth Edition
ASQ Statistics Division

The Desk Reference of Statistical Quality Methods
Mark L. Crossley

Statistical Quality Control Using Excel, Second Edition
Steven M. Zimmerman, PhD and Marjorie L. Icenogle, PhD

Improving Performance Through Statistical Thinking
ASQ Statistics Division

The Quality Improvement Glossary
Donald L. Siebels

The Metrology Handbook
Jay L. Bucher, editor

Failure Mode and Effect Analysis: FMEA From Theory to Execution, Second Edition
D.H. Stamatis

Concepts for R&R Studies, Second Edition
Larry B. Barrentine

To request a complimentary catalog of ASQ Quality Press publications,
call 800-248-1946, or visit our Web site at http://qualitypress.asq.org.

Design of Experiments with MINITAB

Paul G. Mathews

ASQ Quality Press
Milwaukee, Wisconsin

American Society for Quality, Quality Press, Milwaukee 53203
© 2005 by ASQ
All rights reserved. Published 2004
Printed in the United States of America

12 11   5 4

Library of Congress Cataloging-in-Publication Data

Mathews, Paul G., 1960–
    Design of experiments with MINITAB / Paul G. Mathews.
        p. cm.
    Includes bibliographical references and index.
    ISBN 0-87389-637-8 (hardcover, case binding : alk. paper)
        1. Statistical hypothesis testing. 2. Experimental design. 3. Minitab. 4.
    Science—Statistical methods. 5. Engineering—Statistical methods. I. Title.

    QA277.M377 2004
    519.5'7—dc22   2004020013

ISBN 0-87389-637-8

Publisher: William A. Tony
Acquisitions Editor: Annemieke Hytinen
Project Editor: Paul O'Mara
Production Administrator: Randall Benson
Special Marketing Representative: David Luth

ASQ Mission: The American Society for Quality advances individual, organizational, and community excellence worldwide through learning, quality improvement, and knowledge exchange.

Attention Bookstores, Wholesalers, Schools and Corporations: ASQ Quality Press books, videotapes, audiotapes, and software are available at quantity discounts with bulk purchases for business, educational, or instructional use. For information, please contact ASQ Quality Press at 800-248-1946, or write to ASQ Quality Press, P.O. Box 3005, Milwaukee, WI 53201-3005.

To place orders or to request a free copy of the ASQ Quality Press Publications Catalog, including ASQ membership information, call 800-248-1946. Visit our Web site at www.asq.org or http://qualitypress.asq.org.

 Printed on acid-free paper

Quality Press
600 N. Plankinton Avenue
Milwaukee, Wisconsin 53203
Call toll free 800-248-1946
Fax 414-272-1734
www.asq.org
http://qualitypress.asq.org
http://standardsgroup.asq.org
E-mail: authors@asq.org

AMERICAN SOCIETY
FOR QUALITY

Table of Contents

CD Contents
    Example Problem Data
    Chapter Problems
    Classroom Exercises and Labs
    Excel Experiment Design Files
    MINITAB Experiment Design Files
    MINITAB v14 Macros

Preface

WHAT IS DOE?

Design of experiments (DOE) is a methodology for studying any response that varies as a function of one or more independent variables or *knobs*. By observing the response under a planned matrix of knob settings, a statistically valid mathematical model for the response can be determined. The resulting model can be used for a variety of purposes: to select optimum levels for the knobs; to focus attention on the crucial knobs and eliminate the distractions caused by minor or insignificant knobs; to provide predictions for the response under a variety of knob settings; to identify and reduce the response's sensitivity to troublesome knobs and interactions between knobs; and so on. Clearly, DOE is an essential tool for studying complex systems and it is the only rigorous replacement for the inferior but unfortunately still common practice of studying one variable at a time (OVAT).

WHERE DID I LEARN DOE?

When I graduated from college and started working at GE Lighting as a physicist/engineer, I quickly found that statistical methods were an integral part of their design, process, and manufacturing operations. Although I'd had a mathematical statistics course as an undergraduate physics student, I found that my training in statistics was completely inadequate for survival in the GE organization. However, GE knew from experience that this was a major weakness of most if not all of the entry-level engineers coming from any science or engineering program (and still is today), and dealt with the problem by offering a wonderful series of internal statistics courses. Among those classes was my first formal training in DOE—a 20-contact-hour course using Hicks, *Fundamental Concepts of Design of Experiments.* To tell the truth, we spent most of our time in that class solving DOE problems with pocket calculators because there was little software available at the time. Although to some degree the calculations distracted me from the bigger DOE picture, that course made the power and efficiency offered by DOE methods very apparent. Furthermore, DOE was part of the GE Lighting culture—if your work plans didn't incorporate DOE methods they didn't get approved.

During my twelve years at GE Lighting I was involved in about one experiment per week. Many of the systems that we studied were so complex that there was no other possible way of doing the work. While our experiments weren't always successful, we did learn from our mistakes, and the designs and processes that we developed benefited greatly from our use of DOE methods. The proof of our success is shown by the longevity of our findings—many of the designs and processes that we developed years ago are still in use today, even despite recent attempts to modify and improve them.

Although I learned the basic designs and methods of DOE at GE, I eventually realized that we had restricted ourselves to a relatively small subset of the available experiment designs. This only became apparent to me after I started teaching and consulting on DOE to students and corporate clients who had much more diverse requirements. I have to credit GE with giving me a strong foundation in DOE, but my students and clients get the credit for really opening my eyes to the true range of possibilities for designed experiments.

WHY DID I WRITE THIS BOOK?

The first DOE courses that I taught were at GE Lighting and Lakeland Community College in Kirtland, Ohio. At GE we used RS1 and MINITAB for software while I chose MINITAB for Lakeland. The textbooks that I chose for those classes were Montgomery, *Design and Analysis of Experiments* and Hicks, *Fundamental Concepts in the Design of Experiments,* however, I felt that both of those books spent too much time describing the calculations that the software took care of for us and not enough time presenting the full capabilities offered by the software. Since many students were still struggling to learn DOS while I was trying to teach them to use MINITAB, I supplemented their textbooks with a series of documents that integrated material taken from the textbooks with instructions for using the software. As those documents became more comprehensive they evolved into this textbook. I still have and occasionally use Montgomery; Box, Hunter, and Hunter, *Statistics for Experimenters;* Hicks; and other DOE books, but as my own book has become more complete I find that I am using those books less and less often and then only for reference.

WHAT IS THE SCOPE OF THIS BOOK?

I purposely limited the scope of this book to the basic DOE designs and methods that I think are essential for any engineer or scientist to understand. This book is limited to the study of quantitative responses using one-way and multi-way classifications, full and fractional factorial designs, and basic response-surface designs. I've left coverage of other experiment designs and analyses, including qualitative and binary responses, Taguchi methods, and mixture designs, to the other books. However, students who learn the material in this book and gain experience by running their own experiments will be well prepared to use those other books and address those other topics when it becomes necessary.

SAMPLE-SIZE CALCULATIONS

As a consultant, I'm asked more and more often to make sample-size recommendations for designed experiments. Obviously this is an important topic. Even if you choose the perfect experiment to study a particular problem, that experiment will waste time and resources if it uses too many runs and it will put you and your organization at risk if it uses too few runs. Although the calculations are not difficult, the older textbooks present little or no instruction on how to estimate sample size. To a large degree this is not their fault—at the time those books were written the probability functions and tables required to solve sample-size problems were not readily available. But now most good statistical and DOE software programs provide that information and at least a rudimentary interface for sample-size calculations. This book is unique in that it presents detailed instructions and examples of sample-size calculations for most common DOE problems.

HOW COULD THIS BOOK BE USED IN A COLLEGE COURSE?

This book is appropriate for a one-quarter or one-semester course in DOE. Although the book contains a few references to calculus methods, in most cases alternative methods based on simple algebra are also presented. Students are expected to have good algebra skills—no calculus is required.

As prerequisites, students should have completed either: 1) a one-quarter or semester course in statistical methods for quality engineering (such as with Ostle, Turner, Hicks, and McElrath, *Engineering Statistics: The Industrial Experience*) or 2) a one-quarter or semester course in basic statistics (such as with one of Freund's books) and a one-quarter or semester course in statistical quality control covering SPC and acceptance sampling (such as with Montgomery's *Statistical Quality Control*). Students should also have good Microsoft Windows skills and access to a good general statistics package like MINITAB or a dedicated DOE software package.

Students meeting the prerequisite requirements should be able to successfully complete a course using this textbook in about 40 classroom/lab hours with 40 to 80 hours of additional time spent reading and solving homework problems. Students must have access to software during class/lab and to solve homework problems.

WHY MINITAB?

Although most DOE textbooks now present and describe the solutions to DOE problems using one or more software packages, I find that they still tend to be superficial and of little real use to readers and students. I chose to use MINITAB extensively in this book for many reasons:

- The MINITAB program interface is designed to be very simple and easy to use. There are many other powerful programs available that don't get used much because they are so difficult to run.

- Despite its apparent simplicity, MINITAB also supports many advanced methods.

- In addition to the tools required to design and analyze experiments, MINITAB supports most of the other statistical analyses and methods that most users need, such as basic descriptive and inferential statistics, SPC, reliability, GR&R studies, process capability, and so on. Why buy, learn, and maintain multiple software packages when one will suffice?

- MINITAB has a powerful graphics engine with an easy to use interface. Most graph attributes are easy to configure and can be edited after a graph is created. All but a few of the graphs in this book were originally created in MINITAB.

- MINITAB has a simple but powerful integrated sample-size calculation interface that can solve the most common sample-size problems. This eliminates the need to buy and learn another program that is dedicated to sample-size calculations. MINITAB can also be used to solve many more complex sample-size problems that are not included in the standard interface.

- MINITAB has a very simple integrated system to package a series of instructions to form an executable macro. If you can drive a mouse you can write a MINITAB macro. MINITAB macros are easy to edit, customize, and maintain and can be made even more powerful with the higher-level MINITAB macro programming language. All of the custom analysis macros that are described in this book are provided on the CD-ROM included with the book.

- MINITAB is relatively free of bugs and errors, and its output is accurate.

- MINITAB has a very large established user base.

- MINITAB's printed documentation, online help, and technical support are all excellent.

- MINITAB Incorporated is a large company that will be around for many years.

- Although price should not be a primary factor in selecting statistical or DOE software, MINITAB is priced competitively for both single users and network installations.

Despite its dedication to MINITAB, I've successfully taught DOE from this book to students and clients who use other software packages. Generally the user interfaces and outputs of those packages are similar enough to those of MINITAB that most students learn to readily translate from MINITAB into their own program.

I've tried to use the conventions chosen in the MINITAB documentation to present MINITAB references throughout the book. MINITAB commands, buttons, text box labels, and pull-down menus are indicated in **boldface**. MINITAB columns like $c1$, $c2$, . . . are indicated in typewriter (Courier) font. MINITAB file names and extensions are indicated in *italics*. Variable names are capitalized and displayed in the standard font.

HOW ARE THE BOOK AND SUPPLEMENTARY CD-ROM ORGANIZED?

Since many readers and students who would consider this book have rusty statistical skills, a rather detailed review of graphical data presentation methods, descriptive statistics, and inferential statistics is presented in the first three chapters. Sample-size calculations for basic confidence intervals and hypothesis tests are also presented in Chapter 3. This is a new topic for many people and this chapter sets the stage for the sample-size calculations that are presented in later chapters.

Chapter 4 provides a qualitative introduction to the language and concepts of DOE. This chapter can be read superficially the first time, but be prepared to return to it frequently as the topics introduced here are addressed in more detail in later chapters.

Chapters 5 through 7 present experiment designs and analyses for one-way and multi-way classifications. Chapter 7 includes superficial treatment of incomplete designs, nested designs, and fixed, random, and mixed models. Many readers/students postpone their study of much of Chapter 7 until after they've completed the rest of this book or until they have need for that material.

Chapter 8 provides detailed coverage of linear regression and the use of variable transformations. Polynomial and multivariable regression and general linear models are introduced in preparation for the analysis of multivariable designed experiments.

Chapters 9, 10, and 11 present two-level full factorial, fractional factorial, and response-surface experiment designs, respectively. The analysis of data from these experiments using multiple regression methods and the prepackaged MINITAB DOE analyses is presented. Although the two-level plus centers designs are not really response-surface designs, they are included in the beginning of Chapter 11 because of the new concepts and issues that they introduce.

The supplementary CD-ROM included with the book contains:

* Data files from the example problems in the book.

* Descriptions of simple experiments with toys that could be performed at home or in a DOE class. There are experiments involving magic dice, three different kinds of paper helicopters, the strength of rectangular wooden beams, and

catapults. Paper helicopter templates are provided on graph paper to simplify the construction of helicopters to various specifications.

- MINITAB macros for analyzing factorial, fractional factorial, and response-surface designs.

- MINITAB macros for special functions.

- A standard set of experiment design files in MINITAB worksheets.

- Microsoft Excel experiment design files with integrated simulations.

RUNNING EXPERIMENTS

No matter how hard you study this book or how many of the chapter problems or simulations you attempt, you'll never become a proficient experimenter unless you actually run lots of experiments. In many ways, the material in this book is easy and the hard things—the ones no book can capture—are only learned through experience. But don't rush into performing experiments at work where the results could be embarrassing or worse. Rather, take the time to perform the simple experiments with toys that are described in the documents on the supplementary CD-ROM. If you can, recruit a DOE novice or child to help you perform these experiments. Observe your assistant carefully and honestly note the mistakes that you both make because then you'll be less likely to commit those mistakes again under more important circumstances. And always remember that you usually learn more from a failed experiment than one that goes perfectly.

Acknowledgments

I want to thank my mentors and coworkers from GE for introducing me to and convincing me of the power and necessity of statistical methods in general and DOE in particular. I also must thank my clients who challenged my DOE knowledge and skills, built the experiments that I recommended, and found success in these methods. And my many students—from whom I learned so much—have my great appreciation and deserve an apology for having to suffer through the many crude drafts and errors present in the early versions of this book.

In particular, I'd like to acknowledge Bill Lake, Dan Sommers, the Cleveland Section of ASA, Jack Strok, Gary Allen, Larry Mead, Alan Greszler, Stephanie Harrington, Nancy Robinson, Jan Lewandowski, Chuck Hayes, Dale Arstein, Norm Bresky, and Angela Lunato.

I thank my assistant Rebecca Malnar for helping run experiments, prepare graphs, analyze data, select examples and problems, and for suffering through the many hours of classes/labs and proofreading that went into this book.

I gratefully acknowledge Annemieke Hytinen and Paul O'Mara at ASQ Quality Press for their patience and support and Leayn and Paul Tabili at New Paradigm Prepress and Graphics who deserve special mention for their fantastic production work.

Most of all, I must thank my wife Kathy, who tolerated my late-night and weekend writing binges, read new paragraphs and sections of the book that I was excited about, made uncountable suggestions, recommendations, and corrections, and generally supported me in many different ways through the years that it took to complete this work.

I apologize to and beg the forgiveness of any student, customer, or author whose work I used here but failed to acknowledge.

1

Graphical Presentation of Data

1.1 INTRODUCTION

Always plot your data! A plot permits you to explore a data set visually, and you will often see things in a plot that you would have missed otherwise. For example, a simple histogram of measurement data can show you how the data are centered, how much they vary, if they fall in any special pattern, and if there are any outliers present. These characteristics are not obvious when data are presented in tabular form.

Usually we plot data with a specific question in mind about the distribution location, variation, or shape. But plotting data also lets us test assumptions about the data that we've knowingly or unknowingly made. Only after these assumptions are validated can we safely proceed with our intended analysis. When they're not valid, alternative methods may be necessary.*

1.2 TYPES OF DATA

Data can be qualitative or quantitative. Qualitative data characterize things that are sorted by type, such as fruit (apples, oranges, pears, . . .), defects (scratches, burrs, dents, . . .), or operators (Bob, Henry, Sally, . . .). Qualitative data are usually summarized by counting the number of occurrences of each type of event.

Quantitative data characterize things by size, which requires a system of measurement. Examples of quantitative data are length, time, and weight. Design of experiments (DOE) problems involve both types of data, and the distinction between them is important.

---

* Stuart Hunter, one of the demi-gods of design of experiments, tells his students that the first step of data analysis is to "DTDP" or *draw the damned picture.*

1.3 BAR CHARTS

Bar charts are used to display qualitative data. A bar chart is constructed by first determining the different ways the subject can be categorized and then determining the number of occurrences in each category. The number of occurrences in a category is called the frequency and the category or type is called the class. A bar chart is a plot of frequency versus class. Bar lengths correspond to frequencies, that is, longer bars correspond to higher frequencies. Pareto charts are a well known form of bar chart.

Example 1.1
   The following table indicates types of paint defects produced in a car door painting operation and the corresponding frequencies. Construct a bar chart of the defect data.

Defect Type	Frequency
Scratches	450
Pits	150
Burrs	50
Inclusions	50
Other	300

Solution: The bar chart of defect data is shown in Figure 1.1.

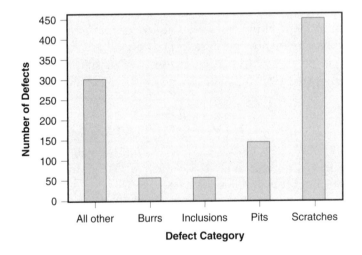

Figure 1.1 Bar chart.

1.4 HISTOGRAMS

The most common graphical method used to present quantitative data is the histogram. Although histograms are very useful for displaying large data sets they are less useful for smaller sets, for which other methods should be considered. Histograms are time-intensive to construct by hand but are supported by most data analysis software packages.

Data to be plotted on a histogram must be quantitative. The data should be sorted into an appropriate number of classes determined by the size of the data set. Large data sets can use more classes. Each class is defined by an upper and lower bound on the measurement scale. Classes should have the same class width, except for the largest and smallest classes, which may be left open to collect outliers. Classes must be contiguous and span all possible data values.

A histogram is similar in presentation to a bar chart except that the categorical scale is replaced with a measurement scale. Bars drawn on a histogram are constructed so that the bar width (along the measurement scale) spans the class width and the bar height is proportional to the class frequency. Open classes may use the same bar width as the other bars even though their width is different.

Example 1.2

Construct a histogram for the following data set:

$$\{52, 88, 56, 79, 72, 91, 85, 88, 68, 63, 76, 73, 86, 95, 12, 69\}.$$

Solution: The largest and smallest values are 95 and 12, although the 12 seems quite low compared to the other values. A simple design for classes is to make classes of the 50s, 60s, and so on. This scheme results in the following table:

Class Lower Limit	Class Upper Limit	Data	Frequency
$-\infty$	49	12	1
50	59	52, 56	2
60	69	68, 63, 69	3
70	79	79, 72, 76, 73	4
80	89	88, 85, 88, 86	4
90	99	91, 95	2

The histogram constructed from the data in the class limits and frequency columns is shown in Figure 1.2.

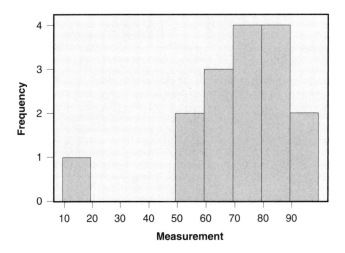

Figure 1.2   Histogram.

1.5 DOTPLOTS

Histograms of small data sets can look silly and/or be misleading. A safe, simple, and fast alternative for the graphical presentation of small data sets is the dotplot. As simple as they are, dotplots are still used in some advanced statistical techniques.

A dotplot is made by constructing a number line spanning the range of data values. One dot is placed along the number line for each data value. If a value is repeated, the dots are stacked. Sometimes with very large data sets, each dot might represent several points instead of one point.

Example 1.3
Construct a dotplot of the data from Example 1.2. Use one dot for each point.

Solution: The dotplot of the data from Example 1.2 is shown in Figure 1.3.

1.6 STEM-AND-LEAF PLOTS

Stem-and-leaf plots are constructed by separating each data value into two pieces: a stem and a leaf. The stems are often taken from the most significant digit or digits of the data values and the leaves are the least significant digits. Stems are collected in a column and leaves are attached to their stems in rows. It's easiest to explain the stem-and-leaf plot with an example.

Example 1.4
Construct a stem-and-leaf plot of the data from Example 1.2.

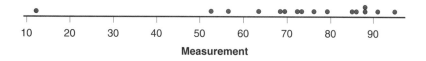

Figure 1.3　Dotplot.

Figure 1.4　Stem-and-leaf plot.

Solution: *The stem-and-leaf plot of the data from Example 1.2 is shown in Figure 1.4. The classes are the 10s, 20s, and so on, through the 90s.*

The design of the stems for a stem-and-leaf plot is up to the user, but stems should be of equal class width. An alternative design for the stems in the example problem would be to break each class of width 10 into two classes of width five. For example, the class 7– could be used to collect leaves from data values from 70 to 74, the class 7+ could collect the leaves from data values from 75 to 79, and so on. This would be a poor choice for this data set though, as the data set is too small for the large number of classes in this design. The best choice for this data set is probably the original one shown in Figure 1.4.

Stem-and-leaf plots are simple to construct, preserve the original data values, and provide a simple histogram of the data. These characteristics make them a very useful and popular preliminary data analysis tool. Some people use stem-and-leaf plots to record data as they're collected in addition to or instead of writing the data in tabular form. However, like the other graphical data presentations, stem-and-leaf plots suffer from loss of information about the order of the data.

1.7 BOX-AND-WHISKER PLOTS

Boxplots, or box-and-whisker plots, provide another wonderful tool for viewing the behavior of a data set or comparing two or more sets. They are especially useful for small data sets when a histogram could be misleading. The boxplot is a graphic presentation that divides quantitative data into quarters. It is constructed by identifying five

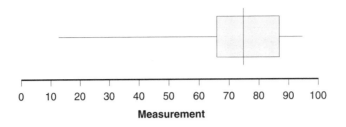

Figure 1.5   Box-and-whisker plot.

statistics from the data set: the largest and smallest values in the data set, x_{max} and x_{min}; the median of the entire data set $\tilde{x}$; and the two quartiles Q_1 and Q_2. The lower quartile Q_1 is the median of all data values less than $\tilde{x}$. Similarly, the upper quartile Q_3 is the median of all data values greater than $\tilde{x}$. The boxplot is constructed along a quantitative number line that spans the range of the data. A line is drawn at the median and then a rectangular box with ends at the quartiles is added. The box contains 50 percent of the observations in the data set and has length equal to the interquartile range (IQR):

$$IQR = Q_3 - Q_1$$

which is a measure of variation in the data set. Whiskers are drawn from the ends of the box at Q_3 and Q_1 to x_{max} and x_{min}, respectively. Each of the whiskers spans 25 percent of the observations in the data set.

Example 1.5

Construct a box-and-whisker plot of the data from Example 1.2.

Solution: The five statistics required to construct the boxplot are $x_{min} = 12$, $Q_1 = 65.5$, $\tilde{x} = 74.5$, $Q_3 = 87$, and $x_{max} = 95$. These values were used to construct the boxplot shown in Figure 1.5. The median determines the position of the center line, the quartiles determine the length of the box, and the maximum and minimum values determine the ends of the whiskers.

There are many variations on boxplots. For example, some boxplots add the mean of the data set as a circle to complement the median as a measure of location. Another common variation on boxplots is to plot possible outlying data points individually instead of including them in really long whiskers. Points are often considered to be outliers if they fall more than 1.5 times the IQR beyond the ends of the box.

1.8 SCATTER PLOTS

All of the plots discussed to this point are used to present one variable at a time. Often it is necessary to see if two variables are correlated, that is, if one variable affects

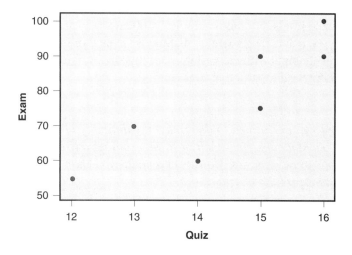

Figure 1.6   Scatter plot of quiz scores versus exam scores.

another. A simple way to do this is provided by a scatter plot—a two-dimensional (x, y) plot with one variable plotted on each axis. If a causal relationship between x and y is suspected, then we generally plot the cause on the horizontal or x axis and the response on the vertical or y axis. Different symbols or colors for plotted points can also be used to distinguish observations that come from different treatments or categories.

Example 1.6

Construct a scatter plot of the quiz and exam score data in the following table and interpret the plot.

Quiz	12	14	13	15	15	16	16
Exam	55	60	70	75	90	90	100

Solution: The scatter plot is shown in Figure 1.6. This plot shows that when quiz scores are high, exam scores also tend to be high, but that there is a large amount of random variation in the relationship.

1.9 MULTI-VARI CHARTS

When a single response is studied as a function of two or more variables, the usual graphical presentation methods for one-way classifications like boxplots, dotplots, and so on, may not be able to resolve the complex structure of the data. An alternative method called a multi-vari chart is specifically designed for cases involving two or more classifications. Multi-vari charts often use combinations of separate graphs distinguished by the different variable levels, but more complex problems may also employ different line styles, symbol styles, colors, and so on, to distinguish even more variables. In such cases, it may take several attempts with the variables arranged in different ways to find the best multi-vari chart to present a particular data set.

Example 1.7

An experiment was performed to determine the difficulty of the questions on a certification exam. Ten students from each of three exam review courses were randomly selected to take one of two quizzes. Construct a multi-vari chart for the quiz score data in Table 1.1 and interpret the chart.

Solution: The multi-vari chart of the two-way classification data is shown in Figure 1.7. The chart suggests that quiz 2 was easier than quiz 1 and that the students in class 3 did better than the students in class 2, who did better than the students in class 1. The random scatter in the individual observations appears to be uniform across quizzes and classes.

Table 1.1 Quiz score data by class and quiz.

Student	Class 1		Class 2		Class 3	
	Quiz 1	Quiz 2	Quiz 1	Quiz 2	Quiz 1	Quiz 2
1	87	86	81	97	84	100
2	82	92	85	93	96	91
3	78	82	85	92	86	102
4	85	85	80	88	92	99
5	73	97	96	88	83	101

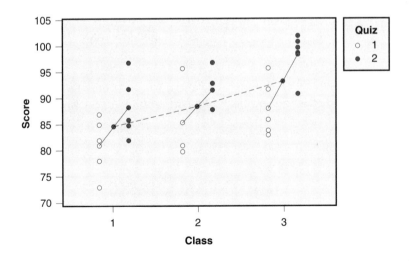

Figure 1.7 Multi-vari chart of quiz scores by class and quiz.

1.10 AN INTRODUCTION TO MINITAB

While all of the graphical techniques presented in this chapter can be prepared by hand, most people have access to personal computers and some kind of statistical software. When working with large data sets, software can save considerable time and, in turn, the time savings and increased speed of analysis permits the analyst to pursue avenues of investigation that might not otherwise be possible. Many of the analysis techniques we will consider were conceived long before they could be practically performed.

This text uses MINITAB 14 to demonstrate graphical and statistical data analyses and DOE techniques. There is nothing sacred about MINITAB. The author chose MINITAB because of its broad user base, ease of use, and reasonable price. If you're using another program besides MINITAB, your program probably offers similar functions that are accessed in a similar manner.

MINITAB has two modes for submitting commands: a command line mode and a mouse-activated pull-down menu environment. Many people will find the mouse/menu environment easier to use, however, this text uses both modes since the command line mode lends itself better to fine-tuning complicated analyses and to writing macros. Most experienced MINITAB users are adept at both methods. See MINITAB's **Help** menu for more information about creating and using MINITAB macros.

1.10.1 Starting MINITAB

There are at least three ways to start MINITAB depending on how your computer is set up. Any one of the following methods should work:

- Double-click the MINITAB icon on the desktop.

- Start MINITAB from the **Start> All Programs** menu.

- Find the executable MINITAB file (for example, *mtb14.exe*) using Windows Explorer and double-click the file.

If you expect to use MINITAB a lot and there's not already a MINITAB shortcut on the desktop, create one by dragging the program from the **Start> All Programs> Minitab 14** menu to the desktop or by right-clicking on the desktop and adding a new shortcut to the MINITAB 14 program.

1.10.2 MINITAB Windows

MINITAB organizes your work in several specialized windows. These MINITAB windows, the menu bar, and the tool bars are shown in Figure 1.8. The two most important windows, the ones that you will use most often, are the Session window and the Worksheet window. The Session window is where you enter typed commands to MINITAB and where any text output from MINITAB will be sent. The Worksheet is where you enter, manipulate, and observe your data. Use the mouse to move between windows or use CTRL+D to move to the Worksheet and CTRL+M to move to the Session window. If you lose a window, look for it in MINITAB's **Window** menu.

Although you will probably do most of your work in the Session and Worksheet windows, MINITAB has several other important windows to help organize your work. The Project Manager window, also shown in Figure 1.8, provides a convenient way to view all of these windows, to navigate between them, and to find information within them. The left panel of the Project Manager provides an overview of all of the information that MINITAB keeps in a project using a directory tree or folder format. In addition to the Session and Worksheets folders, MINITAB keeps: all of the graphs that you create in the Graphs folder; a history of all of the commands that you submit in the History window; the Related Documents folder that allows you to keep a list of non-MINITAB files, Web sites, and so on that are relevant to the project; and a simple word-processing environment called the Report Pad where you can write reports with integrated graphics and other outputs from MINITAB. The right panel of the Project Manager shows details of the item selected from the left panel. There are several special toolbars that you can turn on from the **Tools> Toolbars** menu. Two such toolbars are turned on in Figure 1.8—the **Graph Annotation** toolbar, which allows you to add text, lines, and so on, to a graph, and the **Worksheet** editing toolbar, which allows you to insert rows and columns in a worksheet, and so on.

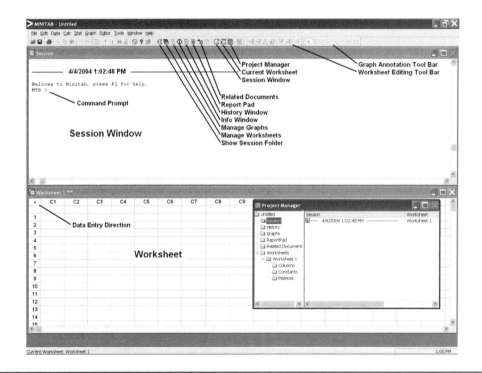

Figure 1.8   The MINITAB environment.

1.10.3 Using the Command Prompt

When MINITAB starts for the first time after installation, it is configured so that all commands must be submitted with the mouse from the pull-down menus. An alternative method of submitting commands is to type the commands at the MINITAB command prompt in the Session window. Before you can type commands, it's necessary to enable the MINITAB command prompt. Do this by clicking the mouse once anywhere in the Session window and then selecting **Editor> Enable Command Language** from the pull-down menu. The MINITAB command prompt **mtb>** will appear at the bottom of the Session window. With the command prompt enabled you can still submit commands with the mouse or by typing commands directly at the command prompt. When you submit a command with the mouse, the corresponding typed commands are automatically generated and appear in the Session window just as if you had typed them there yourself. So with the command prompt turned on you can continue to submit commands with the mouse but you will eventually learn MINITAB's command language just by inspecting the commands as they appear on the screen.

There are many benefits to learning MINITAB's command language. For example, any commands that you type at the **mtb>** prompt or that appear in the Session window after you submit them with the mouse can be repeated by copying and pasting them back into the command line. This saves lots of time, especially when you need to repeat a complicated series of commands that you ran hours or even days earlier. If necessary, you can modify commands before you run them just by editing the necessary lines before you hit the Enter key.

MINITAB commands have formal descriptive names; however, MINITAB allows these names to be abbreviated by the first four letters of the formal name. For example, the **regression** command can be abbreviated with **regr** and the **histogram** command can be abbreviated with **hist**.

1.10.4 Customizing MINITAB

MINITAB permits the user to customize the MINITAB environment from the **Tools> Options** menu. For example, you can set MINITAB to always start with the command prompt enabled from the **Tools> Options> Session Window> Submitting Commands** menu. And while you're there, it's helpful to change the color of the **mtb>** prompt to red or some other conspicuous color so you can find the prompt in the Session window more easily.

By default, MINITAB 14 uses a light gray border around its graphs. This might look good, but if you're sensitive to how much ink is used when you print graphs you can set the fill pattern type to N (none) from the **Tools> Options> Graphics> Regions** menu. You'll have to change the fill pattern in all three regions: **Figure**, **Graph**, and **Data**, to be certain that none of the background areas of your graphs get ink.

Another customization that you should consider is to increase the number of graphs that MINITAB allows to be open at one time. To prevent graphs from taking up too much RAM on older computers, MINITAB's default is to allow up to 15 graphs to be open at once, but there are some DOE operations that create more than 15 graphs, and computers have so much RAM now that the 15-graph limit is not necessary. Consider increasing the number of allowed open graphs from 15 to 30. You can do this from the **Tools> Options> Graphics> Graph Management** menu.

1.10.5 Entering Data

Data are typically entered from the keyboard into the Data window or Worksheet. The Worksheet is organized in columns and rows. Rows are numbered along the left-hand side of the screen and columns are indicated by their generic column names like C1 and C2. There is room for a user-defined column name below each of the column identifiers. Column names can be up to 31 characters long, can contain letters and numbers and limited special characters, but must not start or end with a blank space. Characters in names can be mixed upper- or lowercase but MINITAB does not distinguish between cases. Column names must be unique. Columns can be referenced by either their custom names or by their generic column names.

Although the MINITAB Worksheet looks like a spreadsheet (for example, Excel), the cells in the Worksheet cannot contain equations. All of the values entered into the spreadsheet must be numeric data, text data, or date/time data in an acceptable MINITAB date/time format.

Most mathematical and statistical operations in MINITAB are column operations. Operations are performed by referencing the column identifier (for example, C8) or the custom column name. Column names must be placed in single quotes (for example, 'Length') when you use the name in an operation. If you're submitting commands by menu/mouse, MINITAB will insert the necessary quotes for you. If you've named a column you can still refer to it by number (for example, C8) but MINITAB will show the column name instead in all of its outputs.

To enter column names and data within the body of the worksheet, use the up, down, left, and right arrow keys or the mouse to position the entry cursor in the desired field. Type each field's value with the keyboard or numeric keypad and move from cell to cell within the worksheet using the arrow keys. You must remember to exit a field after typing its contents to finish loading the data into the worksheet. You can enter successive values across a row or down a column by hitting the Enter key on the keyboard. Toggle the entry direction from rows to columns or columns to rows by clicking the entry direction arrow in the upper left hand corner of the Data window. The direction of the arrow, right or down, indicates which way the cursor will move when you hit the Enter key.

There are other ways to enter data into MINITAB. MINITAB will read correctly formatted data from worksheets created by other spreadsheet programs using the **File> Open Worksheet** menu. Data may also be read from a space- or tab-delimited text file using the **File> Other Files> Import Special Text** menu. Copy and paste operations can also be used to enter data into the Worksheet.

MINITAB has operations for numeric, text, and date/time data, but each column must contain only one kind of data. When text data are entered into a column of a worksheet, MINITAB identifies the column as text by appending the characters $-T$ to the generic column name, such as $C8-T$. Similarly, MINITAB identifies columns containing date/time data by appending the $-D$ characters to their generic column names, such as $C9-D$. Whether columns contain numeric text, or date/time data, only the generic column names are used in MINITAB column operations.

1.10.6 Graphing Data

MINITAB has a powerful and easy to use graphics engine that allows you to edit and customize almost every feature of a graph. Most of the graphs in this book were originally created using MINITAB.

To graph data in a MINITAB worksheet, select the type of graph that you want from the **Graph** menu and MINITAB will display a *graph gallery* showing the available styles for that type of graph. Select the appropriate graph style from the graph gallery and MINITAB will open a window allowing you to indicate what data to graph and how to display it. If, after you've created your graph, you want to modify it, you can right-click on the feature you want to change and then specify the changes. There are also text and drawing tools that you can use to customize your graph. Use **Tools> Toolbars> Graph Annotation Tools** to access these tools. If you add data to an existing data set for which you've already made a graph, you can update the old graph simply by right-clicking on it and selecting **Update Graph Now**.

Example 1.8

Use MINITAB to create a histogram of the data from Example 1.2.

Solution: The data were entered into column c1 *of the MINITAB worksheet. The histogram was created by: 1) selecting* **Graph> Histogram** *from the menu bar, 2) selecting a* **Simple** *histogram style from the graph gallery, and 3) specifying column* c1 *in the* **Graph Variables** *window. These steps and the resulting histogram are captured in Figure 1.9. The corresponding* **hist** *command also appears in the Session window.*

1.10.7 Printing Data and Graphs

To print the contents of the Session window, click anywhere in it and then select **File> Print Session Window**. If you only want to print a section of the Session window, use the mouse to select the desired section, then select **File> Print Session Window** and turn on the **Selection** option. If necessary, you can edit the Session window before printing it. If MINITAB won't let you edit the Session window, enable editing by turning on **Editor> Output Editable**.

Print a worksheet by clicking anywhere in the worksheet and then selecting **File> Print Worksheet**. You can also create a hard copy of your data by printing the data to

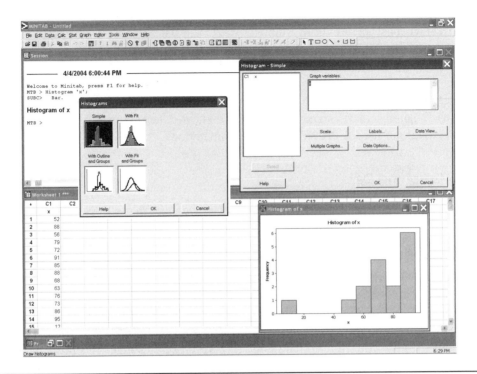

Figure 1.9 Creating a histogram with MINITAB.

the Session window using **Data> Display Data** or the **print** command and then printing the data from the Session window. This gives you the option of formatting the data by editing it in the Session window before you print it.

Print graphs by clicking on them and then selecting **File> Print Graph**. You can also use **Edit> Copy Graph** and **Paste** to make a copy of a graph in the Report Pad or in another word processor like Word. You can even edit graphs pasted into those documents without starting MINITAB by double-clicking on them in the document.

1.10.8 Saving and Retrieving Information

MINITAB saves all of your work in a single file called a project file. The project file contains all worksheets, the contents of the Session window, all graph windows, the History window, and so on. Project files have the extension *.mpj* and are created using the **File> Save Project** or **File> Save Project As** pull-down menus. You will have to indicate the directory in which you want to store the file and an appropriate file name. MINITAB file names follow the usual naming conventions for your operating system. Open an existing project file with the **File> Open** command.

Older versions of MINITAB kept data from a MINITAB worksheet in a separate file with the *.mtw* extension. MINITAB 14 preserves this capability so if you want to save only the data from a worksheet, for example, to start a new project with existing data, use the **File> Save Current Worksheet** or **File> Save Current Worksheet As** commands. If there are multiple worksheets in the project, MINITAB saves only the current worksheet, which is the one with three asterisks after the worksheet name in the title bar. Make sure that the correct worksheet is current before you overwrite an existing worksheet with **File> Save Current Worksheet**.

Open an existing project file with the **File> Open** command and read an existing worksheet into a project with the **File> Open Worksheet** command. Only one project can be open at a time but a project can contain several worksheets.

MINITAB's default directory path is to the directory of the open project file. MINITAB honors some DOS file commands like **cd** (change directory) and **dir** (directory) at the command prompt. Use these commands to change the default directory and view the files in the default directory, respectively. These commands will be useful later on when we discuss MINITAB macros.

Although MINITAB saves all graphs created in a project in the *.mpj* project file, you may want to save a graph separately in its own file. Save a MINITAB graph by clicking on the graph and selecting **File> Save Graph As**. MINITAB will prompt you for the directory path and file name for the graph. By default, MINITAB will create the graphics file in its proprietary graphics format with a *.mgf* extension in the default directory. You can also save graphs in other common formats like *.jpg* and *.png*. (Use *.png* files instead of *.jpg* files because they are very compact, scalable, and have better screen and print resolution.) You can read an existing MINITAB graphics file (*.mgf*) into a project to be viewed or edited with the **File> Open Graph** command. Graphics files of type *.jpg* and *.png* cannot be opened or edited in MINITAB.

1.10.9 MINITAB Macros

Eventually you will create a series of MINITAB commands that you need to run on a regular basis, either using the mouse/menu or by typing commands directly at the **mtb>** prompt. MINITAB anticipates this need and provides a convenient environment to capture those commands in an easy-to-call macro. MINITAB supports three different types of macros: exec, global, and local macros, but only the simplest type—exec macros— will be described here in any detail. The MINITAB **Help** menu contains extensive instructions for the use of all three types of macros.

The easiest way to create a MINITAB macro is to use the mouse/menu or typed commands to perform the commands that you want in the macro. After all of the commands have been executed, use the mouse to select those commands in the MINITAB History window. Select commands by clicking and dragging over them from right to left, then position the mouse over the selected commands, right-click, and select **Save As**. Save the selected commands with a file name of your choice using the *.mtb* file extension, for example, *MyMacro.mtb*. The best place to save the file is the *.../Minitab 14/Macros* folder because it is the default folder that MINITAB looks in to find your macros. After you've saved your macro, you can edit it using Notepad.* In addition to

---

* If you're using a foreign-language version of Notepad, MINITAB will probably not be able to run the macro. You'll either have to install the U.S. version of Notepad or use a different text editor.

using Notepad to edit MINITAB commands, it's always wise to insert comments into your macros such as: instructions for use, descriptions of the expected data structures, author, version, change history, and so on. Use a pound sign (#) to indicate the beginning of a comment. Comments can be on lines all by themselves or can follow a command on the same line. Anything on a line that follows a # is treated as a comment.

Run *.mtb* macros from the **File> Other Files> Run an Exec** menu or with the **exec** command at the command prompt. Both methods allow you to run a macro a specified number of times. For example, the following **exec** command runs *MyMacro.mtb* ten times:

```
mtb > exec 'mymacro.mtb' 10
```

Example 1.9

Write a MINITAB exec macro that: 1) creates a random normal data set of size n = 40 from a population with $\mu = 300$ and $\sigma = 20$ and 2) creates a histogram, dotplot, and boxplot of the data.

Solution: *The necessary steps were performed using the* **Calc> Random Data> Normal,** **Graph> Histogram,** **Graph> Dotplot,** *and* **Graph> Boxplot** *menus. The resulting commands were copied from the History window and saved in the macro file practicegraphs.mtb. Some unnecessary subcommands of the* **histogram** *and* **boxplot** *commands were removed from the macro to keep it as simple as possible.*

```
random 40 c1;
  normal 300 20.
histogram c1
dotplot c1
boxplot c1
```

The only data that MINITAB exec macros can access are data in MINITAB's columns, constants, and matrices. Another type of MINITAB macro, the local macro, is much more flexible than exec macros; only has access to the project data passed to it in its calling statement; can define and use its own variables; supports complex program structures like loops, conditionals, input/output, calls to other local macros, calls to most MINITAB functions, and so on; and has the structure of a freestanding subroutine. Local macros use the *.mac* extension and are called from the MINITAB command prompt using the % operator. For example,

```
mtb > %dothis k1 c1 c2
```

calls local macro *dothis.mac* and passes it the data in constant k1 and columns c1 and c2. If any of these data are changed within the macro, the changes will be adopted as the macro runs. Local macros should be placed in the *.../Minitab 14/Macros* folder or it will be necessary to use the change directory command **cd** to specify the folder where the macros are located. Like exec macros, open local macros in Notepad to view or edit them. Many of the custom macros provided on the CD-ROM distributed with this book are local macros. Descriptions and instructions for use are included in comments at the beginning of each macro.

1.10.10 Summary of MINITAB Files

MINITAB reads and writes files of many types for different kinds of information. They are distinguished by the file extension that is appended to each of the file names. The following file extensions are used:

- Files with the extension *.mpj* are MINITAB project files that store all of the work from MINITAB sessions.

- Files with the extension *.mtw* are MINITAB worksheets where data are stored in MINITAB format.

- Files with the extension *.dat* are ASCII data files that MINITAB and other programs (for example, Excel) can read and write.

- Files with the extension *.mtb* and *.mac* are MINITAB macro files.

- Files with the extension *.mgf* are MINITAB graphics files.

2

Descriptive Statistics

2.1 INTRODUCTION

Data collected from a process are usually evaluated for three characteristics: location (or central tendency), variation (or dispersion), and shape. Location and variation are evaluated quantitatively, that is with numeric measures, and the distribution shape is usually evaluated qualitatively such as by interpreting a histogram.

Since it is usually impossible or impractical to collect all the possible data values from a process, a subset of the complete data set must be used instead. A complete data set is referred to as a *population* and a subset of the population is called a *sample*. Whereas a population is characterized by single measures of its location and variation, each sample drawn from a population will yield a different measure of these quantities. Measures of location and variation determined from a population are called *parameters* of the population. Measures of location or variation determined from samples are called *descriptive statistics*. Descriptive statistics determined from sample data are used to provide estimates of population parameters.

The purpose of this chapter is to introduce the descriptive statistics that are important to the methods of designed experiments.

2.2 SELECTION OF SAMPLES

Samples should be *representative* of the population from which they are drawn. A sample is representative of its population when its location, variation, and shape are good approximations to those of the population. Obviously it's important to select good samples, so we must consider the process used to draw a sample from a population. For lack of a better method, the technique used most often is to draw individuals for a sample randomly from all of the units in the population. In *random sampling,* each individual in the population has the same chance of being drawn for the sample. Such samples are referred to as *random samples.* A common reason that designed experiments fail is that samples are not drawn randomly and are not representative of the population from which they were drawn. Randomization can be painful and expensive but there are few practical alternatives.

2.3 MEASURES OF LOCATION

Two measures of location or central tendency of a sample data set are commonly used: the sample mean $\bar{x}$ and the sample median $\tilde{x}$. The sample mean is used more often and almost exclusively in DOE since it provides a better estimate for the population mean μ than does the median. However, the median is very easy to determine and still finds some useful applications, particularly in the presentation of some types of graphs.

2.3.1 The Median

The median of a data set is the data set's middle value when the data are organized by size from the smallest to the largest value. The median is determined from the observation in the median position given by:

$$\frac{n+1}{2}$$

where n is the size of the sample. For a data set containing an odd number of values, the median will be equal to the middle value in the data set. For a set containing an even number of data points, the median position falls between two values in the data set. In this case, the median is determined by averaging those two values.

Example 2.1
   Find the median of the data set {16, 14, 12, 18, 9, 15}.

   Solution: The data, after ordering them from smallest to largest, are: {9, 12, 14, 15, 16, 18}. *Since the sample size is n = 6 the median position is*

$$\frac{n+1}{2} = \frac{6+1}{2} = 3.5$$

The median falls between the third and fourth data points, which have values 14 *and* 15, *so the median is* $\tilde{x} = 14.5$.

2.3.2 The Mean

The sample median uses only one, or perhaps two, of the values from a data set to determine an estimate for the population mean μ. The sample mean, indicated by $\bar{x}$, provides a better estimate for μ because it uses all of the sample data values in its calculation. The sample mean is determined from:

$$\bar{x} = \frac{1}{n} \sum_{i=1}^{n} x_i \qquad (2.1)$$

where the x_i are the individual values in the sample and the summation is performed over all n of the values in the sample.

Example 2.2

Find the mean of the sample {16, 14, 12, 18, 9, 15}.

Solution: The sample mean is given by:

$$\bar{x} = \frac{1}{6}(16+14+12+18+9+15) = 14$$

2.4 MEASURES OF VARIATION

The most common statistics used to measure variation of sample data are the range R and the standard deviation s. Another measure of variation—important in the interpretation of boxplots—is the interquartile range or IQR that was introduced in Section 1.7. All three of these measures of variation can be used to estimate the population standard deviation σ.

2.4.1 The Range

The range is the simplest measure of variation of a data set. The range is equal to the difference between the largest and smallest values of a sample:

$$R = x_{max} - x_{min} \qquad (2.2)$$

By definition the range is always positive.

The range can be used to estimate the population standard deviation σ from:

$$\sigma \simeq \frac{R}{d_2} \qquad (2.3)$$

where d_2 is a special constant that depends on the size of the sample. Some useful values of d_2 are given in Table 2.1.

Table 2.1 Some values of $d_2(n)$.

n	2	3	4	5	6	7	8	9	10	15	20
d_2	1.128	1.693	2.059	2.326	2.534	2.704	2.847	2.970	3.078	3.472	3.735

Equation 2.3 shows the approximate equality of σ and R/d_2 using the "$\simeq$" binary relation. The equality is approximate because σ is a parameter and R is a statistic. An alternative and commonly used notation for the same relationship is:

$$\hat{\sigma} = \frac{R}{d_2} \tag{2.4}$$

where the caret (^) over the parameter σ indicates that $\hat{\sigma}$ is an estimator for σ. We usually refer to the ^ symbol as a "hat." For example, $\hat{\sigma}$ is pronounced "sigma-hat." All of the following expressions show correct use of the ^ notation: $\mu \simeq \hat{\mu}$, $\sigma \simeq \hat{\sigma}$, $\hat{\mu} = \bar{x}$, and $\hat{\sigma} = s$.

We won't use ranges very often in this book but there are some historical DOE analyses, like the analysis of gage error study data, where the range was used instead of the standard deviation because of its ease of calculation. Some of these range-based methods are still in use but they are really obsolete and should be replaced with more accurate methods now that computation is no longer a challenge.

Example 2.3

Find the range of the sample data set $\{16, 14, 12, 18, 9, 15\}$ and use it to estimate the population standard deviation.

Solution: The largest and smallest values in the sample are 18 and 9, so the range is:

$$R = 18 - 9 = 9$$

The sample size is $n = 6$ which has a corresponding d_2 value of $d_2 = 2.534$. The estimate for the population standard deviation is:

$$\hat{\sigma} = \frac{R}{d_2} = \frac{9}{2.534} = 3.55$$

2.4.2 The Standard Deviation

For small sample sizes ($n \le 10$), the range provides a reasonable measure of variation. For larger samples ($n > 10$), however, the sample standard deviation provides a better estimate of σ than the range because it tends to be more consistent from sample to sample. The sample standard deviation is a bit difficult to calculate, but most calculators now provide this function. *Even if you are comfortable with standard deviation calculations, don't skip lightly over this section. The concept of the standard deviation and its calculation are fundamental to DOE and will show up over and over again.*

The sample standard deviation s is determined by considering the deviation of the data points of a data set from the sample mean $\bar{x}$. It should be clear that s will be a better estimator of σ than R since s takes all of the data values into account, not just the two most extreme values. The deviation of the ith data point from $\bar{x}$ is:

$$\varepsilon_i = x_i - \bar{x} \tag{2.5}$$

The sample standard deviation is given by:

$$s = \sqrt{\frac{\sum_{i=1}^{n}\varepsilon_i^2}{n-1}} \tag{2.6}$$

Why do we need such a complicated measure of variation? Why can't we just take the mean of the deviations? Try it. The mean of the deviations is given by:

$$\bar{\varepsilon} = \frac{1}{n}\sum_{i=1}^{n}\varepsilon_i = 0 \tag{2.7}$$

That $\bar{\varepsilon} = 0$ is just a consequence of the way the sample mean $\bar{x}$ is determined. Since about half of the data values must fall above $\bar{x}$ and half below $\bar{x}$, then roughly half of the ε_i are positive, half are negative, and their mean must be, by definition, equal to zero. To avoid this problem, it's necessary to measure the unsigned size of each deviation from the mean. We could consider the unsigned ε_is by taking their absolute value:

$$\bar{\varepsilon} = \frac{1}{n}\sum_{i=1}^{n}\left|\varepsilon_i\right| \tag{2.8}$$

This quantity is called the *mean deviation* but it's not used very often because the standard deviation provides a more meaningful measure of variation for most physical problems.

The population standard deviation σ is calculated in almost the same way as the sample standard deviation:

$$\sigma = \sqrt{\frac{\sum_{i=1}^{N}\varepsilon_i^2}{N}} \tag{2.9}$$

where $\varepsilon_i = x_i - \mu$ and N is the population size. The reason that N is used here instead of $N-1$ is subtle and has to do with the fact that μ is a parameter of the population. This distinction might become clearer to you in the next section. It is rare that we know all of the x_is in a population so we don't usually get to calculate σ. Rather, we estimate it from R and s calculated from sample data.

The square of the standard deviation is called the *variance* and is indicated by σ^2 or s^2. The variance is actually a more fundamental measure of variation than the standard

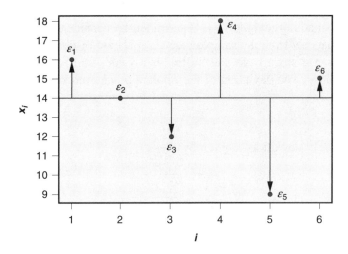

Figure 2.1 Plot of x_is and corresponding ε_is for Example 2.4.

deviation; however, variance has units of the measurement squared and people find the standard deviation easier to use because it has the same units as the measurement values. For example, if measurements are made in inches, the mean and standard deviation of the measurements will be in inches but the variance will be in inches squared. Despite this problem with units, variances have special properties (yet to be seen) that give them a crucial role in the analysis and interpretation of designed experiments.

Example 2.4

For the sample data set $x_i = \{16, 14, 12, 18, 9, 15\}$ plot the observations, indicate the ε_i in the plot, calculate the ε_i, and use them to determine the sample standard deviation.

Solution: The $n = 6$ observations are plotted in Figure 2.1. The sample mean is $\bar{x} = 14$ and the differences between the mean and the observed values are the ε_i indicated with arrows in the figure. The ε_i are $\{2, 0, -2, 4, -5, 1\}$. Note that the ε_i are signed and roughly half are positive and half are negative. The sample standard deviation is:

$$s = \sqrt{\frac{\sum_{i=1}^{n} \varepsilon_i^2}{n-1}}$$

$$= \sqrt{\frac{(2)^2+(0)^2+(-2)^2+(4)^2+(-5)^2+(1)^2}{(6-1)}}$$

$$= 3.16$$

2.4.3 Degrees of Freedom

The calculation of the sample mean by Equation 2.1 is achieved by summing the x_is over all n values in the data set and then dividing by n. Dividing by n makes sense; there are n of the x_is that must be added together so dividing

$$\sum_{i=1}^{n} x_i$$

by n gives the mean value of the x_is. Since the calculation of the mean involves n x_i values which are all free to vary, we say that there are n degrees of freedom (indicated by df or v) for the calculation of the sample mean.

The sample variance s^2 is given by taking the square of Equation 2.6:

$$s^2 = \frac{1}{n-1} \sum_{i=1}^{n} \varepsilon_i^2 \tag{2.10}$$

Taking the sum of all n of the ε_i^2s makes sense, but the reason for dividing the result by $n-1$ instead of n is not obvious. Dividing by $n-1$ is necessary because of the way the ε_is are determined in Equation 2.5. Since calculation of the ε_is requires prior calculation of $\bar{x}$, as soon as the first $n-1$ of them are calculated, the nth one, the last one, is not free to vary. To demonstrate this, suppose that a data set of size $n = 5$ has $\bar{x} = 3$ and that the first four data values are $\{x_1, x_2, x_3, x_4\} = \{3, 3, 3, 3\}$. Obviously the last value must be $x_5 = 3$ since it has to be consistent with the sample mean. Apparently knowledge of $\bar{x}$ and the first $n-1$ of the ε_is fixes ε_n. This means that only the first $n-1$ of the ε_is are free to vary so there are only $n-1$ degrees of freedom available to calculate the sample variance. We say that the remaining degree of freedom was *consumed* by the necessary prior calculation of $\bar{x}$. Typically, each statistic calculated from sample data consumes one degree of freedom from the original data set. A consequence of this is that in more complicated problems the appropriate denominator in a variance calculation might be $n-2$, $n-3$, and so on, and the frequent use of $n-1$ just corresponds to a common but special case.

It requires some practice and experience to become comfortable with the concept of degrees of freedom, however, the management of degrees of freedom in experiments will play an important role in their planning, design selection, and analysis.

2.4.4 The Calculating Form for the Standard Deviation

The equation for the standard deviation given in Equation 2.6 is not practical for calculations because it requires the initial calculation of $\bar{x}$ before the ε_i can be determined. Imagine having to enter the x_is of a very large data set into a calculator to determine $\bar{x}$ and then having to enter the x_is again to calculate the ε_i! Thankfully there is an easier method. By substituting the definition of ε_i given by Equation 2.5 into Equation 2.6, another useful form for the standard deviation is obtained:

$$\begin{aligned} s &= \sqrt{\frac{\sum(x_i - \bar{x})^2}{n-1}} \\ &= \sqrt{\frac{n\sum x_i^2 - (\sum x_i)^2}{n(n-1)}} \end{aligned} \tag{2.11}$$

This is called the calculating form for the sample standard deviation because it is simpler to use to calculate s than Equation 2.6. Use of the calculating form requires three quantities: the sample size n, the sum of the data values Σx_i, and the sum of the squares of the data values Σx_i^2. Calculators and spreadsheets keep track of these values in three special memory locations as the data are entered. Once data entry is complete and the user requests the sample standard deviation, the calculator uses the values in these memories and Equation 2.11 to determine s. This method avoids the need for the calculator to store all of the data values in memory as they're entered.

The calculating form for the standard deviation is practical but it does not provide the physical insight of Equation 2.6. Both methods are important to understand and both will be used frequently—that of Equation 2.6 when it is critical to understand the physical meaning of the standard deviation and that of Equation 2.11 when a calculation is required. Many statistics and DOE textbooks only show the calculating form and students are on their own to figure out what it means. This book uses both forms and you will make constant reference to them. Take the time to learn them and understand them.

Example 2.5

Use the calculating formula for the standard deviation (Equation 2.11) to find the standard deviation of the data set in Example 2.4.

Solution: We have $n = 6$, $\sum_{i=1}^{6} x_i = 84$, and $\sum_{i=1}^{6} x_i^2 = 1226$ so:

$$s = \sqrt{\frac{6(1226) - (84)^2}{6(6-1)}} = 3.16$$

which is in agreement with the standard deviation found by the defining equation.

2.5 THE NORMAL DISTRIBUTION

At the beginning of this chapter it was stated that we must always consider three characteristics of the data taken from a process: location, variation, and shape. We have learned how to calculate statistics from sample data to estimate the location and variation parameters of distributions, but we have yet to address the issue of distribution shape. Although there are many probability distributions that play important roles in DOE, one of the most important distributions is the normal probability distribution. The normal distribution, also referred to as the *bell-shaped curve,* is shown in Figure 2.2. The distribution of the errors, or *noise,* in most of the problems that we will consider in this book is expected to follow a normal distribution.

The equation that gives the height of the normal curve in Figure 2.2 as a function of x is:

$$\varphi(x; \mu, \sigma) = \frac{1}{\sqrt{2\pi}\sigma} e^{-\frac{1}{2}\left(\frac{x-\mu}{\sigma}\right)^2} \tag{2.12}$$

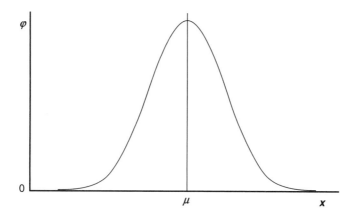

Figure 2.2 The normal distribution or bell-shaped curve.

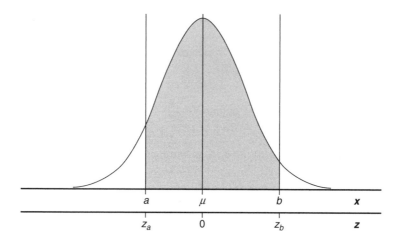

Figure 2.3 x and z limits for calculating the area under the normal curve.

where μ is the mean and σ is the standard deviation of the normal distribution. This function is called the *probability density function* of the normal distribution. We expect to see lots of data values where the probability density function is large and few where it is small.

In practice, we don't have to deal with Equation 2.12 at all. What we are really concerned about is the probability that x falls within a specified range of values. The normal curve is scaled so that the total area under it is exactly 1. Then the probability that x will be in the interval $a < x < b$ is given by the area under the curve in the corresponding vertical slice as in Figure 2.3. For those with a little calculus background, this probability is given by:

$$\Phi\left(a < x < b; \mu, \sigma\right) = \int_a^b \varphi\left(x; \mu, \sigma\right) dx \qquad (2.13)$$

where the Greek symbol Φ stands for the *cumulative* normal probability distribution.

Cumulative normal probability calculations using Equation 2.13 are not pleasant, but since these calculations have to be done so frequently an alternative method for determining normal probabilities has been developed. Notice that x only appears in combination with μ and σ in Equation 2.12. This suggests that instead of working with x, we can use in its place the transformed value:

$$z = \frac{x - \mu}{\sigma} \qquad (2.14)$$

The z value corresponding to x has a very important interpretation: the magnitude of z indicates how many standard deviations x falls away from μ. If the z value for an x is negative, then $x < \mu$. If the z value is positive, then $x > \mu$. Equation 2.14 can also be solved for x to express it in terms of μ, σ, and z:

$$x = \mu + z\sigma \qquad (2.15)$$

Example 2.6

If a normal distribution has $\mu = 40$ and $\sigma = 5$, find the z value that corresponds to the measurement value $x = 50$.

Solution: The z value corresponding to $x = 50$ is given by:

$$z = \frac{x - \mu}{\sigma} = \frac{50 - 40}{5} = 2.0$$

The value of z indicates that $x = 50$ falls 2.0 standard deviations above the mean μ. Another way of indicating this is:

$$x = \mu + z\sigma = 40 + 2\left(5\right) = 50$$

When the z values have been calculated for both the upper and lower bounds of x, we find the probability of x falling in this range by:

$$\Phi\left(a < x < b; \mu, \sigma\right) = \Phi\left(z_a < z < z_b\right) \qquad (2.16)$$

where

$$z_a = \frac{a - \mu}{\sigma}$$

and

$$z_b = \frac{b - \mu}{\sigma}$$

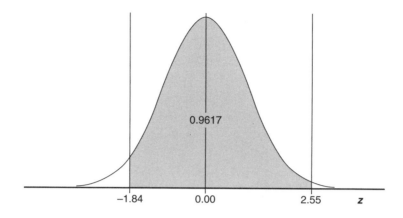

0.9617

−1.84	0.00	2.55 *z*

Figure 2.4 $\Phi(-1.84 < z < 2.55) = 0.9617$.

The mean of the z distribution is always $\mu_z = 0$ and the standard deviation is always $\sigma_z = 1$. $\Phi(z)$ is called the standard normal curve because the measurement values of x have been standardized by converting them into z values.

Special tables of normal probabilities have been prepared as a function of z. The normal table in Appendix A.2 gives the area under the normal curve (that is, the probability) to the left of the indexed z value. You often have to look up the normal curve areas for two or more z values to solve a single problem.

Example 2.7

Find the normal probability $\Phi(-1.84 < z < 2.55)$ and plot the area under the curve corresponding to it.

Solution: From the table of normal probabilities, the area under the normal curve from $z = -\infty$ to $z = 2.55$ is 0.9946 and the area from $z = -\infty$ to $z = -1.84$ is 0.0329 so $\Phi(-1.84 < z < 2.55) = 0.9946 - 0.0329 = 0.9617$. The relevant area under the normal curve is shown in Figure 2.4.

Example 2.8

A process characteristic has $\mu = 50$, $\sigma = 4.2$, and is normally distributed. If the specification limits are USL/LSL = 58/44, find the fraction of the product that meets the specification (or the probability that an observation chosen at random falls inside the specification) and plot the area under the curve that corresponds to it.

Solution: We must solve the normal probability problem $\Phi(44 < x < 58; 50, 4.2)$. The z value corresponding to the lower and upper limits of x are

$$z = \frac{44-50}{4.2} = -1.43$$

and

$$z = \frac{58-50}{4.2} = 1.90,$$

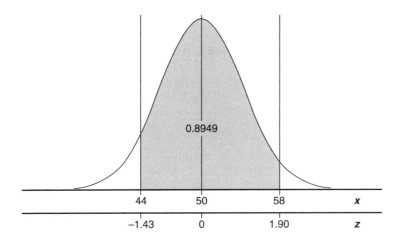

Figure 2.5 $\Phi(44 < x < 58; 50, 4.2) = 0.8949.$

respectively. Then the original problem in x units has the same probability as $\Phi(-1.43 < z < 1.90)$. From the table of normal probabilities $\Phi(-1.43 < z < 1.90) = 0.9713 - 0.0764 = 0.8949$. The corresponding area under the curve is shown in Figure 2.5.

Many people struggle with the concept of the standard deviation and only know standard deviations as numbers, but the standard deviation has a simple interpretation in the context of the normal distribution. If you study the shape of the normal curve, you'll notice that it is curved downward in the middle and curved upward in its tails. The points on the shoulders of the normal curve where the curvature changes from downward to upward are called *inflection points* and the distance that they fall from the mean is equal to one standard deviation. This is a nice concept to understand because it provides a mechanical interpretation for the standard deviation.

2.6 COUNTING

A common problem that is encountered in statistics in general, and in certain DOE applications, involves counting the number of events or occurrences that meet certain conditions. Special notations are used for these problems and they are introduced quickly here because they are used frequently throughout the book. If you require more information or review, consult any basic statistics textbook.

2.6.1 Multiplication of Choices

If a series of k decisions must be made, where the first decision can be made in a_1 different ways, the second decision can be made in a_2 different ways, . . . , and the kth decision can be made in a_k different ways, then the total number of ways all k decisions can be made is:

$$N = a_1 a_2 \cdots a_k \qquad (2.17)$$

This is called the *multiplication of choices* rule.

Example 2.9

An experiment with three variables has two levels of the first variable, four levels of the second variable, and five levels of the third variable. How many runs will there be in the experiment if all possible configurations of the three variables must be built?

Solution: The total number of unique runs in the experiment is:

$$N = 2 \times 4 \times 5 = 40$$

2.6.2 Factorials

If there are n objects in a set, and all n of them are to be picked sequentially without replacement, then there are n ways to make the first choice, $n - 1$ ways to make the second choice, ... , and one way to make the nth choice. By the multiplication of choices rule, the total number of ways the choices can be made is:

$$\begin{aligned} N &= n \times (n-1) \times (n-2) \times \cdots \times 3 \times 2 \times 1 \qquad (2.18) \\ &= n! \end{aligned}$$

where $n!$ is read "n factorial." By definition, $0! = 1$ because there is only one way to pick no objects.

Example 2.10

Four operators are to measure parts for a gage error study. If each operator is to complete his measurements before the next operator starts, how many possible orderings are there for the operators to make their measurements?

Solution: The total number of ways that the four operators can make their measurements is:

$$4! = 4 \times 3 \times 2 \times 1 = 24$$

2.6.3 Permutations

If the factorial problem is modified so that only the first r objects are drawn from the set of n possible objects, then the total number of ways that the r objects can be drawn is:

$$_nP_r = n(n-1)(n-2)\cdots(n-r+1) = \frac{n!}{(n-r)!} \qquad (2.19)$$

where the permutation operation $_nP_r$ is read "*n* pick *r*." Permutations take into consideration the different orderings of the *r* objects and for this reason the objects must be distinct from each other. Permutation calculations are not used very often in DOE but they are the precursor to the next counting operation that is very important—combinations.

Example 2.11

Three operators of ten possible operators are to be used in a gage error study. How many different orderings are there for operators to take their measurements?

Solution: The total number ways the operators can take their measurements is:

$$_{10}P_3 = \frac{10!}{(10-3)!} = \frac{10!}{7!} = \frac{10\times9\times8\times7!}{7!} = 10\times9\times8 = 720$$

2.6.4 Combinations

There are many applications for combination operations in DOE so study this section carefully. As in the permutation problem, suppose that we wish to draw *r* objects from a set of *n* possible objects but that we don't care about the order in which the objects are drawn. Since there are *r*! ways to arrange the same *r* objects, the permutation calculation overcounts the total number of ways by *r*! so:

$$\binom{n}{r} = \frac{_nP_r}{_rP_r} = \frac{n!}{r!(n-r)!} \qquad (2.20)$$

where $\binom{n}{r}$ indicates the combination operation. $\binom{n}{r}$ is also sometimes written $_nC_r$ to be consistent with the permutation notation but $\binom{n}{r}$ is preferred.

It's easy to confuse permutations with combinations. One silly problem that might help clarify the difference has to do with the letters in words. If four letters are chosen from the 26 possible letters of the alphabet without replacement (that is, once a letter is drawn it cannot be drawn again), then the permutation calculation gives the number of different four-letter words: $_{26}P_4 = 358{,}800$, and the combination calculation gives the number of possible four-letter sets where the order of the four letters doesn't matter: $\binom{26}{4} = 14{,}950$. The difference between the two calculations is a multiplicative factor of $4! = 24$ because there are 4! different ways to arrange the four letters once they are picked. The permutation is larger because different orderings of the same letters make different words. The combination is smaller because the letters chosen are important but not their order. Note that if the letters are chosen with replacement (that is, once a letter is drawn it can be drawn again) then by the multiplication of choices rule there are $26^4 = 456,976$ different four letter words that can be created.

Example 2.12

How many different ways are there to pick three operators from ten for a gage error study?

Solution: *Since we probably don't care about the order in which the operators are chosen, the total number of ways we can pick three of ten operators is:*

$$\binom{10}{3} = \frac{10!}{3!7!} = 120$$

Notice that this answer is $3! = 6$ *times smaller than the answer in Example 2.11 because there are six different ways to arrange the three operators once they are chosen and in this problem all six of the ways are considered to be equivalent.*

Example 2.13

An experiment is performed to compare six different types of material $\{1, 2, 3, 4, 5, 6\}$. *How many different tests to compare all possible pairs of means must be performed?*

Solution: *The means that must be compared are* $12, 13, \ldots, 56$ *where* 12 *indicates the first versus second material,* 13 *indicates the first versus third material, and so on. The total number of tests that must be performed is:*

$$\binom{6}{2} = \frac{6!}{2!4!} = 15$$

Example 2.14

An experiment has five variables or factors $\{A, B, C, D, E\}$. *How many possible main effects (that is, one variable at a time), two-factor, three-factor, four-factor, and five-factor interactions are there? Enumerate them.*

Solution: *The effects and the number of them by type are shown in Table 2.2.*

Table 2.2   Effects and the number of them by type for a five-variable experiment.

Effect Type	Number	Effect List
Main effects	$\binom{5}{1} = 5$	*A, B, C, D, E*
Two-factor interactions	$\binom{5}{2} = 10$	*AB, AC, AD, AE, BC, BD, BE, CD, CE, DE*
Three-factor interactions	$\binom{5}{3} = 10$	*ABC, ABD, ABE, ACD, ACE, ADE, BCD, BCE, BDE, CDE*
Four-factor interactions	$\binom{5}{4} = 5$	*ABCD, ABCE, ABDE, ACDE, BCDE*
Five-factor interactions	$\binom{5}{5} = 1$	*ABCDE*

2.7 MINITAB COMMANDS TO CALCULATE DESCRIPTIVE STATISTICS

Once data have been entered into a column of a MINITAB worksheet, specific descriptive statistics for the column can be calculated from the **Calc> Column Statistics** menu. A nice summary of the most common descriptive statistics is provided by the **Stat> Basic Statistics> Display Descriptive Statistics** command. This command can also be invoked with the **describe** command at the command prompt. Other commands available from the command prompt are **mean**, **stdev**, **range**, **count**, and others.

Example 2.15

Use MINITAB to calculate the mean, standard deviation, and range of the data from Example 2.2.

Solution: The data were entered into column C1 *of the MINITAB worksheet. Then the* **describe**, **mean**, **stdev**, *and* **range** *commands were used to analyze the data. The commands were issued from the pull-down menus but the output from the Session window in Figure 2.6 also shows the command syntax used to issue the commands from the* **mtb>** *prompt.*

```
MTB > Describe C1.

Descriptive Statistics: C1


Variable          N       Mean     Median    TrMean      StDev    SE Mean
C1                6      14.00      14.50     14.00       3.16       1.29

Variable     Minimum    Maximum         Q1         Q3
C1              9.00      18.00      11.25      16.50

MTB > Mean C1.

Mean of C1

    Mean of C1 = 14.000
MTB > StDev C1.

Standard Deviation of C1

    Standard deviation of C1 = 3.1623
MTB > Range C1.

Range of C1

    Range of C1 = 9.000
```

Figure 2.6 Descriptive statistics calculations with MINITAB.

MINITAB has two functions for calculating normal probabilities. The **cdf** function, which can also be invoked from the **Calc> Probability Distributions> Normal** menu by selecting the **Cumulative probability** button, finds the normal probability in the left tail of the normal distribution for a specified mean, standard deviation, and x value. The syntax for the **cdf** command function is:

> mtb > cdf x;
>
> subc > normal $\mu\,\sigma$.

The **invcdf** function, which is invoked from the same menu by selecting the **Inverse cumulative probability** button, finds the x value that corresponds to a specified left-tail area. The command syntax is:

> mtb > invcdf p;
>
> subc > normal $\mu\,\sigma$.

where p is the left-tail area under the normal curve. For both functions, the default values of the mean and standard deviation are $\mu = 0$ and $\sigma = 1$, which corresponds to the standard normal (z) distribution. MINITAB has similar **cdf** and **invcdf** functions for many other common probability distributions.

MINITAB also has the ability to determine the normal curve amplitude $\varphi(x;\, \mu,\, \sigma)$ given in Equation 2.12, which can be used to plot the normal curve. The normal curves in Figures 2.3, 2.4, and 2.5 were drawn using this function. To make a normal curve plot, use MINITAB's **set** command or **Calc> Make Patterned Data> Simple Set of Numbers** to create a column in the MINITAB worksheet containing x values that run from the smallest to the largest values of interest using a suitably small increment. Then use MINITAB's **pdf** function to find the corresponding $\varphi(x;\, \mu,\, \sigma)$ values. The command syntax for the **pdf** function is:

> mtb > pdf c1 c2;
>
> subc > normal $\mu\,\sigma$.

where the column of x values is in c1 and the resultant $\varphi(x;\, \mu,\, \sigma)$ values are output in c2. You can also access the **pdf** function from the **Calc> Probability Distributions> Normal** menu by selecting the **Probability density** button. After both columns have been created, plot φ versus x using the **plot** command with the **connect** option or use the **Graph> Scatterplot> With Connect Line** menu and in **Data View> Data Display**, turn **Connect** on and **Symbols** off.

Example 2.16

Use MINITAB to plot the normal curve that has $\mu = 400$ and $\sigma = 20$. Add vertical reference lines to the plot at $x = 370$ and $x = 410$ and find the probability that x falls in this interval. Add this information to the plot.

```
MTB > CDF 370;
SUBC>   Normal 400 20.
```

Cumulative Distribution Function

Normal with mean = 400.000 and standard deviation = 20.0000

```
        x    P( X <= x )
 370.0000        0.0668
```

```
MTB > CDF 410;
SUBC>   Normal 400 20.
```

Cumulative Distribution Function

Normal with mean = 400.000 and standard deviation = 20.0000

```
        x    P( X <= x )
 410.0000        0.6915
```

Figure 2.7   Example normal probability calculations with MINITAB.

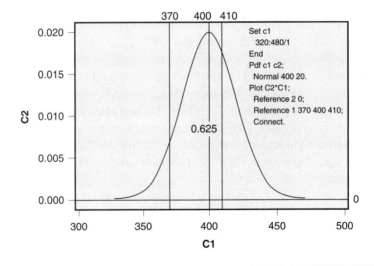

Figure 2.8 $\Phi(370 < x < 410; 400, 20) = 0.625$.

Solution: The normal probability calculations are shown in Figure 2.7. The required normal probability is given by $\Phi(370 < x < 410; 400, 20) = 0.6915 - 0.0668 = 0.6247$. Figure 2.8 shows the MINITAB commands to create the graph and the corresponding graphical output. The graph was constructed using the **Calc> Make Patterned Data> Simple Set of Numbers, Calc> Probability Distributions> Normal**, and **Graph> Scatterplot** menus but these commands could have also been typed directly at the command prompt.

3

Inferential Statistics

3.1 INTRODUCTION

We collect data to learn about processes. The characteristics of a process that we typically want to know are its parameters, μ and σ, and possibly the shape of its distribution. But the task of determining the parameters of a population is at least impractical if not impossible and certainly not economical. As a compromise, we calculate statistics from sample data and use them to estimate the parameters of the population. The statements about parameters that we construct from statistics are called inferences. In this chapter we will consider two methods of statistical inference: hypothesis tests and confidence intervals. These methods are the workhorses for the analysis of designed experiments.

If a sample is drawn that is representative of its population, then a statistic calculated from the sample should be a reasonable approximation to the corresponding population parameter. For example, we expect that $\bar{x}$ is a reasonable estimate for μ. A statistic, a single number, calculated from a sample is called a *point estimate.* In the absence of more or better data, a point estimate is the best available estimate for a parameter, but under reasonably common conditions it is possible to supplement the point estimate with a statement about the uncertainty of the estimate. Such statements take the form, "We are highly confident that the unknown parameter falls within a certain range of values based on the statistic calculated from sample data." These statements are called confidence intervals.

Another type of inference, the hypothesis test, is used to determine which of two complementary statements about a parameter is supported by sample data. If appropriate and sufficient data are collected from a population, then a statistical estimate of its parameter will be consistent with one or the other of the two statements. We conclude a hypothesis test with a statement like, "The sample data support the hypothesis that the parameter is equal to such and such a value."

3.2 THE DISTRIBUTION OF SAMPLE MEANS (R KNOWN)

In order to use the sample mean to make inferences about the unknown population mean, we need to understand how $\bar{x}$ and μ are related. Consider the following *gedanken experiment*.* Suppose that a random sample of size n is drawn from a population with mean μ_x and standard deviation σ_x. (Since a measurement is indicated by the symbol x, then the subscript x on μ and σ indicates that we're talking about the mean and standard deviation of the population of measurements. This notation helps avoid ambiguity and prevents confusion later on.) Since about half of the measurements from the sample should be greater than μ_x and the remaining half should be less than μ_x we expect that the sample mean $\bar{x}$ should fall pretty close to the population mean μ_x. If we repeat the experiment, we'll get a different sample mean, but it should still be pretty close to μ_x. Now imagine (the gedanken part) repeating this process many times. That is, suppose that we draw many random samples from the same population, each of size n, and calculate the mean of each sample. If these many sample means are used to create a histogram, we will obtain a picture of the distribution of sample means that has its own mean $\mu_{\bar{x}}$, its own standard deviation $\sigma_{\bar{x}}$, and its own shape.

Figure 3.1 shows the results of a computer simulation of such a gedanken experiment. The upper histogram was created from 1000 random observations taken from a normal distribution with $\mu_x = 100$ and $\sigma_x = 10$. The lower histogram was created from the means of 1000 random samples of size $n = 16$ taken from the same population. In order to use sample means to make inferences about population means we must understand how these two distributions are related to each other.

The distribution of sample means behaves differently under different conditions, but in many cases it is described by the *central limit theorem:*

Theorem 3.1 *(The Central Limit Theorem) The distribution of sample means is normal in shape with mean $\mu_{\bar{x}} = \mu_x$ and standard deviation*

$$\sigma_{\bar{x}} = \sigma_x / \sqrt{n}$$

if either 1) the distribution of the population is normal, or 2) the sample size is large.

The central limit theorem specifies the location, variation, and shape of the distribution of sample means. (It also makes clear the need for the different subscripts.) The central limit theorem relates the variation of the population (σ_x) to the variation of the distribution of the sample means ($\sigma_{\bar{x}}$). Furthermore, it specifies that the distribution of $\bar{x}$s is contracted relative to the distribution of the xs by a factor of $\sqrt{n}$.

---

* Gedanken is the German word for *thought*. Gedanken experiments are impractical to perform but provide an important and useful way of thinking about a problem. What were once gedanken experiments in statistics are now easily performed using computer simulations but we still refer to them as gedanken experiments.

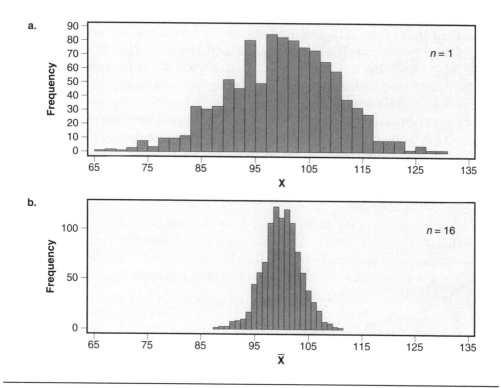

Figure 3.1 Distribution of a population (a) and sample means (b).

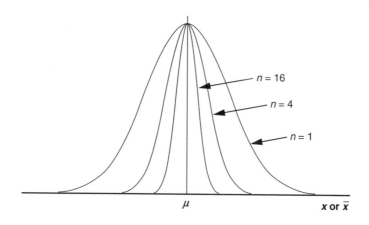

Figure 3.2 Effect of sample size on distribution of sample means.

For large sample sizes the contraction factor will be substantial and the distribution of sample means will be very tight. For smaller sample sizes the distribution of sample means will be broader, but always narrower than the distribution of the *x*s. The effect of different sample sizes on the distribution of sample means is shown in Figure 3.2.

There are two conditions under which the use of the central limit theorem is justified. There are many practical problems that meet one or both of these conditions so the central limit theorem is widely used. Under the first condition, the population being sampled must be normally distributed and the population standard deviation must be known. If this condition is the one invoked to justify the use of the central limit theorem, the population distribution should be tested for normality using the normal probability plotting method described in Section 3.11.

The second condition that justifies the use of the central limit theorem is when the sample size is large, say greater than about $n = 30$. This case doesn't require the normality of the population, although normality helps make conclusions drawn from the central limit theorem more valid. It seems strange that the distribution of the xs could be pathological and that the distribution of the $\bar{x}$s will still be normal, but that's one of the powers of the central limit theorem.

One of the applications of the central limit theorem is to construct an interval that contains a specified fraction of the sample means drawn from a population. The population mean and standard deviation, μ and σ_x, must be known in order to do this. (Since $\mu = \mu_x = \mu_{\bar{x}}$ we can safely drop the unnecessary subscripts from μ.) The interval can be expressed as:

$$\Phi(\mu - z_{\alpha/2}\sigma_{\bar{x}} < \bar{x} < \mu + z_{\alpha/2}\sigma_{\bar{x}}; \mu, \sigma_{\bar{x}}) = 1 - \alpha \tag{3.1}$$

where Φ is the cumulative normal distribution and $z_{\alpha/2}$ is the z value with tail area of $\alpha/2$ under one tail of the normal distribution. The interval is shown in Figure 3.3. Note the use of the dual axes in the figure. One axis shows the scaling of the distribution in $\bar{x}$ units and the other in standard z units according to the standardizing transformation:

$$z = \frac{\bar{x} - \mu}{\sigma_{\bar{x}}} \tag{3.2}$$

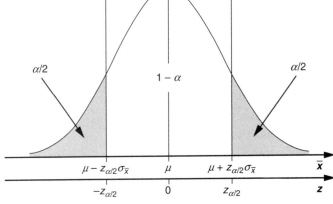

Figure 3.3   Interval containing $(1 - \alpha)$ 100% of the sample means.

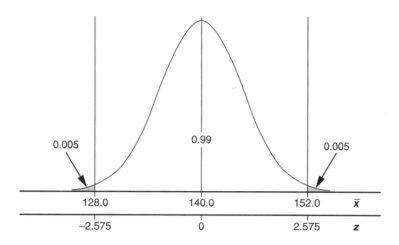

Figure 3.4 Interval containing 99 percent of the sample means.

Note that the area in each of the tails, outside the interval determined by Equation 3.1, is $\alpha/2$ which leaves the area $1 - \alpha$ inside the interval.

Example 3.1

Construct an interval that contains 99 percent of the sample means for samples of size n = 15 drawn from a normal population with $\mu = 140$ and $\sigma = 18$.

Solution: *The population is normally distributed and σ_x is known, so use of the central limit theorem is justified. The interval of interest is given by Equation 3.1. Since $1 - \alpha = 0.99$ we have $\alpha = 0.01$. A table of normal probabilities gives $z_{\alpha/2} = z_{0.005} = 2.575$. The required interval is:*

$$\Phi(140 - 2.575(\frac{18}{\sqrt{15}}) < \bar{x} < 140 + 2.575(\frac{18}{\sqrt{15}}); \mu = 140, \sigma_{\bar{x}} = \frac{18}{\sqrt{15}}) = 1 - 0.01$$

$$\Phi(128.0 < \bar{x} < 152.0; 140, 4.65) = 0.99$$

The distribution of $\bar{x}$s and the interval are shown in Figure 3.4.

3.3 CONFIDENCE INTERVAL FOR THE POPULATION MEAN (σ KNOWN)

The interval given by Equation 3.1 is useful when the population mean is known. Equation 3.1 actually contains two inequalities which provide constraints on $\bar{x}$. These inequalities are $\mu - z_{\alpha/2}\sigma_{\bar{x}} < \bar{x}$ and $\bar{x} < \mu + z_{\alpha/2}\sigma_{\bar{x}}$, which can be solved for μ and used to construct a new interval:

$$\Phi(\overline{x} - z_{\alpha/2}\sigma_{\overline{x}} < \mu < \overline{x} + z_{\alpha/2}\sigma_{\overline{x}}) = 1 - \alpha \qquad (3.3)$$

Note that this interval is centered on the sample mean, which can be determined from sample data, and provides upper and lower bounds for the true but possibly unknown population mean. By design, the range indicated by these bounds has probability $1 - \alpha$ of containing the true mean of the population so $(1 - \alpha)$ 100% of the intervals constructed from sample means using Equation 3.3 should contain the true population mean. Consequently, the interval given by Equation 3.3 is called a $(1 - \alpha)$ 100% confidence interval for μ.

Example 3.2

Construct a 95 percent confidence interval for the true population mean when a sample of size n = 8 yields $\overline{x}$ = 58.4. The population is normally distributed and its standard deviation is known to be σ = 6.8.

Solution: Since the population is normally distributed, the central limit theorem is justified. The interval required is given by Equation 3.3 with $1 - \alpha$ = 0.95 so α = 0.05. From a table of normal probabilities $z_{\alpha/2} = z_{0.025}$ = 1.96 so:

$$\Phi(58.4 - 1.96(\tfrac{6.8}{\sqrt{8}}) < \mu < 58.4 + 1.96(\tfrac{6.8}{\sqrt{8}})) = 1 - 0.05$$

$$\Phi(53.7 < \mu < 63.1) = 0.95$$

Hence, there is a 95 percent probability that the population mean lies between 53.7 and 63.1.

3.4 HYPOTHESIS TEST FOR ONE SAMPLE MEAN (σ KNOWN)

3.4.1 Hypothesis Test Rationale

A very important statistical inference technique called a hypothesis test can be performed using the description of the distribution of sample means provided by the central limit theorem. This particular hypothesis test is critical to the development of DOE methods and has all of the same basic elements as other hypothesis tests, so study it carefully.

Suppose we wish to determine if the unknown mean of a population has a certain value or if it differs from this value. These statements are written:

$$H_0 : \mu = \mu_0$$
$$H_A : \mu \neq \mu_0$$

where μ is the true but unknown mean of the population, μ_0 is the value we think μ might have, and H_0 and H_A are complementary statements about the relationship between μ

and μ_0. H_0 and H_A are called the *null* and *alternative* hypotheses, respectively. The problem is to select one of these hypotheses over the other—that is, to accept one hypothesis and reject the other. This is done using sample data taken from the population to determine which of the two hypotheses the data support.

To avoid the wrath of real statisticians, it's necessary to point out that when we do hypothesis testing, H_0 is not so important and the condition that we're really interested in is described by H_A. That is, the goal of any hypothesis test is really to accept or not accept H_A, and we never really should accept H_0. The reason has to do with the motivation for testing and how we structure the hypotheses to be tested. H_0 is supposed to represent the status quo—a condition that everyone knows about and that we can't personally benefit from. In contrast, H_A is supposed to represent an unexpected result—the new product that our managers have been frantic for, the invention that will make us all rich, or the brilliant new observation that will win us a Nobel Prize. Clearly, hypothesis tests are all about H_A, so our decisions really should be limited to accepting or not accepting H_A.

Carl Sagan (1996) brilliantly summarized the correct strategy used to formulate and test hypotheses. He suggested that hypotheses should be constructed this way: H_0: *something ordinary happens* versus H_A: *something extraordinary happens,* and that our decision of which hypothesis to accept based on experimental data should be based on the rule, "Extraordinary claims require extraordinary evidence." It's correct to note that while Sagan provides a clear criterion for accepting or rejecting H_A, he provides no opportunity to accept H_0.

These observations imply that there are four acceptable forms for stating the conclusions of a hypothesis test:

- On the basis of the sample data we can reject H_0.

- On the basis of the sample data we can accept H_A.

- On the basis of the sample data we cannot reject H_0.

- On the basis of the sample data we cannot accept H_A.

Although the third and fourth cases seem to imply that since the data don't support H_A we should accept H_0, accepting H_0 is not a valid option and we often say instead that the test is inconclusive, that the result is not statistically significant, or that we reserve judgment.

Throughout this book we will make decisions using the hypothesis testing method and try to always use the correct language to state conclusions; however, it's frustrating to have to replace the relatively simple statement, "We accept H_0," with one of the more confusing but technically correct alternatives like, "We can't reject H_0 so we reserve judgment."

Example 3.3

A drug company wishes to compare a new drug under development with a drug that is already established in the marketplace. What hypotheses should they use to compare the two drugs?

Solution: The hypotheses that the drug company should use to guide their tests depend on the purpose of the new drug. If the new drug is supposed to be better than the old one, then appropriate hypotheses would be H_0: the two drugs are equivalent versus H_A: the new drug is better than the old one. If, however, the purpose of the new drug is to serve as a substitute or direct replacement for the old drug, that is, if the two drugs are supposed to be equivalent, then the hypotheses to be tested are H_0: the new drug is different from the old one versus H_A: the new drug is equivalent to the old one. The latter case is appropriately called an equivalence test. In both cases, in order for the new drug to serve its purpose, the drug company hopes that its testing provides evidence that they can reject H_0 and accept H_A or else they don't have a product.

3.4.2 Decision Limits Based on Measurement Units

Suppose that a representative sample of size n is drawn from a population being studied. We require an appropriate statistic that can be calculated from these data and used to make a decision about which hypothesis to accept. The obvious (but not only) choice of statistic is the sample mean $\bar{x}$. If $\bar{x}$ falls close to μ_0 then we will accept H_0 or reserve judgment. If $\bar{x}$ falls far enough away from μ_0 we will reject H_0 and accept H_A. When the conditions for the central limit theorem are satisfied, the range of $\bar{x}$ values for which we accept H_0 is given by the interval in Equation 3.1 with $\mu = \mu_0$:

$$\Phi(\mu_0 - z_{\alpha/2}\sigma_{\bar{x}} < \bar{x} < \mu_0 + z_{\alpha/2}\sigma_{\bar{x}}; \mu_0, \sigma_{\bar{x}}) = 1 - \alpha \qquad (3.4)$$

If $\bar{x}$ falls outside this interval we reject H_0 and say that the result is *statistically significant*.

Example 3.4

We are interested in determining if the mean of a population is different from $\mu = 80.0$. The population is normally distributed with $\sigma = 6.2$. A sample of size $n = 8$ is drawn and found to have a sample mean of $\bar{x} = 78.2$. Is there evidence to indicate that the population mean is different from $\mu = 80.0$? Work with $\alpha = 0.01$ and make a graph representing the solution.

Solution: The hypotheses being tested are:

$$H_0 : \mu = 80.0$$
$$H_A : \mu \neq 80.0$$

The acceptance region for the null hypothesis is given by Equation 3.4 with $z_{0.005} = 2.575$:

$$\Phi(80.0 - 2.575(\tfrac{6.2}{\sqrt{8}}) < \bar{x} < 80.0 + 2.575(\tfrac{6.2}{\sqrt{8}}); \mu = 80.0, \sigma_{\bar{x}} = \tfrac{6.2}{\sqrt{8}}) = 1 - 0.01$$

$$\Phi(74.4 < \bar{x} < 85.6; 80.0, 2.19) = 0.99$$

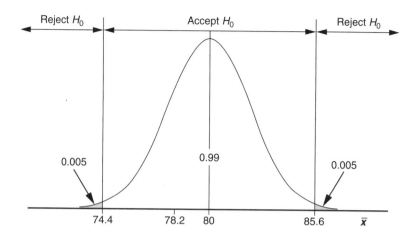

Figure 3.5 Hypothesis test using $\bar{x}$ units.

Since the sample mean $\bar{x} = 78.2$ easily falls inside this interval, we must accept the null hypothesis H_0: $\mu = 80.0$ or reserve judgment. The graph representing the solution is shown in Figure 3.5.

3.4.3 Decision Limits Based on Standard (z) Units

Instead of calculating the acceptance interval for H_0: $\mu = \mu_0$ in $\bar{x}$ units, a shortcut can be taken. This involves selecting α and finding the corresponding acceptance interval in z units. The acceptance interval, given by Equation 3.4 and expressed in standard units, is:

$$\Phi(-z_{\alpha/2} < z < z_{\alpha/2}) = 1 - \alpha \qquad (3.5)$$

The hypothesis test is performed by transforming the sample mean into standard units using Equation 3.2 and comparing this z value to the $\pm z_{\alpha/2}$ values that define the acceptance interval. If this z value falls inside the interval of Equation 3.5, we accept H_0 or reserve judgment, otherwise we reject H_0 and accept H_A.

Example 3.5

Reconsider Example 3.4 but make your decision on the basis of the transformed sample mean. Graph the situation showing both $\bar{x}$ and z axes.

Solution: *The transformed sample mean is:*

$$z = \frac{\bar{x} - \mu_0}{\sigma_{\bar{x}}} = \frac{78.2 - 80.0}{(6.2 / \sqrt{8})} = -0.82$$

The accept region for H_0 with $\alpha = 0.01$ is:

$$\Phi(-2.575 < z < 2.575) = 0.99$$

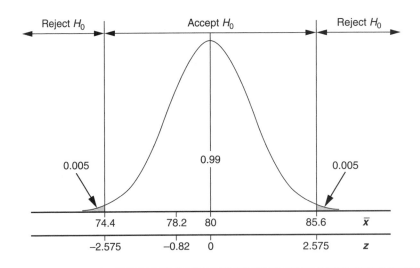

Figure 3.6   Hypothesis test using standard (z) units.

We see that z falls in the acceptance region so we must accept H_0: $\mu = 80.0$ or reserve judgment. The situation is graphed in Figure 3.6.

3.4.4 Decision Limits Based on the *p* Value

In the preceding section, the use of the z value to make a hypothesis test decision was described. The z statistic was calculated from the sample mean and then compared to critical z values indicated by $\pm z_{\alpha/2}$. Then, the decision to accept or reject the null hypothesis test was based on where the z statistic fell with respect to the acceptance interval. Although this method of making a decision is correct, it requires that we keep a table of critical $z_{\alpha/2}$ values handy. As we consider more hypothesis tests for different conditions and statistics, there will be many new probability distributions that will have their own tables of critical values. Instead of dealing with so many tables of critical values, there is a simple, concise, and universal way of making hypothesis test decisions that is very important to DOE. This method involves the calculation of a quantity called the *p value*.

The *p* value for a hypothesis test is calculated from the experimental test statistic under the assumption that the null hypothesis is true. The *p* value is related to the tail area under the distribution that characterizes the test statistic relative to the specific value of the test statistic obtained from the sample data. *p* values are compared directly to α so, to be fair, when α is split between two tails of the $\bar{x}$ distribution, the *p* value also gets contributions from both tails. Since the normal distribution that characterizes the distribution of $\bar{x}$s is symmetric, the *p* value is just twice the normal distribution tail area relative to the experimental test statistic $\bar{x}$ or its corresponding z value. That is:

$$1 - p = \Phi\left(-z_{p/2} < z < +z_{p/2}\right) \tag{3.6}$$

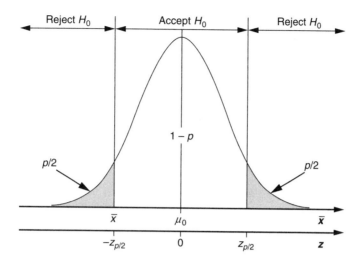

Figure 3.7 Definition of the p value.

where

$$z_{p/2} = \frac{\bar{x} - \mu_0}{\sigma_{\bar{x}}} \tag{3.7}$$

Figure 3.7 shows the relationship between $\bar{x}$, its corresponding z value, and the p value.

Once the p value is known, the decision to accept or reject the null hypothesis is made using the following rules:

- If $p < \alpha$ then reject H_0.

- If $p > \alpha$ then accept H_0 or reserve judgment.

Instead of memorizing these rules, just remember that when the p value is very small, the test statistic $\bar{x}$ must fall far away from μ_0 so we should reject H_0: $\mu = \mu_0$, and when the p value is very large, the test statistic must fall close to μ_0 so we should accept H_0 or reserve judgment.

A helpful way to think about the p value is to recognize that it measures how unusual the experimental test statistic is given that H_0 was true. The p value's size corresponds to the probability of obtaining the observed test statistic, or something even more unusual, if H_0 was true. This means that when p is very small, the observed statistic would be a rare event if H_0 was true, so H_0 is more likely to be false. And when p is large, a value like the observed statistic is an expected result if H_0 was true, so we should accept H_0 or reserve judgment.

Example 3.6

Perform the hypothesis test for Example 3.4 using the p value method.

Solution: From Example 3.5 we have $z_{p/2} = -0.82$ *so the p value is determined from:*

$$1 - p = \Phi(-0.82 < z < +0.82) = 0.59$$

and $p = 1 - 0.59 = 0.41$. *The p value is the shaded area under the curve shown in Figure 3.8. Since we are working with* $\alpha = 0.01$ *we have* $(p = 0.41) > (\alpha = 0.01)$ *so we must accept* H_0 *or reserve judgment.*

Initially, p values may seem abstract; however, their use is very common, so it is essential to become completely comfortable with their use and interpretation. The reasons that they are so important are:

- The p value provides a clear and concise summary of the significance of the experimental data. There is no need to specify the conditions of the test, the type of data collected, or the statistic used in the test.

- The p value is perfectly general and can be applied to hypothesis tests of every type. Even if you don't recognize the hypothesis test being used, its p value behaves like every other p value.

- In many technical journals, experimental p values are considered to be important enough to be included prominently in abstracts. A common question after describing an experiment to a knowledgeable experimenter is, "What is the p value?"

- In DOE, especially in computer analyses of DOE problems, the p value is commonly provided for a number of relevant statistics.

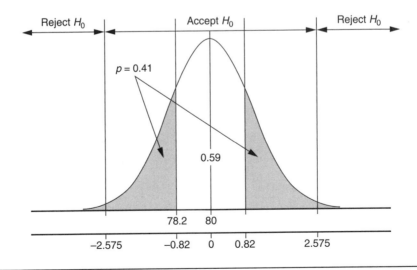

Figure 3.8 Hypothesis test using p value.

There is a trap associated with the use of p values that you must be careful to avoid. Since the decision to accept or reject the null hypothesis is made by comparing the experimental p value to α, it is essential that the value of α be chosen before the data are collected, and based on economic or business requirements. Otherwise, if you pick α after the data are collected and analyzed, you might be tempted to influence the decision to accept or reject H_0 with your choice of α.* This practice is unethical but quite common and gives statisticians and statistical methods a bad reputation.

Example 3.7

A sample drawn from a population yields a mean that gives $p = 0.014$ under the null hypothesis. What decision is made if $\alpha = 0.05$? If $\alpha = 0.01$?

Solution: For $\alpha = 0.05$ we have $(p = 0.014) < (\alpha = 0.05)$ so we must reject H_0. For $\alpha = 0.01$ we have $(p = 0.014) > (\alpha = 0.01)$ so we must accept H_0 or reserve judgment.

3.4.5 Type 1 and Type 2 Errors

Hypothesis tests are fallible. We never know, until it's too late, when an incorrect hypothesis testing decision is made, but the probability of making incorrect decisions can be controlled. Study for a moment the distribution of sample means and the accept and reject regions for H_0 in Figure 3.3. Note that the distribution of $\bar{x}$s is infinite in width and that the acceptance interval for H_0 has a finite width. This means that there is always a small probability of drawing a sample whose mean falls in the reject region even when the null hypothesis is true. *Rejecting the null hypothesis when it is true is called a Type 1 error.* The probability of committing a Type 1 error is given by α, as in Equation 3.4, and the area under the normal curve corresponding to α is shown in Figure 3.6. A convenient way to think about Type 1 errors is as false alarms where the alarm indicates that you should reject H_0 in favor of H_A.

Now consider the situation shown in Figure 3.9 where the mean of the population μ has shifted to a value larger than the hypothesized mean μ_0. In this case, H_0 is false, since $\mu \neq \mu_0$, but there is a significant probability of accepting H_0, that is, of drawing a sample with a mean that falls in the acceptance interval for H_0. *Accepting the null hypothesis when it is false is called a Type 2 error.* The probability of committing a Type 2 error, β, is given by the area under the distribution of sample means inside the acceptance region for H_0:

$$\beta = \Phi(\mu_0 - z_{\alpha/2}\sigma_{\bar{x}} < \bar{x} < \mu_0 + z_{\alpha/2}\sigma_{\bar{x}}; \mu, \sigma_{\bar{x}}) \qquad (3.8)$$

where $\mu \neq \mu_0$. A convenient way to think about Type 2 errors is as missed alarms.

---

* By choosing α after collecting the data in order to influence the result of a test, you will go to statistics hell. Statistics hell is crowded and we will probably see each other there.

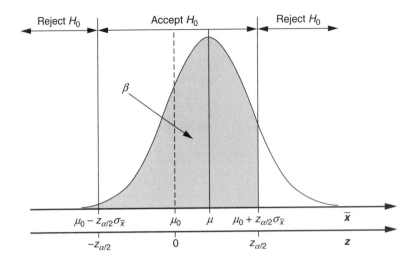

Figure 3.9   Type 2 error situation.

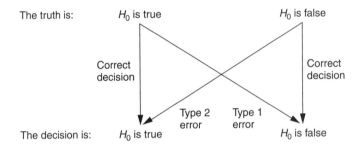

Figure 3.10   Decisions in hypothesis tests.

Figure 3.10 summarizes the decisions and errors that can occur when performing hypothesis tests.

Example 3.8

The hypotheses H_0: $\mu = 0.600$ versus H_A: $\mu \neq 0.600$ are to be tested on the basis of a random sample of size $n = 16$ taken from a normal population with $\sigma = 0.020$ at a significance level of $\alpha = 0.05$. Find the probability of committing a Type 2 error if the true population mean is $\mu = 0.608$.

Solution: The acceptance limits for H_0 are given by:

$$\Phi(\mu_0 - z_{\alpha/2}\sigma_{\bar{x}} < \bar{x} < \mu_0 + z_{\alpha/2}\sigma_{\bar{x}}) = 1 - \alpha$$

$$\Phi\left(0.600 - 1.96\left(\tfrac{0.020}{\sqrt{16}}\right) < \bar{x} < 0.600 + 1.96\left(\tfrac{0.020}{\sqrt{16}}\right)\right) = 1 - 0.05$$

$$\Phi\left(0.590 < \bar{x} < 0.610\right) = 0.95$$

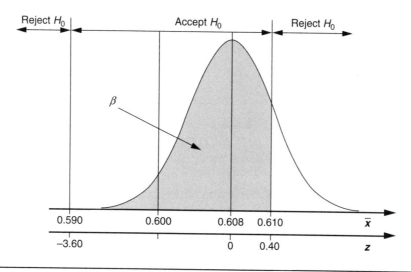

Figure 3.11 Type 2 error situation.

According to Equation 3.8, the Type 2 error probability is given by:

$$\beta = \Phi(\mu_0 - z_{\alpha/2}\sigma_{\bar{x}} < \bar{x} < \mu_0 + z_{\alpha/2}\sigma_{\bar{x}}; \mu, \sigma_{\bar{x}})$$
$$= \Phi(0.590 < \bar{x} < 0.610; 0.608, 0.005)$$
$$= \Phi(-3.60 < z < 0.40)$$
$$= 0.6554$$

This situation is shown in Figure 3.11.

Since the Type 2 error can occur in any case in which $\mu \neq \mu_0$, it is common to construct a plot of β as a function of μ called an operating characteristic (OC) curve. OC curves are useful for studying the size of Type 2 errors as μ deviates from μ_0. OC curves are also useful for comparing the performance of hypothesis tests using different choices of sample size and Type 1 error probability.

3.4.6 One-Tailed Hypothesis Tests

All of the confidence intervals and hypothesis tests discussed so far have been two-sided or two-tailed tests where α is split evenly between the two tails of the normal distribution. But one-sided intervals and tests also exist. In a one-sided test, all of α is committed to one side or tail of the normal distribution. Similarly, the p value for a one-tailed test only gets a contribution from one side of the distribution.

The hypotheses for one-sided tests for the mean are H_0: $\mu = \mu_0$ and H_A: $\mu < \mu_0$ or H_A: $\mu > \mu_0$. (These tests are summarized in Table 3.2 on page 74.)

Example 3.9

Repeat the hypothesis test for Example 3.4 using a one-sided test using H_A: $\mu < 80$.

*   **Solution:** The hypotheses are H_0: $\mu = 80$ versus H_A: $\mu < 80$. For $\alpha = 0.01$ we have $z_\alpha = z_{0.01} = 2.33$ so (using Table 3.2 on page 74) the acceptance interval for H_0 is given by:*

$$P(-2.33 < z < \infty) = 1 - \alpha$$

The sample mean, $\bar{x} = 78.2$, in standard units is $z = -0.82$, which falls in the acceptance interval so we must accept H_0: $\mu = 80.0$. The p value for the test is given by the area under the t distribution to the left of $\bar{x} = 78.2$ or $t = -0.82$:

$$p = \Phi(-\infty < z < -0.82) = 0.2061$$

This situation is shown in Figure 3.12.

3.5 THE DISTRIBUTION OF SAMPLE MEANS (σ UNKNOWN)

3.5.1 Student's *t* Distribution

The central limit theorem can be used to construct confidence intervals and perform hypothesis tests involving the population mean, but it is not valid when the population standard deviation is unknown and the sample size is small. As long as the population being sampled is normally distributed, then the sample standard deviation s can be

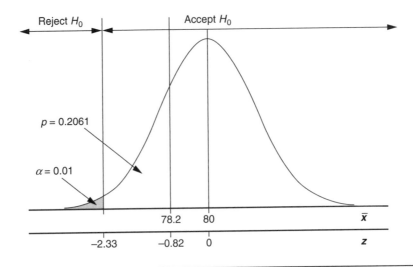

Figure 3.12   One-sided hypothesis test for the mean.

used to approximate σ. Under these conditions, the distribution of sample means is given by *Student's t distribution.*

Theorem 3.2 *The distribution of a random variable:*

$$t = \frac{\bar{x} - \mu}{s / \sqrt{n}} \tag{3.9}$$

where $\bar{x}$ is the mean and s is the standard deviation of a sample of size n taken from a normal population with mean μ and standard deviation σ follows a Student's t distribution with $v = n - 1$ degrees of freedom.

Values of $t_{p,v}$ where p indicates the right tail area are given in Appendix A.3.

Student's t distribution is shown in Figure 3.13. It looks a lot like the normal distribution except it's a bit broader and flatter, reflecting the additional variability introduced by using the estimator s in place of the exact but unknown value of σ. The exact shape of the t distribution depends on the number of degrees of freedom (v or df) for the calculation of s. For the situation described in this section we have

$$s = \sqrt{\sum \varepsilon^2 / (n-1)}$$

so $v = n - 1$, however, the number of degrees of freedom for the t distribution may be different for other problems. The distribution of sample means according to Student's t distribution is flat and broad for small v, gets narrower as v increases, and actually becomes normal as v approaches infinity. In practice, $v \geq 30$ is close enough to ∞ that the t distribution looks pretty much normal and we use the normal distribution anyway.

Before we can use Student's t distribution it's necessary to confirm that the distribution of the population being sampled is normal. In many types of problems, the population only needs to be approximately normal for the use of the t distribution to be justified. Certainly for small sample sizes you need to be careful about the normality of

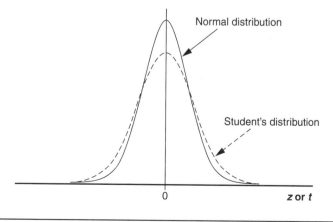

Figure 3.13 Comparison of the normal and student's t distributions.

the population, but as the sample size increases, the normality requirement becomes less strict. Don't be surprised to see some pretty strange looking distributions declared to be approximately normal so that the *t* distribution can be used.

3.5.2 A One-Sample Hypothesis Test for the Population Mean (s Unknown)

Just as the central limit theorem is used to construct an interval that describes the distribution of sample means when σ is known, Student's *t* distribution is used to construct a similar interval when σ is unknown. The interval defining the distribution of $\bar{x}$s about a known population mean μ is given by:

$$P(\mu - t_{\alpha/2,v}(s/\sqrt{n}) < \bar{x} < \mu + t_{\alpha/2,v}(s/\sqrt{n}); \mu, \sigma_{\bar{x}}) = 1 - \alpha \qquad (3.10)$$

where $v = n - 1$ is the *t* distribution degrees of freedom. This interval, with $\mu = \mu_0$, is useful for constructing hypothesis testing limits for sample means. Sample means are transformed into standardized *t* units for hypothesis tests using the transformation given by Equation 3.9 with $\mu = \mu_0$:

$$t = \frac{\bar{x} - \mu_0}{s/\sqrt{n}}, \qquad (3.11)$$

and can be tested with the acceptance interval:

$$P(-t_{\alpha/2,v} < t < t_{\alpha/2,v}) = 1 - \alpha \qquad (3.12)$$

Example 3.10
   A sample of size n = 10 drawn from a normal population with unknown standard deviation is found to have $\bar{x} = 18.8$ and s = 2.1. Test the null hypothesis H_0: $\mu = 20.0$ against the alternative hypothesis H_A: $\mu \neq 20.0$ at the $\alpha = 0.01$ level and determine the p value for the test.

   Solution: *The acceptance interval for H_0 is given by Equation 3.12 with $t_{\alpha/2,v} = t_{0.005,9} = 3.25$:*

$$P(-3.25 < t < 3.25) = 0.99$$

The standardized value of the sample mean given by Equation 3.11 is:

$$t = \frac{18.8 - 20.0}{2.1/\sqrt{10}} = -1.81$$

Since this t value falls inside the acceptance region, we must accept H_0: $\mu = 20.0$ or reserve judgment. This situation is shown in Figure 3.14. The area under the curve of the t distribution corresponding to the p value is shaded in the figure. Generally, due to

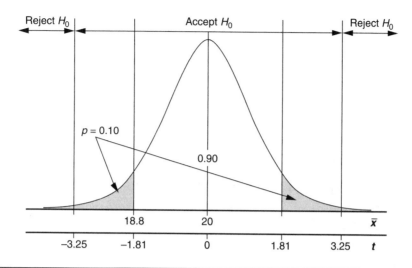

Figure 3.14 Hypothesis test for one sample mean with Student's *t* distribution.

the limitations of published t tables, it is difficult to determine exact p values but in this case we get lucky and a t table gives $t_{0.05,9} = 1.83$ so we have, for this problem, $p \simeq 0.10$. Most statistical software packages provide the exact p values for t tests.

3.5.3 A Confidence Interval for the Population Mean (σ Unknown)

Student's *t* distribution can be used to construct a confidence interval for an unknown population mean based on $\bar{x}$ and *s* determined from sample data. The interval is derived from Equation 3.10 by solving the two inequalities

$$\mu - t_{\alpha/2}(s/\sqrt{n}) < \bar{x}$$

and

$$\bar{x} < \mu + t_{\alpha/2}(s/\sqrt{n})$$

for μ. The resulting expression:

$$P(\bar{x} - t_{\alpha/2,v}(s/\sqrt{n}) < \mu < \bar{x} + t_{\alpha/2,v}(s/\sqrt{n})) = 1 - \alpha \qquad (3.13)$$

where $v = n - 1$ is the $(1 - \alpha)$ 100% confidence interval for μ based on a sample mean $\bar{x}$.

Example 3.11

Construct a 95 percent confidence interval for the true population mean based on the sample from Example 3.10.

Solution: Since $1 - \alpha = 0.95$ *we have* $\alpha = 0.05$ *and* $t_{\alpha/2,\nu} = t_{0.025,9} = 2.262$. *The confidence interval, as defined by Equation 3.13, is:*

$$P(18.8 - 2.262(2.1/\sqrt{10}) < \mu < 18.8 + 2.262(2.1/\sqrt{10})) = 1 - 0.05$$
$$P(17.3 < \mu < 20.3) = 0.95$$

Hence, the probability of μ *falling in the interval 17.3 to 20.3 is 95 percent.*

3.6 HYPOTHESIS TESTS FOR TWO MEANS

Situations that require a test of two independent continuous populations for a possible difference between their means are very common. The specific form of test used is dependent on two conditions: 1) whether the two population standard deviations are known or unknown and 2) whether the two population standard deviations are equal or unequal. This means that there are four different two-sample tests for location. All of these tests require that the two populations follow normal or at least approximately normal distributions. When the distributions are not normal they should be transformed to at least approximate normality using an appropriate mathematical transformation such as a logarithm, square root, reciprocal, square, or power transform. If a successful transformation that recovers the normality of the two distributions cannot be found, then the nonparametric Mann-Whitney test should be used.

3.6.1 Two Independent Samples (σ_1^2 and σ_2^2 Known)

Suppose that we are trying to determine if two independent populations have the same or different means while the two standard deviations, σ_1 and σ_2, are known and not necessarily equal. The appropriate hypotheses: H_0: $\mu_1 = \mu_2$ versus H_A: $\mu_1 \neq \mu_2$, can be tested using the test statistic:

$$z = \frac{\overline{x}_1 - \overline{x}_2}{\sqrt{\frac{\sigma_1^2}{n_1} + \frac{\sigma_2^2}{n_2}}} \tag{3.14}$$

The acceptance interval for the null hypothesis is given by:

$$\Phi(-z_{\alpha/2} < z < z_{\alpha/2}) = 1 - \alpha \tag{3.15}$$

3.6.2 Two Independent Samples (σ_1^2 and σ_2^2 Unknown But Equal)

It's common to encounter hypothesis tests for two sample means in which σ_1 and σ_2 are unknown but probably equal. When two populations have equal standard deviations, we say that they are *homoscedastic* which literally means *constant variation* from the Latin. If the sample sizes n_1 and n_2 are both large enough to satisfy the central limit theorem, then the z test described above will still work with $\sigma_1 \simeq s_1$ and $\sigma_2 \simeq s_2$. But if one or both of the sample sizes are too small to satisfy the central limit theorem, then a two-sample t test must be used instead of the z test. The two-sample t test requires that the two samples come from independent, normal, and homoscedastic populations. The two-sample t test statistic is:

$$t = \frac{\bar{x}_1 - \bar{x}_2}{s_\varepsilon \sqrt{\frac{1}{n_1} + \frac{1}{n_2}}} \tag{3.16}$$

where

$$s_\varepsilon = \sqrt{\frac{\sum_{i=1}^{n_1} \varepsilon_{1i}^2 + \sum_{j=1}^{n_2} \varepsilon_{2j}^2}{(n_1 - 1) + (n_2 - 1)}} = \sqrt{\frac{(n_1 - 1)s_1^2 + (n_2 - 1)s_2^2}{n_1 + n_2 - 2}} \tag{3.17}$$

is an estimate for the common population standard deviation for the two samples. s_ε is often called the pooled standard deviation or the standard error. The term

$$\sqrt{\frac{1}{n_1} + \frac{1}{n_2}}$$

in the denominator of the test statistic is just the old central limit theorem contraction factor determined for two pooled but independent samples. The acceptance interval for H_0 is given by:

$$P(-t_{\alpha/2, v} < t < t_{\alpha/2, v}) = 1 - \alpha \tag{3.18}$$

where the Student's t distribution has $v = n_1 + n_2 - 2$ degrees of freedom. The two lost degrees of freedom are consumed by calculation of $\bar{x}_1$ and $\bar{x}_2$.

Example 3.12

Samples are drawn from two processes that are supposed to be making parts of the same size. The samples yield the following statistics: $n_1 = 8$, $\bar{x}_1 = 220$, $s_1^2 = 190$, and $n_2 = 13$, $\bar{x}_2 = 195$, $s_2^2 = 420$. Are the means of the two processes the same or is there evidence that they are different?

Solution: The hypotheses to be tested are H_0: $\mu_1 = \mu_2$ versus H_A: $\mu_1 \neq \mu_2$. Since the population variances are unknown, the two-sample t test is appropriate, however, to proceed it's necessary to assume that the two populations are normally distributed and have equal variances. These assumptions should be checked with the methods from Sections 3.8 and 3.11. The pooled standard deviation determined from the two samples is:

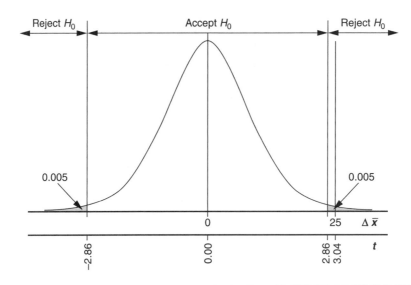

Figure 3.15   Hypothesis test to compare two population means.

$$S_\varepsilon = \sqrt{\frac{(8-1)190+(13-1)420}{8+13-2}}$$
$$= 18.0$$

The test statistic is:

$$t = \frac{220-195}{18.0\sqrt{\frac{1}{8}+\frac{1}{13}}} = 3.04$$

With $\alpha = 0.01$, the acceptance interval for H_0 with $v = 8 + 13 - 2 = 19$ degrees of freedom is:

$$P(-2.861 < t < 2.861) = 0.99$$

Since the test statistic, $t = 3.04$, falls outside the acceptance interval we must reject H_0 and accept H_A: $\mu_1 \neq \mu_2$. The distribution of the t test statistic and the acceptance interval are shown in Figure 3.15.

3.6.3 Two Independent Samples (σ_1^2 and σ_2^2 Unknown and Unequal)

If the two populations being tested for a possible difference between their means are normally distributed but their standard deviations are unknown and probably unequal, then the hypothesis test for H_0: $\mu_1 = \mu_2$ versus H_A: $\mu_1 \neq \mu_2$ must be performed using a modified form of the original two-sample t test. Two such methods are available. The first method, called Hsu's method, uses the t statistic:

$$t = \frac{\bar{x}_1 - \bar{x}_2}{\sqrt{\frac{s_1^2}{n_1} + \frac{s_2^2}{n_2}}} \tag{3.19}$$

where the acceptance interval for H_0 is given by:

$$P\left(-t_{\alpha/2,v} < t < t_{\alpha/2,v}\right) = 1 - \alpha \tag{3.20}$$

and v is the smaller of the two values $n_1 - 1$ and $n_2 - 1$ or $v = \min(n_1 - 1, n_2 - 1)$. The second method, called the Satterthwaite or Welch method, uses the same t statistic and acceptance interval as Hsu's method but the degrees of freedom for the t distribution are given by:

$$v = \frac{\left(\frac{s_1^2}{n_1} + \frac{s_2^2}{n_2}\right)^2}{\frac{1}{n_1-1}\left(\frac{s_1^2}{n_1}\right)^2 + \frac{1}{n_2-1}\left(\frac{s_2^2}{n_2}\right)^2} \tag{3.21}$$

This expression usually gives a fractional value for v that requires interpolation of the t tables, which is only practically implemented using software. The value of Satterthwaite's v is bounded by the degrees of freedom for Hsu's method and the degrees of freedom from the two-sample t test, assuming homoscedastic variances:

$$\min\left(n_1 - 1, n_2 - 1\right) < v < n_1 + n_2 - 2 \tag{3.22}$$

Because Hsu's method uses an integer value of v that can be found in any t table it is the easier of the two methods to use but it tends to be more conservative. The Satterthwaite method is more accurate but computationally difficult. The Satterthwaite method is the preferred method of analysis when it is available.

3.6.4 Paired Samples

When two different methods are used to measure the same experimental units for the purpose of testing for a bias between them, the appropriate analysis is the paired-sample t test. The hypotheses tested are H_0: $\Delta\mu = 0$ versus H_A: $\Delta\mu \neq 0$ where $\Delta\mu$ is the true but unknown difference between the measurement methods. In this test, differences between the units being measured are not important but differences between pairs of measurements made on the same units are.

The experimental data consist of two sets of observations taken on the same n units. It is essential that the identity of the measurement pairs be preserved. The paired-sample t test is performed by calculating the difference between each pair of observations:

$$\Delta x_i = x_{1i} - x_{2i} \tag{3.23}$$

where 1 and 2 indicate the measurement method and i indicates the unit being measured. The test statistic is:

$$t = \frac{\overline{\Delta x_i}}{s_{\Delta x} / \sqrt{n}} \tag{3.24}$$

where

$$\overline{\Delta x_i} = \frac{1}{n} \sum_{i=1}^{n} \Delta x_i \tag{3.25}$$

is the mean difference between the pairs of measurements and

$$s_{\Delta x} = \sqrt{\frac{1}{n-1} \sum_{i=1}^{n} \left(\Delta x_i - \overline{\Delta x_i} \right)^2} \tag{3.26}$$

is the standard deviation of the differences between the measurements. The acceptance interval for H_0 is:

$$P(-t_{\alpha/2,v} < t < t_{\alpha/2,v}) = 1 - \alpha \tag{3.27}$$

where $v = n - 1$. Close examination of these equations reveals that the paired-sample t test is equivalent to the one-sample t test of the Δx_i.

Example 3.13

Eight parts were measured by two operators for the purpose of determining if there was a bias between the operators. Each operator measured each part one time. The data are shown in the table below. Is there evidence of a difference between the operators at $\alpha = 0.05$?

i	1	2	3	4	5	6	7	8
x_{1i}	44	62	59	29	78	79	92	38
x_{2i}	46	58	56	26	72	80	90	35

Solution: *The following table shows the differences between the eight paired observations:*

i	1	2	3	4	5	6	7	8
Δx_i	-2	4	3	3	6	-1	2	3

The mean and standard deviation of the Δx_i are:

$$\overline{\Delta x_i} = \frac{1}{8}(-2+4+3+3+6-1+2+3) = 2.25$$

$$s_{\Delta x} = \sqrt{(-2-2.25)^2 + \cdots + (3-2.25)^2} = 2.60$$

The t test statistic is:

$$t = \frac{2.25}{2.60/\sqrt{8}} = 2.45$$

The p value for the test, determined from the t distribution with $v = 9$ degrees of freedom, is:

$$p = 1 - P(-2.45 < t < 2.45) = 0.037$$

Since $(p = 0.037) < (\alpha = 0.05)$ we must conclude that there is a statistically significant difference between the values reported by the two operators.

3.7 INFERENCES ABOUT ONE VARIANCE (OPTIONAL)

The confidence interval and hypothesis test for one variance based on the χ^2 (chi-square) distribution described in this section are not commonly used when considering DOE problems, but the χ^2 distribution is the basis for the F test presented in the next section. Students can skip this section without compromising their ability to analyze DOE problems.

3.7.1 The Distribution of Sample Variances

Recall the gedanken experiment that we used to develop the arguments that led to the central limit theorem. Imagine that instead of calculating the sample mean for each of our many samples drawn from the same population, we calculate the sample variances s^2 and study how they behave. The expected distribution of sample variances is shown in Figure 3.16. Just as the distribution of $\bar{x}$s requires the use of the z transform to use the central limit theorem, the distribution of the sample variances s^2 has its own transform scale given by χ^2. The following theorem describes the relationship between s^2 and χ^2 and the shape of their distribution:

Theorem 3.3 *The distribution of a random variable:*

$$\chi^2 = \frac{(n-1)s^2}{\sigma^2} \tag{3.28}$$

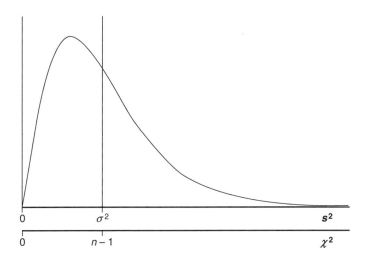

Figure 3.16   Distribution of sample variances.

is chi-square with $v = n - 1$ degrees of freedom where s^2 is the sample variance deter-
mined from a sample of size n drawn from a normal population with variance σ^2.

This theorem can be used to construct an interval that contains a specified fraction of the sample variances drawn from a normal population with variance σ^2:

$$P(\frac{\chi^2_{\alpha/2,v}\sigma^2}{n-1} < s^2 < \frac{\chi^2_{1-\alpha/2,v}\sigma^2}{n-1}) = 1-\alpha \tag{3.29}$$

where the subscripts indicate the left-tail areas under the χ^2 distribution. This interval is the basis for hypothesis tests for one sample variance and it's from this interval that the confidence interval for the population variance is derived. Values of $\chi^2_{p,v}$ where p indicates the left-tail area are given in Appendix A.4.

It can be shown that the mean of the χ^2 distribution occurs when $s^2 = \sigma^2$ or $\chi^2 = n - 1$, that is: $\mu_{\chi^2} = n - 1$. Notice how these conditions are manifested in Figure 3.16. This is a very important clue to help get the correct values of χ^2 from tables when you're trying to construct a confidence interval or perform a hypothesis test using the χ^2 distribution.

There are two important warnings that need to be made clear about using the χ^2 distribution. First, whereas the central limit theorem is fairly robust regarding deviations from normality of the population being sampled, the χ^2 distribution is *very* sensitive to the normality requirement. Small deviations from normality in the population can have large adverse effects on the behavior of the sample variances. This means that the population must be rigorously normal to use the χ^2 distribution. The normality of the population should always be checked carefully using the techniques described in Section 3.11 before attempting to make use of the χ^2 distribution to characterize sample variances.

The other important characteristic to remember about the χ^2 distribution is that it is asymmetric, and when you look up χ^2 values, either in a table or via software, you must know if the tabulated values are indexed by their left- or right-tail areas. Unfortunately, there is no standardization here and both methods are equally common. Since most people use more than one statistics book or software package, it's very likely that you will encounter tables indexed both ways. There's no way to avoid this problem— just be careful that you look up the correct values. MINITAB and the χ^2 table in this book both index the χ^2 distribution by left-tail area. Excel indexes the χ^2 distribution by right-tail area. Remember that the mean of the χ^2 distribution is $\mu_{\chi^2} = n - 1$. This can help you make sure that you get the correct value of χ^2 from the left or right tail as needed.

3.7.2 Hypothesis Test for One Sample Variance

A hypothesis test for one sample variance could be performed from Equation 3.29, but it's easier to work this kind of problem directly in the χ^2 transform space. If the hypotheses to be tested are H_0: $\sigma^2 = \sigma^2_0$ versus H_A: $\sigma^2 \neq \sigma^2_0$, then the null hypothesis is accepted if the test statistic χ^2 given by:

$$\chi^2 = \frac{(n-1)s^2}{\sigma_0^2}$$

(3.30)

falls within the interval:

$$P(\chi^2_{\alpha/2,v} < \chi^2 < \chi^2_{1-\alpha/2,v}) = 1 - \alpha$$

(3.31)

where the χ^2 distribution has $v = n - 1$ degrees of freedom. The χ^2 distribution and hypothesis test decision limits are shown in Figure 3.17.

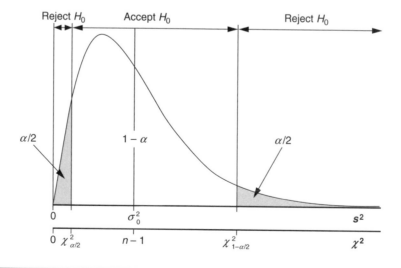

Figure 3.17 Chi-square distribution and hypothesis test decision limits.

Example 3.14

Determine if the null hypothesis H_0: $\sigma^2 = 75.0$ can be rejected if a sample of size $n = 14$ drawn from a normal population yields a sample variance of $s^2 = 97.0$. Graph the distribution and the acceptance interval for H_0. Use $\alpha = 0.01$ and H_A: $\sigma^2 \neq 75.0$.

Solution: *With $\alpha = 0.01$ and $v = 14 - 1 = 13$ we have $\chi^2_{\alpha/2,v} = \chi^2_{0.005,13} = 3.565$ and $\chi^2_{1-\alpha/2,v} = \chi^2_{0.995,13} = 29.82$ so the acceptance interval for the null hypothesis is given by Equation 3.31:*

$$P(3.565 < \chi^2 < 29.82) = 0.99$$

The test statistic is:

$$\chi^2 = \frac{(14-1)97.0}{75.0} = 16.81$$

which falls easily inside the acceptance interval so we must accept H_0: $\sigma^2 = 75$ or reserve judgment. The chi-square distribution and acceptance interval are shown in Figure 3.18.

3.73 Confidence Interval for the Population Variance

The confidence interval for the population variance is derived from Equation 3.29 by solving the two inequalities:

$$\frac{\chi^2_{\alpha/2,v}\sigma^2}{n-1} < s^2 \quad \text{and} \quad s^2 < \frac{\chi^2_{1-\alpha/2,v}\sigma^2}{n-1}$$

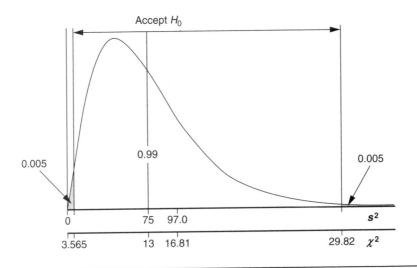

Figure 3.18   Hypothesis test for one sample variance.

for σ^2. This results in the two-sided $(1 - \alpha)$ 100% confidence interval for the unknown population variance:

$$P\left(\frac{(n-1)s^2}{\chi^2_{1-\alpha/2,v}} < \sigma^2 < \frac{(n-1)s^2}{\chi^2_{\alpha/2,v}}\right) = 1 - \alpha \tag{3.32}$$

Example 3.15

A sample of size n = 20 drawn from a normal population has a sample variance of $s^2 = 42.0$. Construct the 95 percent confidence interval for the true population variance.

Solution: We have $v = 19$ and $1 - \alpha = 0.95$ so $\alpha = 0.05$. From an appropriate table of chi-squared probabilities $\chi^2_{\alpha/2,v} = \chi^2_{0.025,19} = 8.91$ and $\chi^2_{1-\alpha/2,v} = \chi^2_{0.975,19} = 32.85$. The required confidence interval is given by Equation 3.32:

$$P\left(\tfrac{(20-1)42.0}{32.85} < \sigma^2 < \tfrac{(20-1)42.0}{8.91}\right) = 0.95$$

$$P(24.3 < \sigma^2 < 89.6) = 0.95$$

Consequently, there is a 95 percent probability that the population variance falls between 24.3 and 89.6. We can also take the square root of each term on the left-hand side to obtain the confidence interval for the population standard deviation:

$$P(4.93 < \sigma < 9.47) = 0.95$$

3.8 Hypothesis Tests for Two Sample Variances

Many of the statistical analyses of DOE problems involve the comparison of two sample standard deviations or variances. The statistic used to make such comparisons is given by the ratio of the two variances and follows a new distribution called the F distribution.

Theorem 3.4 *The distribution of the random variable:*

$$F = \frac{s_1^2}{s_2^2} \tag{3.33}$$

is the F distribution with $v_1 = n_1 - 1$ numerator and $v_2 = n_2 - 1$ denominator degrees of freedom where s_1^2 and s_2^2 are the sample variances of random samples of size n_1 and n_2 taken from two normal populations with equal variance, that is, $\sigma_1^2 = \sigma_2^2$.

Since s_1^2 and s_2^2 are estimates of the same variance σ^2 we expect $F \simeq 1$ but some variation of F above and below 1 will occur. Very large and very small values of F are rare. While the detailed shape of the F distribution depends on the sample sizes n_1 and n_2, the general shape of the F distribution is shown in Figure 3.19.

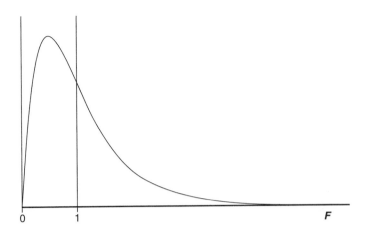

Figure 3.19 Sampling distribution of $F = (s_1/s_2)^2$.

The F distribution can be used to perform a hypothesis test for a difference between two population variances. The relevant hypotheses are $H_0: \sigma_1^2 = \sigma_2^2$ versus $H_A: \sigma_1^2 \neq \sigma_2^2$. The test is performed by constructing the ratio of sample variances as given by Equation 3.33. The distribution of this test statistic follows an F distribution with $v_1 = n_1 - 1$ and $v_2 = n_2 - 1$ degrees of freedom for the numerator and denominator, respectively. The acceptance interval for H_0 is given by:

$$P(F_{\alpha/2} < F < F_{1-\alpha/2}) = 1 - \alpha \tag{3.34}$$

where, as usual, the subscripts indicate left-tail areas and the F values are taken from an appropriate table. The F distribution and the acceptance interval are shown in Figure 3.20.

Example 3.16

Test to see if the population variances for the samples in Example 3.12 are different.

Solution: *The F statistic is:*

$$F = \frac{s_1^2}{s_2^2} = \frac{420}{190} = 2.21$$

and has $v_1 = 13 - 1 = 12$ and $v_2 = 8 - 1 = 7$ degrees of freedom. With $\alpha = 0.10$ the critical F values are $F_{\alpha/2, v_1, v_2} = F_{0.05, 12, 7} = 0.343$ and $F_{1-\alpha/2, v_1, v_2} = F_{0.95, 12, 7} = 3.57$ so the acceptance interval for H_0 is given by:

$$P(0.343 < F < 3.57) = 0.90$$

The test statistic falls inside this interval so we must accept the null hypothesis $H_0: \sigma_1^2 = \sigma_2^2$ or reserve judgment. This situation is shown in Figure 3.21.

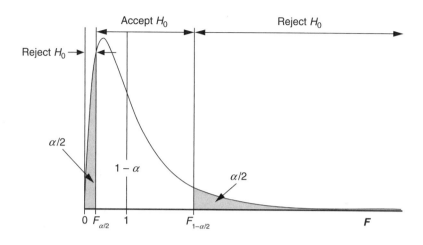

Figure 3.20   *F* distribution and hypothesis testing limits.

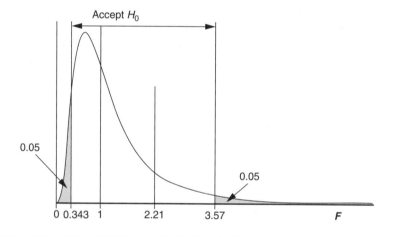

Figure 3.21   Hypothesis test for a difference between two population variances.

The *F* test performed in Example 3.16 is a two-tailed test. Two-tailed *F* tests are actually rare. In most cases, we will perform the one-tailed hypothesis test of H_0: $\sigma_1^2 = \sigma_2^2$ versus H_A: $\sigma_1^2 > \sigma_2^2$. The *F* statistic is still calculated from sample data as given by Equation 3.33, but since the choice of the subscripts is arbitrary, we almost always take s_1^2 to be the larger of the two sample variances. This means that only the values of *F* from the right tail of the *F* distribution need to be provided in tables. The acceptance interval for H_0 for the one-tailed test is:

$$P(0 < F < F_{1-\alpha}) = 1 - \alpha \tag{3.35}$$

where $1 - \alpha$ is the usual left-tail area.

Example 3.17

Repeat the F test from Example 3.16 using a one-tailed test at $\alpha = 0.05$.

Solution: The F statistic is the same as it was before: $F = 2.21$. The critical value of $F_{0.05}$ from the right tail of the F distribution is also still $F_{0.95} = 3.57$. This means that the test statistic $F = 2.21$ falls within the acceptance interval $P(0 < F < 3.57) = 0.95$ and we must conclude that $\sigma_1^2 = \sigma_2^2$ or reserve judgment.

Like the χ^2 distribution, the F distribution has two characteristics that are important to understand. First, the F distribution is very sensitive to the normality of the populations being sampled, more so than the tests for means that require normality. If the populations deviate from normality, especially if the sample sizes are small, then the F test can become unreliable. Be careful to test your data for normality using the techniques described in Section 3.11 before performing an F test.

The other important characteristic of the F distribution is that it is skewed, which means that you must be careful to pick the correct value of F from the tables. Thankfully, we usually set up our F test with the larger variance over the smaller one so that we only need critical values of F from the right tail. It's still very important to understand how your tables or software access F values. Most published tables reference F values by the right-tail area but some reference by left-tail area. The F table provided in Appendix A.5 indexes F by right-tail area, MINITAB indexes by left-tail area, and Excel indexes by right-tail area. There is no way of standardizing the tables and software so it is always your responsibility to make sure that you get the correct values.

3.9 QUICK TESTS FOR THE TWO-SAMPLE LOCATION PROBLEM

The two-sample z and t tests for location are very powerful but they are a little difficult to perform. If a computer and appropriate software are not available, they require at least a calculator, pencil, paper, and appropriate tables of critical values. There are other tests available for the two-sample location problem—tests that are very easy to perform—requiring just simple observation and maybe the ability to count to seven. Statisticians usually don't talk about these tests because they are their tricks of the trade, the magic that makes them appear so knowledgeable.

Two quick tests for the two-sample location problem will be presented here. Study these tests carefully. Despite their apparent crudeness they are very important tests to add to your bag of statistical tricks. These methods are especially easy to apply when data are displayed in graphical form so they are often the first methods used for analysis. Both tests are very easy to learn and they provide a great way to introduce the philosophy and procedures of hypothesis testing to people with limited statistical and technical skills. They also have numerous applications in the analysis of designed experiments.

3.9.1 Tukey's Quick Test

Tukey's quick test is a nonparametric test for the two-sample location problem named after John Tukey who invented it. (Nonparametric tests use test statistics that are not estimates of the parameters being tested. Nonparametric test statistics are usually calculated from counts or ranks of the data.) Tukey's quick test may be used in any situation where the two-sample *t* test is appropriate and in some situations where the assumptions for the two-sample *t* test are violated. The primary advantages of Tukey's quick test are its simplicity and the broad scope of problems that it covers. It's biggest disadvantage is its weak power, that is, its low sensitivity to small location differences, compared to the two-sample *z* and *t* tests.

The hypotheses for Tukey's quick test are $H_0: \tilde{\mu}_1 = \tilde{\mu}_2$ versus $H_A: \tilde{\mu}_1 \neq \tilde{\mu}_2$ where $\tilde{\mu}$ indicates a population median. If the populations being sampled are symmetric (such as the normal distribution) then the tests of medians become tests of means. The test is performed by drawing random samples from the two populations of interest. The samples should each be of size $n \geq 5$ and of equal or approximately equal (±20 percent) size. Combine the two data sets and order them from smallest to largest while maintaining the identity of the observations (that is, you have to keep track of which population each value was drawn from). It's easiest to perform the test if the pooled ordered data are presented graphically using separate dotplots or stem-and-leaf plots for each data set. To justify the use of Tukey's quick test, the two data sets must be slipped from each other, that is, one data set must contain the largest value and the other set must contain the smallest value. It's likely that at least some of the observations in the two data sets will overlap with each other. The test statistic *T* is the number of observations from the two non-overlapping or slipped regions in the tails of the ordered data sets. *T* will get two contributions, one from the observations that fall below the overlapping region from the sample that tends to have lower values and another from the observations that fall above the overlapping region from the sample that tends to have higher values. The decision to accept or reject H_0 is based on the size of *T*. If $T \leq 6$ we must accept H_0 or reserve judgment. Any time $T \geq 7$ we can reject H_0 and conclude that there is evidence that the medians are different at $\alpha = 0.05$. Of course the more slipped points there are, the stronger the evidence is that H_0 is false. Table 3.1 summarizes the decisions and corresponding *p* values appropriate for different ranges of *T*.

Table 3.1 Critical values of Tukey's two-sample quick test for location.

T	*p*	Decision ($\alpha = 0.05$)
$0 \leq T \leq 6$	$p > 0.05$	Accept H_0 or reserve judgment
$7 \leq T \leq 9$	$p \leq 0.05$	Reject H_0
$10 \leq T \leq 12$	$p \leq 0.01$	Reject H_0
$T \geq 13$	$p \leq 0.001$	Reject H_0

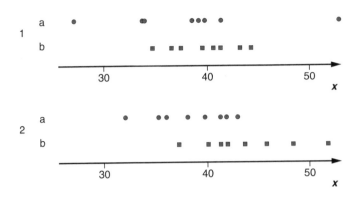

Figure 3.22   Dotplots for two examples of Tukey's quick test.

Example 3.18

Use Tukey's quick test to decide if there is evidence that the samples shown in Figure 3.22 come from populations that have different locations. There are two independent problems in the Figure, 1 and 2, and all samples are random samples from their respective populations.

Solution: In Figure 3.22, samples 1a and 1b are not slipped because 1a contains both the largest and the smallest observations. Tukey's quick test cannot be used to make a decision about a potential difference in location for this case. Samples 2a and 2b are slipped, so Tukey's quick test can be used to study these data. The test statistic is $T = 3 + 4 = 7$ which meets the critical rejection condition of $T \geq 7$ for $\alpha = 0.05$ so we can conclude that there is a difference in location between these two populations.

Example 3.19

Light bulb walls blacken over time, which decreases their light output. A design change is attempted to decrease the blackening. If the original design is A and the new design is B, samples of the two designs ordered from blackest to cleanest show:

$$\{AAAAABAAAABBBABABABBBB\}$$

Determine if the design improvement was effective.

Solution: The ordered data show that the two data sets are slipped. The five worst bulbs are As and the four best bulbs are Bs so the test statistic is $T = 9$. This means that we can reject the null hypothesis at $\alpha = 0.05$ and conclude that the new bulbs are cleaner.

Example 3.20

Manufacturer B claims to make transistors with higher gain than manufacturer A. Determine if their claim is true if the gain values measured on 10 transistors selected randomly from each manufacturer's product are:

Mfg	Gain
A	44, 41, 48, 33, 39, 51, 42, 36, 48, 47
B	51, 54, 46, 53, 56, 43, 47, 50, 56, 53

Solution: The data sets are independent and of the same size. The pooled data, ordered from smallest to largest, are:

$$\{33, 36, 39, 41, 42, \textbf{43}, 44, \textbf{46}, 47, \textbf{47}, 48, 48, \textbf{50}, 51, \textbf{51}, \textbf{53}, 53, \textbf{54}, \textbf{56}, \textbf{56}\}$$

*where the plain font indicates manufacturer A and the bold font indicates manufacturer B. The two data sets are slipped since manufacturer A has the smallest gain (33) and manufacturer B has the largest gain (**56**). The data sets are overlapped from **43** to 51 so there are five slipped points at the low end {33, 36, 39, 41, 42} and five slipped points at the high end {**53**, **53**, **54**, **56**, **56**}. The tied pair {51, **51**} determines the upper end of the overlapped region but cancel each other out so **51** does not count as a slipped point. The test statistic is $T = 5 + 5 = 10$ which means that we can reject H_0 at $\alpha = 0.01$ and conclude that the transistor gain values do not have the same location.*

3.9.2 Boxplot Slippage Tests

Although Tukey's quick test can be used for both large and small sample sizes, it's more likely that boxplots rather than dotplots will be used to present data from large data sets. There are two simple quick tests for the two-sample location problem based on box-plots, called *boxplot slippage tests*. These tests are based on a nonparametric test called the two-sample Smirnov test. Like Tukey's quick test, the boxplot slippage tests technically are tests of medians but when the populations are both symmetric they become tests of means. These tests work in a manner similar to the Tukey quick test—they are based on slippage between features of boxplots constructed from two data sets. Although the tests don't rigorously require that the populations being sampled are normal, have equal standard deviations, and have samples of equal size, they are safest and most effective if these conditions are met.

For the first boxplot slippage test, both samples should be of size $n \geq 5$ if the populations being sampled are normal, and larger if they are not. Boxplots should be constructed for the samples on the same measurement scale, preferably with the boxplots appearing side by side on the same page. If the null hypothesis $H_0: \tilde{\mu}_1 = \tilde{\mu}_2$ is true, then we would expect the two boxplots to be substantially overlapped with each other. However, if the boxes of the two boxplots are completely slipped from each other, that is, do not overlap, then there is sufficient evidence to reject H_0 and conclude that there is a difference in location between the two populations. The Type 1 error rate for the first boxplot slippage test is about $\alpha = 0.05$ when the two populations are normal and the samples are both of size $n = 5$. The Type 1 error rate drops as the sample size increases.

For the second boxplot slippage test, both samples should be of size $n \geq 30$ if the populations being sampled are normal, and larger if they are not. If the null hypothesis

H_0: $\tilde{\mu}_1 = \tilde{\mu}_2$ is true, then we would expect both medians to fall inside of the other sample's boxes. However, if one or both of the medians fall outside of the other sample's box there is sufficient evidence to reject H_0 and conclude that there is a difference in location between the two populations. The Type 1 error rate for the second boxplot slippage test is about $\alpha = 0.05$ when the two populations are normal and the samples are both of size $n = 30$. The Type 1 error rate drops as the sample size increases.

Like their nonparametric sister, the Tukey quick test, the boxplot slippage tests are not as powerful as the parametric z and t tests for location. Despite this weakness, the boxplot slippage tests are so easy to use that it becomes difficult not to use them whenever a pair of boxplots appears side by side in the same plot. The boxplot slippage tests are also very easy to apply when comparing more than two treatments; however, since comparing k treatments involves $\binom{k}{2}$ tests you must stay conscious of the inflated Type 1 error rate associated with performing so many tests.

Example 3.21

Use the boxplot slippage tests to evaluate the boxplots in Figure 3.23 if a) $n_1 = n_2 = 12$ *and b)* $n_1 = n_2 = 40$.

Solution: a) The boxplots suggest that the populations being sampled have comparable standard deviations, are probably at least symmetric if not normally distributed, and the sample sizes are large enough to justify the use of the first boxplot slippage test. The boxes are overlapped with each other so there is insufficient evidence to conclude that there is a difference in location between the two populations. A more sensitive test, like a two-sample t test, might be able to detect a difference between the population means.

b) The sample size is large enough to justify the second boxplot slippage test. The second sample's median falls outside of the first sample's box so there is sufficient evidence to conclude that there is a difference in location between the two populations.

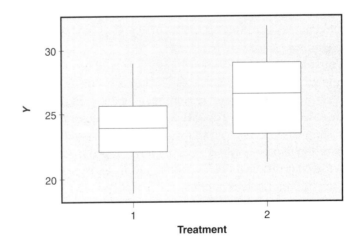

Figure 3.23 Boxplots of two samples to be tested for a difference in location.

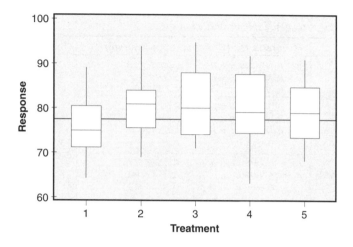

Figure 3.24 Multiple comparisons using the first boxplot slippage test.

Example 3.22

An experiment was performed to test for differences in location between five different treatments. Random samples of size n = 12 were drawn from each treatment and then boxplots were constructed for the responses. The boxplots are shown in Figure 3.24. Is there evidence of a location difference between any pair of treatments?

Solution: *All five samples were of size n = 12 so the first boxplot slippage test is appropriate. By inspection of Figure 3.24, the boxplots all appear to be reasonably symmetric and of comparable size so the assumptions required to validate the use of the first boxplot slippage test appear to be satisfied.*

A single line is drawn across the boxplots in Figure 3.24 that passes through all five boxes. This indicates that all pairs of boxes are overlapped so, at least according to the first boxplot slippage test, there is no evidence for any location differences between the treatments, however, a more sensitive test method might be able to identify a smaller difference than the boxplot slippage test is capable of detecting.

3.10 GENERAL PROCEDURE FOR HYPOTHESIS TESTING

This chapter has provided a very short review of some of the most important hypothesis tests for DOE problems. A more complete collection of hypothesis tests is presented in Table 3.2. Don't be confused or intimidated by the table. All of the hypothesis tests there involve the same basic steps so if you can perform one of them you can perform any of them. The general steps in any hypothesis test are:

1. Choose null and alternate hypotheses for a population parameter. Set up the hypotheses to put the burden of proof on the data.

Table 3.2 Hypothesis tests for means and variances.

Test	H_0 versus H_A: (H_0 Acceptance Interval)	Test Statistic
One mean σ known	$\mu = \mu_0$ versus $\mu \neq \mu_0$: $(-z_{\alpha/2} \leq z \leq z_{\alpha/2})$ $\mu = \mu_0$ versus $\mu < \mu_0$: $(-z_{\alpha} \leq z < \infty)$ $\mu = \mu_0$ versus $\mu > \mu_0$: $(-\infty < z \leq z_{\alpha})$	$z = \dfrac{\bar{x} - \mu_0}{\sigma/\sqrt{n}}$
One mean σ unknown	$\mu = \mu_0$ versus $\mu \neq \mu_0$: $(t_{\alpha/2} \leq t \leq t_{\alpha/2})$ $\mu = \mu_0$ versus $\mu < \mu_0$: $(-t_{\alpha} \leq t < \infty)$ $\mu = \mu_0$ versus $\mu > \mu_0$: $(-\infty < t \leq t_{\alpha})$	$t = \dfrac{\bar{x} - \mu_0}{s/\sqrt{n}}$ $v = n - 1$
Two means Independent samples σs known	$\mu_1 = \mu_2$ versus $\mu_1 \neq \mu_2$: $(-z_{\alpha/2} \leq z \leq z_{\alpha/2})$ $\mu_1 = \mu_2$ versus $\mu_1 < \mu_2$: $(-z_{\alpha} \leq z < \infty)$ $\mu_1 = \mu_2$ versus $\mu_1 > \mu_2$: $(-\infty < z \leq z_{\alpha})$	$z = \dfrac{\bar{x}_1 - \bar{x}_2}{\sqrt{\dfrac{\sigma_1^2}{n_1} + \dfrac{\sigma_2^2}{n_2}}}$
Two means Independent samples σs unknown but equal	$\mu_1 = \mu_2$ versus $\mu_1 \neq \mu_2$: $(-t_{\alpha/2} \leq t \leq t_{\alpha/2})$ $\mu_1 = \mu_2$ versus $\mu_1 < \mu_2$: $(-t_{\alpha} \leq t < \infty)$ $\mu_1 = \mu_2$ versus $\mu_1 > \mu_2$: $(-\infty < t \leq t_{\alpha})$	$t = \dfrac{\bar{x}_1 - \bar{x}_2}{s_{pooled}\sqrt{\dfrac{1}{n_1} + \dfrac{1}{n_2}}}$ $s_{pooled} = \sqrt{\dfrac{(n_1 - 1)s_1^2 + (n_2 - 1)s_2^2}{n_1 + n_2 - 2}}$ $v = n_1 + n_2 - 2$
Two means Independent samples σs unknown, unequal	$\mu_1 = \mu_2$ versus $\mu_1 \neq \mu_2$: $(-t_{\alpha/2} \leq t \leq t_{\alpha/2})$ $\mu_1 = \mu_2$ versus $\mu_1 < \mu_2$: $(-t_{\alpha} \leq t < \infty)$ $\mu_1 = \mu_2$ versus $\mu_1 > \mu_2$: $(-\infty < t \leq t_{\alpha})$	$t = \dfrac{\bar{x}_1 - \bar{x}_2}{\sqrt{\dfrac{s_1^2}{n_1} + \dfrac{s_2^2}{n_2}}}$ $v = \min(n_1 - 1, n_2 - 1)$ $v = \dfrac{\left(\dfrac{s_1^2}{n_1} + \dfrac{s_2^2}{n_2}\right)^2}{\dfrac{1}{n_1 - 1}\left(\dfrac{s_1^2}{n_1}\right)^2 + \dfrac{1}{n_2 - 1}\left(\dfrac{s_2^2}{n_2}\right)^2}$
One mean Paired samples σ unknown	$\Delta\mu = 0$ versus $\Delta\mu \neq 0$: $(-t_{\alpha/2} \leq t \leq t_{\alpha/2})$ $\Delta\mu = 0$ versus $\Delta\mu < 0$: $(-t_{\alpha} \leq t < \infty)$ $\Delta\mu = 0$ versus $\Delta\mu > 0$: $(-\infty < t \leq t_{\alpha})$	$\Delta x_i = x_{1i} - x_{2i}$ $t = \dfrac{\Delta\bar{x}}{s_{\Delta x}/\sqrt{n}}$ $v = n - 1$
One variance	$\sigma^2 = \sigma_0^2$ versus $\sigma^2 \neq \sigma_0^2$: $(\chi_{\alpha/2}^2 \leq \chi^2 \leq \chi_{1-\alpha/2}^2)$ $\sigma^2 = \sigma_0^2$ versus $\sigma^2 < \sigma_0^2$: $(0 < \chi^2 \leq \chi_{1-\alpha}^2)$ $\sigma^2 = \sigma_0^2$ versus $\sigma^2 > \sigma_0^2$: $(\chi_{\alpha}^2 \leq \chi^2 < \infty)$	$\chi^2 = \dfrac{(n-1)s^2}{\sigma_0^2}$ $v = n - 1$
Two variances	$\sigma_1^2 = \sigma_2^2$ versus $\sigma_1^2 \neq \sigma_2^2$: $(F_{1-\alpha/2} \leq F \leq F_{\alpha/2})$ $\sigma_1^2 = \sigma_2^2$ versus $\sigma_1^2 < \sigma_2^2$: $(0 < F \leq F_{\alpha})$	$F = \dfrac{s_2^2}{s_1^2}$ $v_2 = n_2 - 1$ $v_1 = n_1 - 1$

Notes:
1) All populations being sampled are normally distributed.
2) The χ^2 distribution is indexed by left-tail area.
3) The F distribution is indexed by right-tail area.

2. Specify α, the Type 1 error probability, also referred to as the significance level of the test.

3. Determine an appropriate statistic that can be used to test the hypotheses.

4. Determine the sampling distribution of the statistic.

5. Construct the null hypothesis acceptance interval for the test statistic under the assumption that the null hypothesis is true.

6. Collect the required data.

7. Determine if the data satisfy any assumptions made about the population from which they were drawn.

8. Calculate the test statistic, compare it to the acceptance interval, and reject H_0 or reserve judgment.

Get in the habit of performing a hypothesis test by graphing the relevant sampling distribution under the null hypothesis. (Remember, always DTDP!) Then add the acceptance interval, relevant areas under the curve, and the sample statistic to the graph. With some practice, all of the hypothesis tests in the tables and other more advanced tests become simple to perform.

3.11 TESTING FOR NORMALITY

3.11.1 Normal Probability Plots

Since most of the hypothesis tests and confidence intervals introduced in this chapter and many of the new methods to come require that the populations being sampled are normal or at least approximately normal, we require a test to determine if, based on sample data, there is evidence that populations being sampled are not normally distributed. That is, we need to be able to test the hypotheses H_0: *x is normally distributed* versus H_A: *x is not normally distributed.* Although a histogram with a superimposed normal curve can provide clues about whether a population might be normal or not, a much more sensitive graphical method of judging normality is provided by a *normal probability plot,* or *normal plot.* A normal plot essentially straightens out the expected bell-shape of the histogram and the superimposed normal curve so that if the sample does indeed come from a normal population then the plotted points from the sample should fall reasonably close to the straight line. The reason that normal plots are preferred over histograms for judging normality is: 1) they are much more useful for interpreting small samples ($n < 200$) and 2) our eyes are more sensitive to deviations from a straight line than the corresponding deviations from the compound curvature of the normal distribution's bell shape. Normal plots of nonnormal data show curves, hooks, and gaps that are usually easy to distinguish from a straight line while histograms of the same data may still look surprisingly bell-shaped.

Example 3.23

Interpret the three histograms and the associated normal plots in Figure 3.25.

Solution: The first histogram looks like it's well described by the superimposed normal curve and the points in the associated normal plot appear to fall along a substantially straight line so the first data set is probably at least approximately normal. The second histogram appears to have its left shoulder truncated and the normal plot shows substantial curvature, which also suggests that this data set is not normal. The third histogram looks flat across the top with truncated shoulders and the normal plot shows an "S" shape, which also suggests that this data set is not normal.

To understand the rationale of the normal probability plot, suppose that we plotted the usual standardized z values given by

$$z_i = \frac{x_i - \overline{x}}{s}$$

versus the corresponding x_i for all n observations in a sample. Of course, since the z_i are determined directly from the x_i, the plotted points would fall on a perfectly straight line regardless of whether or not the population was normal. However, we can make the z values independent of the x_i by associating each x_i with a normal distribution z value determined from the relative position of each observation in the sample. These z values

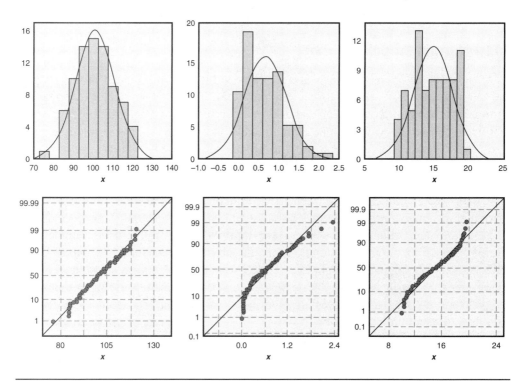

Figure 3.25 Histograms and normal plots for three data sets.

are indicated by z_{p_i}, where, as usual, the subscript on z indicates the left-tail area of the standard normal distribution, that is, $p_i = \Phi(-\infty < z < z_{p_i})$, and the p_i have yet to be determined. The normal plot is constructed by plotting the points (x_i, z_{p_i}) on linear-linear graph paper or by plotting the points (x_i, p_i) on special normal probability paper.

There are several methods available to determine the p_i values for normal plots. The exact values of p_i are difficult to calculate but there are simple approximations that are quite accurate. In the approximate method of *mid-band* positions, the p_i are given by:

$$p_i = \left(\frac{i - 1/2}{n} \right) \tag{3.36}$$

where $i = 1$ corresponds to the smallest x_i, $i = 2$ corresponds to the second smallest x_i, . . . , and $i = n$ corresponds to the largest x_i. The use of the mid-band positions to construct normal plots is easiest to explain by example.

Example 3.24

Test the following sample for normality: $\{22, 25, 32, 18, 23, 15, 30, 27, 19, 23\}$.

Solution: *The ordered data values* x_i*, the midband positions* p_i*, and the corresponding* z_{pi} *values are shown in the following table. Since each observation represents 10 percent of the population, the first observation is associated with the smallest 10 percent of the population and so* $p_1 = 0.05$*. The rest of the* p_i *are determined in the same way—from the midpoints of ten contiguous bands that are each associated with 10 percent of the population. The normal probability plot is shown in Figure 3.26. The z and x scales are both linear. The data plot as an approximately straight line so we conclude that the population being sampled is normal or at least approximately normal. (To be rigorously correct, considering the form of the hypotheses being tested, we have to say that we can't reject* H_0: *x is normally distributed.)*

i	1	2	3	4	5	6	7	8	9	10
x_i	15	18	19	22	23	23	25	27	30	32
p_i	0.05	0.15	0.25	0.35	0.45	0.55	0.65	0.75	0.85	0.95
z_{pi}	-1.645	-1.036	-0.675	-0.385	-0.126	0.126	0.385	0.675	1.036	1.645

Although the mid-band probability plotting positions given by Equation 3.36 are easy to understand, calculate, and use, more accurate probability plotting positions are available but are more difficult to calculate. The method usually implemented in software is the method of *median ranks* given by:

$$p_i = \frac{i - \frac{3}{8}}{n + \frac{1}{4}} \tag{3.37}$$

Generally, when sample sizes are large, there is very little difference between probability plots created using these two methods. Although the differences may become

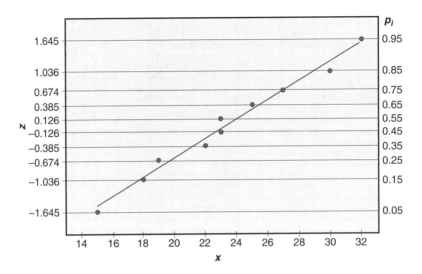

Figure 3.26   Normal probability plot.

noticeable for small data sets, they are usually not so large that they affect the interpretation of the probability plot.

In practice, especially when the sample size is large, a normal plot frequently suggests that the population being studied might not be normal. The implications of a nonnormal population depend on the type of analysis to be performed using statistics calculated from the sample data. That is, in some cases the population must be rigorously normal and in other cases it only needs to be approximately normal. For example, if the purpose of checking for normality is to justify the use of the t test for location, the t test is rather insensitive to even rather large deviations from normality, so approximate normality will suffice. If, however, the purpose of the normal plot is to justify the use of the normal distribution to estimate the population fraction defective relative to specification limits, then the distribution must be rigorously normal to provide any confidence in the result. It's unfortunate that the interpretation of normal plots is subjective, but that subjectivity is caused by the wide range of sensitivity of different analysis methods to the normality assumption and is not at all the fault of the normal plot itself.

3.11.2 Quantitative Tests for Normality

Although most of the normality testing needs for DOE are satisfied by simple normal probability plots, quantitative tests for normality are also available. There are many such tests: the Kolmogorov-Smirnov test, the Lillifors test, the Wilk-Shapiro test, the Ansari-Bradley test, the Anderson-Darling test, and others. Although personal preferences vary, the Anderson-Darling test is currently popular. The details of these tests are outside of the scope of this book but most statistical software packages, including MINITAB, support some or all of these methods.

Each quantitative test for normality has a unique test statistic and a corresponding p value. Although the test statistics and their critical values vary, the p values are all interpreted the same way. When the p value for a quantitative test for normality is relatively large ($p > 0.05$) then we can accept H_0: x *is normally distributed.* When the p value is relatively small ($p \leq 0.01$) then we must reject H_0 and conclude that the distribution is not normal. For intermediate p values ($0.01 < p < 0.05$), the tests may be inconclusive. If the situation only requires approximate normality, such as for a z or t test for location, then a p value in this range probably doesn't indicate a serious problem. If, however, the situation requires rigorous normality, such as for a χ^2 or F test for variances, then more data should be collected to clarify the situation.

3.12 HYPOTHESIS TESTS AND CONFIDENCE INTERVALS WITH MINITAB

MINITAB has the ability to perform all of the hypothesis tests and confidence intervals presented in this chapter and many more. The MINITAB commands for the key hypothesis tests and confidence intervals will be presented in this section. Example problems are included to demonstrate MINITAB's command syntax and outputs. In each case, MINITAB requires that the relevant data are loaded into a column or columns of the worksheet. For simplicity it will be assumed that the data are loaded in column C1 of the current MINITAB worksheet. If two data sets are required, they will be in columns C1 and C2.

3.12.1 Confidence Interval for μ When σ is Known

When the conditions for the central limit theorem are satisfied (that is, if the sample size is large or if the population being sampled is normal and σ is known) the $(1 - \alpha)$ 100% confidence interval is given by Equation 3.3. MINITAB can construct this confidence interval using the **onez** command:

```
mtb > onez c1;
subc > sigma σ.
```

where σ is the known population standard deviation and the sample data are in column C1. The default confidence level is 95 percent but this can be changed with the **confidence** subcommand. There is also a subcommand called **alternative** for one-sided confidence intervals. Note that the semicolon and the period at the end of the commands are required. If you forget a semicolon or period, MINITAB prints a warning that the command is incomplete and waits for you to complete it. Just type a period at the new **subc>** prompt and hit Enter to continue. The **onez** command can also be accessed with the mouse from the **Stat> Basic Stats> 1-Sample Z** menu.

Example 3.25

Construct a 99 percent confidence interval for μ using the following data set: {175, 158, 146, 139, 159, 146, 175, 158, 150}. *The population being sampled is normal and its standard deviation is known to be* $\sigma = 15$.

Solution: The MINITAB output shown in Figure 3.27 indicates that the confidence interval is $\Phi(143.34 < \mu < 169.10) = 0.99$.

3.12.2 Hypothesis Tests for One Sample Mean (σ Known)

When the conditions for the central limit theorem are satisfied, Section 3.4 outlines the hypothesis tests for one sample mean. To perform a hypothesis test for one sample mean with MINITAB you must specify μ_0 for the null hypothesis, the known population standard deviation σ, and the column in which the sample data reside. The command to perform the test is the same **onez** command (or the **Stat> Basic Stats> 1-Sample Z** menu) that was used to construct the confidence interval for μ with the additional **test** subcommand. MINITAB's command syntax is:

$$\text{mtb> onez c1;}$$
$$\text{subc> sigma } \sigma;$$
$$\text{subc> test } \mu_0;$$
$$\text{subc> alternative } tails.$$

where *tails* is -1 for a left-tailed test, 1 for a right-tailed test, or 0 for a two-tailed test, which is the default. The output from MINITAB's **onez** command with the **test** subcommand is the same as the output for confidence intervals with the addition of the z and p values corresponding to the test statistic. The **confidence** subcommand can be

```
MTB > print c1

Data Display

C1
    175    158    146    139    159    146    175    158    150

MTB > OneZ c1;
SUBC>    Sigma 15;
SUBC>    Confidence 99.

One-Sample Z: C1

The assumed sigma = 15

Variable          N      Mean    StDev   SE Mean       99.0% CI
C1                9    156.22    12.57      5.00  ( 143.34,   169.10)
```

Figure 3.27 Ninety-nine percent confidence interval with MINITAB.

used but it only affects the confidence interval—it does not affect the z or p values for the hypothesis test in any way.

Example 3.26

A random sample taken from a normal population with $\sigma = 40$ yields the following data: {532, 533, 455, 491, 515, 505, 525, 488, 488, 404, 420, 429, 465, 471, 490, 473, 447, 478, 513, 512}. *Perform hypothesis tests of H_0: $\mu = 500$ using a two-tailed test and use the one-tailed test with H_A: $\mu < 500$. Use $\alpha = 0.05$ for both tests.*

*Solution: Since the conditions for the central limit theorem are satisfied, the z test is appropriate. The MINITAB **onez** command was used to generate the output in Figure 3.28. The z value for the test is $z = -2.05$. For the two-tailed test the corresponding p*

```
MTB > print c2

Data Display


C2
    532    533    455    491    515    505    525    488    488    404
    420    429    465    471    490    473    447    478    513    512

MTB > OneZ C2;
SUBC>   Sigma 40;
SUBC>   Test 500.

One-Sample Z: C2

Test of mu = 500 vs mu not = 500
The assumed sigma = 40

Variable          N        Mean     StDev    SE Mean
C2               20      481.70     36.88       8.94

Variable              95.0% CI             Z        P
C2          (   464.17,    499.23)    -2.05    0.041


MTB > OneZ C2;
SUBC>   Sigma 40;
SUBC>   Test 500;
SUBC>   Alternative -1.

One-Sample Z: C2

Test of mu = 500 vs mu = 500
The assumed sigma = 40

Variable          N        Mean     StDev    SE Mean
C2               20      481.70     36.88       8.94

Variable      95.0% Upper Bound         Z        P
C2                       496.41     -2.05    0.020
```

Figure 3.28   Two-tailed z test for one sample mean with MINITAB.

value is p = 0.041, which is less than α = 0.05 so we must reject the null hypothesis and conclude that μ ≠ 500. For the one-tailed test the p value is p = 0.020, which is less than α = 0.05 so again we must conclude that μ ≠ 500.

3.12.3 Normal Probability Plots with MINITAB

Use MINITAB's **Stat> Basic Stats> Normality Test** menu or the **normtest** command, for example:

```
mtb> normtest C1
```

to create a normal probability plot of sample data. This command also reports the results of the Anderson-Darling test. Normal plots can also be generated from the **Graph> Probability Plot** menu (or the **pplot** command); this method allows the specific type of distribution to be selected from a long list of possible distributions.

Testing data for normality is a common and necessary step in the analysis of DOE problems. Since normal plots are so tedious to construct by hand, make sure you are comfortable with MINITAB's capabilities for probability plotting—you're going to do lots of them.

Example 3.27
Use MINITAB to construct the normal probability plot of the data from Example 3.24. Interpret the normal plot.

Solution: The example data were entered into column c3 *of a MINITAB worksheet and the normal plot was constructed from the **Stat> Basic Stats> Normality Test** menu. The probability plot, shown in Figure 3.29, shows that the plotted points tend to follow the straight line drawn through them so it appears that the data might come from a normal population. The Anderson-Darling test p value (p = 0.945) confirms this conclusion.*

3.13 SAMPLE-SIZE CALCULATIONS

Too often we're faced with having to calculate confidence intervals and perform hypothesis tests using arbitrarily chosen sample sizes. When the standard deviation of a population is known, or an estimate of it is available, it is possible to calculate a sample size that will meet specified conditions. This is a much more desirable approach to performing experiments that will be analyzed with confidence intervals and hypothesis tests and ensures that we don't make mistakes like substantially over- or undersampling.

There are two potential problems with implementing the sample-size calculation methods presented here: we must know the population standard deviation and we have to be sampling from normal populations. Even when these conditions are not strictly met, however, the methods presented here still provide valuable guidance for sample-size selection.

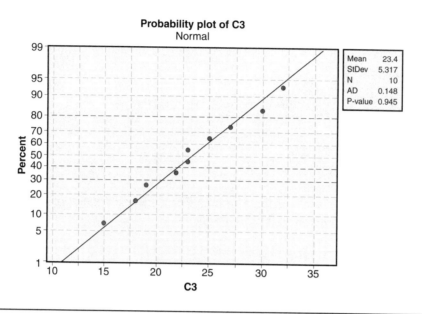

Figure 3.29　Normal plot of example data using MINITAB's **Stat> Basic Stats> Normality Test** menu.

3.13.1 Sample-Size Calculations for Confidence Intervals

The purpose of calculating a confidence interval from sample data to estimate a population parameter is to provide the information needed to make a data-based decision about the management of the process. We have seen that the width of a confidence interval decreases as the number of observations increases. It would seem that collecting lots of data to make the resulting confidence interval very narrow would be desirable, but we can't generally afford to waste time and resources collecting superfluous data. So how wide should a confidence interval be? In general, a confidence interval should be just narrow enough so that a single unique management action is indicated from one end of the confidence interval to the other. Sample sizes that give intervals that are tighter than necessary are wasteful of time and resources. Sample sizes that give intervals that are too wide cannot be used to determine the single appropriate management action that should be taken on the process. In fact, a confidence interval calculated from too few data will be so wide that two, three, or more management actions might be indicated across the span of the interval.

It should be apparent that if we can identify the confidence interval width that just barely indicates a unique management action then we should be able to determine the sample size required to obtain an interval of just that width. It is the purpose of this section to introduce the sample-size calculations necessary to determine a confidence interval with a specified width. This provides protection from the risks associated with over- and undersampling.

Confidence Interval for One Population Mean

The $(1 - \alpha)$ 100% confidence interval for the population mean μ given by Equation 3.3 has the form:

$$\Phi\left(\bar{x} - \delta < \mu < \bar{x} + \delta\right) = 1 - \alpha \tag{3.38}$$

where

$$\delta = z_{\alpha/2}\sigma_x / \sqrt{n}$$

is called the maximum error of the estimate. For a specified value of δ the smallest required sample size must meet the condition:

$$n \geq \left(\frac{z_{\alpha/2}\sigma}{\delta}\right)^2 \tag{3.39}$$

In order to make use of Equation 3.39, the distribution of the population being sampled must be normal and the population standard deviation σ must be known. If σ is not known then it will be estimated by the sample standard deviation of the experimental data. In this case, the t distribution with $n - 1$ degrees of freedom should be used instead of the z distribution in Equation 3.39. This equation is *transcendental* (that is, both sides will depend on n) and will have to be solved for n by iteration. It will still be necessary to estimate σ to complete the sample-size calculation. Of course, the validity of the sample size obtained will depend on the accuracy of the σ estimate.

Example 3.28

Find the sample size required to estimate the population mean to within ±0.8 with 95 percent confidence if measurements are normally distributed with standard deviation σ = 2.3.

Solution: We have δ = 0.8, σ = 2.3, and α = 0.05. The sample size must meet the condition:

$$n \; \geq \left(\frac{z_{0.025}\sigma}{\delta}\right)^2$$

$$\geq \left(\frac{1.96 \times 2.3}{0.8}\right)^2$$

$$\geq 31.8$$

which indicates that n = 32 is the smallest sample size that will deliver a confidence interval with the desired width.

Example 3.29

Find the sample size required to estimate the population mean to within ±100 with 95 percent confidence if measurements are normally distributed. The population *standard deviation is unknown but from knowledge of similar processes it is expected to be about $\hat{\sigma} = 80$.*

Solution: *We have $\delta = 100$, $\hat{\sigma} = 80$, and $\alpha = 0.05$. The sample size required must meet the condition:*

$$n \geq \left(\frac{t_{0.025}\hat{\sigma}}{\delta} \right)^2$$

If the sample size is very large then $t_{0.025} \simeq (z_{0.025} = 1.96)$ and the sample size would be:

$$n \geq \left(\frac{1.96 \times 80}{100} \right)^2$$
$$\geq 3$$

Obviously $n = 3$ doesn't meet the large sample-size condition. By trial and error, when $n = 5$ then $t_{0.025,4} = 2.776$ and:

$$(n = 5) \geq \left(\frac{2.776 \times 80}{100} \right)^2$$
$$\geq 4.93$$

This calculation indicates that the smallest sample size that will deliver a confidence interval with the required width is $n = 5$ although the accuracy of this sample size depends on the accuracy of the σ estimate.

Confidence Interval for the Difference between Two Population Means

The $(1 - \alpha)$ 100% confidence interval for the difference between two population means $\Delta\mu = \mu_1 - \mu_2$ has the form:

$$\Phi\left(\Delta\bar{x} - \delta < \Delta\mu < \Delta\bar{x} + \delta \right) = 1 - \alpha \tag{3.40}$$

where $\Delta\bar{x} = \bar{x}_1 - \bar{x}_2$. For a specified value of δ, the required sample size must meet the condition:

$$n \geq 2 \left(\frac{z_{\alpha/2}\sigma}{\delta} \right)^2 \tag{3.41}$$

In order to make use of this interval, the distribution of x_1 and x_2 must be normal and the population standard deviations σ_1 and σ_2 must be known and equal.

Example 3.30

What sample size should be used to determine the difference between two population means to within ± 6 of the estimated difference with 99 percent confidence? The populations are normal and both have standard deviation $\sigma = 12.5$.

Solution: *We have δ = 6, σ = 12.5, and α = 0.01. The required sample size is:*

$$n \geq 2\left(\frac{z_{\alpha/2}\sigma}{\delta}\right)^2$$

$$\geq 2\left(\frac{2.575 \times 12.5}{6}\right)^2$$

$$\geq 58$$

3.13.2 Sample-Size Calculations for Hypothesis Tests

As in the case of confidence intervals, it is also possible to over- or undersample when collecting data for a hypothesis test. With sufficient input information an appropriate sample size can be calculated before any data are collected.

In addition to specifying the significance level α for a hypothesis test, it is necessary to specify the size of the effect or discrepancy that we want to detect and the corresponding probability of detecting that effect. The probability of detecting a specified difference is called the *power* of the test P and is related to the Type 2 error probability as $P = 1 - \beta$. Tests that are more sensitive to small differences are said to be more powerful than tests that are less sensitive to the same differences.

Hypothesis Test for One Population Mean

The hypotheses to be tested are H_0: $\mu = \mu_0$ versus H_A: $\mu \neq \mu_0$ or alternatively, H_0: $\delta = 0$ versus H_A: $\delta \neq 0$ where $\delta = |\mu - \mu_0|$. Figure 3.30a shows the distribution of $\bar{x}$ when H_0 is true and Figure 3.30b shows the distribution of $\bar{x}$ when H_A is true. From these figures and by equating the z values at the accept/reject boundary, it can be shown that the

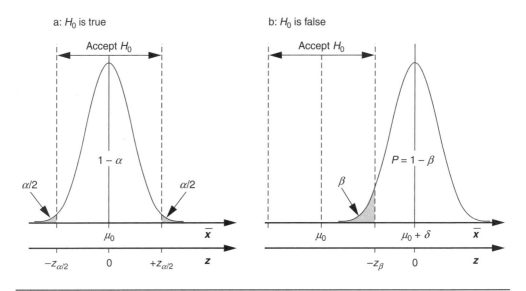

Figure 3.30 Distributions of $\bar{x}$ when H_0 is true and false.

sample size required to reject H_0: $\mu = \mu_0$ with probability $P = 1 - \beta$ when μ is shifted from $\mu = \mu_0$ to $\mu = \mu_0 \pm \delta$ is given by:

$$n \geq \left(\frac{\left(z_{\alpha/2} + z_\beta \right) \sigma_x}{\delta} \right)^2 \tag{3.42}$$

where $z_{\alpha/2}$ and z_β are both positive. For one-tailed tests replace $z_{\alpha/2}$ with z_α.

For the sample size given by Equation 3.42 to be valid, the population that we are sampling from must be normal and we must know the value of σ_x. When σ_x is not known it must be estimated from the sample data, and $z_{\alpha/2}$ and z_β must be replaced with the corresponding t values. This gives a transcendental sample-size condition that must be solved by iteration.

If n is given instead of the power, then β and P can be found by solving Equation 3.42 for z_β:

$$z_\beta = \frac{\delta \sqrt{n}}{\sigma_x} - z_{\alpha/2} \tag{3.43}$$

The quantity:

$$\lambda = \frac{\delta \sqrt{n}}{\sigma_x} = \frac{\delta}{\sigma_x / \sqrt{n}} \tag{3.44}$$

is called the noncentrality parameter. It provides a relative measure of the size of the shift δ in the hypothesized mean.

In the derivation of Equation 3.42, the signs associated with $z_{\alpha/2}$, z_β, and δ were dropped to simplify presentation of the equation. As a result, the sign of z_β given in Equation 3.43 is uncertain and it may not be immediately clear whether β is actually the left- or right-tail area relative to z_β.

Example 3.31

Determine the sample size required to detect a shift from $\mu = 30$ to $\mu = 30 \pm 2$ with probability $P = 0.90$. Use $\alpha = 0.05$. The population standard deviation is $\sigma_x = 1.8$ and the distribution of x is normal.

Solution: *The hypotheses being tested are H_0: $\mu = 30$ versus H_A: $\mu \neq 30$. The size of the shift that we want to detect is $\delta = 2$ and $\sigma_x = 1.8$. Since $z_{\alpha/2} = z_{0.025} = 1.96$ and $z_\beta = z_{0.10} = 1.28$, the sample size required for the test is:*

$$n \geq \left(\frac{\left(z_{\alpha/2} + z_\beta \right) \sigma_x}{\delta} \right)^2$$

$$\geq \left(\frac{(1.96 + 1.28) 1.8}{2} \right)^2$$

$$\geq 8.5 \rightarrow 9$$

Example 3.32

  Find the power of the z test in Example 3.31 when n = 9.

  Solution: *From Equation 3.43, the z_β value is given by:*

$$z_\beta = \frac{\delta\sqrt{n}}{\sigma_x} - z_{\alpha/2}$$
$$= \frac{2\sqrt{9}}{1.8} - 1.96$$
$$= 1.37$$

From a z table, $z_{0.0853} = 1.37$ so $\beta = 0.0853$ and $P = 0.9147$.

Example 3.33

  Find the sample size for Example 3.31 if the actual population standard deviation is unknown but estimated to be $\hat{\sigma}_x = 1.8$.

  Solution: *The required sample size is the smallest value of n that meets the condition:*

$$n \geq \left(\frac{\left(t_{\alpha/2} + t_\beta \right) \hat{\sigma}_x}{\delta} \right)^2$$

where the t distribution has n − 1 degrees of freedom. From the following table, the sample size must be n = 11.

n	$\left(\frac{\left(t_{\alpha/2} + t_\beta \right) \hat{\sigma}_x}{\delta} \right)^2$
9	11.1
10	10.8
11	10.5
12	10.3

Hypothesis Test for the Difference between Two Population Means

The hypotheses to be tested are H_0: $\mu_1 = \mu_2$ versus H_A: $\mu_1 \neq \mu_2$ or alternatively, H_0: $\delta = 0$ versus H_A: $\delta \neq 0$ where $\delta = |\mu_1 - \mu_2|$. The sample size required to reject H_0 with probability $P = 1 - \beta$ for a specified difference between the means δ is given by:

$$n \geq 2 \left(\frac{\left(z_{\alpha/2} + z_\beta \right) \sigma_x}{\delta} \right)^2 \tag{3.45}$$

where n is the sample size that must be drawn from each population and $z_{\alpha/2}$ and z_β are both positive. For this calculation to be valid, the populations we are sampling from must be normal and σ_1 and σ_2 must be known and equal. For one-sided tests, replace $z_{\alpha/2}$ with z_α. If n is given instead of the power then find β and P by solving Equation 3.45 for z_β. If σ_x is unknown and must be estimated from the data, $z_{\alpha/2}$ and z_β must be replaced with the corresponding t values and the transcendental sample-size condition must be solved by iteration. Since the t distribution will have $2n - 2$ degrees of freedom, the approximation of the t distribution with the z distribution is often justified.

Example 3.34

Determine the common sample size required to detect a difference between two population means of $|\mu_1 - \mu_2| = \delta = 8$ with probability $P = 0.95$. Use $\alpha = 0.01$. The common population standard deviation is $\sigma_x = 6.2$ and the distributions of x_1 and x_2 are normal.

Solution: The hypotheses to be tested are H_0: $\delta = 0$ versus H_A: $\delta \neq 0$. We want to detect a difference between the two means of $\delta = 8$ with probability $P = 0.95$ so we have $\beta = 1 - P = 0.05$ so $z_\beta = z_{0.05} = 1.645$. For the two-tailed test we need $z_{\alpha/2} = z_{0.005} = 2.575$ so the required sample size is:

$$n \geq 2\left(\frac{(z_{\alpha/2} + z_\beta)\sigma_x}{\delta}\right)^2$$

$$\geq 2\left(\frac{(2.575 + 1.645)6.2}{8}\right)^2$$

$$\geq 22$$

Sample-Size Calculations for Hypothesis Tests and Confidence Intervals with MINITAB

MINITAB provides basic sample-size calculations for hypothesis testing problems. In addition to the tests outlined above, MINITAB also provides for the σ-unknown cases but an estimate of σ is still necessary. Access MINITAB's sample-size functions from the **Stat>Power and Sample Size** menu and select the **Calculate Sample Size for Each Power** option. Enter the power values as fractions and not percentages, for example, as 0.95 and not 95. MINITAB uses $\alpha = 0.05$ by default but you can change α from the **Options** menu. In all cases, MINITAB assumes that the distributions being sampled are normal.

MINITAB's hypothesis test sample-size calculator can also be used to calculate sample sizes for confidence intervals. Notice that the sample-size equations for hypothesis tests reduce to the sample-size calculations for the corresponding confidence intervals when $z_\beta = 0$. Apply this choice for confidence interval calculations in MINITAB by setting the power in the hypothesis test calculator to $P = 1 - \beta = 0.50$.

Example 3.35

Use MINITAB to find the sample size for Example 3.31.

Solution: For the one-sample hypothesis test for the mean with $P = 0.90$, $\alpha = 0.05$, $\sigma = 1.8$, and $\delta = 2$, MINITAB gave the output in Figure 3.31. MINITAB confirms that the necessary sample size is $n = 9$ and the exact power is $P = 0.9152$.

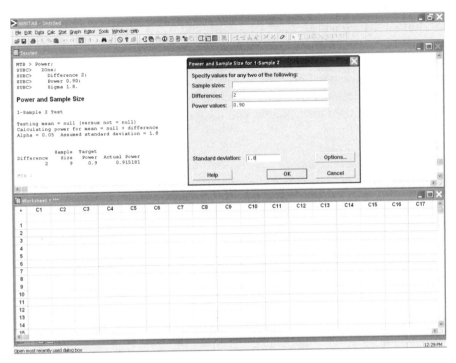

Figure 3.31   Sample-size calculation for test of one sample mean with MINITAB.

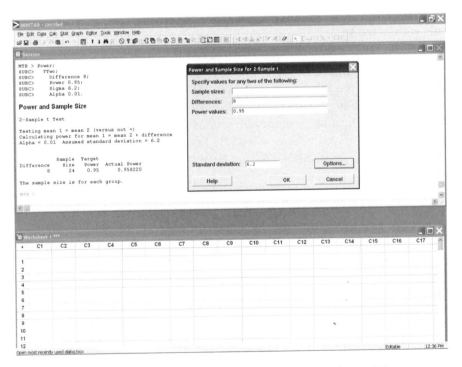

Figure 3.32   Sample-size calculation for test of two sample means with MINITAB.

Example 3.36

Use MINITAB to find the sample size for the two-sample test for means in Example 3.34.

*Solution: MINITAB does not calculate the sample size for the two-sample z test problem but it does do the two-sample t test problem, which should give nearly the same answer. For the two-sample t test with $\alpha = 0.01$, $\sigma_x = 6.2$, and $P = 0.95$ with $\delta = 8$, the required sample size according to MINITAB is $n = 24$. (Set the $\alpha = 0.01$ value in the **Options** menu.) This value is only slightly larger than the sample size that was calculated in Example 3.34. The MINITAB commands and the corresponding output are shown in Figure 3.32.*

4

DOE Language and Concepts

4.1 INTRODUCTION

Like any highly technical discipline, DOE is rife with acronyms and language that may intimidate the novice. The purpose of this chapter is to provide an introduction to the many terms, concepts, and administrative issues of DOE, hopefully in a nonintimidating manner. Don't expect to understand all of the aspects of DOE presented in this chapter the first time you read it. Many of the nuances only become apparent after years of experience and study. But it doesn't take years to demonstrate success with DOE. After reading this chapter you should have sufficient understanding of DOE language and concepts to proceed to the consideration of designed experiments and their applications.

4.2 DESIGN OF EXPERIMENTS: DEFINITION, SCOPE, AND MOTIVATION

Design of experiments (DOE) is a formal structured technique for studying any situation that involves a response that varies as a function of one or more independent variables. DOE is specifically designed to address complex problems where more than one variable may affect a response and two or more variables may interact with each other. DOE replaces inferior methods such as the traditional but unfortunately still common method of studying the effect of one variable at a time (OVAT). Compared to DOE, the OVAT method is an inefficient use of resources and is incapable of detecting the presence of or quantifying the interactions between variables.

DOE is used wherever experimental data are collected and analyzed. It's use is expected in all branches of scientific research but DOE is becoming ever more widespread in engineering, manufacturing, biology, medicine, economics, sociology, psychology, marketing, agriculture, and so on. Most technical publications in any discipline expect that some form of designed experiment will be used to structure any experimental investigation. Researchers who don't use DOE methods don't get published.

The popularity of DOE is due to its tremendous power and efficiency. When used correctly, DOE can provide the answers to specific questions about the behavior of a system, using an optimum number of experimental observations. Since designed experiments are structured to answer specific questions with statistical rigor, experiments with too few observations won't deliver the desired confidence in the results and experiments with too many observations will waste resources. DOE gives the answers that we seek with a minimum expenditure of time and resources.

4.3 EXPERIMENT DEFINED

A simple model of a process is shown in Figure 4.1. Processes have inputs that determine how the process operates and outputs that are produced by the process. The purpose of an experiment is to determine how the inputs affect the outputs. Experiments may be performed to document the behavior of the inputs and corresponding outputs for scientific purposes, but the goal of engineering experimentation is to learn how to control the process inputs in order to produce the desired outputs. Process inputs are called variables, factors, or predictors and process outputs are called responses.

Every experiment involves the observation of both the inputs (the variables) and the outputs (the responses). The action taken by the experimenter on the inputs determines whether the experiment is passive or active. When the experimenter merely observes the system and records any changes that occur in the inputs and the corresponding outputs, the experiment is passive. This type of experimentation can be costly, time-consuming, and unproductive. When the experimenter intentionally varies the inputs, then the experiment is active. Active experimentation, done under controlled conditions in a logical structured manner, is a tremendously powerful tool and is the type of experimentation used in DOE.

4.4 IDENTIFICATION OF VARIABLES AND RESPONSES

Perhaps the best way to identify and document the many variables and responses of a process is to construct a modified cause-and-effect diagram. Consider the example shown in Figure 4.2. The problem of interest is the performance of a two-part epoxy used

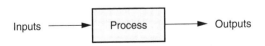

Figure 4.1 Simple model of a process.

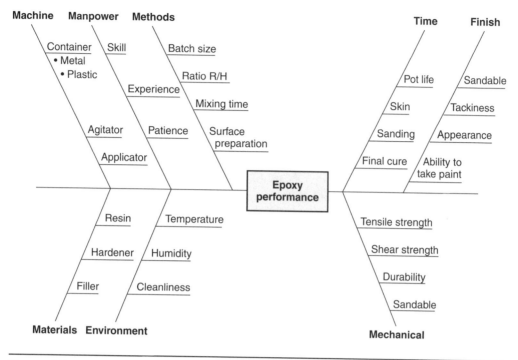

Figure 4.2 Cause-and-effect diagram for epoxy performance.

to bond materials together. The process inputs are shown on the left and the responses are shown on the right. Note that this diagram is just an elaboration of the simple process model in Figure 4.1. MINITAB has the ability to create traditional cause-and-effect diagrams (the left side of Figure 4.2) from the **Stat> Quality Tools> Cause and Effect** menu.

It is very important to keep a cause-and-effect diagram for an experiment. The cause-and-effect diagram:

- Provides a convenient place to collect ideas for new variables.

- Serves as a quick reference tool when things go wrong and quick decisions are necessary.

- Summarizes all of the variable considerations made over the life of the experiment.

- Provides an excellent source of information for planning new experiments.

- Quickly impresses managers with the complexity of the problem.

The cause-and-effect diagram should be updated religiously as new variables and responses are identified.

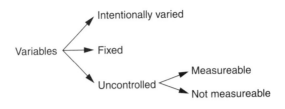

Figure 4.3 Disposition of the experimental variables.

Every process has a multitude of variables and all of them play a role in an experiment. Some variables are intentionally varied by the experimenter to determine their effect on the responses, others are held constant to ensure that they do not affect the responses, and some variables are ignored with the hope that they will have little or no effect on the responses. If the experiment design is a good one, if it is carried out carefully, and if the assumptions regarding uncontrolled variables are met, then the experimenter may learn something about the problem. This classification of process variables is summarized in Figure 4.3. A cause-and-effect diagram can be augmented by using different colored highlighters to classify variables into intentionally varied, fixed, and uncontrolled classes.

4.5 TYPES OF VARIABLES

The inputs to a process are referred to as variables, factors, or predictors. Each variable in an experiment has its own unique settings referred to as levels or treatments. The relationship between the levels of a variable determines whether the variable is qualitative or quantitative. The levels of a qualitative variable differ in type. For example, in the epoxy problem the resin variable may have three qualitative levels determined by manufacturer: Manufacturer A, Manufacturer B, and Manufacturer C. A quantitative variable has levels that differ in size. For example, the epoxy batch-size variable may appear in the experiment at four quantitative levels: 50, 100, 150, and 200 cc. An advantage of a quantitative variable is that the experiment results may be used to interpolate between the levels of the variable included in the experiment. For example, the behavior of the 50, 100, 150, and 200 cc batches could be used to predict how a batch of size 120 cc would behave.

Some experiments include only a single design variable but many of the experiments that we will be interested in will contain two or more variables. Although an experiment with more than one variable can contain a mixture of qualitative and quantitative variables, experiments built with just quantitative variables generally offer more design possibilities. Sometimes it is possible, and generally it is desirable, to redefine a qualitative variable so that it becomes quantitative. This may take some imagination, but with practice and out of necessity it often becomes possible. Methods of redefining a qualitative variable into a quantitative variable are discussed later in this chapter.

4.6 TYPES OF RESPONSES

Whenever possible, the response of an experiment should be quantitative. Any appropriate measurement system may be used but it should be repeatable and reproducible. This text will not rigorously treat binary or count responses although MINITAB has the ability to analyze them. The basic experiment design considerations are the same for these responses but the statistical analyses are different and sample sizes will be much larger. See Agresti (2002), Christensen (1997), or your neighborhood statistician or DOE consultant for help.

Sometimes it's possible to define a severity rating for a binary success/failure type response that approximates a quantitative response. For example, if the response is the cleanliness of a utensil after it is machine washed, then a severity rating of zero to 10 might be used to indicate the range of cleanliness from completely clean to really filthy instead of a simple binary response. The information content of this simple multi-level response is much greater than the binary response and may be sufficient to allow the response to be treated as if it were quantitative. This will give the analysis more power and permit the sample size to be reduced.

Example 4.1

An experiment was designed to study several design variables for a one-time-use chemical indicator. Each indicator contains six strips of paper that are reactive to a specific chemical. In the presence of the chemical in the form of a vapor, the strips quickly turn from white to black. The six strips in the indicator are arranged in series along a torturous diffusion path so that each strip changes color in succession under continuous exposure to the chemical. The purpose of the experiment was to determine the geometry of the torturous path so that: 1) all six of the strips would change color when the indicator was exposed to a known high concentration of the chemical for a specified time and 2) none of the strips would change color when the indicator was exposed to a known low concentration of the chemical for a specified time. In the original concept of the experiment, sample indicators would be run under the two test conditions and judged to either pass or fail the relevant test; however, the sample size for this experiment was found to be prohibitively large. To solve this problem, the response was modified from the original pass/fail binary response to a pseudo-continuous measurement response. A series of 12 indicators was exposed to the chemical for increasing and evenly spaced periods of time to create a 12-step pseudo-quantitative scale that spanned the full range of the response from all white strips to all black strips. These 12 strips were used as the standard against which experimental strips were compared to determine their degree of color change. With this new and improved measurement scale, the number of runs required to study the torturous path variables was significantly reduced.

Most experiments are performed for the purpose of learning about a single response; however, multiple responses can be considered. For example, in the epoxy performance problem, suppose that the primary goal of the experiment is to increase the strength of the cured epoxy without compromising the pot life, viscosity, or sandability characteristics. This will require that all of the responses are recorded during the execution of the experiment and that models be fitted for each response. An acceptable solution to the problem must satisfy all of these requirements simultaneously. This type of problem is common and is completely within the capability of the DOE method.

4.7 INTERACTIONS

When a process contains two or more variables, it is possible that some variables will interact with each other. An interaction exists between variables when the effect of one variable on the response depends on the level of another variable. Interactions can occur between two, three, or more variables but three-variable and higher-order interactions are usually assumed to be insignificant. This is generally a safe assumption although there are certain systems where higher-order interactions are important.

With practice, two-factor interactions between variables can often be identified by simple graphs of the experimental response plotted as a function of the two involved variables. These plots usually show the response plotted as a function of one of the variables with the levels of the other variable distinguished by different types of lines or symbols. Multi-vari charts are also useful for identifying variable interactions.

The management of interactions between variables is a strength of the DOE method and a weakness of the one-variable-at-a-time (OVAT) method. Whereas DOE recognizes and quantifies variable interactions so that they can be used to understand and better manage the response, the OVAT method ignores the interactions and so it will fail in certain cases when the effects of those interactions are relatively large. DOE's success comes from its consideration of all possible combinations of variable levels. OVAT fails because it relies on a simple but flawed algorithm to determine how the variables affect the response. In some cases, OVAT will obtain the same result as DOE, but in many other cases its result will be inferior.

Example 4.2
Two variables, A and B, can both be set to two states indicated by –1 and +1. Figures 4.4a and b show how the responses Y_1 and Y_2 depend on A and B. Use these figures to determine if there is an interaction between the two variables and to demonstrate how DOE is superior to OVAT if the goal is to maximize the responses.

Solution: In Figure 4.4a, the line segments that connect the two levels of B are substantially parallel, which indicates that the levels of B do not cause a change in how A affects the response, so there is probably no interaction between A and B in this case. In Figure 4.4b, the line segments that connect levels of B diverge, which indicates that the chosen level of B determines how A affects the response, so there is probably an interaction between A and B.

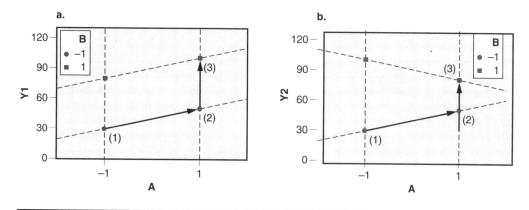

Figure 4.4 Two-variable examples without interaction (a) and with interaction (b).

The weakness of the OVAT method is that it follows a limited decision path through the design space that may or may not lead to the optimal solution. In an experiment to study the situations in Figures 4.4a and b, if the starting point in the OVAT process is point (1) in both cases, and the first step in the experiment is to investigate the effect of variable A, followed by a second step to investigate B, then the desired maximal response is obtained in Figure 4.4a but not in b. In Figure 4.4a, where there is no interaction between variables A and B, the optimal solution is obtained regardless of which variable is studied first. But in Figure 4.4b, where there is an interaction between A and B, the maximal solution is obtained only if those variables are studied in the right order. By contrast, the DOE method investigates all four possible configurations in the design space so it is guaranteed to find the maximal solution whether or not A and B interact.

4.8 TYPES OF EXPERIMENTS

Two of the primary considerations that distinguish experiment designs are the number of design variables that they include and the complexity of the model that they provide. For a specified number of design variables, there could be many experiment designs to choose from, but the extreme designs that span all of the others are called screening experiments and response surface experiments. Screening experiments are used to study a large number of design variables for the purpose of identifying the most important ones. Some screening experiments can evaluate many variables with very few experimental runs. For example, the Plackett-Burman designs can handle seven variables in eight runs, eleven variables in twelve runs, and designs for more variables are available. Screening experiments use only two levels of each design variable and cannot resolve interactions between pairs of variables—a characteristic which can make these designs quite risky.

Response-surface experiments are more complex and difficult to administrate than screening experiments, so they generally involve just two to five variables. Every variable in a response surface design must be quantitative and three or more levels of each variable will be required. The benefit of using so many variable levels is that response surface designs provide very complex models that include at least main effects, two-factor interactions, and terms to measure the curvature induced in the response by each design variable.

There is an intermediate set of experiment designs that falls between screening experiments and response surface experiments in terms of their complexity and capability. These experiments typically use two levels of each design variable and can resolve main effects, two-factor interactions, and sometimes higher-order interactions. When the design variables are all quantitative, a select set of additional runs with intermediate variable levels can be included in these designs to provide a test for, but not complete resolution of, curvature in the response. The existence of this family of intermediate designs should make it apparent that there is actually a discrete spectrum of experiment designs for a given number of experimental variables, where the spectrum is bounded by screening and response surface designs.

When faced with a new situation where there is little prior knowledge or experience, the best strategy may be to employ a series of smaller experiments instead of committing all available time and resources to one large experiment. The first experiment that should be considered is a screening experiment to determine the most influential variables from among the many variables that could affect the process. A screening experiment for many variables will usually identify the two or three significant variables that dominate the process. The next step in the series of experiments would be to build a more complex experiment involving the key variables identified by the screening experiment. This design should at least be capable of resolving two-factor interactions, but often the chosen design is a response surface design which can more completely characterize the process being studied. Occasionally when such a series of experiments is planned, the insights provided by the early experiments are sufficient to indicate an effective solution to the problem that initiated the project, victory can be declared, and the experimental program can be suspended.

4.9 TYPES OF MODELS

There have been many references to a *model* to be constructed from experimental data. The word *model* refers to the mathematical description of how the response behaves as a function of the input variable or variables. A good model explains the systematic behavior of the original data in some concise manner. The specific form of the model depends on the type of design variable used in the experiment. If an experiment contains a single qualitative design variable set to several different treatment levels, then the model consists of the treatment means. There will be as many means for the model as there are treatments in the experiment. If an experiment contains a single quantitative variable that covers a range of values, then the model will consist of an equation that relates the response to the quantitative predictor. Experiments that involve qualitative predictors are usually analyzed by analysis of variance (ANOVA). Experiments that involve quantitative predictors are usually analyzed by regression. Experiments that combine both qualitative and quantitative variables are analyzed using a special regression model called a *general linear model.*

Any model must be accompanied by a corresponding description of the errors or discrepancies between the observed and predicted values. These quantities are related by:

$$y_i = \hat{y}_i + \varepsilon_i \tag{4.1}$$

where y_i represents the ith observed value of the response, $\hat{y}_i$ represents the corresponding predicted value from the model, and ε_i represents the difference between them. The ε_i are usually called the *residuals.* In general, the relationship between the data, model, and error can be expressed as:

$$Data \rightarrow Model + Error\ Statement \tag{4.2}$$

At a minimum, the error statement must include a description of the shape or distribution of the residuals and a summary measure of their variation. The amount of error or residual variation is usually reported as a standard deviation called the *standard error of the model* indicated with the symbol $\hat{\sigma}_\varepsilon$ or s_ε. When the response is measured under several different conditions or treatments, which is the usual case in a designed experiment, then it may be necessary to describe the shape and size of the errors under each condition.

Most of the statistical analysis techniques that we will use to analyze designed experiments demand that the errors meet some very specific requirements. The most common methods that we will use in this book, regression for quantitative predictors and ANOVA for qualitative predictors, require that the distribution of the errors is normal in shape with constant standard deviation under all experimental conditions. When the latter requirement is satisfied, we say that the distribution of the errors is *homoscedastic.* A complete error statement for a situation that is to be analyzed by regression or ANOVA is, "The distribution of errors is normal and homoscedastic with standard error equal to s_ε," where s_ε is some numerical value. If the distribution of errors does not meet the normality and homoscedasticity requirements, then the models obtained by regression and ANOVA may be incorrect.* Consequently, it is very important to check assumptions about the behavior of the error distribution before accepting a model. When these conditions are not met, special methods may be required to analyze the data.

---

* When the standard deviations of the errors are different under different conditions (for example, treatments) we say that the error distributions are *heteroscedastic.*

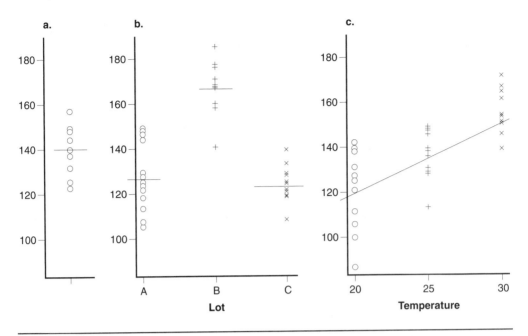

Figure 4.5   Three experiments and three models.

Example 4.3

   A manufacturer wants to study one of the critical quality characteristics of his process. He draws a random sample of n = 12 units from a production lot and measures them, obtaining the distribution of parts shown in Figure 4.5a. The mean of the sample is $\bar{x}$ = 140 and the standard deviation is s = 10. A normal plot of the sample data (not shown) indicates that the observations are normally distributed. From this information, identify the data, model, and the error statement.

   Solution: *The data values are the n = 12 observations, which can be indicated with the symbol y_i where i = 1, 2, . . . , 12. The model is the one number, $\hat{y}_i = \bar{y}$ = 140, that best represents all of the observations. The error values are given by $\varepsilon_i = y_i - \bar{y}$ and are known to be normally distributed with standard deviation $\sigma_\varepsilon \simeq 10$. These definitions permit Equation 4.2 to be written:*

$$y_i = \bar{y} - \varepsilon_i \tag{4.3}$$

Example 4.4

   The manufacturer in Example 4.3 presents his data and analysis to his engineering staff and someone comments that there is considerable lot-to-lot variation in the product. To test this claim, he randomly samples n = 12 units from three different lots. The data are shown in Figure 4.5b. The three lot means are $\bar{y}_A$ = 126, $\bar{y}_B$ = 165, and $\bar{y}_C$ = 123 and the standard deviations are all about s_ε = 10. Normal plots of the errors *indicate that each lot is approximately normally distributed. From this information, identify the data, model, and the error statement.*

   Solution: *The data are the n = 12 observations drawn from the k = 3 lots indicated by the symbol y_{ij} where i indicates the lot (A, B, or C) and j indicates the observation (1 to 12) within a lot. The model consists of the three means $\bar{y}_A = 126$, $\bar{y}_B = 165$, and $\bar{y}_C = 123$. The error statement is, "The errors are normally distributed with constant standard deviation $\sigma_\varepsilon \simeq 10$."*

Example 4.5

   After reviewing the data and analysis described in Example 4.4, someone realizes that the part temperatures were different for the three lots at a critical point in the process. They decide to run an experiment by making parts at different temperatures. n = 12 parts were made at 20, 25, and 30C in completely randomized order and the data are shown in Figure 4.5c. They use linear regression to fit a line to the data and obtain y = 60 + 3T where T is the temperature. The errors calculated from the difference between the observed values and the predicted values (that is, the fitted line) are approximately normal and have $\sigma_\varepsilon \simeq 10$. From this information, identify the data, model, and the error statement.

   Solution: *The data are the 36 sets of paired (T_i, y_i) observations. The model is given by the line y = 60 + 3T. The error statement is, "The errors are normally distributed with constant standard deviation $\sigma_\varepsilon \simeq 10$."*

Models involving quantitative predictors are written in the form of an equation. These models may be empirical or based on first principles depending on the needs of the analyst. The goal of an empirical model is to provide an accurate description of the response independent of the physical mechanisms that cause the predictors to affect the response. Empirical models tend to be arbitrary. A model based on first principles gets its functional form from the mechanistic theory that relates the predictors to the response. First-principles models may be based on very crude to highly accurate analytical study of the problem. It may be safe to extrapolate a first-principles model but empirical models should never be extrapolated.

Whether an empirical or first-principles model is fitted to data depends on the motivation of the experimenter. A scientist who wants to demonstrate that data follow some theoretical formula will, of course, have to use the first-principles approach. This may involve some heroics to transform the formula into a form that can be handled by the software. On the other hand, a manufacturing engineer probably doesn't care about the true form of the relationship between the response and the predictors and is usually willing to settle for an effective empirical model because it gets the job done. He would still be wise to stay conscious of any available first-principles model because it will suggest variables, their ranges of suitable values, and other subtleties that might influence the design of the experiment even if time or model complexity prohibit the use of the first-principles model. When a first-principles model is available, it is almost always preferred over an empirical model, even if the empirical model provides a slightly better fit to the data.

Example 4.6

An experiment is performed to study the pressure of a fixed mass of gas as a function of the gas volume and temperature. Describe empirical and first-principles models that might be fitted to the data.

Solution: In the absence of any knowledge of the form of the relationship between the gas pressure (P) and its volume (V) and temperature (T), an empirical model of the form:

$$P = a + bV + cT + dVT \tag{4.4}$$

might be attempted where a, b, c, and d are coefficients to be determined from the data. For the first-principles model, the kinetic theory of gases suggests that an appropriate model would be:

$$P = \frac{aT}{V} \tag{4.5}$$

where a is a coefficient to be determined from the data. Although both models might fit the data equally well, the second model would be preferred because it is suggested by the theoretical relationship between P, T, and V.

So why are we so concerned about models? What's the purpose for building them in the first place? These questions are also asking about our motivation for doing designed experiments. The purpose of any designed experiment and its corresponding model is to relate the response to its predictors so that the response can be optimized by better management of the predictors. Some of the reasons to build a model are:

- To determine how to maximize, minimize, or set the response to some target value.

- To learn how to decrease variation in the response.

- To identify which predictor variables are most important.

- To quantify the contribution of predictor variables to the response.

- To learn about interactions between predictor variables.

- To improve the operation of a process by learning how to control it better.

- To simplify complex operating procedures by focusing attention on the most important variables and by taking advantage of previously unrecognized relationships between predictor variables and between them and the response.

4.10 SELECTION OF VARIABLE LEVELS

The selection of the variable levels for a designed experiment is a very serious issue. Many experiments fail because the levels of one or more variables are chosen incorrectly. Even when a variable level is chosen badly and much of the data are lost, the DOE method can often recover lots of information from the surviving data. This is one aspect of the robustness provided by DOE.

4.10.1 Qualitative Variable Levels

For qualitative variables the choice of levels is not so critical. Just be sure that each level is practical and should give valid data. For the epoxy example, do not consider Manufacturer C in your experiment if you know that their resin has an inherent problem when used in your process. If, however, you don't know why their resin is a problem and it's much cheaper than the others, you may want to use it in your experiment anyway. The experiment may show that with the correct choice of other variables, Manufacturer C's resin is perfect for the job and will save you money.

Sometimes it's possible to redefine a qualitative variable as a quantitative variable. For example, the old classification of Manufacturer A, B, and C for resin would change if it was determined that the only difference between resins was quantitative, such as if the resins only differed in wax content, say 1, 1.3, and 3 percent. If this is the case, an experiment designed to resolve the effects of wax content might predict improved epoxy performance with two percent wax. Now you're in a position to compromise and use the best wax, A, B, or C, or inquire about a special resin with two percent wax, or mix resins to get two percent wax. Always try to redefine a qualitative variable to make it quantitative. Even if you don't choose to analyze it or interpret it in this way, it provides increased understanding of how the variable behaves.

Sometimes qualitative variables can have only two levels: yes or no. Many process variables behave like this—you either do the step in the process or you don't. For example, if surface preparation in the epoxy example is done by sanding, then the surface might be sanded or not sanded.

4.10.2 Quantitative Variable Levels

The selection of levels for quantitative variables can become quite complicated. The most important issue is the choice of the highest and lowest levels. These levels must be safe, that is, the product obtained at these levels should be useful or at least the process should be able to operate at these levels. This tends to force the choice of levels to be narrow so there's less risk of losing runs or doing damage. If, however, the levels are chosen too close together, you may see no difference between them and you may miss something important outside of the range of experimentation. Experimenters are always trying to guess the highest and lowest safe levels for variables so that they have a high likelihood of seeing measurable effects on the responses. This is often a difficult and nerve-wracking task and it's very important to include the experts, operators, and managers who are knowledgeable of and responsible for the process because they are the ones most likely to offer valuable guidance.

To emphasize the importance of picking the highest and lowest levels of quantitative variables in an experiment, suppose that there are five variables in an experiment. If the safe range of operation for each variable is known, but only one half of that range is used just to be really safe, then the five-variable experiment will only cover $(1/2)^5 =$ 0.031 or three percent of the possible design space. The chances of finding a good design are significantly reduced by using too narrow a range for the variables. This is a very common mistake made by novice experimenters.

When three or more levels of a quantitative variable are used in an experiment, there are several ways to choose the spacing between levels. The most common choice for a three-level quantitative variable is to use three equally spaced levels, often denoted with the coded values -1, 0, and $+1$ or just $-$, 0, and $+$. For example, if the batch-size variable in the epoxy example uses three levels of 50, 100, and 150cc, then the levels are referred to using the codes -1, 0, and $+1$, respectively.

When the increment between levels is constant, we say that we have a linear scale for that variable. It is also possible to design level selections using other schemes. For example, levels can be selected on the basis of squares (for example, 1, 4, 9) or on a log scale (for example, 3, 6, 12). In each case, the three levels are still referenced with the codes -1, 0, and $+1$. The use of special scaling for levels is usually based on the experimenter's understanding of the response and its expected dependence on the study variable.

4.11 NESTED VARIABLES

Sometimes it is impossible or impractical for the levels of one variable to be expressed within each level of another variable. In this case we say that one variable is *nested* within another. For example, suppose we are interested in a manufacturing process in which two machines (x_1 : A or B) are supposed to be producing the same material and that each machine has eight heads or stations (x_2 : 1 to 8) that are all supposed to perform the exact same operation. (Since the product that flows into these two machines gets separated into 16 separate but hopefully identical channels, this is called a multiple stream process.) It's not logical to try to compare pairs of heads with other pairs of heads, such as the two heads with $x_2 = 1$ on machines A and B with the two heads $x_2 = 2$, since they are physically different heads. The comparison is just not meaningful. Instead, we say that heads are nested within machines and treat each head as the unique one that it is. In order to un-nest the heads it would be necessary to redefine the head variable as having 16 levels (x_2 : 1 to 16) and physically move the heads to each of the 16 different positions on the two machines. Ouch!

Another example of nesting is when two manufacturers (x_1 : A or B) are each asked to provide three different lots of material for evaluation. Someone might choose to identify each manufacturer's lots with identification numbers 1, 2, and 3 (x_2 : 1, 2, 3), but lot 1 from manufacturer A has no relationship to lot 1 from manufacturer B other than that they have the same identification number. It would be just as appropriate, and perhaps clearer, to identify the lots as 1, 2, and 3 for manufacturer A and 4, 5, and 6 for manufacturer B. Regardless of how the lots are numbered, they are nested within manufacturers.

4.12 COVARIATES

Figure 4.3 shows that all of the variables in an experiment can be classified as intentionally controlled at desired levels, held constant, or uncontrolled. An uncontrolled quantitative variable that can be measured during the experiment is called a covariate. Common covariates are variables like temperature, atmospheric pressure, humidity, and line voltage. If the covariate has no influence on the response then it is not of any consequence, but in many cases it is unclear if the covariate is important or not. All known variables that are uncontrolled during the experiment are covariates and should be measured and recorded. Then when the statistical analysis of the experimental data is performed, the effect of these covariates can be removed from the response. Generally, the effect of the covariate should have a very small if not unmeasurable effect on the response. If the effect of a covariate becomes too large it can interfere with estimates of the effects of other variables.

Covariates must be continuous (that is, quantitative) variables. They are always analyzed using regression methods. For this reason, the word *covariate* is also used to refer to quantitative variables that are intentionally varied in the experiment, even if they only appear at two discrete levels, because they are also analyzed with regression methods.

4.13 DEFINITION OF *DESIGN* IN
DESIGN OF EXPERIMENTS

The word *design* in the phrase *design of experiments* refers to the way in which variables are intentionally varied over many runs in an experiment. Once the experimental variables are identified and the levels of each variable are chosen, the experiment can be designed. Usually the experiment design is expressed in the form of two matrices: a *variables matrix* and a *design matrix*. Consider the epoxy example. Suppose the variables to be considered are batch size, resin manufacturer, and mixing time and that it has been decided to use two levels for each variable. The following variables matrix shows one possible way to select variable levels:

Level	x_1 : Batch size	x_2 : Resin	x_3 : Mixing time
−	50cc	A	1 minute
+	150cc	B	3 minutes

The purpose of this matrix is to clearly define the experimental variables and their levels. Note the use of the generic variable names x_1, x_2, and x_3. Their use permits references to variables without knowing their names or the context. (Sometimes the letters

A, B, and *C* are used instead of x_1, x_2, and x_3. Some people prefer to use x_1, x_2, . . . to indicate quantitative variables and *A, B,* . . . to indicate qualitative variables but there's no standardized convention for assigning generic names to variables.)

Now, using the – and + notation, an experiment design is shown in the design matrix:

Std	Run	x_1	x_2	x_3
1	4	–	–	–
2	6	–	–	+
3	2	–	+	–
4	7	–	+	+
5	8	+	–	–
6	1	+	–	+
7	3	+	+	–
8	5	+	+	+

This experiment has eight runs. The *Std* or *standard order* column uses an integer to identify each unique configuration of x_1, x_2, and x_3. Each row, called a *run* or a *cell* of the experiment, defines a different set of conditions for the preparation of an epoxy sample. For example, run number 3 is to be made with levels $(x_1, x_2, x_3) = (-, +, -)$ or with a 50cc batch size, Manufacturer B's resin, and a one minute mixing time. This particular design is called a 2^3 full factorial design because there are three variables, each at two levels, and the experiment requires $2^3 = 8$ runs.

The standard order column identifies the logical order of the experimental runs. The actual runs of the experiment must not be performed in this order because of the possibility of confusing one of the study variables with a lurking variable, that is, an uncontrolled and unobserved variable that changes during the experiment and might affect the response. The order of the experimental runs is always randomized, such as the order shown in the *Run* or *run order* column. Randomization doesn't provide perfect protection against lurking variables, but it is often effective so we always randomize. Randomization is so important that it is considered to be part of the experiment design—any design is incomplete if a suitable randomization plan has not been identified.

The matrix of experimental runs is often organized by standard order in the planning and analysis stages of DOE, but is best organized by random run order when the experiment is being constructed. This simplifies the job of the person who actually has to build the experiment, and decreases the chances of making a mistake.

4.14 TYPES OF DESIGNS

There are many different kinds of experiment designs. Generally they can be classified into large groups with strange names: factorials, 2^n factorials, fractional factorials, central

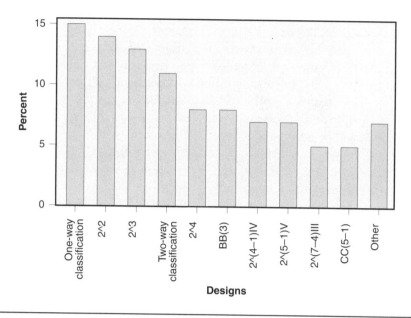

Figure 4.6 Pareto analysis of experiment designs.

composite, Box-Behnken, and Plackett-Burman. There are also hybrid designs which combine characteristics from two or more of these groups. But as complicated as all of this sounds, only a handful of designs are used for the majority of experiments. You'd never guess this from looking at a DOE textbook. The books are always full of all kinds of big elaborate experiment designs because those are the fun ones for the authors to talk and write about. Figure 4.6 is a Pareto chart that attempts to convey how often specific designs get built. (The data are fictional and definitely change from experimenter to experimenter, and technology to technology, but you get the idea.) The figure shows that there are less than a dozen designs that account for nearly all of the experiments that get built, and all of the remaining cases fall into the "Other" category. This book will attempt to focus on the "vital few" designs.

4.15 RANDOMIZATION

It is usually impossible to construct all of the runs of an experiment simultaneously, so runs are typically made one after the other. Since uncontrolled experimental conditions could change from run to run, the influence of the order of the runs must be considered.

Even a simple experiment with one variable at two levels would be easiest to build if all of its runs were done in a convenient order (for example, 11112222); however, such run order plans run the risk of mistakenly attributing the effect of an unobserved variable that changes during the experiment to the experimental variable. The accepted method of protecting against this risk is to randomize the run order of the levels of the experimental variable (for example, 21121221). By randomizing, the effects of any unobserved systematic changes in the process unrelated to the experimental variable are uniformly and randomly distributed over all of the levels of the experimental variable. This inflates the error variability observed within experimental treatments, but it does not add bias to the real and interesting differences between treatments. As an example of this concept, an experiment with a single classification variable with several levels that are run in random order is called a *completely randomized design*. Completely randomized designs will be presented in detail in Chapter 5.

Sometimes you must include a variable in an experiment even though you're not interested in detecting or making claims about differences between its levels. For example, an experiment to compare several operators might require so many parts that raw material for the parts must come from several different raw material lots. If the lot-to-lot differences are not important, then the experiment could be run using one lot at a time, one after the other. To be able to make valid claims about differences between operators, each operator would have to make parts using material from each lot and the operator order would have to be randomized within lots. For example, if there were four operators and three material lots, the following run order plan might be considered:

Run Order	1	2	3	4	5	6	7	8	9	10	11	12
Lot	A	A	A	A	B	B	B	B	C	C	C	C
Operator	2	1	3	4	4	3	2	1	2	4	3	1

In this experiment, called a *randomized block design,* the raw material lots define blocks of runs, and operator is the study variable. Because the blocks (that is, the raw material lots) are not run in random order, it is not safe to interpret any observed differences between them because the differences could be due to unobserved variables that change during the experiment. Since the operators are run in random order, it is safe to interpret differences between them as being real differences between operators. Even though the randomized block design has two variables, it is considered to be a one-variable experiment because claims can be made about only one of the two variables—always the study variable, which *must* be run in random order. Despite the loss of information about differences between the levels of the blocking variable, the use of blocking often increases the sensitivity of the experiment to differences between the levels of the study variable.

To summarize:

- If you intend to makes claims about differences between the treatment levels of a variable, then the run order of the treatment levels must be randomized.

- If a variable must be included in an experiment but you don't intend to make claims about differences between its levels, then the levels do not need to be randomized. Instead, the levels of the variable are used to define blocks of experimental runs.

Example 4.7

   Contamination introduced during a powder dry process forms insoluble particles in the dried powder. A powder drying process introduces contamination that forms insoluble particles into the powder. When the powder is dissolved, these particles eventually clog a critical filter. An alternative drying schedule is proposed that should reduce the amount of contamination. Describe a run order plan for an experiment to compare the amount of insoluble particles formed in the two processes. A sample-size calculation based on historical process information indicates that 10 observations will be required from each drying process.

   Solution: The simplest way to run the experiment would be to configure the drying system for the first process and then to complete all 10 trials before reconfiguring the system for the second process and its 10 trials. The run order would be 11111111112222222222. However, due to possible changes in raw material, temperature, humidity, concentration of the contaminant, the measurement process, and so on, during the experiment, the 20 experimental trials should be performed in random order, such as: 22122121211122111212. Then if one or more unobserved variables do change and have an effect on the response, these effects will be randomly but uniformly applied to both treatments and not affect the true difference between the treatments.

Example 4.8

   Suppose that the three-variable epoxy experiment described in Section 4.13 was built in the standard run order indicated in the table and that a significant effect due to x_1 was detected. What can you conclude about the effect of x_1 on the response from this experiment?

   Solution: Because the experimental runs were not performed in random order, there is a chance that the observed effect that appears to be caused by x_1 is really due to an unobserved variable. No safe conclusion can be drawn from this experiment about the effect of x_1 on the response. Although the experiment design is a good one, its usefulness is compromised by the failure to randomize the run order.

Example 4.9*

   A student performed a science fair project to study the distance that golf balls traveled as a function of golf ball temperature. To standardize the process of hitting the golf balls, he built a machine to hit balls using a five iron, a clay pigeon launcher, a piece of plywood, two sawhorses, and some duct tape. The experiment was performed using three sets of six Maxfli golf balls. One set of golf balls was placed in hot water held at 66C for 10 minutes just before they were hit, another set was stored in a freezer at −12C overnight, and the last set was held at ambient temperature (23C). The distances in yards that the golf balls traveled are shown in Table 4.1, but the order used to collect the observations was not reported. Create dotplots of the data and interpret the differences between the three treatment means assuming that the order of the observations

---

* *Source:* "The Effect of Temperature on the Flight of Golf Balls." John Swang. The National Student Research Center. Used with permission.

Table 4.1   Flight distance of golf balls versus temperature.

Temp	Trial					
	1	2	3	4	5	6
66*C*	31.50	32.10	32.18	32.63	32.70	32.00
−12*C*	32.70	32.78	33.53	33.98	34.64	34.50
23*C*	33.98	34.65	34.98	35.30	36.53	38.20

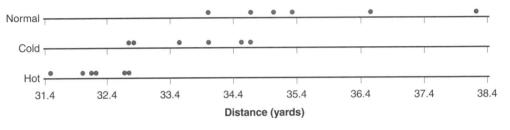

Figure 4.7   Golf ball distance versus temperature.

was random. How does your interpretation change if the observations were collected in the order shown—all of the hot trials, all of the cold trials, and finally all of the ambient temperature trials?

***Solution:** Dotplots for the distances versus the three golf ball temperature treatments are shown in Figure 4.7. The dotplots and Tukey's quick test suggest that the treatment means are all different from each other and that the balls at ambient temperature traveled the farthest. If the order of the observations was indeed random, then this conclusion is probably justified; if, however, the observations were taken in the order shown: hot, cold, then normal temperature, the steady increase in the distance suggests that something else might have been changing during the experiment that caused the golf balls to travel farther on later trials. If the run order was not randomized then it's not safe to conclude from these data that golf balls are sensitive to temperature. Given the lack of information about the run order, this experiment cannot be used to support claims about the effect of temperature on golf ball flight distance.*

There are low-tech and high-tech ways to determine the random order of runs for an experiment. When the experiment is presented in its logical or standard order, each cell is assigned a number indicating its position in the experiment: 1, 2, 3, and so on. Low-tech randomization can be done by writing those numbers on slips of paper, one number per slip, and pulling them from a hat to determine the random run order. Decks of cards and dice can also be used.

High-tech randomization uses a computer with random number generating capability to assign the run order for the cells. MINITAB can be used to create a random run order for an experiment with some of the tools from its **Calc> Random Data** menu. For example, the **Calc> Random Data> Sample from Columns** function can be used to sample, without replacement, from the column showing the experiment's standard order into a new column for the random order. For convenience, the experiment design worksheet should then be sorted (use **Data> Sort**) by the random order column so that the runs are shown in the correct randomized order.

It's important to validate your randomization plan before beginning an experiment. This can be done by analyzing your experiment using the run order as the response. If any of the design variables are found to be good predictors for the random order of the runs, then the randomization wasn't effective and should be performed again.

Randomization is often hard to do and painful but you have no choice—you must randomize. Randomize any variable that you intend to make claims about and use variables that you can't or don't need to randomize to define blocks. It's often easy and tempting to compromise the randomized run order. Don't! Be especially careful if someone else is running the experiment for you. Make sure that they understand that the order of the runs *must* be performed in the specified order. If it is ever necessary to deviate from the planned run order of an experiment, make sure to keep careful records of the actual run order used so that the effect of the change in run order can be assessed.

4.16 REPLICATION AND REPETITION

The design matrix of an experiment determines what terms the model will be capable of resolving, but the sensitivity of the analysis to small variable effects is determined by the number of times each experimental run is built. Generally, the more times the runs of an experiment design are built the greater will be the sensitivity of the experiment.

There are two different ways that the runs of an experiment design can be repeated. When consecutive units are made without changing the levels of the design variables between units, these like units are called *repetitions*. When two or more like units are produced in an experiment, but at different times spaced throughout the experiment and not as consecutive units, these like units are called *replicates*.

DOE novices usually have difficulty using and understanding the word *replicate* because it is used as both a noun and a verb and is even pronounced differently in the two cases. As a noun, the word *replicate* (*-cate* rhymes with *kit*) is used to refer to each set of unique runs that make up a complete experiment design. As a verb, we *replicate* (*-cate* rhymes with *late*) an experiment design by building replicates.

At first it might seem that the use of repetitions and replicates would give similar, if not identical, results, but that is usually not the case. Indeed, the values of the response for both repetitions and replicates will be nearly identical if the process is stable, but replication almost always leads to greater variation in the response due to changes in uncontrolled variables. Despite this apparent disadvantage of replication over repetition, replication generally provides a more realistic measure of the inherent noise in the process and is the preferred way to increase the number of runs in an experiment. The difference in the values associated with repetitions and replicates is made clear by how they are treated in statistical analyses; repeated runs are averaged whereas individual replicated observations are preserved, so repetitions do comparatively little to increase the sensitivity of an experiment to small variable effects.

The number of replicates required for an experiment is often chosen arbitrarily, based on historical choices or guidelines, but should instead be determined by an objective sample-size calculation similar to those performed in Chapter 3. The inputs required to complete such sample size calculations are: 1) an estimate of the inherent error variation in the process, 2) the size of the smallest variable effect considered to be practically significant, and 3) knowledge of the model to be fitted to the experimental data. When one or more of these values are unknown, they should be estimated by considering prior experience with similar processes, information from preliminary experiments, or expert opinion.

It is very important that the number of replicates per cell in the experiment design be held constant. An unequal number of replicates throws off the balance of the experiment and can lead to biased or even incorrect conclusions. The balance of the experiment is referred to as its *orthogonality* and we say that an unbalanced experiment has suffered some loss of orthogonality. There is a rigorous mathematical meaning to the term orthogonality, but we will only use the term in a binary sense to address the issue of whether the experiment is balanced or not. Often an experiment intended to have an equal number of replicates suffers from some loss of units due to breakage or early product failure. Some experiments, especially those that are replicated several times, can tolerate lost units, but recovering the integrity of an experiment with a substantial loss of orthogonality requires finesse and experience. Some recommendations on how to deal with a few lost units will be presented in this book, but plan on replacing lost units if it's at all possible, and consult with your neighborhood statistician when it's not.

Some experiments can be fractionally replicated. Fractionally replicated experiments use only certain runs, such as one half or one quarter of all of the possible runs. If they are carefully designed, these experiments can be very efficient but they do have limitations, such as the inherent confounding (or aliasing) of variables and interactions. If the confounding is managed correctly, a fractionally replicated experiment can provide most of the information that a fully replicated experiment would reveal.

The randomization of replicates can take two forms: complete randomization and limited randomization. In complete randomization, all runs of all replicates are eligible to be run at any time. With limited randomization, all of the runs of each replicate are completed before the next replicate is started, with the runs within each replicate peformed in random order. This approach, called *blocking on replicates,* has the advantage that biases between the blocked replicates, that would otherwise be attributed to experimental noise, can be isolated in the experiment analysis. By isolating the block biases the experimental error is reduced which increases the sensitivity of the experiment to small variable effects. This advantage makes blocking on replicates the preferred practice over complete randomization.

4.17 BLOCKING

Often while preparing a designed experiment to study one or more variables, another important variable, a nuisance variable, is identified that cannot be held constant or randomized. If during the course of the experiment this variable's level changes which has a corresponding effect on the response, these changes in the response will inflate the noise in the experiment making it less sensitive to small but possibly important differences between the levels of the study variables. Rather than tolerate the additional noise introduced by this nuisance variable, the experimental runs should be built in subsets called blocks, where each block uses a single level of the nuisance variable. The usual method of assigning runs to blocks is to build one or more complete replicates of the experiment design within each block. Then when the statistical analysis of the data is performed, the blocking variable is included in the model so that any differences between the nuisance variable's levels are accounted for. This approach isolates the variation caused by the nuisance variable and recovers the full sensitivity of the experiment design.

Although a blocking variable is included in the statistical analysis of an experiment, we usually don't test to see if there are differences between its levels. Such tests would be unsafe because, since the levels of the blocking variable are not typically run in random order, there may be other unidentified variables changing during the experiment that are the real cause of the apparent differences between levels. When a study variable cannot be randomized and must be run in blocks, we must be very careful to guarantee that the experimental conditions are as constant as possible and we must stay conscious of the risk that our conclusions about differences between blocks might be wrong. If we really need to determine if there are differences between the levels of some variable, then we have no choice—its levels must be run in random order. If we don't need to determine if there are differences between the levels of some variable, then we can treat it as a blocking variable.

We almost always want to construct the runs of our experiments in random order; however, in many cases this is impossible or impractical. For example, in the epoxy problem, imagine that a large-scale operation required a full day to clean out all of the equipment to make the change from resin *A* to resin *B*. Running the experiment with a random choice of resin from run to run is desirable from an experimental standpoint, but the many days required to change resins is definitely not practical. One choice is to perform all of the experimental runs with one resin before switching to another. Then only one changeover is required and the experiment will be completed quickly. In this case, we say that the resin variable is run in two blocks and that resin is a blocking variable. The danger of this approach is that if a steady trend or shift occurs in the process during the experiment that is unrelated to the differences between resins *A* and *B*, the trend will be misattributed to differences between the resins. If the purpose of the experiment is to study variables other than resin, then it is appropriate to run resin in blocks. But if the purpose of the experiment is to measure the differences between the resins, then there is no choice—resins *must* be run in random order. This is always the case for blocking variables—effects attributed to blocking variables may have other causes and until the variable is run in random order you cannot be certain of the real cause of the observed effect.

It is common to have several nuisance variables dealt with in blocks in a single experiment in order to study a single independent variable. Even though an experiment might contain many variables, it still is often called a single-variable experiment because only one variable is randomized and all the others are used to define blocks. Such an experiment is still considered to be a one-variable experiment because there's only one variable for which safe conclusions can be drawn.

When an experiment gets so large that it cannot be completed at one time, it should be built in blocks defined, for example, by days or shifts. Then if there are differences between the blocks, the differences can be accounted for in the analysis without decreasing the sensitivity of the original design. When even a single replicate of a design it too big to build at one time, the design can often be broken into fractional replicates, such as two half-fractions or four-quarter fractions, so that the number of runs in a block or blocks defined by these fractional replicates are more reasonable in size.

In some designs, blocks can be analyzed independently as they are built and then the results of several blocks can be combined to improve the analysis. Another advantage of blocking is that occasionally a single block or just a few blocks of a large experiment might be built, analyzed, and found to answer all relevant questions so that the remaining blocks do not have to be constructed. Use this to your advantage! There is no better way to earn brownie points with management than to announce that the last half of an experiment does not have to be built and that a process can again be used to produce saleable product instead of experimental units.

Example 4.10

Describe a blocking and randomization plan for the three-variable eight-run experiment design from Section 4.13 if the experiment requires three replicates and only twenty runs can be completed in a day.

Solution: Since the full experiment requires 24 runs and only 20 runs can be completed in a day, it is necessary to build the experiment over at least a two-day period. To account for possible differences between the morning of the first day, the afternoon of the first day, and the morning of the second day, the experiment will be built in three blocks. Each block will contain a single replicate of the eight-run experiment design with the runs within blocks in random order. Table 4.2 suggests a possible blocking and randomization plan. The numbers in the columns for blocks 1, 2, and 3 indicate the run order within the blocks.

Example 4.11

Suppose that management decides that the experiment from Example 4.10 will take too much time to complete. As a compromise, they decide that all of the runs from resin manufacturer A will be done first, followed by all of the runs from manufacturer B, so that the experiment can be completed in a single day. Describe a blocking and randomization plan for the new experiment and discuss how the analysis and conclusions will differ from the original plan.

Solution: The new experiment will be built with two blocks of twelve runs each, defined by manufacturer (x_2). The study variables will be batch size (x_1) and mixing time (x_3). This two-variable experiment requires $2 \times 2 = 4$ runs per replicate. Since each

Table 4.2 Blocking and randomization plan for a 24-run experiment in three blocks.

Run	x_1	x_2	x_3	Block 1	Block 2	Block 3
1	−	−	−	3	8	5
2	−	−	+	2	1	3
3	−	+	−	8	7	6
4	−	+	+	5	5	7
5	+	−	−	4	6	4
6	+	−	+	6	2	8
7	+	+	−	7	4	1
8	+	+	+	1	3	2

block will contain twelve runs there will be three replicates per block. If the experimental conditions within blocks are expected to be stable, then the twelve runs within each block could be completely randomized. If other variables may cause differences within the original two blocks, however, then each block should consist of three sub-blocks defined by replicates of the four-run experiment. Generally, the latter choice is preferred.

4.18 CONFOUNDING

Sometimes, by accident or design, an experiment is constructed so that two variables have the same levels for each run in the experiment; that is, if our variables are x_1 and x_2, then $x_1 = x_2$. When this happens, it becomes impossible to separate the effects of the two variables. It's like having two input knobs on a machine that are always locked together. When one is changed, the other changes with it so that the true cause of any change in the output cannot be determined. When two variables are coupled or locked together like this we say that the two variables are *confounded* or *aliased*. Confounding should be avoided when possible, but sometimes it's necessary to design an experiment with some confounding of the variables. For example, there are certain designs where a variable is intentionally confounded with an interaction, such as $x_1 = x_{23}$.

Variables can still be confounded and not have exactly the same settings. Suppose that one variable x_1 has levels ± 1 and a second variable x_2 has corresponding levels ∓ 1. That is, whenever the first variable is +1, the second is −1, and vice versa. A concise way of writing this relationship is $x_1 = -x_2$. These two variables are still confounded with each other because the settings of one variable determine the settings of the other. Confounding is an issue of the ability of one variable to predict another. Ideally we want our experimental variables to be independent of each other, that is, no variable should be predictable from another variable or combination of variables. We *design* experiments so that the variables are independent, that is, not confounded.

Confounding of variables is not a simple binary state. Two variables can be independent of each other (that is, not confounded), perfectly confounded with each other, or they can fall in some intermediate state between the two extremes. Some small degree of confounding is tolerable under most circumstances, but large amounts of confounding can cause problems. One way that minor confounding can appear in an experiment is when a well designed experiment, in which all of the variables are independent, loses some experimental runs. There are safe ways to handle some missing data, but an experiment with lots of missing runs will have to be supplemented with new runs or run again from scratch.

The order of the runs in an experiment is another variable that is always present but often overlooked. When the levels of a variable change in some systematic way from the start to the end of the experiment (for example, AAAABBBBCCCC) we say that the variable is confounded with the run order. When a variable is confounded with the run order, it is unsafe to attribute an observed effect to that variable because another unobserved variable, called a lurking variable, that changes during the experiment could have been the real cause of the effect. Because we can never be certain that there are no lurking variables present, we must assume that they are there and protect ourselves from them. We do this by randomizing the run order so that the effects of any lurking variables are not confounded with the experimental variables.

4.19 OCCAM'S RAZOR AND EFFECT HEREDITY

Most statistical analyses of data from designed experiments involve many model terms. Some of these terms are main effects, some are two-factor and higher-order interactions, sometimes when there are quantitative variables a model may have quadratic terms, and other terms are possible. Usually the first model fitted to an experimental data set includes all possible terms in the model, but many of these terms turn out to be statistically insignificant. Rather than reporting the full model with all of its inherent complexity, we usually fit a simplified or reduced model including just those terms that are statistically significant. This practice comes from a recommendation by a 15th-century philosopher named Occam who basically said, "The simplest model that explains the data is probably the best model." This adage is called *Occam's razor.* Occam's razor says that if we have to choose between two models for the same data set, one more complex than the other, the simpler of the two models is more likely to be the correct one. For example, suppose that two models are fitted to the data from a scatter plot where the first model is a simple linear model and the second model contains a quadratic term. If both models fit the data equally well, then the linear model is preferred over the quadratic model because it is simpler.

Another important concept related to Occam's razor is the concept of *effect heredity.* Effect heredity appears in the context of interactions between variables. Effect heredity says that it's more likely that a two-factor interaction will be significant if both of its factors are significant, it's less likely that a two-factor interaction will be significant if only one of its factors is significant, and it's unlikely that a two-factor interaction will be significant if neither of its factors is significant. This concept becomes especially important when we interpret analyses from some of the designs from Chapter 10.

4.20 DATA INTEGRITY AND ETHICS

DOE is a data-driven decision-making tool. The advantage of using data to make decisions is that data are objective—or at least they are supposed to be. Since one or more people usually have access to experimental data and are in a position to knowingly or unknowingly edit, censor, or bias observations, it is possible that the objectivity of the data will be compromised. Everyone who has contact with the data must understand that it is absolutely critical to preserve its integrity.

If you recognize the name David Baltimore it should be because he won a Nobel Prize in virology in 1975, but it's more likely that you would recognize his name because it's forever linked to an infamous case where the integrity of experimental data was called into question. In 1983, David Baltimore got funding from the National Institutes of Health (NIH) for an important experiment in immunology. The lab work was so difficult that it was performed at two different labs at MIT, one operated by David Baltimore and the other operated by Theresa Imanishi-Kari. Baltimore did not personally supervise or perform any of the lab work himself, but he was the most prestigious author of the paper that reported the experimental results (Weaver, 1986). After the results were published, another researcher working in Imanishi-Kari's lab questioned the validity of some of the experimental data. A hearing was held at Tufts University Medical School that exonerated Baltimore, Imanishi-Kari, and the people who worked in their labs, but then other people picked up and expanded on the initial accusation. The accusations grew from simple mismanagement of the data to claims of malicious manipulation and fabrication of data, which carried a criminal fraud charge. Further investigations were carried out at MIT; the NIH; a new special operation, created in part by the Baltimore case, at NIH called the Office of Scientific Integrity (OSI); the congressional subcommittee on oversight and investigation of the House Energy and Commerce Committee, which was responsible for funding the NIH; and eventually a reorganized version of the OSI called the Office of Research Integrity (ORI) in the Department of Health and Human Services. Throughout these investigations, many of them badly managed, Baltimore and Imanishi-Kari were crucified by the press and shunned by the scientific community. Nine years after the initial challenge to their Cell paper, a special panel appointed by the ORI Departmental Appeals Board dropped all charges against Baltimore and Imanishi-Kari. They acknowledged that there was some sloppy record keeping in lab notebooks and some misleading descriptions of the methods used in the Cell paper but there was no evidence of fraud and no indication that the claims in the paper were in error. In the absence of all of the attention, whatever mistakes were made in the Cell paper would have been resolved by the normal progression of science. Ironically, David Baltimore's Nobel Prize that drew special attention to the infamous Cell paper will always be his second claim to fame after his unfortunate role in this story.

During my junior year of college, I performed a lab experiment in physical electronics with my lab partner, Steve. The experiment was very complex so Steve and I split up the task of recording the variable settings and the corresponding response. A week later—the night before the lab report was due, of course—we discovered that we had both forgotten to record one of the independent variables that we adjusted during the experiment. Without the missing values we couldn't complete the lab report. Being the creative students that we were, and having few other choices, Steve and I created a graph of the theoretical relationship between the response and the independent variables. Then we plotted fictitious points along this curve and worked backward to create the column of missing settings. Of course we drew the points along the curve with lots of experimental error. We didn't want to make unreasonably strong claims about the relationship—only that the relationship was roughly as the theory predicted.

A few days after turning in our reports, Steve and I were called to a special meeting with the lab professor to discuss our results. When we met with him, Steve and I were initially relieved to find out that our fakery hadn't been detected, but then shocked to realize that the professor was completely thrilled with our work! No other students had ever successfully obtained the expected relationship between the response and the independent variables! The experiment had essentially been a study of noise! We quickly admitted that we had faked the data and luckily got away with passing grades and a verbal reprimand; however, in any other environment it's unlikely that the commission of such an act would be dealt with so lightly. Nowadays, in most workplaces, someone caught faking data would probably be fired, maybe even prosecuted, and certainly ostracized by their peers like Baltimore and Imanishi-Kari.

The moral of these stories is that you should not fake or in any other way compromise the integrity of your data. If you do, you put yourself and your whole organization at risk and you will probably be caught and held accountable. Whether you get caught or not, you will certainly go to data hell. Like statistics hell, the line to get into data hell is very long and we will probably see each other there.

4.21 GENERAL PROCEDURE FOR EXPERIMENTATION

The following procedure outlines the steps involved in planning, executing, analyzing, and reporting an experiment:

1. Prepare a cause-and-effect analysis of all of the process inputs (variables) and outputs (responses).

2. Document the process using written procedures or flowcharts.

3. Write a detailed problem statement.

4. Perform preliminary experimentation.

5. Design the experiment.

6. Determine the sample size and the blocking and randomization plan.

7. Run the experiment.

8. Perform the statistical analysis of the experimental data.

9. Interpret the statistical analysis.

10. Perform a confirmation experiment.

11. Report the results of the experiment.

Each of these steps is described in detail in the following sections. The descriptions include a list of the activities that must be considered, recommendations for who should be involved in these activities, and an estimate of how much time is required. The time estimates are appropriate for someone proficient in DOE methods. Novices will probably take longer to complete each step if they have to do any research and review.

The cast of characters involved in the DOE process and their primary functions on the DOE team are:

- The DOE project leader, who has the primary responsibility for the project.

- The operators, who run the process.

- The technicians or machine adjusters, who maintain the equipment and implement significant process changes or upgrades.

- The design engineer, who has knowledge of how the product is supposed to work.

- The process engineer, who has knowledge of how the process is supposed to run.

- The manager/customer, for whose benefit the experiment is being performed.

- The DOE statistical specialist, who will support the DOE project leader on complicated statistical issues as necessary.

Table 4.3 provides a summary of which DOE team members are required for each activity.

4.21.1 Step 1: Cause-and-Effect Analysis

The first step in preparing for a new designed experiment or recovering from a poorly implemented one is to complete a cause-and-effect analysis. The purpose of this analysis is to create a catalog of all of the possible variables that affect the process. The traditional variable categories: methods, manpower, machines, material, and environment, provide a good starting point. All variables, including ones that are not and can not be included in the experiment, should be added to the list. Try to identify every possible source of variation. If late in an experiment you discover that you've overlooked an important variable, you should have at least listed the source of the problem in your cause-and-effect analysis.

In addition to creating a list of the input variables, it's also important to create a complete list of all of the possible responses. Although most experiments tend to focus on a single response, there are usually secondary responses that must at least meet some constraints, if not aggressive performance requirements. A modified cause-and-effect

Table 4.3 Cast of characters and their responsibilities.

Activity	Project Leader	Operators	Technicians	Design Engineer	Process Engineer	Manager/ Customer	Statistical Specialist
1. Cause-and-effect analysis	✓	✓	✓	✓	✓	✓	
2. Document the process	✓	✓	✓	✓	✓		
3. Problem statement	✓	Review	Review	Review	Review	Review	Review
4. Preliminary experiment	✓	✓	✓	✓	✓		
5. Design the experiment	✓						Support
6. Randomization plan	✓						Support
7. Run the experiment	✓	✓	✓	✓	✓		
8. Analyze the data	✓						Support
9. Interpret the model	✓	✓	✓				Support
10. Confirmation experiment	✓						
11. Report the results	✓			Review	Review	Review	

diagram, such as the example in Figure 4.2, page 95, is a good way to incorporate the variables and responses into one document.

The initial cause-and-effect diagram that you create to document a process should evolve as your understanding of the system changes and improves. Try to keep photocopies of the most current diagram handy so you can add to it as you get new ideas. The modified cause-and-effect diagram is also a great way to get a new DOE team member up to speed on the process or to show an anxious manager that you have command of the situation.

Although an initial modified cause-and-effect diagram can be started by a single person, most likely the DOE project team leader, it is essential that all of the people involved in the process contribute to this step. Inputs from the operators and technicians who run the process on a daily basis are critical because they are often the only ones aware of special but important variables. The design and process engineering people are important because they must provide the more technical and theoretical viewpoint. The manager of the organization that owns and operates the process should be involved to make sure that all of the requirements of the process, including broader requirements that might not be known or obvious to the others, are addressed. If the customer of the process cannot be involved or consulted at this stage, the manager is also responsible for representing his or her viewpoint.

The initial creation of the modified cause-and-effect diagram can happen in a relatively short period of time, but the document is rarely complete in its early stages. It is just so easy to overlook secondary or even important variables or responses that you must expect to spend quite a bit of time spread out over several days or even weeks to develop a complete analysis. And always update this document on a regular basis as new variables and interpretations of the system are discovered.

4.21.2 Step 2: Document the Process

The process to be studied should be documented in the form of written procedures or flowcharts. The documentation should be sufficiently complete that someone unfamiliar with the particular process but reasonably skilled in the art could operate the process and reproduce the results of an experiment. If this documentation doesn't exist, it is well worth taking the time to create it. If the documentation already exists, it is wise to review it carefully for discrepancies between the perceived and real processes. It's likely that the problems or issues that instigated a DOE study of the system were caused by a lack of understanding of the system. This is the time to resolve as many issues as possible before proceeding to the next step in the DOE procedure.

In addition to the instructions required to operate the process, historical records of the performance of the process should also be reviewed and summarized. It is almost pointless to consider performing a designed experiment on a process that is out of statistical control, so locating up-to-date and relevant control charts or other evidence that confirms that the process is in control is very important. If this evidence doesn't exist or hasn't been compiled, you should take the opportunity to complete this step instead of just assuming that everything is OK.

In many cases, the creation of new procedures or the review of existing procedures will uncover potentially serious gaps in the system. For example, it may be discovered that one or more operators really don't understand how the process is supposed to operate. These issues must be identified and resolved before proceeding to the next step in the DOE process.

If the independent variables and/or response are quantitative, then calibration records and gage error study data should be checked to confirm that all of the necessary measurements and settings are accurate and precise. If this evidence doesn't exist, then it may be worth the time to address the most serious concerns if not all of them.

All of the owners/managers of the process should be involved in documenting the process. This includes the operators who run the process, the technicians or machine adjusters who troubleshoot and maintain the process on a daily basis, and the design and/or process engineers who have overall responsibility for the process.

It's relatively rare that a process is sufficiently documented prior to performing a designed experiment. Usually something important among the many procedures, process performance records, calibration records, and gage error study results that are necessary to completely document the process is inadequate or completely missing. If these things are all available and up-to-date, this step of the DOE process might happen quickly, but it's more likely that many hours of preparation will be necessary before this step can be considered complete. Often these activities uncover the problem or problems that initiated considerations for performing a designed experiment in the first place. If effective solutions can be found to these problems, it may not be necessary to continue to the next step in the DOE process.

4.21.3 Step 3: Write a Detailed Problem Statement

Most DOE projects involve many people who come from different levels and parts of the organization. These people often have very different perceptions of the purpose of the specific DOE project. For example, the expectations of an upper manager who will only see the final report from a DOE project may be completely different from those of an operator who has to run the process. The purpose of a DOE problem statement is to unambiguously define the scope and goals of the experimental program for everyone involved.

The DOE problem statement should be a written document that is circulated for comments, formally reviewed, and signed off like a contract between the DOE project team and the manager that they report to. The problem statement should include:

- A description of the response or responses to be studied and their relevant goals or constraints.

- An estimate of the smallest practically significant change in the response that the experiment is expected to detect for the purpose of sample-size calculations.

- A presentation of any relevant theory or physical model for the problem that might provide additional insight into its behavior.

- A description of relevant historical data or other experiments that were performed to study the problem.

- A list of the possible experimental variables. This list does not need to be complete or even accurate at this point in the DOE process, but it helps identify the scope of the variables that will be considered. Preliminary assignments of variables to the following categories should be made: 1) a variable intended for active experimentation, 2) a variable that will be held constant throughout the experiment, or 3) a variable that cannot be controlled and may or may not be measured during the experiment.

- A list of expected and possible interactions between design variables.

- Citation of evidence of gage capability for experimental variables and responses.

- Citation of evidence that the process is in control.

- Estimates of the personnel, amount of time, and material required to perform the experiment.

- A list of the assumptions that will be made to simplify the design, execution, and analysis of the experiment.

- Identification of questions that must be answered, such as by preliminary experimentation, before a large designed experiment is undertaken.

The DOE problem statement is usually drafted by the DOE project team leader, but the draft should be reviewed by all of the people on the project team. Their changes and recommendations should be considered and incorporated into the document if appropriate. Because there are so many people involved and because this document sets the stage for most of the later steps in a DOE project, this step can be very time-consuming; however, if the problem statement is accurate and well written, the DOE project will be more likely to succeed.

4.21.4 Step 4: Preliminary Experimentation

Often the only way to fill knowledge gaps identified in the DOE problem statement is to perform some preliminary experiments, either in the lab or on the actual process to be studied. Successful preliminary experimentation is critical to decreasing the risks of a large designed experiment. These preliminary experiments usually take the form of small sets of runs to investigate one variable or procedure at a time.

The purpose of preliminary experimentation is to:

- Gain experience with new experimental variables.

- Confirm that there are no unidentified variables.

- Confirm that the classification of each variable as fixed, experimental, or uncontrolled is appropriate.

- Identify the safe upper and lower bounds for experimental variables.

- Investigate the need for an intermediate level of a quantitative variable to detect or quantify curvature in a response.

- Confirm that the procedures used to operate the process are accurate.

- Confirm that the operators and equipment function correctly and as expected.

- Estimate the standard deviation of the response so that a sample-size calculation can be done.

Preliminary experiments should use no more than 10 to 15 percent of the total resources allocated for an experiment. The scope of preliminary experiments should be limited to those questions that must be resolved before the full experiment can be performed. It's often difficult to decide how much preliminary experimentation is necessary. If an insufficient amount of preliminary experimentation is done, problems will appear later in the DOE process. Besides wasting time, some committed experimental resources will possibly become useless.

Excessive preliminary experimentation can also cause a DOE project to fail. Although most preliminary experiments appear to be simple and innocent, there are often unexpected surprises that consume time, materials, and perhaps most importantly the patience of the managers waiting for results. Always decide in advance of beginning any preliminary experiments how much of your resources will be expended. When those resources are gone, it's time to push on to the next step in the program. In some extreme cases, the results of preliminary experiments may also cause you to back up several steps in the DOE process or even to abandon the DOE project completely.

Which preliminary experiments to run must be decided by the DOE project leader, the operators, the technicians, and the design and process engineers. After all preliminary experiments are completed, all of these people must be convinced that they understand the product and process well enough to guarantee that the primary experiment can be built successfully. The amount of time required to perform preliminary experiments is very dependent on the process being studied and the number and complexity of issues that have to be resolved.

4.21.5 Step 5: Design the Experiment

The goal of an experiment is to extract an appropriate model from an experimental data set that can be used to answer specific questions about the process being studied. This relationship is shown in Figure 4.8. Although the execution of an experiment flows as in the figure, the process of selecting an experiment design actually flows backward. The questions to be answered determine the model that is necessary, the model determines

Figure 4.8 Relationship between the experiment design, data, model, and answers.

the data to be collected, and the experiment design defines the organization and structure of the data.

Section 4.13 indicated that there are two parts to every experiment design: the variables matrix, which identifies the experimental variables and their levels, and the design matrix, which identifies the combination of variable levels that will be used for the experimental runs. Both of these matrices must be completely defined in this step of the DOE process. Use the information collected in the previous steps of the DOE process to determine which variables to include in an experiment and what levels each variable will have. Then, based on this information and the number and nature of the design variables, that is, whether they are qualitative, quantitative, or a mixture of the two types, and how many levels of the variables there are, select an appropriate experiment design. For example, the experiment design may be: a one-way or multi-way classification design with qualitative variables, a two-level screening design, a factorial design to model main effects and interactions, a response surface design to account for curvature in the response, or a hybrid design involving both qualitative and quantitative variables. Once the design has been chosen, the matrix of experimental runs and a fictional response (for example, random normal) should be created and analyzed to confirm that the desired model can indeed be fitted to the data.

The DOE project leader should have enough information collected at this point in the DOE process that he or she can specify the variables and experimental design matrices, however, they may still find it necessary to consult with the appropriate experts on the process if there are still ambiguities with respect to some of the variables or their levels. And if there are too many variables and/or variable levels in the experiment, it may be necessary to consult with the statistical specialist and/or reconvene the whole project team to identify a more practical design. In the majority of the cases, when the previous steps in the DOE process have been completed successfully, the specification of an appropriate experiment design should take the DOE project leader less than one hour.

4.21.6 Step 6: Sample Size, Randomization, and Blocking

The tasks of determining the sample size and the randomization and blocking plans for an experiment are often considered to be a part of the experiment design step, but these tasks are so important, so interrelated, and so frequently botched, that they deserve to be elevated to a separate DOE process step of their own. These tasks are also usually performed after an experiment design has been chosen, but they may raise issues that force you to reconsider that choice.

After the experiment design, has been chosen a sample-size calculation should be performed to determine the number of replicates of the design necessary to make the experiment sufficiently sensitive to practically significant effects. If the indicated total number of runs exhausts the available time and resources, it may be necessary to revise or perhaps even abandon the original plan. The total number of runs required and the rate at which they can be produced will also factor into blocking considerations.

All experimental variables are either randomized or used to define blocks. If you intend to make claims about the effect of a variable, then that variable must be randomized. If the experiment is blocked, then the study variables must be randomized within blocks. The role of blocking variables is limited to reducing the variability associated with sources of noise that would reduce the sensitivity of the experiment if they were overlooked. If the experiment is to be built in blocks, randomize the order of the blocks and randomize runs involving study variables within blocks. Confirm that the randomization and blocking plan is effective by analyzing the intended order of the experimental runs as if it were the experimental response. If any of the design variables or other important terms in the model can predict the run order, then the randomization wasn't effective and you will have to re-randomize the runs or modify the randomization plan. Use this opportunity to confirm that the blocking plan didn't interfere with the intended model, such as by confounding a blocking variable with a study variable or an important interaction between study variables.

After the randomization plan is validated, data sheets should be created for the operators. These data sheets should indicate the settings of the experimental runs, with room to record the response and any special notes. To avoid confusing the operators, the order of the runs on the data sheets should be the randomized run order. If the experiment is to be built in blocks, separate data sheets can be created for each block. The team members who will participate in actually building the experiment should review the data collection sheets to make sure that they are correct and understood.

The DOE project leader is responsible for determining the randomization and blocking plan, but it may be necessary for him or her to consult with the statistical specialist, technicians, or process engineer to determine practical strategies for the plan. Simple experiments take only a few minutes to randomize and block but a complicated experiment may take several hours. In severe cases, the difficulties associated with randomization and blocking may require reconsideration of the experiment design.

4.21.7 Step 7: Run the Experiment

An experiment should not be run unless there is consensus among the key people involved that everything is ready. There is so much preparation and investment involved that no one wants to start an experiment prematurely. Even after a large experiment is started, you may realize that some aspect of the process was not considered and it may be necessary to suspend the experiment until the issue is resolved. Sometimes this can be done immediately after the problem is discovered, but when a clear and effective solution is not apparent it's usually better to walk away, regroup, and come back another day.

When the experiment is being performed, great care has to be taken to follow the correct procedures for the process, to honor the randomization plan, to maintain the identity of the parts, and to make sure that all of the data are faithfully and accurately recorded. Any unusual events or conditions should be clearly noted. These observations will be crucial later on if it becomes necessary to explain outliers in the data set.

All of the key people required to operate the process must be available to run the experiment. If a crucial person is missing, you're better off waiting until that person becomes available. This may or may not include the process engineer depending on how unusual some of the experimental runs are. If the operators and technicians have been properly trained and prepared to run the experiment, the DOE project leader should be able to sit back, observe, and only take action if someone becomes confused or if some unexpected event occurs.

4.21.8 Step 8: Analyze the Data

Before performing any analysis of the experimental data, the accuracy of the recorded data values should be confirmed by checking each recorded value in the worksheet against the original data record. All discrepancies must be resolved before any analysis is performed.

The experimental data should be analyzed using MINITAB or some other suitable statistical software package. When possible, the raw data should be plotted in some meaningful way. The full model, including all relevant main effects, interactions, and other terms, should be run and a complete set of residuals diagnostic plots should be created, including plots of the residuals versus each of the design variables, residuals versus fitted values, and residuals versus the run order. A normal probability plot of the residuals should also be created. Special consideration should be given to outliers or highly influential observations. It may be necessary to compare outliers detected in the statistical analysis to records or notes of unusual conditions that occurred during the experiment. Outliers must not be dropped from the data set without correlation to a clear special cause.

If the full model is excessively complex, a simplified model should be created. Both models, the full model and the simplified model, should be retained in their complete form because it is usually necessary to report both of them. The full model is important because it will probably include terms that are testable but not statistically significant, which can be of as much or even greater importance than the terms that are statistically significant.

The statistical analysis of the data should be done by the DOE project leader with support from the DOE statistical specialist if necessary. The analysis of a simple experiment should take less than an hour. More complicated experiments might require several different models and so may take several hours to analyze.

4.21.9 Step 9: Interpret the Results

Before attempting to interpret any model, the residuals diagnostic plots should be evaluated for normality, homoscedasticity, and independence. Only after these conditions and any other requirements are found to be valid should the statistical model be interpreted. If only one model was constructed from the data, the interpretation of the model will probably be straightforward. When there are several possible models to consider, it will be necessary to compare several different aspects of each to determine which is the best fit to the data. When the best model is identified, a corresponding error statement must be constructed.

When an acceptable model and error statement are found, the model should be interpreted relative to the goals of the experiments. For example, if there were specific numerical goals for the response, then valid ranges of the experimental variables that meet those goals should be identified. Several different strategies for achieving the target response might be possible. When an experimental variable is quantitative, be careful not to extrapolate the predicted response outside the range of experimentation.

The interpretation of the statistical model should be done by the DOE project leader with support from the DOE statistical specialist, if necessary. The interpretation of the model for a simple experiment will generally be straightforward and take less than an hour but more complicated problems may take several hours to interpret.

4.21.10 Step 10: Run a Confirmation Experiment

Despite the most diligent efforts and attention to detail, occasionally you will find that you can't duplicate the results of a successful experiment. To protect yourself and the organization from irreproducible results, you should always follow up a designed experiment with a confirmation experiment. The purpose of a confirmation experiment is to demonstrate the validity of the model derived from the designed experiment. The confirmation experiment may be quite small, perhaps consisting of just a single crucial condition, but it should address the most important claims or conclusions from the full experiment. It should be run well after the original experiment and under typical operating conditions. If the conclusions from the original experiment were robust, then the confirmation experiment will successfully reproduce the desired results. However, if something was overlooked or changed from the time the original experiment was performed, then the variable or changes need to be identified and incorporated into the analysis. *Never* report the results from the original experiment until the confirmation experiment has been successfully run.

The confirmation experiment is usually designed by the DOE project leader and is performed by the operators who run the process. The experiment usually doesn't take too long or consume a large amount of resources unless its results are inconsistent with the original experiment. If the confirmation experiment requires an unusual combination of variable levels, it may be necessary for the process engineer to consult or even participate in the confirmation experiment.

4.21.11 Step 11: Report the Experiment

Many organizations compile a report of an experiment in the form of slides, for example, in the form of a PowerPoint presentation. The eleven-step procedure provides an effective outline for such a presentation. It can also serve as a checklist that makes it relatively easy to confirm that all aspects of the experiment have been appropriately documented.

If a designed experiment must be documented in a written report, most organizations have a standard report format that must be used. If a standard format has not been established, the following report organization is effective:

1. *Findings.* An executive summary of the experiment summarizing the design, the analysis, and the results. This section should be no longer than just a few sentences.

2. *Background.* Some technical background on the process to be studied, a description of the problem, and a statement of the purpose of the experiment. This section should be no more than one page long.

3. *Experiment design.* A description of the experiment design and the randomization and blocking plan that was used. It may also be necessary to justify the sample size that was used.

4. *Data.* A table of the experimental data with a description of the table and its organization. Special mention should be made of missing values and any observations that have associated special causes. The location of the original data in its paper or electronic form should be indicated.

5. *Statistical analysis.* A description of the statistical analysis with explicit references to all of the computer analyses and supporting graphs. Discussion of the analysis can also be integrated into this section.

6. *Recommendations.* A recommendations section should be included in the report if a follow-up study is required or if there are any ambiguities remaining after the analysis is complete. This section may also include a focused interpretation of the analysis to address a specific problem or goal of the experiment, for example, to optimize a response.

The formal report should be written by the DOE project leader, but the report should be reviewed and approved by those members of the team who have the technical skills to understand it. Most designed experiments can be reported in detail in three to 10 pages with attached figures. Someone skilled in the art of DOE report writing will require about one to 1.5 hours per page to write the report.

Example 4.12

The following report is presented as an example of a well-written report of a designed experiment.

Report: Analysis of an Experiment to Compare Two Lubricants in a Cutting Operation

Author: Paul Mathews, Mathews Malnar and Bailey, Inc.

For: Dan M., Engineering Manager, XYZ Cutoff Inc.

Date: 22 November 1999

Findings: An experiment was performed to compare the standard lubricant (LAU-003) to a recommended replacement lubricant (LAU-016) in the brake-bar cutting operation to determine if the new lubricant would allow more cuts between blade resharpenings. The new lubricant was confirmed to deliver about 16 more cuts (131 versus 147) on average than the old lubricant ($p = 0.005$) and no adverse effects were observed. The 95 percent confidence interval for the increase in the number of cuts with LAU-016 was $P(6.3 < \Delta\mu < 25.7) = 0.95$ or between five percent to 20 percent relative to LAU-003. Based on these results, it is recommended that LAU-003 be replaced with LAU-016 in the brake-bar cutting operation.

Background: Brake bars are cut using carbide-tipped circular saws lubricated with LAU-003. Saws must be resharpened when burrs on the perimeter of the cut approach the allowed tolerances for the cut surface. LAU has suggested that saws lubricated with LAU-016 instead of LAU-003 would make more cuts between resharpenings. Decreased downtime and resharpening costs would more than offset the minor price increase for LAU-016. The purpose of this experiment is to: 1) demonstrate that LAU-016 delivers more cuts between resharpenings than LAU-003 and 2) confirm that there are no adverse effects associated with the use of LAU-016.

Preparation: A cause-and-effect analysis and operating procedure review were performed to identify factors that might influence the number of cuts delivered in the brake-bar cutting operation. These analyses identified the following factors that were thought to deserve special attention or comment:

- Methods

  - The brake-bar cutting operation is automated so there should be no variation in the methods used.

  - LAU-003 and LAU-016 are delivered in dry form and mixed with mineral oil. Both lubricants were mixed according to LAU's instructions.

  - LAU-003 lubricant is continuously filtered and eventually replaced on an established schedule; however, that schedule is not rigorously followed. For this experiment, new batches of both lubricants were prepared and used for about 10 percent of their scheduled life before the experimental runs were performed.

  - The lubricant tank was drained and refilled between trials that required a lubricant change. No attempt was made to flush out lubricant that was adsorbed on machine surfaces.

Continued

- All saw blade resharpenings were performed in-house on the Heller grinder by Tony E. Tony also confirmed the critical blade tooth specs before a blade was released for the experiment.

- Material

  - The steel stock used for brake bars is thought to be consistent from lot to lot so no attempt was made to control for lots. The order of the experimental runs was randomized to reduce the risk of lot-to-lot differences.

  - Saw blades tend to have a 'personality' so each blade was run two times— once with LAU-003 and once with LAU-016.

  - LAU lubricants tend to be very consistent from batch to batch and batches are very large, so single batches of both lubricants were used in the experiment.

  - 10 randomly selected saw blades were used for the experiment.

  - Standard-grade mineral oil provided by LAU was used to mix the lubricants.

- Manpower

  - Bob P. is the primary operator of the brake-bar cutting operation so all experimental runs were performed by him. Bob also mixed the lubricants, switched the lubricants between trials, and monitored the cutting operation to determine when a blade had reached its end of life. Bob documented all of these steps in the brake-bar cutting operation log book.

  - Tony E. resharpened blades and confirmed that they met their specs.

- Machines

  - All blades were sharpened on the Heller grinder.

  - All cuts were made with the dedicated brake bar cutter.

  - The number of cuts was determined from the counter on the brake bar cutter.

Experiment Design: Each saw blade was used once with each lubricant so the experiment is a paired-sample design that can be analyzed using a paired-sample t test. The sample size ($n = 10$) was determined by prior calculation to deliver a 90 percent probability of detecting a 10 percent increase in the life of the saw blades using LAU-016. The standard deviation for the sample-size calculation was estimated from LAU-003 historical data. The lubricant type was run in completely random order by randomly choosing a blade from among those scheduled and available for use with the required lubricant.

Experimental Data: The experiment was performed over the period 14–18 October 1999. The experimental data are shown in Figure 4.9 in the order in which they were collected. Blade #9 broke a carbide tip during its first trial so it was repaired, resharpened, and put back into service. Broken tips are random events thought to be unrelated to the lubricant so the first observation of blade #9 was omitted from the analysis. There were no other special events recorded during the execution of the experiment. The original record of these data is in the brake-bar operation logbook.

Continued

Row	Rand	Std	Blade	Lube	Cuts	
1	1	15	5	2	162	
*	2	9	9	1	*	Broken Tip
2	2	11	1	2	145	
3	3	4	4	1	117	
4	4	9	9	1	135	
5	5	13	3	2	145	
6	6	2	2	1	124	
7	7	3	3	1	131	
8	8	20	10	2	147	
9	9	12	2	2	146	
10	10	16	6	2	134	
11	11	7	7	1	130	
12	12	19	9	2	142	
13	13	8	8	1	134	
14	14	6	6	1	138	
15	15	5	5	1	123	
16	16	18	8	2	161	
17	17	1	1	1	139	
18	18	17	7	2	139	
19	19	14	4	2	149	
20	20	10	10	1	139	

Figure 4.9 Number of cuts by lubricant and blade.

Statistical Analysis: The experimental data are plotted by lubricant type and connected by blade in Figure 4.10. The plot clearly shows that the number of cuts obtained using LAU-016 is, on average, greater than the number of cuts obtained with LAU-003.

The data were analyzed using a paired-sample t test with **Stat> Basic Stats> Paired t** in MINITAB V13.1. The output from MINITAB is shown in Figure 4.11. The mean and standard deviation of the difference between the number of cuts obtained with LAU-016 versus LAU-003 was $\overline{\Delta x} = 16.0$ and $s = 13.5$. This result was statistically significant with $p = 0.005$. The Δx_i were analyzed graphically (not shown) and found to be at least approximately normal and homoscedastic with respect to run order as required for the paired-sample t test. The 95 percent confidence interval for the increase in the mean number of cuts is given by:

$$P\left(6.3 < \Delta\mu < 25.7\right) = 0.95$$

Relative to the mean number of cuts observed with LAU-003, the 95 percent confidence interval for the fractional increase in the mean number of cuts is given by:

$$P\left(0.05 < \frac{\Delta\mu}{\overline{x}_{003}} < 0.20\right) = 0.95$$

Continued

Continued

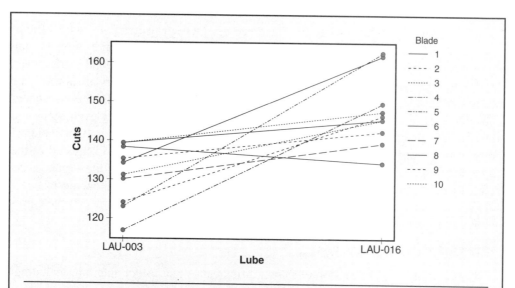

Figure 4.10 Number of cuts versus lubricant by blade.

```
Paired T-Test and CI: LAU-016, LAU-003

Paired T for LAU-016 - LAU-003

                N      Mean     StDev    SE Mean
LAU-016        10    147.00      8.77      2.77
LAU-003        10    131.00      7.54      2.39
Difference     10     16.00     13.50      4.27

95% CI for mean difference: (6.34, 25.66)
T-Test of mean difference = 0 (vs not = 0): T-Value = 3.75   P-Value = 0.005
```

Figure 4.11 Paired-sample *t* test for cuts.

Although the lower bound of the 95 percent confidence interval falls below the 10 percent target increase in the number of cuts, the true magnitude of the increase is still relatively uncertain but large enough to justify the change from LAU-003 to LAU-016.

Conclusions: The experiment indicated that LAU-016 provides a greater number of brake-bar cuts than LAU-003, and no adverse effects associated with the use of LAU-016 were observed. Based on these results, it is recommended that LAU-016 be used to replace LAU-003. Blade life should continue to be monitored after the lubricant change has been implemented to confirm that the life improvement with LAU-016 is maintained.

4.22 EXPERIMENT DOCUMENTATION

There are so many people and activities involved in a DOE project that it can be difficult to keep all of the associated documents organized. Perhaps the best way is to use a ring binder with twelve tabs or dividers. The first eleven tabs should correspond to the eleven steps of the DOE procedure and the 12th is for everything else. Some organizations issue the DOE project leader a standardized project binder or open a special folder on a shared computer hard drive at the beginning of a project. Then, as the eleven steps are addressed, the project leader and team members are responsible for seeing that copies of the appropriate documents are added to the binder or folder. This also keeps all of the relevant information in one place so everyone on the project and in the organization knows where to go and has at least some sense of the organization of the material.

The following list describes the general contents of each section of a complete project binder for an experimental program:

1. Cause-and-effect analysis

   - Copies of each revision of the modified cause-and-effect diagram, including a list of contributors to each one.

   - Relevant notes about any significant changes or additions to the cause-and-effect diagram.

   - Preliminary classification of variables into categories: possible design variable, variable to be held fixed, uncontrolled variable.

2. Process documentation

   - Copies or references to the original and final versions of the process procedures.

   - Copies or references to control charts documenting the state of the process.

   - Copies or references to relevant process capability analyses.

   - Copies or references to GR&R study results.

   - Completed checklist of relevant calibration records.

   - Completed checklist of operator training records and/or proficiency test results.

   - Completed checklist of relevant maintenance items.

3. Problem statement

   - Copies of each revision to the DOE problem statement.

   - Copy of the final DOE problem statement with appropriate approvals (for example, initials or signatures) required prior to proceeding with the experimental program.

4. Preliminary experiments

   - List of specific questions or issues to be resolved with preliminary experiments. (This list may already exist in the problem statement.)

   - Summary statement of the purpose and results of each preliminary experiment.

   - Original data records, notes, and analysis from each preliminary experiment.

   - Notes on any follow-up actions taken as a result of findings from preliminary experiments.

5. Experiment design

   - Final classification of each input variable from the cause-and-effect analysis into one of the following categories: experimental variable, variable to be held fixed, uncontrolled variable not recorded, or uncontrolled variable recorded.

   - Copies of the variable and design matrices.

   - Copy of the sample-size calculation or other sample-size justification.

   - Copy of the analysis of a simulated response demonstrating that the desired model can be fitted from the design. (This may be postponed and done in combination with the validation of the randomization and blocking plan in the next step.)

6. Randomization and blocking plan

   - Description of and justification for the randomization and blocking plan.

   - Copy of analysis validating the randomization plan (for example, analysis of run order as the response).

   - Copies of the actual data sheets (with the runs in random order) to be used for data collection.

7. Experiment records

   - Copies of any required formal authorizations to build the experiment.

   - Copies of all original data records.

   - Copies of all notes taken during the execution of the experiment.

8. Statistical analysis

   - Copy of the experimental data after transcription into the electronic worksheet.

- Copies of the analyses of the full and refined models, including the residuals analysis.

- Copies of any alternative models considered.

- Copies of any special notes or observations from the analysis concerning unusual observations, and so on, and any related findings from follow-up activities.

9. Interpretation

- Written interpretation of the statistical analysis with references to graphs and tables.

- Explanation of special applications of the final model, for example, optimization, variable settings to achieve a specified value of the response, and so on.

- Description of any special conditions or observations that might indicate the need for a follow-up experiment or influence the direction of the confirmation experiment.

- If appropriate, a brief statement about the strengths and/or weaknesses of the process, experiment, and/or analysis.

- Recommendations for the next step in the experimental project, for example, proceed to a confirmation experiment, run more replicates of the original experiment, perform another designed experiment, and so on.

10. Confirmation experiment

- Description of and justification for the confirmation experiment.

- Copies of the original data records, statistical analysis, and interpretation of the confirmation experiment.

- Summary statement about the success or failure of the confirmation experiment and implications for the goals of the experimental project.

11. Report

- Copy of the final experiment report (written and/or slide presentation) and distribution list.

- Copies of any comments or follow-up to the report.

- List of recommendations and/or warnings for anyone who might reconsider this problem in the future.

4.23 WHY EXPERIMENTS GO BAD

Despite the most careful planning, preparation, execution, and analysis, experiments still go bad. In fact, more experiments probably go wrong than right. It's safe to say that someone with lots of DOE experience has a better chance of getting an experiment right the first time, but even the best experimenter runs an unsuccessful experiment now and then. Hopefully this won't happen to you too often but as with every other type of problem that occurs, consider it to be an opportunity for improvement. Remember that there's usually more to be learned from an experiment that has gone bad than one that goes perfectly. Experiments are expected to deliver surprises but not surprises of career-ending magnitude.

The general procedure outlined in the preceding section consists of just 11 steps. Every one of those 11 steps contains numerous places where an experiment can fail. It might seem strange that most of this book is dedicated to steps 5 and 7, as those are probably the easiest ones to get right.

One of the crucial skills that distinguishes an experienced experimenter from a novice is the experienced experimenter's attention to detail coupled with the ability to recognize, among the many factors competing for attention, those important but subtle factors that can cause an experiment to fail. Experienced experimenters develop a special type of experimental sense or conscience that borders on intuition. Novices have this sense, too, but they have to learn to listen to it, develop it, and trust it. If you're new to DOE, take special note of the problems that cause your experiments to fail and try to identify the first moment that you became aware of them. Usually you'll find that you had some early sense that a problem existed but didn't fully appreciate its significance at the time. With practice, you'll get better at recognizing and reacting to those problems in time to minimize the damage to your experiments.

Here's a short list of some mistakes that can lead you astray:

- Inexperienced experimenter

- The presence of the experimenter changes the process

- Failure to identify an important variable

- Picked the wrong variables for the experiment

- Failure to hold a known variable fixed

- Failure to record the value of a known but uncontrollable variable

- Failure to block on an influential variable

- Poor understanding of the process and procedures

- Multiple processes in use

- Failure to consult the operators and technicians

- Failure to identify significant interactions
- Failure to recognize all of the responses
- Ambiguous operational definition for one or more variables or for the response.
- Inadequate repeatability and reproducibility (R&R) to measure the responses
- Failure to do any or enough preliminary experimentation
- Exhausted resources and patience with too much preliminary experimentation
- Picked variable levels too close together
- Picked variable levels too far apart
- Wrong experiment design (overlooked interactions, curvature, or first principles)
- One experiment instead of several smaller ones
- Several small experiments instead of a single larger one
- Not enough replicates
- Too many replicates
- Repetitions instead of replicates
- Failure to randomize
- Randomization plan ignored by those building the experiment
- Failure to record the actual run order
- Critical person missing when the experiment is run
- Data recording or transcription errors
- Failure to record all of the data
- Lost or confused data records
- Failure to maintain part identity
- Error in setting variable levels
- Deviations from variable target levels
- Unanticipated process change during experiment
- Equipment not properly maintained
- Failure to complete the experiment in the allotted time (for example, before a shift change)

- Failure to note special occurrences

- Wrong statistical analysis

- Failure to check assumptions (normality, equality of variances, lack of fit, and so on)

- Failure to specify the model correctly in the analysis software

- Mistreatment of experimental runs that suffered from special causes

- Mistreatment of lost experimental runs

- Failure to refine the model

- Misinterpretation of results

- Extrapolation outside of experimental boundaries

- Failure to perform a confirmation experiment

- Inadequate resources to build a confirmation experiment

- Inadequate documentation of the results

- Inappropriate presentation of the results for the audience

5

Experiments for One-Way Classifications

5.1 INTRODUCTION

When one variable appears at two levels in an experiment (for example, Manufacturer A versus B) the two-sample t test can be used to test for a difference between the means of the two levels. When a similar experiment has three or more levels (for example, Manufacturer A, B, C, and so on) you might be tempted to use the two-sample t test to test all possible pairs of levels (A versus B, A versus C, B versus C, and so on) but this is risky and a better method of analysis, called analysis of variance (ANOVA), is preferred. ANOVA employs a single statistical test to simultaneously compare all possible pairs of means to see if there are differences between them. It might seem strange that the word *variance* would appear in a test for means, but the technique really does use the F test for two variances to test for differences among three or more treatment means in a clever and safe way.

An experiment to test for differences between the means of several different levels of a single variable involves a *one-way* classification and we analyze one-way classification data using *one-way ANOVA,* which is the topic of this chapter. As you would expect, more complex experiments involving two or more classification variables are called two-way and multi-way classification designs and are analyzed using two-way and multi-way ANOVA, which are considered in Chapter 6. And while the ANOVA method is generally used to treat qualitative classification variables, it can also be used with quantitative variables so ANOVA appears again in the presentation of linear regression methods in Chapter 8.

5.2 ANALYSIS BY COMPARISON OF ALL POSSIBLE PAIRS MEANS

Suppose that in an experiment involving several different levels or treatments of a single variable, we wish to determine whether one or more pairs of treatments have means that are different from each other. That is, we want to test the hypotheses:

$$H_0 : \mu_q = \mu_r \text{ for all possible pairs of treatments} \tag{5.1}$$

versus:

$$H_A : \mu_q \neq \mu_r \text{ for one or more pairs of treatments} \tag{5.2}$$

If we try to test these hypotheses using multiple two-sample t tests there will be:

$$\binom{k}{2} = \frac{k!}{2!(k-2)!} = \frac{k(k-1)}{2} \tag{5.3}$$

tests to perform. These tests are certainly feasible but there's a serious risk associated with this approach. If the significance level for each two-sample t test is α, then the probability of *not* committing a Type 1 error on a test is $1 - \alpha$. Since we have to do $\binom{k}{2}$ tests, the probability of not committing *any* Type 1 errors is given by:

$$1 - \alpha_{total} = (1-\alpha)^{\binom{k}{2}} \tag{5.4}$$

where α_{total} is the probability of committing a Type 1 error on at least one of the tests.* α_{total} can become very large, especially when there are many tests to perform, so the use of multiple t tests must be reconsidered. An alternative method, one that either replaces the multiple two-sample t tests with a single test or that reduces the overall error rate to a reasonable value, is required.

Example 5.1

An experiment is to be performed to test five treatments for differences between their means. Determine the overall Type 1 error probability for multiple comparisons if a significance level of $\alpha = 0.05$ is used for each two-sample t test. List the pairs of means to be compared.

Solution: There will be $\binom{5}{2} = 10$ pairs of means to be compared: {12, 13, 14, 15, 23, 24, 25, 34, 35, 45}, so:

$$1 - \alpha_{total} = (1 - 0.05)^{10} = 0.60 = 1 - 0.40$$

---

* The approximation $(1 - x)^n \approx 1 - nx$ if and only if $|x| \ll 1$ implies that $\alpha_{total} \approx k(k-1)\alpha/2$ or that α_{total} is approximately equal to the α value for individual tests times the number of tests.

or $\alpha_{total} = 0.40$. α_{total} is seriously inflated by making so many multiple comparisons relative to the α selected for a single t test. This level of risk is entirely unacceptable!

5.3 THE GRAPHICAL APPROACH TO ANOVA

Consider the one-way classification data of $k = 9$ treatments shown in Table 5.1 and the corresponding boxplots in Figure 5.1. Each of the $k = 9$ samples is of size $n = 9$ and is drawn from a normal population. If we choose to use multiple two-sample t tests to check for differences between the treatment means, there would be $\binom{9}{2} = 36$ tests to perform. With $\alpha = 0.05$ for individual tests, the overall Type 1 error rate is $\alpha_{total} = 1 - 0.95^{36}$ or about 84 percent, which is obviously unacceptable.

Table 5.1 Sample data from nine treatments.

Observation	Treatment								
	1	2	3	4	5	6	7	8	9
1	80.9	78.2	76.2	80.6	78.3	74.5	83.7	86.6	83.1
2	78.3	81.8	78.7	84.3	83.1	79.0	80.3	83.6	77.9
3	77.8	83.5	79.5	80.5	78.9	79.7	80.8	85.6	77.9
4	76.6	84.2	75.3	77.2	83.4	83.1	83.6	83.9	79.9
5	82.2	75.7	82.2	82.6	81.0	76.4	83.4	86.0	83.7
6	74.5	81.4	78.7	79.1	77.8	80.2	78.6	77.0	80.5
7	80.5	78.0	74.2	83.7	77.4	80.9	82.8	80.0	81.4
8	77.0	81.9	84.1	81.9	78.4	81.2	73.6	84.2	74.8
9	82.5	83.2	83.7	77.9	78.1	84.0	82.7	76.7	86.1

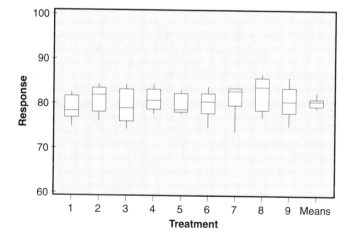

Figure 5.1 Boxplots of treatments with all means equal.

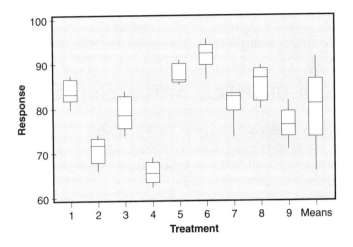

Figure 5.2 Boxplots of treatments with unequal means.

Now inspect the last boxplot in Figure 5.1. This boxplot was constructed from the $k = 9$ treatment means. One of the characteristics of boxplots is that they tend to get larger with sample size, but in this case each of the ten boxplots in the figure is constructed from nine observations. The boxplot of sample means is obviously much smaller than the other nine boxplots—but this is just a consequence of the central limit theorem, which says that the distribution of the sample means for samples drawn from a single population is contracted by a factor of $\sqrt{n}$ relative to the distribution of that population. That is:

$$\sigma_{\bar{y}} = \frac{\sigma_y}{\sqrt{n}}$$

So, as expected, the boxplot of sample means in Figure 5.1 appears to be smaller than most of the other boxplots by about a factor of $\sqrt{9} = 3$. Now consider the boxplots in Figure 5.2. Again, there are $k = 9$ different treatments shown, all of size $n = 9$ and with about the same amount of variation as the boxplots in Figure 5.1, but these boxplots clearly have means that are different from each other. Notice the effect of the different means on the last boxplot, which again shows the distribution of sample means; it is inflated to a size much larger than that of any of the individual boxplots, which contradicts the prediction of the central limit theorem. This contradiction, which is based on the relative size of the boxplot of sample means, confirms our observation that there are signficant differences between the treatment means.

Figures 5.1 and 5.2 suggest a new graphical method of checking for differences between pairs of means for many different treatments; if the distribution of sample means is contracted by the expected factor of $\sqrt{n}$ as predicted by the central limit theorem, then there are probably no significant differences between any of the population means. If, however, the distribution of sample means is not contracted by the expected amount, then one or more of the populations being sampled must have a mean that is significantly different from the others. This graphical test is the basis of the ANOVA method.

5.4 INTRODUCTION TO ANOVA

5.4.1 The ANOVA Rationale

The failure of the method of multiple comparisons to test for differences between k treatment means was due to the application of $\binom{k}{2}$ separate tests. A single test that compares all of the means simultaneously is required to avoid this problem. Such a test is provided by the *analysis of variance* (ANOVA).

To understand how ANOVA works, consider the following situation. Suppose k random samples, all of size n, are drawn from the *same* normal population so that the samples are guaranteed to have the same population mean and variance. Let $x = \{1, 2, \ldots, k\}$ distinguish the different samples and y indicate the measurement response. If the variance of the population is σ_y^2, then the central limit theorem describes the distribution of the sample means, so the variance of the distribution of sample $\bar{y}$s is:

$$\sigma_{\bar{y}}^2 = \frac{\sigma_y^2}{n} \tag{5.5}$$

If we solve this expression for σ_y^2 we get:

$$\sigma_y^2 = n\sigma_{\bar{y}}^2 \tag{5.6}$$

Of course σ_y^2 and $\sigma_{\bar{y}}^2$ are usually unknown, but we can estimate them both from the sample data. An estimate of σ_y^2 could be made from the sample variance of any one of the k samples, but a better estimate can be made by averaging all k sample variances. This technique, combining the variances from different treatments, is called pooling, and we say that the k sample variances are pooled to estimate the common population variance. The pooled sample variance is also called the error variance because it measures the random error variability within samples. If the variance of the ith sample is s_i^2, given by:

$$s_i^2 = \frac{1}{n-1}\sum_{j=1}^{n}(y_{ij} - \bar{y}_i)^2 = \frac{1}{n-1}\sum_{j=1}^{n}\varepsilon_{ij}^2 \tag{5.7}$$

then the pooled or error variance is:

$$s_\varepsilon^2 = \frac{1}{k}\sum_{i=1}^{k}s_i^2 \tag{5.8}$$

The quantity $\varepsilon_{ij} = y_{ij} - \bar{y}_i$ is the discrepancy or error between an observation and its treatment mean. Since s_i^2 measures the amount of error variation within the ith treatment, then s_ε^2 measures the amount of variation that occurs *within* treatments, based on information from all of the treatments. Note that s_ε^2 is an estimate for σ_y^2. It is this quantity that determines the nominal size of the boxplots in Figures 5.1 and 5.2.

A second estimate of σ_y^2 can be determined from the variance of the distribution of the k sample means. If the ith sample mean is $\bar{y}_i$, then the grand mean is:

$$\bar{\bar{y}} = \frac{1}{k}\sum_{i=1}^{k}\bar{y}_i \tag{5.9}$$

and the variance of the $\bar{y}_i$s is given by:

$$s_{\bar{y}}^2 = \frac{\sum_{i=1}^{k}\left(\bar{y}_i - \bar{\bar{y}}\right)^2}{k-1} \tag{5.10}$$

This is the quantity that determines the size of the boxplots of sample means in Figures 5.1 and 5.2. Combined with Equation 5.6, Equation 5.10 gives us a second estimate of σ_y^2 given by $\sigma_y^2 \simeq ns_{\bar{y}}^2$, as determined from the variation that occurs *between* treatment levels.

Now for the magic! We have two estimates for σ_y^2—one given by the variation *within* samples:

$$\hat{\sigma}_y^2 = s_\varepsilon^2 \tag{5.11}$$

and another given by the variation *between* samples:

$$\hat{\sigma}_y^2 = ns_{\bar{y}}^2 \tag{5.12}$$

The ratio of the two estimates of σ_y^2:

$$F = \frac{\hat{\sigma}_y^2}{\hat{\sigma}_y^2} = \frac{ns_{\bar{y}}^2}{s_\varepsilon^2} \tag{5.13}$$

follows an F distribution with $k - 1$ numerator and $k(n - 1)$ denominator degrees of freedom. There are $k - 1$ degrees of freedom for the numerator because $k - 1$ sample means are used to calculate $s_{\bar{y}}^2$. There are $k(n - 1)$ degrees of freedom for the denominator because k sample variances, each with $n - 1$ degrees of freedom, are used to calculate the error variance s_ε^2. If all of the necessary conditions are met, those that make the central limit theorem work and the claim that all of the k samples have the same population mean, then we expect this F ratio to be $F = 1$. If, however, we relax the condition that all of the samples come from the same population, then if one or more of the population means is different from the others, $s_{\bar{y}}^2$ will be inflated and our F ratio will become larger than $F = 1$. In practice, if $F \simeq 1$ then we accept the claim that all treatment means are equal (or reserve judgement) and if $F \gg 1$ then we reject the claim that all treatment means are equal.

Example 5.2

The means and the variances of the $k = 9$ samples from Figure 5.1 are shown in the following table. Use these statistics to perform the ANOVA to test the claim that the nine samples come from populations with the same mean.

i	1	2	3	4	5	6	7	8	9
n_i	9	9	9	9	9	9	9	9	9
$\bar{y}_i$	78.9	80.9	79.2	80.9	79.6	79.9	81.1	82.6	80.6
s_i^2	7.56	8.41	12.9	6.14	5.39	9.04	10.9	14.3	11.9

Solution: The error variance is given by:

$$\begin{aligned}
s_\varepsilon^2 &= \tfrac{1}{9}\Sigma_{i=1}^9 s_i^2 \\
&= \tfrac{1}{9}\left(7.56 + 8.41 + \cdots + 11.9\right) \\
&= \tfrac{1}{9}\left(86.7\right) \\
&= 9.63
\end{aligned}$$

The grand mean is:

$$\begin{aligned}
\bar{\bar{y}} &= \tfrac{1}{9}\Sigma_{i=1}^9 \bar{y}_i \\
&= \tfrac{1}{9}\left(724\right) \\
&= 80.4
\end{aligned}$$

and the variance of the sample means is given by:

$$\begin{aligned}
s_{\bar{y}}^2 &= \tfrac{1}{9-1}\Sigma_{i=1}^9\left(\bar{y}_i - \bar{\bar{y}}\right)^2 \\
&= \tfrac{1}{8}\left[\left(78.9 - 80.4\right)^2 + \left(80.9 - 80.4\right)^2 + \cdots + \left(80.6 - 80.4\right)^2\right] \\
&= \tfrac{1}{8}\left(10.45\right) \\
&= 1.31
\end{aligned}$$

The F ratio for the ANOVA is:

$$F = \frac{ns_{\bar{y}}^2}{s_{\varepsilon}^2}$$

$$= \frac{9 \times 1.31}{9.63}$$

$$= 1.22$$

F = 1.22 is very close to the expected F = 1 value which suggests that there are no differences between any of the k = 9 population means, but to be rigorous we need to find the critical value of F that determines the accept/reject boundary for the hypotheses. The F distribution has $df_{numerator} = k - 1 = 9 - 1 = 8$ degrees of freedom and $df_{denominator} = k (n - 1) = 9 (9 - 1) = 72$ denominator degrees of freedom. At a significance level of $\alpha = 0.05$ we have $F_{0.05,8,72} = 2.07$. Since $(F = 1.22) < (F_{0.05} = 2.07)$ we must conclude that there are no significant differences between the means of the nine populations.

5.4.2 ANOVA Assumptions and Validation

The conditions required to validate the use of the ANOVA method are:

- The populations being sampled are normally distributed.
- The populations being sampled are homoscedastic.
- The observations are independent.

When these conditions are satisfied, the hypotheses can be expressed as: H_0: *All samples come from essentially the same population* versus H_A: *One or more pairs of treatments have population means that are different from each other.* ANOVA is not particularly sensitive to deviations from some of these conditions so the usual method of checking them is the rather subjective evaluation of various plots of the residuals. The plots that are usually constructed are:

- A histogram of the residuals.
- A normal probability plot of the residuals.
- A plot of the residuals by treatment.
- A plot of the residuals versus the order of the experimental runs.
- A plot of the residuals versus the treatment means.

The purpose of the histogram and normal probability plot is primarily to evaluate the assumption that the populations being sampled are normally distributed. The normal plot is worth more attention than the histogram, especially when there are few observations, because normal plots are much more sensitive to deviations from normality than histograms. Although individual normal plots could be constructed of the data from each treatment to test the normality requirement, if the homoscedasticity assumption is also satisfied then a single normal plot of the combined residuals is sufficient to test the normality of all of the treatments at once. The single normal plot of the residuals also has many more points on it than the individual normal plots would, so it is much easier to interpret.

DOE novices frequently make the mistake of attempting to evaluate the normality requirement by creating a single histogram or normal plot of all of the response values instead of the residuals; however, the normality requirement applies to the distribution of the residuals within treatments—not to the distribution of the response taken over all treatments. ANOVA can tolerate—and is in fact designed to detect—differences between the treatment means, so the normal plot of the *response* is allowed to be far from normal.

The purpose of the plot of the residuals by treatment is to provide a test of the assumption that the populations being studied are homoscedastic. If the dotplots of the different treatments appear to have about the same amount of scatter, then the homoscedasticity assumption is probably satisfied. This is certainly a subjective evaluation, and it takes some practice to calibrate your eye to know when there might be a violation of the homoscedasticity requirement. Keep in mind that just as the multiple comparisons of all possible pairs of means involves $\binom{k}{2}$ tests, there will also be $\binom{k}{2}$ pairs of treatments to evaluate for homoscedasticity and, more importantly, that your eye will naturally be drawn to the most outrageously different pair of treatments. Don't rush to the conclusion that the treatments are heteroscedastic without strong evidence, because the ANOVA method isn't particularly sensitive to this requirement. And if you're still uneasy about judging treatment homoscedasticity from the residuals plot, consider using a quantitative method like Bartlett's or Levene's test. These methods do for the treatment variances what ANOVA does for the treatment means.* That is, they test the hypotheses H_0: $\sigma_q^2 = \sigma_r^2$ for all possible pairs of treatments versus H_A: $\sigma_q^2 \neq \sigma_r^2$ for at least one pair of treatments.†

The purpose of the plot of residuals versus the order of the observations is to evaluate the assumption that the residuals are independent and homoscedastic with respect to run order. This plot is essentially a run chart of residuals, which should display an approximately constant mean of $\bar{\varepsilon} = 0$ and constant residual variance throughout the experiment. If the only systematic difference between observations is due to a possible difference between the treatment means, and if the order of the observations is randomized with respect to treatments as it is supposed to be, then this plot should display no patterns or structure. If, however, there is a pattern in the residuals with respect to the order of the observations, then there must be some unidentified cause for that pattern that is not accounted for in the analysis. The presence of such a pattern could invalidate the ANOVA conclusions.

The purpose of the plot of residuals versus the treatment means or fits is to evaluate the assumption that the residuals are homoscedastic with respect to the magnitude

---

* Levene's test actually uses ANOVA to analyze a transformation of the residuals to evaluate treatment homoscedasticity!

† Both Bartlett's test and the modified Levene's test are available in MINITAB from the **Stat> ANOVA> Test for Equal Variances** menu. The modified Levene's test is preferred over other methods because it is more robust in cases of deviations from normality.

of the response. To some degree, this plot is redundant to the plot of residuals by treatment, but it can provide important clues about how to manage heteroscedasticity if the residual variance is simply related to the size of the treatment means.

Since ANOVA is relatively insensitive to deviations from the normality and homoscedasticity conditions, the validation of both of these conditions is frequently performed by inspection of boxplots of the treatments. The validity of the normality condition can be judged by checking for the tendency of the boxplots to be symmetric and to have reasonably sized whiskers relative to the size of the boxes. Be careful not to focus on the detailed structure of individual boxplots but, instead, look for common behavior in all of the boxplots. For example, if all of the boxplots suggest that the residual distribution is skewed, then the normality assumption is probably violated. Or if the boxplots are wildly different in size, then the treatments may be heteroscedastic. As was pointed out before, don't get lured into overreacting to the worst-case pair of treatments— focus on the overall behavior of all of the boxplots. The independence assumption can't be evaluated by inspecting boxplots because boxplots don't present any information about the order of the observations; however, when the order of the runs in an experiment is correctly and faithfully randomized, then it's common to assume independence without checking to see if the condition is actually met.

If there are any observations that are outliers in the data set, they will be apparent in one or more of the residuals diagnostic plots. Don't be tempted to omit outliers from the data set because they are proof that there are unexplained sources of variation in the process being studied. By definition, outliers are rare events, so if there are several of them they probably aren't outliers and they probably have a common cause. The standard diagnostic plots can provide clues about the nature of the outliers, but it may be necessary to consider other variables that were outside the scope of the original experiment. If a cause for the outliers cannot be determined and they truly appear to be random events, their presence could compromise the ANOVA because of violations of the ANOVA assumptions. A safe approach to take in this case is to analyze the data set with and without the ouliers present. If the two analyses give the same results, then the outliers haven't had any influence and the analysis including the outliers should be reported. If the two analyses give different results, it will be necessary to investigate the process and the experiment in more detail to find the cause of the outliers before valid conclusions can be drawn.

Example 5.3

The residuals diagnostic graphs in Figure 5.3 were created following the one-way ANOVA of the data set in Table 5.1. Use these graphs to determine if the ANOVA assumptions are satisfied.

Solution: Figure 5.3a shows boxplots of the data by treatment. The boxplots are all comparable in size which suggests that the residuals are homoscedastic with respect to treatments. The boxplots also appear to be roughly symmetric so the residuals might be normally distributed.

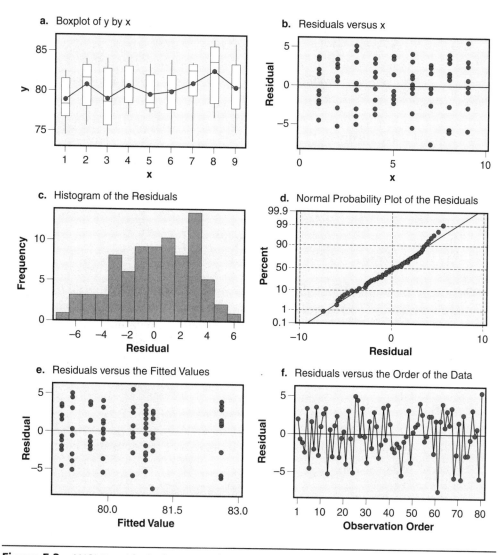

Figure 5.3 ANOVA residuals diagnostics for the data from Table 5.1.

Figure 5.3b shows dotplots of residuals versus treatments. Although there is some variability in the amount of scatter present in the different treatments, there are no glaring differences so the residuals are probably homoscedastic with respect to treatments.

Figure 5.3c shows a histogram of the residuals. The residuals appear to follow the expected bell-shaped normal curve and there is no evidence of outliers. The normal probability plot of the residuals in Figure 5.3d shows that they fall along an approximately straight line, which supports the claim that the residuals are normally distributed.

Figure 5.3e shows a plot of the residuals versus the predicted values (that is, the treatment means). The amount of variation in the residuals appears to be comparable whether the magnitude of the response is large or small so the residuals are probably homoscedastic with respect to the predicted values.

Figure 5.3f shows a run chart of the residuals.* The run chart does not show any patterns so the residuals are probably mutually independent. The residuals also appear to be homoscedastic with respect to run order.

5.4.3 The ANOVA Table

There is one more sample variance that can be calculated from the data. The total variance in the data set can be calculated by considering all of the kn units' deviations from the grand mean $\bar{\bar{y}}$:

$$s_{total}^2 = \frac{1}{kn-1}\sum_{i=1}^{k}\sum_{j=1}^{n}\left(y_{ij}-\bar{\bar{y}}\right)^2 \tag{5.14}$$

There is a very important relationship between the three variances: s_{total}^2, s_ε^2, and $s_{\bar{y}}^2$. The total variance s_{total}^2 is actually divided into two parts. The total variance within samples is measured by s_ε^2 and the variance between samples is measured by $s_{\bar{y}}^2$. Welcome to ANOVA! The partitioning of the total variance into within and between components is of fundamental importance. It will be seen explicitly in the next section that the partitioning of variances is determined by the following equation:

$$(kn-1)s_{total}^2 = (k-1)ns_{\bar{y}}^2 + k(n-1)s_\varepsilon^2 \tag{5.15}$$

The different variances and their associated degrees of freedom are summarized in an ANOVA table:

Source	df	$\hat{\sigma}_y^2$	F
Treatment	$k-1$	$ns_{\bar{y}}^2$	$F = \frac{ns_{\bar{y}}^2}{s_\varepsilon^2}$
Error	$k(n-1)$	s_ε^2	
Total	$kn-1$	s_{total}^2	

Example 5.4
Construct the ANOVA summary table for the data from Figure 5.1.

Solution: The only piece of information that hasn't been calculated already is the total variance. The total variance is given by:

---

* The actual order of the observations was not indicated with the data in Table 5.1 so, for demonstration purposes, the run chart was constructed using the order of the stacked observations in the table. For real problems, the real randomized run order must be used to construct the residuals run chart.

$$s^2_{total} = \frac{1}{kn-1}\sum_{i=1}^{k}\sum_{j=1}^{n}\left(y_{ij}-\bar{\bar{y}}\right)^2$$

$$= \frac{1}{9\times 9-1}\sum_{i=1}^{9}\sum_{j=1}^{9}\left(y_{ij}-80.4\right)^2$$

$$= 9.83$$

The ANOVA table is then:

Source	df	$\hat{\sigma}^2_y$	F
Treatment	8	11.73	1.22
Error	72	9.62	
Total	80	9.83	

5.5 THE SUM OF SQUARES APPROACH TO ANOVA CALCULATIONS

The method used to determine the three variances s^2_{total}, s^2_{ε}, and $s^2_{\bar{y}}$ in the previous section was by the use of the defining forms of the variances. These variances were identified as the total, within-sample, and between-sample variations. This section is devoted to the development of the general forms for these variances. These forms are very important and you should study this section carefully. The corresponding calculating forms will be introduced in the next section and although they are less physically meaningful than the general forms presented here, the calculating forms do provide a simpler method of implementing the ANOVA calculations.

The calculation of the total variance for the data sets considered in the hypothetical examples was done with Equation 5.14:

$$s^2_{total} = \frac{1}{kn-1}\sum_{i=1}^{k}\sum_{j=1}^{n}\left(y_{ij}-\bar{\bar{y}}\right)^2 \tag{5.16}$$

For the moment, just consider the double summation. Addition and subtraction of the same quantity inside the summation will not change its value, so by adding and subtracting $\bar{y}_i$ we have:

$$\sum_{i=1}^{k}\sum_{j=1}^{n}\left(y_{ij}-\bar{\bar{y}}\right)^2 = \sum_{i=1}^{k}\sum_{j=1}^{n}\left(y_{ij}-\bar{y}_i+\bar{y}_i-\bar{\bar{y}}\right)^2 \tag{5.17}$$

By rewriting this summation as:

$$\sum_{i=1}^{k}\sum_{j=1}^{n}\left(y_{ij}-\bar{\bar{y}}\right)^2 = \sum_{i=1}^{k}\sum_{j=1}^{n}\left(\left(y_{ij}-\bar{y}_i\right)+\left(\bar{y}_i-\bar{\bar{y}}\right)\right)^2 \tag{5.18}$$

and expanding the square, the following expression is obtained:

$$\sum_{i=1}^{k}\sum_{j=1}^{n}\left(y_{ij}-\bar{\bar{y}}\right)^2 = \sum_{i=1}^{k}\sum_{j=1}^{n}(y_{ij}-\bar{y}_i)^2 + n\sum_{i=1}^{k}\left(\bar{y}_i-\bar{\bar{y}}\right)^2 \tag{5.19}$$

This equation is of primary importance and is the key to all of the more complex ANOVA and linear regression techniques that follow it. The equation says that the total variation in the data, as measured with the total sum of squares, is partitioned into two parts: a sum of squares due to variation *within* treatments plus a sum of squares due to variation *between* treatments. These three summations are fundamentally important and deserve individual attention. They are referred to generically as sums of squares, abbreviated *SS,* and specifically by the following identifications:

$$SS_{total} = \sum_{i=1}^{k}\sum_{j=1}^{n}(y_{ij}-\bar{\bar{y}})^2 \tag{5.20}$$

$$SS_{error} = \sum_{i=1}^{k}\sum_{j=1}^{n}(y_{ij}-\bar{y}_i)^2 \tag{5.21}$$

and

$$SS_{treatments} = n\sum_{i=1}^{k}\left(\bar{y}_i-\bar{\bar{y}}\right)^2 \tag{5.22}$$

The total sum of squares term SS_{total} provides a measure of all of the variation present in the data set because it considers the deviation of each data point in the set from the grand mean. The error sum of squares term SS_{error} or SS_{ε} measures the variation of each data point from its treatment-level mean. This is a measure of the variation within treatments and so must be random or error variation. Finally, the treatment sum of squares term $SS_{treatments}$ provides a measure of variation between treatments by considering the deviation of each treatment-level mean from the grand mean. This quantity measures the amount of variation introduced by differences between the treatment means. The partitioning of the variation according to Equation 5.19 is shown graphically in Figures 5.4, 5.5, and 5.6.

The sums of squares terms are easily calculated in appropriate computer programs and are even more easily calculated using special calculating forms. The defining and calculating forms of these equations are derived in and behave the same way as the defining and calculating forms for the standard deviation. The definitions for the sums of squares given by Equations 5.20, 5.21, and 5.22 permit Equation 5.19 to be rewritten as:

$$SS_{total} = SS_{error} + SS_{treatments} \tag{5.23}$$

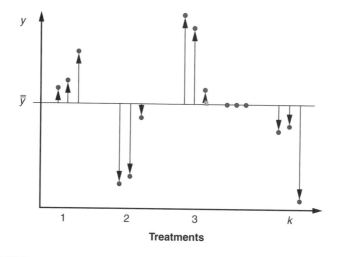

Figure 5.4 Total variation in the data set.

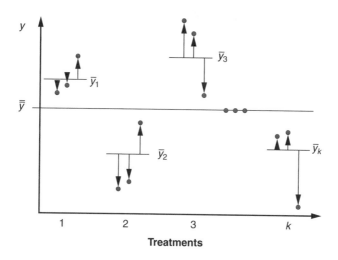

Figure 5.5 Variation within treatments.

While the sums of squares quantify the variation due to different sources, another set of relations characterizes the number of degrees of freedom associated with each sum of squares. The total number of degrees of freedom is, as always, the total number of observations minus one:

$$df_{total} = kn - 1$$

This quantity is partitioned according to the following relation:

$$kn - 1 = k(n-1) + (k-1) \tag{5.24}$$

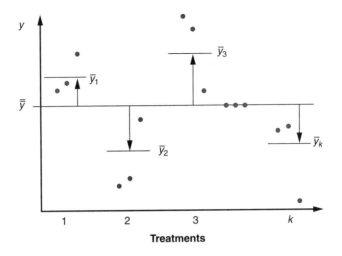

Figure 5.6   Variation between treatments.

The quantities $k(n-1)$ and $(k-1)$ are associated with the number of degrees of freedom available to estimate the *within* treatment-level variation and the *between* treatment-level variation, respectively, so we write:

$$df_{error} = k(n-1) \tag{5.25}$$

and

$$df_{treatments} = k - 1 \tag{5.26}$$

The partitioning of the total degrees of freedom can then be expressed as:

$$df_{total} = df_{error} + df_{treatments} \tag{5.27}$$

Finally, by constructing the respective ratios of *SS* to *df* from the partitioned quantities in Equations 5.23 and 5.27 and identifying the ratios with the variances defined in Equations 5.14, 5.8, 5.10, and we have:

$$s_{total}^2 = \frac{SS_{total}}{df_{total}} \tag{5.28}$$

$$s_{\varepsilon}^2 = \frac{SS_{error}}{df_{error}} \tag{5.29}$$

and

$$ns_{\bar{y}}^2 = \frac{SS_{treatments}}{df_{treatments}} \tag{5.30}$$

These three variances are referred to as *mean squares,* abbreviated *MS,* but they are just the variances that characterize the total, within-treatment, and between-treatment variation. They are specifically referred to as MS_{total}, MS_{error}, and $MS_{treatments}$, respectively.

The sums of squares, degrees of freedom, mean squares, and *F* statistics are usually summarized in an ANOVA table, which has the following form:

Source	df	SS	MS	F
Treatment	$k-1$	$SS_{treatment}$	$SS_{treatment} / df_{treatment}$	$MS_{treatment} / MS_{error}$
Error	$k(n-1)$	SS_{error}	SS_{error} / df_{error}	
Total	$kn-1$	SS_{total}	SS_{total} / df_{total}	

Note that the treatment and error terms in the degrees of freedom column add to the total degrees of freedom. Likewise, the treatment and error terms in the sum of squares column add to the total sum of squares; however, the mean square treatment and error terms *do not* add like the others. Remember that the mean squares are always variances.

5.6 THE CALCULATING FORMS FOR THE SUMS OF SQUARES

The sum of squares calculations described by Equations 5.20, 5.21, and 5.22 are analogous to the defining formula for the standard deviation. They are useful because they are insightful, but they involve excessive calculations. An alternative form of these three equations is available analogous to the calculating form of the standard deviation. These are the forms used most often for both hand calculation and in software. If your intention is to understand what ANOVA does and you trust your software to get it right, then you're done and you could skip the rest of this section. However, if you want to understand how your software works or if you feel the need to implement ANOVA on your own, you definitely need to read this section (and get a life). The section is short and the special dot notation introduced here is used in later chapters so it's worth reading.

A special notational convention is commonly used when describing the calculating forms for the sums of squares. This notation is referred to as the *dot* notation because a dot is used to indicate summation over a subscript. For example, since y_{ij} represents the *j*th replicate of *n* replicates within the *i*th sample or treatment level of *k* treatment levels, the dot notation can be used to indicate the sum of the *i*th treatment level's observations:

$$y_{i\bullet} = \sum_{j=1}^{n} y_{ij} \qquad (5.31)$$

In this manner, the *i*th treatment-level mean is $\bar{y}_{i\bullet}$. The sum of all of the *kn* observations is given by:

$$y_{\bullet\bullet} = \sum_{i=1}^{k} \sum_{j=1}^{n} y_{ij} \tag{5.32}$$

and the grand mean, formerly indicated with the symbol $\bar{\bar{y}}$ can be written as $\bar{y}_{\bullet\bullet}$, where the two dots indicate summation over i and j and the bar indicates that the mean is taken after the summations. (The single bar over y indicates that the mean is taken over both dotted variables.) Using this notation, the following calculating formulas are used to determine the sums of squares:

$$SS_{total} = \sum_{i=1}^{k} \sum_{j=1}^{n} y_{ij}^2 - \frac{y_{\bullet\bullet}^2}{kn} \tag{5.33}$$

$$SS_{treatment} = \frac{1}{n} \sum_{i=1}^{k} y_{i\bullet}^2 - \frac{y_{\bullet\bullet}^2}{kn} \tag{5.34}$$

and

$$SS_{error} = SS_{total} - SS_{treatment} \tag{5.35}$$

Some DOE textbooks only show the calculating forms, usually in dot notation. Back before software was generally available for ANOVA, most experimenters did calculations by hand or wrote their own code and the calculating forms were the only way to go. But now there are so many software packages to do these calculations that no one has to write their own anymore and the need for the calculating forms has substantially gone away. This means that the emphasis on the ANOVA calculations has shifted back to the defining forms for conceptual reasons but the authors of those old DOE books have not taken the time nor had the motivation to make the change.

5.7 ANOVA FOR UNBALANCED EXPERIMENTS

An experiment that has an unequal number of observations for its treatments is said to be an *unbalanced* experiment. This situation is generally undesirable, but can happen for a variety of reasons: by design to put emphasis on certain important treatments, when some units are lost during construction of the experiment, or for other reasons beyond the experimenter's control. The ANOVA calculations for unbalanced experiments are malicious—plan to leave them to your software. If you really want to see how the calculations are done, see Montgomery (1991).

Be careful interpreting boxplots and dotplots of residuals versus treatments for homoscedasticity in unbalanced experiments because the size of boxplots and the scatter of dotplots increase with sample size, which might cause the residuals to appear to be heteroscedastic with respect to treatments when they really aren't. Small differences in sample size, such as when a few runs are lost in a balanced experiment, have little effect on the sizes of boxplots and dotplots so interpret them in the usual manner. The assumption that residuals are homoscedastic with respect to treatments can be checked more rigorously when the sample sizes are different by using quantitative tests like Bartlett's and Levene's tests.

5.8 AFTER ANOVA: COMPARING THE TREATMENT MEANS

5.8.1 Introduction

ANOVA is used to avoid the inflation of the Type 1 error rate that occurs with the use of multiple two-sample *t* tests between all possible pairs of treatment means. All ANOVA does, however, is indicate if there are differences between one or more pairs of treatment means—it does not indicate which pairs are different. Special post-ANOVA methods of analysis have been developed to identify the different pairs, *but these methods should only be invoked after ANOVA indicates that there really are significant differences between treatments.* Perhaps, not surprisingly, many of these post-ANOVA methods are variations on the two-sample *t* test method that we went out of the way to avoid at the beginning of this chapter. You might want to review the calculations for the two-sample *t* test in Section 3.6 before proceeding.

Multiple comparisons of treatment means after ANOVA is a controversial topic. (This is one of the things that statisticians get in bar fights about.) The multiple two-sample *t*-tests that we worked so hard to avoid can actually be used with some modifications. Many formal methods exist, all with their own strengths and weaknesses, but we can address most problems with just a handful of them. Hopefully your experiments will be well designed and executed and the differences between the treatments will be easy to spot; however, these post-ANOVA methods are essential to detect subtle differences between treatments. Always start by looking at boxplots or dotplots of the raw data, then look at boxplots or dotplots of the sample means, and finally resort to a formal multiple comparisons test. Most statistical software, like MINITAB, supports several different multiple comparisons tests. Use one method, use several, use none—it's your choice. But always use an appropriate method of analysis to identify the significant differences between treatments.

5.8.2 Bonferroni's Method

Many of the available post-ANOVA multiple comparisons methods are variations on a technique introduced by Bonferroni. Bonferroni argued that the overall Type 1 error rate for multiple *t* tests could be kept tolerably low by using an appropriately small α for individual tests. The overall error rate for all of the tests is called the *family* error rate α_{family}. Bonferroni took the family error rate for the $\binom{k}{2}$ multiple comparisons of *k* treatment means to be the sum of the individual testing errors:

$$\alpha_{family} = \binom{k}{2}\alpha \tag{5.36}$$

Then α for individual tests must be:

$$\alpha = \frac{\alpha_{family}}{\binom{k}{2}} \tag{5.37}$$

where we can pick α_{family} to be acceptably low, such as $\alpha_{family} = 0.05$.

The t test statistic for the Bonferroni comparison of the ith and jth treatment means is given by:

$$t = \frac{\bar{y}_i - \bar{y}_j}{s_\varepsilon \sqrt{\frac{1}{n_i} + \frac{1}{n_j}}} \tag{5.38}$$

where s_ε is the standard error of the ANOVA. The acceptance interval for the two-sided test of H_0: $\mu_i = \mu_j$ is given by:

$$P\left(-t_{\alpha/2} \leq t \leq t_{\alpha/2}\right) = 1 - \alpha \tag{5.39}$$

where α is given by Equation 5.37 and the t distribution has degrees of freedom equal to the error degrees of freedom from the ANOVA. Similar arguments can be used to construct a Bonferroni confidence interval for the true difference between two treatment means:

$$P\left(\Delta\bar{y}_{ij} - t_{\alpha/2}s_\varepsilon\sqrt{\frac{1}{n_i} + \frac{1}{n_j}} < \Delta\mu_{ij} < \Delta\bar{y}_{ij} + t_{\alpha/2}s_\varepsilon\sqrt{\frac{1}{n_i} + \frac{1}{n_j}}\right) = 1 - \alpha \tag{5.40}$$

where $\Delta\bar{y}_{ij} = \bar{y}_i - \bar{y}_j$ and $\Delta\mu_{ij} = \mu_i - \mu_j$. Bonferroni multiple comparisons are often performed from confidence intervals by rejecting H_0 if the relevant Bonferroni confidence interval does not contain zero.

If the Bonferroni acceptance interval for hypothesis tests and the confidence interval look familiar, they should, because they're exactly the same as the expressions used for the two-sample t test. The only difference between the two cases is in their values of α.

Most of the post-ANOVA methods presented in this section assume that all possible pairs or a well-defined subset of all possible pairs of treatments are to be compared; however, sometimes only certain comparisons that are known in advance are important. In these situations it is common to use Bonnferroni's method to reduce the family error rate only by the number of predetermined tests to be performed. This approach still protects the family error rate while improving the sensitivity of the smaller but necessary set of tests to small differences between the treatments.

Compared to other, more popular, post-ANOVA multiple comparisons methods, Bonferroni's method is conservative, which makes it less sensitive to small but significant differences between treatment means. Bonferroni's method is still invoked frequently, however, because of its simplicity. Also, be aware that variations on Bonferroni's method that also go by other names are sometimes still called Bonferroni's method.

Example 5.5

An experiment to compare all possible pairs of k = 4 treatments using n = 8 observations per treatment is to be performed. Find Bonferroni's value of α for individual tests and the critical t value for two-sided tests if the family error rate for the tests is to be $\alpha_{family} = 0.05$.

Solution: There will be $\binom{4}{2} = 6$ multiple comparisons to be performed. The value of α for each test to deliver $\alpha_{family} = 0.05$ is:

$$\alpha = \frac{0.05}{6} = 0.00833$$

There will be kn = 32 observations in the experiment, with $df_\varepsilon = 32 - 1 - 3 = 28$ error degrees of freedom for the ANOVA. The critical t value for performing hypothesis tests and constructing confidence intervals will be $t_{\alpha/2, df_\varepsilon} = t_{0.00417, 28} = 2.839$.

5.8.3 Sidak's Method

A variation on Bonferroni's method attributed to Sidak or Dunn proposes that if the error for a single *t* test of two treatments is α, then the probability of making a correct decision for that test is $1 - \alpha$, and the probability of making correct decisions for all $\binom{k}{2}$ multiple comparisons of *k* treatments is:

$$1 - \alpha_{family} = (1 - \alpha)^{\binom{k}{2}} \qquad (5.41)$$

where α_{family} is the overall or family error rate. If we choose a specific low value of α_{family}, then α for individual tests must be:

$$\alpha = 1 - (1 - \alpha_{family})^{1/\binom{k}{2}} \qquad (5.42)$$

The *t* test and confidence interval formulas for the Sidak method are the same as for the two-sample *t* test and Bonferroni's method—only the α value for individual tests is different.

Sidak's α isn't as simple as Bonferroni's α, but the additional complexity is not an issue when the methods are implemented in software. When α_{family} is small and the number of paired comparisons is small, then the Bonferroni and Sidak α values are almost equal. When α_{family} is larger and/or the number of tests is large the α values will differ considerably. The Sidak method is less conservative than Bonferroni's method; that is, the Sidak method offers a higher probability (that is, power) of rejecting H_0: $\mu_i = \mu_j$ when there is a relatively small difference between the means. This makes the Sidak method somewhat preferred over Bonferroni's method.

Example 5.6

Find the α for individual tests using Sidak's method of multiple comparisons and the critical t value for two-sided tests from Example 5.5.

Solution: The value of Sidak's α for individual tests that delivers $\alpha_{family} = 0.05$ is:

$$\alpha = 1 - \left(1 - \alpha_{family}\right)^{1/\binom{k}{2}}$$
$$= 1 - \left(1 - 0.05\right)^{1/6}$$
$$= 0.00851$$

and as before there will be $df_\varepsilon = 28$. The critical t value is $t_{0.00425, 28} = 2.831$.

5.8.4 Duncan's Multiple Range Test

Another post-ANOVA test known for its sensitivity to small differences between treatment means is Duncan's multiple range test. This test requires that the sample sizes for the treatments are equal or at least approximately equal. It potentially tests all possible pairs of treatment means; however, the individual tests are performed in a sequence that helps protect against Type 1 errors.

Here's the procedure for Duncan's multiple range test:

1. Start a tree diagram with the first node consisting of the k treatment means ordered from smallest to largest.

2. Create two branches from the first node—one of the $k - 1$ smallest means and the other of the $k - 1$ largest means.

3. Continue the pattern of creating two branches from each node of p means— one with the $p - 1$ smallest means and the other with the $p - 1$ largest means—until the last level of branches contains just two means at each node.

4. Calculate the range R of the p means at each node of the tree diagram.

5. Starting from the first node, compare the range R of the p means at that node to Duncan's least significant range:

$$R_p = \frac{s_\varepsilon r_{\alpha, p, df_\varepsilon}}{\sqrt{n}} \tag{5.43}$$

where s_ε is the standard error of the ANOVA, n is the number of observations in each treatment, and values of $r_{\alpha,p,df_\varepsilon}$ are tabulated in Appendix A.6 for $\alpha = 0.05$. $r_{\alpha,p,df_\varepsilon}$ depends on the significance level α, the number of treatments p at the node, and the number of error degrees of freedom df_ε for the ANOVA.

a. If $R > R_p$ conclude that the two extreme means at that node are significantly different from each other and continue testing the next pair of nodes along that branch of the tree.

b. If $R < R_p$ conclude that there are no significant differences between any of the means at that node and suspend testing of all other nodes along that branch of the tree.

Although the procedure for Duncan's test might appear to be complicated, the calculations and necessary comparisons are actually quite easy to perform. The suspension of further testing in step 5b helps prevent contradictions, but even this step is not foolproof and sometimes Duncan's method can give some confusing results.

Example 5.7

An ANOVA for four treatments indicates that there are significant differences among the means ($p = 0.016$). There are $n = 8$ observations in each treatment, the treatment means are $\{39, 38, 36, 43\}$, and the standard error is $s_\varepsilon = 41$. Use Duncan's method with $\alpha = 0.05$ to determine which pairs of means are different.

Solution: There are $N = 4 \times 8 = 32$ observations in the data set, so the error degrees of freedom for the ANOVA is $df_\varepsilon = 32 - 1 - 3 = 28$. The nodes on the tree diagram that must be considered are: $\{36, 38, 39, 43\}$, $\{36, 38, 39\}$, $\{38, 39, 43\}$, $\{36, 38\}$, $\{38, 39\}$, and $\{39, 43\}$. The least significant ranges for $p = 4, 3,$ and 2 means are given by:

$$R_4 = \frac{4.1 \times 3.14}{\sqrt{8}} = 4.55$$

$$R_3 = \frac{4.1 \times 3.04}{\sqrt{8}} = 4.41$$

$$R_2 = \frac{4.1 \times 2.90}{\sqrt{8}} = 4.20$$

where the $r_{0.05,p,df_\varepsilon}$ values were taken from Appendix A.6 with $df_\varepsilon = 28$. The evaluations of the various nodes in the tree diagram are shown in Figure 5.7. The only significant ranges, shown in bold font, indicate that the treatments with means 36 and 43 are different from each other (which we already knew because the ANOVA was significant) and the treatments with means 38 and 43 are different from each other. Further subsets of $\{36, 38, 39\}$ were not considered because the range across this set was not significant.

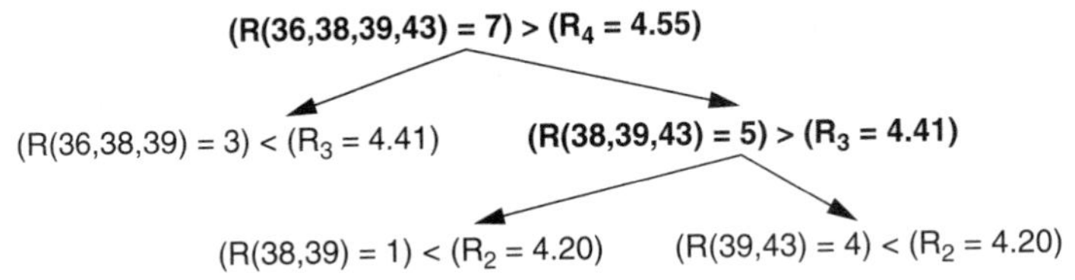

$$(R(36,38,39,43) = 7) > (R_4 = 4.55)$$

$$(R(36,38,39) = 3) < (R_3 = 4.41) \qquad (R(38,39,43) = 5) > (R_3 = 4.41)$$

$$(R(38,39) = 1) < (R_2 = 4.20) \qquad (R(39,43) = 4) < (R_2 = 4.20)$$

Figure 5.7   Calculations for Duncan's multiple range test.

5.8.5 Tukey's Multiple Comparisons Test

Duncan's multiple range test is powerful but difficult to perform because there are so many sets of treatment means to consider and different critical values at each step in the analysis. A popular compromise to Duncan's test is Tukey's honest significant difference (HSD) test (also called the Tukey-Kramer test or Tukey's multiple comparisons test). Like the other tests described, Tukey's HSD test considers all possible pairs of treatment means. Although Tukey's test is less powerful than Duncan's (that is, less sensitive to small differences between treatment means), it involves fewer calculations, is easier to report, and is quite popular.

The critical value of Tukey's HSD test is:

$$w_\alpha = \frac{s_\varepsilon Q_{\alpha, k, df_\varepsilon}}{\sqrt{n}} \tag{5.44}$$

where $Q_{\alpha, k, df_\varepsilon}$ is the critical value of the *Studentized range distribution* (given in Appendix A.7 for $\alpha = 0.05$). $Q_{\alpha, k, df_\varepsilon}$ depends on the significance level α, the number of treatments k, and the number of error degrees of freedom for the ANOVA df_ε. If the difference between any pair of means $\Delta \bar{y}_{ij}$ exceeds w_α, then we can conclude that those means are significantly different from each other. w_α can also be used to determine $(1 - \alpha)$ 100% confidence intervals for the differences between pairs of treatment means. These confidence intervals have the form:

$$P\left(\Delta \bar{y}_{ij} - w_\alpha < \Delta \mu_{ij} < \Delta \bar{y}_{ij} + w_\alpha\right) = 1 - \alpha \tag{5.45}$$

where $\Delta \bar{y}_{ij} = \bar{y}_i - \bar{y}_j$ and $\Delta \mu_{ij} = \mu_i - \mu_j$.

Example 5.8
    Repeat Example 5.7 using Tukey's multiple comparisons test at $\alpha = 0.05$. Construct 95 percent confidence intervals for those means with significant differences between them.

    Solution: *From the table of the Studentized range distribution in Appendix A.7 with $k = 4$ treatments and $df_\varepsilon = 28$ we have $Q_{0.05, 4, 28} \approx 3.89$ so:*

$$w_{0.05} = \frac{4.1 \times 3.89}{\sqrt{8}} = 5.64$$

Table 5.2 Results for Tukey's multiple comparisons tests.

Means	R	$R > W_{0.05}$
{36, 38}	2	no
{36, 39}	3	no
{36, 43}	7	yes
{38, 39}	1	no
{38, 43}	5	no
{39, 43}	4	no

Table 5.2 shows the magnitude of the difference between each possible pair of means. The only difference that is significant is between the pair {36, 43}. This result is different from that of Duncan's method, which is more sensitive to small differences between treatment means.

The 95 percent confidence interval for the difference between 36 and 43 is given by:

$$P(36 - 43 - 5.64 < \Delta\mu < 36 - 43 + 5.64) = 0.95$$

$$P(-12.64 < \Delta\mu < -1.36) = 0.95$$

This interval does not contain zero, which is consistent with the conclusion that the two treatment means are different from each other.

5.8.6 Dunnett's Test

Sometimes, instead of making post-ANOVA comparisons of all $\binom{k}{2}$ pairs of treatment means, the only comparisons of interest are those between a control treatment and the $k - 1$ test treatments. Since there are fewer comparisons necessary in this case, the α for individual tests does not need to be reduced as substantially as in the cases where all tests are performed. One of the more popular methods of performing comparisons with a control treatment is Dunnett's test. Dunnett's test uses the same t statistic as Bonferroni's method (Equation 5.38), but the critical t values of Dunnett's test are special values that are not given in this book. See Montgomery (1991) or Box, Hunter, and Hunter (1978) for details on using Dunnett's method or just specify Dunnett's method in MINITAB's **Stat> ANOVA> One-Way** or **Stat> ANOVA> One-Way (Unstacked) Comparisons** menu. MINITAB reports the Dunnett confidence intervals for the differences between the test and control means, so reject H_0: $\mu_i = \mu_{control}$ for those confidence intervals that do not contain zero.

5.9 ANOVA WITH MINITAB

MINITAB can accept one-way ANOVA data in two different formats. The first format, which is used by the **Stat> ANOVA> One-Way** menu, requires that all of the response values are stacked in a single column with an associated column that distinguishes the different treatments. The treatment identifier column can contain numeric, text, or date/time values; however, there are some ANOVA diagnostics that will not accept text data, so numerical and date/time values are preferred. The second format, which is used by the **Stat> ANOVA> One-Way (Unstacked)** menu, requires that each treatment appear in its own column. The stacked format is preferred over the unstacked format because it is easily generalized to multi-way classification designs and it allows the observations to be entered into the Worksheet in their (hopefully) randomized run order. The latter point is important because it allows MINITAB to display an extra diagnostic plot of the residuals versus the run order that can be used to assess the independence assumption.

Configure MINITAB for one-way ANOVA from the **Stat> ANOVA> One-Way** or **Stat> ANOVA> One-Way (Unstacked)** menu depending on the format of your data. For stacked data you will have to specify the experimental response in the **Response:** input box and the treatment identifier column in the **Factor:** input box. In the unstacked case, you will have to specify the columns containing the experimental responses in the **Responses (in separate columns):** input box. Use the **Graphs** menu to select ANOVA graphical diagnostics: **Boxplots of data**, **Histogram of residuals**, **Normal plot of residuals**, **Residuals versus fits**, **Residuals versus order** (**One-Way** menu only), and enter the treatment variable in the **Residuals versus the variables:** input box. If you suspect that there is other structure in the residuals that will not be apparent in the default diagnostic plots, turn on **Store residuals** so that you can do your own follow-up analysis after you run the ANOVA.

If the residuals plots leave any uncertainty about the validity of the assumption that the residuals are homoscedastic, use the **Stat> ANOVA> Test for Equal Variances** menu to perform Bartlett's and Levene's tests for the homogeneity of error variances. MINITAB reports quantitative results of the tests in the Session window and it also creates a graph of the confidence intervals for the population standard deviations. As in other cases, if two confidence intervals are slipped from each other then there's probably reason to believe that the populations are heteroscedastic and that the ANOVA may be compromised. The p values for Bartlett's and Levene's tests are also reported in both the Session window and in the graphical display of the confidence intervals. Levene's method is preferred over Bartlett's because it is more robust to deviations from normality. MINITAB actually uses the *modified Levene's test* which has been shown to be superior to the original form of Levene's test.

Since ANOVA only indicates if there are any statistically significant differences between the treatment means and not which pairs of treatments are different, it's necessary to use post-ANOVA multiple comparisons tests to identify the pairs of treatments that are significantly different. MINITAB offers four types of post-ANOVA multiple comparisons tests:

- Tukey's method, or the Tukey-Kramer method if the experiment is unbalanced, is used to compare all possible pairs of treatments while controlling the family error rate.

- Fisher's method is used to compare all possible pairs of treatments using a specified error rate for individual tests. Use this method with the appropriate Bonferroni corrected α if only a subset of all possible comparisons is of interest.

- Dunnett's method is used to compare a specified control treatment to all other treatments while controlling the family error rate.

- Hsu's method compares the best treatment—the one with the lowest or highest mean—to all other treatments while controlling the family error rate.

Configure MINITAB for post-ANOVA comparisons from the **Comparisons** menu in the **Stat> ANOVA> One-Way** or **Stat> ANOVA> One-Way (Unstacked)** menu.

For each of the post-ANOVA comparisons methods, MINITAB reports confidence intervals for the difference between the relevant pairs of treatment means. If the confidence interval for the difference between two treatment means does not contain zero, then conclude that those treatment means are significantly different from each other. MINITAB reports both the numerical values of the confidence bounds and a graphical display of the confidence intervals that makes it easy to interpret the complete sequence of tests.

MINITAB's ANOVA output also provides another simple graphical presentation that's useful for quick post-ANOVA multiple comparisons testing. MINITAB calculates and plots the 95 percent confidence intervals for the population means for all of the treatments. Since ANOVA requires that the treatments are homoscedastic, the pooled standard deviation s_ε is used to construct these intervals so they all have the same width. If the 95 percent confidence intervals for two treatments are slipped from each other, conclude that those means are significantly different. Compared to other methods, this method tends to be rather insensitive to differences between treatments so its primary advantage is its simple presentation.

Example 5.9

Use MINITAB to perform the ANOVA for the data from Table 5.1 and follow-up with Tukey's HSD test with a family error rate of $\alpha_{family} = 0.05$.

Solution: The MINITAB ANOVA output is shown in Figure 5.8. The F value from the ANOVA is $F = 1.22$, which falls very close to the $F = 1$ value we expect if there are no differences between the means. The p value for the ANOVA is $p = 0.300$. These values both indicate that there are no significant differences between any pairs of treatment means. The residuals diagnostic plots, shown in Figure 5.3, indicate that the residuals are normally distributed and homoscedastic with respect to treatments, fitted values, and run order as required by the ANOVA method. To be technically rigorous, since the ANOVA does not indicate the presence of any significant differences between treatment means, we shouldn't interpret any of the post-ANOVA multiple comparisons tests. However, for the purpose of this example, the 95 percent confidence intervals in Figure 5.8 indicate that all of the intervals are overlapped, confirming that there are no significant differences between any pairs of means, and Tukey's multiple comparisons also give the same result since all of the confidence intervals for the differences between all pairs of means contain zero.

```
One-way ANOVA: Y versus X

Source   DF      SS     MS     F      P
X         8   93.86  11.73  1.22  0.300
Error    72  692.34   9.62
Total    80  786.20

S = 3.101   R-Sq = 11.94%   R-Sq(adj) = 2.15%


                                Individual 95% CIs For Mean Based on Pooled StDev
Level  N    Mean   StDev   ------+---------+---------+---------+---
1      9  78.922   2.744   (-----------*---------)
2      9  80.878   2.910            (---------*----------)
3      9  79.178   3.589   (---------*---------)
4      9  80.867   2.486            (---------*----------)
5      9  79.600   2.308       (---------*---------)
6      9  79.889   3.002       (---------*----------)
7      9  81.056   3.297            (---------*----------)
8      9  82.622   3.787                  (---------*---------)
9      9  80.589   3.455            (---------*---------)
                                ------+---------+---------+---------+---
                                    78.0      80.0      82.0      84.0


Pooled StDev = 3.101


Tukey 95% Simultaneous Confidence Intervals
All Pairwise Comparisons among Levels of X

Individual confidence level = 99.79%


X = 1 subtracted from:
X    Lower   Center  Upper   ------+---------+---------+---------+---
2   -2.717   1.956   6.628          (---------*---------)
3   -4.417   0.256   4.928       (---------*--------)
4   -2.728   1.944   6.617          (--------*--------)
5   -3.994   0.678   5.350       (--------*---------)
6   -3.705   0.967   5.639       (--------*---------)
7   -2.539   2.133   6.805          (--------*---------)
8   -0.972   3.700   8.372             (---------*---------)
9   -3.005   1.667   6.339          (--------*---------)
                                ------+---------+---------+---------+---
                                    -5.0      0.0       5.0      10.0


X = 2 subtracted from:

X    Lower   Center  Upper   ------+---------+---------+---------+---
3   -6.372  -1.700   2.972   (---------*--------)
4   -4.683  -0.011   4.661      (--------*--------)
5   -5.950  -1.278   3.394    (--------*--------)
6   -5.661  -0.989   3.683    (--------*--------)
7   -4.494   0.178   4.850      (--------*---------)
8   -2.928   1.744   6.417         (--------*---------)
9   -4.961  -0.289   4.383     (--------*---------)
                                ------+---------+---------+---------+---
                                    -5.0      0.0       5.0      10.0
```

Figure 5.8   MINITAB's ANOVA and Tukey pairwise comparisons for data from Table 5.1.   *Continued*

Continued

```
X = 3 subtracted from:

X    Lower   Center  Upper    ------+---------+---------+---------+---
4   -2.983   1.689   6.361          (--------*---------)
5   -4.250   0.422   5.094       (--------*--------)
6   -3.961   0.711   5.383       (--------*---------)
7   -2.794   1.878   6.550          (---------*--------)
8   -1.228   3.444   8.117             (--------*---------)
9   -3.261   1.411   6.083          (---------*--------)
                                 ------+---------+---------+---------+---
                                    -5.0       0.0       5.0       10.0


X = 4 subtracted from:

X    Lower   Center  Upper    ------+---------+---------+---------+---
5   -5.939  -1.267   3.405       (--------*---------)
6   -5.650  -0.978   3.694       (--------*--------)
7   -4.483   0.189   4.861        (--------*---------)
8   -2.917   1.756   6.428          (---------*--------)
9   -4.950  -0.278   4.394        (--------*---------)
                                 ------+---------+---------+---------+---
                                    -5.0       0.0       5.0       10.0


X = 5 subtracted from:

X    Lower   Center  Upper    ------+---------+---------+---------+---
6   -4.383   0.289   4.961       (---------*--------)
7   -3.217   1.456   6.128        (--------*--------)
8   -1.650   3.022   7.694          (--------*--------)
9   -3.683   0.989   5.661        (--------*--------)
                                 ------+---------+---------+---------+---
                                    -5.0       0.0       5.0       10.0


X = 6 subtracted from:

X    Lower   Center  Upper    ------+---------+---------+---------+---
7   -3.505   1.167   5.839       (--------*---------)
8   -1.939   2.733   7.405         (--------*---------)
9   -3.972   0.700   5.372       (--------*---------)
                                 ------+---------+---------+---------+---
                                    -5.0       0.0       5.0       10.0


X = 7 subtracted from:

X    Lower   Center  Upper    ------+---------+---------+---------+---
8   -3.105   1.567   6.239          (--------*--------)
9   -5.139  -0.467   4.205        (--------*--------)
                                 ------+---------+---------+---------+---
                                    -5.0       0.0       5.0       10.0


X = 8 subtracted from:

X    Lower   Center  Upper    ------+---------+---------+---------+---
9   -6.705  -2.033   2.639       (--------*--------)
                                 ------+---------+---------+---------+---
                                    -5.0       0.0       5.0       10.0
```

5.10 THE COMPLETELY RANDOMIZED DESIGN

Suppose that an experiment is to be performed to study three different treatments: A, B, and C, and that six observations will be made under each treatment condition. Table 5.3 shows some run orders that could be used to collect the experimental data. In the first run order plan, the observations are taken in order by treatment—all of the As, followed by all of the Bs, followed by all of the Cs. In the third run order plan, the observations are taken in completely random order. A one-way classification experiment like this, where the treatments are taken in random order, is called a *completely randomized design*. The second run order plan is a compromise between these two extremes. Obviously, the easiest and cheapest run order plan is the first one because it involves the fewest changes to the process. Likewise, the third run order plan would be the most difficult and expensive one because it involves the most changes to the process. But cost and ease of construction must not be the only factors that determine the choice of run order.

If the only variable that changes during the example experiment is the study variable and all other sources of variation are fixed, then all three of the run orders in Table 5.3 will deliver comparable results. Suppose, however, that there is an unidentified variable that changes during the execution of the experiment and that these changes affect the response. Such variables are called *lurking* variables because we can never be certain when they are present. Lurking variables, like other variables, may be qualitative or quantitative. As we will see, lurking variables can be tolerated when they're managed correctly and disastrous when they're not.

Table 5.4 shows the candidate run orders again with a lurking variable that changes state during the experiment. How does the presence of the lurking variable affect our experiment under the different run orders? To answer this question, let's assume that

Table 5.3 Some run order choices for a one-way classification experiment.

								— Run Order ➝										
Plan	1	2	3	4	5	6	7	8	9	10	11	12	13	14	15	16	17	18
1	A	A	A	A	A	A	B	B	B	B	B	B	C	C	C	C	C	C
2	A	A	A	B	B	B	C	C	C	A	A	A	B	B	B	C	C	C
3	C	B	C	A	A	B	C	C	C	A	B	B	A	A	B	C	A	B

Table 5.4 Some run order choices and a lurking variable.

								— Run Order ➝										
Plan	1	2	3	4	5	6	7	8	9	10	11	12	13	14	15	16	17	18
1	A	A	A	A	A	A	B	B	B	B	B	B	C	C	C	C	C	C
2	A	A	A	B	B	B	C	C	C	A	A	A	B	B	B	C	C	C
3	C	B	C	A	A	B	C	C	C	A	B	B	A	A	B	C	A	B
Lurking variable	1	1	1	1	1	1	1	1	2	2	2	2	2	2	2	3	3	3

there are no differences between treatments A, B, and C, and that the lurking variable tends to increase the response as its state increases from 1 to 2 to 3. Under the first run order plan, the changes in the response caused by the lurking variable will be misattributed to differences between treatments: treatment A will appear to have a low mean, treatment B will appear to have an intermediate mean, and treatment C will appear to have a high mean. Under the third run order plan, where the runs are taken in random order, the effects of the lurking variable will, at least to some degree, average out across the treatments. This will make the treatment means fall closer together—which more accurately represents the truth of the situation—than they did under the first run order plan. This same observation applies whether the treatment means are equal or not, that is, a lurking variable can cause erroneous biases to appear in the treatment means if it is correlated to the treatments. We can conclude that using a random run order for the experimental treatments will desensitize an experiment to the effects of lurking variables and more accurately predict the real differences between treatment means.

Figure 5.9 shows three ANOVAs of simulated data taken under the run order plans of Table 5.3. $Y1(X1)$ was taken under plan 1, $Y2(X2)$ was taken under plan 2, and $Y3(X3)$ was taken under plan 3. The exact same Y values were used in all three cases and there were no real differences between the treatment means, but in each case the effect of a lurking variable, in this case a simple positive linear drift related to the run order, was superimposed on the response Y. That is, each original Y value has added to it a contribution from a lurking variable that increases monotonically with run order. In the absence of the lurking variable, the three ANOVAs would be identical, independent of run order, and show that there are no significant differences between treatment means. However, the presence of the linearly increasing lurking variable changes the ANOVA results. In the first ANOVA, because the lurking variable is strongly confounded with the treatments, there appears to be a large difference between the treatment means ($F = 72.42$, $p = 0.000$). In the second ANOVA, because plan 2 breaks up the run order a bit, the ANOVA does not detect any significant differences between treatments ($F = 2.21$, $p = 0.144$) but there is still some hint of an increase in the response in order of A, B, C from the 95 percent confidence intervals. In the third ANOVA, the completely randomized design has protected us from the lurking variable and we obtain the correct answer—that there are no significant differences between the treatment means ($F = 0.64$, $p = 0.543$).

Although randomization helps protect against lurking variables, it doesn't completely compensate for their effect. The variation caused by a lurking variable is still present in the experimental data and will always inflate the error variability. This will tend to make the ANOVA less sensitive to small differences between the treatment means. If the lurking variable could be held constant or if its variation could be accounted for in the model then the potential sensitivity of the completely randomized design would be completely recovered.

Despite the added costs and difficulties, randomization of the run order is the accepted method for managing the risks of lurking variables. If we could be certain that

```
One-way ANOVA: Y1 versus X1

Source   DF      SS       MS      F       P
X1        2   489.32   244.66   72.42   0.000
Error    15    50.67     3.38
Total    17   540.00


S = 1.838   R-Sq = 90.62%   R-Sq(adj) = 89.36%


                             Individual 95% CIs For Mean Based on Pooled StDev
Level   N    Mean    StDev   ------+---------+---------+---------+---
A       6   3.192    1.629   (---*---)
B       6   9.877    2.130                     (---*---)
C       6  15.959    1.716                                  (---*---)
                             ------+---------+---------+---------+---
                                 4.0       8.0      12.0      16.0

Pooled StDev = 1.838


One-way ANOVA: Y2 versus X2

Source   DF      SS      MS      F       P
X2        2   123.2   61.6    2.21    0.144
Error    15   417.8   27.9
Total    17   541.0


S = 5.278   R-Sq = 22.77%   R-Sq(adj) = 12.48%


                             Individual 95% CIs For Mean Based on Pooled StDev
Level   N    Mean    StDev   -----+---------+---------+---------+----
A       6   6.466    5.294   (----------*----------)
B       6  10.254    5.155           (-----------*----------)
C       6  12.836    5.381              (----------*-----------)
                             -----+---------+---------+---------+----
                                 4.0       8.0      12.0      16.0

Pooled StDev = 5.278


One-way ANOVA: Y3 versus X3

Source   DF      SS      MS      F       P
X3        2    34.1   17.1    0.64    0.543
Error    15   401.8   26.8
Total    17   435.9


S = 5.175   R-Sq = 7.83%   R-Sq(adj) = 0.00%


                             Individual 95% CIs For Mean Based on Pooled StDev
Level   N    Mean    StDev   -+---------+---------+---------+--------
A       6  10.192    4.799        (------------*------------)
B       6  11.043    5.821          (------------*-----------)
C       6   7.792    4.842   (------------*------------)
                             -+---------+---------+---------+--------
                             3.5       7.0      10.5      14.0

Pooled StDev = 5.175
```

Figure 5.9 ANOVA of the same response with a superimposed trending lurking variable.

all of the non-study variables in an experiment were accounted for and held constant then we would be justified in using a more convenient run order. No one can anticipate all of the lurking variables, however, so the only solution is to randomize. This conclusion is so universally accepted that if you don't randomize, your results will not be accepted or believed, at least by people knowledgeable in designed experiments. Do experienced people compromise the randomness of the run order in really difficult situations? Yes, they do. But they make every attempt to randomize when it's possible and they make prominent disclaimers about the results of their experiments when it's not. Managers and customers tend to forget these disclaimers though, and after you get burned by lurking variables once or twice you will be much more ready to adopt the position, "We either randomize or we don't do the experiment."

In addition to being sensitive about randomization in your own experiments, you must learn to be critical of other people's experiments, too. This includes experiments that are in the planning stages and completed experiments that are ready to be analyzed. If the DOE environment in which you work is mature, then randomization is already a way of life and everyone understands and accepts the need to randomize. In less mature environments, however, people tend to be lax about randomization. If you work in the latter environment, or if there are DOE novices around who haven't been initiated into the joys of fatal lurking variables (fatal to experiments, hopefully not careers), make sure that you always check that their randomization plan was appropriate and that it was followed. If it wasn't, then walk away or at least make a big deal out of it and make your concerns known. As your DOE skills improve and you become recognized as an expert within the organization, people with weaker skills will seek your help. Make your expectations known early: "I will work with you but only if you randomize."

An important variation on the completely randomized design is the randomized block design, which will be described in detail in Chapter 6. Randomized block designs offer a significant performance improvement over completely randomized designs when lurking variables are present. In a randomized block design, the levels of the study variable are randomized within blocks of runs that are run consecutively. If the blocks are defined correctly, the experiment can tolerate large differences between blocks but the conditions within each block will be relatively homogeneous. The blocking variable is included in the ANOVA, now a two-way ANOVA, to isolate the variation associated with differences between blocks.

Table 5.5 shows a randomized block design for our example problem where the blocks are defined by replicates. This design would significantly improve the performance of our experiment in the presence of a lurking variable. If you are planning a one-way classification experiment and suspect that there might be lurking variables present in

Table 5.5 Run order for a randomized block design.

							—— Run Order ——➤											
Plan	1	2	3	4	5	6	7	8	9	10	11	12	13	14	15	16	17	18
4	A	C	B	A	B	C	B	C	A	C	A	B	C	A	B	B	A	C
Block	1			2			3			4			5			6		

your process—in other words, always—then improve the sensitivity of the experiment by using a randomized block design.

MINITAB doesn't have a menu to create the completely randomized design so you will have to do it yourself. The following procedure describes the necessary steps:

1. Use **Calc> Make Patterned Data> Simple Set of Numbers** (or the **set** command) to create a column for the treatments.

2. Use **Calc> Make Patterned Data> Simple Set of Numbers** to create a column for the standard order of the runs.

3. Use **Calc> Random Data> Sample From Columns** (or the **sample** command) to randomize the numbers from the standard order column into a new column for the random run order.

4. Use **Stat> ANOVA> One-Way** (or the **oneway** command) to validate the random run order by performing a one-way ANOVA treating the run order as the response. If the treatments are significantly different (that is, if the ANOVA F statistic is significant) then the run order is not sufficiently random and you should try another run order.

5. Use **Data> Sort** (or the **sort** command) to sort the standard order, random order, and treatment columns by the random order column. This puts the runs in the order that they must be made and makes the printed worksheet easier to follow for the person who has to run the experiment.

6. Add an empty column to the worksheet for the response and go run the experiment.

This procedure is implemented in a custom MINITAB macro called *makeoneway.mac* found on the CD-ROM included with this book.

5.11 ANALYSIS OF MEANS

An alternative method for analyzing one-way classification data is the *analysis of means* (ANOM). This important technique has the advantage of presenting its output in a graphical format that looks very much like a control chart. Quality managers, engineers, and technicians who are less familiar with ANOVA are usually comforted by the familiarity of this method of presentation. If the results of ANOVA and ANOM agree, as they often do, and if the statistical skills of the customer of the experiment are weak, you may prefer to report the analysis by ANOM instead of or in addition to ANOVA.

The hypotheses of ANOM are subtly different from those of ANOVA. Where ANOVA tests for differences between all possible pairs of treatment means, ANOM tests each treatment mean against the grand mean of the data set. The ANOM hypotheses are:

$$H_0 : \mu_i = \mu_0 \text{ for all treatments}$$
$$H_A : \mu_i \neq \mu_0 \text{ for at least one treatment}$$

where μ_0 is the common population mean for all of the treatments. This approach reduces the total number of tests that have to be performed to just one per treatment.

The ANOM procedure involves determining the grand mean $\bar{\bar{y}}$ and the within-treatment standard deviation s_ε from the sample data set. (This is the same standard error as that of the ANOVA.) Then upper and lower acceptance (or decision) limits for the null hypothesis, much like control limits for a control chart, are calculated from:

$$\left(UDL \,/\, LDL\right)_{\bar{y}} \;=\; \bar{\bar{y}} \pm \left(h_{\alpha,k,df_\varepsilon} s_\varepsilon \sqrt{\tfrac{(k-1)}{nk}}\right) \tag{5.46}$$

where k is the number of treatments, n is the number of observations per treatment, and $h_{\alpha,k,df_\varepsilon}$ comes from the table of critical values for one-way ANOM in Appendix A.8. Once the decision limits have been determined, a plot of the treatment means versus the treatment identifier is created and lines are added at $\bar{\bar{y}}$, *UDL*, and *LDL*. Any treatment means that fall outside of the decision limits are considered to be different from the grand mean of the data set.

The assumptions of ANOM, that the residuals are normal, homoscedastic, and independent, are the same as those for ANOVA and should be checked in the same way. The ANOVA and ANOM models and residuals are exactly the same so you can use the ANOVA graphical diagnostics to check the ANOM assumptions.

MINITAB's ANOM functions are available from the **Stat> ANOVA> Analysis of Means** menu. MINITAB can analyze one-way and two-way classification data by ANOM when the observations are quantitative and meet the usual assumptions about the behavior of the residuals. MINITAB also supports ANOM for data that follow a binomial distribution (for example, defectives data) and for data that follow a Poisson distribution (for example, defects data). All of MINITAB's ANOM functions require that the experiments are balanced, with no missing observations.

Example 5.10

Use analysis of means to analyze the data from Table 5.1 and compare the results to those from ANOVA.

Solution: The graphical output from MINITAB's one-way ANOM for the data from Table 5.1 is shown in Figure 5.10. The figure indicates that the treatment means are not significantly different from the grand mean of the data set. The residuals analysis from the ANOVA, shown in Figure 5.3, still applies and confirms that the assumptions for ANOM are satisfied.

5.12 RESPONSE TRANSFORMATIONS

5.12.1 Introduction

For the ANOVA method to be valid, the distribution of the model residuals must be normal and homoscedastic with respect to the treatment groups. These conditions can be

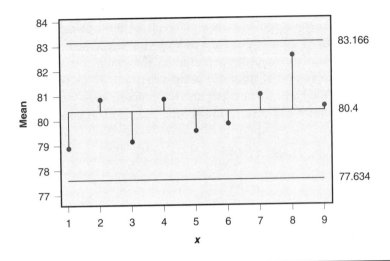

Figure 5.10   One-way ANOM for the data from Table 5.1.

checked from the normal probability plot of the residuals and from plots of residuals versus treatment or from a simple boxplot of the data by treatment. Although the ANOVA is fairly robust to deviations from normality and homoscedasticity, there are still situations where the discrepancy may be large enough that some doubt is cast on the validity of the ANOVA. In many cases these discrepancies can be resolved or at least alleviated by applying a mathematical transformation to the original data values. The purpose of this section is to describe the use of transformations to recover the normality and homoscedasticity requirements that validate the use of ANOVA.

A transformation is a mathematical operation or function applied to the quantitative response to convert the original raw data values y_i into some new set of values y_i'. In general:

$$y_i' = f(y_i) \tag{5.47}$$

If a transformation is beneficial then the conditions required to validate the use of ANOVA (normality and homoscedasticity of residuals) will be better satisfied by the transformed data than by the original observations. Always check the residuals diagnostic plots after transforming your observations to confirm that the transform was effective.

Some transformations are very simple, such as adding a constant to each value of the response or multiplying the response by a constant. Unfortunately, these simple transforms don't affect the normality or homoscedasticity problems that we wish to address. What we need are transformations that affect responses of different sizes to different degrees. Although there are an infinite number of transforms possible, the most popular transforms used for badly behaved one-way classification data are the logarithm, square root, reciprocal, square, and power transforms. These transforms are effective because their strength, that is, the amount that they change the raw data values, depends on the size of the raw data value. For example, a square root transform applied to a raw data value of $y = 0.90$ returns a new value $y' = 0.95$ whereas the same transform applied to $y = 9$ returns a new value of $y' = 3$. In this case, not only are the relative changes between the original and transformed values very different, the directions of the changes are different, too. Other transforms have similar effects.

Many DOE practitioners invoke transformations to recover the desired behavior of the residuals without considering the mechanism that causes the undesirable behavior. When chosen correctly, these somewhat arbitrary transformations are generally valid, but it is always preferable to select a transform based on an appropriate first-principles argument. That is, if the theoretical behavior of the response suggests a specific transformation then that transformation is probably the best one to use. If the theoretically suggested transform doesn't help, then it's appropriate to resort to the transform that best addresses the problem with the residuals. This approach puts the onus for identifying appropriate transformations on the technical experts: the physicists, chemists, engineers, and so on, who know the theoretical aspects of the system the best. It also provides some job security—it helps guarantee that all of us non-statisticians won't be replaced by real statisticians. Always try to leverage your technical expertise by supplementing your skills, not replacing them, with statistical methods.

After a suitable transformation is identified, it is wise to perform independent ANOVA analyses on both the original and transformed data, including full analyses of the residuals. If the ANOVA results from the two methods agree, then there is little benefit to the transform and the ANOVA of the original values should be reported. If the ANOVA results disagree and if the conditions of normality and homoscedasticity of the residuals are better satisfied for the transformed values, then the results based on the transformed values should be reported.

One disadvantage of using a transform is that it is often difficult to think in terms of the new units for the response. For example, if your response is a measurement in *inches* and a log transform is indicated, then the units of the transformed response are *log(inches)*. Few people can think in terms of these strange new units. Even though this can make transformations difficult to work with, remember that the underlying mechanism causing the variation in the residuals is probably inducing normally distributed random errors. If there's something causing the distribution of the errors of a response measured in *log(inches)* to be normal, but we happen to measure the response in inches, then that's just the way things are and the log transform is a necessary complication.

5.12.2 The Logarithmic Transform

ANOVA requires that the distribution of errors be homoscedastic across all of the treatment groups. Occasionally when there are large differences between the treatment means, the standard deviations of the treatments are proportional to their treatment means. In this case, the appropriate transformation for the data is to take the logarithm of the response, $y' = \log(y)$. Either the common log (log) or the natural log (ln) are appropriate.

As with all transformations, diagnostic plots of the residuals should be checked to confirm that the transformation was effective.

The standard error of the log-transformed response requires special interpretation. If the common log (*log*) was used to transform the data, then approximately $(1 - \alpha)\,100\%$ of the population of observations should fall in the interval given by:

$$P\left(\bar{y}10^{-t_{\alpha/2}s_\varepsilon} < y < \bar{y}10^{+t_{\alpha/2}s_\varepsilon}\right) = 1 - \alpha \tag{5.48}$$

where s_ε is the standard error of the ANOVA and the *t* distribution has degrees of freedom equal to the error degrees of freedom from the ANOVA. If the natural log (*ln*) was used to transform the data then the corresponding interval is:

$$P\left(\bar{y}e^{-t_{\alpha/2}s_\varepsilon} < y < \bar{y}e^{+t_{\alpha/2}s_\varepsilon}\right) = 1 - \alpha \tag{5.49}$$

Example 5.11
Use one-way ANOVA to analyze the data in Table 5.6. There are five treatments, each with n = 12 observations, and the runs were performed in completely random order. Within what range of values should 95 percent of the population fall?

Solution: Boxplots of the original data are shown in Figure 5.11a. Some of the five treatment groups have very different standard deviations from the others so the ANOVA method cannot be used to analyze these data, at least not in their original form. Figure 5.11a suggests that the standard deviations of the treatments are proportional to the treatment means, so a log transform might be appropriate. Figure 5.11b shows boxplots of the common log-transformed data. These boxplots suggest that the transformed data are homoscedastic and at least approximately normally distributed so ANOVA is probably appropriate. Figure 5.12 shows the ANOVA for the transformed data. The F statistic

Table 5.6   Log transform example data.

Observation	A	B	C	D	E
1	31	6	10	35	45
2	36	9	15	19	36
3	11	11	21	17	49
4	24	9	9	24	32
5	37	6	29	18	47
6	16	8	32	20	89
7	18	11	28	33	47
8	20	5	27	24	27
9	18	12	16	40	58
10	20	4	16	24	73
11	13	9	20	10	66
12	23	6	32	14	77

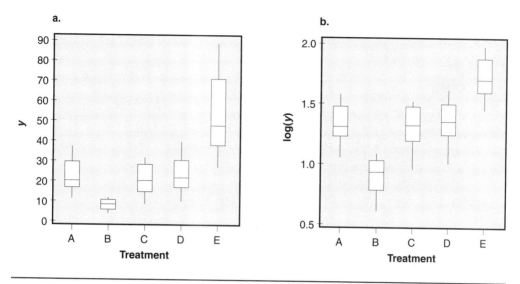

Figure 5.11 Boxplots of original and log-transformed data.

```
One-way ANOVA: log(y) versus Treatment

Source      DF      SS       MS      F      P
Treatment    4    4.1015   1.0254  36.67  0.000
Error       55    1.5380   0.0280
Total       59    5.6395

S = 0.1672    R-Sq = 72.23%    R-Sq (adj) = 70.75%


                                Individual 95% CIs For Mean Based on
                                Pooled StDev
Level   N     Mean    StDev   ----+---------+---------+---------+-----
A       12   1.3192   0.1637                     (--*--)
B       12   0.8803   0.1507   (--*---)
C       12   1.2928   0.1889               (--*--)
D       12   1.3347   0.1717               (--*---)
E       12   1.7052   0.1585                          (--*--)
                                ----+---------+---------+---------+-----
                                0.90      1.20      1.50      1.80

Pooled StDev = 0.1672
```

Figure 5.12 ANOVA of log-transformed data.

is very large, indicating that there are significant differences between the treatments. The 95 percent confidence intervals for the treatment means suggest that the mean of treatment B is lower than the others and that the mean of treatment E is higher than the others. There are no significant differences between treatments A, C, and D. The treatment means in their original measurement units can be recovered by applying the *inverse log transform* (10^y) *to the means reported in the ANOVA output.* For example, the first treatment mean in original measurement units is* $10^{1.3192} = 20.9$. *The standard error of the ANOVA model is*

$$s_\varepsilon = \sqrt{0.0280} = 0.1672$$

and is determined from $df_\varepsilon = 55$ *error degrees of freedom. Equation 5.48 with* $\alpha = 0.05$ *gives the interval that should contain approximately 95 percent of the population. Since* $t_{0.025,55} = 2.00$ *the 95 percent interval for observations is:*

$$P\left(\bar{y}10^{-t_{\alpha/2}s_\varepsilon} < y < \bar{y}10^{+t_{\alpha/2}s_\varepsilon}\right) = 1 - \alpha$$
$$P\left(\bar{y}10^{-2.00(0.1672)} < y < \bar{y}10^{+2.00(0.1672)}\right) = 0.95$$
$$P\left(0.46\bar{y} < y < 2.16\bar{y}\right) = 0.95$$

This interval seems rather wide, but the width of the boxplots in Figure 5.11a confirms that there's lots of variation in these treatments.

5.12.3 Transforming Count Data

If the response of an experiment is a count of the number of occurrences then the response is probably distributed according to the Poisson distribution. The standard deviation of a Poisson-distributed random variable is related to the Poisson mean by:

$$\sigma = \sqrt{\mu} \qquad (5.50)$$

so samples drawn from Poisson populations clearly will not be homoscedastic if there are differences between the population means. Poisson distributions are also skewed, especially when the mean count is low ($\mu < 20$), so a transformation of the raw count data must address both the heteroscedasticity and nonnormality issues. An appropriate transformation for Poisson-distributed data is the square root:

$$y_i' = \sqrt{y_i} \qquad (5.51)$$

A related and slightly better transformation for count data is:

$$y_i' = \frac{1}{2}\left(\sqrt{y_i} + \sqrt{y_i + 1}\right) \qquad (5.52)$$

---

* The inverse transform actually delivers the geometric mean in original measurement units rather than the usual arithmetic mean. The geometric mean is a more appropriate measure of location for data with this kind of behavior.

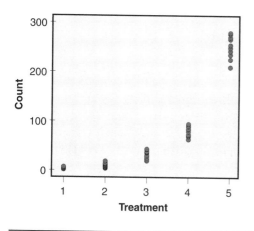 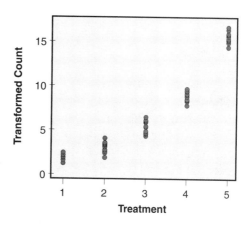

Figure 5.13 Original and transformed count data.

This transformation is available in MINITAB as the **ftc** function. Invoke this function with:

```
mtb> let c2 = ftc(c1)
```

or from the **Calc> Calculator** menu using the **Transform count** function. Both of these transformations are very effective at recovering the homoscedasticity and normality conditions for Poisson data as required by the ANOVA method.

The transformation methods for count data mentioned here are all relatively crude and there are better methods of analysis but they are beyond the scope of this book. See Neter et al. (1996) or Agresti (2002) for more information on the analysis of count data.

Example 5.12

*To demonstrate the effectiveness of the transformation for count data given in Equation 5.52, five random Poisson-distributed data sets were created using MINITAB's **Calc> Probability Distributions> Random Data> Poisson** function. The data sets were all of size $n = 20$ and had Poisson means of $\mu = \{3, 9, 27, 81, 243\}$. The original count data and the transformed count data are plotted by treatment in Figure 5.13. The figure clearly shows that the transform solves the heteroscedasticity problem in the original data. Normal plots of the residuals (not shown) from the one-way ANOVA analysis of the transformed data confirm that the residuals are at least approximately normally distributed.*

5.12.4 Transforming Fraction Data

Occasionally, a response y_i is encountered that can only take on fractional values $0 \le y_i \le 1$. These responses often follow a binomial distribution where the fraction y_i is determined from the ratio of the number of observed successes d_i to the number of trials n_i:

$$y_i = \frac{d_i}{n_i} \tag{5.53}$$

The binomial distribution can have substantial asymmetry and the binomial standard deviation is related to the binomial mean, so these cases can also suffer from heteroscedasticity. The appropriate transformation of the raw fractional values depends on the uniformity of the sample size n_i and the nominal size and range of the observations. The transformations that might effectively normalize the distribution of errors and recover at least approximate homoscedasticity are:

- If the number of trials n_i is the same or nearly the same for each observation and if all of the fractional observations are small, say $y_i < 0.20$, then attempt a square root transform:

$$y_i' = \sqrt{y_i} \tag{5.54}$$

- If the number of trials n_i is the same for each observation and if all of the observations are close to unity, say $y_i > 0.80$, then try transforming the raw data by taking the square root of the complement of the response:

$$y_i' = \sqrt{1 - y_i} \tag{5.55}$$

- If the fractional values span the full range $0 < y_i < 1$ then try the arcsin transform:

$$y_i' = \arcsin\left(\sqrt{y_i}\right) \tag{5.56}$$

The transform in Equation 5.56 is available in MINITAB as the **ftp** function. Invoke this function from the **Calc> Calculator** menu using the **Transform proportion** function or with:

```
mtb> let c3 = ftp(c1,c2)
```

where c1 is a column of the number of trials n_i for each sample and c2 is a column of the number of successes d_i found in the trials.

If one of these or some other transform does not recover the normality and homoscedasticity of the residuals, then get help from your local neighborhood statistician. The transformation methods for fractions mentioned here are all relatively crude and there are better methods of analysis but they are beyond the scope of this book. See Neter et al. (1996) or Agresti (2002) for more information on the analysis of proportions.

5.12.5 The Rank Transform

In some extreme cases it will be impossible to identify a suitable transform that recovers the normality of the residuals. In these cases it may be appropriate to transform the raw data values by replacing them with their rank order within the complete data set. Use MINITAB's **Sort> Rank** function to determine the ranks corresponding to values of the response. Then ANOVA can be used to analyze the ranks to determine if there are statistically significant differences between treatments; however, the interpretation of the size of the differences can be difficult.

The rank transform for one-way classification data is the basis for the Kruskal-Wallis test, which is the nonparametric analog to one-way ANOVA. The Kruskal-Wallis test statistic is itself a transformation of the ANOVA *F* statistic determined from the analysis of the ranks. The Kruskal-Wallis test is appropriate for independent random samples from continuous populations that have the same shape (that is, not necessarily normal) and standard deviation. If the distributions are skewed then the Kruskal-Wallis test is a test of medians, but if the distributions are symmetric then it is a test of means.

Another nonparametric analysis option for one-way classifications is Mood's median test. Mood's median test is less sensitive to outliers than the Kruskal-Wallis test but it is also less powerful, that is, it is not as sensitive to small differences between treatment means. When the ANOVA assumptions are satisfied, ANOVA is more powerful than both of the nonparametric methods.

Access the Kruskal-Wallis test in MINITAB from **Stat> Nonparametrics> Kruskal-Wallis** and Mood's median test from **Stat> Nonparametrics> Mood's Median Test**. In both cases use the ANOVA residuals diagnostic graphs to validate the assumptions that the samples come from populations that have the same shape and standard deviation.

5.13 SAMPLE SIZE FOR ONE-WAY ANOVA

As with all other sample-size calculations for hypothesis tests (see Chapter 3), the ANOVA sample-size calculation requires that the experimenter know the desired significance level α, the population standard deviation σ, the number of treatments in the study k, and the desired probability or power P of detecting the smallest practically significant difference δ between a pair of treatment means. The complement of the power is the Type 2 error rate $\beta = 1 - P$. This information is sufficient to uniquely determine the number of replicates n required for an experiment.

It is very important that the sample size be determined from the specific needs of the experiment. If the sample size is chosen arbitrarily rather than by calculation, then the sample size may be too small or too large. If the sample size is too small, then practically significant effects of size δ might be present and not detected. If the sample size is too large, then a statistically significant difference might be reported when the corresponding effect size δ is smaller than is practically significant. Remember, a sample-size calculation equates a practically significant difference with a statistically significant difference.

In Chapter 3 it was shown that the sample size for the two-sample *t* test is given by:

$$n \geq 2\left(\frac{\sigma}{\delta}\right)^2 \left(t_{\alpha/2,v} + t_{\beta,v}\right)^2 \tag{5.57}$$

where $v = n_1 + n_2 - 2$ is the number of error degrees of freedom. By direct analogy, the condition for the sample size for the one-way ANOVA problem is:

$$n \geq 2\left(\frac{\sigma}{\delta}\right)^2 \left(t_{\frac{\alpha}{k(k-1)},v} + t_{\beta,v}\right)^2 \qquad (5.58)$$

where the nightmarish significance value

$$\frac{2\alpha}{k(k-1)}$$

comes from Bonferroni's $\binom{k}{2}$ correction for multiple comparisons tests. The number of error degrees of freedom is given by the error degrees of freedom for the one-way ANOVA:

$$v = df_\varepsilon = k(n-1) \qquad (5.59)$$

That v depends on n means that Equation 5.58 is transcendental and will have to be solved by iteration. Since the t distribution approaches the normal distribution as v gets large, a good first guess for the sample size is given by:

$$n \simeq 2\left(\frac{\sigma}{\delta}\right)^2 \left(z_{\frac{\alpha}{k(k-1)}} + z_\beta\right)^2 \qquad (5.60)$$

This guess will tend to err on the small side of the correct n, but a second or third iteration is usually sufficient to identify the appropriate sample size.

While Equation 5.58 does deliver useful sample sizes for the one-way ANOVA problem, it really gives the sample size for Bonferroni post-ANOVA multiple comparisons. A more accurate form of sample-size calculation specifically for the ANOVA F statistic will be presented in Chapter 7, but in most cases the two methods return comparable if not the same sample size.

Example 5.13

A completely randomized one-way experiment is to be run with $k = 5$ different treatments. The process standard deviation is known to be $\sigma = 4.2$. If we want 90 percent probability of detecting a difference of $\delta = 10$ between a pair of treatment means, how many replicates n must be run? Use a significance level of $\alpha = 0.05$.

Solution: For the first iteration, suppose that the number of replicates is large enough that Equation 5.60 is valid. Then we have

$$z_{\frac{\alpha}{k(k-1)}} = z_{\frac{0.05}{5(4)}} = z_{0.0025} = 2.81,$$

$z_\beta = z_{0.10} = 1.28$, *and:*

$$n \simeq 2\left(\tfrac{\sigma}{\delta}\right)^2 \left(z_{\frac{\alpha}{k(k-1)}} + z_\beta \right)^2$$

$$\simeq 2\left(\tfrac{4.2}{10}\right)^2 \left(z_{0.0025} + z_{0.10} \right)^2$$

$$\simeq 2\left(\tfrac{4.2}{10}\right)^2 \left(2.81 + 1.28 \right)^2$$

$$\simeq 5.90$$

Since n must be an integer, we have to round up to $n \geq 6$. For the next iteration with n = 6 we have $v = k\,(n-1) = 5\,(6-1) = 25$,

$$t_{\frac{\alpha}{k(k-1)}, v} = t_{\frac{0.05}{5(4)}, 25} = t_{0.0025, 25} = 3.08,$$

and $t_{\beta, v} = t_{0.10, 25} = 1.32$. If we substitute all of these values into Equation 5.58 we have:

$$n \geq 2\left(\tfrac{\sigma}{\delta}\right)^2 \left(t_{\frac{\alpha}{k(k-1)}, v} + t_{\beta, v} \right)^2$$

$$\geq 2\left(\tfrac{4.2}{10}\right)^2 \left(3.08 + 1.32 \right)^2$$

$$\geq 6.83$$

which of course rounds up to $n \geq 7$. With n = 7 we have $v = k\,(n-1) = 5\,(7-1) = 30$,

$$t_{\frac{\alpha}{k(k-1)}, v} = t_{0.0025, 30} = 3.03,$$

and $t_{\beta, v} = t_{0.10, 30} = 1.31$. Equation 5.58 gives us:

$$n \geq 2\left(\tfrac{4.2}{10}\right)^2 \left(3.03 + 1.31 \right)^2$$

$$\geq 6.65$$

which rounds up to $n = 7$ again. Further iterations are unnecessary, so we can conclude that the solution converges to $n = 7$. Thus, the experiment requires $n = 7$ observations for each of the $k = 5$ treatments to meet the specified conditions.

Example 5.13 demonstrates that the amount of work required to determine the number of replicates for an ANOVA problem can be intimidating. Thankfully, MINITAB can do sample-size calculations for one-way ANOVA. Access MINITAB's ANOVA sample-size capability from the **Stat> Power and Sample Size> One-Way ANOVA** menu. Enter the **Number of Levels** (k), **Values for the Maximum Difference Between Means** (δ), **Power Values** (P), and **Sigma** (σ) and MINITAB will respond with the smallest sample size *n* that meets these conditions. By default, MINITAB uses $\alpha = 0.05$ but this value can be changed in the **Options** menu.

Example 5.14
    Use MINITAB to determine the sample size for Example 5.13.

    ***Solution:** From the **Stat> Power and Sample Size> One-Way ANOVA** menu we set the **Number of Levels** to k = 5, **Values for the Maximum Difference Between Means** to δ = 10, **Power Values** to P = 0.90, and **Sigma** to σ = 4.2. The resulting MINITAB output is shown in Figure 5.14. MINITAB confirms that the required sample size is n = 7 and the exact power delivered is P = 0.9279. MINITAB's algorithm for determining the sample size is more accurate than the procedure described above, so don't be surprised if there is a small discrepancy between the two methods. Trust MINITAB's answer more than the manual iterative method.*

5.14 DESIGN CONSIDERATIONS FOR ONE-WAY CLASSIFICATION EXPERIMENTS

- Use a balanced experiment design with the same number of observations in each treatment.

- Decide in advance how large a difference between treatments is practically significant and perform a sample-size calculation to determine the number of replicates required to detect such a difference.

- Validate the random order of the runs and make sure that they are followed when the experiment is built.

```
MTB > Power;
SUBC>   OneWay 5;
SUBC>     MaxDifference 10;
SUBC>     Power 0.90;
SUBC>     Sigma 4.2.

Power and Sample Size

One-way ANOVA

Sigma = 4.2  Alpha = 0.5  Number of Levels = 5

           Sample  Target  Actual   Maximum
SS Means     Size   Power   Power  Difference
      50        7  0.9000  0.9279  10

The sample size is for each level.
```

Figure 5.14   MINITAB output from example power calculation.

- Evaluate the ANOVA residuals graphically to confirm that they are normally distributed and homoscedastic with respect to the different treatments, the magnitude of the response, and the run order.

- If the residuals are not normally distributed or heteroscedastic, consider the use of a mathematical transform to recover the normality and homoscedasticity conditions.

- If there are lurking or nuisance variables that affect the process during the execution of the experiment, use a randomized block design (Chapter 6) instead of the completely randomized design.

- Use post-ANOVA multiple comparisons tests to determine which treatments are different from each other if the ANOVA indicates that there are indeed differences.

6

Experiments for Multi-Way Classifications

6.1 INTRODUCTION

During preparation for a one-way classification experiment, a second classification variable is often identified that could affect the response being studied. This second variable might take the form of:

- *Days.* The experimental runs might have to be performed over several days.

- *Operators.* The experimental runs might have to be collected by different operators.

- *Material.* The experimental runs might have to be made using material from different lots.

- *Temperature.* There might be reason to consider investigating the effect of different temperatures.

- *Equipment.* There might be reason to test for a difference between two or more machines.

- *Methods.* There may be two or more ways to operate the process.

One strategy for managing an unavoidable second variable in an experiment would be to ignore it, but this would be naive and risky. If the second variable does affect the response, then by ignoring it we might confuse its effect with the first variable or its effect might inflate the standard error of the model, which would make it harder to detect differences between the levels of the first variable. If, however, two experimental variables are incorporated into an experiment correctly, these and other problems can be avoided and sometimes we can get the added benefit of learning about differences between the levels of both variables. Obviously we require a structured method for the design and analysis of experiments that involve two-way classifications.

It shouldn't come as a surprise that the method of analysis of two-way classification experiments is by two-way ANOVA, or that the methods for designing and analyzing two-way classification experiments can be extended to multi-way classifications.

6.2 RATIONALE FOR THE TWO-WAY ANOVA

The purpose of this section is to establish the relationship of the various problems that have been encountered in earlier chapters and to extend the use of the ANOVA method to two-way classifications. But before considering experiments with two or more variables, it is necessary to introduce new notation. This notation is used to review the sample variance calculation of Chapter 3 and the one-way ANOVA of Chapter 5 before introducing the two-way ANOVA.

6.2.1 No-Way Classification

When a sample is taken from a single population then the sample data values differ only due to random variation. If the mean of the population being sampled is μ then the deviation of the ith observation from μ can be expressed as:

$$\varepsilon_i = y_i - \mu \tag{6.1}$$

Since μ is generally unknown, we approximate it with $\bar{y}$ or $\bar{y}_\bullet$ using the dot notation introduced in Chapter 5. In this manner the ε_i can be written:

$$\varepsilon_i = y_i - \bar{y}_\bullet \tag{6.2}$$

The amount of random or error variation is quantified by the sample variance:

$$s_\varepsilon^2 = \frac{\sum_{i=1}^{n} \varepsilon_i^2}{n-1} \tag{6.3}$$

The simple model given by Equation 6.1 partitions the information contained in the data into two components: a component common to all of the data values $\bar{y}$ and a random or error component ε_i unique to each observation. This type of partitioning is fundamental in this and the more complex models to follow.

Example 6.1
Find the error variance of the following no-way classified data set:

i	1	2	3	4	5
y_i	55	52	59	61	58

Solution: *The mean of the data set is:*

$$\bar{y} = \frac{1}{n}\sum_{i=1}^{n} y_i$$
$$= \frac{1}{5}(55+52+59+61+58)$$
$$= 57$$

The errors are given by the differences between the observed values and the mean:

i	1	2	3	4	5
y_i	55	52	59	61	58
ε_i	-2	-5	2	4	1

Notice that $\sum \varepsilon_i = 0$ *as required. The error variance is given by:*

$$s_\varepsilon^2 = \frac{1}{n-1}\sum_{i=1}^{n} \varepsilon_i^2$$
$$= \frac{1}{5-1}\left((-2)^2 + (-5)^2 + (2)^2 + (4)^2 + (1)^2\right)$$
$$= 12.5$$

6.2.2 One-Way Classification

The one-variable experiments of Chapter 5 were analyzed using one-way ANOVA. A model for the individual data values analogous to the no-way classification model of Equation 6.1 can be written:

$$y_{ij} = \mu_i + \varepsilon_{ij} \qquad (6.4)$$

where μ_i is the population mean of the ith of k treatments and ε_{ij} is the deviation of the jth of n replicates from its treatment mean. It is helpful to break μ_i into two components: a constant term μ common to all of the observations, and a term that quantifies the ith treatment's deviation from μ called the treatment *effect*. The ith treatment effect is identified with the symbol α_i. In this manner, μ_i may be written:

$$\mu_i = \mu + \alpha_i \qquad (6.5)$$

Note that by definition, $\bar{\mu}_\bullet$ and $\bar{\alpha}_\bullet = 0$. Thus, the null hypothesis for the one-way ANOVA problem may be written as H_0: $\mu_i = \mu$ or H_0: $\alpha_i = 0$ for all i from 1 to k. With this new form for μ_i the model may be written:

$$y_{ij} = \mu + \alpha_i + \varepsilon_{ij} \tag{6.6}$$

This equation shows that data values can be partitioned into three components: a component due to the grand mean μ, a component due to the treatment effect α_i, and a random or error component ε_{ij}.

Since μ and the α_i are generally unknown, they are approximated with

$$\hat{\mu} = \bar{y}_{\bullet\bullet} \tag{6.7}$$

and

$$\hat{\alpha}_i = \bar{y}_{i\bullet} - \bar{y}_{\bullet\bullet} \tag{6.8}$$

so the experimental ε_{ij} are expressed:

$$\varepsilon_{ij} = y_{ij} - \bar{y}_{\bullet\bullet} - \hat{\alpha}_i \tag{6.9}$$

Two variances are required to quantify the one-way ANOVA problem: one for the variation between treatments and one for the error variation within treatments. Respectively, these variances are:

$$s_{\bar{y}}^2 = \frac{\sum_{i=1}^k \hat{\alpha}_i^2}{k-1} \tag{6.10}$$

and

$$s_{\varepsilon}^2 = \frac{\sum_{i=1}^k s_i^2}{k} \tag{6.11}$$

where the sample variance of the ith treatment is:

$$s_i^2 = \frac{\sum_{j=1}^n \varepsilon_{ij}^2}{n-1} \tag{6.12}$$

The F statistic for the one-way ANOVA is determined from:

$$F = \frac{n s_{\bar{y}}^2}{s_{\varepsilon}^2} \tag{6.13}$$

with $(k-1)$ and $k(n-1)$ numerator and denominator degrees of freedom, respectively.

Study these last four equations carefully. They summarize the one-way ANOVA of Chapter 5, but this time the variation between treatments $s_{\bar{y}}^2$ is expressed in terms of the α_i, the deviations of treatments from the grand mean. Although these equations provide the rationale for the one-way ANOVA, the preferred method of calculation still involves the sums of squares, degrees of freedom, and mean squares that were introduced in Chapter 5.

Example 6.2

Determine the treatment effects (α_i) and the model errors (ε_{ij}) for the following data set. The data are classified by one variable with three levels. Use the treatment effects and the errors to determine the ANOVA F statistic and determine if it's significant at $\alpha = 0.05$.

Treatment (i)	1	1	1	1	2	2	2	2	3	3	3	3
Response (y_{ij})	14	17	13	12	20	21	16	15	25	29	24	22

Solution: The model consists of the three treatment means which are:

$$\bar{y}_{1\bullet} = \frac{1}{4}(14+17+13+12) = 14$$

$$\bar{y}_{2\bullet} = \frac{1}{4}(20+21+16+15) = 18$$

$$\bar{y}_{3\bullet} = \frac{1}{4}(25+29+24+22) = 25$$

The grand mean is:

$$\bar{y}_{\bullet\bullet} = \frac{1}{3}(14+18+25) = 19$$

The differences between the treatment means and the grand mean are the treatment effects, that is $\hat{\alpha}_i = \bar{y}_i - \bar{y}_{\bullet\bullet}$:

$$\hat{\alpha}_1 = 14 - 19 = -5$$

$$\hat{\alpha}_2 = 18 - 19 = -1$$

$$\hat{\alpha}_3 = 25 - 19 = 6$$

Notice that the mean treatment effect is $\bar{\alpha}_i = \frac{1}{3}(-5 - 1 + 6) = 0$ as required. The model errors are given by the differences between the individual observations and their treatment means, that is $\varepsilon_{ij} = y_{ij} - \bar{y}_{i\bullet}$. After subtracting the treatment mean from each observation, the effects and errors are summarized in the following table:

Treatment (i)	1	1	1	1	2	2	2	2	3	3	3	3
Response (y_{ij})	14	17	13	12	20	21	16	15	25	29	24	22
Treatment mean $(\bar{y}_{i\bullet})$	14	14	14	14	18	18	18	18	25	25	25	25
Grand mean $(\bar{y}_{\bullet\bullet})$	19	19	19	19	19	19	19	19	19	19	19	19
Treatment effect $(\hat{\alpha}_i)$	−5	−5	−5	−5	−1	−1	−1	−1	6	6	6	6
Error (ε_{ij})	0	3	−1	−2	2	3	−2	−3	0	4	−1	−3

The numerator of the ANOVA F statistic is given by:

$$ns_{\bar{y}}^2 = \frac{n\sum_{i=1}^{k}\hat{\alpha}_i^2}{k-1}$$

$$= \frac{4\left((-5)^2+(-1)^2+(6)^2\right)}{3-1}$$

$$= 124$$

and the denominator is given by:

$$s_{\varepsilon}^2 = \frac{\sum_{i=1}^{k}s_i^2}{k}$$

$$= \frac{1}{k(n-1)}\sum_{i=1}^{k}\sum_{j=1}^{n}\varepsilon_{ij}^2$$

$$= \frac{1}{3(4-1)}\left((0)^2+(3)^2+\cdots+(-3)^2\right)$$

$$= 7.33$$

The F ratio is:

$$F = \frac{ns_{\bar{y}}^2}{s_{\varepsilon}^2}$$

$$= \frac{124}{7.33}$$

$$= 16.9$$

which is much larger than the value of F = 1 that we expect if there are no differences between the treatment means. The critical F value with k − 1 = 3 − 2 = 2 numerator degrees of freedom and k (n − 1) = 3 (4 − 1) = 9 denominator degrees of freedom is $F_{0.05}$ = 4.26. Since (F = 16.9) > ($F_{0.05}$ = 4.26) we must conclude that there are significant differences between the treatment means. The normality, homoscedasticity, and independence assumptions should be checked, and a multiple comparisons test could be used to determine which treatment means are different from the others.

6.2.3 Two-Way Classification

Consider the general two-way classification shown in Table 6.1 where there are *a* different levels of the first variable *A* indicated in columns and *b* different levels of the second variable *B* indicated in rows. y_{ij} is the observation taken at the *i*th level of *A* and the *j*th level of *B*. To keep the analysis simple, there is no replication although replication is possible and probably likely. For now don't worry about replication—let your software deal with it.

One of the first exploratory data analysis techniques to try with the two-way classified data is to construct boxplots using just one variable at a time. Two sets of boxplots are required. The first set is constructed from the data classified according to *A* and the second set is constructed from the same data classified according to *B*. Additional boxplots showing the distribution of sample means could be added to each

Table 6.1   Observations in a two-way classification.

y_{ij}		A				
		1	2	3	. . .	a
	1	y_{11}	y_{21}	y_{31}	. . .	y_{a1}
	2	y_{12}	y_{22}	y_{32}	. . .	y_{a2}
B	3	y_{13}	y_{23}	y_{33}	. . .	y_{a3}
	⋮	⋮	⋮	⋮	⋮	⋮
	b	y_{1b}	y_{2b}	y_{3b}	. . .	y_{ab}

set to help determine, by eye, if there are any differences between the treatment means. This analysis is exactly the same as that used for the one-way ANOVA problem except that it has to be carried out twice.

While boxplots or dotplots are useful in looking for differences between treatments for one-way classifications, they are inadequate for the two-way classification problem. The problem is that the boxplots organized by one variable at a time will be inflated if there is significant variation due to the other variable. Since the effect of a second variable is to spread out the points in boxplots organized by the first variable, the usual visual tests for differences between boxplots, such as the box slippage test, lose power. The only solution to this problem is to proceed with the two-way ANOVA, which separates the effects of both variables so that small differences between the levels of both variables can be detected.

The two-way classification model for individual data values can be written:

$$y_{ij} = \mu_{ij} + \varepsilon_{ij} \tag{6.14}$$

where μ_{ij} is the population mean of the observations taken at the ith level of A and the jth level of B, and ε_{ij} is the difference between this mean and the observation y_{ij}.* As was done in the one-way case, the μ_{ij} can be broken down into components: one due to the common constant term μ, one due to the A effect α_i, and the last due to the B effect β_j. In component form the μ_{ij} can be written as:

$$\mu_{ij} = \mu + \alpha_i + \beta_j \tag{6.15}$$

Since $\bar{\mu}_{..}$ must be equal to μ we must also have $\bar{\alpha}_{.} = 0$ and $\bar{\beta}_{.} = 0$. This model for μ_{ij} can be used to rewrite Equation 6.14:

$$y_{ij} = \mu + \alpha_i + \beta_j + \varepsilon_{ij} \tag{6.16}$$

This model clearly shows how the different sources of variation affect the observations.

---

* Equation 6.14 describes the model for the two-way classification problem with one replicate. When there is more than one replicate, the model will be $y_{ijk} = \mu_{ij} + \varepsilon_{ijk}$ where the subscript k accounts for the replicates.

The terms μ, α_i, and β_j that appear in Equation 6.16 are parameters that must be estimated with appropriate statistics determined from the experimental data. μ is not usually of any special concern; however, the α_i and β_j are the subjects of hypothesis tests to determine if there are significant variable effects. These tests are: H_0: $\alpha_i = 0$ for all i versus H_A: $\alpha_i \neq 0$ for at least one i and H_0: $\beta_j = 0$ for all j versus H_A: $\beta_j = 0$ for at least one j. The ANOVA F test is used to determine if significant variable effects are present.

Estimates for μ, α_i, and β_j can be calculated from the data:

$$\hat{\mu} = \overline{y}_{..} \tag{6.17}$$

$$\hat{\alpha}_i = \overline{y}_{i.} - \overline{y}_{..} \tag{6.18}$$

$$\hat{\beta}_j = \overline{y}_{.j} - \overline{y}_{..} \tag{6.19}$$

Finally, the ε_{ij} may be written as:

$$\begin{aligned} \varepsilon_{ij} &= y_{ij} - \hat{\mu}_{ij} \\ &= y_{ij} - \overline{y}_{..} - \hat{\alpha}_i - \hat{\beta}_j \end{aligned} \tag{6.20}$$

There are three variances that must be determined in this problem to test for A and B effects: the variance associated with differences between the means of the columns (A), the variance associated with differences between the means of the rows (B), and the error variance. The variances associated with the two study variables, A and B, are analogous to the variance $s_{\overline{y}}^2$ determined in the one-way ANOVA problem, so we'll call them s_A^2 and s_B^2:

$$s_A^2 = \frac{\sum_{i=1}^{a} \hat{\alpha}_i^2}{a-1} \tag{6.21}$$

and

$$s_B^2 = \frac{\sum_{j=1}^{b} \hat{\beta}_j^2}{b-1} \tag{6.22}$$

The last variance is the error variance calculated from the ε_{ij}:

$$s_\varepsilon^2 = \frac{\sum_{i=1}^{a} \sum_{j=1}^{b} \varepsilon_{ij}^2}{(a-1)(b-1)} \tag{6.23}$$

The denominator of the expression for s_ε^2 is cryptic. Basically the degrees of freedom not consumed by s_A^2 or s_B^2 are left to estimate the error. Since there are $df_{total} = ab - 1$

total degrees of freedom, $df_A = a - 1$ degrees of freedom associated with A, and $df_B = b - 1$ degrees of freedom associated with B, the number of error degrees of freedom are:

$$
\begin{aligned}
df_\varepsilon &= (ab-1)-(a-1)-(b-1) \\
&= ab-a-b+1 \\
&= a(b-1)-(b-1) \\
&= (a-1)(b-1)
\end{aligned}
\tag{6.24}
$$

Now we have the variances required to determine if there are significant effects due to the two variables in the two-way experiment. The F statistic for A is given by:

$$
F_A = \frac{bs_\alpha^2}{s_\varepsilon^2}
\tag{6.25}
$$

with $df_A = a - 1$ and $df_\varepsilon = (a - 1)(b - 1)$ degrees of freedom for the numerator and denominator, respectively. The b term in the numerator is the correction for the central limit theorem contraction because each $\hat{\alpha}_i$ is determined from the mean of b observations. We saw the same thing in the one-way analysis where the variance in the numerator of the F ratio (Equation 6.13) was $ns_{\bar{y}}^2$ because there were n observations to determine each $\bar{y}$. Similarly, the F statistic for B is:

$$
F_B = \frac{as_\beta^2}{s_\varepsilon^2}
\tag{6.26}
$$

with $df_B = b - 1$ and $df_\varepsilon = (a - 1)(b - 1)$ degrees of freedom for the numerator and denominator, respectively.

Example 6.3

For the following two-way classification problem, determine the A and B effects and use them to determine the corresponding F statistics. Are they significant at $\alpha = 0.01$?

	y_{ij}	1	2	3	4
		A			
	1	18	42	34	46
B	2	16	40	30	42
	3	11	35	29	41

Solution: There are a = 4 levels of A and b = 3 levels of B in the experiment. The row and column means and the grand mean are:

			A			
y_{ij}		**1**	**2**	**3**	**4**	**Mean**
B	**1**	18	42	34	46	$\bar{y}_{\bullet 1} = 35$
	2	16	40	30	42	$\bar{y}_{\bullet 2} = 32$
	3	11	35	29	41	$\bar{y}_{\bullet 3} = 29$
	Mean	$\bar{y}_{1\bullet} = 15$	$\bar{y}_{2\bullet} = 39$	$\bar{y}_{3\bullet} = 31$	$\bar{y}_{4\bullet} = 43$	$\bar{y}_{\bullet\bullet} = 32$

The A and B effects are the differences between the column and row means and the grand mean, respectively:

			A				
y_{ij}		**1**	**2**	**3**	**4**	**Mean**	$\hat{\beta}_j$
B	**1**	18	42	34	46	$\bar{y}_{\bullet 1} = 35$	$\hat{\beta}_1 = 3$
	2	16	40	30	42	$\bar{y}_{\bullet 2} = 32$	$\hat{\beta}_2 = 0$
	3	11	35	29	41	$\bar{y}_{\bullet 3} = 29$	$\hat{\beta}_3 = -3$
	Mean	$\bar{y}_{1\bullet} = 15$	$\bar{y}_{2\bullet} = 39$	$\bar{y}_{3\bullet} = 31$	$\bar{y}_{4\bullet} = 43$	$\bar{y}_{\bullet\bullet} = 32$	
	$\hat{\alpha}_i$	$\hat{\alpha}_1 = -17$	$\hat{\alpha}_2 = 7$	$\hat{\alpha}_3 = -1$	$\hat{\alpha}_4 = 11$		

Notice that the mean A and B effects are $\bar{\alpha} = 0$ and $\bar{\beta} = 0$ as required. The effect variances are given by:

$$s_A^2 = \tfrac{1}{a-1} \textstyle\sum_{i=1}^{a} \hat{\alpha}_i^2$$
$$= \tfrac{1}{4-1}\left(\left(-17\right)^2 + \left(7\right)^2 + \left(-1\right)^2 + \left(11\right)^2 \right)$$
$$= 153.3$$

and

$$s_B^2 = \tfrac{1}{b-1} \textstyle\sum_{j=1}^{b} \hat{\beta}_j^2$$
$$= \tfrac{1}{3-1}\left(\left(3\right)^2 + \left(0\right)^2 + \left(-3\right)^2 \right)$$
$$= 9.0$$

The last quantity that we need in order to determine the F statistics is the error variance s_ε^2. This requires that we calculate the deviations of individual observations from their predicted values, but the predicted values are complex because they are a function of both A and B. The individual errors are given by Equation 6.20. For example, the first observation y_{11} has an error of:

$$\varepsilon_{11} = y_{11} - \hat{y}_{11}$$
$$= y_{11} - \left(\bar{y}_{\bullet\bullet} + \hat{\alpha}_1 + \hat{\beta}_1 \right)$$
$$= 18 - \left(32 - 17 + 3 \right)$$
$$= 0$$

This particular point is exactly predicted by the model since its error is zero, but other observations aren't so lucky. The errors for all of the observations are:

		\multicolumn{4}{c}{A}			
	ε_{ij}	1	2	3	4
	1	0	0	0	0
B	2	1	1	−1	−1
	3	−1	−1	1	1

Notice that the row and column sums add up to zero as required. The error variance is given by:

$$s_\varepsilon^2 = \frac{1}{(a-1)(b-1)} \sum_{i=1}^a \sum_{j=1}^b \varepsilon_{ij}^2$$
$$= \frac{1}{(4-1)(3-1)} \left((0)^2 + (0^2) + \cdots + (1)^2 \right)$$
$$= 1.33$$

Finally, the F ratio for A is:

$$F_A = \frac{b s_\alpha^2}{s_\varepsilon^2}$$
$$= \frac{3 \times 153.3}{1.33}$$
$$= 346$$

and the F ratio for B is:

$$F_B = \frac{a s_\beta^2}{s_\varepsilon^2}$$
$$= \frac{4 \times 9.0}{1.33}$$
$$= 27.1$$

There are $df_A = 4 - 1 = 3$ degrees of freedom associated with A, $df_B = 3 - 1 = 2$ degrees of freedom associated with B, and $df_\varepsilon = 11 - 3 - 2 = 6$ error degrees of freedom. Notice that these degrees of freedom are just the denominators used to determine the required variances s_A^2, s_B^2, and s_ε^2, respectively. At $\alpha = 0.01$ the critical values of F are $F_{0.01,3,6} = 9.78$ for the test for A and $F_{0.01,2,6} = 10.92$ for the test for B. Both F_A and F_B

exceed their critical values by a lot so they are highly significant. The normality assumption and the equality of variances assumption should be checked and then a multiple comparisons test could be used to determine which treatments are different from the others.

6.3 THE SUMS OF SQUARES APPROACH FOR TWO-WAY ANOVA (ONE REPLICATE)

The approach taken in Section 6.2.3 to solving the two-way classification problem has conceptual value but the sums of squares approach is more concise and offers additional insight into the two-way ANOVA problem. The following analysis is applicable to the two-way classification problem with one replicate. When there are two or more replicates, the equations shown here must be modified to include another summation over replicates. The interpretation of the ANOVA results, which will be discussed later, depends on the nature of the design variables and the order of the experimental runs.

The ANOVA calculations by the sums of squares method for the two-way classification problem are analogous to the calculations for the one-way problem. Consider a balanced two-way classification experiment with a levels of the first variable A, b levels of the second variable B, and one observation for each (A, B) combination. The total sum of squares for the experiment is:

$$SS_{total} = \sum_{i=1}^{a}\sum_{j=1}^{b}\left(y_{ij} - \bar{y}_{\bullet\bullet}\right)^2 \tag{6.27}$$

By adding and subtracting $\bar{y}_{i\bullet}$ and $\bar{y}_{\bullet j}$ within the parentheses and manipulating the summations, the total sum of squares becomes:

$$SS_{total} = \sum_{i=1}^{a}\sum_{j=1}^{b}\left(y_{ij} - \bar{y}_{i\bullet} - \bar{y}_{\bullet j} - \bar{y}_{\bullet\bullet}\right)^2 + b\sum_{i=1}^{a}\left(\bar{y}_{i\bullet} - \bar{y}_{\bullet\bullet}\right)^2 + a\sum_{j=1}^{b}\left(\bar{y}_{\bullet j} - \bar{y}_{\bullet\bullet}\right)^2 \tag{6.28}$$

In terms of the sums of squares, this equation may be written:

$$SS_{total} = SS_{\varepsilon} + SS_A + SS_B \tag{6.29}$$

where the respective order of the terms in the two equations has been maintained. The summations may be simplified to determine the calculating forms:

$$SS_{total} = \sum_{i=1}^{a}\sum_{j=1}^{b}\left(y_{ij} - \bar{y}_{\bullet\bullet}\right)^2 = \sum_{i=1}^{a}\sum_{j=1}^{b}y_{ij}^2 - \frac{y_{\bullet\bullet}^2}{ab} \tag{6.30}$$

$$SS_A = b\sum_{i=1}^{a}\left(\bar{y}_{i\bullet} - \bar{y}_{\bullet\bullet}\right)^2 = \frac{1}{b}\sum_{i=1}^{a}y_{i\bullet}^2 - \frac{y_{\bullet\bullet}^2}{ab} \tag{6.31}$$

$$SS_B = a\sum_{j=1}^{b}\left(\bar{y}_{\bullet j} - \bar{y}_{\bullet\bullet}\right)^2 = \frac{1}{a}\sum_{j=1}^{b}y_{\bullet j}^2 - \frac{y_{\bullet\bullet}^2}{ab} \tag{6.32}$$

and

$$SS_\varepsilon = \sum_{i=1}^{a}\sum_{j=1}^{b}\left(y_{ij} - \bar{y}_{i\bullet} - \bar{y}_{\bullet j} - \bar{y}_{\bullet\bullet}\right)^2 = SS_{total} - SS_A - SS_B \tag{6.33}$$

The degrees of freedom are also partitioned:

$$ab - 1 = (a-1)(b-1) + (a-1) + (b-1) \tag{6.34}$$

or in terms of the *df* notation:

$$df_{total} = df_\varepsilon + df_A + df_B \tag{6.35}$$

where

$$
\begin{aligned}
df_A &= a-1 \\
df_B &= b-1 \\
df_\varepsilon &= (a-1)(b-1) \\
df_{total} &= ab-1
\end{aligned}
\tag{6.36}
$$

All of the information regarding the sums of squares and their degrees of freedom for the two-way ANOVA problem with one replicate are summarized in Table 6.2. The mean squares due to different sources are calculated in the usual way, from the ratios of the sums of squares to the associated degrees of freedom: $MS_i = SS_i/df_i$, and the F statistics are ratios of the A and B mean squares to the error mean squares: $F_i = MS_i/MS_\varepsilon$.

6.4 INTERACTIONS

In any process with two or more important variables there is a chance that variables will interact with each other. When two variables interact, the effect of one variable on the

Table 6.2 Two-way ANOVA table with one replicate.

Source	df	SS	MS	F
A	df_A	SS_A	MS_A	F_A
B	df_B	SS_B	MS_B	F_B
Error	df_ε	SS_ε	MS_ε	
Total	df_{total}	SS_{total}		

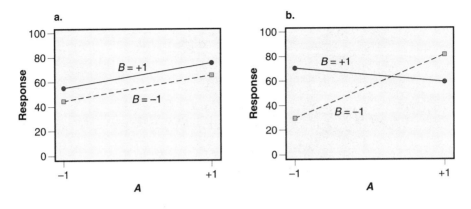

Figure 6.1   Two-way classifications without and with interactions.

response depends on the level of the other variable. To see what this means, consider the two situations in Figure 6.1. In both cases two variables, *A* and *B,* are considered at two levels, −1 and +1. In Figure 6.1a the effect of *A* is to increase the response as *A* changes from its −1 to +1 level, and the effect of *B* is to increase the response as *B* changes from −1 to +1. Notice that the size of the increase in the response when *A* changes is independent of the level of *B*. Likewise, the size of the increase in the response when *B* changes is independent of the level of *A*. These observations indicate that there is no interaction between *A* and *B*.

Now consider the situation shown in Figure 6.1b. Notice that the effect of *A* on the response depends on the level of *B* and the effect of *B* depends on the level of *A*. This type of behavior occurs when a significant interaction exists between two variables. Obviously this is a more complex case than in Figure 6.1a, but fortunately ANOVA has the ability to detect and quantify the presence of an interaction if the correct experiment design and analysis are used.

Graphs like those in Figure 6.1 are often called interaction plots because they can be used to check for the presence of interactions between variables. Generally, when the lines in an interaction plot are parallel there is no interaction between the variables and when the lines diverge there is an interaction between the variables. When there are more than two levels of one or more variables in an experiment, there can be many sets of line segments to observe for parallelism. In these cases check each set of line segments defined by the horizontal plotting axis. If all of the lines in each set are roughly parallel then there is no evidence of interactions between the variables.

Example 6.4

Interpret the interaction plots from the 3 × 3 *experiments in Figure 6.2. (These represent two different experiments.) Is there evidence of significant main effects? Interactions?*

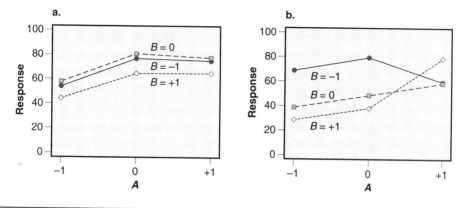

Figure 6.2 Example interaction plots.

Solution: *Figure 6.2a suggests that there are significant main effects. The response at the –1 level of A appears to be biased low compared to when A = 0 or 1. There also appear to be significant differences between the levels of B. The levels of B that deliver the lowest to highest values of the response are +1, –1, and then 0. The line segments between A = –1 to 0 and from A = 0 to +1 are substantially parallel so there is probably not a significant interaction between A and B.*

Figure 6.2b is not as simple. There appear to be significant main effects associated with A and B but there is also a significant interaction between the two variables indicated by the diverging line segments between A = 0 to 1. It is difficult to form a simple statement describing the dependence of the response on A and B.

Interactions between variables are very common in engineering and manufacturing problems so it is important to use experiment designs that can handle them. Although the relative frequency of significant interactions varies from experiment to experiment, it's not uncommon to find that about one-quarter of the possible two-factor interactions are significant. When an experiment contains many variables, the number of possible two-factor interactions is large and some of them will very likely be significant. In fact, many of the problems with processes that cause people to resort to DOE methods are caused by unrecognized interactions between variables.

When the two-factor interaction is included in the two-way ANOVA, the sums of squares partition according to:

$$SS_{total} = SS_A + SS_B + SS_{AB} + SS_\varepsilon \tag{6.37}$$

where SS_{AB} is the sum of squares associated with the interaction. There is a corresponding relationship for the degrees of freedom:

$$df_{total} = df_A + df_B + df_{AB} + df_\varepsilon \tag{6.38}$$

If there are a levels of variable A, b levels of variable B, and n replicates then:

$$\begin{aligned}
df_A &= a-1 \\
df_B &= b-1 \\
df_{AB} &= (a-1)(b-1) \\
df_\varepsilon &= ab(n-1) \\
df_{total} &= abn-1
\end{aligned}$$

(6.39)

Table 6.3 summarizes the two-way ANOVA table, including the interaction term. The mean squares and F statistics are calculated in the usual way. F_{AB} allows us to test the hypotheses H_0: *there is no interaction between A and B* versus H_A: *there is an interaction between A and B.*

Equation 6.37 shows how the sums of squares are partitioned when an interaction is considered in the analysis, but exactly how is the interaction sum of squares calculated? Consider the simple case of a two-way classification problem with three levels of the first variable A, two levels of the second variable B, and n replicates as shown in the following table:

			A	
$y_{ij\bullet}$		**1**	**2**	**3**
B	**1**	$y_{11\bullet}$	$y_{21\bullet}$	$y_{31\bullet}$
	2	$y_{12\bullet}$	$y_{22\bullet}$	$y_{32\bullet}$

where i indicates the A treatment, j indicates the B treatment, and the observations are summed over the n replicates. Remember that we determined the effects of A and B by calculating the means of the observations grouped by the columns and rows, respectively. The interaction effect is determined in the same manner except that the groupings are taken along diagonals. The first contribution to the interaction term comes from the difference between the sums of diagonals taken from the first two columns:

$$\left[\left(y_{11\bullet} + y_{22\bullet} \right) - \left(y_{12\bullet} + y_{21\bullet} \right) \right]^2$$

Table 6.3 Two-way ANOVA table with interaction.

Source	df	SS	MS	F
A	df_A	SS_A	MS_A	F_A
B	df_B	SS_B	MS_B	F_B
AB	df_{AB}	SS_{AB}	MS_{AB}	F_{AB}
Error	df_ε	SS_ε	MS_ε	
Total	df_{total}	SS_{total}		

Two more contributions come from the difference of the sums of diagonals from the first and third and the second and third columns, which gives:

$$SS_{AB} = \frac{1}{abn}\left[\left[\left(y_{11\bullet} + y_{22\bullet} \right) - \left(y_{12\bullet} + y_{21\bullet} \right) \right]^2 \right.$$
$$+ \left[\left(y_{11\bullet} + y_{32\bullet} \right) - \left(y_{12\bullet} + y_{31\bullet} \right) \right]^2$$
$$\left. + \left[\left(y_{21\bullet} + y_{32\bullet} \right) - \left(y_{22\bullet} + y_{31\bullet} \right) \right]^2 \right] \tag{6.40}$$

Now that we know how the interaction sum of squares is calculated, where do the interaction degrees of freedom come from? Remember that the row and column means must be calculated to determine the row and column effects. This means that as soon as a pair of cells are picked from a row of the 3 × 2 table (for example, $y_{11\bullet}$ and $y_{21\bullet}$), the remaining cells are not free to vary because they must be consistent with the row and column means. The two cells chosen, any two will do, correspond to the two degrees of freedom required to estimate the interaction effect.

With some thought it should be apparent that the number of degrees of freedom for a two-factor interaction corresponds to the number of cells left after striking out one row and one column from the two-way classification table. The row and column being struck out account for the degrees of freedom consumed by the calculation of the row and column means. (The one cell where the struck out row and column intersect corresponds to the grand mean of the data set.) In general, the degrees of freedom associated with any interaction are equal to the degrees of freedom associated with the main effects involved in the interaction, so for the two-way case we have $df_{AB} = (a - 1)$ $(b - 1)$. This rule applies to higher-order interactions as well. For example, in a three-way classification problem with variables A, B, and C, with a, b, and c levels, respectively, the three-factor interaction will consume $df_{ABC} = (a - 1)(b - 1)(c - 1)$ degrees of freedom.

Example 6.5

Determine the sum of squares and degrees of freedom for the interaction for the following data set:

y_{ij}		A		
		1	**2**	**3**
B	**1**	29, 33	46, 48	36, 32
	2	24, 22	48, 44	26, 22

Solution: The sum of squares for the interaction term is given by:

$$SS_{AB} = \tfrac{1}{12}\Big[\big[(29+33+48+44)-(24+22+46+48)\big]^2$$
$$+\big[(29+33+26+22)-(24+22+36+32)\big]^2$$
$$+\big[(46+48+26+22)-(48+44+36+32)\big]^2\,\Big]$$
$$= 44.7$$

There will be $df_{AB} = (3-1)(2-1) = 2$ degrees of freedom to determine the interaction effect.

Compare the two-way ANOVA tables for the single replicate case ($n = 1$) in Table 6.2 to the replicated case ($n > 1$) in Table 6.3. Specifically, note that their error degrees of freedom are different. If the model including the main effects and the interaction from Table 6.3 is applied to the single replicate situation, then the number of degrees of freedom to estimate the error is:

$$df_\varepsilon = ab(n-1) = ab(1-1) = 0 \tag{6.41}$$

This means that after fitting a model for main effects and the interaction there will be no information left to estimate the error variability so it will be impossible to perform any of the usual F tests. This problem can only be resolved by compromising the model. Occam and the principle of effect heredity suggest that of the three potential terms in a two-way classification model—A, B, and AB—we expect that the main effects will be more important than the two-factor interaction. If we're willing to assume that A and B don't interact (an assumption that cannot be checked using information from the experiment), then we can drop the AB interaction term from the model because we expect it to be insignificant or at least the weakest term in the model. Then the sum of squares and degrees of freedom associated with the interaction will be pooled with the error estimate. In this case, since $SS_\varepsilon = 0$ and $df_\varepsilon = 0$ when the interaction term is included in the model, the interaction sum of squares and degrees of freedom will form the error estimate when the interaction term is dropped from the model. The validity of the F tests for A and B will depend on the validity of the assumption of no AB interaction, but this is a necessary risk in allowing the F tests for A and B to be completed.

There are two ways to address the risk associated with the assumption that there is no AB interaction in the single replicate two-way classification problem. If an independent estimate of the standard deviation of the experimental response is available, such as from historical data, it can be compared to the standard error of the model given by $s_\varepsilon = \sqrt{MS_\varepsilon}$ using an F test. If the two error estimates are found to be comparable, then there is reason to conclude that the interaction is not significant and that the F statistics are accurate. If the standard error of the model is significantly larger than the independent estimate, then there is reason to believe that the interaction might be significant and that the F statistics for A and B might be compromised. The data used to create the independent estimate must be carefully chosen so that they provide comparable errors to those expected in the experiment. This requirement is hard to guarantee and makes this approach difficult to defend.

The second way to test the assumption that there is no *AB* interaction is simply to use two or more replicates in the two-way classification design. This approach is preferred over the use of an independent estimate of the error because there is always the risk that the data used to form the independent estimate will not be representative of the errors present during the experiment. It's always preferred to create an error estimate for testing hypotheses from the experimental data.

So what strategy for interactions should you use to analyze two-way ANOVAs? If the experiment is replicated, you should definitely include the interaction term in the model. If there is an interaction present and you choose to ignore it, then the sum of squares and degrees of freedom associated with the interaction will be pooled with the error. If the ignored interaction is significant, then pooling it with the error will decrease the sensitivity of the experiment, perhaps so much that significant variable effects will be hidden in the noise. If you include the interaction term in the model and it is not statistically significant, then you can always rerun the analysis leaving the interaction out.

Example 6.6

Evaluate the data from Example 6.3 for an interaction between A and B.

Solution: Since the two-way classification experiment only involves a single repli-cate, there aren't enough error degrees of freedom to include the AB interaction and the main effects in the model, so no formal quantitative test for the AB interaction can be performed. A superficial evaluation for the AB interaction can be made, however, using interaction plots as shown in Figure 6.3. The interaction plots show that the line segments connecting the levels of B and A in the plots are substantially parallel to each other so there is probably no significant AB interaction in this case. To confirm this

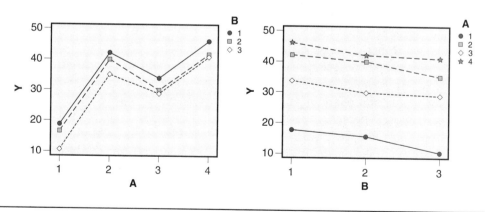

Figure 6.3 Interaction plots of data from Example 6.3.

result rigorously, the experiment should be repeated using two or more replicates of the 4×3 *factorial design.*

6.5 INTERPRETATION OF TWO-WAY EXPERIMENTS

6.5.1 Introduction

We've considered the statistical analysis of the two-way classification experiment, but there are actually four different interpretations possible for the same analysis. Which interpretation is appropriate is determined by the nature of the study variables and the order in which the data are collected. All four interpretations could be considered for one data set, but only one of the four interpretations is valid.

Suppose that we wish to study a manufacturing process where five different material lots are to be processed by three different operators. Clearly this is a two-way classification problem, but whether we can learn if there are differences between the lots, or differences between the operators, or differences between both lots and operators, or nothing about differences between lots or operators is determined by the order of the experimental runs.

If all three operators are on the job at the same time and the lots are processed in order (Lot 1, Lot 2, . . . , Lot 5) with each part being made by a randomly chosen operator, then *lot* is a blocking variable and *operator* is the treatment variable. The distinction is that the level of the treatment variable (the operator) is determined randomly whereas the levels of the blocking variable (the lot) are not random. This distinction is crucial because this experiment permits the operators to be compared to each other, but lots cannot be compared because successive lots are not necessarily run under the same conditions. The benefit of including lot as a blocking variable in the analysis is that it permits the ANOVA to remove any variation caused by differences between lots along with any additional variation caused by unidentified variables that were confounded with lots. This type of experiment is called a *randomized block* design because the levels of the study variable are (and must be) randomized while the levels of the second variable are used to define blocks.

In another scenario, suppose that the three operators work successive shifts and material from the five lots can be stockpiled so that material from the different lots can be processed in random order. This is another randomized block design where *lot* is the treatment variable and *operator* is the blocking variable. This experiment would be used to learn about differences between lots with any difference caused by the blocking variable (operator) removed. This experiment cannot be used to determine if there are differences between the operators because they work under potentially different conditions. Any apparent difference between operators could be due to some other unidentified cause.

A third way to interpret the same data is appropriate if the lots and operators are both completely randomized. This could be done if random parts from all five lots were given to random operators in random order. This type of experiment is called a 5×3

factorial experiment and it has the ability to identify differences between lots and operators in the same experiment.

The fourth way to interpret the experiment is appropriate if neither lots nor operators are randomized. This is probably the easiest way to run the experiment but because neither of the variables are randomized, the experiment can't be used to draw any safe conclusions about differences between levels of lots or operators. In effect, both of the variables are blocking variables.

For all four of these situations, the data are exactly the same and the ANOVA, which doesn't account for the order of the experimental runs, will give exactly the same results. It is the experimenter's responsibility to see that the correct randomization plan is used to support the goals of the experiment and to see that the correct interpretation of the results is made.

6.5.2 The Randomized Complete Block Design

The *randomized complete block design* is one of the most commonly used experiment designs. It is intended to deal with two variables with the distinction that one of the variables is the true subject of the study and the second variable is a possible source of nuisance variation, that is, the second variable is a known or potential source of variation in the process that cannot be eliminated from the experiment. The variable being studied is referred to as the treatment or study variable and the nuisance variable is used to define blocks of runs in the experiment. The treatment variable levels must appear in random order within blocks, hence the word *randomized* in the experiment name. This distinction can be confusing, and it's often difficult to differentiate between the treatment variable and the blocking variable. The word *complete* in the experiment's name indicates that each block contains all of the treatments. When the same number of runs or replicates of each treatment is used in each block, the experiment is said to be *balanced*.

The levels of a blocking variable should be chosen so that the observations within blocks are as much alike as possible but large differences between the blocks are allowed—the ANOVA analysis can account for that. When there is more than one nuisance variable in an experiment, they should all be blocked. These multi-way classification designs are still analyzed with ANOVA using very similar methods to the two-way classification problem.

Both *F* ratios are reported when the experiment is a two-way factorial design, but it is common to leave the *F* ratio for the blocking variable out of the ANOVA table if the experiment is a randomized block design. This helps prevent an inappropriate attempt to interpret the *F* statistic for blocks. Remember that the ANOVA cannot tell you which interpretation is correct. You must base your interpretation on the run order that was employed in the experiment.

Example 6.7

The yield of a machining process is to be studied as a function of one of the critical machine controls (that is, a knob). It is suspected that raw material for the machine also affects its yield but it is not easy to change from one lot of raw material to another.

Describe how a randomized block experiment design would be constructed to study the yield.

Solution: There are two variables that potentially affect the yield: the knob and the raw material. The knob setting is to be the study variable in the experiment. There is no or little choice about what lots are submitted to the process and it is not easy to change from one lot to another, so raw material should be treated as a blocking variable. To control the nuisance variation caused by differences in the raw material lots, raw material lots can be run sequentially as blocks. Then the knob setting must be changed randomly within blocks to determine its affect on the yield.

Example 6.8

Three different degreasing solutions are to be considered for cleaning wire. It is suspected that contamination on the surface of the wire varies in composition and consistency from day to day. Describe how a randomized block design would be used to identify the best degreasing solution.

Solution: Since degreasing solution is the study variable it is necessary to randomize the order in which the solutions are used. The composition and consistency of the wire contamination apparently changes slowly, so all three degreasing solutions should be used in random order each day for several days. The interpretation of the two-way analysis will treat degreasing solution as the study variable and days as blocks.

6.5.3 *a* × *b* Factorial Experiments

In a randomized block design, the levels of the study variable are randomized within blocks and it's only safe to interpret the effect of the study variable. When the levels of both of the variables in a two-way classification design can be and are completely randomized, however, then both variables are effectively study variables and it's safe to interpret both of their effects. These designs, where the levels of both variables are selected in random order, are called *a* × *b* *factorial* designs where *a* and *b* indicate the number of levels of the variables.

The randomized block design and the two-way factorial design only differ from each other in the way that their variable levels are randomized, but the ANOVA doesn't take this distinction into account so the ANOVA reports for the two designs will be exactly the same. This means that the correct interpretation of the ANOVA is left up to the person doing the interpretation. And as a word of warning, if you become your organization's internal DOE consultant, make sure that you fully investigate and understand the nature of each variable in every experiment you are asked to analyze to determine which are study variables and which are blocking variables.

Example 6.9

A two-way classification experiment is being designed. The potential run orders being considered for the experiment are shown in Table 6.4. Identify the experiment design and describe what can be learned from the experiment for each planned run order.

Table 6.4 Two-way experiment with different potential run orders.

Plan	Variable	\multicolumn{12}{c}{Run Order}

Plan	Variable	1	2	3	4	5	6	7	8	9	10	11	12
1	A	1	1	1	1	2	2	2	2	3	3	3	3
	B	1	2	3	4	1	2	3	4	1	2	3	4
2	A	1	1	1	1	2	2	2	2	3	3	3	3
	B	1	4	3	2	2	3	1	4	3	2	4	1
3	A	2	3	1	1	3	2	2	1	3	1	2	3
	B	1	1	1	2	2	2	3	3	3	4	4	4
4	A	2	3	2	1	1	2	3	1	3	2	1	3
	B	2	4	3	1	2	1	1	4	2	4	3	3

Solution: The experiment involves two variables, A and B, with three levels of A and four levels of B. All possible combinations of A and B are included in each run order plan so the design is balanced. The first run order plan systematically changes the levels of both A and B so neither variable is randomized. This run order plan should not be used.

In the second run order plan, the levels of A are changed systematically and the levels of B are set randomly within each block of runs defined by A. All four possible levels of B are considered within each block. This is a randomized block design where A is the blocking variable and B is the study variable. The ANOVA table will report F statistics for both A and B, but only F_B should be interpreted. If F_A is found to be significant, there might be real differences between the levels of A but the differences could also be caused by an unidentified variable confounded with A.

In the third run order, plan the levels of B are changed systematically and the levels of A are set randomly within blocks defined by the levels of B. This is another randomized block design where A is the study variable and B is the blocking variable.

In the fourth run order plan, both variables A and B are set in random order. This experiment is a two-way factorial design, so claims can be made about both variables. This experiment delivers the most information about the system being studied but it may not be necessary or possible to use this run order plan.

6.6 FACTORIAL DESIGNS

In general, regardless of the number of classification variables, the ANOVA technique can be used to analyze multi-way classification problems. There will be two-way interactions between each pair of variables and there will potentially be three-way and higher-order interactions to consider. If the number of classification variables in an experiment is k then there will be $\binom{k}{1}$ main effects, $\binom{k}{2}$ two-way interactions, $\binom{k}{3}$ three-way interactions, and so on. The number of degrees of freedom for any interaction is always equal to the product of the number of degrees of freedom of the main effects involved in the interaction. Thankfully, in most engineering situations three-way and higher-order interactions are rare, so much so that we usually assume that they are insignificant. Still, always obtain the opinion of an expert on the process and seriously consider the possibility of three-way and higher interactions.*

If a full-factorial experiment with k classification variables is built with two or more replicates, then all of the interactions between two variables, three variables, and up to the single k-factor interaction can be included in the model. It's wise to analyze the full model to see if any of the higher-order interactions are significant. When they aren't, which is usually the case, these terms should be dropped from the model. Their degrees of freedom and associated sums of squares are then added to or pooled with the error degrees of freedom and error sum of squares. The resulting model is simpler to explain, especially to less skilled people like managers, who are often easily confused, and is more intuitively pleasing. Recall the rule from Chapter 4, Occam's razor, that states "the simplest model that explains the data is the best model." Take this as a mandate to simplify your models as much as you can. When you do find it necessary to report a three-factor or higher-order interaction make sure you have plenty of data to support your claim. You will likely find lots of opposition to the claim of a significant high-order interaction so be prepared for a fight.

A factorial experiment that has the same number of replicates for each cell in the design is said to be a *balanced* experiment. When all possible $a \times b \times \ldots$ cells are included in the design, the factorial design is said to be *full*. Balanced full factorial experiments are among the best-behaved designs and some of the easiest to analyze.

Example 6.10

A $3 \times 4 \times 5$ full-factorial experiment with two replicates is planned. Determine how many degrees of freedom there will be for each term in the model if the model includes main effects and two- and three-factor interactions. How many error degrees of freedom will there be? How many error degrees of freedom will there be if we omit the three-factor interaction from the model?

Solution: Table 6.5 shows the degrees of freedom for the three-way classification design. If the three-factor interaction is retained in the model, there will be $df_\varepsilon = 60$ error degrees of freedom. If we assume that the three-factor interaction is not significant, then it can be dropped from the model. Then the $df_{ABC} = 24$ degrees of freedom used for the three-way interaction can be pooled with the error. This would give $df_\varepsilon = 84$ error degrees of freedom. The sum of squares associated with the ABC interaction would also be pooled with the error sum of squares.

---

* In some technologies, the higher-order interactions are very important. For example, in fields involving human behavior (for example, psychology, marketing, and so on) an experimenter might be especially interested in detecting a four-factor or higher-order interaction.

Table 6.5 Degrees of freedom for the $3 \times 4 \times 5$ factorial design with two replicates.

Source	df
A	2
B	3
C	4
AB	6
AC	8
BC	12
ABC	24
ε	60
Total	119

6.7 MULTI-WAY CLASSIFICATION ANOVA WITH MINITAB

6.7.1 Two-Way ANOVA with MINITAB

Two-way classification experiments can be analyzed from three different menus in MINITAB: **Stat> ANOVA> Two-way**, **Stat> ANOVA> Balanced ANOVA**, and **Stat> ANOVA> General Linear Model**. **Stat> ANOVA> Two-way** is the simplest to run but it also has the fewest options. **Stat> ANOVA> Balanced ANOVA** offers more analysis options but is limited to balanced full-factorial designs without any missing or extra observations. If the experiment is unbalanced then you will have to do the analysis using **Stat> ANOVA> General Linear Model**. **Stat> ANOVA> General Linear Model** is also the only one of the three methods that provides extensive post-ANOVA multiple comparisons.

Only **Stat> ANOVA> Two-way** will be described here in detail; however, once you learn to run it then **Stat> ANOVA> Balanced ANOVA** and **Stat> ANOVA> General Linear Model** are relatively easy to figure out. By default, **Stat> ANOVA> Two-way** includes the interaction term in the model but there is an option to drop it. Generally the model for a two-way classification experiment should include the interaction term, which should only be dropped if it is found to be insignificant.

Access MINITAB's two-way ANOVA capability from the **Stat>ANOVA>Two-way** menu. Specify the **Response** and the two experimental variables as **Rows** and **Columns**. There is no distinction between **Rows** and **Columns** so it's not important to get the variables in any special order. By default, MINITAB includes the interaction term in the model but you can omit it by selecting the **Fit Additive Model** option. You can also invoke the two-way ANOVA by typing the **twoway** command at the MINITAB command prompt:

```
mtb> twoway c1 c2 c3;
subc> additive.
```

where the response is in column c1 and the two classification variables are in columns c2 and c3. The **additive** subcommand excludes the interaction term from the model.

As for any ANOVA, residuals diagnostic graphs should always be used to check the ANOVA assumptions. The necessary graphs should be turned on in the **Stat>ANOVA> Two-way** menu by clicking the **Graphs** button. All of the graphs should be selected: the histogram of residuals, the normal plot of residuals, residuals versus fits, residuals versus run order, and residuals versus both classification variables.

Example 6.11

Use MINITAB to perform the two-way ANOVA for the data from Example 6.3 and confirm the manual calculations from the example.

Solution: The output from MINITAB's Session window is shown in Figure 6.4. The experiment only contains one replicate so there is no interaction term in the model. The ANOVA table shows that the A and B effects are highly significant, with p values of p = 0.000 and p = 0.001, respectively. The 95 percent confidence intervals for the treatments show that all of the rows are different from each other and all of the columns are different from each other. The standard error of the model is

$$s_\varepsilon = \sqrt{MS_{error}} = \sqrt{1.33} = 1.15$$

The F values associated with A and B and the standard error are in excellent agreement with the manual calculations from Example 6.3. Residuals diagnostics are not shown because there are too few error degrees of freedom to show any meaningful patterns.

Example 6.12

Use MINITAB to perform the two-way ANOVA for the data from Example 6.5. Include the interaction term in the model and compare the interaction sum of squares calculated in Example 6.5 to the value reported by MINITAB. Refine the model if appropriate and evaluate the residuals to confirm that the ANOVA assumptions are satisfied.

Solution: The two-way ANOVA output is shown in Figure 6.5. The interaction sum of squares was found to be $SS_{AB} = 44.67$ which is in excellent agreement with the value that was determined manually. The interaction term was not significant ($p = 0.089$) so the ANOVA was run again without it. The second ANOVA shows that there are significant A ($p = 0.000$) and B ($p = 0.004$) effects. The confidence intervals for the treatment means indicate that treatment level 2 of variable A is significantly different from treatment levels 1 and 3. The confidence intervals also confirm that the two treatment levels of variable B are different from each other, which was expected because the B effect was significant. The residuals diagnostic plots in Figure 6.6 indicate that the residuals are normally distributed and homoscedastic with respect to A, B, the run order, and the fitted values, as required by the ANOVA method.

```
MTB > print c1-c3
```

Data Display

```
Row   Y   A   B
  1   18   1   1
  2   16   1   2
  3   11   1   3
  4   42   2   1
  5   40   2   2
  6   35   2   3
  7   34   3   1
  8   30   3   2
  9   29   3   3
 10   46   4   1
 11   42   4   2
 12   41   4   3
```

```
MTB > Twoway 'Y' 'A' 'B';
SUBC>   Means 'A' 'B'.
```

Two-way ANOVA: Y versus A, B

```
Source   DF    SS      MS       F       P
A         3   1380   460.000   345.00   0.000
B         2     72    36.000    27.00   0.001
Error     6      8     1.333
Total    11   1460
```

```
S = 1.155   R-Sq = 99.45%   R-Sq(adj) = 99.00%
```

```
                 Individual 95% CIs For Mean Based on Pooled StDev
A   Mean   ---+---------+---------+---------+------
1    15    (-*-)
2    39                                  (-*-)
3    31                       (-*-)
4    43                                    (-*-)
           ---+---------+---------+---------+------
           16.0      24.0      32.0      40.0
```

```
                 Individual 95% CIs For Mean Based on Pooled StDev
B   Mean     +---------+---------+---------+---------
1    35                              (-----*-----)
2    32                  (-----*-----)
3    29      (-----*-----)
             +---------+---------+---------+---------
            27.5      30.0      32.5      35.0
```

Figure 6.4 Two-way ANOVA for data from Example 6.3.

Example 6.13

Bone anchors are used by surgeons to repair torn rotator cuffs. A bone anchor consists of a threaded and/or barbed bullet-shaped insert that is screwed into a hole drilled into the shoulder bone near the site of the torn tendon. The torn tendon is attached to an exposed eyelet on the anchor using sutures. If the repair is successful, the tendon will

Data Display

```
Row   Y  A  B
  1  29  1  1
  2  33  1  1
  3  46  2  1
  4  48  2  1
  5  36  3  1
  6  32  3  1
  7  24  1  2
  8  22  1  2
  9  48  2  2
 10  44  2  2
 11  26  3  2
 12  22  3  2
```

Two-way ANOVA: Y versus A, B

```
Source        DF       SS       MS      F      P
A              2   920.67  460.333  76.72  0.000
B              1   120.33  120.333  20.06  0.004
Interaction    2    44.67   22.333   3.72  0.089
Error          6    36.00    6.000
Total         11  1121.67

S = 2.449   R-Sq = 96.79%   R-Sq(adj) = 94.12%


                 Individual 95% CIs For Mean Based on Pooled StDev
A   Mean    ------+---------+---------+---------+---
1   27.0    (----*---)
2   46.5                              (---*----)
3   29.0      (---*----)
            ------+---------+---------+---------+---
               28.0      35.0      42.0      49.0


                 Individual 95% CIs For Mean Based on Pooled StDev
B      Mean    -----+---------+---------+---------+----
1   37.3333                          (-------*--------)
2   31.0000    (-------*-------)
               -----+---------+---------+---------+----
                  30.0      33.0      36.0      39.0
```

Two-way ANOVA: Y versus A, B

```
Source  DF       SS       MS      F      P
A        2   920.67  460.333  45.65  0.000
B        1   120.33  120.333  11.93  0.009
Error    8    80.67   10.083
Total   11  1121.67

S = 3.175   R-Sq = 92.81%   R-Sq(adj) = 90.11%


                 Individual 95% CIs For Mean Based on Pooled StDev
A   Mean    -------+---------+---------+---------+--
1   27.0    (-----*----)
2   46.5                              (----*-----)
3   29.0       (----*-----)
            -------+---------+---------+---------+--
                28.0      35.0      42.0      49.0
```

Figure 6.5 Two-way ANOVA for Example 6.5.   *Continued*

Continued

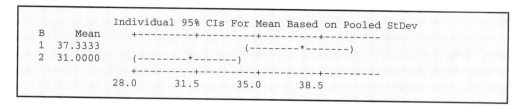

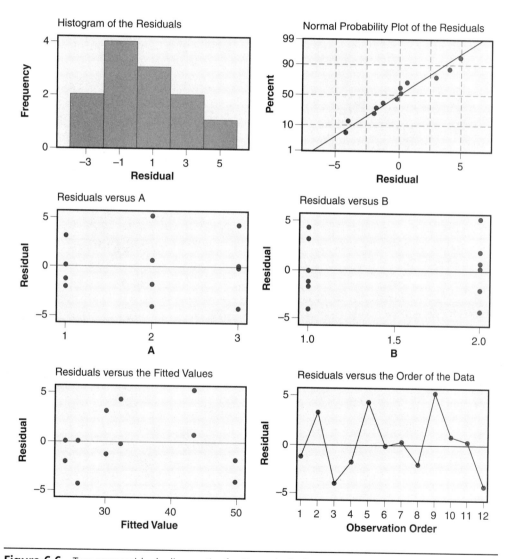

Figure 6.6 Two-way residuals diagnostics for Example 6.12.

eventually reattach to the adjacent bone while is it stabilized by the sutures and anchor. One of the problems with bone anchors is that under high loads they can pull out of the bone. Anchors with high pull-out force are preferred.

An experiment was performed to compare the pull-out forces of two standard (A, B) and one experimental (E) bone anchor. To improve the repeatability of the pull-out force measurements, the anchors were tested in high- and low-density foam (HD and LD, respectively) that simulates high- and low-density (that is, normal and osteoporotic) bone instead of real bone, which can be too variable in mechanical properties. Eight anchors of each type were used with each type of foam and the run order was randomized. The experimental data are shown in the order that they were collected in Table 6.6. The response is the pull-out force measured in newtons. Analyze the pull-out force data and determine if there is evidence that the experimental bone anchor has a higher pullout strength than the standard anchors.

Solution: *The experiment design is a 2×3 two-way classification design with eight replicates. The experimental data were entered into a MINITAB worksheet in the order that they are shown in the table. Figure 6.7 shows the interaction plots created with* **Stat> ANOVA> Interactions Plot** *of pull-out force versus anchor and foam type. The plots show that there is a significant difference in the pull-out force between the low- and high-density foams and that the experimental anchor does appear to deliver a higher pull-out force than the two standard anchors. The divergence in the line segments of the plots suggests that there is probably a significant interaction between the anchor and foam types. Most importantly, the experimental anchor appears to have a much higher pull-out force in LD foam than the other two anchor types but the difference is smaller in HD foam.*

Table 6.6   Bone anchor pull-out force by anchor and foam type.

Run	Foam	Anchor	Force	Run	Foam	Anchor	Force	Run	Foam	Anchor	Force
1	HD	A	191	17	LD	A	81	33	HD	E	203
2	HD	E	194	18	HD	A	198	34	HD	A	196
3	LD	B	75	19	LD	A	98	35	LD	B	64
4	LD	E	146	20	HD	B	178	36	LD	E	130
5	HD	B	171	21	LD	B	77	37	LD	E	132
6	LD	A	79	22	LD	E	138	38	HD	E	209
7	HD	B	188	23	HD	E	202	39	HD	B	180
8	LD	B	76	24	HD	A	193	40	LD	A	85
9	LD	E	136	25	HD	B	169	41	HD	A	182
10	HD	A	195	26	LD	B	63	42	LD	B	67
11	HD	E	207	27	LD	A	90	43	LD	A	88
12	LD	A	86	28	HD	E	194	44	HD	B	191
13	LD	B	71	29	HD	A	191	45	LD	B	70
14	LD	E	145	30	LD	E	132	46	HD	E	197
15	HD	B	184	31	HD	B	172	47	HD	A	205
16	HD	E	195	32	LD	A	86	48	LD	E	143

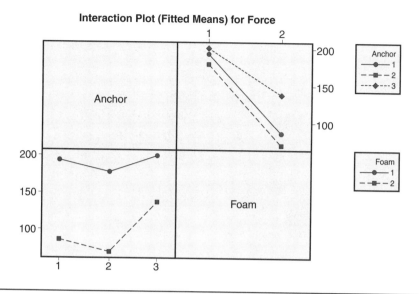

Figure 6.7 Interaction plots of pull-out force versus foam and anchor type.

The statistical analysis could be done in MINITAB several different ways, but the **Stat> ANOVA> General Linear Model** *method was chosen because it offers extensive post-ANOVA multiple comparisons tests that we need to determine if the experimental anchor outperforms the standard anchors under all conditions. The analysis is shown in Figure 6.8. The ANOVA confirms that there are significant differences between the foam types (p = 0.000), between the anchor types (p = 0.000), and that there is a significant interaction between foam and anchor (p = 0.000). The Tukey's post-ANOVA multiple comparisons test shows that the experimental (E) and first standard (A) anchors are not significantly different in HD foam (p = 0.3907); however, these anchors are significantly different in the LD foam (p = 0.000). The experimental anchor outperforms the second standard anchor (B) in both HD (p = 0.000) and LD (p = 0.000) foams. The graphical residuals analysis from the two-way model is shown in Figure 6.9. The graphs show that the residuals were normally distributed and homoscedastic with respect to the design variables, the run order, and the predicted values, as required by the ANOVA method.*

6.7.2 Creating and Analyzing Factorial Designs in MINITAB

Factorial designs can be created and analyzed several different ways using MINITAB. You can always create your own matrix of runs for a factorial design and then analyze the data manually in MINITAB using the tools in **Stat> ANOVA**. MINITAB also has extensive tools for factorial designs in **Stat> DOE> Factorial**. If you have a custom or preexisting experiment design and want to analyze it using MINITAB's prepackaged DOE analysis tools, you will have to specify the design to MINITAB from **Stat> DOE> Factorial> Define Custom Factorial Design**. After the design is defined, you can analyze it with **Stat> DOE> Factorial> Analyze Factorial Design**. If you want MINITAB

```
General Linear Model: Force versus Anchor, Foam

Factor      Type Levels Values
Anchor      fixed      3 A B E
Foam        fixed      2 HD LD

Analysis of Variance for Force, using Adjusted SS for Tests

Source        DF     Seq SS     Adj SS      Adj MS       F      P
Anchor         2      16084      16084        8042  194.58  0.000
Foam           1     103324     103324      103324 2499.94  0.000
Anchor*Foam    2       5556       5556        2778   67.21  0.000
Error         42       1736       1736          41
Total         47     126699

S = 6.42887   R-Sq = 98.63%   R-Sq(adj) = 98.47%

Tukey Simultaneous Tests
Response Variable Force
All Pairwise Comparisons among Levels of Anchor*Foam

Anchor = A
Foam   = HD subtracted from:

Level                Difference      SE of               Adjusted
Anchor*Foam          of Means     Difference   T-Value    P-Value
A        LD            -107.2         3.214     -33.37     0.0000
B        HD             -14.7         3.214      -4.59     0.0006
B        LD            -123.5         3.214     -38.42     0.0000
E        HD               6.3         3.214       1.94     0.3907
E        LD             -56.1         3.214     -17.46     0.0000


Anchor = A
Foam   = LD subtracted from:

Level                Difference      SE of               Adjusted
Anchor*Foam          of Means     Difference   T-Value    P-Value
B        HD             92.50         3.214     28.776     0.0000
B        LD            -16.25         3.214     -5.055     0.0001
E        HD            113.50         3.214     35.309     0.0000
E        LD             51.12         3.214     15.905     0.0000


Anchor = B
Foam   = HD subtracted from:

Level                Difference      SE of               Adjusted
Anchor*Foam          of Means     Difference   T-Value    P-Value
B        LD            -108.7         3.214     -33.83     0.0000
E        HD             21.0          3.214       6.53     0.0000
E        LD            -41.4          3.214     -12.87     0.0000


Anchor = B
Foam   = LD subtracted from:

Level                Difference      SE of               Adjusted
Anchor*Foam          of Means     Difference   T-Value    P-Value
E        HD            129.75         3.214     40.36      0.0000
E        LD             67.37         3.214     20.96      0.0000


Anchor = E
Foam   = HD subtracted from:

Level                Difference      SE of               Adjusted
Anchor*Foam          of Means     Difference   T-Value    P-Value
E        LD            -62.38         3.214     -19.40     0.0000
```

Figure 6.8 Analysis of bone anchor pull-out force versus anchor and foam type.

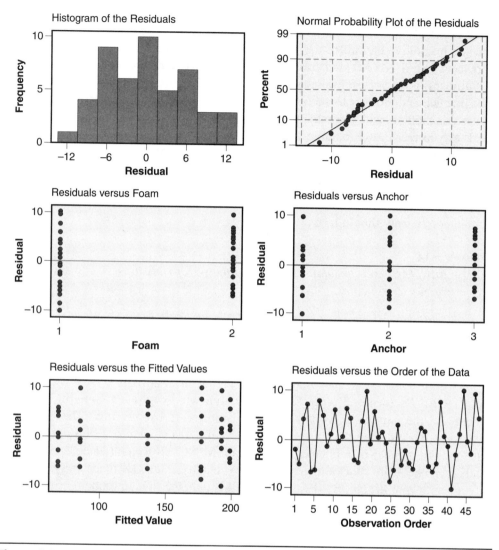

Figure 6.9   Residuals diagnostics from analysis of bone anchor pull-out force.

to create a new factorial design, use **Stat> DOE> Factorial> Create Factorial Design** to specify your new design and then use **Stat> DOE> Factorial> Analyze Factorial Design** to perform the analysis. These three modes of using MINITAB cover most of the permutations of factorial designs and preferences of DOE practitioners.

The purpose of this section is not to provide a comprehensive presentation of MINITAB's capabilities to design and analyze factorial experiments. Rather, the goal is to give you enough information so that you can manually enter and analyze a factorial experiment in MINITAB or use MINITAB in its automatic mode to create and analyze a new design. Some people prefer to design and analyze their own experiments, others like the canned capabilities that MINITAB offers. MINITAB also supports intermediate design and analysis activities.

Creating the Matrix of Experimental Runs

You can manually enter all of the variable-level settings of a design into a MINITAB worksheet, but MINITAB's **set** command (or **Calc> Make Patterned Data> Simple Set of Numbers**) is very useful to create the columns of experimental runs. It does take a little practice and thought to successfully specify the **set** command parameters. If you do use this method, and you may be forced to when the design is nonstandard, a good check as you create each column of the run matrix is to do a **count** of the number of runs in that column. Each design variable should have the same number of entries N. Once the matrix of runs is completed, another good test to confirm that the design is specified correctly is to calculate the correlation matrix of the design variables with MINITAB's **correlation** command (or **Calc> Basic Stats> Correlation**). All of the correlation coefficients should be exactly $r = 0$.*

Example 6.14

*Use MINITAB's **set** command to create a matrix of runs for a $3 \times 8 \times 5$ factorial design with $n = 2$ replicates.*

*Solution: The MINITAB commands to create the matrix of experimental runs and the first few resulting runs are shown in Figure 6.10. Notice that each **set** command generates a column with $N = 240$ values.*

The easiest way to create balanced complete factorial designs is from MINITAB's **Stat> DOE> Factorial> Create Factorial Design** window. Select **General Factorial Design** and the number of variables in the **Number of Factors** box. Then click the **Designs** button and enter the names of your variables, the number of levels of each variable, and the number of replicates. If you want MINITAB to treat each replicate as a block, then check the **Block on Replicates** box. Finally, click **OK** twice and MINITAB will generate your design. By default, MINITAB puts the runs in random order. If you want the runs in standard order you can override the random default setting in the **Options** menu or sort the runs after the design is created.

If you've used MINITAB to create a factorial design with the runs in random order, you can put them back into standard order by sorting by the **StdOrder** column in the worksheet. Use MINITAB's **sort** function to do this (or the **Data> Sort** menu). Alternatively, we've provided a custom macro on the CD-ROM included with this text called *unrandomize.mac*. The macro requires that you specify as its inputs columns of: the standard order, the random order, the response (optional), and the design variables. There is an optional **blocks** subcommand that will preserve the blocking specified in an indicated column. The macro overwrites the original columns by putting the runs back into standard order. Be careful to save your work before running the macro in case you don't like the results. Open the *unrandomize.mac* file for details on the use of the macro.

---

* By default, MINITAB's correlation command (**corr**) also reports the corresponding p values. These complicate the output in the Session window. Use the **nopvalue** subcommand to suppress the p values in the output.

```
MTB > set c1
DATA> (1:3)80
DATA> end
MTB > set c2
DATA> 3(1:8)10
DATA> end
MTB > set c3
DATA> 24(1:5)2
DATA> end
MTB > set c4
DATA> 120(1:2)
DATA> end
MTB > print c1-c4
```

Data Display

```
Row   C1   C2   C3   C4
  1    1    1    1    1
  2    1    1    1    2
  3    1    1    2    1
  4    1    1    2    2
  5    1    1    3    1
  6    1    1    3    2
  7    1    1    4    1
  8    1    1    4    2
```

Figure 6.10   MINITAB commands to generate the $3 \times 8 \times 5 \times 2$ run matrix.

Sometimes you may use MINITAB to generate a design that is in standard order or you may manually enter the runs in standard order. If you want to generate a random order for the runs with randomization across all replicates:

1. Create a column containing the numbers from 1 to N for the standard order. You can use the **set** command (or **Calc> Make Patterned Data> Simple Set of Numbers**) to do this. This column is necessary as the source for random run order numbers and so that you can recover the standard order at a later time if desired.

2. Create a column for the randomized run order using the **sample** command (or **Calc> Random Data> Sample from Columns**). Specify the number of samples to be drawn as the total number of runs N, the column containing the standard order as the input, and an empty column for the randomized output.

3. Sort the runs by the random run order column using the **Data> Sort** menu or the **sort** command.

This simple procedure randomizes across all of the runs in the experiment. If you want to randomize within blocks, so that each block is completed before the next block is started, you will have to unstack the blocks, apply this procedure to each block separately, and then restack the blocks. Alternatively, we have provided a macro with this text called *randomize.mac*. With *randomize.mac* you must specify a column containing the standard order, an empty column that will contain the randomized run order, the response (optional), and the design variables. There is also a **blocks** subcommand that will permit you to randomize the run order within specified blocks. Open the *randomize.mac* file for details on the use of the macro.

Analyzing the Data

MINITAB can analyze balanced experiments with one or more classification variables from the **Stat> ANOVA> Balanced ANOVA** menu or from the **Stat> ANOVA> General Linear Model** menu. The general linear model can also handle unbalanced experiments, that is, experiments with an unequal number of replicates in each cell. In either case, enter the response in the **Response** window and the design variables in the **Model** window. Include any interactions you want in the **Model** window in the form *A*B*. For example, if you have a three-variable factorial design and want to include two-factor and three-factor interactions in the model, then type the following terms in the **Model** window: *A B A*B A*C B*C A*B*C*. Be sure to create and check the appropriate diagnostic plots from the **Graphs** menu. Other details on the use of MINITAB for variations on factorial designs are described elsewhere in this chapter.

Instead of manually configuring the analysis of a factorial experiment as described in the preceding paragraph, you can use MINITAB's prepackaged analysis routines instead. If you created your own matrix of experimental runs in a MINITAB worksheet, you will first have to specify the design to MINITAB from **Stat> DOE> Factorial> Define Custom Factorial Design**. If you created the design from **Stat> DOE> Factorial> Create Factorial Design**, then MINITAB already understands the design and you will not have to define it. The analysis of the experiment is performed from **Stat> DOE> Factorial> Analyze Factorial Design**. Indicate the response in the **Responses** window and the diagnostic plots required to check the assumptions in the **Graphs** menu. In the **Terms** menu you need to enter each term that you want in the model into the **Selected Terms:** list. There are several ways to do this: you can double-click terms to move them from one list to the other, you can select terms with the mouse and then click the left or right arrows to move them, or you can specify the highest order for the terms that you want in the model from the **Include terms in the model up through order:** window. Entering a 1 here includes only main effects in the model, a 2 puts main effects and two-factor interactions in the model, and so on. If your experiment was built in blocks and there is a column for blocks in the worksheet, leave the **Include blocks in the model** box checked. Then MINITAB will include blocks as an additional qualitative term in the model so you can control for possible differences between the blocks.

Example 6.15

An experiment was performed by a Web site developer to study the amount of time two different Internet Web domain registrars (A : 1, 2) required to activate three different types of domains (B : 1, 2, 3). Two replicates of the six-run design were performed and the replicates were submitted as blocks 12 hours apart. After the registration requests were submitted, each Web address was checked once per hour to determine when it was activated. Table 6.7 shows the results of a 2×3 factorial experiment with two replicates. The data are shown in the order in which they were taken. Enter the data into a MINITAB worksheet and use Stat> DOE> Factorial> Define Custom Factorial Design to define the

Table 6.7 2 × 3 factorial design with two replicates.

Run	Block	A	B	Y
1	1	1	1	57
2	1	2	1	75
3	1	1	3	46
4	1	2	3	78
5	1	2	2	69
6	1	1	2	68
7	2	2	1	97
8	2	2	3	83
9	2	1	1	81
10	2	1	3	64
11	2	2	2	83
12	2	1	2	60

design. Analyze the data using **Stat> DOE> Factorial> Analyze Factorial Design.** Include main effects, two-factor interactions, and a term for the blocks in the model.

Solution: The data were transcribed into a MINITAB worksheet and the design was defined from **Stat> DOE> Factorial> Define Custom Factorial Design.** A and B were declared as **Factors** and the Run and Block columns were declared as the columns for the run order and blocking, respectively, in the **Design** menu. After the design was defined, the data were analyzed from **Stat> DOE> Factorial> Analyze Factorial Design.** The response, the activation time in hours, was called Y and diagnostic plots were selected. In the **Terms** menu, the AB interaction term and a term for the blocks were added to the model. MINITAB generated the output shown in Figure 6.11. The model shows that there is a significant difference between the two levels of A ($p = 0.014$) and that the first (A = 1) registrar processes applications faster. There is a hint that there might be a difference between the two blocks ($p = 0.052$). The diagnostic plots are shown in Figure 6.12 and all of the ANOVA assumptions (homoscedasticity, normality of residuals, independence) appear to be met.

6.8 DESIGN CONSIDERATIONS FOR MULTI-WAY CLASSIFICATION DESIGNS

- If the variables in a multi-way classification design are all easy to randomize, then perform the experimental runs in completely random order and interpret the experiment as a multi-way factorial design.

- If one of the variables in a multi-way classification design is difficult to randomize or can't be randomized, then use that variable to define blocks of runs. Be sure to randomize the levels of the study variables within blocks and do not attempt to interpret the ANOVA *F* statistic of the blocking variable.

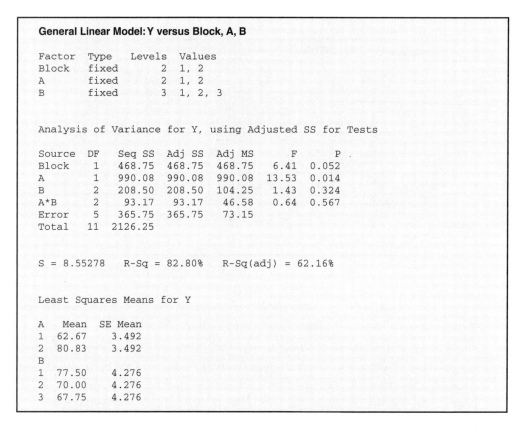

General Linear Model: Y versus Block, A, B

```
Factor   Type   Levels  Values
Block    fixed       2  1, 2
A        fixed       2  1, 2
B        fixed       3  1, 2, 3


Analysis of Variance for Y, using Adjusted SS for Tests

Source  DF   Seq SS   Adj SS   Adj MS      F      P .
Block    1   468.75   468.75   468.75   6.41  0.052
A        1   990.08   990.08   990.08  13.53  0.014
B        2   208.50   208.50   104.25   1.43  0.324
A*B      2    93.17    93.17    46.58   0.64  0.567
Error    5   365.75   365.75    73.15
Total   11  2126.25


S = 8.55278   R-Sq = 82.80%   R-Sq(adj) = 62.16%


Least Squares Means for Y

A    Mean  SE Mean
1   62.67    3.492
2   80.83    3.492
B
1   77.50    4.276
2   70.00    4.276
3   67.75    4.276
```

Figure 6.11 MINITAB output generated with **Stat> DOE> Factorial> Analyze Factorial Design**.

- Look for opportunities to improve the sensitivity of any experiment by identifying one or more blocking variables.

- Even if there are no obvious process variables that can be used to define blocks, sets of consecutive runs in an experiment can still be treated as blocks. For example, the runs in an experiment can be broken up into a first half and a second half, or a first third, middle third, and last third, and so on. This blocking structure will help account for unexpected variability present during the experiment without adding much complexity or otherwise compromising the experiment.

- It is often appropriate and always wise to complete the runs for each replicate of a design before starting the runs from another replicate. Then each complete replicate can be treated as a separate block.

- If there is no chance that an interaction exists between the two variables in a two-way classification design, then it is safe to run a single replicate of the

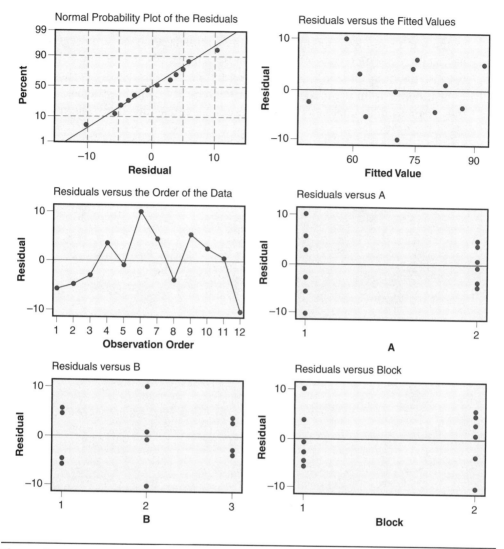

Figure 6.12 Residuals diagnostic plots for Example 6.15.

experiment design. If, however, there may be or is known to be an interaction between the two variables, then the only way to resolve the interaction is by building two or more replicates.

- Include two-factor and higher-order interactions in the analysis of multi-way classification designs, and use Occam to drop those interactions that are not statistically significant. Remember that the model must be hierarchical—a model that contains any high-order interaction must contain all of the simpler terms that can be derived from that interaction. For example, a model that includes *ABC* must also include *AB, AC, BC, A, B,* and *C.*

- Build two or more replicates of a two-way classification design to allow formal testing for a two-factor interaction. A single replicate may be sufficient for testing three- or more-way classification designs for two-factor interactions because the rarity of significant higher-order interactions usually permits them to be dropped from the model. Then the degrees of freedom associated with those higher-order interactions can be used to estimate the experimental error.

7

Advanced ANOVA Topics

The purpose of this chapter is to present some special topics involving designs for qualitative experimental variables:

- Special multi-way classification designs
- Fixed versus random variables
- Nested variables
- Sample-size and power calculations

This chapter can be skipped without compromising your ability to understand the material in later chapters, although those chapters do make use of some of the sample-size and power methods presented here.

7.1 INCOMPLETE FACTORIAL DESIGNS

Consider the 3×3 factorial design shown in Table 7.1a. The ✓ marks indicate which runs are built. Since all of the runs are checked, we use the adjective *full* to describe the experiment. One replicate of this full design will require $3 \times 3 = 9$ runs. When two or more replicates are run, the model can include two-factor interactions. The full model requires:

$$df_{model} = (3-1)+(3-1)+(3-1)(3-1) = 8 \qquad (7.1)$$

Table 7.1   Complete and incomplete factorial designs.

a.		B			b.		B		
		B_1	B_2	B_3			B_1	B_2	B_3
	A_1	✓	✓	✓		A_1	✓	×	✓
A	A_2	✓	✓	✓	A	A_2	✓	✓	×
	A_3	✓	✓	✓		A_3	×	✓	✓

degrees of freedom. Now consider the factorial design in Table 7.1b. The runs marked with multiplication signs are omitted from the experiment so there are only six runs required. This experiment can still be analyzed for main effects but because some of the cells are missing, it is not possible to test for interactions. Since the experiment does not include all possible $a \times b$ runs it is called an *incomplete* design. The number of runs in each row and each column are the same so the experiment is still balanced. That makes this design a *balanced incomplete design*. The benefit of incomplete designs like this is that they are smaller and cheaper to run than a complete design, but their success depends on the validity of the assumption that interactions are not significant. If there are significant interactions between the variables in an incomplete design, there will be errors in the main effects and the unresolved effect of the interaction will inflate the standard error of the model making it more difficult to detect differences between the levels of the study variables.

Analyze incomplete designs from MINITAB's **Stat> ANOVA> General Linear Model** menu. Specify the response in the **Response** window and include each of the design variables in the **Model** window. If you attempt to include interactions in the model, MINITAB will respond with an error indicating that the structure of the data is incorrect for the model you have specified.

7.2 LATIN SQUARES AND OTHER SQUARES

The concept of an incomplete design can be extended to three-way and higher-way classification problems. The benefit of considering these designs is that they can significantly reduce the number of runs required in an experiment. Their disadvantage is that they cannot resolve any of the interactions. In fact, if an incomplete design is used and there is a significant interaction between two or more variables, then you will get erroneous results from the ANOVA for the main effects. You must be certain that there are no significant interactions before you consider an incomplete design.

A 3×3 factorial design requires nine experimental runs. Suppose that a third variable C is introduced into a 3×3 two-way design in the pattern shown in Table 7.2. For example, the run labeled C_2 in the B_1 column and A_1 row is made in configuration (A_1, B_1, C_2). Notice that each level (that is, subscript) of each variable appears only once at each level of the other variables. This design is called a *Latin Square*. As with the other incomplete designs, the Latin Square cannot test for the presence of interactions.

Table 7.2 Three variable Latin Square design.

			B	
		B_1	B_2	B_3
	A_1	C_2	C_3	C_1
A	A_2	C_3	C_1	C_2
	A_3	C_1	C_2	C_3

Where does the Latin Square design come from? A $3 \times 3 \times 3$ full-factorial design would require 27 runs. The Latin Square uses only one third of these runs. Not just any nine runs of the 27 possible runs can be used in a Latin Square. The runs chosen must meet certain conditions necessary to make the experiment balanced. There are two other nine-run experiments that also meet the balanced and incomplete conditions that can be constructed from the remaining 18 runs. All three of these nine-run experiments combine to form the $3 \times 3 \times 3$ full-factorial design. This concept of incomplete designs is considered in much more detail in Chapter 10.

All Latin Square designs contain exactly three variables and have at least three levels of each variable. Each variable in a Latin Square must have the same number of levels. For example, a 4×4 Latin Square will require 16 runs and will have four levels of each of the three design variables, a 5×5 Latin Square will require 25 runs and will have five levels of each of the three design variables, and so on.

A 4×4 Latin Square design can be modified to include a fourth design variable. This is called a Graeco-Latin Square. A 5×5 design can be further modified to include a fifth variable. This design is called a hyper-Graeco-Latin square. These designs are not discussed here, but see Hicks (1993) for more information on these designs.

Certain types of processes are well suited to the use of Latin Squares and other square designs but you may do DOE for a long time before you find the need to use them. Their lack of the ability to test for interactions between variables makes them unsuitable for many processes.

Analyze Latin Square designs from MINITAB's **Stat> ANOVA> General Linear Model** menu. Specify the response in the **Response** window and include each of the design variables in the **Model** window. If you attempt to include interactions in the model, MINITAB will respond with an error indicating that the structure of the data is incorrect for the model you have specified.

Example 7.1

A Latin Square experiment was run with three levels of each variable A, B, and C. Two replicates were run and the data are shown in Table 7.3. Use MINITAB's general linear model capability to analyze the experiment. Use a post-ANOVA multiple comparisons method to identify significant differences if necessary.

Solution: The ANOVA analysis by GLM is shown in Figure 7.1. The ANOVA shows that there are no significant A ($p = 0.925$) or C ($p = 0.227$) effects but there is a statistically significant B effect ($p = 0.001$). Tukey's multiple comparisons of B show that

Table 7.3 3×3 Latin Square experiment.

A	B	C	Data	
1	1	1	63	52
1	2	2	73	67
1	3	3	78	82
2	1	2	66	60
2	2	3	63	62
2	3	1	92	73
3	1	3	59	46
3	2	1	49	73
3	3	2	99	79

```
General Linear Model: Y versus A, B, C

Factor   Type   Levels   Values
A        fixed     3     1, 2, 3
B        fixed     3     1, 2, 3
C        fixed     3     1, 2, 3


Analysis of Variance for Y, using Adjusted SS for Tests

Source   DF    Seq SS    Adj SS    Adj MS       F       P
A         2     12.33     12.33      6.17     0.08   0.925
B         2   2210.33   2210.33   1105.17    14.02   0.001
C         2    268.00    268.00    134.00     1.70   0.227
Error    11    867.33    867.33     78.85
Total    17   3358.00

S = 8.87967   R-Sq = 74.17%   R-Sq(adj) = 60.08%

Tukey Simultaneous Tests
Response Variable Y
All Pairwise Comparisons among Levels of B
B = 1  subtracted from:

     Difference      SE of              Adjusted
B    of Means    Difference   T-Value   P-Value
2        6.833       5.127     1.333     0.4072
3       26.167       5.127     5.104     0.0009


B = 2  subtracted from:

     Difference      SE of              Adjusted
B    of Means    Difference   T-Value   P-Value
3        19.33       5.127     3.771     0.0080
```

Figure 7.1 MINITAB analysis by general linear model of Latin Square experiment.

there is evidence that level 3 of B is significantly different from level 1 ($p = 0.0009$) and from level 2 ($p = 0.0080$). The analysis of residuals (not shown) indicates that they are normally distributed and homoscedastic with respect to A, B, C, and the predicted values as required. The order of the experimental runs is not indicated so we must assume that the independence condition is satisfied.

7.3 FIXED AND RANDOM VARIABLES

In Chapters 5 and 6 it was assumed that the levels of the qualitative variables being studied were fixed. Recall from the discussion of fixed and random variables in Chapter 4 that if a variable has discrete, known, and forever identifiable levels, then that variable is said to be *fixed*. If the levels of a variable that are included in an experiment are only a sample of many possible levels of that variable, then the variable is said to be *random*. The distinction between fixed and random variables is very important because, from a practical standpoint, there is a difference between the actions taken when a random variable is significant versus when a fixed variable is significant, and from a computational standpoint the tests for statistical significance of fixed and random variables are different.

When a variable is fixed, the purpose of ANOVA is to determine if there are significant differences between its levels. If the F statistic for a fixed variable is significant, then we compare the treatment means to find out which pairs are different and take appropriate action on those differences.

When a variable is random, the reason for including only a sample of its many possible levels in an experiment is economic—it's impractical or impossible to consider all possible levels when the number of levels is very large or the levels themselves are constantly changing. The few levels of a random variable that do appear in an experiment serve to estimate the variance associated with the distribution of the population of levels. Then a formal test can be performed to determine if this variance is different from zero or not. The hypotheses tested for a random variable A are: H_0: $\sigma_A^2 = 0$ versus H_A: $\sigma_A^2 > 0$. If the F statistic for a random variable is significant, we solve the expected mean squares equations to estimate the unknown variance. There's no reason to consider comparisons of pairs of means when a variable is random because such comparisons are inappropriate and it's impossible or impractical to account for all possible treatment pairs.

7.3.1 One-Way Classification (Fixed Variable)

In Chapter 5 we saw that the one-way ANOVA F statistic is given by:

$$F = \frac{n s_{\bar{y}}^2}{s_\varepsilon^2}$$

(7.2)

When there are no differences between the a treatment means, both the numerator and denominator are estimates of the population variance σ_y^2 and we expect to get $E(F) = \hat{\sigma}_y^2/\hat{\sigma}_y^2 = 1$.* However, when there are differences between the treatment means, $ns_{\bar{y}}^2$ is inflated. The amount that it increases determines the size of the F statistic and consequently what our chances are of detecting the presence of the differences.

To determine how $E(F)$ behaves, we need to study the things that contribute to $ns_{\bar{y}}^2$. If the a treatment effects are given by $\mu_i - \mu = \alpha_i$, then the expected value of the numerator of the F statistic is:

$$E(MS_A) = \sigma_\varepsilon^2 + \frac{n}{a-1}\sum_{i=1}^{a}\alpha_i^2 \tag{7.3}$$

The subscript A indicates the treatment variable and is used here in anticipation of multi-way classification problems. $E(MS_A)$ is the expected mean square associated with the classification variable A. The first term in $E(MS_A)$, σ_ε^2, is the error variance that comes from the usual inherent random sampling error in the response. The second term is the variance that measures the scatter of the a treatment means about the grand mean μ. $n\sum_{i=1}^{a}\alpha_i^2$ is the sum of squares SS_A and $a-1$ is the corresponding degrees of freedom. Notice that by definition $\sum_{i=1}^{a}\alpha_i = 0$. Since the denominator of F is an estimate of the error variance, its expected mean square is:

$$E(MS_\varepsilon) = \sigma_\varepsilon^2 \tag{7.4}$$

The important quantities for the one-way fixed-effects ANOVA are summarized in the following table:

Source	df	$E(MS)$	F
A	$a-1$	$\sigma_\varepsilon^2 + \frac{n}{a-1}\sum_{i=1}^{a}\alpha_i^2$	$\frac{MS_A}{MS_\varepsilon}$
$Error(\varepsilon)$	$a(n-1)$	σ_ε^2	
Total	$an-1$		

The expected value of F is:

$$E(F) = \frac{E(MS_A)}{E(MS_\varepsilon)}$$

$$= \frac{\sigma_\varepsilon^2 + \frac{n}{a-1}\sum_{i=1}^{a}\alpha_i^2}{\sigma_\varepsilon^2}$$

$$= 1 + \frac{n\sum_{i=1}^{a}\alpha_i^2}{(a-1)\sigma_\varepsilon^2} \tag{7.5}$$

---

* Here the $E(\ )$ indicates the expectation value function which returns a parameter. A better known example is $E(\bar{y}) = \mu$. In this case, F is a statistic determined from a sample data set. $E(F)$ is the expected value of the statistic.

where the F distribution has $df_A = a - 1$ numerator and $df_\varepsilon = a\,(n - 1)$ denominator degrees of freedom. Notice that when the null hypothesis is true (H_0: $\alpha_i = 0$ for all i), then the F ratio reduces to $E(F) = 1$ as required. Equation 7.5 is sometimes written:

$$E(F) = 1 + \frac{\lambda}{a-1} \qquad (7.6)$$

where

$$\lambda = \frac{n \sum_{i=1}^{a} \alpha_i^2}{\sigma_\varepsilon^2} \qquad (7.7)$$

is called the F distribution *noncentrality parameter*. The noncentrality parameter measures how much the expected F distribution is shifted to higher F values when some of the $\alpha_i \neq 0$.

Example 7.2

A completely randomized experiment to study five fixed treatments is performed using six replicates. Find the expected mean square for the treatment and error and the expected F value if $\alpha_1 = \alpha_2 = \alpha_3 = 0$, $\alpha_4 = 3$, $\alpha_5 = -3$, and $\sigma_\varepsilon^2 = 10$.

Solution: *Notice that $\sum_{i=1}^{a} \alpha_i = 0$ as required. The expected mean square for treatments is:*

$$\begin{aligned} E(MS_A) &= \sigma_\varepsilon^2 + \tfrac{n}{a-1}\sum_{i=1}^{a}\alpha_i^2 \\ &= 10 + \tfrac{6}{5-1}\left(0^2 + 0^2 + 0^2 + 3^2 + (-3)^2\right) \\ &= 37 \end{aligned}$$

The expected mean square for error is:

$$E(MS_\varepsilon) = \sigma_\varepsilon^2 = 10$$

The expected F value is:

$$E(F) = \frac{E(MS_A)}{E(MS_\varepsilon)} = \frac{37}{10} = 3.7$$

which is large compared to $F = 1$ so there should be a reasonable probability of detecting the differences between the treatment means. The calculation of this probability will be presented later in this chapter.

7.3.2 Two-Way Classification (Both Variables Fixed)

When there are two classification variables A and B with a levels of A, b levels of B, and n replicates, the expected mean squares are as given in the following table:

Source	df	$E(MS)$	F
A	$a-1$	$\sigma_\varepsilon^2 + \frac{bn}{a-1}\sum_{i=1}^{a}\alpha_i^2$	$\frac{MS_A}{MS_\varepsilon}$
B	$b-1$	$\sigma_\varepsilon^2 + \frac{an}{b-1}\sum_{j=1}^{b}\beta_j^2$	$\frac{MS_B}{MS_\varepsilon}$
AB	$(a-1)(b-1)$	$\sigma_\varepsilon^2 + \frac{n}{(a-1)(b-1)}\sum_{i=1}^{a}\sum_{j=1}^{b}\gamma_{ij}^2$	$\frac{MS_{AB}}{MS_\varepsilon}$
$Error(\varepsilon)$	$ab(n-1)$	σ_ε^2	
Total	$abn-1$		

where the γ_{ij} are measures of the interaction effects.* Notice that MS_ε is the error term for determining the F statistics for A, B, and the AB interaction. Thankfully, MINITAB does all of these calculations for us. The only reason that this relatively simple problem is presented in this section is to scare the heck out of you and make you realize that your only chance of dealing with $E(MS)$ calculations is to rely on your software.

7.3.3 One-Way Classification (Random Variable)

The hypotheses tested for an experiment with a single random variable A are: H_0: $\sigma_A^2 = 0$ versus H_0: $\sigma_A^2 \neq 0$. The expected mean square associated with A is given by:

$$E(MS_A) = \sigma_\varepsilon^2 + n\sigma_A^2 \tag{7.8}$$

The $E(MS_\varepsilon)$ for the error is still σ_ε^2 so the expected F value for the one-way ANOVA is:

$$E(F_A) = \frac{E(MS_A)}{E(MS_\varepsilon)} = \frac{\sigma_\varepsilon^2 + n\sigma_A^2}{\sigma_\varepsilon^2} = 1 + n\left(\frac{\sigma_A}{\sigma_\varepsilon}\right)^2 \tag{7.9}$$

where the F distribution has $df_A = a - 1$ numerator and $df_\varepsilon = a(n - 1)$ denominator degrees of freedom. In this simple case there are no surprises and the ANOVA calculations are essentially the same as they were in the case of a fixed variable. The difference is that when A is random, MS_A provides an estimate for the variance of the population of levels of A, whereas when A is fixed, MS_A is a measure of the net effect due to location differences between the discrete treatments. The important quantities for the one-way random-effects ANOVA are summarized in the following table:

Source	df	$E(MS)$	F
A	$a-1$	$\sigma_\varepsilon^2 + n\sigma_A^2$	$\frac{MS_A}{MS_\varepsilon}$
$Error(\varepsilon)$	$a(n-1)$	σ_ε^2	
Total	$an-1$		

---

* The interaction term γ_{ij} is often written $(\alpha\beta)_{ij}$.

When a one-way classification experiment is run with a random variable, the value of σ_A^2 is usually estimated from the experimental mean squares by solving $E(MS_A)$ for σ_A^2. This gives:

$$\hat{\sigma}_A^2 = \frac{1}{n}\left(MS_A - MS_\varepsilon\right) \tag{7.10}$$

Similar calculations are done to isolate estimates for the different variances in more complex designs involving random design variables. These variances are appropriately called *variance components*. MINITAB also calculates and reports the variance components for experiments that involve random variables.

Example 7.3

An experiment was performed to estimate the variability in the amount of time it takes operators to assemble the transmission of a vacuum cleaner. The operators who perform this operation change from day to day so a random sample of six operators was used in the experiment. Each operator was unknowingly timed while they assembled eight transmissions. The ANOVA sums of squares were $SS_{Operator} = 5500$ and $SS_\varepsilon = 11760$. Complete the ANOVA table and determine if there is evidence of significant differences between operators. Estimate the variability in the assembly time within operators and the variability between operators. The measurement times were reported in seconds.

Solution: The completed ANOVA table is:

Source	df	SS	MS	F
Operators	5	5500	1100	3.93
Error	42	11760	280	
Total	47	17260		

From MINITAB, $F_{0.0052,5,42} = 3.93$, so the p value for the ANOVA F statistic is $p = 0.0052$ which indicates that the operator variance is statistically significant. The experiment design is a one-way classification with a random variable so Equation 7.10 indicates that the variance associated with the population of operator biases is:

$$\hat{\sigma}_A^2 = \frac{1}{n}\left(MS_A - MS_\varepsilon\right)$$

$$= \frac{1}{8}\left(1100 - 280\right)$$

$$= 103$$

The standard deviation associated with the distribution of operators,

$$\hat{\sigma}_A = \sqrt{103} = 10 \text{ seconds,}$$

is a measure of the variation between operators. The standard error of the model,

$$s_\varepsilon = \sqrt{MS_\varepsilon} = \sqrt{280} = 16.7 \text{ seconds},$$

is an estimate of the amount of variability within operators.

Occasionally it is necessary to determine confidence intervals for σ_A^2 and σ_ε^2 from the one-way random-effects ANOVA. The distribution of the statistic s_ε^2 follows a χ^2 distribution with $a\,(n-1)$ degrees of freedom so the confidence interval for σ_ε^2 is given by:

$$P\left(\frac{a(n-1)}{\chi_{1-\alpha/2}^2} s_\varepsilon^2 < \sigma_\varepsilon^2 < \frac{a(n-1)}{\chi_{\alpha/2}^2} s_\varepsilon^2 \right) = 1 - \alpha \tag{7.11}$$

This interval is *very* sensitive to deviations from the required normality of the distribution of the ε_i so the normality condition should be checked very carefully. If a confidence interval is required when the distribution of the ε_i has tails that are lighter or heavier than a normal distribution, see Hoaglin, Mosteller, and Tukey (1991) for approximate corrected intervals.

The confidence interval for σ_A^2 is rather complicated because the estimate of σ_A^2 involves the difference between two mean squares, as in Equation 7.10. An approximate confidence interval for σ_A^2 developed by Tukey and Williams is given by:

$$P\left(\frac{(a-1)}{n\chi_{1-\alpha/2}^2}\left(MS_A - F_{1-\alpha/2}MS_\varepsilon\right) < \sigma_A^2 < \frac{(a-1)}{n\chi_{\alpha/2}^2}\left(MS_A - F_{\alpha/2}MS_\varepsilon\right) \right) = 1 - \alpha \tag{7.12}$$

where the χ^2 distribution has $a-1$ degrees of freedom and the F distribution has $a-1$ numerator and $a\,(n-1)$ denominator degrees of freedom. Both the F and χ^2 distributions are indexed by their left tail areas. This interval is also very sensitive to the normality assumption.

Example 7.4
Find 95 percent confidence intervals for the variance components from Example 7.3.

Solution: *The problem involves a = 6 operators who each take n = 8 measurements. The confidence interval for σ_ε^2 is given by Equation 7.11 with $s_\varepsilon^2 = MS_\varepsilon = 280$, $\chi_{42,0.025}^2 = 35.5$, and $\chi_{42,0.975}^2 = 61.8$:*

$$P\left(\tfrac{6(8-1)}{61.8} \times 280 < \sigma_\varepsilon^2 < \tfrac{6(8-1)}{35.5} \times 280 \right) = 0.95$$

$$P\left(190.3 < \sigma_\varepsilon^2 < 331.3 \right) = 0.95$$

$$P\left(13.8 < \sigma_\varepsilon < 18.2 \right) = 0.95$$

The confidence interval for σ_A^2 is given by Equation 7.12 with $MS_A = 1100$, $\chi_{0.025,5}^2$ = 0.831, $\chi_{0.975,5}^2 = 12.8$, $F_{0.025,5,42} = 0.162$, and $F_{0.975,5,42} = 2.89$:

$$P\left(\tfrac{6-1}{8\times12.8}\left(1100 - 2.89\times280\right) < \sigma_A^2 < \tfrac{6-1}{8\times0.831}\left(1100 - 0.162\times280\right)\right) = 0.95$$

$$P\left(14.2 < \sigma_A^2 < 793\right) = 0.95$$

$$P\left(3.8 < \sigma_A < 28.2\right) = 0.95$$

The confidence interval for σ_A is rather wide compared to that for σ_ε because it is based on fewer degrees of freedom. This observation should serve as a warning to anyone attempting to estimate the variance associated with a random variable using an experiment with relatively few levels of that variable.

7.3.4 Two-Way Classification (One Fixed and One Random Variable)

When an experiment design contains at least one fixed and one random variable, the model is called a *mixed* model. The $E(MS)$ values and F tests for the mixed model with one fixed (A) and one random (B) variable are given in the following table:

Source	df	$E\left(MS\right)$	F
A	$a-1$	$\sigma_\varepsilon^2 + n\sigma_{AB}^2 + \tfrac{bn}{a-1}\sum_{i=1}^a \alpha_i^2$	$\tfrac{MS_A}{MS_{AB}}$
B	$b-1$	$\sigma_\varepsilon^2 + n\sigma_{AB}^2 + an\sigma_B^2$	$\tfrac{MS_B}{MS_{AB}}$
AB	$(a-1)(b-1)$	$\sigma_\varepsilon^2 + n\sigma_{AB}^2$	$\tfrac{MS_{AB}}{MS_\varepsilon}$
$Error(\varepsilon)$	$ab(n-1)$	σ_ε^2	
$Total$	$abn-1$		

$E(MS_A)$ gets contributions from three different sources. The first contribution is the usual one from the error variance σ_ε^2, the third contribution is the expected one from A's treatment effects α_i, but the additional contribution from the AB interaction might be a surprise. In order to construct an F test for A that is only sensitive to the α_i, the F test must take the form:

$$E\left(F_A\right) = \frac{E\left(MS_A\right)}{E\left(MS_{AB}\right)}$$

$$= \frac{\sigma_\varepsilon^2 + n\sigma_{AB}^2 + \tfrac{bn}{a-1}\sum_{i=1}^a \alpha_i^2}{\sigma_\varepsilon^2 + n\sigma_{AB}^2}$$

$$= 1 + \frac{\tfrac{bn}{a-1}\sum_{i=1}^a \alpha_i^2}{\sigma_\varepsilon^2 + n\sigma_{AB}^2} \tag{7.13}$$

This is necessary so that if H_0: $\alpha_i = 0$ for all i is true, then the expected value of F_A is still $E(F_A) = 1$.

$E(MS_B)$ also gets an unexpected contribution from the AB interaction so its F test must also be constructed using MS_{AB} as the error term:

$$
\begin{aligned}
E(F_B) &= \frac{E(MS_B)}{E(MS_{AB})} \\
&= \frac{\sigma_\varepsilon^2 + n\sigma_{AB}^2 + an\sigma_B^2}{\sigma_\varepsilon^2 + n\sigma_{AB}^2} \\
&= 1 + \frac{an\sigma_B^2}{\sigma_\varepsilon^2 + n\sigma_{AB}^2}
\end{aligned}
\tag{7.14}
$$

If H_0: $\sigma_B^2 = 0$ is true, then the expected value of the F_B statistic is $E(F_B) = 1$. When this type of design is run, it is common to solve the $E(MS)$ equations to estimate the variance components $\hat{\sigma}_B^2$ and $\hat{\sigma}_{AB}^2$.

7.3.5 Two-Way Classification (Both Variables Random)

When both variables in a two-way classification design are random, the *EMS* values and F tests are as given in the following table:

Source	df	$E(MS)$	F
A	$a-1$	$\sigma_\varepsilon^2 + n\sigma_{AB}^2 + bn\sigma_A^2$	$\frac{MS_A}{MS_{AB}}$
B	$b-1$	$\sigma_\varepsilon^2 + n\sigma_{AB}^2 + an\sigma_B^2$	$\frac{MS_B}{MS_{AB}}$
AB	$(a-1)(b-1)$	$\sigma_\varepsilon^2 + n\sigma_{AB}^2$	$\frac{MS_{AB}}{MS_\varepsilon}$
$Error(\varepsilon)$	$ab(n-1)$	σ_ε^2	
Total	$abn-1$		

Notice that the error term for the F test of A is $MS_{\varepsilon(A)} = MS_{AB} = \sigma_\varepsilon^2 + n\sigma_{AB}^2$. The use of this error term is necessary to isolate the contribution of A to the F statistic so that the F statistic is specifically sensitive to A. The error term for the F test of B is also $MS_{\varepsilon(B)} = MS_{AB}$ for the same reason.

Example 7.5

A gage error study was run using four operators (A, B, C, D) and eight parts (1, 2, . . . , 8). The operators and parts for the study were chosen randomly from among many possible operators and parts. Each operator measured each part twice. The data are shown in the Table 7.4 with the pairs of observed values separated with commas. Use MINITAB to determine if there are significant differences between the operators, if

Table 7.4 Gage error study data.

Operator	Part							
	1	2	3	4	5	6	7	8
A	65, 68	60, 63	44, 45	75, 76	63, 66	59, 60	81, 83	42, 42
B	62, 63	56, 56	38, 43	68, 71	57, 57	55, 53	79, 77	32, 37
C	64, 65	60, 61	46, 46	73, 71	63, 62	57, 60	78, 82	44, 42
D	71, 69	65, 66	50, 47	78, 78	65, 68	65, 62	90, 85	39, 41

there is evidence of an operator-by-part interaction, and estimate the variances associated with the operators, parts, and error.

Solution: MINITAB's GLM function (**Stat> ANOVA> General Linear Model**) *was used to analyze the gage error data and produced the results shown in Figure 7.2. The GLM was configured by entering Part, Op, and Part*Op in the* **Model** *window, Part and Op were entered in the* **Random Factors** *window,* **Display expected mean squares and variance components** *was selected in the* **Results** *window, and residuals diagnostic plots were selected in the* **Graphs** *window. The residuals diagnostic plots (not shown) indicated that the residuals were normally distributed and homoscedastic with respect to parts, operators, and the predicted values as required. The ANOVA table, shown in Figure 7.2, indicates that there are significant differences between the operators (* $p = 0.000$ *) and parts (* $p = 0.000$ *). There is no significant operator*part interaction (* $p = 0.164$ *). The* **Expected Mean Squares, using Adjusted SS** *portion of the report indicates the equations that determine the different E(MS) terms. For example, the E(MS) equation for parts is:*

$$E\left(MS_{Parts}\right) = (4) + 2(3) + 8(1)$$

The numbers in parentheses indicate the sources of the different variances so this equation means:

$$E\left(MS_{Parts}\right) = \sigma_{\varepsilon}^2 + 2\sigma_{Part*Op}^2 + 8\sigma_{Part}^2$$

The system of E(MS) equations is solved and estimates of the variances associated with parts, operators, the part*operator interaction, and error are reported at the bottom of the output. The corresponding standard deviations for these terms were manually calculated and added to the MINITAB output in the figure. (Additional columns (**6SD** *and* **6SD/Tol** *) were also manually calculated and added to the MINITAB output to provide a comparison to another MINITAB GR&R analysis method to be described next.)*

In the analysis of gage error studies, the variance components reported in the GLM output are more important than the F statistics. The variances associated with the operators and error are used to determine related quantities called the appraiser variation (AV) and equipment variation (EV), respectively. These quantities are intervals with

General Linear Model: Y versus Part, Op

```
Factor  Type    Levels  Values
Part    random       8  1, 2, 3, 4, 5, 6, 7, 8
Op      random       4  1, 2, 3, 4

Analysis of Variance for Y, using Adjusted SS for Tests

Source   DF     Seq SS     Adj SS   Adj MS       F      P
Part      7   10683.98   10683.98  1526.28  336.67  0.000
Op        3     587.92     587.92   195.97   43.23  0.000
Part*Op  21      95.20      95.20     4.53    1.46  0.164
Error    32      99.50      99.50     3.11
Total    63   11466.61

S = 1.76334   R-Sq = 99.13%   R-Sq(adj) = 98.29%

Unusual Observations for Y

Obs        Y      Fit   SE Fit  Residual  St Resid
 21  38.0000  40.5000   1.2469   -2.5000     -2.01 R
 22  43.0000  40.5000   1.2469    2.5000      2.01 R
 31  32.0000  34.5000   1.2469   -2.5000     -2.01 R
 32  37.0000  34.5000   1.2469    2.5000      2.01 R
 61  90.0000  87.5000   1.2469    2.5000      2.01 R
 62  85.0000  87.5000   1.2469   -2.5000     -2.01 R

R denotes an observation with a large standardized residual.

Expected Mean Squares, using Adjusted SS

    Source  Expected Mean Square for Each Term
1   Part    (4) + 2.0000 (3) + 8.0000 (1)
2   Op      (4) + 2.0000 (3) + 16.0000 (2)
3   Part*Op (4) + 2.0000 (3)
4   Error   (4)

Error Terms for Tests, using Adjusted SS

                              Synthesis
                              of Error
    Source   Error DF  Error MS  MS
1   Part        21.00      4.53  (3)
2   Op          21.00      4.53  (3)
3   Part*Op     32.00      3.11  (4)

Variance Components, using Adjusted SS

Tolerance = 100

           Estimated   Standard
Source         Value  Deviation    6SD   6SD/Tol
Part         190.219      13.79   82.8     0.828
Op            11.965       3.46   20.8     0.208
Part*Op        0.712       0.84    5.1     0.051
Error          3.109       1.76   10.6     0.106
```

Figure 7.2   Gage error study analysis using MINITAB's general linear model.

width $\pm 3\hat{\sigma}$ so they should contain approximately 99.7 percent of their respective populations. That is, $AV = 6\hat{\sigma}_{Op}$ is the width of an interval that should contain 99.7 percent of the operator biases and $EV = 6\hat{\sigma}_\varepsilon$ is the width of an interval that should contain 99.7 percent of the instrument precision errors. A measurement system is generally deemed acceptable if its AV and EV are both less than 10 percent of the part tolerance. A measurement system is considered to be marginal if either AV or EV or both are between 10 and 30 percent of the tolerance, and is considered to be rejectable if either AV and EV or both are greater than 30 percent of the tolerance. The same 10 percent and 30 percent requirements are placed on the combined AV and EV called the gage error (GRR) given by:

$$GRR = \sqrt{AV^2 + EV^2} \tag{7.15}$$

When the part or process variation $PV = 6\sigma_{Parts}$ is small compared to the tolerance, it is usually preferred as the basis of comparison for EV and AV.

Gage error problems are so common that MINITAB contains a set of prepackaged gage error study analysis functions that perform the ANOVA with detailed numerical and graphical analyses. MINITAB's **Stat> Quality Tools> Gage Study> Gage R&R Study (Crossed)** function expects that two or more operators have measured several parts at least two times each. The experiment must be balanced, there can be no missing observations, and operators and parts are treated as random variables. The tolerance width should be entered in the **Process Tolerance:** field in the **Options** window. MINITAB reports the part, operator, and error variations relative to the total observed variation and relative to the tolerance.

Example 7.6

Use one of MINITAB's gage error functions to perform the analysis of the gage error data from Example 7.5. Use a tolerance width of 100 measurement units in the analysis.

Solution: The gage error analysis was performed using Stat> Quality Tools> Gage Study> Gage R&R Study (Crossed) with the Process Tolerance: set to 100 units. MINITAB's output is shown in Figures 7.3 and 7.4. The variance components shown in Figure 7.3 are exactly the same values as were reported by the GLM in Figure 7.2. The column labeled %Contribution (of Varcomp) shows the relative contribution of each variance component to the total variation observed in the experiment. The StdDev (SD) column shows the standard deviations associated with each source term, calculated by taking the square roots of the variance components. The Study Var (6*SD) column indicates that the total gage error is GRR = 23.8, the equipment variation is EV = 10.6, appraiser variation is AV = 21.4, part variation is PV = 82.8, and total variation is TV = 86.1 where all values are in measurement units. The %Study Var (%SV) column shows the size of these variations relative to the total variation. The %Tolerance (SV/Toler) column shows the EV, AV, PV, and TV relative to the tolerance. All of these values are

Gage R&R Study - ANOVA Method

Gage R&R for Y

Gage name: GR&R Example
Date of study:
Reported by: Paul Mathews
Tolerance: 100
Misc:

Two-Way ANOVA Table With Interaction

Source	DF	SS	MS	F	P
Part	7	10684.0	1526.28	336.669	0.000
Op	3	587.9	195.97	43.228	0.000
Part # Op	21	95.2	4.53	1.458	0.164
Repeatability	32	99.5	3.11		
Total	63	11466.6			

Gage R&R

		%Contribution
Source	VarComp	(of VarComp)
Total Gage R&R	15.786	7.66
Repeatability	3.109	1.51
Reproducibility	12.677	6.15
Op	11.965	5.81
Op*Part	0.712	0.35
Part-To-Part	190.219	92.34
Total Variation	206.005	100.00

		Study Var	%Study Var	%Tolerance
Source	StdDev (SD)	(6 * SD)	(%SV)	(SV/Toler)
Total Gage R&R	3.9732	23.8393	26.68	23.84
Repeatability	1.7633	10.5801	12.29	10.58
Reproducibility	3.5605	21.3629	24.81	21.36
Op	3.4591	20.7543	24.10	20.75
Op*Part	0.8438	5.0630	5.88	5.06
Part-To-Part	13.7920	82.7519	96.09	82.75
Total Variation	14.3529	86.1173	100.00	86.12

Number of Distinct Categories = 4

Figure 7.3 GR&R study analysis with MINITAB.

in near-perfect agreement with the values that were manually calculated and added to the MINITAB output in Figure 7.2.

Since the total gage error is about 24 percent of the tolerance, this measurement system is only marginal at best. The reproducibility is about twice the size of the repeatability so the first action that should be taken to improve the measurement system

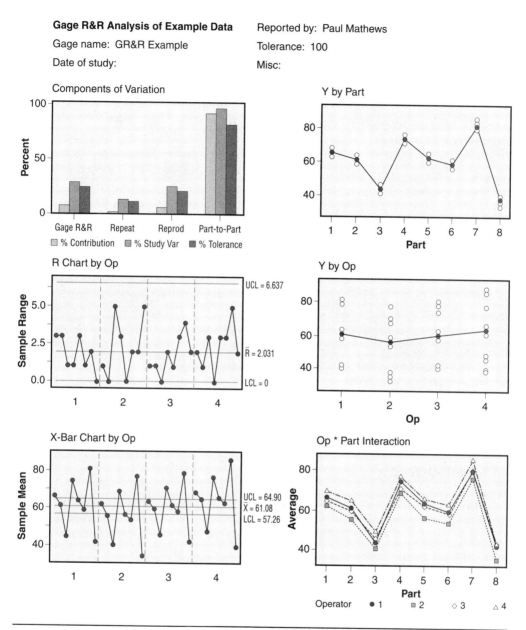

Figure 7.4 GR&R study graphical analysis with MINITAB.

is to consider the causes of differences between operators and identify possible remedies like operator training.

Figure 7.4 shows the graphical analysis of the gage error study. The first graph shows the relative sources of variability in the study. All of the comparisons indicate that part variation is the largest source of variation in the experiment followed by *reproducibility and then repeatability. This is a desirable condition—it indicates that the measurement system errors are relatively small compared to the part variation so that differences between reported measurements reflect real differences in part size. The second graph (middle left) shows the range chart by part and operator. All of the ranges are in control as they should be and the operators appear to be homoscedastic with respect to measurement precision. The third graph (bottom left) is an x-bar chart by operator and part. Its control limits are very tight because they are calculated only from the repeatability. Most of the plotted points are out of control because the part-to-part variation is much larger than the variation due to repeatability. This is another desireable characteristic of a good measurement system. The fourth graph (upper right) shows the measurement values by part. There are substantial differences between parts, and the variation within parts caused by measurement system errors is homoscedastic and relatively small compared to the part-to-part differences, as desired. The fifth graph (middle right) shows the measurement values by operator. Although the differences between operators are subtle, the graph shows that operators 1 and 3 have comparable means but operator 2 tends to report lower values than the others and operator 4 tends to report higher values than the others. These visually small operator-to-operator differences are the source of the marginal reproducibility variation relative to the tolerance. The last graph (lower right) is the operator-by-part interaction graph. The line segments between adjacent parts are substantially parallel indicating that there is no evidence of an interaction between operator and part.*

7.4 NESTED DESIGNS

7.4.1 Nested Variables

Sometimes the levels of one variable are unique within the levels of another. For example, a manufacturing operation may have three shifts per day and three operators on each shift named Al, Bob, and Chuck, but obviously the same three operators don't work all three shifts. They only share the same names. In this case, we say that operators are nested within shifts and we designate this condition with the notation *Operator(Shift)*. (Think of this as a function—identifying a specific operator requires knowledge of the shift.) Other common examples of nested variables are *Lot(Material)*, *Head(Machine)*, and *Part(Machine)*. In a chemical powder processing operation, a single batch of powder might be broken into several hoppers then further subdivided into small bags. This is designated *Bag(Hopper(Batch))*.

7.4.2 Two-Stage Nested Design: *B(A)*

The simplest nested design is the two-stage design designated *B(A)*. The first stage *A* is the larger and more encompassing variable. The second stage *B* is nested within the first. The analysis of the nested design depends on whether *A* and *B* are random or fixed variables.

The ANOVA table for the two-stage nested design when both A and B are fixed is:

Source	df	E (MS)	F
A	$a-1$	$\sigma_\varepsilon^2 + \frac{bn}{a-1}\sum_{i=1}^a \alpha_i^2$	$\frac{MS_A}{MS_\varepsilon}$
$B(A)$	$a(b-1)$	$\sigma_\varepsilon^2 + \frac{n}{a(b-1)}\sum_{i=1}^a\sum_{j=1}^b \beta_{j(i)}^2$	$\frac{MS_{B(A)}}{MS_\varepsilon}$
$Error(\varepsilon)$	$ab(n-1)$	σ_ε^2	
$Total$	$abn-1$		

The ANOVA table for the two-stage nested design when A is fixed and B is random is:

Source	df	E (MS)	F
A	$a-1$	$\sigma_\varepsilon^2 + n\sigma_{B(A)}^2 + \frac{bn}{a-1}\sum_{i=1}^a \alpha_i^2$	$\frac{MS_A}{MS_{B(A)}}$
$B(A)$	$a(b-1)$	$\sigma_\varepsilon^2 + n\sigma_{B(A)}^2$	$\frac{MS_{B(A)}}{MS_\varepsilon}$
$Error(\varepsilon)$	$ab(n-1)$	σ_ε^2	
$Total$	$abn-1$		

The ANOVA table for the two-stage nested design when both A and B are random is:

Source	df	E (MS)	F
A	$a-1$	$\sigma_\varepsilon^2 + n\sigma_{B(A)}^2 + bn\sigma_A^2$	$\frac{MS_A}{MS_{B(A)}}$
$B(A)$	$a(b-1)$	$\sigma_\varepsilon^2 + n\sigma_{B(A)}^2$	$\frac{MS_{B(A)}}{MS_\varepsilon}$
$Error(\varepsilon)$	$ab(n-1)$	σ_ε^2	
$Total$	$abn-1$		

7.4.3 Analysis of Nested Designs in MINITAB

Nested designs can be analyzed in MINITAB from **Stat> ANOVA> General Linear Model**, **Stat> ANOVA> Balanced ANOVA**, and **Stat> ANOVA> Fully Nested ANOVA**. The latter method is only suitable when the variables are all random and hierarchically nested, that is, when each new variable is nested within the preceding variable such as *Bag(Hopper(Batch))*. **General Linear Model** is a more general tool than **Balanced ANOVA** and has more options and post-ANOVA analysis capabilities. There are, however, some situations in which you should use **Balanced ANOVA** instead of **General Linear Model**. See the MINITAB documentation for details on these methods.

Example 7.7

    An experiment was performed to study the homogeneity of a multicomponent dry powder prepared in a batch blending process. The response to be studied was the

Blend Homogeneity Study Data: Cup(Tote(Batch))

		Batch 1		Batch 2		Batch 3	
Tote	Cup						
1	1	12.8	12.5	11.2	11.3	11.5	11.7
1	2	12.8	12.2	11.2	11.0	11.5	11.3
2	1	13.0	13.0	12.3	12.4	11.3	11.5
2	2	12.9	12.8	12.3	12.0	11.3	11.4
3	1	13.5	13.5	10.7	10.5	11.6	11.7
3	2	13.5	13.4	10.4	10.9	11.4	11.2
4	1	12.9	12.5	11.8	11.5	11.2	11.0
4	2	13.2	12.7	12.1	11.8	11.1	11.2

Figure 7.5   Blend homogeneity study data.

concentration of the active ingredient. The normal method of handling a 1000-pound batch of blended material is to dump 250 pounds of the blend into each of four totes. Then the material is vacuum-transferred from the totes into half-pound cups. For the experiment, three random batches were studied. Two cups were randomly drawn from each tote and two samples from each cup were assayed to determine the concentration of the active ingredient. The percentage concentration data are shown in Figure 7.5. (The data were formatted for convenient printing. In the MINITAB spreadsheet, the 48 observations must be in one column with corresponding batch, tote, cup, and sample-number columns.) Analyze the nested design and determine how much each nested variable contributes to the total variability of the blends.

   Solution: The experiment is a hierarchically nested design with Sample(Cup(Tote (Batch))). The data were analyzed using Stat> ANOVA> Fully Nested ANOVA and the analysis is shown in Figure 7.6. The ANOVA table indicates that the batch variance is significantly different from zero ($p = 0.002$), that the tote variance is significantly different from zero ($p = 0.000$), and that the cups taken from totes are homogeneous ($p = 0.478$). The variance components analysis shows that 74 percent of the total variation in the experiment was associated with batch-to-batch differences, 22 percent of the total variation was associated with tote-to-tote differences, and zero percent of the total variation was associated with cup-to-cup differences. The sample-to-sample differences accounted for 3.7 percent of the total variability. Since cups from the same totes were found to be homogeneous, the 3.7 percent sample-to-sample variability is probably indicative of the precision error of the assay method.

7.5 POWER CALCULATIONS

7.5.1 Comments on Notation

Since we are considering some relatively complicated experiment designs and there will be several F tests in a single experiment, we will freely use subscripts to identify

```
Nested ANOVA: Y versus A, B, C

Analysis of Variance for Y

    Source     DF           SS          MS       F        P
    A:Batch     2      25.1829     12.5915   13.897    0.002
    B:Tote      9       8.1544      0.9060   25.139    0.000
    C:Cup      12       0.4325      0.0360    1.000    0.478
    Error      24       0.8650      0.0360
    Total      47      34.6348

Variance Components

    Source    Var Comp.   % of Total        StDev
    A:Batch       0.730        74.23         0.855
    B:Tote        0.218        22.11         0.466
    C:Cup        -0.000*        0.00         0.000
    Error         0.036         3.66         0.190
    Total         0.984                      0.992

    * Value is negative, and is estimated by zero.

Expected Mean Squares

    1 A:Batch   1.00(4) + 2.00(3) + 4.00(2) + 16.00(1)
    2 B:Tote    1.00(4) + 2.00(3) + 4.00(2)
    3 C:Cup     1.00(4) + 2.00(3)
    4 Error     1.00(4)
```

Figure 7.6 Blend homogeneity analysis.

which model term the degrees of freedom (*df*), sum of squares (*SS*), mean square (*MS*), and *F* test statistic (*F*) are referring to. For example, a term *A* in a model will have df_A, SS_A, MS_A, and F_A. The symbol MS_ε will always indicate the error variance of the model so $E(MS_\varepsilon) = \sigma_\varepsilon^2$. Sometimes, depending on the design of the experiment and the nature of the variables, the *F* statistic for *A* might be given by $F_A = MS_A / MS_\varepsilon$ but in other cases the error term (that is, mean square) in the denominator of F_A might be something other than MS_ε. When the error term is something other than MS_ε, $MS_{\varepsilon(A)}$ will be used to indicate the mean square error estimate for the *A* term in the model. In general, the *F* statistic for *A* is $F_A = MS_A / MS_{\varepsilon(A)}$ and in special but common cases $MS_{\varepsilon(A)} = MS_\varepsilon$.

When the power for a nested design is considered, the usual notation like *B(A)* will be used to indicate that levels of *B* are nested within levels of *A*. Even if a term only shows *B*, if *B* is nested within *A* then *B* implies *B(A)*. When interactions between a nested variable and other variables are considered, they can be identified in several different ways. For example, an interaction between *B* (*A*) and another variable *C* can be written: *BC*, *B*×*C*, *B(A)C*, *B(A)*×*C*, *CB*, *C*×*B*, *CB(A)*, and *C*×*B(A)*. We'll try to be consistent, but be aware that other textbooks and software use different conventions. For example, in Example 7.15, you will see the *BC* interaction appear as *BC* in this text, *B*×*C* in MINITAB's GLM **Model** window, and *C*×*B(A)* in MINITAB's Session window output. All these expressions refer to the same term, but different expressions are used in different contexts. Sorry for the confusion. Get used to it.

7.5.2 General Introduction to Power Calculations

The power P of an experiment is the probability that it will detect a difference δ between two levels of a variable if such a difference exists. Let's call the variable to be studied A. The power depends on the number of levels of A, whether A is fixed or random, the number of levels of other variables in the experiment, the number of replicates, and the Type 1 error rate α.

The quantity δ is called the *least significant difference*. It is the smallest difference between two levels of a variable that is still considered to be large enough that we would want to detect it. The value used for δ in power and sample-size calculations must be chosen by someone who knows the process being studied well and understands the implications of differences between variable levels.

The power P is the probability that the experiment will detect a difference between two levels of a variable of size δ. Values of P and δ always come in a pair. A typical target value for the power of an experiment is $P = 0.90$ although $P = 0.80$ may be used in higher risk situations and $P = 0.95$ or 0.99 may be used when it is very important to detect a difference of size δ. Since the power P is the probability of detecting the difference δ between two levels of a variable, the complement of the power $\beta = 1 - P$ is the Type 2 error rate or the probability of not detecting the difference δ.

There are two steps to any power calculation for ANOVA. First, you must determine the critical value F_α that determines the accept/reject bound for the hypotheses $H_0: \delta = 0$ versus $H_A: \delta \neq 0$. This requires you to specify the model that will be fitted to the data so that the numerator and denominator degrees of freedom for the F test can be determined. When $\delta = 0$ the expected F value is $E(F) = 1$ and we call this F distribution the *central F distribution*. The central F distribution is the usual F distribution that we are used to working with. The central F distribution and α, the tail area under it to the right of F_α, are shown in Figure 7.7a.

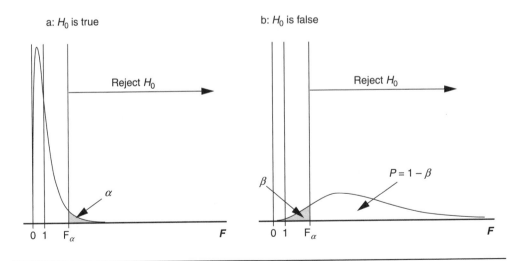

Figure 7.7 Central and noncentral F distributions for ANOVA power calculations.

The second step in the power calculation is to consider the expected F value when $\delta \neq 0$. This value of F will be larger than $F = 1$ so the distribution of experimental F values obtained is called the *noncentral F distribution*. When $\delta \neq 0$, the probability of finding an experimental F value that falls in the reject region for H_0, that is $P\ (F_\alpha < F < \infty;\ \delta \neq 0)$, is called the power of the test P. The power is the area under the noncentral F distribution to the right of F_α as shown in Figure 7.7b. The values of α and P meet the condition:

$$F_\alpha = F_{P,\lambda} \tag{7.16}$$

where λ is a measure of the noncentrality of F when $\delta \neq 0$. F_α and $F_{P,\lambda}$ have the same number of numerator and denominator degrees of freedom.* In general, the noncentrality parameter λ is related to the expected F value for A by:

$$E\left(F_A\right) = 1 + \frac{\lambda}{df_A} \tag{7.17}$$

where

$$\lambda = \frac{E\left(SS_A\right)}{E\left(MS_{\varepsilon(A)}\right)} \tag{7.18}$$

The forms of $E(SS_A)$ and $E(MS_{\varepsilon(A)})$ depend on the experiment design and the model to be fitted. MINITAB can be used to make the necessary calculations for these quantities and to make calculations for both the central and noncentral F distributions.

Sometimes, after an experiment has been performed, you may be asked to calculate the post-experiment power of the ANOVA. The post-experiment power of the ANOVA F test for a fixed variable A is given by Equation 7.16 with:

$$\lambda = \frac{SS_A}{MS_{\varepsilon(A)}} = F_A df_A \tag{7.19}$$

where the necessary values come directly from the experimental ANOVA table. This power corresponds to the probability of rejecting H_0: $\mu_i = \mu_j$ under the assumptions that: 1) the population treatment means are equal to the experimental treatment means and 2) that $MS_{\varepsilon(A)}$ is equal to the true error variance associated with A. Since these assumptions are often unlikely to be true, the use of the post-experiment power is not usually recommended.

---

* If the numerator and denominator degrees of freedom are df_A and $df_{\varepsilon(A)}$, respectively, then these F values may also be indicated $F_{\alpha,df_A,df_{\varepsilon(A)}}$ and $F_{P,df_A,df_{\varepsilon(A)},\lambda}$.

7.5.3 Factorial Designs with All Variables Fixed

Suppose that we intend to build a balanced full-factorial experiment with one or more qualitative design variables that all have fixed levels. If the variable of interest A has a levels and we want to detect a difference δ between two of those levels, then the non-centrality parameter given by Equation 7.18 becomes:

$$\lambda = \frac{N}{2a}\left(\frac{\delta}{\sigma_\varepsilon}\right)^2 \tag{7.20}$$

where N is the total number of runs in the experiment. The power is determined from Equation 7.16 where the central and noncentral F distributions have $a - 1$ numerator and df_ε denominator degrees of freedom. The value of df_ε must be calculated from:

$$df_\varepsilon = df_{total} - df_{model} \tag{7.21}$$

MINITAB's **invcdf** function (or the **Calc> Probability Distributions> F** menu) can be used to determine F_α with $a - 1$ and df_ε degrees of freedom. Then the **cdf** function can be used to find the power P from Equation 7.16.

The quantity δ in Equation 7.20 is determined by the treatment effects α_i that in turn determine SS_A. If the first (arbitrary) treatment has an effect $\alpha_1 = \delta/2$, the second has $\alpha_2 = -\delta/2$, and all of the other α_i equal zero, then the largest difference between two levels of A is $\alpha_1 - \alpha_2 = \delta$. These definitions meet the requirement that $\Sigma \alpha_i = 0$.

Example 7.8
A 3×5 full-factorial experiment is built with $n = 3$ replicates. Both variables are fixed and the model must include the interaction term. Find the power to detect a difference $\delta = 4$ between two levels of the first variable if $\sigma_\varepsilon = 2.4$. Use $\alpha = 0.05$.

Solution: The total number of runs is $N = 3 \times 5 \times 3 = 45$. The model will require $df_{model} = 2 + 4 + (2 \times 4) = 14$ degrees of freedom so there will be $df_\varepsilon = 44 - 14 = 30$ error degrees of freedom. The critical value of F is $F_{0.05,2,30} = 3.3158$. The noncentrality parameter is:

$$\lambda = \frac{45}{2 \times 3}\left(\frac{4}{2.4}\right)^2 = 20.8$$

The value of the power P that satisfies the condition given in Equation 7.16, that is, $F_{P,2,30,20.8} = 3.3158$, is $P = 0.979$. The MINITAB calculations to complete this power calculation are shown in Figure 7.8.

When there are two or more fixed variables in an experiment, the power to detect differences between the levels of the different variables generally differs. Even when we

```
MTB > invcdf 0.95;
SUBC> f 2 30.

Inverse Cumulative Distribution Function

F distribution with 2 DF in numerator and 30 DF in denominator

P(X <= x)           x
     0.95   3.31583

MTB > cdf 3.3158;
SUBC> f 2 30 20.8.

Cumulative Distribution Function

F distribution with 2 DF in numerator and 30 DF in denominator and
     noncentrality parameter 20.8

       x       P(X <= x)
   3.3158    0.0207932
```

Figure 7.8   MINITAB power calculation for Example 7.8.

want to detect the same difference δ between a pair of levels from each of two or more variables, the power depends on the number of levels those variables have. The difference in the power is due to the different number of observations taken for each level of the different variables. For example, in a 3×5 experiment with $n = 4$ replicates there are a total of 60 observations. There will be $60/3 = 20$ observations at each level of the three-level variable and $60/5 = 12$ observations at each level of the five-level variable, so the power to detect a difference δ between two levels will be greater for the three-level variable than the five-level variable.

Example 7.9

Find the power to detect the difference $\delta = 4$ between two levels of the second (five-level) variable from Example 7.8.

Solution: The noncentrality parameter is:

$$\lambda = \frac{45}{2 \times 5}\left(\frac{4}{2.4}\right)^2 = 12.5$$

The model will still require 14 *degrees of freedom and the error degrees of freedom will still be $df_\varepsilon = 30$ but there will be $5 - 1 = 4$ degrees of freedom for the numerator of the F statistic. The critical accept/reject value for H_0 is $F_{0.05} = 2.6896$. The power determined from $F_{P,12.5} = 2.6896$ is $P = 0.7485$. This value is lower than the power for the first (three-level) variable because there are fewer observations at each level of the second (five-level) variable.*

7.5.4 Factorial Designs with Random Variables

Power and sample-size calculations for experiments with random variables are more complicated and less easy to characterize in general terms than when all of the variables are fixed. When an experiment contains all fixed variables, the error term for all of the F tests is σ_ε^2. When an experiment contains a random variable, however, the error terms for the F tests are complex and often different for each term. Several common cases will be considered in this section and then a general method for determining the power using MINITAB's ability to calculate $E(MS)$ terms for different models will be presented.

One-Way Classification (Random Variable)

The purpose of a one-way classification problem with a single random design variable is to provide a test for the hypotheses:

$$H_0 : \sigma_A^2 = 0 \text{ versus } H_A : \sigma_A^2 > 0 \qquad (7.22)$$

and to permit estimation of the variance σ_A^2 associated with the population of levels of A. If the experiment is balanced so that there are n observations taken at each of the a levels of A, then the expected F value for the hypothesis test is given by Equation 7.9 and the critical value of the accept/reject bound for H_0 will be $F_{\alpha, df_A, df_\varepsilon}$ where $df_A = a - 1$ and $df_\varepsilon = a (n - 1)$. It can be shown that the distribution of:

$$F_A' = \frac{F_A}{F_\alpha} \qquad (7.23)$$

follows the F distribution with $a (n - 1)$ numerator and $a - 1$ denominator degrees of freedom. The power for the hypothesis test is given by:

$$P = P\left(0 < F < E\left(F_A'\right)\right) \qquad (7.24)$$

where:

$$E\left(F_A'\right) = \frac{E\left(F_A\right)}{F_\alpha} \qquad (7.25)$$

Software such as MINITAB is usually used to determine the required F values and probabilities because they are usually difficult to find in a standard table of the F distribution.

Example 7.10
An experiment to study one random design variable uses a random sample of eight treatment levels with five observations per treatment. The standard deviation within treatments is known to be $\sigma_\varepsilon = 50$. Find the power to reject H_0: $\sigma_A = 0$ at $\alpha = 0.05$ when $\sigma_A = 30$.

Solution: *From Equation 7.9 the expected F_A value is:*

$$E\left(F_A\right) = 1 + 5\left(\frac{30}{50}\right)^2 = 2.8$$

and the critical F value for the hypothesis test is $F_{0.05,7,32} = 2.313$. This gives:

$$E\left(F_A'\right) = \frac{E\left(F_A\right)}{F_\alpha} = \frac{2.8}{2.313} = 1.21$$

so the power is given by:

$$P = P\left(0 < F < 1.21; 32, 7\right) = 0.573$$

This result might be easier to understand in terms of inequalities: the probability of rejecting H_0: $\sigma_A = 0$ is $P \geq 0.573$ when $\sigma_A \geq 30$.

Two-Way Classification (One Fixed and One Random Variable)

The sample-size calculations for the two-way classification design with A fixed and B random follows the same basic patterns as the one-way classification problems with fixed and random variables, respectively. The hypotheses to test for significant A effects when A is a fixed variable are H_0: $\alpha_i = 0$ for all i versus H_A: $\alpha_i \neq 0$ for at least one i. If we want power P to detect a difference δ between two levels of A then the noncentrality parameter is:

$$\lambda = \frac{bn}{2}\left(\frac{\delta}{\sigma_{\varepsilon(A)}}\right)^2 \tag{7.26}$$

where, from Section 7.3.4, $\sigma_{\varepsilon(A)}^2 = E(MS_{AB}) = \sigma_\varepsilon^2 + n\sigma_{AB}^2$. The power meets the condition given in Equation 7.16 where the central and noncentral F distributions have $a - 1$ numerator and $(a - 1)(b - 1)$ denominator degrees of freedom, respectively.

The hypotheses to test the random variable B are H_0: $\sigma_B^2 = 0$ versus H_A: $\sigma_B^2 > 0$. If we want power P to reject H_0 for some specified nonzero value of σ_B^2 then:

$$E\left(F_B'\right) = \frac{E\left(F_B\right)}{F_\alpha} = \frac{1 + \frac{an\sigma_B^2}{\sigma_\varepsilon^2 + n\sigma_{AB}^2}}{F_\alpha} \tag{7.27}$$

and the power is given by:

$$P = P\left(0 < F < E\left(F_B'\right)\right) \tag{7.28}$$

where the central F distribution has $(a - 1)(b - 1)$ numerator and $b - 1$ denominator degrees of freedom.

Example 7.11

An experiment was designed to determine which of three different container materials (polyethylene, polypropylene, or PVC) gives the longest shelf life for a powdered chemical. Since there could be significant variation between powder lots, four random lots were used. Samples from each batch of powder were placed into three cups made from each material. The same amount of material was loaded into each cup. The filled cups were put into storage together for six months, then the powder was assayed to determine the amount that had been inactivated during storage. The assay error for the inactivated amount is known to be $\sigma_\varepsilon = 0.8\%$ and no interaction is expected between the materials and lots. Find the power to detect a difference between the materials of $\delta = 1.0\%$ in the amount of inactivated powder.

Solution: The material variable (A) is fixed with a = 3 levels and chemical powder lot (B) is a random variable with b = 4 levels. There are n = 3 replicates, we have $\sigma_\varepsilon = 0.8$, and since no interaction between the cup materials and powder lots is expected we have $\sigma_{AB} = 0$. The noncentrality parameter for a difference $\delta = 1.0$ between levels of material (A) is given by Equation 7.26:

$$\lambda = \frac{4 \times 3}{2}\left(\frac{1.0}{0.8}\right)^2 = 9.38$$

where:

$$\sigma_{\varepsilon(A)} = \sqrt{\sigma_\varepsilon^2 + n\sigma_{AB}^2} = \sqrt{0.8^2 + 3(0)^2} = 0.8:$$

There will be a − 1 = 2 degrees of freedom for the numerator of F_A and (a − 1) (b − 1) = 2 × 3 = 6 degrees of freedom for the denominator. If we use $\alpha = 0.05$, then from MINITAB the accept/reject bound for the null hypothesis is $F_{0.05,2,6} = 5.143$. The power, determined from $F_{P,2,6,9.38} = 5.143$, is P = 0.448. This power is relatively low and more than n = 3 cups from each powder lot should be used to increase the power.

Two-Way Classification (Both Variables Random)

The two-way classification problem where both variables are random is an important problem because this design is used frequently, for example, in the design of gage error studies. The classic gage error study uses three operators who are randomly chosen from among the many operators who make measurements and ten parts chosen randomly but with sufficient variation to be representative of the full range of observations to be expected. Each operator measures each part two or more times. The purpose of the study is to quantify: 1) the variance associated with the measuring instrument (also called the precision or repeatability), 2) the variance associated with differences between operators (also called the reproducibility), and 3) the variance associated with the interaction between operators and parts. The variance associated with parts can also be determined but this value is not generally used or useful. It's necessary to use a sample of parts to determine the repeatability and reproducibility but the sample is too small to indicate anything meaningful about the distribution of parts.

When there are preliminary data available to estimate the standard deviation associated with the repeatability, a power calculation can be performed to determine the sensitivity of the gage error study. Section 7.3.5 shows the *EMS* values and *F* test calculations for the two-way classification problem when both variables are random. The expected *F* value to determine if the variable *A* is statistically significant is given by:

$$E(F_A) = \frac{E(MS_A)}{E(MS_{AB})}$$

$$= \frac{\sigma_\varepsilon^2 + n\sigma_{AB}^2 + bn\sigma_A^2}{\sigma_\varepsilon^2 + n\sigma_{AB}^2}$$

$$= 1 + \frac{bn\sigma_A^2}{\sigma_\varepsilon^2 + n\sigma_{AB}^2} \tag{7.29}$$

where the *F* distribution has $a - 1$ numerator and $(a - 1)(b - 1)$ denominator degrees of freedom. The power is determined, as before, with Equation 7.24.

Notice that the power calculation requires knowledge of or at least an estimate for σ_ε^2 and σ_{AB}^2; however, it is common to assume that $\sigma_{AB}^2 = 0$. If this assumption is not true, the discrepancy will be discovered when the experimental data are analyzed.

Example 7.12

A gage error study is being planned to evaluate the use of a micrometer to measure parts with specification 0.200 ± 0.050 inches. Three random operators and ten parts are to be used in the study. Each operator will measure each part twice in random order. Preliminary data indicate that the precision error inherent in the use of the micrometer is 0.0022 inches and the opinion is that there will be no operator-by-part interaction. For the measurement system (instrument and operators measuring parts of this type) to be valid, the repeatability and reproducibility standard deviations, σ_ε and σ_{Op}, respectively, must meet the conditions:

$$(6\sigma_\varepsilon) \leq (Tolerance / 10) \quad and \quad (6\sigma_{Op}) \leq (Tolerance / 10)$$

Determine the power of this test design to detect the maximum allowable reproducibility variation.

Solution: The maximum allowable variation due to operators is:

---

* The repeatability and reproducibility conditions applied in gage error studies require that 99.7 percent of the expected errors span a range narrower than 10 percent of the tolerance. If the errors are normally distributed, then the interval will be ±3σ wide or 6σ ≤ *Tolerance*/10.

$$\sigma_{Op} \leq \frac{0.10 \times Tolerance}{6}$$

$$\leq \frac{0.10 \times 0.100}{6}$$

$$\leq 0.00167$$

The hypotheses to be tested are H_0: $\sigma_{Op} = 0$ versus H_A: $\sigma_{Op} > 0$ and we want to find the power of the design to reject H_0 when $\sigma_{Op} = 0.00167$. If we assume that there is no operator-by-part interaction then $\sigma_{Op*Part} = 0$. If we let variable A indicate operators and variable B indicate parts, then $a = 3$, $b = 10$, and $n = 2$. The ANOVA F statistic will have $df_A = a - 1 = 2$ numerator and $df_{\varepsilon(A)} = (a - 1)(b - 1) = 18$ denominator degrees of freedom. The critical value of F for the accept/reject bound with $\alpha = 0.05$ is $F_{0.05,2,18} = 3.5546$. The expected F_A' value is:

$$E(F_A') = \frac{1 + \frac{bn\sigma_A^2}{\sigma_\varepsilon^2 + n\sigma_{AB}^2}}{F_\alpha}$$

$$= \frac{1 + \frac{10 \times 2 \times (0.00167)^2}{(0.0022)^2 + 2(0)^2}}{3.5546}$$

$$= 3.52$$

The power is given by:

$$P = P(0 < F < 3.52; 18, 2) = 0.756$$

This means that the experiment design will deliver about a 76 percent chance of rejecting H_0: $\sigma_{Op} = 0$ if $\sigma_{Op} = 0.00167$. This power is relatively low, especially considering how much emphasis is put on the results of gage error studies like this.

Example 7.13

Consider a relatively risky gage error study which uses only two operators and ten parts, and each operator measures each part twice.* If the measurement repeatability is just barely acceptable with $EV = 6\sigma_\varepsilon = Tolerance/10$, determine the power to reject H_0: $\sigma_{Op} = 0$ when $AV = 6\sigma_{Op} = Tolerance/10$. Include the operator-by-part interaction in the model but assume that it is not significant. Use $\alpha = 0.05$.

__Solution:__ The F test for an operator effect will have $df_A = a - 1 = 1$ numerator and $df_{\varepsilon(A)} = df_{AB} = (a - 1)(b - 1) = 1 \times 9 = 9$ denominator degrees of freedom. The critical value of F for the accept/reject bound with $\alpha = 0.05$ is $F_{0.05,1,9} = 5.117$. With $\sigma_{Op} = \sigma_\varepsilon = Tolerance/(10 \times 6)$ and $\sigma_{Op*Part} = 0$ the expected F_A' value is:

---

* This problem is intended to serve as a warning to people who use this popular design for gage error studies. The problem is stated in a very general way so that its conclusions are applicable to many cases.

$$E\left(F_A'\right) = \frac{1 + \frac{bn\sigma_{Op}^2}{\sigma_\varepsilon^2 + n\sigma_{Op\times Part}^2}}{F_\alpha}$$

$$= \frac{1 + \frac{10\times2\times\left(Tolerance/(10\times6)\right)^2}{\left(Tolerance/(10\times6)\right)^2 + 2(0)^2}}{5.117}$$

$$= 4.10$$

The power is given by:

$$P = P\left(0 < F < 4.10; 9, 1\right) = 0.633$$

The low power indicates that the relatively small gage error study is rather insensitive to significant reproducibility variation. The number of parts, operators, and measurements used in this study are common practice, yet most people don't understand the high risks associated with this design.

7.5.5 Nested Designs

B(A): Both Variables Fixed

For the nested design $B(A)$, when both A and B are fixed, the error terms for F_A and $F_{B(A)}$ are both σ_ε^2. In this case the same methods used to determine the power for factorial designs with fixed variables are used to determine the power for nested designs with fixed variables except that the degrees of freedom for the denominator of the F test changes. Write out the table of the degrees of freedom for each term to be included in the model and solve for the power using the appropriate values.

B(A): *A* Fixed and *B* Random

The sample-size calculations for a nested design $B(A)$ when A is fixed and B is random follow the same basic patterns as the one-way classification problems with fixed and random variables, respectively. The hypotheses to test for significant A effects when A is a fixed variable are H_0: $\alpha_i = 0$ for all i versus H_A: $\alpha_i \neq 0$ for at least one i. If we want power P to detect a difference δ between two levels of A, then the noncentrality parameter is:

$$\lambda = \frac{bn}{2}\left(\frac{\delta}{\sigma_{\varepsilon(A)}}\right)^2 = \frac{bn}{2}\left(\frac{\delta^2}{\sigma_\varepsilon^2 + n\sigma_{B(A)}^2}\right) \tag{7.30}$$

and the power meets the condition given in Equation 7.16 where the central and noncentral F distributions have $a - 1$ numerator and $a(b - 1)$ denominator degrees of freedom, respectively.

The hypotheses to test the random variable B are H_0: $\sigma_B^2 = 0$ versus H_A: $\sigma_B^2 > 0$. If we want power P to reject H_0 for some specified nonzero value of σ_B^2 then:

$$E\left(F_B'\right) = \frac{1 + n\left(\frac{\sigma_{B(A)}}{\sigma_\varepsilon}\right)^2}{F_\alpha} \tag{7.31}$$

where the central F distribution has $ab(n-1)$ numerator and $b-1$ denominator degrees of freedom. The power is given by Equation 7.24.

Example 7.14

In the experiment from Example 7.11, there could be significant differences in the cup material from lot to lot. An experiment was designed to determine which of three different container materials (polyethylene, polypropylene, or PVC) gives the longest shelf life for a powdered chemical. Since there could be significant lot-to-lot variation within materials, four random lots were used from each material. Samples from the same batch of powder were placed into three cups made from each lot. The same amount of material was loaded into each cup. The filled cups were put into storage together for six months. After six months, the powder was assayed to determine the amount that had been inactivated during storage. The assay error for the inactivated amount is known to be $\sigma_\varepsilon = 0.8\%$. Find the power to detect a difference between the materials of $\delta = 1.0\%$ in the amount of inactivated powder assuming that $\sigma_{B(A)}^2 = 0$.

Solution: The material variable (A) is fixed with $a = 3$ levels and lot (B) is a random variable nested within materials with $b = 4$ levels. There are $n = 3$ replicates, we have $\sigma_\varepsilon = 0.8$, and we need to find the power to detect a difference $\delta = 1.0$ between levels of material (A). The noncentrality parameter is given by Equation 7.30:

$$\lambda = \frac{4 \times 3}{2}\left(\frac{1.0}{0.8}\right)^2 = 9.38$$

There will be $a - 1 = 2$ degrees of freedom for the numerator of F_A and $a(b-1) = 9$ degrees of freedom for the denominator of F_A. If we use $\alpha = 0.05$, then from MINITAB the accept/reject bound for the null hypothesis is $F_{0.05,2,9} = 4.26$. The power, determined from $F_{P,2,9,9.38} = 4.26$ is $P = 0.631$.

B(A): Both Variables Random

When both A and $B(A)$ are random, the expected F ratio for A is:

$$E\left(F_A\right) = \frac{\sigma_\varepsilon^2 + n\sigma_{B(A)}^2 + bn\sigma_A^2}{\sigma_\varepsilon^2 + n\sigma_{B(A)}^2} = 1 + \frac{bn\sigma_A^2}{\sigma_\varepsilon^2 + n\sigma_{B(A)}^2} \tag{7.32}$$

where F_A will have $a - 1$ numerator and $a(b-1)$ denominator degrees of freedom. The power can be calculated from Equation 7.24 with:

$$E\left(F_A'\right) = \frac{1 + \frac{bn\sigma_A^2}{\sigma_\varepsilon^2 + n\sigma_{B(A)}^2}}{F_\alpha} \tag{7.33}$$

and $a\,(b-1)$ numerator and $a-1$ denominator degrees of freedom. Note that this calculation will require estimates of both σ_ε^2 and $\sigma_{B(A)}^2$.

The expected F ratio for $B\,(A)$ is:

$$E\left(F_B\right) = \frac{\sigma_\varepsilon^2 + n\sigma_{B(A)}^2}{\sigma_\varepsilon^2} = 1 + \frac{n\sigma_{B(A)}^2}{\sigma_\varepsilon^2} \tag{7.34}$$

where F_B will have $a\,(b-1)$ numerator and $df_\varepsilon = ab\,(n-1)$ denominator degrees of freedom. The power can be calculated from Equation 7.24 with:

$$E\left(F_B'\right) = \frac{1 + \frac{n\sigma_{B(A)}^2}{\sigma_\varepsilon^2}}{F_\alpha} \tag{7.35}$$

and $ab\,(n-1)$ numerator and $a\,(b-1)$ denominator degrees of freedom.

7.5.6 General Method to Determine the Power for a Fixed Variable

The following procedure can be used to determine the power for a fixed variable in a specified design. MINITAB is used to determine the equations for the expected mean squares and to solve the central and noncentral F distributions to determine the power.

1. Enter the experiment design into columns of a MINITAB worksheet. Replicate the experiment as many times (n) as are required. The total number of runs in the experiment is N.

2. Select an open column for the response; let's call it Y. Set all of the N rows in the column to zeros, that is, for as many rows as there are runs.

3. Determine the design variable, let's call it X, that we want to determine the power for and the δ between two of its levels that we want to detect with power P. Set Y for all of the runs of one level of X to $Y = -\delta/2$ and all of the runs of another level of X to $Y = +\delta/2$. There should be N/a runs with $Y = -\delta/2$, another N/a runs with $Y = \delta/2$, and the remaining $(a-2)\,N/a$ should be $Y = 0$.

4. Open MINITAB's GLM menu and set up the GLM to analyze Y as a function of X and any other design variables. Be sure to specify terms as fixed or random and indicate all of the interactions to be included in the model. Click the **Results** button and check the box for **Display expected mean squares and variance components.** Click **OK** to run the GLM. The resulting ANOVA table

will have many zeros in it and MINITAB will report an error "Denominator of *F*-Test is zero."

5. In the **Adj SS** (adjusted *sums of squares*) column of the ANOVA table, find SS_X. (This should be the only nonzero SS in the column.) Also find df_X.

6. In the **Error Terms for Tests, using Adjusted SS** table find the term *X* in the **Source** column and the corresponding error degrees of freedom $df_{\varepsilon(X)}$ for the *F* test for *X*. In the **Synthesis of Error MS** column of the same table, note the term (a number in parentheses) that provides the mean square error for the *F* test of *X* (for example, 5). Find the row number in the **Expected Mean Square for Each Term** column of the **Expected Mean Squares, using Adjusted SS** table that corresponds to the (numbered) error term for the *F* test of *X* called $E(MS_{\varepsilon(X)})$. Read the equation for the expected mean square [for example, (6)+2.000000(5)] which gives $E(MS_{\varepsilon(X)})$. Use this equation and the definitions for the various terms to write out the mean square error in terms of the different variances.

7. Use known or estimated variances to determine the numerical value for $E(MS_{\varepsilon(X)})$.

8. Determine the noncentrality parameter from:

$$\lambda = \frac{SS_X}{E\left(MS_{\varepsilon(X)}\right)} \tag{7.36}$$

9. Use MINITAB to find the critical value of F_α for the null hypothesis H_0: *there is no variable effect* using the degrees of freedom associated with df_X in the numerator and $df_{\varepsilon(X)}$ in the denominator.

10. Use MINITAB to find the power from $F_\alpha = F_{P,\lambda}$ with df_X and $df_{\varepsilon(X)}$ degrees of freedom.

Example 7.15
   A is a fixed variable with three levels, B is a fixed variable with four levels nested within each level of A [hence B(A)], and C is a random variable with five levels. Two full replicates of the experiment are built. The variance associated with the response is $\sigma_\varepsilon^2 = 120$. Include the AC and BC [technically B(A)×C] interactions in the model. Assume that the BC interaction has associated variance $\sigma_{BC}^2 = 20$ and that the AC interaction has variance $\sigma_{AC}^2 = 200$. Find the power to detect a difference $\delta = 20$ between two levels of B within one of the levels of A.

   Solution: The general method for determining power can be used to solve this problem:

   1. The matrix of $3 \times 4 \times 5 \times 2 = 120$ experimental runs was entered into a MINITAB worksheet.

   2. A column of 120 zeros was created for the response Y in an open column.

3. For one level of B within one level of A, $c \times n = 5 \times 2 = 10$ of the zeros were changed to $-\delta/2 = -10$ and for a second level of B within the same level of A, another 10 values were changed to $+\delta/2 = 10$.

4. MINITAB's GLM menu was opened and the model terms were set to A, B(A), C, A×C, and B×C. C was entered as a random variable. In the **Results** menu of the GLM menu, the box for **Display expected mean squares and variance components** was checked. The resulting output is shown in Figure 7.9.

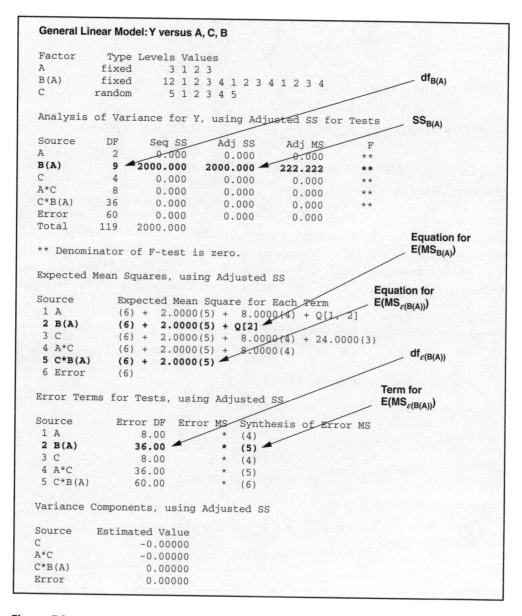

Figure 7.9 MINITAB GLM output for Example 7.15.

5. *From the MINITAB output in the Session window,* $SS_{B(A)} = 2000$ *and* $df_{B(A)} = 9$.

6. *From the table* **Error Terms for Tests, using Adjusted SS** *in the B(A) row,* $df_{\varepsilon(B(A))} = 36$ *and* $E(MS_{\varepsilon(B(A))}) = \sigma_{\varepsilon}^2 + 2\sigma_{BC}^2$.

7. *From the values given in the problem statement,* $E(MS_{\varepsilon(B(A))}) = \sigma_{\varepsilon}^2 + 2\sigma_{BC}^2$
   $= 120 + 2\,(20) = 160$.

8. *The noncentrality parameter is:*

$$\lambda = \frac{SS_{B(A)}}{E\left(MS_{\varepsilon(B(A))}\right)} = \frac{2000}{160} = 12.5$$

9. *From MINITAB (see Figure 7.10), the critical value for the accept/reject bound for* H_0 *is* $F_{0.05,9,36} = 2.1526$.

10. *From MINITAB (see Figure 7.10),* $F_{0.566,9,36,12.5} = 2.1526$ *so the power is* $P = 0.566$.

7.5.7 General Method to Determine the Power for a Random Variable

The following procedure can be used to determine the power for a random variable in a specified design. Some designs are very complicated and you may not be able to use this procedure. The use of MINITAB is described to determine the equations for the expected mean squares; however, if the *E(MS)* equations for your design were presented in this chapter you can get them from the appropriate table. Whether you use MINITAB or the

```
MTB > invcdf 0.95;
SUBC> f 9 36.

Inverse Cumulative Distribution Function

F distribution with 9 DF in numerator and 36 DF in denominator

P( X <= x )            x
   0.9500        2.1526

MTB > cdf 2.1526;
SUBC> f 9 36 12.5.

Cumulative Distribution Function

F distribution with 9 DF in numerator and 36 DF in denominator
Noncentrality parameter 12.5

        x      P( X <= x )
   2.1526        0.4338
```

Figure 7.10   MINITAB calculations of *F* values for Example 7.15.

tables, you must be able to specify the numerical values of df_X and $df_{\varepsilon(X)}$ and write the equations for MS_X and $MS_{\varepsilon(X)}$.

1. Enter the experiment design into columns of a MINITAB worksheet. Replicate the experiment as many times as required. The total number of runs in the experiment is N.

2. Select an open column for the response; let's call it Y. Use the random data command to put N random normal values into Y. The values you obtain are not important, they just need to be in the column for MINITAB to complete the calculations.

3. In the **Stat> ANOVA> General Linear Model** menu, configure the GLM to analyze Y as a function of X and any other design variables or desired model terms. Be sure to specify variables as fixed or random and indicate all of the interactions to be included in the model. Click the **Results** button and check the box for **Display expected mean squares and variance components.** Click **OK** twice to run the GLM.

4. Locate the variable for the power calculation X in the **Source** column of the **Expected Mean Squares** portion of the output. The corresponding equation in the **Expected Mean Squares for Each Term** column is $E(MS_X)$. Each number in parentheses corresponds to the variance of a term from the model as defined in the **Source** column.

5. Locate the variable for the power calculation X in the **Source** column of the **Analysis of Variance** portion of the output. The corresponding value in the **DF** column is df_X.

6. Locate the variable for the power calculation X in the **Source** column of the **Error Terms for Tests** portion of the output. The corresponding value in the **Error DF** column is $df_{\varepsilon(X)}$. The number in parentheses in the **Synthesis of Error MS** column indicates which mean square serves as the denominator of F_X. Match this number to the numbered **Source** term in the **Expected Mean Squares** portion of the output. The corresponding mean square equation is $MS_{\varepsilon(X)}$.

7. Calculate the expected value of the F statistic for X:

$$E\left(F_X\right) = \frac{E\left(MS_X\right)}{E\left(MS_{\varepsilon(X)}\right)} \tag{7.37}$$

for the desired value of $\sigma_X^2 \neq 0$. This F distribution has df_X and $df_{\varepsilon(X)}$ degrees of freedom. It may be necessary to estimate several other variances in addition to σ_ε^2 to complete this calculation.

8. Use MINITAB's **invcdf** function to determine the critical accept/reject bound for H_0: $\sigma_X^2 = 0$ versus H_A: $\sigma_X^2 > 0$ from $F_{\alpha, df_X, df_{\varepsilon(X)}}$.

9. Determine the numerical value for:

$$E(F_X') = \frac{E(F_X)}{F_\alpha}$$ (7.38)

10. Use MINITAB's **cdf** function to determine the power P from:

$$P = P\left(0 < F < E(F_X'); df_{\varepsilon(X)}, df_X\right)$$ (7.39)

Example 7.16

   A 5×8 *full-factorial experiment with two replicates is built. Both variables, A and B, respectively, are random variables. The error variance is $\sigma_\varepsilon^2 = 0.04$ and the variance associated with the interaction is $\sigma_{AB}^2 = 0.08$. Use the general method with MINITAB to find the power to reject H_0: $\sigma_A^2 = 0$ if $\sigma_A^2 = 0.1$ at $\alpha = 0.05$.*

   Solution: *The general method for determining the power for a random variable can be used to solve this problem:*

   1. *The $5 \times 8 \times 2$ matrix of experimental runs was entered into two columns of a MINITAB worksheet. There are a total of $N = 80$ runs.*

   2. *$N = 80$ random standard normal numbers were put into a column Y in the worksheet.*

   3. *MINITAB's GLM function was configured with A, B, and A×B specified as model terms. A and B were specified as random terms.* **Display expected mean squares and variance components** *was selected in the* **Results** *window and the GLM was run. The output of the GLM is shown in Figure 7.11.*

   4. *From the definitions in the* **Source** *column of the* **Expected Mean Squares** *portion of the output the model variances are identified as:*

$$
\begin{aligned}
(1) &= \sigma_A^2 \\
(2) &= \sigma_B^2 \\
(3) &= \sigma_{AB}^2 \\
(4) &= \sigma_\varepsilon^2
\end{aligned}
$$

   In the **Expected Mean Square for Each Term** *column $E(MS_A)$ is given by:*

$$
\begin{aligned}
E(MS_A) &= (4) + 2(3) + 16(1) \\
&= \sigma_\varepsilon^2 + 2\sigma_{AB}^2 + 16\sigma_A^2
\end{aligned}
$$

   5. *From the* **Analysis of Variance** *portion of the output, $df_A = 4$.*

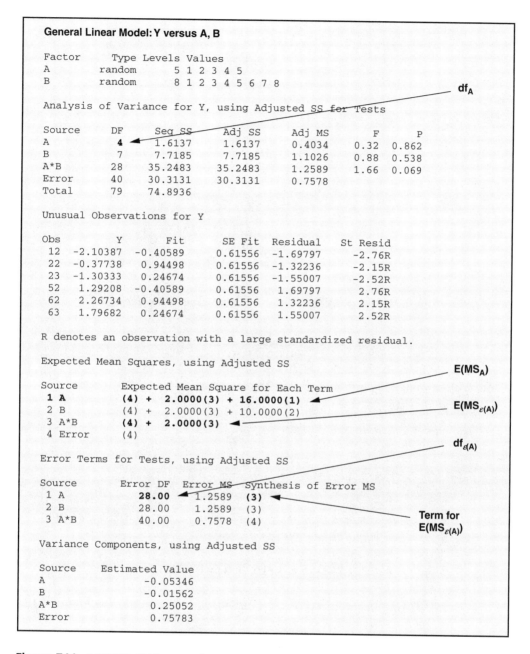

General Linear Model: Y versus A, B

```
Factor      Type Levels Values
A         random     5 1 2 3 4 5
B         random     8 1 2 3 4 5 6 7 8
```
                                                                         dfₐ

Analysis of Variance for Y, using Adjusted SS for Tests

```
Source      DF      Seq SS      Adj SS      Adj MS        F       P
A            4      1.6137      1.6137      0.4034     0.32    0.862
B            7      7.7185      7.7185      1.1026     0.88    0.538
A*B         28     35.2483     35.2483      1.2589     1.66    0.069
Error       40     30.3131     30.3131      0.7578
Total       79     74.8936
```

Unusual Observations for Y

```
Obs        Y          Fit      SE Fit  Residual    St Resid
 12   -2.10387    -0.40589     0.61556  -1.69797     -2.76R
 22   -0.37738     0.94498     0.61556  -1.32236     -2.15R
 23   -1.30333     0.24674     0.61556  -1.55007     -2.52R
 52    1.29208    -0.40589     0.61556   1.69797      2.76R
 62    2.26734     0.94498     0.61556   1.32236      2.15R
 63    1.79682     0.24674     0.61556   1.55007      2.52R
```

R denotes an observation with a large standardized residual.

Expected Mean Squares, using Adjusted SS

                                                                  E(MSₐ)

```
Source        Expected Mean Square for Each Term
1 A           (4) +  2.0000(3) + 16.0000(1)
2 B           (4) +  2.0000(3) + 10.0000(2)
3 A*B         (4) +  2.0000(3)
4 Error       (4)
```
                                                                  E(MS_{ε(A)})

                                                                  df_{ε(A)}

Error Terms for Tests, using Adjusted SS

```
Source        Error DF  Error MS  Synthesis of Error MS
1 A             28.00    1.2589      (3)
2 B             28.00    1.2589      (3)
3 A*B           40.00    0.7578      (4)
```
                                                                  Term for
                                                                  E(MS_{ε(A)})

Variance Components, using Adjusted SS

```
Source     Estimated Value
A              -0.05346
B              -0.01562
A*B             0.25052
Error           0.75783
```

Figure 7.11   MINITAB GLM output for Example 7.16.

6. *From the **Error Terms for Tests** portion of the output, $df_{\varepsilon(A)} = 28$. The mean square for the denominator of F_A is given by term (3) which is $E(MS_{AB})$. From the **Expected Mean Squares** portion of the output:*

$$E\left(MS_{\varepsilon(A)}\right) = E\left(MS_{AB}\right)$$
$$= 4 + 2(3)$$
$$= \sigma_{\varepsilon}^2 + 2\sigma_{AB}^2$$

7. *The expected value of F_A is given by:*

$$E\left(F_A\right) = \frac{E\left(MS_A\right)}{E\left(MS_{AB}\right)}$$
$$= \frac{\sigma_{\varepsilon}^2 + 2\sigma_{AB}^2 + 16\sigma_A^2}{\sigma_{\varepsilon}^2 + 2\sigma_{AB}^2}$$
$$= 1 + \frac{16\sigma_A^2}{\sigma_{\varepsilon}^2 + 2\sigma_{AB}^2}$$

With $\sigma_{\varepsilon}^2 = 0.04$, $\sigma_{AB}^2 = 0.08$, and $\sigma_A^2 = 0.1$ the expected value of F_A is:

$$E\left(F_A\right) = 1 + \frac{16 \times 0.1}{0.04 + 2 \times 0.08} = 9.0$$

8. *With $\alpha = 0.05$, $df_A = 4$, and $df_{\varepsilon(A)} = 28$ the critical value for the accept/reject bound for H_0: $\sigma_A^2 = 0$ is $F_{0.05,4,28} = 2.7141$.*

9. *The numerical value of $E(F_A')$ is:*

$$E\left(F_A'\right) = \frac{E\left(F_A\right)}{F_\alpha} = \frac{9.0}{2.7141} = 3.316$$

10. *The power is determined from the F distribution with $df_{\varepsilon(A)} = 28$ numerator and $df_A = 4$ denominator degrees of freedom:*

$$P = P\left(0 < F < 3.316; 28, 4\right) = 0.8744$$

The MINITAB calculations of $F_{0.05,4,28}$ and the power are shown in Figure 7.12.

```
MTB > invcdf 0.95;
SUBC> f 4 28.
```

Inverse Cumulative Distribution Function

F distribution with 4 DF in numerator and 28 DF in denominator

```
P( X <= x )           x
    0.9500        2.7141
```

```
MTB > cdf 3.316;
SUBC> f 28 4.
```

Cumulative Distribution Function

F distribution with 28 DF in numerator and 4 DF in denominator

```
        x      P( X <= x )
    3.3160        0.8744
```

Figure 7.12 MINITAB calculations of *F* values for Example 7.16.

8

Linear Regression

8.1 INTRODUCTION

The input variables of a process that may be set at the user's discretion are referred to as independent variables. Independent variables are the knobs of a process—the controls that you use to make adjustments to the process. In previous chapters the input variables were qualitative—they could only be set to discrete qualitative levels. In this chapter the knobs are quantitative and continuous—they can be set to an infinite number of levels between upper and lower bounds or limits.

As in the earlier chapters, we will still be considering quantitative responses. Since responses are controlled or set by manipulation of the independent variables, the responses are called dependent variables. In general, the variable x will be used to refer to an independent variable and the variable y will refer to a response. Our problem in this chapter is to determine a statistically sound linear equation that relates y to x of the form $y = b_0 + b_1 x$ where b_0 and b_1 are statistics to be determined from the sample data.

8.2 LINEAR REGRESSION RATIONALE

Consider the simple measurement response y_i plotted in Figure 8.1a. If the only distinction between the observations is the order or time at which they were taken, then the y_i should all be estimates of a single population mean. We usually characterize a measurement response like this by calculating the sample mean $\bar{y}$ and sample standard deviation s or variance s^2. To be complete we should also state the shape of the distribution of the errors or discrepancies ε_i between the mean and the individual observations. The usual assumption is that the errors are normally distributed but, as with all assumptions, this should be tested.

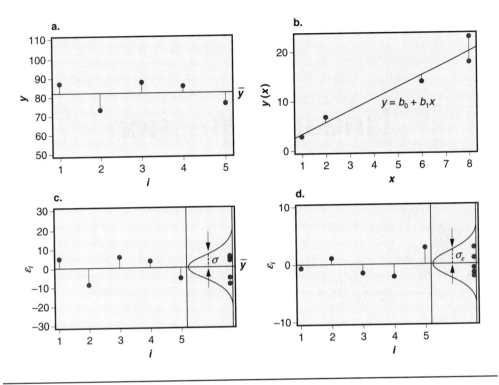

Figure 8.1 Errors in simple measurement data and a scatter plot.

A simple model for the y_i in Figure 8.1a may be written as:

$$y_i = \hat{y} + \varepsilon_i \qquad (8.1)$$

where, as we said, the logical choice for $\hat{y}$ is the sample mean $\bar{y}$. The corresponding sample variance is:

$$s^2 = \frac{\sum_{i=1}^{n} \varepsilon_i^2}{n-1} \qquad (8.2)$$

where $\varepsilon_i = y_i - \bar{y}$. The ε_i and their distribution are shown in Figure 8.1c.

Although it might seem to be a trivial question, you might ask why the sample mean $\bar{y}$ was the correct value to use for $\hat{y}$. Is there another choice, another condition, that could be used to provide a model for the y_i? Since the purpose of the model is to accurately describe the y_i, then we would expect the model to deliver small errors (that is, ε_i), but how should we go about making the errors small? A logical choice is to pick $\hat{y}$, which might now be different from $\bar{y}$, so that the error variance s^2 calculated with $\varepsilon_i = y_i - \hat{y}$ is minimized. Note that from Equation 8.2 this is equivalent to minimizing $\sum \varepsilon_i^2$ because the sample size n is constant. It can be shown, empirically or by calculus, that the value of $\hat{y}$ that minimizes s^2 and $\sum \varepsilon_i^2$ happens to be $\hat{y} = \bar{y}$. The calculus operation that delivers this solution is:

$$\frac{d}{d\hat{y}} \sum \varepsilon_i^2 = 0 \tag{8.3}$$

This is called the *method of least squares* because the method minimizes the error sum of squares.* This analysis confirms that the sample mean $\bar{y}$ is also the value of $\hat{y}$ that minimizes the error variance and the error sum of squares.

Now consider the scatter diagram of Figure 8.1b. The dependent variable y appears to increase linearly with respect to the independent variable x so there might be an underlying causal relationship between x and y of the form:

$$y = \beta_0 + \beta_1 x \tag{8.4}$$

where the parameters β_0 and β_1 are the y axis intercept and slope, respectively. Since we typically have sample data and not the complete population of (x_i, y_i) observations, we cannot expect to determine β_0 and β_1 exactly—they will have to be estimated from the sample data. Our model, to be determined from the sample data, will have the same form as Equation 8.4:

$$y_i = b_0 + b_1 x_i + \varepsilon_i \tag{8.5}$$

where b_0 and b_1 are estimates of the parameters β_0 and β_1, respectively, and the ε_i measure the discrepancy between the individual data points y_i and the predicted y_i values given by:

$$\hat{y}_i = b_0 + b_1 x_i \tag{8.6}$$

Then for any choice of b_0 and b_1, the ε_i may be determined from:

$$\varepsilon_i = y_i - \hat{y}_i = y_i - \left(b_0 + b_1 x_i \right) \tag{8.7}$$

These errors or discrepancies, also called the *model residuals,* are shown in Figure 8.1d for the model fitted to the data in Figure 8.1b.

Although Equation 8.7 allows us to calculate the ε_i for a given (x_i, y_i) data set once b_0 and b_1 are specified, there are still an infinite number of b_0 and b_1 values that could be used in the model. Clearly the choice of b_0 and b_1 that provides the best fit to the data should make the ε_i or some function of them small. Although many conditions can be stated to define best fit lines by minimizing the ε_i, by far the most frequently used condition to define the best fit line is the one that minimizes $\sum \varepsilon_i^2$. That is, the best fit line for the (x_i, y_i) data, called the *linear least squares regression line,* corresponds to the

---

* If you don't know calculus—and you're not expected to—Equation 8.3 defines a mathematical condition that can be solved to show that $\bar{y}$ is the unique choice of $\hat{y}$ that minimizes the sample variance s^2. This makes $\bar{y}$ the best fit to the data.

choice of b_0 and b_1 that minimizes $\Sigma \varepsilon_i^2$. The calculus solution to this problem, which is analogous to the solution for the simple measurement response in Equation 8.3, is given by the simultaneous solution to the two equations:

$$\tfrac{\partial}{\partial b_0} \Sigma \varepsilon_i^2 = 0 \quad \text{and} \quad \tfrac{\partial}{\partial b_1} \Sigma \varepsilon_i^2 = 0 \tag{8.8}$$

The method of fitting a line to (x_i, y_i) data using the solution to Equations 8.8 is called *linear regression*. The word *linear* refers to the straight-line relationship that describes *y* as a function of *x*. The word *regression* means "returning to an earlier state," which refers to the implied causality of the relationship between *y* and *x*. That is, the value taken on by the dependent variable *y* (the result) is *caused* by the independent variable *x* (the earlier state). The values b_0 and b_1 are called the *regression coefficients*. They are statistics determined from sample data just like the sample mean $\bar{y}$ is a statistic determined from a simple set of measurement values.

The error variance for linear least squares regression is given by:

$$s_\varepsilon^2 = \frac{\sum_{i=1}^{n} \varepsilon_i^2}{n-2} \tag{8.9}$$

where *n* is the number of (x_i, y_i) observations and s_ε is called the standard error of the model. Equation 8.9 is obviously analogous to the error variance calculated for the simple measurement response in Equation 8.2 except for the $n - 2$ in the denominator. Recall that the reason for using $n - 1$ instead of *n* in the denominator of Equation 8.2 was to account for the loss of one degree of freedom associated with the calculation of the sample mean $\bar{y}$ from the experimental data. When $\bar{y}$ is calculated from a set of *n* observations then only the first $n - 1$ of the observations are free to vary when the error variance is calculated. Likewise, Equation 8.9 has $n - 2$ in the denominator because two degrees of freedom are consumed by the calculation of the regression coefficients b_0 and b_1 from the experimental data. b_0 and b_1 are statistics calculated from the (x_i, y_i) data just like $\bar{y}$ is a statistic calculated from the y_i data.

Think of the error variance s_ε^2 in the regression problem in the same way as you think of the sample variance s^2 used to quantify the amount of variation in simple measurement data. Whereas the sample variance characterizes the scatter of observations about a single value $\hat{y}_i = \bar{y}$, the error variance in the regression problem characterizes the distribution of values about the line $\hat{y}_i = b_0 + b_1 x_i$. s_ε^2 and s^2 are close cousins; they are both measures of the errors associated with different models for different kinds of data.

Example 8.1
   A matrix of (b_0, b_1) regression coefficients was considered as fits to the following data:

i	1	2	3	4	5
x_i	1	2	6	8	8
y_i	3	7	14	18	23

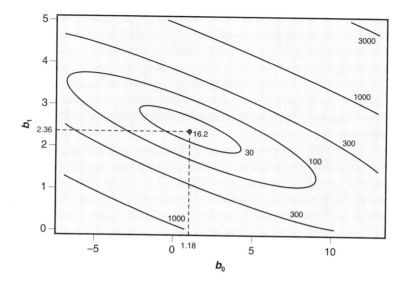

Figure 8.2 Contours $\sum \varepsilon_i^2$ versus b_0 and b_1.

The error sum of squares $\sum \varepsilon_i^2$ was evaluated for each (b_0, b_1) case and then the results were used to create the contour plot of $\sum \varepsilon_i^2$ as a function of b_0 and b_1, shown in Figure 8.2. Interpret the contour plot, indicate the equation of the line that provides the best fit to the data, and calculate the standard error of the model.

Solution: The contour plot shows that $\sum \varepsilon_i^2$ decreases toward the center of the plot where the fit is best. The point at the very center where $(b_0, b_1) = (1.18, 2.36)$ minimizes $\sum \varepsilon_i^2$ so $y = 1.18 + 2.36x$ is the best fit line. The standard error of the model is given by:

$$s_\varepsilon = \sqrt{\frac{1}{n-2} \sum \varepsilon_i^2} = \sqrt{\frac{16.2}{5-2}} = 2.32$$

which is the smallest possible standard error for all possible choices of b_0 and b_1.

8.3 REGRESSION COEFFICIENTS

With the condition to determine the b_0 and b_1 values that provide the best fit line for the (x_i, y_i) data, namely the minimization of $\sum \varepsilon_i^2$, we proceed to determine b_0 and b_1 in a more rigorous manner. This can be explained in two ways, either graphically for those without calculus experience or by using simple differential calculus.

The calculus method that determines the unique values of b_0 and b_1 that minimize $\sum \varepsilon_i^2$ requires that we solve the simultaneous equations:

$$\frac{\partial}{\partial b_0} \sum_{i=1}^{n} \varepsilon_i^2 = 0 \tag{8.10}$$

and

$$\frac{\partial}{\partial b_1} \sum_{i=1}^{n} \varepsilon_i^2 = 0 \tag{8.11}$$

From these equations the resulting values of b_0 and b_1 are best expressed in terms of sums of squares:

$$b_1 = \frac{SS_{xy}}{SS_x} \tag{8.12}$$

and

$$b_0 = \bar{y} - b_1 \bar{x} \tag{8.13}$$

where

$$SS_x = \sum_{i=1}^{n} \left(x_i - \bar{x} \right)^2 \tag{8.14}$$

$$SS_y = \sum_{i=1}^{n} \left(y_i - \bar{y} \right)^2 \tag{8.15}$$

$$SS_{xy} = \sum_{i=1}^{n} \left(x_i - \bar{x} \right)\left(y_i - \bar{y} \right) \tag{8.16}$$

and $\bar{x}$ and $\bar{y}$ are the usual means. These sums of squares will be useful shortly and are worth the pain to introduce here. Take a careful look at them. SS_x and SS_y are just the sums of squares required to determine the variances of the x and y values. That is:

$$s_x^2 = \frac{SS_x}{n-1} \tag{8.17}$$

and

$$s_y^2 = \frac{SS_y}{n-1} \tag{8.18}$$

Similarly, using the sum of squares notation, we can write the error sum of squares for the regression as:

$$SS_\varepsilon = \sum \varepsilon_i^2 \tag{8.19}$$

and the standard error as:

$$s_\varepsilon = \sqrt{\frac{\sum \varepsilon_i^2}{n-2}} = \sqrt{\frac{SS_\varepsilon}{df_\varepsilon}} \tag{8.20}$$

Another important implication of Equations 8.12 and 8.13 is that the point $(\bar{x}, \bar{y})$ must fall on the best-fit line. This is just a consequence of the way the sums of squares are calculated—relative to $\bar{x}$ for SS_x and relative to $\bar{y}$ for SS_y.

Example 8.2

Using the data from Example 8.1, find the error sum of squares for slopes $b_1 = 0$, 1, 2, 3, and 4 using the point $(\bar{x}, \bar{y})$ as an anchor point. Construct the plot of $\sum \varepsilon_i^2$ versus b_1 and use the plot to estimate the value of b_1 that provides the best fit to the data.

Solution: The anchor point given by $(\bar{x}, \bar{y})$ is positioned at:

$$\bar{x} = \frac{1}{5}(1+2+6+8+8) = 5$$

and

$$\bar{y} = \frac{1}{5}(3+7+4+18+23) = 13$$

Consider the case when the slope is $b_1 = 2$. The value of b_0 is given by Equation 8.13:

$$b_0 = \bar{y} - b_1\bar{x} = 13 - 2(5) = 3$$

so the predicted values of y_i are given by:

$$\hat{y}_i = 3 + 2x_i$$

The following table shows the data with the predicted values of the response $\hat{y}_i$, the corresponding values of the ε_i, their squares, and all of the necessary sums.

i	1	2	3	4	5	**Sums**
x_i	1	2	6	8	8	25
y_i	3	7	14	18	23	65
$\hat{y}_i$	5	7	15	19	19	65
ε_i	−2	0	−1	−1	4	0
ε_i^2	4	0	1	1	16	22

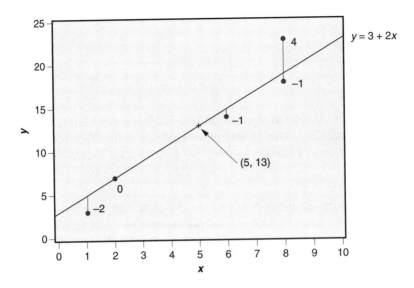

Figure 8.3   Line $y = 3 + 2x$ and errors ε_i.

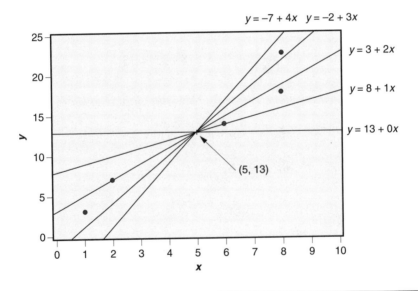

Figure 8.4   Data set and lines with slopes from $b = 0$ to 4.

The data values, $(\bar{x}, \bar{y})$, the line defined by $\hat{y}_i = 3 + 2x_i$, and the errors ε_i are shown in Figure 8.3. The error sum of squares for this model is $SS_\varepsilon = \Sigma \varepsilon_i^2 = 22$. The lines and analyses for the other slopes are summarized in the following table and are shown in Figure 8.4.

b_1	0	1	2	3	4
$\sum \varepsilon_i^2$	262	102	22	34	134

Figure 8.5 shows the error variances plotted against the slopes. The plot suggests that the slope that minimizes the error sum of squares is about $b_1 = 2.4$.

Example 8.3

Use the sums of squares method to find the best-fit model for the data in Example 8.1. Determine the error variance and the standard error.

Solution: We require the quantities $\bar{x}$, $\bar{y}$, SS_x, SS_y, and SS_{xy} in order to determine the regression equation and error variance. From Example 8.2, the means of the x_i and y_i are: $\bar{x} = 5.0$ and $\bar{y} = 13.0$. The necessary sums of squares are determined from Equations 8.14, 8.15, and 8.16. The calculations are performed in the following table:

i	x_i	$(x_i - \bar{x})$	$(x_i - \bar{x})^2$	y_i	$(y_i - \bar{y})$	$(y_i - \bar{y})^2$	$(x_i - \bar{x})(y_i - \bar{y})$
1	1	−4	16	3	−10	100	40
2	2	−3	9	7	−6	36	18
3	6	1	1	14	1	1	1
4	8	3	9	18	5	25	15
5	8	3	9	23	10	100	30
Totals	25	0	44	65	0	262	104

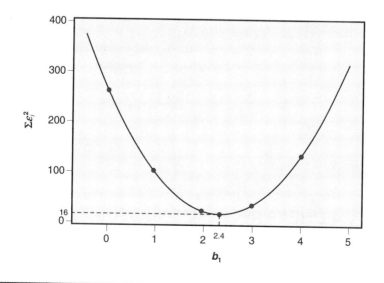

Figure 8.5 Best-fit slope from the minimum of $\sum \varepsilon_i^2$.

so we have $SS_x = 44$, $SS_y = 262$, and $SS_{xy} = 104$. Now from Equation 8.12, the value of the slope in the regression equation is:

$$b_1 = \frac{SS_{xy}}{SS_x} = \frac{104}{44} = 2.36$$

and from Equation 8.13, the value of the y axis intercept is:

$$b_0 = \bar{y} - b_1\bar{x} = 13.0 - 2.36 \times 5.0 = 1.18$$

so the best-fit regression equation is:

$$y = 1.18 + 2.36x$$

The standard error is found from the model residuals, the ε_i, determined from Equation 8.7. The predicted y values and the residuals are shown in the following table:

i	x_i	y_i	$\hat{y}_i$	ε_i	ε_i^2
1	1	3	3.55	−0.55	0.30
2	2	7	5.91	1.09	1.19
3	6	14	15.36	−1.36	1.86
4	8	18	20.1	−2.09	4.37
5	8	23	20.1	2.91	8.46
			Totals	0.00	16.2

From the table, the error sum of squares is $SS_\varepsilon = \sum \varepsilon_i^2 = 16.2$. Since there are $n = 5$ data points in the data set and there are two regression coefficients, there are $df_\varepsilon = 5 - 2 = 3$ degrees of freedom to estimate the error. The error variance is:

$$s_\varepsilon^2 = \frac{SS_\varepsilon}{df_\varepsilon} = \frac{16.2}{(5-2)} = 5.4$$

so the model standard error is $s_\varepsilon = \sqrt{5.4} = 2.32$.

8.4 LINEAR REGRESSION ASSUMPTIONS

A valid linear regression model requires that five conditions are satisfied:

1. The values of x are determined without error.

2. The ε_i are normally distributed with mean $\mu_\varepsilon = 0$ for all values of x.

3. The distribution of the ε_i has constant variance σ_ε^2 for all values of x within the range of experimentation (that is, homoscedasticity).

4. The ε_i are independent of each other.

5. The linear model provides a good fit to the data.

The assumptions for linear regression are comparable to the assumptions for ANOVA with some additions. The first assumption, that the values of x are known exactly, is a necessity for using the techniques described in this chapter. If there is a random error component in the xs, then the linear regression method gives incorrect values for the regression coefficients. One consequence of error in the xs is that the magnitude of the slope of the regression line is underestimated, sometimes badly. This bias can be corrected for some simple problems. See Section 8.13 for more a few more details on this type of problem.

The second assumption, that the errors are normally distributed, should be checked with a normal probability plot. If the errors aren't normal, a transformation of the data may be necessary or other techniques must be considered. As with ANOVA, there are several reasons that the ε_i might not be normally distributed.

The third assumption, that the distribution of errors has constant variance, should be checked with a plot of the errors versus the independent variable x or versus the predicted value of the response $\hat{y}$. These plots should show that the scatter in the ε_i is uniform in magnitude with respect to x or $\hat{y}$. If there is any tendency for the error variance to change with x or $\hat{y}$, then the regression model may be invalid and special techniques should be used to analyze the data. Under certain conditions it is possible to resolve this problem with an appropriate transformation of the data. In other cases it may become necessary to use a technique called weighted regression. Weighted regression places more emphasis on the observations where the error variance is relatively small since those observations provide a better prediction of the response than observations where there is a relatively large amount of variation. The weighted regression calculations are complex but thankfully MINITAB has the ability to do them. Weighted regression is beyond the scope of this book, but see Section 8.14 for a few more details on this type of analysis.

The fourth assumption, that the errors are independently distributed, should be checked by plotting the errors versus the run order. There should be no patterns on this plot. If the errors are truly random, then they should be scattered uniformly about the line $\varepsilon = 0$. Another graphical method for evaluating independence, called a *lag-one* plot, is constructed by plotting each error against the preceding error. If the lag-one plot shows a circular cloud of points, then the errors are probably independent.

The fifth and last assumption, that the linear model provides a good fit to the data, can be checked with one or more of several plots. In extreme cases, the scatter plot of y_i versus x_i will reveal curvature or lack of fit. In more subtle cases, a plot of the residuals versus the predicted values (ε_i versus $\hat{y}_i$) or the residuals versus the independent variable (ε_i versus x_i) will uncover the problem. If these plots show any sign of curvature or systematic deviation from the $\varepsilon = 0$ line, then a different model should be considered. Some less subjective methods of testing for lack of fit are described in Section 8.12.

Related to the issue of lack of fit is the possible effect of outlying observations. Potential outliers are usually easy to spot in the various diagnostic graphs, but a more formal method of testing for outliers is useful. One such method, called *deleted Studentized residuals,* is computationally intensive but quite good at identifying outliers. The deleted Studentized residual associated with an observation is calculated by determining the difference between the observed value of the response and the predicted value when that observation is omitted from the data set, then dividing that difference by the estimated local standard deviation associated with that observation. Obviously, highly influential observations will have large deleted Studentized residuals. The usual method for testing these special residuals for significance is to compare them to the critical value $t_{\alpha/(2n), df_\varepsilon}$ where α is the family error rate, n is the number of observations in the data set, $\alpha/(2n)$ is the Bonferroni corrected Type 1 error rate for individual tests of all n observations, and df_ε is the error degrees of freedom from the regression. Observations with deleted Studentized residuals greater in magnitude than this critical value are probably outliers. A normal probability plot of the deleted Studentized residuals with reference lines at $\pm t_{\alpha/(2n), df_\varepsilon}$ makes it easy to spot potential outliers.

The **Graphs** menu in MINITAB's **Stat> Regression> Regression** menu creates a comprehensive set of residuals diagnostic plots including: the histogram and normal plot of the residuals, a plot of the residuals versus the fits, a plot of residuals versus order of the observations, and a plot of the residuals versus the x_i. The deleted Studentized residuals can also be stored in the worksheet by selecting **Deleted t residuals** from the **Storage** menu.

The primary focus of the assumption-testing methods presented in this section has been on graphical methods; there are, however, analogous quantitative methods available. In most situations, the graphical methods are sufficient, but in more subtle or critical situations the quantitative methods may become necessary. See Neter et al. (1996) or the MINITAB **Help** files for more detail on these methods.

Example 8.4

A regression analysis of fifty observations, collected in random order, was performed. Interpret the post-regression residuals plots in Figure 8.6 to determine if the regression assumptions are satisfied.

Solution: The normal plot of residuals shows that the plotted points fall roughly along a straight line, so the residuals are normal or at least approximately normal. The histogram of residuals is hard to interpret since there are so few observations, but it also shows no evidence to indicate that the residuals deviate from normality. The plot of

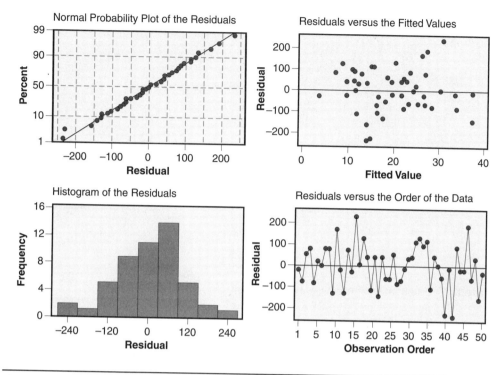

Figure 8.6   Residual plots from MINITAB for Example 8.4.

residuals versus the fitted values shows that the residuals have about the same amount of variation at all levels of the fitted value, that is, it appears that the residuals are homoscedastic with respect to the fitted values. The figure also shows no general tendency for the residuals to swing above and below $\varepsilon = 0$, so there is no evidence of lack of linear fit. The plot of residuals versus run order shows that the residuals are randomly and uniformly distributed about $\varepsilon = 0$, so the residuals appear to be homoscedastic with respect to time. There are no patterns that allow a residual to be predicted from those that precede it, so the errors appear to be independent. All of the assumptions required to validate the use of regression for this problem appear to be satisifed.

8.5 HYPOTHESIS TESTS FOR REGRESSION COEFFICIENTS

The values of the intercept and slope found with Equations 8.13 and 8.12 are actually estimates for the true parameters β_0 and β_1. Luckily these estimates follow well behaved distributions so that as long as the regression assumptions are satisfied and

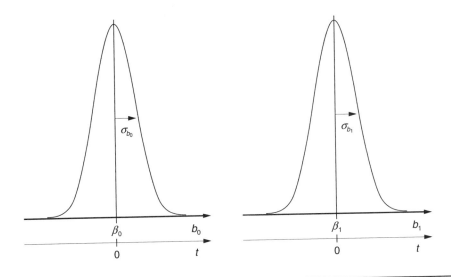

Figure 8.7 Distributions of estimates for β_0 and β_1.

there are error degrees of freedom to determine s_ε, we have the information required to construct confidence intervals and perform hypothesis tests for β_0 and β_1. Hypothetical distributions for b_0 and b_1 are shown in Figure 8.7. Both of these distributions follow Student's t distribution with degrees of freedom equal to the error degrees of freedom.

Although linear regression analysis will always return b_0 and b_1 values, it's possible that one or both of these values could be statistically insignificant. We require a formal method of testing β_0 and β_1 to see if they are different from zero. Hypotheses for these tests are:

$$H_0 : \beta_0 = 0$$
$$H_A : \beta_0 \neq 0$$

and

$$H_0 : \beta_1 = 0$$
$$H_A : \beta_1 \neq 0$$

To perform these tests we need some idea of the amount of variability present in the estimates of β_0 and β_1. Estimates of the variances $\sigma_{b_0}^2$ and $\sigma_{b_1}^2$ are given by:

$$s_{b_0}^2 = s_\varepsilon^2 \left(\frac{1}{n} + \frac{\bar{x}^2}{SS_x} \right) \tag{8.21}$$

and

$$s_{b_1}^2 = s_\varepsilon^2 \left(\frac{1}{SS_x} \right) \tag{8.22}$$

The hypothesis tests can be performed using one-sample t tests with $df_\varepsilon = n - 2$ degrees of freedom with the t statistics:

$$t_{b_0} = \frac{b_0}{s_{b_0}} \tag{8.23}$$

and

$$t_{b_1} = \frac{b_1}{s_{b_1}} \tag{8.24}$$

The $(1 - \alpha)$ 100% confidence intervals for β_0 and β_1 are determined from:

$$P\left(b_0 - t_{\alpha/2} s_{b_0} < \beta_0 < b_0 + t_{\alpha/2} s_{b_0} \right) = 1 - \alpha \tag{8.25}$$

and

$$P(b_1 - t_{\alpha/2} s_{b_1} < \beta_1 < b_1 - t_{\alpha/2} s_{b_1}) = 1 - \alpha \tag{8.26}$$

with $n - 2$ degrees of freedom. Typical computer outputs of linear regression analyses report the quantities b_0, s_{b_0}, and t_{b_0} and the p value for t_{b_0}. The corresponding values for the regression coefficient b_1 are also reported. Some programs also report the confidence intervals for the regression coefficients.

It is very important to realize that the variances of b_0 and b_1, as given in Equations 8.21 and 8.22, are proportional to the standard error of the fit s_ε. This means that if there are any uncontrolled variables in the experiment that cause the standard error to increase, there will be a corresponding increase in the standard deviations of the regression coefficients. This could make the regression coefficients disappear into the noise. Always keep in mind that the model's ability to predict the regression coefficients is dependent on the size of the standard error. Take care to remove or control or account for extraneous variation so that you get the best predictions from your models with the least effort.

Example 8.5

Determine the standard deviations of the regression coefficients for the best-fit line from Example 8.3. Test the regression coefficients at $\alpha = 0.05$ to see if they are different from zero.

Solution: The standard deviations of the regression coefficients are given by Equations 8.21 and 8.22. They are:

$$s_{b_0} = s_\varepsilon \sqrt{\frac{1}{n} + \frac{\bar{x}^2}{SS_x}} = 2.32 \sqrt{\frac{1}{5} + \frac{5^2}{44}} = 2.03$$

$$s_{b_1} = \frac{s_\varepsilon}{\sqrt{SS_x}} = \frac{2.32}{\sqrt{44}} = 0.35$$

The t values for the hypothesis tests of H_0: $\beta_0 = 0$ versus H_A: $\beta_0 \neq 0$ and H_0: $\beta_1 = 0$ versus H_A: $\beta_1 \neq 0$ are given by Equations 8.23 and 8.24. The t values are:

$$t_{b_0} = \frac{b_0}{s_{b_0}} = \frac{1.18}{2.03} = 0.58$$

$$t_{b_1} = \frac{b_1}{s_{b_1}} = \frac{2.36}{0.35} = 6.74$$

The critical t value that these statistics must be compared to is $t_{0.025}$ (since the tests are two-tailed) with $df_\varepsilon = 5 - 2 = 3$ degrees of freedom. This value is $t_{0.025,3} = 3.18$ so the acceptance interval for the null hypotheses is $P(-3.18 < t < 3.18) = 0.95$. Since $t_{b_0} = 0.58$ is within this interval, the value of b_0 from the regression is not statistically significant, that is, $b_0 = 1.18$ is not distinguishable from zero. This means that we have to accept the null hypothesis H_0: $\beta_0 = 0$. Since $t_{b_1} = 6.74$ is very large and falls outside the acceptance interval for H_0 we must conclude that $b_1 = 2.36$ is significantly different from zero, that is, we must reject H_0: $\beta_1 = 0$ in favor of H_A: $\beta_1 \neq 0$.

Example 8.6

Construct confidence intervals for β_0 and β_1 for the best-fit line from Example 8.3.

Solution: The confidence intervals for β_0 and β_1 are determined from Equations 8.25 and 8.26:

$$P(1.18 - 3.18 \times 2.03 < \beta_0 < 1.18 + 3.18 \times 2.03) = 0.95$$
$$P(-5.3 < \beta_0 < 7.6) = 0.95$$

$$P(2.36 - 3.18 \times 0.35 < \beta_1 < 2.36 + 3.18 \times 0.35) = 0.95$$
$$P(1.2 < \beta_1 < 3.5) = 0.95$$

The interval for β_0 contains zero, which could be expected from the preceding example that showed that β_0 was not statistically distinguishable from zero. Even though the t test indicates that β_1 is significantly different from zero, there is still a large degree of uncertainty in its true value.

8.6 CONFIDENCE LIMITS FOR THE REGRESSION LINE

The previous section makes it apparent that the true slope and intercept of a regression line are not exactly known. This means that the regression line $\hat{y} = b_0 + b_1 x$ drawn through the (x, y) data might be the best line to draw based on the limited information available, but that the true line that represents the population of (x, y) could be shifted up or down a bit or that the true slope might be a bit shallower or a bit steeper. The quantities s_{b_0} and s_{b_1} estimate the size of these uncertainties. If we take these two effects together—the shifting up and down of the regression line due to uncertainty in β_0 and changes to the slope so that the line is steeper or more shallow due to uncertainty in β_1, we can determine confidence limits for where we can expect the true line to fall. The $(1 - \alpha)$ 100% confidence interval for the regression line is given by:

$$P\left(\hat{y} - t_{\alpha/2} s_\varepsilon \sqrt{\frac{1}{n} + \frac{(x - \bar{x})^2}{SS_x}} < \mu_{y(x)} < \hat{y} + t_{\alpha/2} s_\varepsilon \sqrt{\frac{1}{n} + \frac{(x - \bar{x})^2}{SS_x}} \right) = 1 - \alpha \qquad (8.27)$$

where $t_{\alpha/2}$ is taken with $df_\varepsilon = n - 2$ degrees of freedom and $\mu_{y(x)}$ is the parameter associated with y at the specified x value. Remember that this interval does not reflect the distribution of individual data points about the regression line—it indicates with $(1 - \alpha)$ 100% confidence where the true regression line might be located. Notice that the confidence limits for the regression can be made arbitrarily tight by taking as many observations for the regression as is required.

Since the calculations for the confidence interval involve limits of the function $y(x)$, there are many values along the regression line that must be evaluated to determine what the bounds look like. This isn't something that you want to do by hand. MINITAB has the ability to construct the confidence intervals from the **Stat> Regression> Fitted Line Plot** menu. You will have to select **Display Confidence Bands** in the **Options** menu to add the confidence limits to the fitted line plot.

Example 8.7
Use MINITAB to construct the 95 percent confidence interval for the regression line from Example 8.2.

*Solution: MINITAB provides the capability to construct confidence intervals for regression models from its **Stat> Regression> Fitted Line Plot** menu. The 95 percent confidence interval for the regression line is shown in Figure 8.8.*

Sometimes after regression for $y(x)$ it is necessary to construct a confidence interval for x for a specified value of y. To construct this interval, you might be tempted to perform the regression of x as a function of y and then to use the method of Equation 8.27 to construct the confidence interval for x, but this approach gives the wrong answer. The correct interval is given by a method called *inverse prediction*. Given the results of a linear regression analysis for $y = f(x)$ of the form $y = b_0 + b_1 x$ determined

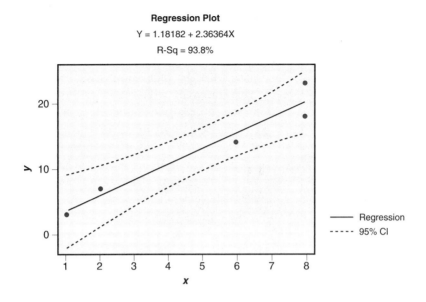

Figure 8.8 95 percent confidence bands for the regression line.

from n observations, the $(1 - \alpha)$ 100% confidence interval for the true value of x that delivers the specified value of y is given by:

$$P\left(\bar{x} + \frac{b_1(y - \bar{y})}{d} - h < \mu_{x(y)} < \bar{x} + \frac{b_1(y - \bar{y})}{d} + h\right) = 1 - \alpha \qquad (8.28)$$

where:

$$h = \frac{t_{\alpha/2} s_\varepsilon}{d} \sqrt{d\left(1 + \frac{1}{n}\right) + \frac{(y - \bar{y})^2}{\sum x^2}} \qquad (8.29)$$

and:

$$d = b_1^2 - \left(t_{\alpha/2} s_{b_1}\right)^2 \qquad (8.30)$$

and the t distribution has $df_\varepsilon = n - 2$ degrees of freedom. See Neter et al. (1996) or Sokal and Rohlf (1995) for more detailed explanations and examples of inverse prediction.

8.7 PREDICTION LIMITS FOR THE OBSERVED VALUES

In the previous section, a confidence interval was described for the position of the true regression line for the population of (x, y) observations. The purpose of this section is to build on that confidence interval to create a new interval that provides prediction bounds for individual observations. The width of the prediction interval combines the uncertainty of the position of the true line as described by the confidence interval with the scatter of points about the line as measured by the standard error.

For a given value of x, the predicted value of y will be $\hat{y} = b_0 + b_1 x$. The fraction of the population of values that should fall within a certain distance of this prediction equation is given by:

$$P\left(\hat{y} - t_{\alpha/2} s_\varepsilon \sqrt{1 + \frac{1}{n} + \frac{(x - \bar{x})^2}{SS_x}} < y(x) < \hat{y} + t_{\alpha/2} s_\varepsilon \sqrt{1 + \frac{1}{n} + \frac{(x - \bar{x})^2}{SS_x}} \right) = 1 - \alpha \qquad (8.31)$$

where $t_{\alpha/2}$ has $df_\varepsilon = n - 2$ degrees of freedom. This interval looks very much like the confidence interval in Equation 8.27 but it has an additional term (1) inside the square root. This term represents the additional variation of individual points about the regression line.

Whereas the confidence interval for the regression line can be made arbitrarily tight by taking many observations, the width of the prediction interval is limited by the standard error of the regression. Notice that when n is very large in Equation 8.31 the prediction interval can be approximated by:

$$P\left(\hat{y} - t_{\alpha/2} s_\varepsilon < y(x) < \hat{y} + t_{\alpha/2} s_\varepsilon \right) < 1 - \alpha \qquad (8.32)$$

This approximate interval will always be narrower than the true prediction interval but the discrepancy between them is small when the sample size is large. The simplification provided by the approximate interval makes it an important, very useful, and actually common practice. It is much easier to make a statement like "95 percent of the observations are expected to fall within $\pm t_{\alpha/2} s_\varepsilon$ of the best-fit line," rather than trying to explain the complex but relatively insignificant behavior of the exact prediction interval.

MINITAB can plot prediction limits along with the best-fit line from the **Stat> Regression> Fitted Line Plot** menu. You will have to select **Display Prediction Bands** in the **Options** menu. Both confidence bands and prediction bands are often shown along with the regression line and the scatterplot of the data.

Example 8.8

Construct a 95 percent prediction interval for y when x = 4 for the model determined in Example 8.2.

Solution: *The predicted value of y at x = 4 is:*

$$\hat{y}(4) = 1.18 + 2.36(4) = 10.6$$

The 95 *percent prediction interval is given by Equation 8.31 with* $\alpha = 0.05$ *where the* t *distribution has* $df_\varepsilon = n - 2 = 5 - 2 = 3$ *degrees of freedom. The required* t *value is* $t_{0.025,3} = 3.18$ *so the prediction interval for* $y(4)$ *is:*

$$P\left(\hat{y} - t_{0.025}s_\varepsilon\sqrt{1 + \frac{1}{n} + \frac{(x-\bar{x})^2}{SS_x}} < y(x) < \hat{y} + t_{0.025}s_\varepsilon\sqrt{1 + \frac{1}{n} + \frac{(x-\bar{x})^2}{SS_x}}\right) = 0.95$$

$$P\left(10.6 - 3.18 \times 2.32\sqrt{1 + \frac{1}{5} + \frac{(4-5)^2}{44}} < y(4) < 10.6 + 3.18 \times 2.32\sqrt{1 + \frac{1}{5} + \frac{(4-5)^2}{44}}\right) = 0.95$$

$$P\left(2.4 < y(4) < 18.8\right) = 0.95$$

That is, 95 *percent of the observations taken at* $x = 4$ *should have values of* y *that fall between* 2.4 *and* 18.8.

Example 8.9

   Determine the approximate prediction interval corresponding to the situation described in Example 8.8.

   Solution: *The approximate* 95 *percent prediction interval is given by:*

$$P\left(\hat{y} - t_{\alpha/2}s_\varepsilon < y(x) < \hat{y} + t_{\alpha/2}s_\varepsilon\right) < 1 - \alpha$$
$$P\left(10.6 - 3.18 \times 2.32 < y(4) < 10.6 + 3.18 \times 2.32\right) < 0.95$$
$$P\left(3.2 < y(4) < 18.0\right) < 0.95$$

This interval is narrower than the exact prediction interval by about 10 *percent but it is so much easier to calculate that it is an appealing compromise. The agreement between the approximate and exact intervals is much better when the number of observations is larger than the* $n = 5$ *case considered here, so the approximation is usually safe to use.*

Example 8.10

   Use MINITAB to construct the 95 *percent prediction interval for observations from Example 8.2.*

   Solution: *The graphical prediction interval can be constructed from MINITAB's* **Stat> Regression> Fitted Line Plot** *menu. The graphical output is shown in Figure 8.9. The values of the prediction interval at* $x = 4$ *are* 2.4 *and* 18.8 *as calculated in Example 8.8.*

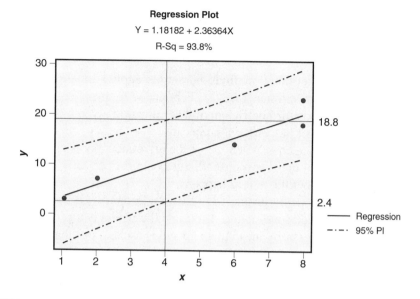

Figure 8.9 95 percent prediction interval for observations.

8.8 CORRELATION

8.8.1 The Coefficient of Determination

A comprehensive statistic is required to measure the fraction of the total variation in the response y that is explained by the regression model. The total variation in y taken relative to $\bar{y}$ is given by $SS_y = \Sigma(y_i - \bar{y})^2$, but SS_y is partitioned into two terms: one that accounts for the amount of variation explained by the straight-line model given by $SS_{regression}$ and another that accounts for the unexplained error variation given by $SS_\varepsilon = \Sigma(y_i - \hat{y}_i)^2 = \Sigma \varepsilon_i^2$. The three quantities are related by:

$$SS_y = SS_{regression} + SS_\varepsilon$$

(8.33)

Consequently, the fraction of SS_y explained by the model is:

$$r^2 = \frac{SS_{regression}}{SS_y}$$

$$= 1 - \frac{SS_\varepsilon}{SS_y}$$

(8.34)

where r^2 is called the coefficient of determination. In practice, r^2 is more easily determined from its calculating form:

$$r^2 = \frac{SS_{xy}^2}{SS_x SS_y} \tag{8.35}$$

The coefficient of determination finds numerous applications in regression and multiple regression problems. Since $SS_{regression}$ is bounded by $0 \leq SS_{regression} \leq SS_y$, there are corresponding bounds on the coefficient of determination given by $0 \leq r^2 \leq 1$. When $r^2 \simeq 0$ the regression model has little value because very little of the variation in y is attributable to its dependence on x. When $r^2 \simeq 1$ the regression model almost completely explains all of the variation in the response, that is, x almost perfectly predicts y. We're usually hoping for $r^2 = 1$, but this rarely happens.

A common mistake made by people who don't understand r^2 is to compare it to an arbitrarily chosen acceptance condition to determine if a model is a good fit to the data. A low r^2 value doesn't necessarily mean that a model is useless, just that the overall performance of the model is poor because of the large amount of random error in the data set. Even if you find a low r^2 value in an analysis, make sure to go back and look at the regression coefficients and their t values. You may find that, despite the low r^2 value, one or more of the regression coefficients is still strong and relatively well known. In the same manner, a high r^2 value doesn't necessarily mean that the model that you've fitted to the data is the right model. That is, even when r^2 is very large, the fitted model may not accurately predict the response. It's the job of *lack of fit* or *goodness of fit* tests, which will be discussed later in this chapter, to determine if a model is a good fit to the data.

Example 8.11

Calculate the values of r^2 for each of the slopes attempted in Example 8.1 and the best-fit line. Plot r^2 versus b_1 and show that the best-fit line corresponds to the maximum value of r^2.

Solution: The following table was developed from the one in Example 8.1:

b_1	0	1	2	2.36	3	4
$\sum \varepsilon_i^2$	262	102	22	16	34	134
s_ε^2	87.3	34.0	7.33	2.32	11.3	44.7
r^2	0	0.611	0.916	0.939	0.870	0.489

The r^2 values were determined from Equation 8.34 where $SS_y = 262$. The r^2 values are plotted against their b_1 values in Figure 8.10. The plot clearly shows that the best-fit line is the one that maximizes r^2. This shows, again, that the best-fit line given by linear regression is the one that has the least error.

8.8.2 The Correlation Coefficient

The correlation coefficient r is given by the square root of the coefficient of determination with an appropriate plus or minus sign. Return for a moment to the calculating

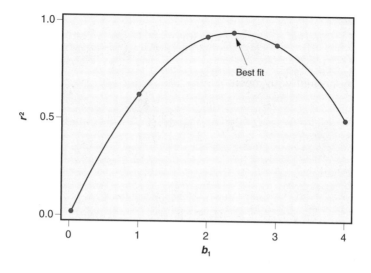

Figure 8.10 r^2 values for different slopes b_1.

form of r^2 given in Equation 8.35. Note that the sum in the numerator SS_{xy} is not actually a sum of squares, hence r can be signed. The sign of r is useful—if r is positive it means that y increases with respect to x, and if it is negative y decreases with respect to x. That is, the sign of r is the same as the sign of the slope of the regression line. Since r is determined from the appropriately signed value of

$$\sqrt{r^2}$$

and r^2 is bounded by $0 \le r^2 \le 1$, then the correlation coefficient is bounded by $-1 \le r \le 1$. Because of the ease of interpreting the coefficient of determination on a zero to 100 percent scale, it is used more frequently as a regression summary statistic than the correlation coefficient.

Whereas linear regression operates under the assumption that the values of x are known exactly, that is, without error, correlation analysis does not require the same assumption and so is more robust than linear regression. In situations where there are known errors in the x as well as the y, or when there is a need to correlate two responses, for example, y_1 and y_2, the appropriate method of analysis is correlation.

8.8.3 Confidence Interval for the Correlation Coefficient

The coefficient of determination r^2 is a statistic that estimates the degree of correlation between x and y. A different data set of (x, y) values will give a different value of r^2. The quantity that such r^2 values estimate is the true population coefficient of determination ρ^2, which is a parameter. When the distribution of the regression model residuals is normal with constant variance, the distribution of r is complicated, but the distribution of:

$$Z = \frac{1}{2}\ln\left(\frac{1+r}{1-r}\right) \tag{8.36}$$

is approximately normal with mean:

$$\mu_z = \frac{1}{2}\ln\left(\frac{1+\rho}{1-\rho}\right) \tag{8.37}$$

and standard deviation:

$$\sigma_z = \frac{1}{\sqrt{n-3}} \tag{8.38}$$

The transformation of r into Z is called *Fisher's Z transformation*. A lookup table relating Z and r is provided in Appendix A.9. This information can be used to construct a confidence interval for the unknown parameter μ_z from the statistic r and the sample size n. The confidence interval is:

$$P\left(Z - \frac{z_{\alpha/2}}{\sqrt{n-3}} < \mu_z < Z + \frac{z_{\alpha/2}}{\sqrt{n-3}}\right) = 1-\alpha \tag{8.39}$$

The inverse of the Z transform then gives a confidence interval for the correlation coefficient of the form:

$$P\left(r_L < \rho < r_U\right) = 1-\alpha \tag{8.40}$$

Fisher's Z transform is accurate when $n \geq 50$ and tolerable when $n \geq 25$. For $10 < n < 25$ a small-sample correction to Fisher's original Z transform should be used. The corrected transform is given by:

$$Z' = Z - \frac{3Z+r}{4(n-1)} \tag{8.41}$$

where Z' has standard deviation

$$\sigma_{Z'} = \frac{1}{\sqrt{n-1}} \tag{8.42}$$

The resulting confidence interval is:

$$P\left(Z' - \frac{z_{\alpha/2}}{\sqrt{n-1}} < \mu_{z'} < Z' + \frac{z_{\alpha/2}}{\sqrt{n-1}}\right) = 1-\alpha \tag{8.43}$$

The transformation from Z' back to r is given by solving Equation 8.41 for r:

$$r = 4(n-1)(Z-Z') - 3Z \qquad (8.44)$$

Example 8.12

A linear regression analysis based on $n = 30$ observations had coefficient of determination $r^2 = 0.828$. The regression assumptions of independent, normal, and homoscedastic residuals were satisfied and the linear model provided a good fit to the data. Find the 95 percent confidence interval for the true population coefficient of determination.

Solution: The sample size is sufficiently large that Fisher's Z transform should provide adequate accuracy for the confidence interval. The correlation coefficient is:

$$r = \sqrt{0.828} = 0.910$$

so the value of Fisher's Z is:

$$
\begin{aligned}
Z &= \frac{1}{2}\ln\left(\frac{1+r}{1-r}\right) \\
&= \frac{1}{2}\ln\left(\frac{1+0.910}{1-0.910}\right) \\
&= 1.528
\end{aligned}
$$

The 95 percent confidence interval for μ_z is then:

$$P\left(Z - \frac{z_{0.025}}{\sqrt{n-3}} < \mu_z < Z + \frac{z_{0.025}}{\sqrt{n-3}}\right) = 1 - 0.05$$

$$P\left(1.528 - \frac{1.96}{\sqrt{30-3}} < \mu_z < 1.528 + \frac{1.96}{\sqrt{30-3}}\right) = 0.95$$

$$P(1.151 < \mu_z < 1.905) = 0.95$$

From the table for $Z(r)$ in Appendix A.9, the values of r that correspond to $Z = 1.151$ and 1.905 are $r = 0.816$ and 0.957, respectively, so our interval for the unknown population correlation coefficient is:

$$P(0.816 < \rho < 0.957) = 0.95$$

Then the confidence interval for the unknown population coefficient of determination is:

$$P(0.666 < \rho^2 < 0.916) = 0.95$$

This example makes it very clear that despite the apparently high experimental coefficient of determination, the relatively small sample size leaves a tremendous amount of uncertainty about the true value of ρ^2. Don't be fooled into a false sense of confidence by a large value of r^2 determined from a small data set.

8.8.4 The Adjusted Correlation Coefficient

In more complex regression problems where many independent variables and possibly interaction terms enter the model, it's unfair to measure the model quality with the coefficient of determination r^2. As more and more terms are carried in a complex model, the r^2 value will always increase. This makes it necessary to penalize r^2 for the additional complexity of the model. This new coefficient of determination, called the *adjusted coefficient of determination, $r^2_{adjusted}$*, is given by:

$$r^2_{adjusted} = 1 - \frac{df_{total}SS_\varepsilon}{df_\varepsilon SS_y} \tag{8.45}$$

$r^2_{adjusted}$ is always smaller than r^2 and is the safer of the two statistics to use when evaluating a complex model.

Example 8.13
Calculate r^2 for the best fit of the data in Example 8.1 using both the defining and calculating forms given in Equations 8.34 and 8.35. Also calculate the adjusted coefficient of determination.

Solution: The sums of squares necessary to determine the correlation coefficients were already determined in Example 8.2. By the defining form of the coefficient of determination:

$$r^2 = 1 - \frac{SS_\varepsilon}{SS_y} = 1 - \frac{16.2}{262} = 0.938$$

Alternatively, by the calculating form:

$$r^2 = \frac{SS_{xy}^2}{SS_x SS_y} = \frac{104^2}{44 \times 262} = 0.938$$

The adjusted coefficient of determination is given by Equation 8.45:

$$r^2_{adjusted} = 1 - \frac{df_{total}SS_\varepsilon}{df_\varepsilon SS_y} = 1 - \frac{4(16.2)}{3(262)} = 0.918$$

8.9 LINEAR REGRESSION WITH MINITAB

MINITAB provides two basic functions for performing linear regression. The first method, accessed from the **Stat> Regression> Fitted Line Plot** menu or with the **fitline** function at the command prompt, is the best place to start to evaluate the quality of the fitted function. The output from **Stat> Regression> Fitted Line Plot** (or **fitline**) includes a scatter plot of the (x_i, y_i) data with the superimposed fitted line, a full ANOVA table, and an abbreviated table of regression coefficients. A comprehensive set of graphical residuals diagnostics can be turned on in the **Graphs** menu and there are options to fit quadratic and cubic models.

MINITAB provides a more comprehensive regression analysis from the **Stat> Regression> Regression** menu. You must specify the columns for the x and the y values, either by name or by column number, or you can invoke the regression command directly from the command line with:

```
mtb> regress c1 1 c2
```

where column `c1` contains the response y and `c2` contains the values of x. The "1" between `c1` and `c2` tells MINITAB that there is only one independent variable. This anticipates multiple linear regression, which involves more than one predictor in the model. A comprehensive set of graphical residuals diagnostics can be turned on from the **Stat> Regression> Regression> Graphs** menu.

MINITAB's **Stat> Regression> Regression** output has two parts. The first part is a table of the regression coefficients and the corresponding standard deviations, t values, and p values. The second part is the ANOVA table, which summarizes the statistics required to determine the regression coefficients and the summary statistics like r^2, r^2_{adj}, and s_ε. There is a p value reported for the slope of the regression line in the table of regression coefficients and another p value reported in the ANOVA table for the ANOVA F test. These two p values are numerically identical and not just by coincidence. There is a special relationship that exists between the t and F distributions when the F distribution has one numerator degree of freedom. This relationship is:

$$F_{\alpha,1,df_\varepsilon} = t^2_{\alpha,df_\varepsilon} \tag{8.46}$$

Because the ANOVA F value and the t value associated with the slope are mathematically equivalent, they also share the same p value.

Example 8.14

Analyze the data from Example 8.1 using MINITAB and explain the output line by line.

Solution: The MINITAB output is shown in Figure 8.11. The agreement between the calculations done above and MINITAB is excellent. The only differences are small ones

```
MTB > Name c3 "RESI1"
MTB > Regress 'y' 1 'x';
SUBC>    Residuals 'RESI1';
SUBC>    Constant;
SUBC>    Brief 2.
```

Regression Analysis: y versus x

```
The regression equation is
y = 1.18 + 2.36 x

Predictor     Coef   SE Coef      T      P
Constant     1.182     2.036   0.58  0.602
x           2.3636    0.3501   6.75  0.007


S = 2.32249   R-Sq = 93.8%    R-Sq(adj) = 91.8%


Analysis of Variance

Source           DF        SS      MS      F      P
Regression        1    245.82  245.82  45.57  0.007
Residual Error    3     16.18    5.39
Total             4    262.00

MTB > print c1-c3
```

Data Display

```
Row   x    y      RESI1
  1   1    3   -0.54545
  2   2    7    1.09091
  3   6   14   -1.36364
  4   8   18   -2.09091
  5   8   23    2.90909
```

Figure 8.11   MINITAB output for data from Example 8.1.

due to round-off error. There are not enough data points to make meaningful residuals plots so they are not shown. MINITAB determines the constant in the linear model to be $b_0 = 1.182$. The constant has standard deviation $s_{b_0} = 2.036$. For the hypothesis test of H_0: $\beta_0 = 0$ versus H_A: $\beta_0 \neq 0$, the t statistic is $t_{b_0} = b_0/s_{b_0} = 0.58$, which, with $df_\varepsilon = 3$ degrees of freedom, is not statistically significant ($p = 0.602$). The t and p values indicate that β_0 is indistinguishable from zero. The slope of the fitted line is $b_1 = 2.3636$ and its standard deviation is $s_{b_1} = 0.3501$. For the hypothesis test of H_0: $\beta_1 = 0$ versus H_A: $\beta_1 \neq 0$, the t statistic is $t_{b_1} = b_1/s_{b_1} = 2.36/0.35 = 6.75$, which is highly significant ($p = 0.007$). The degrees of freedom column indicates that there are $5 - 1 = 4$ total degrees of freedom, 1 regression degree of freedom, and $4 - 1 = 3$ error degrees of freedom. The total amount of variation in the response is $SS_{total} = 262.0$ of which $SS_{regression} = 245.82$ is explained by the linear model and the remaining $SS_\varepsilon = 262.0 - 245.8 = 16.2$ is unexplained or error variation. The mean squares are given by $MS = SS/df$ and their ratio *gives F = 45.57 which is much greater than the F = 1 value we expect if the linear model is not meaningful. The p value for this F with $df_{regression} = 1$ and $df_\varepsilon = 3$ is $p = 0.007$. The standard error of the model is given by:*

$$s_\varepsilon = \sqrt{MS_\varepsilon} = \sqrt{5.39} = 2.322$$

The coefficient of determination is $r^2 = SS_{regression}/SS_{total} = 245.82/262.0 = 0.938$. The ANOVA F value and the t value for the slope are related by $(F = 45.57) = (t^2 = 6.75^2)$ and they share the same p value. The data display at the bottom of the figure shows the x and y values used for the analysis and the model residuals ε_i are reported in the next column.

8.10 TRANSFORMATIONS TO LINEAR FORM

The usefulness of the linear regression analysis is extended tremendously when nonlinear problems can be transformed into linear form. As long as all of the regression assumptions are satisfied by the transformed variables this approach is valid.

As an example, consider a response y that depends on the single independent variable x according to:

$$y = a + bx^2$$

where a and b are to be determined by regression. After the transformation $x' = x^2$ is applied, linear regression can be used to fit a model of the form:

$$y = a + bx'$$

Generally, transformations are applied to x but sometimes, because of the structure of the expected relationship between y and x, it may be easier to apply the transformation to y instead of x. Sometimes it may even be necessary to apply transforms to both x and y variables in the same problem. An infinite number of transformations are possible. The diversity of possible transforms makes the linear regression method one of the most powerful engineering and modeling tools available.

A catalog of some common nonlinear problems that can be linearized by variable transformation is shown in Table 8.1. Some of these functions are plotted in Figure 8.12. Generally, the model attempted should be based on first principles, but if no such first principles model is available you can identify a candidate model by matching your scatter plot with one of the functions from the figure.

MINITAB makes it easy to apply variable transformations to data so that you can still use linear regression to analyze nonlinear problems. Enter the (x, y) data into two columns of the MINITAB worksheet just as you normally would. Then use MINITAB's **let** command (or the **Calc> Calculator** menu) to make the appropriate variable transformation.

Table 8.1   Transformations to linear form.

Function	y'	x'	a'	Linear Form
$y = ae^{bx}$	$\ln y$		$\ln a$	$y' = a' + bx$
$y = ax^b$	$\log y$	$\log x$	$\log a$	$y' = a' + bx'$
$y = a + \dfrac{b}{x}$		$\dfrac{1}{x}$		$y = a + bx'$
$y = \dfrac{1}{a+bx}$	$\dfrac{1}{y}$			$y' = a + bx$
$y = ae^{\frac{b}{x}}$	$\ln y$	$\dfrac{1}{x}$	$\ln a$	$y' = a' + bx'$
$y = ax^2 e^{bx}$	$\ln\left(\dfrac{y}{x^2}\right)$		$\ln a$	$y' = a' + bx$
$n = n_o e^{\frac{-\varphi}{kT}}$	$\ln n$	$\dfrac{1}{kT}$	$\ln n_o$	$y' = a' - \varphi x'$
$j = AT^2 e^{\frac{-\varphi}{kT}}$	$\ln\left(\dfrac{j}{T^2}\right)$	$\dfrac{1}{kT}$	$\ln A$	$y' = a' - \varphi x'$
$f(y) = a + bf(x)$	$f(y)$	$f(x)$		$y' = a + bx'$

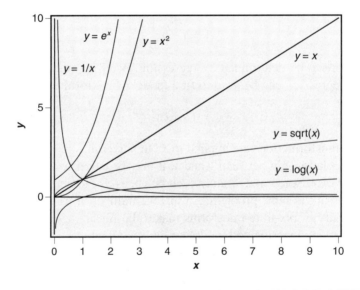

Figure 8.12   Some common functions that can be linearized.

For the example described above, if the x values reside in column $c1$ and the y values in $c2$, then create the column of x^2 values with the command:

```
mtb> let c3 = c1*c1
```

Then perform the regression for y using the x^2 values in column c3 as the independent variable:

```
mtb> regress c2 1 c3
```

Although count and proportion responses can be transformed using the methods presented in Section 5.12 and then analyzed using linear regression, there are better analysis methods available for these kinds of data but they are beyond the scope of this book. See Neter et al. (1996) or Agresti (2002) for help with the analysis of count and proportion responses.

Example 8.15

A dependent variable y is thought to have the following dependence on x:

$$y = ax^b$$

Find an appropriate transformation that linearizes the equation.

Solution: *If we take the natural log of both sides of the equation we have:*

$$\ln y = \ln\left(ax^b\right) = \ln a + b \ln x$$

If we make the substitutions $y' = \ln y$, $a' = \ln a$, and $x' = \ln x$, then our original equation can be written:

$$y' = a' + bx'$$

which is a linear equation.

Example 8.16

The deflection angle θ in radians of a solid cylindrical shaft of diameter D and length L under an applied torque τ is expected to depend on D according to:

$$\theta = \frac{\pi L \tau D^k}{32G}$$

where G is the shear modulus of the material. If an experiment is performed to study the deflection angle as a function of the cylinder diameter for a fixed material, cylinder length L, and applied torque τ, what transformation should be applied to determine k, the exponent of D?

Solution: *The equation for θ must be rewritten to isolate its dependence on D:*

$$\theta = \left(\frac{\pi L \tau}{32G}\right) D^k$$

If we take the natural log of both sides:

$$\ln\left(\theta\right) = \ln\left(\frac{\pi L \tau}{32G}\right) + k \ln\left(D\right)$$

and with the substitutions $\theta' = \ln(\theta)$, $D' = \ln(D)$, and

$$a' = \ln\left(\frac{\pi L \tau}{32G}\right)$$

we have the linear equation:

$$\theta' = a' + kD'$$

If this model is appropriate, then the slope of the line in a plot of θ' versus D' will indicate the value of k.

Example 8.17

A dependent variable y is thought to have the following dependence on x:

$$y = ae^{bx}$$

where e = 2.7182818 is the base of the natural logarithm. Find an appropriate transformation that linearizes the equation.

Solution: If we take the natural log of both sides of the equation we have:

$$\ln y = \ln\left(ae^{bx}\right) = \ln a + bx$$

If we make the substitutions $y' = \ln y$ and $a' = \ln a$ then our original equation can be written:

$$y' = a' + bx$$

which is a linear equation.

Example 8.18

A dependent variable y is thought to have the following dependence on x:

$$y = a + \frac{b}{x}$$

Find an appropriate transformation that linearizes the equation.

Solution: *If we take the reciprocal of the x values then* $x' = 1/x$ *so:*

$$y = a + bx'$$

Example 8.19

In life testing studies, the reliability of a device is its probability of survival to time t. A common model for reliability is the Weibull probability distribution given by:

$$R(t) = e^{-\left(\frac{t}{\eta}\right)^\beta}$$

where η is called the scale factor and β is called the shape factor. Find a transform that linearizes Weibull reliability as a function of time.

Solution: *The first step is to apply a natural log transform to both sides:*

$$\ln(R) = -\left(\frac{t}{\eta}\right)^\beta$$

If we multiply both sides through by -1:

$$-\ln(R) = \left(\frac{t}{\eta}\right)^\beta$$

$$\ln\left(\frac{1}{R}\right) = \left(\frac{t}{\eta}\right)^\beta$$

and if we apply another natural log transform:

$$\ln\left(\ln\left(\tfrac{1}{R}\right)\right) = \ln\left(\left(\tfrac{t}{\eta}\right)^\beta\right)$$

$$= \beta \ln\left(\tfrac{t}{\eta}\right)$$

$$= \beta \ln(t) - \beta \ln(\eta)$$

Finally, if we define $R' = \ln(\ln(1/R))$, $t' = \ln(t)$, and $\eta' = \beta \ln(\eta)$ this equation has the form:

$$R' = \beta t' - \eta'$$

which is linear in t'.

In practice we would put n units up for life test and record their failure times. Then, for the ith failure at time t_i, we estimate the reliability with:

$$\hat{R}_i = 1 - \frac{i}{n+1}$$

If the failure times come from a Weibull population, then the transformed values of $(t_i, \hat{R}_i)$ given by $(t'_i, \hat{R}'_i)$ as defined above should fall along a straight line.

*MINITAB supports Weibull plots of complete failure data from its **Graph> Probability Plot** menu with the **Weibull** option, and plots of censored data from its **Stat> Reliability/ Survival> Distribution Analysis (Right Censoring)** and **Stat> Reliability/Survival> Distribution Analysis (Arbitrary Censoring)** menus.*

8.11 POLYNOMIAL MODELS

The form of a model attempted for $y(x)$ should always be based on an understanding of the first-principles relationship between y and x (that is, the first principles of chemistry, physics, biology, economics, and so on). In many cases a simple linear model is sufficient. In other cases the first-principles relationship might suggest the need to transform one or perhaps both variables before a linear model can be fitted. However, when the (x, y) data display some complex nonlinear behavior and there is no known first-principles explanation for that behavior, it usually becomes necessary to consider a polynomial model. The general form of a polynomial model is:

$$\hat{y} = b_0 + b_1 x + b_2 x^2 + \cdots + b_p x^p \tag{8.47}$$

where the polynomial is said to be of order p. The regression coefficients $b_0, b_1, \ldots,$ b_p are determined using the same algorithm that was used for the simple linear model; the error sum of squares is simultaneously minimized with respect to the regression coefficients. The family of equations that must be solved to determine the regression coefficients is nightmarish, but most of the good statistical software packages have this capability.

Although high-order polynomial models can fit the (x, y) data very well, they should be of the lowest order possible that accurately represents the relationship between y and x. There are no clear guidelines on what order might be necessary, but watch the significance (that is, the p values) of the various regression coefficients to confirm that all of the terms are contributing to the model. Polynomial models must also be hierarchical, that is, a model of order p must contain all possible lower-order terms.

Because of their complexity, it's important to summarize the performance of polynomial models using $r^2_{adjusted}$ instead of r^2. In some cases when there are relatively few error degrees of freedom after fitting a large polynomial model, the r^2 value could be misleadingly large whereas $r^2_{adjusted}$ will be much lower but more representative of the true performance of the model.

Example 8.20

Write out the third-order polynomial model for y (x) and describe how the standard error of the model is calculated.

Solution: The third-order polynomial model for y (x) has the form:

$$\hat{y} = b_0 + b_1 x + b_2 x^2 + b_3 x^3$$

The error sum of squares is given by:

$$SS_\varepsilon = \sum \varepsilon_i^2$$

where

$$\varepsilon_i = y_i - \hat{y}_i = y_i - (b_0 + b_1 x_i + b_2 x_i^2 + b_3 x_i^3)$$

If there are n (x, y) observations in the data set there will be $df_{total} = n - 1$ total degrees of freedom where a degree of freedom is lost to calculate $(\bar{x}, \bar{y})$. Each of the four regression coefficients consumes a degree of freedom but only the first three are independent so $df_{model} = 3$. By subtraction there will be $df_\varepsilon = n - 4$ error degrees of freedom so the standard error of the model will be:

$$s_\varepsilon = \sqrt{\frac{SS_\varepsilon}{df_\varepsilon}} = \sqrt{\frac{\sum_{i=1}^{n} \varepsilon_i^2}{n - 4}}$$

Most statistical software packages and spreadsheets provide functions to perform polynomial regression. In MINITAB, you must construct a column for each power of x that you want to include in the model and then instruct MINITAB to include all of those columns in the model. The **Stat> Regression> Regression** menu or the **regress** command at the command prompt are used to perform the regression calculations.

Example 8.21

Use MINITAB to construct a third-order polynomial model for the following data:

x	8.9	8.7	0.1	5.4	4.3	2.4	3.4	6.8	2.9	5.6	8.4	0.7	3.8	9.5	0.7
y	126	143	58	50	40	38	41	66	47	65	138	49	56	163	45

Solution: The MINITAB commands to fit the third-order polynomial are shown in Figure 8.13. The y values were loaded into column c1 of the MINITAB worksheet and the x values were loaded into column c2. The x^2 and x^3 values were calculated in c3 and c4, respectively. The data and the fitted function are plotted in Figure 8.14. Despite the fact that the model looks like it fits the data well, the regression coefficients are not statistically significant. Another model should be considered such as a lower-order polynomial or perhaps a model involving a transformation.

```
MTB > name c1 'y'
MTB > name c2 'x'
MTB > name c3 'x^2'
MTB > name c4 'x^3'
MTB > let 'x^2'='x'**2
MTB > let 'x^3'='x'**3
MTB > Regress 'y' 3 'x' 'x^2' 'x^3';
SUBC>    Constant;
SUBC>    Brief 2.
```

Regression Analysis: y versus x, x^2, x^3

```
The regression equation is
y = 54.8 - 7.49 x + 0.65 x^2 + 0.143 x^3

Predictor    Coef   SE Coef      T      P
Constant   54.783     7.932   6.91  0.000
x          -7.486     8.138  -0.92  0.377
x^2         0.651     2.150   0.30  0.768
x^3        0.1431    0.1513   0.95  0.365

S = 9.88422   R-Sq = 95.9%   R-Sq(adj) = 94.8%

Analysis of Variance

Source          DF        SS       MS      F      P
Regression       3   25429.3   8476.4  86.76  0.000
Residual Error  11    1074.7     97.7
Total           14   26504.0

Source  DF   Seq SS
x        1  18452.9
x^2      1   6889.2
x^3      1     87.3
```

Figure 8.13 Fitting a third-order polynomial.

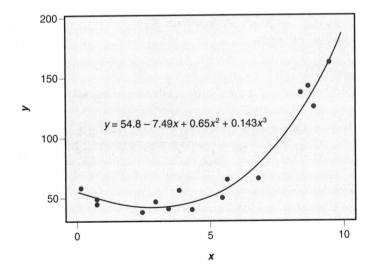

Figure 8.14 Third-order polynomial fitted to example data.

8.12 GOODNESS OF FIT TESTS

Whenever a model is fitted to data it's necessary to test the resulting goodness of the fit. The fit is judged to be good when the mean of observed values of the response y taken at a fixed level of x coincides with the predicted value of y from the model. (See Figure 8.16, page 311, for an example of a linear fit that does not provide a good fit to the data.) Many people are under the misconception that the goodness of fit is indicated by the coefficient of determination r^2, but goodness of fit and correlation are two different issues. While a model with a high r^2 explains much of the observed variation in the response, that model doesn't necessarily provide a good fit to the data.

There are many methods that can be used to judge the goodness of a linear model's fit to data: post-regression graphical diagnostics, the use of a quadratic model, and the linear lack of fit test. MINITAB supports all of these methods. The first method is a simple graphical technique that only requires the proper training and practice to interpret correctly. The last two methods are more formal quantitative methods. The purpose of this section is to present all three of these techniques.

8.12.1 The Quadratic Model As a Test of Linear Goodness of Fit

The quadratic model goodness of fit test for the linear model uses the hypotheses H_0: *there is no curvature in the data* versus H_A: *there is curvature in the data*. The test is performed by fitting a quadratic model to the data:

$$y = b_0 + b_1 x + b_2 x^2 \tag{8.48}$$

where the regression coefficients b_0, b_1, and b_2 are estimates of parameters β_0, β_1, and β_2, respectively. The decision to accept or reject the null hypothesis regarding curvature is based on the significance of the b_2 regression coefficient. That is, the hypotheses can be mathematically expressed as H_0: $\beta_2 = 0$ versus H_A: $\beta_2 \neq 0$ and the test is carried out using the t test method described earlier, where:

$$t_{b_2} = \frac{b_2}{s_{b_2}} \tag{8.49}$$

is compared to $t_{\alpha/2}$ with $df_\varepsilon = n - 3$ degrees of freedom. If t_{b2} is statistically significant then there is evidence that the linear model does not fit the data. If t_{b2} is not statistically significant then the quadratic term can be dropped from the model and the linear model provides a good fit.

The quadratic model for linear lack of fit is especially useful when an independent variable x has just three discrete levels in an experiment. This situation is encountered frequently in designed experiments as we will see in Chapter 11. When there are more than three levels of x in an experiment, the linear lack of fit test is preferred over the quadratic model. The quadratic model may still be effective, but there are some situations in which it will not detect lack of fit that the linear lack of fit test picks up easily.

Example 8.22

Fit the following data with an appropriate model and use scatter plots and residuals diagnostic plots to check for lack of fit.

x	3	3	3	5	5	5	7	7	7	9	9	9	11	11	11
y	65	60	62	86	85	89	100	102	98	109	113	112	117	112	118

Solution: The linear regression model is shown in Figure 8.15. From the coefficient of determination $r^2 = 0.92$ and the highly significant regression coefficients everything looks just great, but the fitted line plot and residuals versus x plot in Figure 8.16 suggest

```
MTB > Regress 'y' 1 'x';
SUBC>   Constant;
SUBC>   Brief 2.

Regression Analysis: y versus x

The regression equation is
y = 49.2 + 6.57 x

Predictor    Coef   SE Coef      T       P
Constant   49.233     4.054   12.14   0.000
x           6.5667    0.5370   12.23   0.000

S = 5.88261    R-Sq = 92.0%    R-Sq(adj) = 91.4%

Analysis of Variance

Source          DF       SS      MS       F       P
Regression       1   5174.5  5174.5  149.53   0.000
Residual Error  13    449.9    34.6
Total           14   5624.4
```

Figure 8.15   Linear fit to data from Example 8.22.

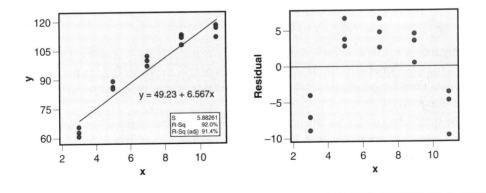

Figure 8.16   Linear fit and residuals diagnostic plot for Example 8.22.

that there might be a problem with curvature. The graphs clearly indicate that the model overpredicts the response y when x is at its extreme values and the model under-predicts y when x takes on intermediate values. Clearly, the linear model is insufficient to express y(x).

Since it appears that there might be significant curvature in y(x), the next step is to fit a quadratic model to the data. The quadratic model has the form given in Equation 8.48 where the squared term quantifies the amount of curvature present. The quadratic model was fitted and is shown in Figure 8.17. From the regression and ANOVA tables, this new model looks much better than the original linear model. The r^2 is much higher, the standard error is smaller, but more importantly, the coefficient of the quadratic term in the model is highly significant. This indicates that there is significant curvature in the data and that the quadratic model really is necessary. The fitted line plot and residuals versus x plot are shown in Figure 8.18. The improvement in the quality of the fit is obvious. These observations all suggest that the quadratic model provides a better fit to the data than the linear model does. The goodness of fit of the quadratic model could be tested by fitting a cubic model to the data and testing the regression coefficient of the x^3 term for statistical significance; however, the two plots suggest that this is an unnecessary step.

```
MTB > name c3 'x^2'
MTB > let 'x^2'='x'*'x'
MTB > Regress 'y' 2 'x' 'x^2';
SUBC>    Constant;
SUBC>    Brief 2.

Regression Analysis: y versus x, x^2

The regression equation is
y = 18.5 + 17.1 x - 0.750 x^2

Predictor       Coef  SE Coef       T      P
Constant      18.483    4.222    4.38  0.001
x             17.067    1.340   12.73  0.000
x^2          -0.75000  0.09440   -7.94  0.000

S = 2.44722   R-Sq = 98.7%   R-Sq(adj) = 98.5%

Analysis of Variance

Source           DF       SS      MS       F      P
Regression        2   5552.5  2776.3  463.57  0.000
Residual Error   12     71.9     6.0
Total            14   5624.4

Source   DF   Seq SS
x         1   5174.5
x^2       1    378.0
```

Figure 8.17   Quadratic fit to data from Example 8.22.

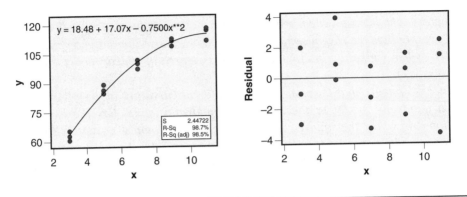

Figure 8.18 Quadratic fit and residuals diagnostic plot for Example 8.22.

8.12.2 The Linear Lack of Fit Test

The linear lack of fit test is a powerful alternative to the quadratic model for testing goodness of fit. The rationale for the linear lack of fit test is relatively simple: the linear lack of fit test contrasts the error estimates from two models for the same data. The first model is the usual regression model. The second model is a one-way classification model fitted using ANOVA where the treatments are defined by the x values.* Because the one-way ANOVA model always has more degrees of freedom than the linear regression model it must always fit the data better, so its error sum of squares must be smaller. Since the residuals from the ANOVA model can only be due to random error about the treatment means, their contribution to the total variability is referred to as *pure error*. In contrast, the linear regression residuals can get contributions from two sources: a contribution from truly random or pure error and a contribution due to biases in the treatment means from the values predicted by the linear model. If the linear model is valid then the treatment means defined by the one-way classification based on x will fall on or near the values predicted by the linear model. If, however, the treatment means differ substantially from the values predicted by the linear model then there is evidence of linear lack of fit and another model— something other than the linear model—should be considered.

The lack of fit test calculations are done by constructing and combining the results of the linear regression and one-way ANOVA models. The allocation of sums of squares for the linear lack of fit test is shown in Figure 8.19 where $SS_{\varepsilon(PureError)}$ is the error sum of squares taken directly from the one-way ANOVA model; that is: $SS_{\varepsilon(PureError)} = SS_{\varepsilon(ANOVA)}$. The sum of squares associated with linear lack of fit is given by the difference between the error sums of squares of the two models:

$$SS_{\varepsilon(LOF)} = SS_{\varepsilon(Regression)} - SS_{\varepsilon(PureError)} \tag{8.50}$$

---

* When repeated observations are not made at identical x values, the observations can still be grouped for the linear lack of fit test according to comparable x values.

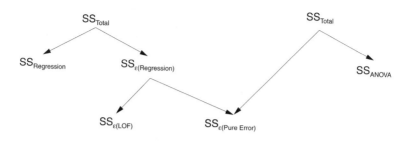

Figure 8.19 Relationship between ANOVA and regression sums of squares.

$SS_{\varepsilon(LOF)}$ is always positive because the ANOVA model is always more complex than the regression model, so $SS_{\varepsilon(PureError)}$ will always be smaller than $SS_{\varepsilon(Regression)}$.

The degrees of freedom for the linear lack of fit calculations also break down according to the tree diagram in Figure 8.19. (Just replace each SS in the figure with df.) The degrees of freedom associated with linear lack of fit are given by the difference between the error degrees of freedom from the two models:

$$df_{\varepsilon(LOF)} = df_{\varepsilon(Regression)} - df_{\varepsilon(PureError)} \qquad (8.51)$$

The mean square associated with lack of fit is given by:

$$MS_{\varepsilon(LOF)} = SS_{\varepsilon(LOF)} / df_{\varepsilon(LOF)} \qquad (8.52)$$

which is tested for significance against the ANOVA (or pure) error mean square:

$$F_{LOF} = MS_{\varepsilon(LOF)} / MS_{\varepsilon(PureError)} \qquad (8.53)$$

If F_{LOF} is statistically significant then we must accept the hypothesis that the linear model does not fit the data and another model—perhaps one with curvature—should be considered. Table 8.2 shows the structure of the new linear regression ANOVA table, which includes the linear lack of fit calculations.

MINITAB supports lack of fit calculations from the **Options> Lack of Fit Tests** menu in **Stat> Regression> Regression**. If two or more observations are taken at each level of x, then use the **Pure Error** option. If the x values are not repeated, then use the **Data Subsetting** option.

Example 8.23

Use MINITAB's pure error lack of fit test option to perform the linear lack of fit test for the data from Example 8.22. Use the results from the linear regression and ANOVA analyses to confirm the lack of fit test results.

Table 8.2 ANOVA table layout with lack of fit.

Source	df	SS	MS	F
Regression	$df_{Regression}$	$SS_{Regression}$	$MS_{Regression}$	$F_{Regression}$
Residual Error	$df_{\varepsilon(Regression)}$	$SS_{\varepsilon(Regression)}$	$MS_{\varepsilon(Regression)}$	
Lack of Fit	$df_{\varepsilon(LOF)}$	$SS_{\varepsilon(LOF)}$	$MS_{\varepsilon(LOF)}$	$F_{\varepsilon(LOF)}$
Pure Error	$df_{\varepsilon(PureError)}$	$SS_{\varepsilon(PureError)}$	$MS_{\varepsilon(PureError)}$	
Total	df_{Total}	SS_{Total}		

```
MTB > Regress 'y' 1 'x';
SUBC>    Constant;
SUBC>    Pure;
SUBC>    Brief 2.

Regression Analysis: y versus x

The regression equation is
y = 49.2 + 6.57 x

Predictor    Coef   SE Coef      T       P
Constant   49.233     4.054   12.14   0.000
x          6.5667    0.5370   12.23   0.000

S = 5.88261   R-Sq = 92.0%   R-Sq(adj) = 91.4%

Analysis of Variance

Source          DF      SS      MS       F       P
Regression       1  5174.5  5174.5  149.53   0.000
Residual Error  13   449.9    34.6
  Lack of Fit    3   391.2   130.4   22.23   0.000
  Pure Error    10    58.7     5.9
Total           14  5624.4
```

Figure 8.20 MINITAB's regression output with lack of fit information.

Solution: The MINITAB regression output showing the results of the pure error lack of fit test is shown in Figure 8.20. The significant lack of fit term ($F_{LOF} = 22.23$, $p_{LOF} = 0.000$) indicates that the linear model does not fit the data.

The linear regression and one-way ANOVA analyses of the data are shown in Figures 8.15, page 310, and 8.21, respectively. The sum of squares associated with lack of fit is given by the difference between the error sums of squares of the two models as in Equation 8.50:

$$SS_{\varepsilon(LOF)} = 449.9 - 58.67 = 391.23$$

Similarly, the degrees of freedom to estimate the lack of fit is given by the difference between the degrees of freedom of the two models as in Equation 8.51:

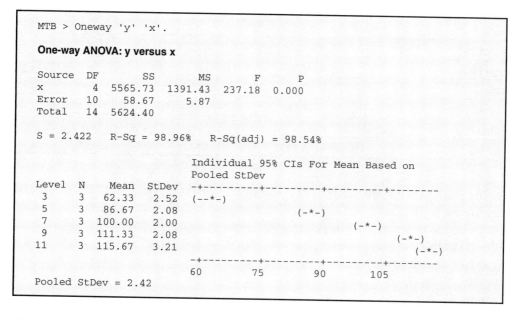

```
MTB > Oneway 'y' 'x'.

One-way ANOVA: y versus x

Source   DF        SS       MS        F        P
x         4   5565.73  1391.43   237.18    0.000
Error    10     58.67     5.87
Total    14   5624.40


S = 2.422   R-Sq = 98.96%   R-Sq(adj) = 98.54%

                         Individual 95% CIs For Mean Based on
                         Pooled StDev
Level  N    Mean   StDev  -+---------+---------+---------+--------
 3     3   62.33   2.52   (--*-)
 5     3   86.67   2.08                  (-*-)
 7     3  100.00   2.00                          (-*-)
 9     3  111.33   2.08                              (-*-)
11     3  115.67   3.21                                 (-*-)
                          -+---------+---------+---------+--------
                          60        75        90       105
Pooled StDev = 2.42
```

Figure 8.21   ANOVA model from Example 8.22.

$$df_{\varepsilon(LOF)} = 13 - 10 = 3$$

The mean square associated with lack of fit is given by Equation 8.52:

$$MS_{\varepsilon(LOF)} = \frac{SS_{\varepsilon(LOF)}}{df_{\varepsilon(LOF)}} = \frac{391.23}{3} = 130.4$$

This mean square is tested for significance by comparing it to $MS_{\varepsilon(PureError)}$ according to Equation 8.53:

$$F_{LOF} = \frac{MS_{\varepsilon(LOF)}}{MS_{\varepsilon(PureError)}} = \frac{130.4}{5.87} = 22.2$$

F_{LOF} has $df_{\varepsilon(LOF)} = 3$ numerator degrees of freedom and $df_{\varepsilon(PureError)} = 10$ denominator degrees of freedom. Its corresponding p value is $p_{LOF} = 0.0001$, which is highly significant. The lack of fit sums of squares, degrees of freedom, mean squares, F, and p values all confirm the results of MINITAB's lack of fit calculations. Evidently there is evidence of lack of fit in the linear model.

The lack of fit test method can be extended to test for lack of fit in any fitted function provided that the observations can be broken up into enough different groups that there are sufficient degrees of freedom to perform the test. As a minimum, the number

Table 8.3 Lack of fit calculations for quadratic model.

Source	df	SS	MS	F	p
Regression	2	5552.5	2776.25	463.5	0.000
Error	12	71.9	5.99		
Lack of Fit	2	13.2	6.6	1.12	0.363
Pure Error	10	58.7	5.87		
Total	14	5624.4			

of groupings according to the x variable must be at least one greater than the number of regression coefficients in the fitted model. For example, to test a quadratic model for lack of fit, the observations must be classified into at least four groups. MINITAB does not support these calculations but they are relatively easy to perform by comparing the regression and ANOVA reports.

Example 8.24

Test the quadratic model for the data from Example 8.22 for lack of fit.

Solution: The quadratic and one-way classification models are given in Figures 8.17, page 311, and 8.21, respectively. The degrees of freedom and sums of squares were taken from these figures and used to construct the ANOVA table showing the lack of fit calculations for the quadratic model in Table 8.3. The relatively small F_{LOF} value and corresponding large p_{LOF} value indicate that there is no evidence of lack of fit in the quadratic model. Apparently the quadratic model is a good fit to the data.

8.13 ERRORS IN VARIABLES

The previous section dealt with the issue of a regression assumption violation—that the linear model did not provide a good fit to the data. Another type of regression assumption violation occurs when there is random error in the independent variable x. This conflicts with the requirement that the x values be known exactly. The consequence of this assumption violation is that the resulting regression coefficients determined using methods from this chapter become biased; however, when the standard deviation of the random error in the x values is known or can be estimated, then the bias in the regression coefficients can be removed using *errors-in-variables* regression analysis.

Consider a situation in which a response y is a linear function of an independent variable x:

$$y_i = a + bx_i + \varepsilon_i \tag{8.54}$$

where the ε_i are normally distributed errors with $\mu_\varepsilon = 0$ and constant variance σ_ε^2. All appears to be fine, except suppose that the x_i are not directly measurable and can only be approximated by an observable quantity w_i:

$$x_i = w_i + u_i \tag{8.55}$$

where the u_i are normally distributed errors with mean $\mu_u = 0$ and constant variance σ_u^2. Since the x_i are not known, we cannot fit $y(x)$ so we must settle for $y(w)$ obtaining:

$$y = a_w + b_w w \tag{8.56}$$

where the subscript w indicates that the regression coefficients are calculated from the (w, y) observations. It can be shown (with difficulty) that the true regression coefficient b is related to b_w by:

$$b = b_w \left(\frac{\sigma_w^2}{\sigma_w^2 - \sigma_u^2} \right) \tag{8.57}$$

where σ_w^2 is the variance of the w observations and σ_u^2 must be known or estimated from repeated x observations or from an independent experiment. Once the corrected value of b is determined, the corrected value of a is given by:

$$a = \bar{y} - b\bar{w} \tag{8.58}$$

and the error variance σ_ε^2 can be recovered from:

$$\sigma_\varepsilon^2 = \sigma_{\varepsilon(y(w))}^2 - b^2 \sigma_u^2 \tag{8.59}$$

where $\sigma_{\varepsilon(y(w))}^2$ is the error variance from the linear fit of $y(w)$.

8.14 WEIGHTED REGRESSION

The linear regression method assumes that the regression model residuals are homoscedastic so that all observations in the data set deserve to be weighted equally in the analysis. When the residuals are heteroscedastic, the observations with greater inherent noise deserve to be weighted less heavily than those observations where the noise is smaller. The usual first approach to dealing with heteroscedastic residuals is to attempt a variable transformation that recovers the homoscedasticity of the residuals, but when such a transform cannot be found, it becomes necessary to introduce weighting factors for each observation. The new array of observations has the form (x_i, y_i, w_i) where the w_i are the weighting factors. The w_i are chosen to be the reciprocals of the local error variance:

$$w_i = \frac{1}{\sigma_i^2} \tag{8.60}$$

The result of applying such weights to observations is that the weighted residuals given by:

$$\varepsilon_i' = \sqrt{w_i} \, \varepsilon_i \tag{8.61}$$

will be homoscedastic, which satisfies the modified regression assumption. This approach is equivalent to minimizing $SS_{\varepsilon'} = \Sigma w_i \varepsilon_i^2$ instead of the usual $SS_\varepsilon = \Sigma \varepsilon_i^2$ with respect to the regression coefficients.

In most cases, the values of the error variance to associate with the observations are unknown and must be determined empirically. When there are many repeated observations at a limited set of x_i values the σ_i^2 can be estimated from each set. When there are not repeated observations but the ε_i appear to be systematically related to the x_i, the usual approach is to try to find a function of the form $\varepsilon_i^2 = f(x_i)$, then to use the resulting function to predict error variances for each observation, and finally to determine the necessary weighting factors from $w_i = 1/\hat{\sigma}_i^2$.

MINITAB's **Stat> Regression> Regression** function allows the column of weights w_i to be specified from its **Options** menu. See MINITAB's **Help** files or Neter et al. (1996) for help with weighted regression.

8.15 CODED VARIABLES

In many situations it is necessary to use coded levels of an independent variable instead of the actual quantitative levels of that variable. This is usually done when only two or three equally spaced levels of a quantitative variable are required. The codes used are just like the transforms used to get from measurement units on an x axis to standard normal z units, or from x to t units, or from sample variance s^2 to χ^2 units. The codes required here are actually much easier to use than any of these transforms. It is generally not necessary to be concerned with coding when there is just one independent variable in a problem. However, as soon as two or more independent variables are involved, coding becomes a necessity.

In many experiments only two levels of a quantitative variable will be considered. Rather than using the values of the quantitative levels in calculations, the two levels are referenced by the codes –1 for the smaller level and +1 for the larger level. This arrangement is shown in Figure 8.22, however, we require a more formal relationship between the two scales. Consider the same situation described in Figure 8.23. The coding makes use of two quantities from the x or original measurement units axis: the midpoint or zero level between the –1 and +1 levels, and the step size from the zero level out to the –1 and +1 levels. Let's let the zero level be denoted x_0 and the step size be denoted Δx. Then

Figure 8.22 Original and coded axes.

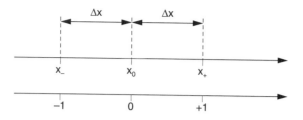

Figure 8.23 Transformation between original and coded values.

it makes sense to let the −1 and +1 levels of x be denoted x_- and x_+, respectively. If we let the coded levels of x be indicated by the symbol x', then we can easily switch from a value in original measurement units to its corresponding coded value with:

$$x' = \frac{x - x_0}{\Delta x} \tag{8.62}$$

And by solving this equation for x we can easily switch from coded units back to measurement units:

$$x = x_0 + x'\Delta x \tag{8.63}$$

This looks messy now, but the use of coded variables is so common that shortly you will do it without thinking about it. The x' notation is also not used universally, it's just been introduced here for clarity, and you will not see it used in this book outside of this chapter. It should also be apparent that the transformation equations that have just been defined are linear equations much like the ones discussed earlier in this chapter. It is possible and entirely appropriate to redraw Figures 8.22 and 8.23 as x–y plots with x on the vertical axis and x' on the horizontal axis, but since the transforms will generally be used in place of the original measurement values it makes sense to think of the two scales in parallel, as they are presented in the figures.

Example 8.25

An experiment is performed with two levels of temperature: 25C and 35C. If these are the −1 and +1 levels of temperature, respectively, then find the coded value that corresponds to 28C.

*   **Solution:** *The zero level of temperature is $x_0 = 30C$ and the step size to the −1 and +1 levels is $\Delta x = 5C$, so the transformation equation to coded units is:*

$$x' = \frac{x - 30}{5}$$

Then the coded value of $x = 28C$ is:

$$x' = \frac{28 - 30}{5} = -0.4$$

The solution is shown graphically in Figure 8.24.

Example 8.26

Use the definitions in the preceding example to determine the temperature that has a coded value of $x' = +0.6$.

Solution: The equation to transform from coded to actual values is:

$$x = 30 + 5x'$$

so the actual temperature that corresponds to the coded value $x' = +0.6$ is:

$$x = 30 + 5(0.6) = 33$$

The solution is shown graphically in Figure 8.25.

8.16 MULTIPLE REGRESSION

When a response has n quantitative predictors such as $y (x_1, x_2, \ldots, x_n)$, the model for y must be created by *multiple regression*. In multiple regression each predictive term in

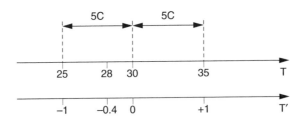

Figure 8.24 Transformation of *T* = 28C to coded units.

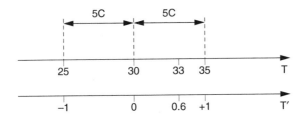

Figure 8.25 Transformation of *T'* = 0.6 coded units back to temperature *T* units.

the model has its own regression coefficient. The simplest multiple regression model contains a linear term for each predictor:

$$y = b_0 + b_1 x_1 + b_2 x_2 + \cdots + b_n x_n \tag{8.64}$$

This equation has the same basic structure as the polynomial model in Equation 8.47 and, in fact, the two models are fitted and analyzed in much the same way. Where the worksheet to fit the polynomial model requires n columns, one for each power of x, the worksheet to fit the multiple regression model requires n columns to account for each of the n predictors. The same regression methods are used to analyze both problems.

Frequently, the simple linear model in Equation 8.64 does not fit the data and a more complex model is required. The terms that must be added to the model to achieve a good fit might involve interactions, quadratic terms, or terms of even higher order. Such models have the basic form:

$$y = b_0 + b_1 x_1 + b_2 x_2 + \cdots + b_{12} x_1 x_2 + \cdots + b_{11} x_1^2 + b_{22} x_2^2 + \cdots \tag{8.65}$$

and must be hierarchical, that is, if a complex term is to be included in the model then all of the simpler terms that can be derived from it must also be present in the model. For example, if a model is to contain a term like $b_{123} x_1 x_2 x_3$ then the model must also contain x_1, x_2, x_3, x_{12}, x_{13}, and x_{23}. Complex equations like this can be fitted in the usual way after a column is created in the worksheet for each term in the model.

The relationship between the levels used in an experiment for the different quantitative predictors plays a role in determining what model can be fitted for the response. Ideally, the predictors should be completely independent of each other. Then each predictor can be included in the model and their effects will be quantified independently. Things become more complicated when predictors are dependent on each other. Suppose that two predictors are perfectly correlated, that is, that the magnitude of their correlation coefficient is unity. A series of models can be constructed that contain either or both variables; however, when both variables are included in the model, it is impossible to determine unique regression coefficients for the predictors. In fact, there are an infinite number of sets of regression coefficients that deliver identical performance. This problem limits the predictive use of the model to those cases in which the correlation between the two predictors is preserved. If the correlation is broken then the model cannot be used because the independent effects of the predictors have not been determined.

An experiment that has correlated quantitative predictors is said to suffer from a form of variable confounding called *colinearity*. Colinearity is a continuous, not binary, characteristic of an experiment design. Generally, we wish to have complete independence between our predictive variables, but sometimes, by design or by chance, some degree of dependence appears between variables. For example, in a passive experiment (that is, where the experimental input and output variables are observed but not controlled) certain predictors may be naturally and uncontrollably correlated. Special analysis methods and interpretations are available for problems that suffer from some colinearity, but the general nature of DOE is to avoid colinearity so that these methods are not necessary.

To demonstrate the difficulties caused by colinearity, consider a simple example. Suppose that a response y depends on two predictors x_1 and x_2, that an experiment is performed in which all of the observations are taken such that $x_1 = x_2$, and that when y is modeled as a function of x_1, an excellent fit of the form $y = 10x_1$ is obtained that meets all of the requirements of the regression method. The response could also be expressed as $y = 10x_2$, or combinations of x_1 and x_2 could be considered, for example: $y = 5x_1 + 5x_2$, $y = -5x_1 + 15x_2$, $y = 20x_1 - 10x_2$, and an infinite number of others are possible. [If you want to check that all of these give the same answer, try an example like $y (x_1, x_2) = y (1, 1)$.] Although these are all excellent models for y, they are all constrained by the condition $x_1 = x_2$. As long as this condition is satisfied then y can be safely predicted from any of these models, but as soon as the correlation between x_1 and x_2 is broken then none of the models can be used. If we are going to go to the trouble of doing an experiment, we would prefer to do it such that the effects of x_1 and x_2 could be determined independently.

The specific intent of DOE is to avoid the problems caused by correlated predictors. Designs that have independent predictors are called *orthogonal* designs. Except for some special cases, these are the designs that will be considered in the remaining chapters of this book. The orthogonality of a design is often evaluated by constructing a matrix of the correlation coefficients (r) between all possible pairs of predictors. Designs that are orthogonal will have $r = 0$ for all pairs of predictors.

Multiple regression can be used to fit both empirical and first-principles models to data; however, the values used in the model for the different predictors depends on which type of model is being fitted. When an empirical model is being fitted and includes an interaction between two independent variables, the variables must first be coded using the methods described in Section 8.15. If variables are not coded then incorrect regression coefficients may be obtained for the main effects and interactions. When a first-principles model is being fitted then the variables may be expressed in their original measurement units. Then the regression coefficients are often equal to physical or material constants suggested by the first-principles model.

Multiple regression can be performed from MINITAB's **Stat> Regression> Regression** menu or with the **regress** command at the command prompt. Each predictor must be created in a separate column of the worksheet before the model can be fitted. This might require you to explicitly create columns for the squares of variables, interactions, and any transformations. Use the **let** command (or **Stat> Calc> Calculator**) to create these columns. The syntax for the regression command from the command prompt is similar to that for regression on one predictor variable. For example, to regress a response in c1 as a function of three predictors in columns c2, c3, and c4 use:

```
mtb > regress c1 3 c2-c4
```

Example 8.27

Analyze the following 2^2 experiment with two replicates using multiple linear regression. Use an empirical model including terms for x_1, x_2, and their interaction.

Compare the model obtained by fitting the original numerical values of the predictors with the model obtained by fitting the transformed values.

x_1	x_2	y
10	40	286,1
10	50	114,91
100	40	803,749
100	50	591,598

     Solution: *The data were entered into a MINITAB worksheet with a single response in each row. Then the x_1 and x_2 columns were multiplied together using the **let** command to create the x_{12} interaction column. Figure 8.26 shows a matrix plot of the response and the three predictors created with **Graph> Matrix Plot**. The first row of plots shows that y appears to increase with respect to x_1 and x_{12} but does not appear to depend on x_2 at all. The plot of x_1 versus x_2 shows that they are independent of each other, the plot of x_1 versus x_{12} shows that they are very strongly correlated, and the plot of x_2 versus x_{12} shows that they are mostly independent of each other.*

     Figure 8.27 shows the data and multiple regression analysis using the original values of the predictors. The correlation matrix of the predictors confirms the observations made from the matrix plot: x_1 and x_2 are independent ($r = 0$), x_1 and x_{12} are strongly correlated ($r = 0.985$), and x_2 and x_{12} are weakly correlated ($r = 0.134$). None of the predictors in the regression analysis are statistically significant. This result is unexpected because of the apparently strong correlations observed between the response and x_1 and x_{12} in the matrix plot.

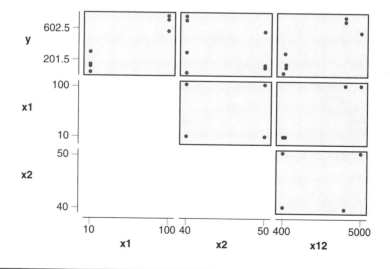

Figure 8.26   Matrix plot of response and uncoded predictors.

```
MTB > print c1-c4

Data Display

Row    y    x1   x2    x12
  1  286    10   40    400
  2    1    10   40    400
  3  114    10   50    500
  4   91    10   50    500
  5  803   100   40   4000
  6  749   100   40   4000
  7  591   100   50   5000
  8  598   100   50   5000

MTB > corr c2-c4;
SUBC> nopvalue.

Correlations: x1, x2, x12

          x1      x2
x2     0.000
x12    0.985   0.134

Cell Contents: Pearson correlation

MTB > regress c1 3 c2-c4

Regression Analysis: y versus x1, x2, x12

The regression equation is
y = 175 + 13.3 x1 - 2.5 x2 - 0.156 x12

Predictor      Coef   SE Coef       T       P
Constant      174.8     520.3    0.34   0.754
x1           13.272     7.321    1.81   0.144
x2            -2.54     11.49   -0.22   0.836
x12         -0.1561    0.1617   -0.97   0.389

S = 102.907   R-Sq = 94.0%   R-Sq(adj) = 89.5%

Analysis of Variance

Source           DF       SS       MS       F       P
Regression        3   666873   222291   20.99   0.007
Residual Error    4    42359    10590
Total             7   709233

Source   DF   Seq SS
x1        1   632250
x2        1    24753
x12       1     9870
```

Figure 8.27   Multiple regression analysis using original values of the predictors.

The regression analysis in Figure 8.27 is flawed because of the strong correlation between x_1 and x_{12}. This correlation is not real—it is an artifact of the use of the original values of the predictors instead of the coded values. The coded values (cx_1, cx_2, cx_{12}) of the predictors were determined by assigning the values -1 and $+1$ to the low and high values of the original predictors, respectively. Figure 8.28 shows the matrix plot of the response and coded predictors and Figure 8.29 shows the corresponding regression *analysis. Figure 8.28 suggests that the response depends only on x_1 and that the predictors are all independent of each other. This is a very different interpretation of the situation than that provided by Figure 8.26. Figure 8.28 provides the correct interpretation because it faithfully represents the true independence of the predictors. The regression analysis in Figure 8.29 confirms that the predictors are all independent ($r = 0$ for all pairs of predictors) and that y only depends on x_1. A comparison of the ANOVA tables and summary statistics from Figures 8.27 and 8.29 shows that they are identical, but the regression analysis in Figure 8.27 completely misses the dependence of y on x_1 because of the colinear predictors.*

Figure 8.26 suggests that y depends rather strongly on x_{12} but any hint of this dependence is missing in Figure 8.28. The correlation between the response and x_{12} in Figure 8.26 is caused by the colinearity of x_{12} and x_1. To determine the interaction between x_1 and x_2 these predictors were just multiplied together. Since x_2 is relatively constant compared to x_1, the x_{12} term determined from $x_{12} = x_1 x_2$ is essentially proportional to x_1. Coding the original values of the predictors eliminates this mathematical difficulty so that the true influence of the interaction on the response can be determined.

This example clearly demonstrates that it is necessary to use coded values for the predictors when using multiple regression to build models with two or more predictors.

Section 8.10 described methods for transforming nonlinear functions into linear form so that they could be analyzed using simple linear regression methods. The same transformation methods may be required to linearize a multiple regression problem, especially when the model to be fitted is a first-principles model of some specific form. If the first-principles model cannot be easily linearized with an appropriate transform, then you will have to settle for an empirical model or get help from your

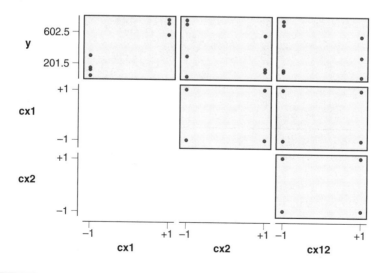

Figure 8.28 Matrix plot of response and coded predictors.

```
MTB > print c1-c7

Data Display

Row     y   x1  x2   x12   cx1   cx2   cx12
  1   286   10  40   400    -1    -1      1
  2     1   10  40   400    -1    -1      1
  3   114   10  50   500    -1     1     -1
  4    91   10  50   500    -1     1     -1
  5   803  100  40  4000     1    -1     -1
  6   749  100  40  4000     1    -1     -1
  7   591  100  50  5000     1     1      1
  8   598  100  50  5000     1     1      1

MTB > corr c5-c7;
SUBC> nopvalue.

Correlations: cx1, cx2, cx12

          cx1      cx2
cx2     0.000
cx12    0.000    0.000

Cell Contents: Pearson correlation

MTB > regress c1 3 c5-c7

Regression Analysis: y versus cx1, cx2, cx12

The regression equation is
y = 404 + 281 cx1 - 55.6 cx2 - 35.1 cx12

Predictor      Coef   SE Coef        T       P
Constant     404.13     36.38    11.11   0.000
cx1          281.13     36.38     7.73   0.002
cx2          -55.63     36.38    -1.53   0.201
cx12         -35.13     36.38    -0.97   0.389

S = 102.907   R-Sq = 94.0%   R-Sq(adj) = 89.5%

Analysis of Variance

Source            DF       SS       MS       F       P
Regression         3   666873   222291   20.99   0.007
Residual Error     4    42359    10590
Total              7   709233

Source   DF   Seq SS
cx1       1   632250
cx2       1    24753
cx12      1     9870
```

Figure 8.29   Multiple regression analysis using coded predictors.

neighborhood statistician. If, however, the first-principles model can be linearized, then the usual multivariable regression analysis can be used. If the resulting first-principles model doesn't fit the data, then the theory behind the model may be invalid or the data may be corrupt or just inappropriate. If a model for the data is still required, an empirical model can always be fitted.

A common type of first-principles model that can be easily linearized is any model that involves only products and ratios of the predictors that are possibly raised to powers. A simple logarithmic transform will convert such models into the linear form necessary for analysis using multiple regression. The powers of the predictors don't need to be known—they will reported as the regression coefficients for the different variables.

8.17 GENERAL LINEAR MODELS

In Chapter 6 we saw that when an experiment contains two or more qualitative variables, the response can be analyzed as a function of those variables using multi-way ANOVA. In the preceding section we saw that when an experiment contains two or more quantitative variables, the response can be fitted as a function of those variables using multiple linear regression. When an experiment contains a combination of qualitative and quantitative variables, however, the usual ANOVA and multiple regression techniques will not work. Experiments that contain both qualitative and quantitative variables are analyzed using a technique called a *general linear model.*

The trick to general linear models is to replace each qualitative variable that normally would be analyzed by ANOVA with an array of quantitative variables that can be analyzed by regression. Let's reconsider the one-way classification problems that were analyzed using one-way ANOVA in Chapter 5. The one-way ANOVA model consists of one mean for each of the k treatment conditions where only the first $k - 1$ means are independent. Now, suppose that we create k indicator variables, one for each of the k treatments, where the first indicator variable takes on the value one for those runs that used the first treatment and zero for all other runs, the second indicator variable is one for those runs that used the second treatment and zero for all other runs, and so on. After indicator variables are created for all of the treatments, the response can be analyzed as a function of any $k - 1$ of them using multiple regression. Only $k - 1$ indicator variables can be included in the model because the last one is always dependent on the others just as the kth treatment mean is dependent on the other $k - 1$ treatment means in ANOVA. Although this method of coding the treatments works, it introduces an undesirable bias in the regression model's constant. This problem is corrected by introducing a minor but important modification to the treatment coding scheme that is demonstrated in Example 8.29. A consequence of this scheme is that the kth treatment's regression coefficient is often not reported, but it can be determined from the negative sum of the other $k - 1$ coefficients. In practice, the software to construct general linear models hides all of the necessary coding of qualitative variables so that although it appears that they are being analyzed using ANOVA, they are actually being analyzed by the equivalent regression methods.

When a general linear model includes an interaction between a qualitative and quantitative variable, the model must also include the main effects of those variables to remain hierachical. The effect of the interaction in the model is that, in addition to the usual slope term associated with the quantitative variable, there will be adjustments to the slope for each level of the qualitative variable.

Example 8.28

Write out the general linear model for a quantitative variable x and a qualitative variable A with three levels A = {1, 2, 3} including the interaction term.

Solution: The general linear model will have the form:

$$y = b_0 + b_1 x + b_{21}(A = 1) + b_{22}(A = 2) + b_{23}(A = 3)$$
$$+ b_{31} x(A = 1) + b_{32} x(A = 2) + b_{33} x(A = 3)$$

where the b_i are regression coefficients and terms like (A = 1) are Boolean expressions that are equal to one when the expression is true, and zero otherwise. The nominal slope of y versus x is indicated by b_1 but the three terms of the form b_{3i} describe corrections to the slope for each A treatment. In practice, the coefficients b_{23} and b_{33} will not be reported but can be determined from $b_{23} = -(b_{21} + b_{22})$ and $b_{33} = -(b_{31} + b_{32})$.

Use MINITAB's **Stat> ANOVA> General Linear Model** function to analyze experiments with both quantitative and qualitative variables. In the **Model** window enter the qualitative and quantitative variables and any other terms that you want to include in the model such as interactions and quadratic terms. By default, MINITAB assumes that any terms that appear in the **Model** window are qualitative variables to be analyzed by ANOVA, so identify the quantitative variables to be analyzed by regression by entering them in the **Covariates** window. MINITAB's **Stat> ANOVA> General Linear Model** function also includes a powerful collection of post-ANOVA comparison tools, excellent residuals diagnostics, and many other advanced capabilities.

Example 8.29

The glass used to construct arc lamps is often doped with materials that attenuate harmful UV radiation; however, these dopants usually decrease the life of the lamp. An experiment was performed to determine which of four doping materials would have the least impact on lamp life. The concentration of each dopant was adjusted to attenuate the UV by the desired amount and then five randomly selected lamps from each of the four treatments were operated to end of life. The experimental life data in hours are shown below. Analyze these data using both one-way ANOVA and regression to demonstrate the equivalence of the two analysis methods.

Obs	A	B	C	D
1	316	309	354	243
2	330	291	364	298
3	311	363	400	322
4	286	341	381	317
5	258	369	330	273

Solution: The data were entered into a MINITAB worksheet and analyzed using **Stat> ANOVA> One-Way**. The results of the ANOVA are shown in Figure 8.30. To perform the same analysis by regression, an indicator variable was created for each treatment using **Calc> Make Indicator Variables**. The resulting indicator variables are shown in Figure 8.31 under the label **Indicator Variables**. These indicator variables are not quite suitable for use in the regression analysis because they are biased, that is, they don't each have an average value of zero. To resolve this problem, the first three columns of indicator variables were retained and modified according to the columns under the label **GLM Coding**. The modification was to change the zero values for runs of treatment D (or ID = 4) in columns A, B, and C to −1 values. This corrects the bias problem, giving each treatment column an average value of zero, and preserves the independence of the treatments.

The regression analysis of lamp life as a function of the correctly coded treatments is shown at the bottom of Figure 8.31. This analysis exactly reproduces the results from the one-way ANOVA, including the values of the standard error and the coefficients of determination. The regression coefficient for treatment D was not automatically reported in the MINITAB output but its value was calculated from the negative sum of

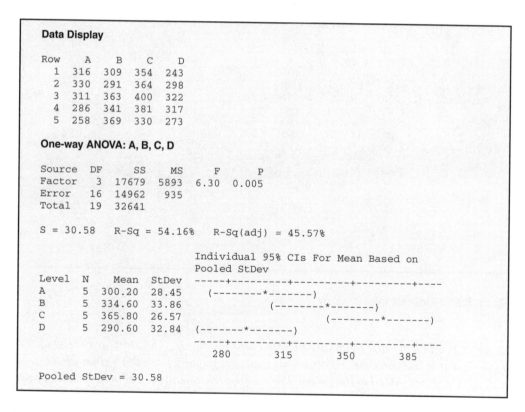

Figure 8.30   Arc lamp life analysis by ANOVA.

Data Display

			| Indicator Variables				| GLM Coding		
Row	Life	ID	A	B	C	D	A	B	C
1	316	1	1	0	0	0	1	0	0
2	330	1	1	0	0	0	1	0	0
3	311	1	1	0	0	0	1	0	0
4	286	1	1	0	0	0	1	0	0
5	258	1	1	0	0	0	1	0	0
6	309	2	0	1	0	0	0	1	0
7	291	2	0	1	0	0	0	1	0
8	363	2	0	1	0	0	0	1	0
9	341	2	0	1	0	0	0	1	0
10	369	2	0	1	0	0	0	1	0
11	354	3	0	0	1	0	0	0	1
12	364	3	0	0	1	0	0	0	1
13	400	3	0	0	1	0	0	0	1
14	381	3	0	0	1	0	0	0	1
15	330	3	0	0	1	0	0	0	1
16	243	4	0	0	0	1	-1	-1	-1
17	298	4	0	0	0	1	-1	-1	-1
18	322	4	0	0	0	1	-1	-1	-1
19	317	4	0	0	0	1	-1	-1	-1
20	273	4	0	0	0	1	-1	-1	-1

Regression Analysis: Life versus A, B, C

```
The regression equation is
Life = 323 - 22.6 A + 11.8 B + 43.0 C

Predictor        Coef   SE Coef       T      P
Constant      322.800     6.838   47.21  0.000
A             -22.60      11.84   -1.91  0.074
B              11.80      11.84    1.00  0.334
C              43.00      11.84    3.63  0.002
D             -32.20                             -(-22.60 + 11.80 + 43.00) = -32.20

S = 30.5798   R-Sq = 54.2%   R-Sq(adj) = 45.6%

Analysis of Variance

Source            DF       SS      MS      F      P
Regression         3  17679.2  5893.1   6.30  0.005
Residual Error    16  14962.0   935.1
Total             19  32641.2
```

Figure 8.31   Arc lamp life analysis by regression.

the other coefficients and manually inserted into the figure. The standard error of the D coefficient is the same as the others so the corresponding t and p values could also be determined and added to the figure. For the first treatment, the regression model predicts that the lamp life is $\overline{Life}_A = 322.8 - 22.6 = 300.2$, which is in exact agreement with the treatment mean reported in the ANOVA. There is also perfect agreement between the two models for the other treatment means, and the regression model constant is exactly equal to the grand mean of the data set.

Example 8.30

An experiment was performed by Swagelok Company in Solon, Ohio, to compare the torques required to tighten nuts on tubing fittings for three different lubricants: LAU, MIS, and SWW. The purpose of the experiment was to determine if one of the lubricants delivered lower tightening torque than the others where a 10 percent difference would be considered significant. The tightening operation is destructive to the nut and fitting so six randomly selected nut and fitting combinations were treated with each lubricant and torques were measured for each nut/fitting combination at 180, 270, 360, and 450 degrees as the nuts were tightened through 450 degrees of rotation. The order of the runs was completely randomized. The experimental data are shown in Figure 8.32. Analyze the torque as a function of lubricant and angle and determine if there are differences between the lubricants.

Solution: A multi-vari chart of the torque data is shown in Figure 8.33. The chart shows that there is an approximately linear relationship between torque and angle with some slight upward curvature. Both LAU and MIS appear to have higher torque than SWW. Unfortunately, the variation in the observations appears to increase in size with the torque. Figure 8.34 shows another multi-vari chart after the torque has been transformed by taking the natural logarithm. The figure shows some weak downward curvature in the torque versus angle curve; however, the transform appears to have successfully recovered the homoscedasticity of the observations about their treatment means.

Data Display					
Row	Unit	Angle	LAU	MIS	SWW
1	1	180	72.1	70.6	53.4
2	1	270	103.6	102.1	80.2
3	1	360	129.9	145.7	112.4
4	1	450	173.9	193.3	138.0
5	2	180	77.2	65.2	49.4
6	2	270	122.6	91.9	70.6
7	2	360	162.9	123.7	100.7
8	2	450	210.1	162.9	135.4
9	3	180	61.1	58.9	53.4
10	3	270	88.9	83.5	80.2
11	3	360	130.3	117.9	122.2
12	3	450	157.8	156.3	153.7
13	4	180	75.8	71.4	50.5
14	4	270	116.4	101.4	72.8
15	4	360	153.0	158.5	106.1
16	4	450	198.4	204.2	129.6
17	5	180	67.3	73.6	57.8
18	5	270	105.4	111.6	85.3
19	5	360	154.1	165.1	120.4
20	5	450	222.5	198.4	154.8
21	6	180	70.6	63.3	51.6
22	6	270	107.6	92.6	71.7
23	6	360	144.9	130.7	108.3
24	6	450	197.3	168.7	147.9

Figure 8.32 Tightening torque data.

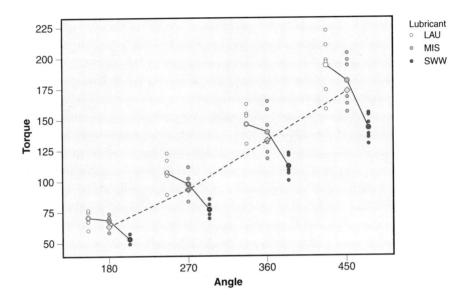

Figure 8.33 Multi-vari chart of torque versus angle by lubricant.

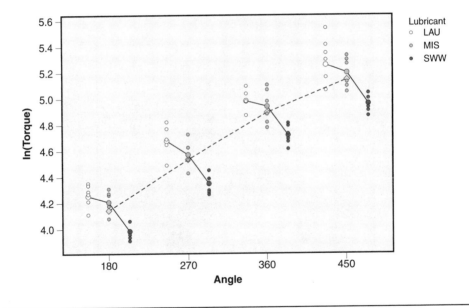

Figure 8.34 Multi-vari chart of ln(*Torque*) versus angle by lubricant.

Because angle is a quantitative variable and lubricant is a qualitative variable it is necessary to use the general linear model method of analysis. In addition to these two variables, there may be an interaction between them, and a quadratic angle term must be included in the model to account for the slight curvature observed in the multi-vari chart. There is also a chance that the nut/fitting combinations used within treatments could be different, so they should also be accounted for in the model.

*The torque data from Figure 8.32 were stacked and columns indicating the lubricant type and nut/fitting unit number for each lubricant were created. Part of the worksheet and output obtained using MINITAB's **Stat> ANOVA> General Linear Model** function are shown in Figure 8.35. The terms included in the model were Lubricant, Unit(Lubricant), Angle, Lubricant*Angle, and Angle*Angle. The nested term Unit (Lubricant) indicates that the nut/fitting units were unique within lubricant treatments. Unit was declared to be a random variable because the nut/fitting combinations were random samples assigned to the different treatments. Angle was declared to be a covariate because it is a quantitative predictor.*

The diagnostic plots in Figure 8.36 show that the residuals are normally distributed and homoscedastic with respect to angle, lubricant, the fitted values, and run order, as required by the analysis method. There is no evidence of lack of fit in the plot of residuals versus angle so the quadratic model is probably appropriate.

The general linear model analysis shows that Lubricant ($p = 0.000$), Unit ($p = 0.000$), Angle ($p = 0.000$), and Angle*Angle ($p = 0.000$) are all highly significant. The only term that is not statistically significant is the Lubricant*Angle interaction ($p = 0.847$). The insignificance of this term means that the torque versus angle curves for all of the lubricants have the same slope. To satisfy Occam we should run the analysis again with the Lubricant*Angle interaction removed from the model because the regression coefficients for the surviving lubricant terms will change; however, in this case the interaction term is so weak that there is little difference between the two models. The overall performance of the model is excellent, with adjusted coefficient of determination $r^2_{adj} = 0.9898$.

The table of regression coefficients was simplified for clarity; the coefficients for the Unit(Lubricant) terms were deleted from the table because they are not of interest and the table was reformatted slightly. The nonreported coefficients for the Lubricant and Lubricant*Angle interaction where Lubricant = SWW, and the corresponding t and p values, were calculated manually and added to the table. Ignoring the insignificant Lubricant*Angle interaction terms, the model can be written:

$$\ln(Torque) = 3.16 + 0.128(Lubricant = LAU) + 0.060(Lubricant = MIS)$$
$$- 0.188(Lubricant = SWW) + 0.0062\,Angle - 0.000004\,Angle^2$$

where expressions like (Lubricant = LAU) are Boolean expressions. The signs of the lubricant coefficients indicate that the SWW lubricant delivers the lowest torque, which is consistent with the multi-vari charts. Since the coefficient of SWW is negative and the other two are positive so that zero falls between them, SWW is very different from the other two lubricants, at least statistically if not practically. The predicted relative differences between torques by lubricant are: $(1 - e^{(0.128-(-0.188))})\,100\% = 37\%$ for LAU relative to SWW, $(1 - e^{(0.060-(-0.188))})100\% = 28\%$ for MIS relative to SWW, and $(1 - e^{(0.128-0.060)})100\% = 7\%$ for LAU relative to MIS. The first two differences are practically significant relative to the goals of the experiment.

Continued

Data Display

Row	Lubricant	Unit	Angle	Torque	ln(Torque)
1	LAU	1	180	72.1	4.27805
2	LAU	1	270	103.6	4.64054
.	.	.	.	.	.
.	.	.	.	.	.
71	SWW	6	360	108.3	4.68491
72	SWW	6	450	147.9	4.99654

General Linear Model: ln(Torque) versus Lubricant, Unit

Factor	Type	Levels	Values
Lubricant	fixed	3	LAU, MIS, SWW
Unit(Lubricant)	random	18	1, 2, 3, 4, 5, 6, 1, 2, 3, 4, 5, 6, 1, 2, 3, 4, 5, 6

Analysis of Variance for ln(Torque), using Adjusted SS for Tests

Source	DF	Seq SS	Adj SS	Adj MS	F	P	
Lubricant	2	1.16643	0.12337	0.06169	13.48	0.000	x Not an exact F-test
Unit(Lubricant)	15	0.49245	0.49245	0.03283	19.39	0.000	
Angle	1	10.02376	0.44326	0.44326	261.83	0.000	
Lubricant*Angle	2	0.00057	0.00057	0.00028	0.17	0.847	
Angle*Angle	1	0.07110	0.07110	0.07110	42.00	0.000	
Error	50	0.08465	0.08465	0.00169			
Total	71	11.83896					

S = 0.0411453   R-Sq = 99.29%   R-Sq(adj) = 98.98%

Term	Coef	SE Coef	T	P	
Constant	3.15664	0.05567	56.70	0.000	
Lubricant					
LAU	0.12826	0.02254	5.69	0.000	
MIS	0.06005	0.02254	2.66	0.010	
SWW	-0.18831	0.02254	-8.35	0.000	-(0.12826+0.06005) = -0.18831
Angle	0.006152	0.000380	16.18	0.000	
Angle*Lubricant					
LAU	-0.000024	0.000068	-0.36	0.722	
MIS	-0.000015	0.000068	-0.21	0.832	
SWW	-0.000039	0.000068	0.57	0.571	-(-0.000024-0.000015) = 0.000039
Angle*Angle	-0.000004	0.000001	*		

Figure 8.35   General linear model for ln(*Torque*).

Continued

```
Unusual Observations for ln(Torque)
Obs  ln(Torque)      Fit   SE Fit  Residual  St Resid
  1     4.27805  4.20724  0.02395   0.07082     2.12 R
 17     4.20916  4.29864  0.02395  -0.08948    -2.67 R
 20     5.40493  5.29323  0.02395   0.11169     3.34 R

R denotes an observation with a large standardized residual.


Expected Mean Squares, using Adjusted SS
                        Expected Mean Square
   Source               for Each Term
 1 Lubricant            (6) + 0.3704 (2) + Q[1]
 2 Unit(Lubricant)      (6) + 4.0000 (2)
 3 Angle                (6) + Q[3, 4]
 4 Lubricant*Angle      (6) + Q[4]
 5 Angle*Angle          (6) + Q[5]
 6 Error                (6)


Error Terms for Tests, using Adjusted SS
   Source           Error DF  Error MS  Synthesis of Error MS
 1 Lubricant           31.57   0.00458  0.0926 (2) + 0.9074 (6)
 2 Unit(Lubricant)     50.00   0.00169  (6)
 3 Angle               50.00   0.00169  (6)
 4 Lubricant*Angle     50.00   0.00169  (6)
 5 Angle*Angle         50.00   0.00169  (6)


Variance Components, using Adjusted SS
                   Estimated   Standard
   Source            Value     Deviation
 Unit(Lubricant)    0.00778    0.0882
 Error              0.00169    0.0411
 Total              0.00947    0.0973
```

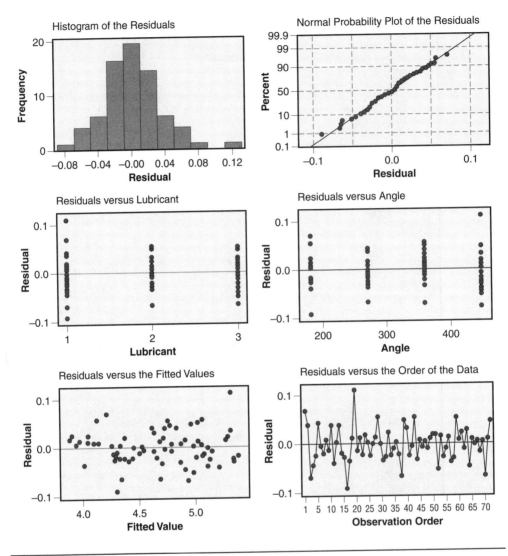

Figure 8.36 Residuals diagnostic plots from the general linear model for ln(*Torque*).

Under other circumstances, the post-ANOVA comparisons of the three lubricants might be carried out using Tukey's, Duncan's, or Hsu's methods; however, MINITAB correctly refuses to attempt these comparisons because of the presence of the random nut/fitting units nested within each lubricant type. The problem is that the apparent differences between lubricants could still be due to the way the 18 nut/fitting units were assigned to the three lubricants and a different randomization or a different set of 18 units could deliver different results. Consequently, the conclusion that there are statistically and practically significant differences between the lubricants is dependent on the untestable assumption that the random assignment of units to lubricants was fair.

From the variance components analysis at the end of Figure 8.35 the standard deviation of variability in ln (torque) associated with random variability in the nut/fitting units is given by:

$$s_{units} = \sqrt{0.00778} = 0.0882$$

The corresponding relative variation in the torques is given by $1 - e^{0.0882} = 0.092$ *or about 9.2 percent. In the same manner, the standard error of the model is:*

$$s_\varepsilon = \sqrt{MS_\varepsilon} = \sqrt{0.00169} = 0.0411$$

and the corresponding relative error variation in the torques is given by $1 - e^{0.0411} = 0.042$ *or 4.2 percent. The combined variation due to both random sources has standard deviation:*

$$s_{total} = \sqrt{0.00778 + 0.00169} = 0.0973$$

and the corresponding combined relative error in the torques is $1 - e^{0.0973} = 0.102$ *or about 10.2 percent. This means that about 95 percent of the observed torques should fall within about ±2 standard deviations or within* $\pm(1 - e^{2 \times 0.0973})\,100\% = \pm21\%$ *of the mean torque.*

8.18 SAMPLE-SIZE CALCULATIONS FOR LINEAR REGRESSION

8.18.1 Sample-Size to Determine the Slope with Specified Confidence

Suppose that we wish to determine the number of (x, y) observations that are required to estimate the true slope β_1 from a regression line fitted to experimental data to within some specified range of values. The regression model will be of the form $y = b_0 + b_1 x$ which approximates the true relationship $y = \beta_0 + \beta_1 x$. The confidence interval for the slope parameter β_1 will have the form:

$$P\left(b_1 - \delta < \beta_1 < b_1 + \delta\right) = 1 - \alpha \tag{8.66}$$

where b_1 is the slope determined from the experimental data, δ is the half-width of the confidence interval for the unknown slope parameter β_1, and α is the usual Type 1 error rate. We know that the distribution of b_1 as an estimate of β_1 is Student's t with degrees of freedom equal to the number of observations minus two. Then we can set:

$$\delta = t_{\alpha/2}\sigma_{b_1} \tag{8.67}$$

where σ_{b_1} can also be estimated from the experimental data. But σ_{b_1} is calculated from:

$$\sigma_{b_1} = \frac{\sigma_\varepsilon}{\sqrt{SS_x}} \tag{8.68}$$

where σ_ε is the standard deviation of the inherent noise in the process and SS_x is:

$$SS_x = \sum_i \left(x_i - \bar{x}\right)^2 \tag{8.69}$$

The value of SS_x is dependent on the number of observations in the data set and the distribution of the x values over the range of interest. In general, if n observations are made at each of k evenly spaced levels of x between some specified bounds of x given by x_{min} and x_{max}, then it can be shown (with difficulty) that:

$$SS_x = \frac{1}{12}(k-1)(k)(k+1)n(\Delta x)^2 \tag{8.70}$$

where

$$\Delta x = \frac{x_{max} - x_{min}}{k-1} \tag{8.71}$$

is the spacing between the k evenly spaced levels of x. Equations 8.67, 8.68, and 8.70 can be solved to obtain the following condition for the sample size:

$$n \geq \frac{12}{k(k-1)(k+1)}\left(\frac{t_{\alpha/2}\sigma_\varepsilon}{\delta\Delta x}\right)^2 \tag{8.72}$$

The inequality is necessary because n must be an integer and exact equality is unlikely. This inequality is also transcendental—both sides depend on n, the number of observations to be taken at each of the k evenly spaced levels of x. The dependence of the right-hand side on n is hidden in the degrees of freedom of $t_{\alpha/2}$. It may be necessary to attempt several values of n before the minimum value that meets the condition in Equation 8.72 is found. A first estimate for the sample size can be obtained by approximating $t_{\alpha/2}$ with $z_{\alpha/2}$. The quantities x_{min}, x_{max}, k, and δ are chosen by the experimenter and σ_ε must be estimated from prior data, data from a related process, or with an educated guess.

All Observations at Two Extreme Levels (*k* = 2)

When all observations are to be concentrated at the two extreme levels of x given by x_{min} and x_{max}, the sample-size condition with $k = 2$ becomes:

$$n \geq 2\left(\frac{t_{\alpha/2}\sigma_\varepsilon}{\delta\Delta x}\right)^2 \tag{8.73}$$

where $\Delta x = x_{max} - x_{min}$. This case is very important because we often want to determine the slope of $y(x)$ with the fewest possible observations and the simplest experiment design. Obviously, the sample size n decreases as Δx increases so we want to pick x_{min} and x_{max} to be as far apart as is practically possible.

Example 8.31

An electrochemical lead sensor outputs a small current that is proportional to the lead concentration in a solution. How many observations must be taken to determine the sensitivity of the sensor if it must operate for lead concentrations from zero to 2000 ppm? Preliminary data indicate that the sensitivity is about 0.002 nA/ppm and the standard error is about $\sigma_\varepsilon = 0.05$ nA. The sample size should be sufficient so that the 95 percent confidence interval for the slope spans ±2 percent of the slope.

Solution: If we can assume that the sensor is linear in the range of interest then we only need to take observations at zero and 2000 ppm, which gives the separation between the levels $\Delta x = 2000$ ppm. We want the half-width of the resultant confidence interval for the slope to be $\delta = 0.02 \times 0.002 = 4 \times 10^{-5}$ nA/ppm so the initial estimate $(t_{0.025} \simeq z_{0.025} = 1.96)$ for the sample size is:

$$
\begin{aligned}
n \;\; &\geq 2\left(\frac{z_{\alpha/2}\sigma_\varepsilon}{\Delta x\delta}\right)^2 \\
&\geq 2\left(\frac{1.96 \times 0.05}{2000 \times 4 \times 10^{-5}}\right)^2 \\
&\geq 3.0
\end{aligned}
$$

This calculation suggests that we might get by with just $n = 3$ observations at 0 ppm and another three observations at 2000 ppm; however, the greater than or equal to condition of Equation 8.73 is not rigorously satisfied. With $2n = 6$ total observations there will only be $2n - 2 = 4$ error degrees of freedom. The corresponding t value is $t_{0.025,4} = 2.78$, which is very different from $z_{0.025} = 1.96$. If we substitute this t value into the right-hand side of Equation 8.73 we get:

$$
\begin{aligned}
2\left(\frac{t_{\alpha/2}\sigma_\varepsilon}{\Delta x\delta}\right)^2 &\simeq 2\left(\frac{2.78 \times 0.05}{2000 \times 4 \times 10^{-5}}\right)^2 \\
&\simeq 6.04
\end{aligned}
$$

Because $n = 3$ is not greater than or equal to 6.04 the $n = 3$ solution is not valid. The following table indicates values of n and the corresponding values of:

$$2\left(\frac{t_{\alpha/2}\sigma_\varepsilon}{\Delta x \delta}\right)^2$$

where the t value has $df_\varepsilon = 2n - 2$ degrees of freedom:

n	df_ε	$t_{0.025}$	$2\left(\frac{t_{\alpha/2}\sigma_\varepsilon}{\Delta x \delta}\right)^2$
3	4	2.776	6.0
4	6	2.447	4.7
5	8	2.306	4.2
6	10	2.228	3.9

The smallest value of n that meets the condition given by Equation 8.73 is n = 5 because 5 ≥ 4.2 is true. This value slightly exceeds the condition defined in Equation 8.73, but will deliver a narrower confidence interval for b than what was initially specified. The solution n = 5 indicates that we need to run n = 5 observations at 0 ppm and another five observations at 2000 ppm to obtain the desired confidence interval for the slope.

Many Uniformly Distributed Observations ($k \to \infty$)

When the values of x within the interval x_{min} to x_{max} cannot be controlled but the observations can be made randomly and uniformly distributed between these bounds, the value of k becomes very large and Δx becomes correspondingly small. (Uniformly distributed doesn't necessarily mean that the observations are evenly spaced—only that all values of x within the range of interest are equally likely.) The sample-size condition given by Equation 8.72 can be manipulated and becomes:

$$N \geq 12 \left(\frac{t_{\alpha/2}\sigma_\varepsilon}{\delta\left(x_{max} - x_{min}\right)}\right)^2 \tag{8.74}$$

where N is the total number of observations taken in the interval from x_{min} to x_{max}. It is very important that the distribution of the observations in the interval from x_{min} to x_{max} be checked carefully, especially with respect to the density of points near the ends of the interval. These points are the largest contributors to information about the slope and they must be well represented in the sample to obtain the desired confidence interval width. If too many of the points fall near the middle of the interval then the value of δ obtained will be larger than intended.

Example 8.32

Find the sample size for Example 8.31 if a total of N observations are to be uniformly distributed in the interval from zero to 2000 ppm.

*   *Solution: If N is so large that $t_{0.025} \simeq z_{0.025}$ then the sample size is given by:*

$$N \geq 12 \left(\frac{1.96 \times 0.05}{4 \times 10^{-5} \times 2000} \right)^2 = 18.0$$

This gives only $df_\varepsilon = 16$ degrees of freedom for the t distribution, so the approximation of $t_{0.025}$ with $z_{0.025}$ is probably only marginally satisfied. After another iteration, the minimum sample size is determined to be $N = 21$.

8.18.2 Sample Size to Determine the Regression Constant with Specified Confidence

The same approach used to determine sample size for the regression slope can be applied to estimate the y axis intercept β_0. Our goal is to determine the minimum sample size necessary to determine a confidence interval for the unknown constant β_0 in $y = \beta_0 + \beta_1 x$. The confidence interval will have the form:

$$P \left(b_0 - \delta < \beta_0 < b_0 + \delta \right) = 1 - \alpha \tag{8.75}$$

where b_0 is the regression constant determined from the experimental data, δ is the half-width of the confidence interval where:

$$\delta = t_{\alpha/2} \sigma_{b_0} \tag{8.76}$$

and α is the Type 1 error probability. The standard error of the estimate of the regression constant is:

$$\sigma_{b_0} = \sigma_\varepsilon \sqrt{\frac{1}{n} + \frac{\bar{x}^2}{SS_x}} \tag{8.77}$$

When Equations 8.76, 8.77, and 8.70 are solved for n we obtain:

$$n \geq \left(\frac{t_{\alpha/2} \sigma_\varepsilon}{\delta} \right)^2 \left(1 + \frac{12}{k(k-1)(k+1)} \left(\frac{\bar{x}}{\Delta x} \right)^2 \right) \tag{8.78}$$

where n is the number of observations taken at each of k evenly spaced levels from x_{min} to x_{max} and Δx is the spacing between the levels. This expression is transcendental because the degrees of freedom for $t_{\alpha/2}$ depend on the sample size. Unfortunately this expression doesn't reduce to anything simpler.

Example 8.33

Determine the sample size required to estimate the true value of the regression constant in Example 8.31 to within $\pm 0.03nA$ with 95 percent confidence. Use observations at $k = 3$ evenly spaced levels of x.

Solution: We have $\sigma_\varepsilon = 0.05nA$, $\delta = 0.03nA$, *and* $\alpha = 0.05$. *With* $k = 3$ *evenly spaced levels, we will have to take n observations at* 0, 1000, *and* 2000 *ppm lead concentrations so* $\Delta x = 1000$ *ppm. Since the same number of observations will be taken at each of these three levels, we will have* $\bar{x} = 1000$ *ppm. These values give the sample-size condition:*

$$n \geq \left(\frac{t_{0.025}(0.05)}{0.03}\right)^2 \left(1 + \frac{12}{2\times3\times4}\left(\frac{1000}{1000}\right)^2\right)$$

$$\geq 4.17 t_{0.025}^2$$

where $t_{0.025}$ *has* $kn - 2$ *degrees of freedom. If n is going to be large, then as a first guess* $t_{0.025} \simeq (z_{0.025} = 1.96)$ *so:*

$$n \geq 4.17(1.96)^2$$

$$\geq 16.0$$

Since the total number of observations will be $nk = 48$, *and* $t_{0.025}$ *with* $df_\varepsilon = 48 - 2 = 46$ *degrees of freedom is approximately equal to* $z_{0.025} = 1.96$, *we can accept this solution. The calculation indicates that it will be necessary to take* $n = 16$ *observations at zero,* 1000, *and* 2000 *ppm lead concentrations to determine the true value of the regression constant to within* $\pm0.03nA$ *with* 95 *percent confidence.*

8.18.3 Sample Size to Determine the Predicted Value of the Response with Specified Confidence

The confidence interval for the true value of the response y determined from the predicted value $\hat{y} = b_0 + b_1 x$ was given in Equation 8.26. If the true value of the response y for some specified value of x must be determined to within some specified amount δ such that:

$$P\left(\hat{y} - \delta < \mu_{y(x)} < \hat{y} + \delta\right) = 1 - \alpha \tag{8.79}$$

then by comparison of the two equations:

$$\delta = t_{\alpha/2}\sigma_\varepsilon \sqrt{\frac{1}{n} + \frac{(x - \bar{x})^2}{SS_x}} \tag{8.80}$$

If n observations are taken at each of k evenly spaced levels of x between x_{min} and x_{max}, then SS_x is given by Equations 8.70 and 8.71. These equations can be solved to determine a condition for the sample size to deliver a confidence interval for $\mu_{y(x)}$ of the desired width:

$$n \geq \left(\frac{t_{\alpha/2}\sigma_\varepsilon}{\delta}\right)^2 \left(1 + \frac{12}{k(k-1)(k+1)}\left(\frac{x - \bar{x}}{\Delta x}\right)^2\right) \tag{8.81}$$

Equation 8.78, which gives the sample size for the confidence interval for the regression constant, is just a special case of this condition with $x = 0$.

8.18.4 Sample Size to Detect a Slope Different from Zero

The sample-size calculations above apply to confidence intervals for the slope, the regression constant, and predicted values. Those calculations assume that you know that the slope, constant, or predicted value is different from zero and that you want to quantify it within a specified range of values with some degree of confidence. A different but frequently encountered sample-size problem for regression is to determine the power necessary to detect a nonzero slope for a given sample size. The hypotheses to be tested are H_0: $\beta_1 = 0$ versus H_A: $\beta_1 \neq 0$. There are two equivalent solutions to this problem available. The first solution is analogous to the relationship between the sample-size solutions for simple confidence intervals and hypothesis tests for one mean where $t_{\alpha/2}$ in the confidence interval solution is simply replaced by $t_{\alpha/2} + t_\beta$ in the hypothesis testing solution. (See Equations 3.39 and 3.42.) The power P for the linear regression to detect the nonzero slope β_1 is given by:

$$P = 1 - P\left(\frac{\beta_1}{\sigma_{b_1}} - t_{\alpha/2} < t < \frac{\beta_1}{\sigma_{b_1}} + t_{\alpha/2}\right)$$
$$= 1 - P\left(\frac{\beta_1\sqrt{SS_x}}{\sigma_\varepsilon} - t_{\alpha/2} < t < \frac{\beta_1\sqrt{SS_x}}{\sigma_\varepsilon} + t_{\alpha/2}\right) \tag{8.82}$$

where

$$\sigma_{b_1} = \sigma_\varepsilon / \sqrt{SS_x} \tag{8.83}$$

The second sample-size calculation to test H_0: $\beta_1 = 0$ versus H_A: $\beta_1 \neq 0$ requires the method of the power of F tests from Chapter 7 where the relevant F test is the regression F test from the regression ANOVA table. This shouldn't be a surprise since the F statistic for the regression is equal to the square of the t_{b_1} statistic for the regression slope.

The expected value of the regression's ANOVA F statistic is given by:

$$E(F) = \frac{E(SS_{regr})}{E(MS_\varepsilon)} + 1 = \lambda + 1 \tag{8.84}$$

where λ is the F distribution noncentrality parameter when $\beta_1 \neq 0$. This equation can be solved for the noncentrality parameter in terms of the distribution of the xs and the expected value of the mean square error:

$$\lambda = \frac{E(SS_{regr})}{E(MS_\varepsilon)} = \frac{\beta_1^2 SS_x}{\sigma_\varepsilon^2} \tag{8.85}$$

where β_1 is the nonzero value of the slope that we wish to detect. The power $P = 1 - \beta$ to reject H_0: $\beta_1 = 0$ is given by the condition:

$$F_\alpha = F_{P,\lambda} \tag{8.86}$$

where the central and noncentral F distributions both have one numerator and df_ε denominator degrees of freedom. This relationship is used to determine the power for a specified sample size. It is transcendental in the sample size, so iterations must be used to determine the correct sample size to achieve a desired value of the power.

Example 8.34
    An experiment is to be performed to determine whether the ramp-up time of a propane-fired heat-treatment furnace depends on the intake/ambient air temperature. The experiment will use three levels of intake air temperature: 15C, 20C, and 25C. A single load of carbon steel will be placed in the furnace for the experiment. The response will be the time required to bring the load to the usual heat-treatment temperature of 930C. What is the power to detect an effect of 10 minutes per degree centigrade if three trials are performed at each level of ambient temperature? Historical data suggest that the variation in the amount of time required to heat a load of this size is $\sigma_\varepsilon = 30$ minutes.

    Solution: *The slope of the ramp-up time versus ambient temperature relationship that we are trying to detect is $\beta_1 = 10$ min/C. There are three equally represented levels of ambient temperature, so SS_x is given by:*

$$\begin{aligned} SS_x &= \Sigma\left(x_i - \bar{x}\right)^2 \\ &= \tfrac{1}{12}(k-1)(k)(k+1)n(\Delta x)^2 \\ &= \tfrac{1}{12}(2)(3)(4)(3)(5)^2 \\ &= 150 \end{aligned}$$

The noncentrality parameter of the F distribution when $\beta_1 = 10$ is:

$$\begin{aligned} \lambda &= \tfrac{\beta_1^2 SS_x}{\sigma_\varepsilon^2} \\ &= \tfrac{10^2(150)}{30^2} \\ &= 16.7 \end{aligned}$$

The regression's ANOVA F test will have $df_{regr} = 1$ numerator degree of freedom and $df_\varepsilon = 9 - 2 = 7$ denominator degrees of freedom. The power for the test is given by:

$$\left(F_{0.05} = 5.59\right) = \left(F_{P,16.7} = F_{0.94,16.7}\right)$$

so the power is P = 0.94. This means that the experiment has a 94 percent chance of delivering a statistically significant (p < 0.05) regression slope if the true slope is $\beta_1 = 10$ min/C. The power will be higher if the slope is larger and lower if the slope is smaller.

Example 8.35

Use the method of Equation 8.82 to confirm the answer to Example 8.34.

Solution: There are $df_\varepsilon = 7$ degrees of freedom for the error so $t_{0.025,7} = 2.365$ and:

$$\begin{aligned}
P &= 1 - P\left(\frac{\beta_1\sqrt{SS_x}}{\sigma_\varepsilon} - t_{\alpha/2} < t < \frac{\beta_1\sqrt{SS_x}}{\sigma_\varepsilon} + t_{\alpha/2}\right) \\
&= 1 - P\left(\frac{10\sqrt{150}}{30} - 2.365 < t < \frac{10\sqrt{150}}{30} + 2.365\right) \\
&= 1 - P(1.72 < t < 6.447) \\
&= 0.94
\end{aligned}$$

The value of the power, P = 0.94, is in agreement with the power found using the method of the ANOVA F test.

8.19 DESIGN CONSIDERATIONS FOR LINEAR REGRESSION

The 11-step general procedure for experimentation introduced in Chapter 4 is appropriate for situations that will be analyzed by linear regression methods. Following are some special considerations for these situations:

- Confirm that the independent variable (x) can be determined exactly. If this condition is not met it will be necessary to use the errors in variables method of Section 8.13.

- Select minimum and maximum values of x that are as far apart as practically possible. This will improve the estimates of the regression coefficients and decrease the number of observations required for the experiment.

- Concentrate a substantial fraction of the observations at or near the minimum and maximum values of x. These observations improve the estimates of the regression coefficients more than observations that fall near the middle of the range of x.

- Use at least three levels of x to permit a lack of fit test. It's best to evenly space the levels. If a transformation of x is anticipated to linearize the model, the transformed x values should be evenly spaced.

- Take at least two replicate readings at each level of x so that a linear lack of fit test can be performed.

- Do the runs in random order. *Do not* perform the runs by systematically increasing or decreasing x.

- If possible, block replicated observations. Include the blocks as a qualitative variable in the model to reduce the effects of extraneous variation and to help identify possible causes for it. Use the general linear model method to do regression on the quantitative variable and ANOVA on the blocking variable.

- Perform a sample-size calculation to determine the necessary rather than an arbitrary number of observations to collect. Consider historical data, data from a related process, or do a preliminary experiment to estimate the standard error of the model required for the calculation.

9

Two-Level Factorial Experiments

9.1 INTRODUCTION

Chapter 6 introduced the general factorial designs where two or more variables could each have two or more levels and all possible combinations of variables were constructed. These designs were designated $a \times b \times c \times \ldots$ designs where each number indicated the number of levels of a variable and all the runs were performed in random order. This chapter introduces a special subset of these factorial designs—those that have only two levels of each variable. These experiments are designated $2 \times 2 \times \ldots \times 2$ or 2^k experiments where k is the number of variables. 2^k is also the number of unique cells or runs in each replicate of the design. When all of the experimental runs are performed in random order, the 2^k experiments have the ability to characterize all of the variables under consideration, and, as with the other factorial designs, they can resolve two-factor and higher-order interactions.

The 2^k experiments are one of the most important and fundamental families of experiments in DOE. In addition to being some of the most commonly run experiments, they also provide the foundation for the more complex designs considered in Chapters 10 and 11, so study these experiments very carefully.

9.2 THE 2^1 FACTORIAL EXPERIMENT

The 2^1 factorial experiment is the simplest of the two-level experiments. Some people would call it trivial, but despite its simplicity the 2^1 factorial experiment still demonstrates many of the important aspects of the analysis common to all two-level factorial experiments.

The 2^1 factorial experiment involves only one variable at two levels. The variable may be qualitative or quantitative—in either case the analysis is the same. This is one of the important characteristics of two-level factorial experiments. When two or more variables are being studied, they can be all qualitative, all quantitative, or a mix of the two types. This flexibility is not preserved when an experiment has one or more qualitative variables at three or more levels.

The two levels of the variable under study are referenced in terms of the coded levels that were introduced back in Chapter 8. These levels are designated –1 and +1 or just – and + and are often called the low and high levels, respectively. The actual physical levels used for the low and high settings are entirely up to the experimenter. The coded values provide a universal way of communicating information about variables. The use of codes also has mathematical benefits that greatly simplify many calculations. These codes are used so frequently that, with experience, their use becomes second nature. You will soon find yourself immediately thinking in terms of appropriate low and high levels for each variable in a 2^k experiment.

In tabular form the 2^1 factorial experiment design may be written:

Run	x_1
1	−1
2	+1

The subscript 1 on x indicates that x_1 is the first independent variable in our experiment in anticipation of more complex experiments with two or more variables. The other variables will be indicated by x_2, x_3, and so on. (MINITAB and some books prefer the use of A for x_1, B for x_2, and so on. This choice is certainly valid, but I like the simplicity of the x_1 notation. Get used to both choices of notation.)

Replicates are used to increase the total number of observations in the 2^1 experiment. When the experiment is replicated, the same number of runs should be used for each level of x_1. For example, this experiment might be replicated four times giving four observations at the $x_1 = -1$ level and four observations at the $x_1 = +1$ level for a total of eight experimental runs. If the same number of runs are not used at each level of x_1, the experiment becomes unbalanced and its validity could be compromised. This issue of balance in the number of runs performed at each level of a variable is a key concept of DOE, and you should always try to preserve this balance if possible. When the number of runs at each level of a variable are not equal, either by accident or by design, special considerations must be made in the analysis. These issues will be addressed later in this chapter.

There are several ways to analyze the response in a 2^1 experiment. Although we could use ANOVA to test for a difference between the response means at the two levels of x_1, the regression methods of Chapter 8 provide a more concise model that can be easily expanded for more complex designs. Chapter 8 suggests the use of the model:

$$y = b_0 + b_1 x_1 \tag{9.1}$$

where y is the measured response and the regression methods of Chapter 8 are used to determine the statistics b_0 and b_1. Here the values of x_1 are limited to the coded values -1 and $+1$ and, if x_1 is quantitative, all of the fractional values in between. Since the actual values of the measurement variable x_1 are not used in Equation 9.1, you are responsible for switching back and forth between the real and coded levels of x_1.

Some discussion of the b_0 coefficient is appropriate because it has special meaning in the interpretation of all of the 2^k experiments. Recall from Chapter 8 that the point $(\bar{x}, \bar{y})$ must fall on the regression line. Since the 2^1 experiment contains the same number of runs at the low and high levels of x_1, the mean level of x_1 in the experiment must be $\bar{x}_1 = 0$. The corresponding response under this condition must be $\bar{y}$, or in terms of the dot notation introduced earlier $\bar{y}_{..}$ where the implied summations are over both levels of x_1 and all replicates. It can be seen by comparing these results that:

$$\begin{aligned} \bar{y} &= b_0 + b_1 \bar{x}_1 \\ &= b_0 + b_1(0) \\ &= b_0 \end{aligned}$$

This is an important observation—the b_0 coefficient in the regression analysis of the 2^1 experiment, and of any balanced 2^k experiment for that matter, corresponds to the grand mean of the response y. In general, the b_0 coefficient will represent the grand mean of the response, and the effects due to $x_1, x_2, \ldots$ can be interpreted as deviations or perturbations from the grand mean. The b_0 term provides a sort of anchor for the response about which all the other terms exhibit their effects.

The effect of x_1 on the response is best seen from a response plot of y versus x_1 as shown in Figure 9.1. Two points are plotted in the figure, one at $(x_1, y) = (-1, \bar{y}_{-\bullet})$ and the other at $(x_1, y) = (+1, \bar{y}_{+\bullet})$, where $\bar{y}_{-\bullet}$ is the mean of all responses at $x_1 = -1$:

$$\bar{y}_{-\bullet} = \frac{1}{n} \sum_{i=1}^{n} y(x_1 = -1) \tag{9.2}$$

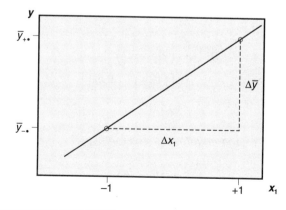

Figure 9.1 Response y versus x_1.

where n is the number of replicates and $\bar{y}_{+\bullet}$ is the mean of all responses at $x_1 = +1$:

$$\bar{y}_{+\bullet} = \frac{1}{n}\sum_{i=1}^{n} y(x_1 = +1) \tag{9.3}$$

From the plot, the slope of the line through these two points is:

$$b_1 = \frac{\Delta \bar{y}}{\Delta x_1} = \frac{\bar{y}_{+\bullet} - \bar{y}_{-\bullet}}{(+1) - (-1)} = \frac{1}{2}\left(\bar{y}_{+\bullet} - \bar{y}_{-\bullet}\right) \tag{9.4}$$

Now that b_0 and b_1 are both uniquely determined from the data, Equation 9.1 can be used to describe how y depends on x_1.

If there are n replicates of the 2^1 experiment then there will be $2n$ total runs or df_{total} = $2n - 1$ where one degree of freedom is consumed, as always, by the grand mean. In this experiment, the grand mean corresponds to the b_0 coefficient. Since the b_1 coefficient also consumes one degree of freedom there will be $df_\varepsilon = 2n - 2$ degrees of freedom for the error estimate, just as in Chapter 8.

Example 9.1
   Determine the regression equation for the following data set. Use the methods described in Section 9.2.

x_1	−1	−1	+1	+1
y	47	51	21	17

   Solution: The b_0 coefficient from the regression model is:

$$
\begin{aligned}
b_0 &= \bar{y}_{\bullet\bullet} \\
&= \tfrac{1}{4}\left(47 + 51 + 21 + 17\right) \\
&= 34.0
\end{aligned}
$$

The b_1 coefficient is given by:

$$
\begin{aligned}
b_1 &= \tfrac{1}{2}\left(\bar{y}_{+\bullet} - \bar{y}_{-\bullet}\right) \\
&= \tfrac{1}{2}\left[\left(\tfrac{21+17}{2}\right) - \left(\tfrac{47+51}{2}\right)\right] \\
&= -15.0
\end{aligned}
$$

This means that the regression equation is given by:

$$
\begin{aligned}
y &= b_0 + b_1 x_1 \\
&= 34 - 15 x_1
\end{aligned}
$$

The data and the regression line are plotted in Figure 9.2.

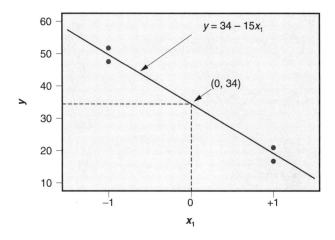

Figure 9.2 Plot of example data and regression fit.

Example 9.2

Use MINITAB's **regress** *command to confirm the regression equation found in Example 9.1. Also determine the standard error and r^2 value.*

Solution: *The MINITAB output is shown in Figure 9.3. The regression equation is the same as was found in the example. The model standard error is $s_\varepsilon = 2.828$ and the coefficient of determination is $r^2 = 0.983$.*

9.3 THE 2^2 FACTORIAL EXPERIMENT

The 2×2 factorial experiment is one of the simplest and yet most profoundly important experiments. Despite its simplicity, it is one of the most commonly run experiments of all types. Its analysis embodies all of the key concepts, mathematics, and interpretation issues of the more complicated designs that are founded on it, so study this design carefully.

The 2×2 or 2^2 factorial experiment has two variables, x_1 and x_2, each at two levels. As before, the coded levels are designated -1 and $+1$ or just $-$ and $+$, and simple transformations are used to convert back and forth between these coded levels and the real measurable levels of a variable. The four unique runs of the 2^2 experiment design may be expressed in tabular form as:

Run	x_1	x_2
1	$-$	$-$
2	$-$	$+$
3	$+$	$-$
4	$+$	$+$

```
MTB > print c1-c2

Data Display

Row  x1   y
  1  -1  47
  2  -1  51
  3   1  21
  4   1  17

MTB > regress c2 1 c1

Regression Analysis: y versus x1

The regression equation is
y = 34.0 - 15.0 x1

Predictor      Coef  SE Coef        T      P
Constant     34.000    1.414    24.04  0.002
x1          -15.000    1.414   -10.61  0.009

S = 2.82843   R-Sq = 98.3%   R-Sq(adj) = 97.4%

Analysis of Variance

Source           DF       SS       MS       F      P
Regression        1   900.00   900.00  112.50  0.009
Residual Error    2    16.00     8.00
Total             3   916.00
```

Figure 9.3 MINITAB output for Example 9.2.

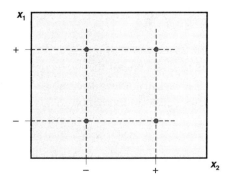

Figure 9.4 2 × 2 factorial design.

or in graphical form as in Figure 9.4. The experiment is performed by selecting a random order of experimentation for the runs, configuring the system to the required (x_1, x_2) levels, and measuring the corresponding responses. If replication is desired, the order of experimentation can be randomized completely by randomizing over all possible runs, or randomization can be limited by blocking on replicates.

The analysis of the 2^2 factorial experiment is carried out by evaluating the effects of variables x_1 and x_2. The effects can be expressed in the form of a linear regression model with two variables:

$$y(x_1, x_2) = b_0 + b_1 x_1 + b_2 x_2 \tag{9.5}$$

where b_0, b_1, and b_2 are regression coefficients to be determined from the data. The effect of x_1 is determined by grouping the responses according to their x_1 levels as shown in Figure 9.5. The coefficient b_1 will then be:

$$b_1 = \frac{\bar{y}_{+\bullet\bullet} - \bar{y}_{-\bullet\bullet}}{2} \tag{9.6}$$

where

$$\bar{y}_{+\bullet\bullet} = \frac{1}{2n} \sum_{i=1}^{n} \sum_{x_2} y(+1, x_2) \tag{9.7}$$

$$\bar{y}_{-\bullet\bullet} = \frac{1}{2n} \sum_{i=1}^{n} \sum_{x_2} y(-1, x_2) \tag{9.8}$$

and n is the number of replicates. The first dot indicates summation over all x_2 levels and the second dot indicates summation over replicates. The choice of -1 and $+1$ for the levels of x_1 clearly makes for easy calculation and interpretation of the b_1 term. The numerator of Equation 9.6 is the change in y:

$$\Delta \bar{y} = \bar{y}_{+\bullet\bullet} - \bar{y}_{-\bullet\bullet} \tag{9.9}$$

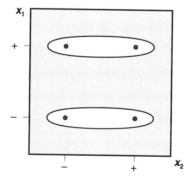

Figure 9.5 Determination of the x_1 effect.

observed over a change of x_1 from -1 to $+1$:

$$\Delta x_1 = +1 - (-1) = 2 \tag{9.10}$$

This interpretation is shown in the plot of y versus x_1 in Figure 9.6.

The coefficient b_2 can be determined in a similar manner. This is done by grouping the responses by their x_2 classification as shown in Figure 9.7. The b_2 coefficient is calculated in the same way as was the b_1 coefficient:

$$b_2 = \frac{\overline{y}_{\bullet+\bullet} - \overline{y}_{\bullet-\bullet}}{2} \tag{9.11}$$

where

$$\overline{y}_{\bullet+\bullet} = \frac{1}{2n} \sum_{i=1}^{n} \sum_{x_1} y(x_1, +1) \tag{9.12}$$

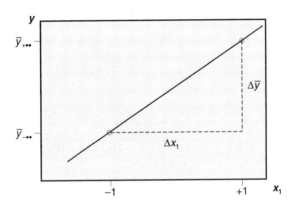

Figure 9.6 Response y versus variable x_1.

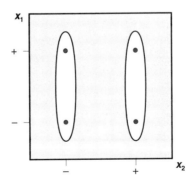

Figure 9.7 Determination of the x_2 effect.

$$\overline{y}_{\bullet-\bullet} = \frac{1}{2n}\sum_{i=1}^{n}\sum_{x_1} y(x_1, -1) \tag{9.13}$$

It is possible and highly desirable to add one more term to the model given by Equation 9.5. In fact, this term and other terms like it are one of the major strengths of the factorial designs. The term to be added is the two-factor interaction term that measures the strength of the interaction between x_1 and x_2. We write the interaction as x_{12} and its regression coefficient as b_{12}. The new model becomes:

$$y(x_1, x_2) = b_0 + b_1 x_1 + b_2 x_2 + b_{12} x_{12} \tag{9.14}$$

In terms of the four cells of the 2×2 experiment, the interaction term is determined by pairing the observations as shown in Figure 9.8. The levels of x_{12} are determined by taking the product of x_1 and x_2:

$$x_{12} = x_1 x_2 \tag{9.15}$$

The coefficient b_{12} is determined in a manner similar to the way that b_1 and b_2 were determined:

$$b_{12} = \frac{(\overline{y}_{++\bullet} + \overline{y}_{--\bullet}) - (\overline{y}_{+-\bullet} + \overline{y}_{-+\bullet})}{2} \tag{9.16}$$

where

$$\overline{y}_{++\bullet} = \frac{1}{n}\sum_{i=1}^{n} y(+1, +1) \tag{9.17}$$

and so on for $\overline{y}_{--\bullet}$, $\overline{y}_{+-\bullet}$, and $\overline{y}_{-+\bullet}$.

In practice, the coefficients b_0, b_1, b_2, and b_{12} are determined using the linear regression function of a suitable computer program. In MINITAB for example, if c1 contains

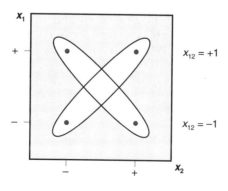

Figure 9.8 Determination of the x_{12} effect.

the response y and the levels of x_1 and x_2 are included in columns c2 and c3, then the interaction levels for x_{12} can be determined with:

$$\text{mtb> let c4=c2*c3}$$

or from the **Calc> Calculator** menu. This performs the simple operation $x_{12} = x_1 \times x_2$ and puts the result in column c4. The regression is carried out with MINITAB's **regress** command:

$$\text{mtb> regress c1 3 c2 c3 c4}$$

or from the **Stat> Regression> Regression** menu. The "3" after c1 indicates to MINITAB that three terms are to be included in the regression model.

Example 9.3

Use the technique presented in Figures 9.5, 9.7, and 9.8 to construct a model for the following data set.

$x_1 \backslash x_2$	-1	$+1$
-1	61, 63	41, 35
$+1$	76, 72	68, 64

Solution: The model we need has the form:

$$y(x_1, x_2) = b_0 + b_1 x_1 + b_2 x_2 + b_{12} x_{12}$$

Since the experiment has the same number of observations at each level of each variable, the grand mean of the data set corresponds to the b_0 coefficient so:

$$b_0 = \bar{y}_{\bullet\bullet\bullet} = \frac{1}{8}\left(61 + 63 + 76 + 72 + 41 + 35 + 68 + 64\right) = 60$$

where the data are y_{ijk} and the i subscript indicates the level of x_1, j indicates the level of x_2, and k indicates the replicate. We can find the b_1 coefficient by taking the data in rows according to the levels of x_1. When $x_1 = -1$ we have a mean response of:

$$\bar{y}_{-\bullet\bullet} = \frac{1}{4}\left(61 + 63 + 41 + 35\right) = 50$$

When $x_1 = +1$ we have a mean response of:

$$\bar{y}_{+\bullet\bullet} = \frac{1}{4}\left(76 + 72 + 68 + 64\right) = 70$$

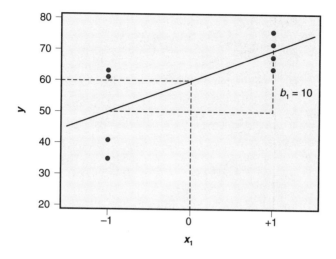

Figure 9.9 Response *y* versus variable x_1.

The data and the response means are plotted in Figure 9.9. As required, the y axis intercept (at $x_1 = 0$) is 60. The slope of the line in the figure, which is the b_1 coefficient, is given by:

$$b_1 = \frac{\bar{y}_{+\bullet\bullet} - \bar{y}_{-\bullet\bullet}}{\Delta x_1} = \frac{70 - 50}{(+1) - (-1)} = 10$$

We can find the b_2 coefficient in a similar manner. If we take the data by columns according to the levels of x_2 we have:

$$\bar{y}_{\bullet-\bullet} = \frac{1}{4}(61 + 63 + 76 + 72) = 68$$
$$\bar{y}_{\bullet+\bullet} = \frac{1}{4}(41 + 35 + 68 + 64) = 52$$

The data and the response means are plotted in Figure 9.10. The b_2 coefficient is:

$$b_2 = \frac{\bar{y}_{\bullet+\bullet} - \bar{y}_{\bullet-\bullet}}{\Delta x_2} = \frac{52 - 68}{(+1) - (-1)} = -8$$

The coefficient for the interaction x_{12} is found by taking the data from the table along the diagonals as shown in Figure 9.8. The data on the falling diagonal corresponds to the $x_{12} = -1$ level. The mean response along this diagonal is:

$$\bar{y}(x_{12} = -1) = \frac{1}{4}(76 + 72 + 41 + 35) = 56$$

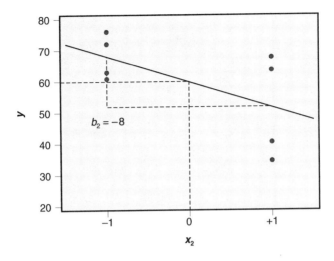

Figure 9.10 Response *y* versus variable x_2.

The data on the rising diagonal corresponding to the $x_{12} = +1$ level gives a mean response of:

$$\bar{y}(x_{12} = +1) = \frac{1}{4}(61 + 63 + 68 + 64) = 64$$

The data and the response means are plotted in Figure 9.11. The b_{12} coefficient is:

$$b_{12} = \frac{\bar{y}(x_{12} = +1) - \bar{y}(x_{12} = -1)}{\Delta x_{12}} = \frac{64 - 56}{(+1) - (-1)} = +4$$

If we put all of this information together, the mathematical model for the response is:

$$y = 60 + 10x_1 - 8x_2 + 4x_{12} \tag{9.18}$$

Example 9.4
Find the model standard error and the coefficient of determination for Example 9.3.

Solution: We need to determine the residuals to find the model standard error. The table below shows the responses y_{ijk} and the predicted values or fits $\hat{y}_{ijk}$. The differences between the observed and predicted values are the residuals according to:

$$\varepsilon_{ijk} = y_{ijk} - \hat{y}_{ijk}$$

The model standard error is calculated from the square root of the sum of the squares of the residuals divided by the appropriate degrees of freedom:

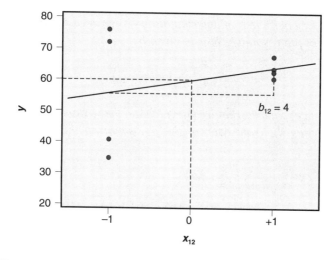

Figure 9.11 Response y versus interaction x_{12}.

$$s_\varepsilon = \sqrt{\frac{SS_\varepsilon}{df_\varepsilon}}$$

where $SS_\varepsilon = \Sigma\varepsilon_{ijk}^2$ and $df_\varepsilon = n - 4$ is the number of degrees of freedom available to estimate the error after calculating the regression coefficients b_0, b_1, b_2, and b_{12}. The following table gives the observed values, the predicted values according to Equation 9.18, the residuals, and the squares of the residuals:

x_1	x_2	y_{ijk}	$\hat{y}_{ijk}$	ε_{ijk}	ε_{ijk}^2
−1	−1	61	62	−1	1
−1	−1	63	62	1	1
−1	+1	41	38	3	9
−1	+1	35	38	−3	9
+1	−1	76	74	2	4
+1	−1	72	74	−2	4
+1	+1	68	66	2	4
+1	+1	64	66	−2	4

The model standard error is:

$$s_\varepsilon = \sqrt{\frac{1+1+9+9+4+4+4+4}{8-4}} = \sqrt{\frac{36}{4}} = 3.0$$

To determine the coefficient of determination r^2, we need to find the amount of total variation present in the response. This is given by:

$$SS_{total} = \sum \left(y_{ijk} - \overline{y}_{...} \right)^2$$

which is just the sum of squares required to calculate the variance (or standard deviation) of the y_{ijk}. Subtracting $\overline{y}_{...}$ from each of the y_{ijk}, squaring the results, and adding the squares, we get:

$$
\begin{aligned}
SS_{total} &= \sum \left(y_{ijk} - 60 \right)^2 \\
&= \left(61 - 60 \right)^2 + \left(63 - 60 \right)^2 + \left(41 - 60 \right)^2 + \cdots \\
&= 1476
\end{aligned}
$$

The coefficient of determination is given by:

$$
\begin{aligned}
r^2 &= 1 - \frac{SS_\varepsilon}{SS_{total}} \\
&= 1 - \frac{36}{1476} \\
&= 0.976
\end{aligned}
$$

The adjusted coefficient of determination is given by:

$$
\begin{aligned}
r^2_{adjusted} &= 1 - \frac{df_{total} \times SS_\varepsilon}{df_\varepsilon \times SS_{total}} \\
&= 1 - \frac{7 \times 36}{4 \times 1476} \\
&= 0.957
\end{aligned}
$$

Example 9.5

   Find and interpret the regression coefficient t values and the corresponding p values for Example 9.3.

   Solution: *We need to determine the regression coefficient standard deviations in order to find their t values. The standard deviations for regression coefficients were defined in Chapter 8. For the constant term, the standard deviation is:*

$$s_{b_0} = s_\varepsilon \sqrt{\frac{1}{n} + \frac{\overline{x}^2}{SS_x}}$$

Since the mean level of each variable is $\overline{x} = 0$, this expression simplifies to:

$$s_{b_0} = \frac{s_\varepsilon}{\sqrt{n}}$$

For the example problem we have:

$$s_{b_0} = \frac{3.0}{\sqrt{8}} = 1.061$$

Also from Chapter 8, the standard deviation of the b_1 coefficient is given by:

$$s_{b_1} = \frac{s_\varepsilon}{\sqrt{SS_x}}$$

where $SS_x = \Sigma(x_i - \bar{x})^2$. Again, since $\bar{x} = 0$ by design and since the x values are either +1 or −1, this expression simplifies to:

$$s_{b_1} = \frac{s_\varepsilon}{\sqrt{n}}$$

so again we have:

$$s_{b_1} = 3/\sqrt{8} = 1.061$$

Similarly, the standard deviations of the b_2 and b_{12} coefficients are also equal to 1.061. (It is common for several of the standard deviations of the regression coefficients in simple designed experiments to be equal.) The t values for the regression coefficients are found by taking the ratio of each coefficient to its standard deviation so we have:

$$t_{b_0} = \frac{b_0}{s_{b_0}} = \frac{60}{1.061} = 56.6$$

$$t_{b_1} = \frac{b_1}{s_{b_1}} = \frac{10}{1.061} = 9.43$$

$$t_{b_2} = \frac{b_2}{s_{b_2}} = \frac{-8}{1.061} = -7.54$$

$$t_{b_{12}} = \frac{b_{12}}{s_{b_{12}}} = \frac{4}{1.061} = 3.77$$

These values correspond to the t values used in hypothesis tests of H_0: the coefficient is zero versus H_A: the coefficient is different from zero. For example, $t_{b_1} = 9.43$ indicates that the coefficient $b_1 = 10$ is 9.43 of its standard deviations greater than zero. This indicates, without much doubt, that the coefficient is different from zero (that is, that H_A should be accepted). The corresponding p value indicates just how much doubt there is in this conclusion. A p value measures the tail area under the t distribution that characterizes the distribution of the experimental regression coefficient outboard of the t value.

*Since the hypothesis test being used is two-tailed, the p value gets contributions from both tails. The degrees of freedom for the t distributions used here are equal to df_ε. The t values for the first three regression coefficients are large enough so that their p values are very near zero. A t table shows that $t_{0.01,4} = 3.75$ so the p value for $t_{b_{12}} = 3.77$ is about $p = 2(0.01) = 0.02$. The exact p values are easiest to find using MINITAB's **invcdf** function or from the **Calc> Probability Distribution** menu. The results of the regression analysis are summarized in the following table:*

Source	b	s	t	p
Constant	60	1.06	57	0.00
x_1	10	1.06	9.4	0.00
x_2	-8.0	1.06	-7.5	0.00
x_{12}	4.0	1.06	3.8	0.02

$df_{total} = 7 \qquad s_\varepsilon = 3.0$

$df_{model} = 3 \qquad r^2 = 0.977$

$df_\varepsilon = 4 \qquad r^2_{adjusted} = 0.957$

Example 9.6

Perform the MINITAB analysis on the data from Example 9.3 and compare it to the summary table above. Construct the necessary plots to check assumptions.

Solution: The analysis by MINITAB of the example data is shown in Figure 9.12. MINITAB confirms all of the values that we calculated manually. The diagnostic plots that must be constructed and the characteristics to check from each of them are: the normal plot of residuals for normality and outlier check; a plot of residuals versus observation order for independence and homoscedasticity; plots of residuals versus independent variables for homoscedasticity; and a plot of residuals versus predicted values for homoscedasticity. There is some redundancy in creating all of these plots; however, there is no harm done by checking them all. The diagnostic plots are shown in Figure 9.13 and they confirm that all necessary conditions are met, although some of the graphs are a little coarse and hard to interpret because of the relatively small number of observations.

9.4 THE 2³ FACTORIAL DESIGN

The 2^3 factorial design has two levels of each of three variables and requires $2 \times 2 \times 2 = 8$ runs. The 2^3 design matrix is shown in Table 9.1. The matrix of runs is generated by alternating between levels –1 and +1 for runs one to eight of variable x_3. Then variable x_2 is generated by alternating pairs of –1s and +1s. Finally, variable x_1 is generated by taking four –1s and then four +1s. Since the same number of –1s and +1s appear in each column, the experiment is balanced. The assignment of the names x_1, x_2, and x_3 to the three columns is arbitrary. The two- and three-factor interactions were added to the table by multiplying the appropriate columns of signs.

The experimental runs in Table 9.1 are organized by their logical or *standard order* indicated by the column labeled *Std.* To prevent the effects of study variables from being

```
MTB > let c4=c2*c3
MTB > corr c2-c4;
SUBC> nopvalue.
```

Correlations: x1, x2, x12

```
        x1      x2
x2    0.000
x12   0.000   0.000
```

```
Cell Contents: Pearson correlation
```

```
MTB > regress c1 3 c2-c4
```

Regression Analysis: y versus x1, x2, x12

```
The regression equation is
y = 60.0 + 10.0 x1 - 8.00 x2 + 4.00 x12
```

```
Predictor    Coef   SE Coef      T       P
Constant   60.000    1.061   56.57   0.000
x1         10.000    1.061    9.43   0.001
x2         -8.000    1.061   -7.54   0.002
x12         4.000    1.061    3.77   0.020
```

```
S = 3    R-Sq = 97.6%    R-Sq(adj) = 95.7%
```

```
Analysis of Variance
```

```
Source           DF        SS       MS       F      P
Regression        3   1440.00   480.00   53.33  0.001
Residual Error    4     36.00     9.00
Total             7   1476.00
```

```
Source   DF   Seq SS
x1        1   800.00
x2        1   512.00
x12       1   128.00
```

Figure 9.12 MINITAB analysis of data from Example 9.3.

confounded with lurking variables, the runs should be performed in *random order,* such as the order shown in the column labeled *Run.* The first run of the experiment (*Run* = 1) must be configured with x_1 at its +1 level, x_2 at its –1 level, and x_3 at its +1 level. Then the process should be operated to generate a part or whatever the output of the process happens to be. After the first run has been completed, the process should be reconfigured for the second run (*Run* = 2) and so on until all eight runs have been completed.

If the 2^3 design is to be replicated, the runs should be randomized either by: 1) randomizing completely over all possible runs or 2) randomizing the order of the runs within each replicate. If the latter method is used, then the replicates can be treated as blocks to protect against lurking variables that change from block to block. This benefit makes blocking on replicates preferred over randomizing over all possible runs.

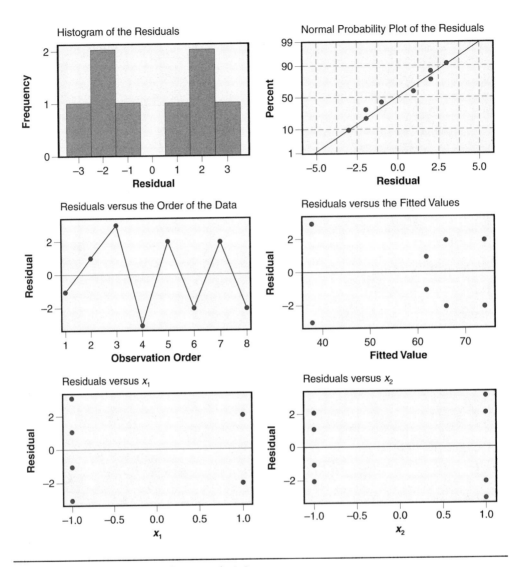

Figure 9.13 Diagnostic plots for Example 9.6.

Table 9.1 Matrix of runs for 2^3 design.

Std	Run	x_1	x_2	x_3	x_{12}	x_{13}	x_{23}	x_{123}
1	8	−	−	−	+	+	+	−
2	3	−	−	+	+	−	−	+
3	2	−	+	−	−	+	−	+
4	6	−	+	+	−	−	+	−
5	5	+	−	−	−	−	+	+
6	1	+	−	+	−	+	−	−
7	4	+	+	−	+	−	−	−
8	7	+	+	+	+	+	+	+

When a 2^3 experiment is blocked on replicates, the blocks constitute a fourth variable that is qualitative. The method of analysis for the blocked 2^3 experiment is to fit a general linear model (GLM), which is available in MINITAB's **Stat> ANOVA> General Linear Model** menu. The use of general linear models is covered in Chapter 7. MINITAB's DOE tools can also analyze the blocked experiment. With either method of analysis, if there are no significant differences between blocks defined by replicates, then the model can be simplified by ignoring the blocking structure. The little bit of added complexity that comes with blocking on replicates is well worth the trouble.

The 2^3 experiment design can be visualized as a cube, as in Figure 9.14, with an experimental run at each of the cube's corners. The numbers in parentheses next to each run correspond to the standard order numbers from Table 9.1. Practice until you become proficient in thinking about 2^k experiments this way. Even when an experiment involves more than three variables, it is still possible and useful to think about the design in terms of just three variables at a time.

A regression analysis of the 2^3 factorial experiment can fit the following model:

$$y = b_0 + b_1 x_1 + b_2 x_2 + b_3 x_3 + b_{12} x_{12} + b_{13} x_{13} + b_{23} x_{23} + b_{123} x_{123} \qquad (9.19)$$

where the bs are all regression coefficients. The b_0 term is referred to as the model's constant; the coefficients b_1, b_2, and b_3 are called the main effects; the b_{12}, b_{13}, and b_{23} terms are two-factor interactions; and b_{123} is a three-factor interaction. In engineering and manufacturing it is rare to encounter a significant three-factor interaction so this term is usually omitted from the model. Then the sum of squares and degrees of freedom associated with the three-factor interaction term are pooled (that is, combined) with the error.

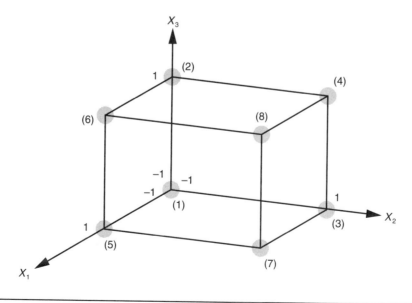

Figure 9.14 2^3 design.

Since all of the design variables in the 2^3 experiment have an equal number of runs at their -1 and $+1$ levels, the average level of each design variable is $\bar{x}_i = 0$ where $i = 1$, 2, 3 indicates the design variable. This means that the constant b_0 in the regression model must be equal to the grand mean of the response, that is, $b_0 = \bar{y}$. While it is appropriate to compare the magnitudes of $b_1, b_2, \ldots, b_{123}$ to each other, b_0 may be several orders of magnitude different than the other regression coefficients. The information contained in b_0 is different in nature from the information contained in the other regression coefficients. It's best to interpret b_0 as a reference value or anchor for the response and the other regression coefficients as perturbations to the response due to the different model terms. For example, the expected values of the response with x_1 at its ± 1 levels are given by $b_0 \pm b_1$, the expected values of the response with x_2 at its ± 1 levels are given by $b_0 \pm b_2$, and so on.

If an experiment uses a single replicate of a 2^3 design then the model in Equation 9.19 will consume all available degrees of freedom. This means that the model given by Equation 9.19 would exactly fit all eight data points without error. Not having an error estimate is a serious problem. Without any degrees of freedom left to estimate error there is no standard error, no regression coefficient standard deviations, no ANOVA F statistic, and so on. There are two ways to resolve this problem. Either the experiment must be replicated to provide additional degrees of freedom to estimate the error, or one or more terms must be eliminated from the model and used to form the error estimate. Since it is rare to find significant three-factor interactions in engineering and manufacturing problems, the three-factor interaction term is usually omitted from the model and becomes the error estimate. This only provides one degree of freedom for the error estimate, but it's a start. After fitting the model with just one degree of freedom for the error estimate, it is likely that other model terms will appear to be insignificant. These terms can also be eliminated from the model and pooled with the error estimate.

As you refine a model, be careful to preserve its hierarchy. This means that in order to keep an interaction term in the model, the main effects contributing to the interaction must be retained in the model whether or not they are statistically significant. If a three-factor or higher-order interaction is to be retained in the model, then all possible lower-order interactions must also be retained.

When can you stop refining a model? To some degree the p values for the regression coefficients can be helpful, but this is really a judgment call that can only be made by the person doing the analysis. One strategy is to keep eliminating terms from the model until the standard error reaches a minimum value. Eliminating a term from the model causes its sum of squares to be combined with the error sum of squares and its single degree of freedom to be added to the error degrees of freedom. If the term is truly insignificant, the effect of the additional error degree of freedom will outweigh the addition to the error sum of squares and the standard error of the model will decrease. If the dropped term is significant, then the addition to the error sum of squares will outweigh the benefit of the additional error degree of freedom and the standard error of the model will increase. There are no hard and fast rules about how far to take the refinements to a model, but remember, *when refining a model, always keep Occam's razor in mind: the best model is probably the simplest one that explains the data.*

Example 9.7

A 2^3 experiment was performed to study the breaking strength of plastic wire ties used for stabilizing and organizing wiring in electrical enclosures. The experimental variables were A: Manufacturer, B: Temperature, and C: Age. The matrix of experimental runs and the breaking strength response are shown in Figure 9.15. The figure also shows the regression analysis using the full model with main effects and two- and three-factor interactions. Use the regression analysis and the sums of squares associated with the different model terms to identify a refined model.

Solution: The regression analysis in Figure 9.15 shows the full model with main effects and two- and three-factor interactions. Since the experiment has only one replicate of the 2^3 design, there are no degrees of freedom left over for the error estimate. Occam says that the most complex factor is the least likely to be important so the three-factor interaction should be the first one omitted from the model. This frees up a single degree of freedom so that an error estimate can be made and p values for regression coefficients can be calculated.

Table 9.2 shows the results of a series of regression analyses, starting from the full model and progressing to the simplest model where all terms have been dropped, where the weakest term in the model was dropped in each successive step. (This analysis was run manually; however, the same analysis can be performed automatically using **Stat> Regression> Stepwise.** *Be careful using automated stepwise regression because it doesn't check to make sure that the models fitted are hierarchical.) The regression coefficient p values, standard errors, and coefficients of determination don't suggest an obvious stopping point for model simplification. The larger models suggest that the B variable doesn't have any affect on the response so all terms involving B should certainly be dropped. The model with A, C, and AC is appealing except that the AC term is weak ($p = 0.107$). However, when AC is dropped from the model, then the C term is no longer statistically significant ($p = 0.080$). The only model with terms that are all statistically significant is the model including only the A variable ($p = 0.026$); however, this model may be oversimplified. The two best candidate models to report appear to be the model with A, C, and AC and the model with only A. Figure 9.16, which shows the r^2 and r^2_{adj} values from Table 9.2 as a function of df_{model}, confirms that there's no abrupt change in the quality of the model as individual model terms are added or removed. Clearly, more data are required to clarify the importance of C in the model.*

9.5 THE ADDITION OF CENTER CELLS TO 2^K DESIGNS

The power of any 2^k experiment, that is, its ability to detect small differences between the ±1 states of each of its variables, can be increased by adding experimental runs. Runs cannot be added to an experiment in an arbitrary manner, however. To preserve the very important balance (that is, orthogonality) of the 2^k designs, it is necessary to add runs by adding complete replicates. Since each replicate requires an additional 2^k runs, replicating a complete experiment design can be expensive. The only other way to add runs to a 2^k experiment without unbalancing it is to add center cells to the design. Center

```
MTB > let c5=c2*c3
MTB > let c6=c2*c4
MTB > let c7=c3*c4
MTB > let c8=c2*c3*c4
MTB > print c1-c8
```

Data Display

```
Row    y    A    B    C    AB   AC   BC   ABC
 1    91    1   -1   -1   -1   -1    1    1
 2   123    1    1    1    1    1    1    1
 3    68   -1   -1   -1    1    1    1   -1
 4   131    1   -1    1   -1    1   -1   -1
 5    85    1    1   -1    1   -1   -1   -1
 6    87   -1   -1    1    1   -1   -1    1
 7    64   -1    1   -1   -1    1   -1    1
 8    57   -1    1    1   -1   -1    1   -1
```

```
MTB > corr c2-c8;
SUBC> nopvalue.
```

Correlations: A, B, C, AB, AC, BC, ABC

```
            A        B        C       AB       AC       BC
B        0.000
C        0.000    0.000
AB       0.000    0.000    0.000
AC       0.000    0.000    0.000    0.000
BC       0.000    0.000    0.000    0.000    0.000
ABC      0.000    0.000    0.000    0.000    0.000    0.000
```

```
Cell Contents: Pearson correlation
```

```
MTB > regress c1 7 c2-c8
```

Regression Analysis: y versus A, B, C, AB, AC, BC, ABC

```
The regression equation is
y = 88.3 + 19.3 A - 6.00 B + 11.2 C + 2.50 AB + 8.25 AC - 3.50 BC + 3.00 ABC

Predictor      Coef    SE Coef      T      P
Constant    88.2500         *      *      *
A           19.2500         *      *      *
B           -6.00000        *      *      *
C           11.2500         *      *      *
AB           2.50000        *      *      *
AC           8.25000        *      *      *
BC          -3.50000        *      *      *
ABC          3.00000        *      *      *

S = *

Analysis of Variance

Source           DF         SS       MS    F    P
Regression        7    5029.500  718.500    *    *
Residual Error    0           *        *
Total             7    5029.500

Source   DF     Seq SS
A         1    2964.500
B         1     288.000
C         1    1012.500
AB        1      50.000
AC        1     544.500
BC        1      98.000
ABC       1      72.000
```

Figure 9.15 Regression analysis of a 2^3 design using the full model.

Table 9.2 Results from fitting a series of reduced models to a 2^3 design.

Term	Coeff	SS	p Values						
A	19.25	2964.5	0.022	0.020	0.008	0.008	0.013	0.026	
B	−6.00	288.0	0.098	0.162	0.142				
C	11.25	1012.5	0.295	0.055	0.034	0.048	0.080		
AB	2.50	50.0	0.166						
AC	8.25	544.5	0.558	0.096	0.072	0.107			
BC	−3.50	98.0	0.222	0.333					
ABC	3.00	72.0							
SS_{model}		5029.5	4957.5	4907.5	4809.5	4521.5	3977.0	2964.5	0
SS_{ε}		0	72.0	122	220	508	1052.5	2065	5029.5
df_{model}		7	6	5	4	3	2	1	0
df_{ε}		0	1	2	3	4	5	6	7
MS_{ε}		*	72.0	61.0	73.3	127	210.5	344.2	718.5
s_{ε}		*	8.5	7.8	8.6	11.3	14.5	18.6	26.8
r^2		1.0	0.986	0.976	0.956	0.899	0.791	0.589	0
r^2_{adj}		*	0.900	0.915	0.898	0.823	0.707	0.521	0

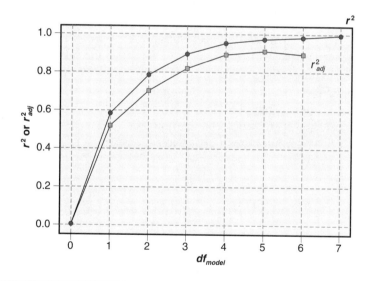

Figure 9.16 r^2 and r^2_{adj} versus df_{model} for wire tie strength example.

cells have all of their variables at their zero level, that is, $(x_1, x_2, \ldots) = (0, 0, \ldots)$. This means that to add center cells to an experiment, all of the variables in the experiment must be quantitative and that a zero level midway between the ± 1 state of each variable must be available. Any number of center cells can be added to an experiment without unbalancing the design.

It may seem strange that the error estimate for a 2^k design with centers can be substantially determined using information from the center cells, especially when an experiment has few or even no error degrees of freedom before the center cells are added. This practice is justified as long as the homoscedasticity assumption, that the distribution of error variability is constant throughout the design space, is satisfied.

The increase in the power of an experiment provided by the addition of center cells is limited. When an experiment has relatively few initial error degrees of freedom, adding center cells can improve the situation significantly. For example, a 2^3 experiment with just one replicate will only have one error degree of freedom if the model includes main effects and two-factor interactions:

$$df_\varepsilon = df_{total} - df_{model} = (8-1)-(3+3) = 1$$

The addition of a few center cell runs can provide the additional error degrees of freedom that make the analysis of the experiment easier and confidence in its interpretation higher. If, however, the 2^3 design has been replicated many times, the additional center cells won't increase the number of error degrees of freedom enough to improve the error estimate significantly.

Although the use of center cells can improve the power of some experiments, the usual reason that center cells are added to 2^k experiments is to allow for a test of curvature in the response between the ±1 levels of quantitative design variables. Since the 2^k experiments only have two levels of each variable, they provide no opportunity to test the assumed linearity between the ±1 states, which is essential if the model is to be used for interpolation. Center cells provide the necessary third state required to test the linearity assumption. Tests for the linearity assumption will be presented in Chapter 11. For the purposes of this chapter, the discussion of center cells will be limited to their contribution to the error degrees of freedom; however, if you are using center cells in a 2^k design, you should definitely read ahead into Chapter 11 to learn how to evaluate your experiment for possible curvature.

9.6 GENERAL PROCEDURE FOR ANALYSIS OF 2^k DESIGNS

Regardless of what software you're using to analyze 2^k designs, or whether you do the analysis step by step or with some off-the-shelf comprehensive analysis package, the same basic steps need to be considered. These steps are:

1. Enter the design matrix of ±1 values into the appropriate columns of the worksheet. Add columns indicating the standard order, run order, blocks, and experimental response. Use an appropriate missing value symbol in the response column to indicate any missing observations. (MINITAB's missing value symbol is an asterisk [*].)

2. Create columns for the two-factor and, if necessary, any desired higher-order interactions by multiplying the appropriate columns of main effects together.

3. Delete any rows/runs that correspond to missing or otherwise seriously compromised observations. Construct the correlation (r) matrix of main effects and interactions. The purpose of constructing and inspecting the correlation matrix is to check the validity and integrity of the experiment design. If the experiment was designed correctly and there were no missing or extra observations, the correlation matrix should have $r = 0$ everywhere except on the diagonal where the row variable and the column variable are the same where $r = 1$. This structure in the correlation matrix is present by design; it is an important characteristic of a well-designed experiment. If there was a mistake creating the matrix of runs or the interactions, or if there were missing or extra runs that unbalanced the experiment, at least some of the off-diagonal correlations will be non-zero. Inspect these cases to determine if any correlations are so high that they compromise the integrity of the experiment. If so, identify and implement appropriate corrective actions before attempting to analyze the experiment.

4. Perform and interpret some type of graphical analysis of the response as a function of the design variables, such as a multi-vari chart for smaller experiments or main effects and interaction plots for larger ones.

5. Analyze the response as a function of the main effects, two-factor interactions, any desired higher-order interactions, and blocks. Interpret the p values of the model terms to determine which terms are significant. Interpret the standard error of the model s_ε and the adjusted coefficient of determination r^2_{adj}.

6. If the model has a large number of terms, create a normal probability plot of the regression coefficient t values. (The t values are used instead of the coefficients themselves because sometimes the coefficients can have different standard errors, so it's more appropriate to compare their t values instead.) Points that plot near $t_i = 0$ correspond to insignificant model terms, and outliers correspond to significant model terms. Add reference lines to the normal plot corresponding to the threshold t values at $\pm t_{\alpha/2, df_\varepsilon}$ to help distinguish between insignificant and significant terms.

7. Perform an analysis of the residuals to validate the analysis method:

   a. Inspect the histogram of residuals for normality and potential outliers.

   b. Inspect the normal probability plot of the residuals for normality and potential outliers.

   c. Inspect the plot of residuals versus run order for homoscedasticity and independence.

   d. Inspect the plot of residuals versus fits for homoscedasticity.

e. Inspect the plot of residuals versus blocks for homoscedasticity.

f. Inspect each plot of the residuals versus the independent variables for homoscedasticity.

8. If a more quantitative test for outliers is required, compare the deleted Studentized residuals for the suspect observations to the Bonferroni corrected critical value $t_{\alpha/(2n),df_\varepsilon}$. Observations whose deleted Studentized residuals are larger in magnitude than this critical value are probably statistical outliers. Attempt to correlate any unusual observations from when the experiment was being performed to the suspected outliers to find grounds for omitting these observations from the data set; however, *never* omit any observations without good cause. Resolve the effects of outliers on the model before accepting a final model.

9. Identify terms that can be omitted from the model without significantly compromising its predictive capability and refine the model. Be careful to preserve the hierarchy of terms in the model. This operation may have to be performed in a series of incremental steps.

10. Accept a refined model, determine its regression coefficients, standard error, and adjusted coefficient of determination, and confirm that the assumptions required of the analysis method are satisfied.

9.7 2^K FACTORIAL DESIGNS IN MINITAB

9.7.1 Creating the 2^k Designs in MINITAB

There are several different ways to create 2^k factorial designs in MINITAB:

- Manually enter all of the ±1 values for each column into the worksheet.

- Copy the design from an existing file, such as the appropriate *2^k.mtw* MINITAB worksheet or the *2^k.xls* Excel worksheet provided on the CD-ROM included with this book.

- Use the **set** command (or the **Calc> Make Patterned Data> Simple Set of Numbers** menu) to create the necessary pattern of ±1 values for each column.

- Use MINITAB's **Stat> DOE> Factorial> Create Factorial Design** menu to specify and create the design.

The first three methods are much less important now that MINITAB contains the **Stat> DOE** tools; however, these methods are still useful in special cases and are certainly worth studying to better understand the 2^k factorial designs. Always check your work carefully if you use any of these methods, because an unidentified mistake at this stage can ruin an experiment. You will also have to create your own randomization and blocking plans for the experimental runs.

The first method above—manually creating the matrix of experimental runs—is only practical for the smallest designs. For example, the 2^2 and 2^3 designs with just four and eight runs, respectively, can be quickly typed into a worksheet and then copy/paste operations can be used to create the desired number of replicates. Any experiments larger than 2^4 are too complicated and time-consuming to create manually, however, and there are just too many opportunities to make mistakes.

Opportunities for using the second method above—copying the design from an existing worksheet—might be more frequent than you think. Relatively few of the 2^k designs are regularly used, so a small collection of designs can be quite comprehensive. The handful of designs included on the CD-ROM will be sufficient for most experiments. And once a new design has been created, it's easy to copy it from its original worksheet and paste it into a new one when that design is required for another experiment.

With some practice, the third method above—creating the matrix of experimental runs with the **set** command (or the **Calc> Make Patterned Data> Simple Set of Numbers** menu)—can be a fast and safe way of creating 2^k designs. A 2^k design will require k calls of the **set** command to create the necessary pattern of ± 1 values for each of the k columns of the design. The **set** command can also be used to create a column for the standard order of the runs and then the **sample** command (or the **Calculate> Random Data> Sample from Columns** menu) can be used to determine the random run order.

The fourth method above—creating the design using the **Stat> DOE> Factorial> Create Factorial Design** menu—is quick, safe, and easy, and designs created by this method are ready to analyze from the **Stat> DOE> Factorial> Analyze Factorial Design** menu. MINITAB takes care of all of the randomization and blocking, too. Designs created by other means can still be analyzed with **Stat> DOE> Factorial> Analyze Factorial Design** if they are first defined in MINITAB using **Stat> DOE> Factorial> Define Factorial Design**. This step creates the necessary hidden links between the worksheet and MINITAB so that the **Stat> DOE> Factorial> Analyze Factorial Design** function can locate the necessary information to complete the analysis.

Example 9.8

*Use MINITAB's **Calc> Make Patterned Data> Simple Set of Numbers** menu or the **set** command to create the 2^4 experiment design.*

*Solution: The first four columns of the MINITAB worksheet were named $x1$, $x2$, $x3$, and $x4$. The following table shows how the inputs to the **Calc> Make Patterned Data> Simple Set of Numbers** menu were set to create the matrix of experimental runs:*

Store patterned data in:	$x1$	$x2$	$x3$	$x4$
From first value:	−1	−1	−1	−1
To last value:	1	1	1	1
In steps of:	2	2	2	2
List each value	8	4	2	1
List the whole sequence	1	2	4	8

*Alternatively, the corresponding **set** commands could be typed at the command prompt in the Session window. For example, to create the x1 column in* C1, *use:*

```
mtb> set c1
data> 1(-1:1/2)8
data> end.
```

*When you use the **Calc> Make Patterned Data> Simple Set of Numbers** menu with the command prompt enabled, these **set** commands will also appear in the Session window. Figure 9.17 shows these commands in the Session window and the resulting matrix of experimental runs. The **set** command was also used to determine the standard order column, and the **sample** command (or the **Calc> Random Data> Sample from Columns** menu) was used to determine a random order for the runs.*

Example 9.9

*Use MINITAB's **Stat> DOE> Factorial> Create Factorial Design** menu to recreate the 2^4 experiment design.*

*Solution: The 2^4 design was created using MINITAB's **Stat> DOE > Factorial> Create Factorial Design** menu. In the **Create Factorial Design** menu, a two-level*

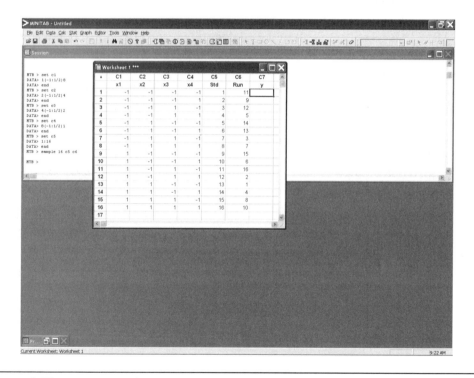

Figure 9.17 Creating the 2^4 design with the **Calc> Make Patterned Data> Simple Set of Numbers** menu or the **set** command.

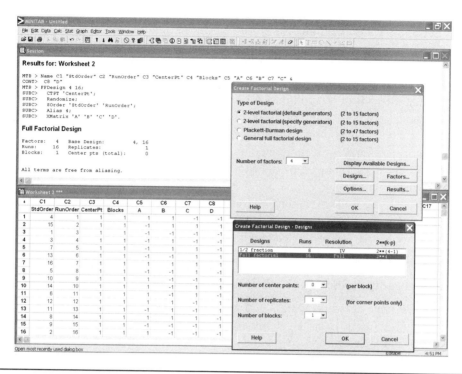

Figure 9.18 Stat> DOE> Factorial> **Create Factorial Design** configuration to create the 2^4 design.

factorial design with four factors was selected. Then in the **Designs** *menu the* **Full factorial** *design was chosen. These instructions and the resulting 16-run experiment design with the runs in random order are shown in Figure 9.18. The* **CenterPt** *and* **Blocks** *columns are special columns required by MINITAB's* **Stat> DOE> Factorial> Analyze Factorial Design** *tool.*

9.7.2 Analyzing the 2^k Factorial Designs with MINITAB

There are at least three different ways to analyze data from a 2^k factorial experiment using MINITAB. The first and easiest way is to use the experiment design and analysis tools provided in MINITAB's **Stat> DOE> Factorial> Analyze Factorial Design** menu. The second way is to use the special experiment analysis macros provided with this text. These are MINITAB local *.mac* macros that include the standard set of analyses along with some special analyses that aren't usually provided but are still easy to implement. The third way to analyze a 2^k experiment in MINITAB is to run the analysis manually, step by step. The three methods give largely the same results.

The two primary MINITAB tools that can be used to perform manual analyses of 2^k designs are the **Stat> Regression> Regression** menu and the **Stat> ANOVA> General Linear Model** menu. Both methods give exactly the same results when they are configured correctly. The primary disadvantages of the **Stat> Regression> Regression** menu are: 1) you must create columns for all of the desired interactions before running the analysis and 2) if the experiment was run in blocks and you want to include a term for blocks in the model, you have to build columns of indicator variables for the blocks using the method of Section 8.17. The advantages of the **Stat> Regression> Regression** menu are that after all of the columns for the interactions and blocks are created: 1) it is easy to create the correlation matrix to check the integrity of the design/experiment, 2) it is very easy to configure the regression analysis, and 3) the algorithm is a little bit more robust to problems with some models than other methods.

The primary disadvantages of the **Stat> ANOVA> General Linear Model** menu are: 1) you have to explicitly type out the desired model, which can be tedious and tricky for larger designs, 2) the algorithm can be sensitive to problems with some models, and 3) there's no easy way to create the correlation matrix. The primary advantages are: 1) the GLM tool is very flexible and can be used to analyze very complex experiments and 2) if the experiment is blocked it's easy to include blocks in the model.

Manual Analysis with Stat> Regression> Regression

To better appreciate the more automated analysis methods, let's consider the manual method of analysis first. Even if you always intend to use MINITAB's integrated DOE analysis tools in the **Stat> DOE** menu, it's useful to consider these steps to better understand what MINITAB is doing. The method described here uses the **Stat> Regression> Regression** approach and is the same method captured in the *mlrk.mac* macros, which will be described in the next section.

The steps in a manual analysis of a 2^k experiment using MINITAB are:

1. Enter the matrix of experimental runs into a new MINITAB worksheet or load the desired design from an existing project or worksheet file if the design already exists. The worksheet should have one column for each variable. Use short but informative names preceded by a generic prefix for the columns such as *x1:Temp, x2:Press, x3:Time, or A:Temp, B:Press, C:Time.*

2. If the experiment was replicated, copy the first replicate into new rows of the original columns for as many replicates as are required. If the experiment was blocked, perhaps on replicates, add a column to uniquely distinguish each block.

3. Enter the response into a single column of the MINITAB worksheet and give it an informative name. Indicate missing values with the "*" missing value symbol. Add a column to the worksheet indicating the run order of the observations.

4. Use the **Calc> Calculator** menu or **let** statements to build all of the two-factor interactions to be included in the model. Higher-order interactions can also be generated but usually aren't. Use the generic variable prefixes to name the interactions, such as *x12, x13, x14, or AB, AC, AD.*

5. If the experiment was blocked, use the **Calc> Make Indicator Variables** menu or the **indicator** command to translate the blocking column with *b* blocks into *b* columns of indicator variables.

6. Create the correlation matrix including all main effects, two-factor interactions, and blocks from the **Stat> Basic Stats> Correlation** menu or with the **correlation** command. You may wish to suppress the obnoxious display of p values for the correlation coefficients by turning off the **Display p-values** option or by using the **nopvalues** subcommand. By design, the correlation matrix should be diagonal with zero correlation between unlike terms (for example, x_1 and x_2) and unity correlation between like terms (for example, x_1 and x_1). Inspect the correlation matrix for non-zero values in the off-diagonal fields, which would indicate errors in an earlier step. Some correlation is expected between the different blocks but these correlations should be symmetric.

7. If there are more than a few missing observations, copy the worksheet to a new worksheet, delete the rows that contain missing observations, then recreate the correlation matrix and inspect it for substantial correlations between model terms. If there are any substantial correlations, the experiment is compromised and remedial actions will have to be taken before it's safe to complete the analysis.

8. In the first $b - 1$ of b columns of indicator variables for the blocks, change all of the zero values in the rows corresponding to the last block to −1s.

9. Use the **Stat> Regression> Regression** menu or the **regress** command to analyze the response as a function of all of the desired main effects, interactions, and blocks. Include only the first $b - 1$ columns of modified block indicators in the model. Open the **Graphs** menu and turn on the appropriate residuals diagnostic plots. Set the **Storage** menu to store the residuals, fits, regression coefficients, and deleted (Studentized) t residuals in case they're needed for further analysis.

10. Inspect the residuals diagnostic plots for normality, homoscedasticity, independence, and the presence of outliers. If any of the observations appear to be outliers, check their deleted (Studentized) t residuals that were stored in step 9. Observations with deleted Studentized residuals of magnitude greater than $t_{\alpha/(2n),df_\varepsilon}$ are probably outliers, where n is the number of observations in the data set and df_ε is the error degrees of freedom.

11. If the model has lots of terms, many of which might be statistically insignificant, create a normal probability plot of the regression coefficient t values to help distinguish the significant coefficients from the insignificant ones. To create this plot, use MINITAB's *block copy* operation to copy the regression coefficient t values from the Session window into a new column of the worksheet.* Omit or delete the t value for the model constant because it's

---

* To use MINITAB's block copy operation, hold down the ALT key and use the mouse to select the desired rectangular area in the Session window. Then use the usual copy and paste operations to put a copy of the selected data into a new column or columns of the worksheet.

fundamentally different from the other coefficients and not of interest here. Then use the **Stat> Basic Stats> Normality Test** or **Graph> Probability Plot** menus, or the **normtest** or **pplot** commands to create the normal plot. The insignificant regression coefficients will appear near the middle of the normal plot with coefficient t values near zero and significant coefficients will appear as outliers. Add reference lines at $\pm t_{\alpha/2, df_\varepsilon}$ to help distinguish between significant and insignificant coefficients.

12. Refine the model by dropping insignificant terms identified from the regression coefficient p values and from the normal plot of the regression coefficients. When there are terms on the borderline of being significant ($p \simeq 0.05$), it may be necessary to refine the model in a series of steps by dropping one term—the weakest term—at each step so that the p values can be watched carefully. If a two-factor interaction is to be retained in the model then both of the corresponding main effects must also be retained, whether or not they are significant, to preserve the hierarchy of terms in the model.

13. Before a refined model can be accepted, the residuals must be checked for: normality; homoscedasticity with respect to the regression predictors, run order, and fitted values; and independence. These checks can be done from the residuals diagnostic graphs.

Analysis with the *mlrk.mac* Macros

The *mlrk.mac* macros provided with this text are MINITAB local *.mac* macros that capture most of the instructions described in the previous section. These macros have some extra features that aren't important for 2^k designs but will be required for the designs in the next two chapters.

The *mlrk.mac* macros are run from the MINITAB command prompt with calling statements like:

```
mtb> %mlr3 "Std" "Run" "Center" "Block" "A" "B" "C" "Y";
subc> terms "AB" "AC" "BC" "AA" "BB" "CC".
```

When the columns of the worksheet are in the necessary order, the calling statement is much simpler, like `mtb> %mlr3 c1-c8`. The "k" in the generic *mlrk.mac* designation indicates the number of variables in the design, so *mlr3.mac* is expecting a three-variable experiment, *mlr4.mac* is expecting a four-variable experiment, and so on. It is up to you to apply the correct *mlrk.mac* macro to your experimental data. The definition and order of the input columns to the *mlrk.mac* macros are identical to the columns created by MINITAB's **Stat> DOE> Factorial> Create Factorial Design** menu, so the *mlrk.mac* macros can be used as an alternative to MINITAB's **Stat> DOE> Factorial> Analyze Factorial Design** method. The optional **terms** subcommand stores the indicated two-factor interactions and quadratic terms in the indicated columns of the worksheet. Storing these columns in the worksheet simplifies the steps required to refine a model after the initial model is fitted with the macro. Descriptions of the data formats and instructions for the use of the *mlrk.mac* macros are given in comments at the beginning of each macro that can be viewed in a text editor like Notepad. As an example, the text of the *mlr3.mac* macro is shown in Figure 9.19.

If the experiment is saturated, that is, if there aren't sufficient degrees of freedom to estimate the error, the *mlrk.mac* macros generate the error: *"Error: Not enough data in column"* in which case you will have to continue the analysis manually with a smaller model from the **Stat> Regression> Regression** or the **Stat> ANOVA> General Linear Model** menus. However, before the error is encountered, the macro completes many of its early steps in the analysis so the new model is relatively easy to configure.

The *mlrk.mac* macros cannot create the normal probability plot of the regression coefficient *t* values because MINITAB doesn't have the ability to store them. After the macro is run, however, you can copy the *t* values from the Session window, paste them back into the worksheet, and then create the normal plot. To simplify this operation, a special macro called *coefftnormplot.mac* was written and is included on the CD-ROM. The inputs to the macro are the column of regression coefficient names, the column of *t* values, and the number of error degrees of freedom. An example calling statement for the macro is:

```
mtb> %coefftnormplot "Coeff" "T" 18
```

The *mlrk.mac* macros also call another custom macro that creates a normal plot of the deleted Studentized residuals, which are useful for identifying statistical outliers. Each observation is identified by its run number and reference lines are displayed at the Bonferroni-corrected critical values given by $\pm t_{\alpha/(2n),df_\varepsilon}$ to assist in the identification of outliers.

Example 9.10

The experimental data from a 2^5 experiment are shown in Figure 9.20. Use the mlr5.mac macro to analyze the data and then interpret the results.

Solution: The experimental data were entered into a MINITAB worksheet and then analyzed using the mlr5.mac macro. The command statement was:

```
mtb> %mlr5 c1-c10;
subc> terms c11-c25.
```

The main effects plot in Figure 9.21 suggests that there might be significant effects associated with B, C, and E. The interactions plot in Figure 9.22 suggests that there might be significant interactions due to BC, CE, and possibly AC. The Session window output is shown in Figure 9.23. The correlation matrix, which was edited for space and clarity, confirms that all of the terms in the model are independent of each other. The terms AA, BB, . . . , and EE are quadratic terms that mlr5.mac attempts to include in the model but cannot because the design is not capable of resolving them, consequently, MINITAB omits them from the regression analysis that follows. The Blocks term was also omitted from the model because there is only one block in the experiment. The

```
macro
mlr3 Std Run Ctr Blo A B C Y;
  terms AB AC BC AA BB CC.

#PGMathews, 18 May 2004, V1.0 for Minitab V14
#Copyright (C) 2004 Mathews Malnar and Bailey, Inc.
#See Mathews, Design of Experiments with Minitab, ASQ Press, 2004 for details.
#This macro performs the analysis of a three variable designed experiment with main
#effects, two-factor interactions, quadratic terms, and blocks.
#The expected input data structure is the standard column format created by Minitab 14's
#Stat> DOE> Factorial> Create Factorial Design or ...> Response Surface> Create Response
#Surface Design menus. The macro is suitable for 2^3 and 2^(3-1) with and without centers,
#3^3, BB(3), and CC(3) designs. When two or more terms are confounded, the first term
#encountered will be retained in the model.

#The 'terms' subcommand will output the calculated interactions and quadratic terms
#into the 6 specified columns. (Be careful because those columns will be overwritten.)
#Then subsequent analyses, such as to refine the model, can be performed using Stat> ANOVA>
#General Linear Model.

#Example calling statement:
#    mtb> %mlr3 c1-c8;
#    subc> terms c9-c14.

mcolumn Std Run Ctr Blo A B C Y
mcolumn AB AC BC AA BB CC
mcolumn ID IDCount Block.1-Block.NumBlo.20 DSR coeff
mconstant NumBlo dfmodel i dfe alphaB tcrit

#Make indicator variable columns for the blocks.
max Blo NumBlo        #Number of blocks
indicator Blo Block.1-Block.NumBlo  #Make indicator columns for blocks

#Calculate the interaction and quadratic terms and construct the correlation matrix.
let AB=A*B
let AC=A*C
let BC=B*C
let AA=A*A
let BB=B*B
let CC=C*C
if terms=1     #name the interactions and quadratic terms
  name AB "AB" AC "AC"  BC "BC" AA "AA" BB "BB" CC "CC"
endif

#If you need to view the p values, remove the ; from the following line and comment out the nopvalues subcommand.
corr A B C AB AC BC AA BB CC Block.1-Block.NumBlo;
  nopvalues.
```

Continued

Figue 9.19　Text of *mlr3.mac* macro.

Continued

```
#Fix the block codes for the last (reference) block. To view the coding convention search Minitab
#Help for "Design matrix used by General Linear Model".
let i=1
while i<NumBlo
    let Block.i=Block.i-Block.NumBlo
    let i=i+1
endwhile

#Create the plots of main effects and interactions.
main Blo A B C;
    response Y.
interact A B C;
    response Y;
    full.

#Run the regression analysis
if NumBlo>1       #then the experiment is blocked
    let NumBlo=NumBlo-1    #Keep the last block out of the model
    let dfmodel=NumBlo+3+3
    regress Y dfmodel Block.1-Block.NumBlo A B C AB AC BC AA BB CC;
        gfourpack;    #residuals diagnostic plots
        gvars Blo A B C;    #residuals vs. blocks and study variables
        tresiduals DSR;    #store the deleted Studentized residuals for outlier analysis
        coeff coeff.
else          #no blocking
    let dfmodel=3+3
    regress Y dfmodel A B C AB AC BC AA BB CC;
        gfourpack;
        gvars A B C;
        tresiduals DSR;
        coeff coeff.
endif

#Create normal plot of deleted Studentized residuals with Bonferroni critical values.
let dfe=count(Y)-count(Y)-count(coeff)    #error degrees of freedom, note coeff includes the constant
let alphaB=1-0.05/count(Y)/2    #Bonferroni corrected t value for alpha=0.05
invcdf alphaB tcrit;
    t dfe.
call normplotDSR DSR Run tcrit

endmacro
```

Row	StdOrder	RunOrder	CP	Blocks	A	B	C	D	E	Y
1	25	1	1	1	1	1	-1	-1	-1	226
2	14	2	1	1	-1	1	1	-1	1	150
3	15	3	1	1	-1	1	1	1	-1	284
4	30	4	1	1	1	1	1	-1	1	190
5	29	5	1	1	1	1	1	-1	-1	287
6	2	6	1	1	-1	-1	-1	-1	1	149
7	23	7	1	1	1	-1	1	1	-1	53
8	28	8	1	1	1	1	-1	1	1	232
9	11	9	1	1	-1	1	-1	1	-1	221
10	24	10	1	1	1	-1	1	1	1	-30
11	20	11	1	1	1	-1	-1	1	1	76
12	31	12	1	1	1	1	1	1	-1	270
13	21	13	1	1	1	-1	1	-1	-1	59
14	22	14	1	1	1	-1	1	-1	1	-32
15	3	15	1	1	-1	-1	-1	1	-1	142
16	17	16	1	1	1	-1	-1	-1	-1	121
17	8	17	1	1	-1	-1	1	1	1	-43
18	32	18	1	1	1	1	1	1	1	200
19	19	19	1	1	1	-1	-1	1	-1	123
20	4	20	1	1	-1	-1	-1	1	1	137
21	5	21	1	1	-1	-1	1	-1	-1	1
22	6	22	1	1	-1	-1	1	-1	1	-51
23	26	23	1	1	1	1	-1	-1	1	187
24	13	24	1	1	-1	1	1	-1	-1	265
25	12	25	1	1	-1	1	-1	1	1	233
26	10	26	1	1	-1	1	-1	-1	1	217
27	18	27	1	1	1	-1	-1	-1	1	71
28	16	28	1	1	-1	1	1	1	1	187
29	27	29	1	1	1	1	-1	1	-1	207
30	7	30	1	1	-1	-1	1	1	-1	40
31	1	31	1	1	-1	-1	-1	-1	-1	179
32	9	32	1	1	-1	1	-1	-1	-1	266

Figure 9.20 Experimental data from a 2^5 experiment.

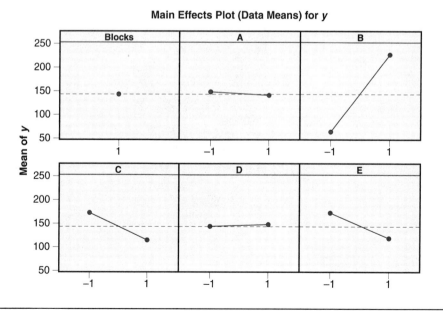

Figure 9.21 Main effects plot from Example 9.10.

Interaction Plot (Data Means) for *y*

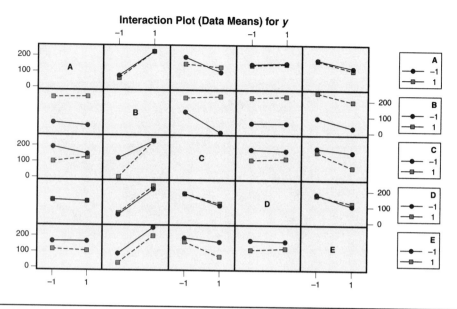

Figure 9.22 Interactions plot from Example 9.10.

regression analysis indicates that there are many statistically significant terms, especially B, C, E, AC, BC, and CE. The standard error of the model is $s_\varepsilon = 19.21$ and the adjusted coefficient of determination is $r^2_{adj} = 0.965$.

The graphical analyses of the residuals created by the macro are shown in Figure 9.24. The residuals diagnostic plots confirm that the residuals are normally distributed and homoscedastic with respect to the run order, the fitted values, and the design variables as required by the ANOVA method. All of the deleted Studentized residuals in the normal plot shown in Figure 9.25 fall inside of the Bonferroni-corrected critical values, so no observations are statistical outliers. The normal plot of the regression coefficient t values in Figure 9.26 was created with the coefftnormplot.mac macro and confirms the conclusions drawn from the regression coefficient p values—there appear to be significant effects due to B, C, E, BC, CE, and AC. The many insignificant model terms stack up in a nice line centered at about $t_i = 0$, which makes the outliers—the statistically significant terms—easy to identify.

*Although the regression model has plenty of error degrees of freedom despite its relatively large size, the model should be simplified by eliminating terms that do not contribute to it. An obvious choice is to eliminate all terms involving D because none of these terms are statistically significant. Other terms also can be dropped from the model. Figure 9.27 shows the regression analysis obtained using **Stat> Regression> Regression** including the statistically significant terms from the original model. It was necessary to retain the statistically insignificant A term in the refined model to preserve the hierarchy of terms since AC is to appear in the model. The new residuals diagnostic plots (not shown) indicated that the residuals were still normal and homoscedastic as required by the regression method.*

Correlations: A, B, C, D, E, AB, AC, AD, AE, BC, BD, BE, CD, CE, DE, AA, BB, CC, DD, EE, Block.1

```
          A   B   C   D   E  AB  AC  AD  AE  BC  BD  BE  CD  CE  DE  AA  BB  CC  DD  EE
B         0
C         0   0
D         0   0   0
E         0   0   0   0
AB        0   0   0   0   0
AC        0   0   0   0   0   0
AD        0   0   0   0   0   0   0
AE        0   0   0   0   0   0   0   0
BC        0   0   0   0   0   0   0   0   0
BD        0   0   0   0   0   0   0   0   0   0
BE        0   0   0   0   0   0   0   0   0   0   0
CD        0   0   0   0   0   0   0   0   0   0   0   0
CE        0   0   0   0   0   0   0   0   0   0   0   0   0
DE        0   0   0   0   0   0   0   0   0   0   0   0   0   0
AA        *   *   *   *   *   *   *   *   *   *   *   *   *   *   *
BB        *   *   *   *   *   *   *   *   *   *   *   *   *   *   *   *
CC        *   *   *   *   *   *   *   *   *   *   *   *   *   *   *   *   *
DD        *   *   *   *   *   *   *   *   *   *   *   *   *   *   *   *   *   *
EE        *   *   *   *   *   *   *   *   *   *   *   *   *   *   *   *   *   *   *
Block.1   *   *   *   *   *   *   *   *   *   *   *   *   *   *   *   *   *   *   *   *
```

Regression Analysis: Y versus A, B, ...

```
* AA is (essentially) constant
* AA has been removed from the equation.

* BB is (essentially) constant
* BB has been removed from the equation.

* CC is (essentially) constant
* CC has been removed from the equation.

* DD is (essentially) constant
* DD has been removed from the equation.

* EE is (essentially) constant
* EE has been removed from the equation.

The regression equation is
Y = 144 - 4.28 A + 82.1 B - 29.9 C + 1.47 D - 27.2 E + 2.78 AB + 14.5 AC
    - 0.09 AD - 1.03 AE + 32.7 BC + 1.41 BD + 0.34 BE + 4.28 CD - 15.8 CE + 5.47 DE
```

Figure 9.23 Output from *mlr5.mac* macro for a 2^5 experiment.

Continued

Continued

Predictor	Coef	SE Coef	T	P
Constant	144.281	3.396	42.49	0.000
A	-4.281	3.396	-1.26	0.225
B	82.094	3.396	24.18	0.000
C	-29.906	3.396	-8.81	0.000
D	1.469	3.396	0.43	0.671
E	-27.219	3.396	-8.02	0.000
AB	2.781	3.396	0.82	0.425
AC	14.531	3.396	4.28	0.001
AD	-0.094	3.396	-0.03	0.978
AE	-1.031	3.396	-0.30	0.765
BC	32.656	3.396	9.62	0.000
BD	1.406	3.396	0.41	0.684
BE	0.344	3.396	0.10	0.921
CD	4.281	3.396	1.26	0.225
CE	-15.781	3.396	-4.65	0.000
DE	5.469	3.396	1.61	0.127

S = 19.2094   R-Sq = 98.2%   R-Sq(adj) = 96.5%

Analysis of Variance

Source	DF	SS	MS	F	P
Regression	15	319388	21293	57.70	0.000
Residual Error	16	5904	369		
Total	31	325292			

Source	DF	Seq SS
A	1	587
B	1	215660
C	1	28620
D	1	69
E	1	23708
AB	1	248
AC	1	6757
AD	1	0
AE	1	34
BC	1	34126
BD	1	63
BE	1	4
CD	1	587
CE	1	7970
DE	1	957

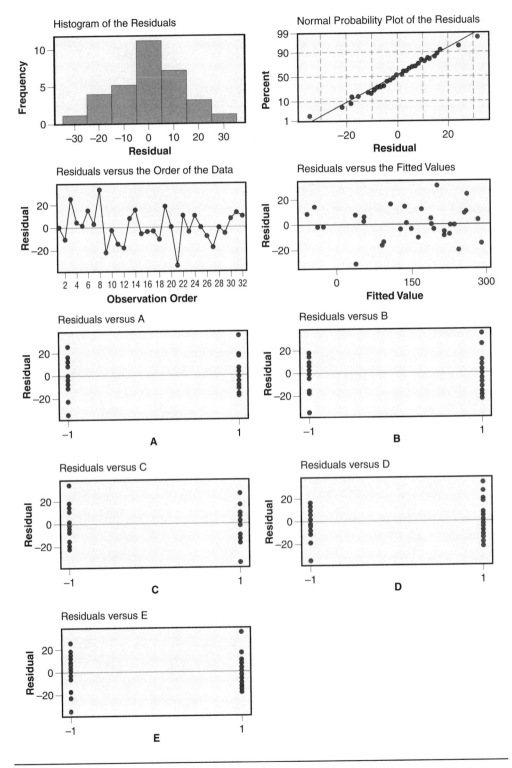

Figure 9.24 Residuals diagnostic plots from a 2^5 experiment.

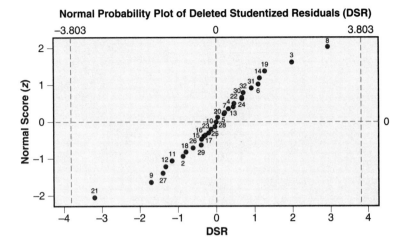

Reference lines indicate Bonferroni-corrected +/− t (0.025/n,df_ε) critical values.

Data labels indicate the run number.

Figure 9.25 Normal probability plot of deleted Studentized residuals.

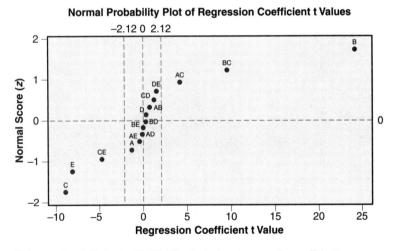

Reference lines indicate +/− t (0.025,df_ε) critical values for regression coefficients.

Figure 9.26 Normal probability plot of regression coefficient *t* values.

```
Regression Analysis: Y versus A, B, C, E, AC, BC, CE

The regression equation is
Y = 144 - 4.28 A + 82.1 B - 29.9 C - 27.2 E + 14.5 AC + 32.7 BC - 15.8 CE

Predictor       Coef   SE Coef       T       P
Constant     144.281     3.200   45.08   0.000
A             -4.281     3.200   -1.34   0.194
B             82.094     3.200   25.65   0.000
C            -29.906     3.200   -9.35   0.000
E            -27.219     3.200   -8.51   0.000
AC            14.531     3.200    4.54   0.000
BC            32.656     3.200   10.20   0.000
CE           -15.781     3.200   -4.93   0.000

S = 18.1033   R-Sq = 97.6%   R-Sq(adj) = 96.9%

Analysis of Variance

Source             DF       SS      MS       F       P
Regression          7   317427   45347  138.37   0.000
Residual Error     24     7866     328
Total              31   325292

Source  DF   Seq SS
A        1      587
B        1   215660
C        1    28620
E        1    23708
AC       1     6757
BC       1    34126
CE       1     7970

Unusual Observations

Obs      A       Y     Fit   SE Fit   Residual   St Resid
  8   1.00  232.00  193.38     9.05      38.63      2.46R
  9  -1.00  221.00  253.88     9.05     -32.88     -2.10R
 21  -1.00    1.00   32.37     9.05     -31.37     -2.00R

R denotes an observation with a large standardized residual.
```

Figure 9.27   Refined model for the 2^5 experiment.

Analysis with MINITAB's DOE Tools (Stat> DOE> Factorial)

You can use MINITAB's **Stat> DOE> Factorial> Create Factorial Design** menu to create a 2^k factorial design that meets your requirements or, if you've created your own matrix of runs for a 2^k experiment, you can use **Stat> DOE> Factorial> Define Factorial Design** to specify the design to MINITAB. After you've created the design and entered the response column but before you consider any quantitative analysis of the data, it's helpful to present the data graphically to get a preview of what variables and model terms might be most important. Use the **Stat> DOE> Factorial> Factorial Plots** menu to create main effects and interaction plots. You will have to specify the response to be analyzed and the terms to consider in the two **Setup** menus. Main effects plots with sloped lines indicate possibly significant main effects. Interaction plots that show diverging line segments indicate possibly significant two-factor interactions.

After the design has been defined and the required responses entered into the worksheet, you can analyze the design with **Stat> DOE> Factorial> Analyze Factorial Design**. The functions provided within MINITAB should be very familiar to you by now. Select the experimental response column in the **Responses:** window and use the **Terms** window to select the terms to be included in the model. Use the arrows to move selected terms back and forth between the **Available Terms:** and the **Selected Terms:** windows or indicate the highest-order terms to be included in the model in the **Include terms in the model up through order:** window. If the experiment was run in blocks, then check the **Include blocks in the model** box to account for possible block-to-block differences.

In the **Graphs** menu, select the usual residuals diagnostic plots including plots of the residuals versus all of the independent variables. You should also consider turning on the normal and/or Pareto effects plots. These plots are very useful for distinguishing between significant and insignificant model terms when you need to refine the model. Significant terms will be outliers on the normal plot of effects and will have long bars on the Pareto chart. Insignificant terms will fall on an approximately straight line near zero on the normal plot and have short bars on the Pareto chart. After you've determined which model terms can safely be omitted from the model, return to the **Terms** window to remove them and rerun the analysis. MINITAB will issue a warning if you attempt to analyze a nonhierarchical model.

9.8 EXTRA AND MISSING VALUES

By design, the 2^k experiments are balanced; they have the same number of observations at the +1 and −1 levels of each design variable. This characteristic gives these designs some very desirable behavior; most importantly, it makes the design variables completely independent of each other. When there are extra or missing observations in a 2^k design, however, the experiment becomes unbalanced, causing many of the model terms to become correlated with each other. This effect can be observed by comparing the correlation matrices of an intact 2^k design with one that has a few missing or extra observations. The primary undesirable consequence of an unbalanced design is that the regression coefficients become biased. This problem is serious enough that some simple strategies have been developed for managing extra or missing observations in 2^k designs. A few practical strategies will be presented here, but more rigorous and even exact methods are available. See Montgomery (1991) or Hoaglin et al. (1991) for details on these methods.

When an experiment has many replicates and there are a few extra observations, the extra values can often be left intact or omitted from the data set at random without substantially affecting the results of the analysis. The latter approach wastes some information that might otherwise improve the error estimate but it does recover the balance of the experiment. If the experiment only has a single replicate plus a few extra observations, the usual approach is to average the duplicated observations, but it's important to recognize that this approach tends to underestimate the size of the standard error because averages tend to behave better than individuals. When there are wildly different numbers of replicates in the various unique cells of the experiment design, the usual approach is to calculate and then fit the cell means. Then the standard error of the cell mean model must be combined with the within-cell variation to obtain a more realistic measure of the inherent noise in the system. The disadvantage to this approach is that it ignores differences in the relative weights that should be applied to the various cells based on the number of observations that they contain. There are rigorous methods for weighting the cell means but they are beyond the scope of this book.

The strategies for managing a few missing observations are a bit different than those for extra observations. The first condition that should be checked is to determine if the missing observations have a common cause or if they are *missing at random* (MAR). If there is a common cause for the missing observations then that cause must be investigated. If the missing observations occur at random then there are some relatively simple remedial actions that can be taken. If the experiment contains several replicates, the difficulties caused by the unbalanced design are often minor and can be ignored. The correlation matrix is helpful in deciding if this might be the case. If that approach is not appropriate, the missing values can be replaced by estimated values. These estimates could be determined from the cell means of the surviving observations or by iteratively replacing the missing observations with their values as predicted by the model until they converge. The latter approach effectively minimizes SS_ε with respect to the missing observations as if they were regression coefficients. These replacement solutions recover the balance of the experiment design but the error degrees of freedom should be reduced by the number of missing observations, and all of the statistics that depend on the error degrees of freedom should be recalculated, including the regression coefficient t and p values. These calculations are relatively easy to perform by copying the sums of squares to a spreadsheet, correcting the degrees of freedom column, then recalculating the mean squares, F statistics, and their p values. The regression coefficient t values can be determined from the square root of the corresponding F statistics because of the identity:

$$t_{p,df_\varepsilon} = \sqrt{F_{p,1,df_\varepsilon}} \tag{9.20}$$

9.9 PROPAGATION OF ERROR

An important application of the model derived from a 2^k experiment is to predict the expected variation in the response y due to variation in the independent variables x_i. Obviously, for a given set of x_i values, the corresponding point estimate of y can be determined from the model; however, random noise in the x_i about their nominal values will tend to cause variation in the y that can also be predicted from the model. This technique, called *propagation of error,* is very important in manufacturing applications where it is important to understand how tolerances on process input variables cause undesirable variation in the process output variables. Propagation of error calculations require some calculus operations; however, the calculus required is very simple and you can probably find someone to help if you don't understand what's going on. The propagation of error method also has important applications with more complex models, such as those we will see in later chapters.

Theorem 9.1 (Propagation of Error) *If a process is configured to some nominal condition indicated by x_i' but each of the x_i suffers from some random variation about x_i' characterized by σ_{x_i}, then the induced variation in y $(x_1, x_2, \ldots, x_k)$ at $(x_1', x_2', \ldots, x_k')$ is given by:*

$$\sigma_y^2 = \sigma_\varepsilon^2 + \sum_{i=1}^{k} \left(\left. \frac{\partial y}{\partial x_i} \right|_{x_i'} \times \sigma_{x_i} \right)^2 \tag{9.21}$$

where σ_ε is the standard error of the model for y.

Example 9.11

A manufacturer of valves used in marine hydraulic steering controls built and analyzed an experiment to study hydraulic pressure leak-back rate as a function of critical valve characteristics. The model that they obtained, after appropriate refinements, was:

$$y = 13 - 0.8x_1 + 2.0x_2 + 1.2x_{12}$$

and had standard error $s_\varepsilon = 0.4$. Control charts of x_1 and x_2 indicated that the normal manufacturing variation in those variables was $\hat{\sigma}_{x_1} = 0.2$ and $\hat{\sigma}_{x_2} = 0.3$. (All quantities are given in standardized units.) Determine the predicted response and the variation induced in y by manufacturing variation in x_1 and x_2 when $(x_1', x_2') = (1, -0.5)$.

Solution: The predicted value of the leak-back rate is given by:

$$\hat{y}(1, -0.5) = 13 - 0.8(1) + 2.0(-0.5) + 1.2(1)(-0.5) = 10.6$$

The values of the required partial derivatives at the specified point are:

$$\left. \frac{\partial y}{\partial x_1} \right|_{(1,-0.5)} = -0.8 + 1.2x_2 \big|_{(1,-0.5)} = -1.4$$

$$\left. \frac{\partial y}{\partial x_2} \right|_{(1,-0.5)} = 2.0 + 1.2x_1 \big|_{(1,-0.5)} = 3.2$$

The expected standard deviation of the leak-back rate due to the propagation of errors in x_1 and x_2 is given by Equation 9.20:

$$
\begin{aligned}
\hat{\sigma}_y\big|_{(1,-0.5)} &= \sqrt{\hat{\sigma}_\varepsilon^2 + \left(\frac{\partial y}{\partial x_1}\Big|_{(1,-0.5)} \times \hat{\sigma}_{x_1}\right)^2 + \left(\frac{\partial y}{\partial x_2}\Big|_{(1,-0.5)} \times \hat{\sigma}_{x_2}\right)^2} \\
&= \sqrt{(0.4)^2 + (-1.4 \times 0.2)^2 + (3.2 \times 0.3)^2} \\
&= \sqrt{0.160 + 0.078 + 0.922} \\
&= \sqrt{1.160} \\
&= 1.08
\end{aligned}
$$

These calculations indicate that the predicted value of the leak-back rate is $\hat{y}$ $(1, -0.5) = 10.6$ and the corresponding standard deviation in the leak-back rate due to manufacturing variation in x_1 and x_2 is expected to be $\hat{\sigma}_y = 1.08$. The variance magnitudes indicate that variation in x_2 is the largest source of induced variation in the leak-back rate, so any effort to reduce variation should be focused on improved control of x_2.

9.10 SAMPLE SIZE AND POWER

There are two approaches that can be used to determine the sample size (that is, the number of replicates) for two-level factorial designs:

- The sample size can be determined so as to deliver a specified power for the ANOVA F test to detect a specified difference between the ±1 levels of a variable.

- The sample size can be determined so as to quantify the regression coefficient associated with a variable to within some specified range with specified confidence.

When the focus of an experiment is on the identification of significant variables, such as in a screening experiment, the sample size and power analysis for the ANOVA F test are appropriate. When the focus of the experiment is on quantifying the regression coefficient associated with a term that is already known or suspected to be significant, then the sample size analysis for the confidence interval is appropriate. These methods have already been presented in Chapters 7 and 8, respectively, but their specific applications to two-level factorial designs will be reviewed here.

9.10.1 Sample Size and Power to Detect Significant Effects

The sample-size and power calculations for an F test to detect a significant difference between the ±1 levels of a variable in a 2^k factorial experiment were presented in Section

7.5.3. Since all k of the design variables are coded to ± 1 levels, then the 2^k factorial design offers the same power to detect a difference δ between the ± 1 levels of each variable. In practice, the choices for the real physical settings of the variables corresponding to the coded ± 1 levels determine the true power for each variable. This means that the power to detect a difference between the ± 1 levels of a variable with two widely separated levels is relatively high compared to the power obtained when the levels are set closer together.

Example 9.12

Calculate the power to determine a difference $\delta = 400$ between the ± 1 levels of the variables in a 2^4 design with six replicates if $\sigma_\varepsilon = 800$. Include main effects and two-factor interactions in the model and use the method of Section 7.5.3 to find the power.

Solution: The experiment requires a total of $N = 6 \times 2^4 = 96$ runs, so there are $df_{total} = 95$ total degrees of freedom. The model will contain $df_{model} = \binom{4}{1} + \binom{4}{2} = 10$ degrees of freedom so there will be $df_\varepsilon = 95 - 10 = 85$ error degrees of freedom. The F statistic for the effect of any of the four design variables will have one numerator and 85 denominator degrees of freedom so, with $\alpha = 0.05$, the critical value of the accept/reject bound for F will be $F_{0.05,1,85} = 3.953$. The power is given by the condition $F_\alpha = F_{P,\lambda}$ where the noncentrality parameter λ is:

$$\lambda = \frac{N}{2a}\left(\frac{\delta}{\sigma_\varepsilon}\right)^2$$
$$= \frac{96}{2(2)}\left(\frac{400}{800}\right)^2$$
$$= 6.0$$

and $a = 2$ is the number of levels of each variable. From $F_{P,6.0} = 3.953$ we find that the power is $P = 0.678$. That is, this experiment will deliver a 67.8 percent chance of detecting the presence of a 400-unit difference between the -1 and $+1$ levels of a design variable if such a difference is present. This power is relatively low and more replicates should be considered.

MINITAB V14 contains a simple power and sample-size calculator for the 2^k designs that can be found in its **Stat> Power and Sample Size> 2-Level Factorial Design** menu. There are several different types of power and sample-size calculations that MINITAB can make. All of these problems require you to specify:

- The number of variables k.

- The number of corner points in the design given by 2^k. (This specification may seem unnecessary right now but the reason will become clear in Chapter 10.)

- The expected value of the model standard error σ_ε.

Then, given any three of the following quantities, MINITAB calculates the fourth quantity:

- The number of replicates n.
- The size of the smallest effect δ.
- The power P.
- The number of center points.

The addition of center points to the 2^k designs will be discussed in detail in Chapter 11. For now, leave the number of center points set to zero.

There is an important option in the **Stat> Power and Sample Size> 2-Level Factorial Design** menu that you will probably have to exercise to get the correct sample-size answers. MINITAB assumes that the model you intend to build will include all possible terms: main effects, two-factor interactions, three-factor interactions, and so on. If you don't want to include some of these terms in the model, such as three-factor and higher-order interactions, then enter the **Design** menu and specify the number of model terms that you want to omit from the model. You will have to calculate this number yourself.

Example 9.13

Use MINITAB's power calculation capability to confirm the answer to Example 9.12.

*Solution: In MINITAB's **Stat> Power and Sample Size> 2-Level Factorial Design** menu the number of variables is $k = 4$, the number of corner points is $2^4 = 16$, the standard deviation is $\sigma_\varepsilon = 800$, the number of replicates is $n = 6$, the effect size is $\delta = 400$, and the number of center points is zero. In the **Design** menu it is necessary to indicate that the three- and four-factor interactions are to be omitted from the model. The number of terms to be omitted is $\binom{4}{3} + \binom{4}{4} = 5$. The MINITAB menus and corresponding output are shown in Figure 9.28. MINITAB confirms that the power is $P = 0.678$ within round-off error.*

Example 9.14

Use MINITAB's power calculation capability to determine the number of replicates of the 2^4 design from Example 9.12 necessary to deliver a power of 90 percent or greater to detect a difference of $\delta = 400$ between the ± 1 levels of a design variable.

*Solution: The sample-size calculation (not shown) was performed by changing the **Stat> Power and Sample Size> 2-Level Factorial Design** menu so that the **Power values:** field was 0.90 and the **Replicates:** field was empty. MINITAB indicates that $n = 11$ replicates of the 2^4 design are required and that the exact power of the experiment to detect an effect $\delta = 400$ will be $P = 0.9094$.*

Whether you have MINITAB or not, there is a simple approximation to the exact method for determining the number of replicates of a 2^k experiment necessary to achieve a specified power. The method is analogous to the relationship between the sample-size calculations for the confidence interval and the hypothesis test for the two-sample t test

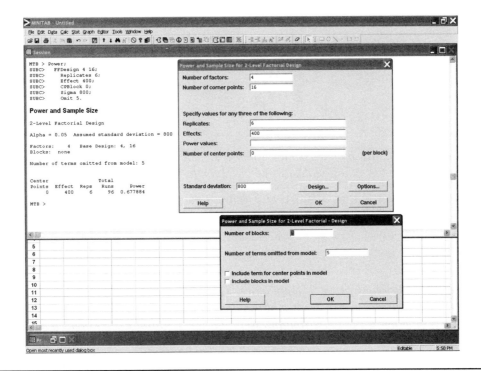

Figure 9.28 Power calculation for 2^4 design.

introduced in Chapter 3. It can be shown that the number of replicates determined in the exact algorithm is approximately:

$$r \geq \frac{1}{2^{k-2}} \left(\left(t_{\alpha/2} + t_\beta \right) \frac{\sigma_\varepsilon}{\delta} \right)^2 \qquad (9.22)$$

where r is the number of replicates, the power is $P = 1 - \beta$, and the t distribution has degrees of freedom equal to the error degrees of freedom of the regression. Although this expression is transcendental, if there are plenty of error degrees of freedom in the model then the t distribution is approximately z. This provides a convenient starting point for iterations and the correct answer is often obtained on the first iteration.

Example 9.15

Use the alternative method to determine a general formula for the number of replicates required for a 2^k experiment that will deliver 90 percent power to detect a difference δ between the ± 1 levels of a variable. Use $\alpha = 0.05$ and assume that there will be enough error degrees of freedom in the model that the t distribution is approximately normal.

Solution: *With $t_{0.025} \simeq z_{0.025} = 1.96$ and $t_{0.10} \simeq z_{0.10} = 1.28$, Equation 9.22 gives:*

$$r \geq \frac{1}{2^{k-2}}(1.96+1.28)^2\left(\frac{\sigma_\varepsilon}{\delta}\right)^2$$

$$\geq \frac{42}{2^k}\left(\frac{\sigma_\varepsilon}{\delta}\right)^2 \qquad (9.23)$$

Example 9.16

Use the alternative method from Example 9.15 to determine the number of replicates required for the situation described in Example 9.14.

Solution: With $k = 4$, $\sigma_\varepsilon = 800$, and $\delta = 400$, Equation 9.23 gives:

$$r \geq \frac{42}{2^4}\left(\frac{800}{400}\right)^2 = 10.5$$

so the experiment requires $r = 11$ replicates. This confirms MINITAB's exact solution. There will be plenty of error degrees of freedom to justify the use of the normal distribution to approximate the t distribution, so no further iterations are required.

9.10.2 Sample Size to Quantify Effects

In Section 8.18 an algorithm was presented to find the sample size required to determine the regression slope parameter to within a specified range of values with specified confidence. This algorithm, with observations taken at coded ±1 levels, so separated by $\Delta x = 2$, is directly applicable to the sample-size problem for two-level factorial experiments. This sample-size calculation applies to all of the variables in the experiment because they all use the same coded ±1 levels.

Under these conditions, to determine the slope parameter β_i for the ith of k variables with confidence $1 - \alpha$ within an interval given by:

$$P\left(b_i - \delta < \beta_i < b_i + \delta\right) = 1 - \alpha \qquad (9.24)$$

where b_i is the estimated value of β_i determined from the regression analysis, the minimum required sample size must meet the condition:

$$n \geq \frac{1}{2}\left(\frac{t_{\alpha/2}\sigma_\varepsilon}{\delta}\right)^2 \qquad (9.25)$$

where $t_{\alpha/2}$ has degrees of freedom equal to the error degrees of freedom of the model. The sample-size problem is not solved yet. Here n is the number of observations that must be taken at the −1 and +1 levels, so the total number of observations in the experiment must meet the condition:

$$r2^k \geq 2n \tag{9.26}$$

where r is the number of replicates of the 2^k design. When these last two conditions are combined, the number of replicates is given by:

$$r \geq \frac{1}{2^k}\left(\frac{t_{\alpha/2}\sigma_\varepsilon}{\delta}\right)^2 \tag{9.27}$$

The smallest value of r that meets this condition is the minimum number of replicates of the experiment required to determine β_i with the specified precision. As before, this condition is transcendental because the degrees of freedom for $t_{\alpha/2}$ depend on the value of r.

Example 9.17

A 2^3 experiment is to be performed to quantify the regression slopes associated with the main effects to within $\delta = 20$ with 95 percent confidence. The standard error of the model is expected to be $\sigma_\varepsilon = 80$. How many replicates of the 2^3 design are required?

Solution: The number of replicates must meet the condition given by Equation 9.27. If the number of replicates is sufficiently large that $t_{0.025} \simeq (z_{0.025} = 1.96)$ then:

$$
\begin{aligned}
r \quad &\geq \tfrac{1}{2^k}\left(\tfrac{t_{\alpha/2}\sigma_\varepsilon}{\delta}\right)^2 \\
&\geq \tfrac{1}{2^3}\left(\tfrac{1.96\times 80}{20}\right)^2 \\
&\geq 8
\end{aligned}
\tag{9.28}
$$

The number of error degrees of freedom for the model with main effects and two-factor interactions is $df_\varepsilon = df_{total} - df_{model} = (8\,(2^3) - 1) - 6 = 57$, so the approximation of $t_{0.025}$ with $z_{0.025}$ is justified and the solution $r = 8$ is valid.

9.11 DESIGN CONSIDERATIONS FOR 2^K EXPERIMENTS

- Pick the ± 1 levels for each variable to be as far apart as is safely and practically possible.

- Block the experiment by replicates and include blocks in the model to control for differences between them. (This requires analysis by general linear model, available either from **Stat> DOE> Factorial> Analyze Factorial Design** or **Stat> ANOVA> General Linear Model**.)

- If all of the design variables in a 2^k experiment are quantitative, consider adding center cells to the design to increase the error degrees of freedom and permit a linear lack of fit test. See Chapters 8 and 11 for details on how to perform the lack of fit test.

- If: 1) all design variables in a 2^k experiment are quantitative, 2) there are very few (≤ 10) error degrees of freedom, and 3) it's too expensive to replicate the entire experiment, then add center cells to increase the error degrees of freedom and the power of the experiment. Use the information from the center cells to do a linear lack of fit test. (See Chapter 11.)

- For 2^k designs with five or more variables consider using the fractional factorial designs of Chapter 10 to reduce the number of runs required by the experiment.

- Use the methods of Chapter 10 to block large 2^k experiments.

- Do a sample-size calculation to determine the number of replicates required for your experiment. Use the appropriate calculation—either one to detect significant effects or one to quantify the regression coefficients using a confidence interval.

10

Fractional Factorial Experiments

10.1 INTRODUCTION

One of the advantages of the factorial designs is their ability to use relatively few experimental runs to estimate many effects. For example, in the 2^5 design with one replicate, the 32 runs are used to determine five main effects, 10 two-factor interactions, and higher-order interactions if necessary. The analysis is done by grouping the 32 runs into two sets of 16 runs each according to the -1 and $+1$ levels of each factor of interest. The regression coefficient for each factor is then calculated from:

$$b_i = \frac{\Delta \bar{y}}{\Delta x_i} = \frac{\bar{y}_+ - \bar{y}_-}{2} \tag{10.1}$$

where the $+$ and $-$ subscripts indicate the x_i factor levels. Different groupings of the same y values are used to determine each effect.

Table 10.1 shows how the size of the 2^k experiments grows with the number of variables and how the available information is used. In the table, df_{model} is determined from the number of main effects plus the number of two-factor interactions, that is:

$$df_{model} = \binom{k}{1} + \binom{k}{2} = \frac{k(k+1)}{2} \tag{10.2}$$

Of course we could consider more complex model terms including three-factor and higher-order interactions; however, those are rarely significant so it is usually safe to ignore them. The table shows that for the larger experiments most of the runs are used to estimate the error. Do we really need so many error degrees of freedom? How many

Table 10.1 Number of runs in factorial experiments.

k	2^k	df_{total}	df_{model}	df_{error}
2	4	3	3	0
3	8	7	6	1
4	16	15	10	5
5	32	31	15	16
6	64	63	21	42
7	128	127	28	99
8	256	255	36	219
9	512	511	45	466
10	1024	1023	55	968

runs are really required to accurately estimate the b_i statistics? If it were possible to cut back on the size of the experiment, which runs would we cut? These are the questions to be addressed in this chapter.

10.2 THE 2^{5-1} HALF-FRACTIONAL FACTORIAL DESIGN

Table 10.1 shows that the 2^k factorial designs get very large as k gets large but the number of terms modeled does not grow as quickly. In general, the number of runs in a single replicate will be 2^k and the number of terms in the model (main effects plus two-factor interactions) will only be $df_{model} = k(k + 1)/2$. For example, the model for a 2^5 experiment requiring 32 runs potentially includes $\binom{5}{0} = 1$ constant, $\binom{5}{1} = 5$ main effects, $\binom{5}{2} = 10$ two-factor interactions, $\binom{5}{3} = 10$ three-factor interactions, $\binom{5}{4} = 5$ four-factor interactions, and $\binom{5}{5} = 1$ five-factor interaction. If we agree that three-, four-, and five-factor interactions are unlikely then all of these terms can be removed from the model and pooled with the error estimate. The model including just the constant, main effects, and two-factor interactions requires only $5 + 10 = 15$ degrees of freedom and there are $32 - 1 = 31$ total degrees of freedom available. This leaves $31 - 15 = 16$ degrees of freedom for the error estimate, which could be considered excessive! This is before any replication is considered and Occam is likely to drop some terms from the model and df_ε will get even larger! What a waste! Clearly, we need a scheme to selectively reduce the number of runs in a large 2^k experiment to get the information that we need with a reasonable amount of work.

If there is indeed an excessive number of error degrees of freedom built into the 2^5 experiment, then let's consider some possible strategies to eliminate some of the runs. As an aggressive but perhaps arbitrary goal let's try to find a way to eliminate one half of the original 32 runs. (For the moment ignore the fact that a 16-run experiment with a 15-term model doesn't leave any degrees of freedom for error. We'll deal with this problem later.) Consider the full 2^5 experiment design in 32 runs shown in Table 10.2. If one half of the runs are to be eliminated, just how do we select them? We might consider randomly selecting the runs to be eliminated but that method has some substantial risks as

Table 10.2 2^5 design with all two-factor interactions.

Run	x_1	x_2	x_3	x_4	x_5	x_{12}	x_{13}	x_{14}	x_{15}	x_{23}	x_{24}	x_{25}	x_{34}	x_{35}	x_{45}
1	−	−	−	−	−	+	+	+	+	+	+	+	+	+	+
2	−	−	−	−	+	+	+	+	−	+	+	−	+	−	−
3	−	−	−	+	−	+	+	−	+	+	−	+	−	+	−
4	−	−	−	+	+	+	+	−	−	+	−	−	−	−	+
5	−	−	+	−	−	+	−	+	+	−	+	+	−	−	+
6	−	−	+	−	+	+	−	+	−	−	+	−	−	+	−
7	−	−	+	+	−	+	−	−	+	−	−	+	+	−	−
8	−	−	+	+	+	+	−	−	−	−	−	−	+	+	+
9	−	+	−	−	−	−	+	+	+	−	−	−	+	+	+
10	−	+	−	−	+	−	+	+	−	−	−	+	+	−	−
11	−	+	−	+	−	−	+	−	+	−	+	−	−	+	−
12	−	+	−	+	+	−	+	−	−	−	+	+	−	−	+
13	−	+	+	−	−	−	−	+	+	+	−	−	−	−	+
14	−	+	+	−	+	−	−	+	−	+	−	+	−	+	−
15	−	+	+	+	−	−	−	−	+	+	+	−	+	−	−
16	−	+	+	+	+	−	−	−	−	+	+	+	+	+	+
17	+	−	−	−	−	−	−	−	−	+	+	+	+	+	+
18	+	−	−	−	+	−	−	−	+	+	+	−	+	−	−
19	+	−	−	+	−	−	−	+	−	+	−	+	−	+	−
20	+	−	−	+	+	−	−	+	+	+	−	−	−	−	+
21	+	−	+	−	−	−	+	−	−	−	+	+	−	−	+
22	+	−	+	−	+	−	+	−	+	−	+	−	−	+	−
23	+	−	+	+	−	−	+	+	−	−	−	+	+	−	−
24	+	−	+	+	+	−	+	+	+	−	−	−	+	+	+
25	+	+	−	−	−	+	−	−	−	−	−	−	+	+	+
26	+	+	−	−	+	+	−	−	+	−	−	+	+	−	−
27	+	+	−	+	−	+	−	+	−	−	+	−	−	+	−
28	+	+	−	+	+	+	−	+	+	−	+	+	−	−	+
29	+	+	+	−	−	+	+	−	−	+	−	−	−	−	+
30	+	+	+	−	+	+	+	−	+	+	−	+	−	+	−
31	+	+	+	+	−	+	+	+	−	+	+	−	+	−	−
32	+	+	+	+	+	+	+	+	+	+	+	+	+	+	+

we will see. Another method might be to eliminate the last sixteen of the thirty-two runs but then we'd lose the ability to detect the effect of x_1. This strategy is definitely unacceptable. A third choice might be to eliminate eight of the sixteen runs with $x_1 = -1$ and eight of the sixteen runs with $x_1 = +1$. This would preserve the ability to resolve the x_1 effect, but then we're back to the original problem—how do we select the eight runs to eliminate from each set of sixteen? A logical method for the selection of these runs is required and hopefully it will have minimal consequences.

Table 10.2 shows all 32 runs of the 2^5 experiment and the 10 two-factor interactions that we would like to determine. An advantage of the factorial designs is that all of the

Table 10.3 Correlation matrix for 2^5 full-factorial design with all two-factor interactions.

	X_1	X_2	X_3	X_4	X_5	X_{12}	X_{13}	X_{14}	X_{15}	X_{23}	X_{24}	X_{25}	X_{34}	X_{35}	X_{45}
X_1	1	0	0	0	0	0	0	0	0	0	0	0	0	0	0
X_2	0	1	0	0	0	0	0	0	0	0	0	0	0	0	0
X_3	0	0	1	0	0	0	0	0	0	0	0	0	0	0	0
X_4	0	0	0	1	0	0	0	0	0	0	0	0	0	0	0
X_5	0	0	0	0	1	0	0	0	0	0	0	0	0	0	0
X_{12}	0	0	0	0	0	1	0	0	0	0	0	0	0	0	0
X_{13}	0	0	0	0	0	0	1	0	0	0	0	0	0	0	0
X_{14}	0	0	0	0	0	0	0	1	0	0	0	0	0	0	0
X_{15}	0	0	0	0	0	0	0	0	1	0	0	0	0	0	0
X_{23}	0	0	0	0	0	0	0	0	0	1	0	0	0	0	0
X_{24}	0	0	0	0	0	0	0	0	0	0	1	0	0	0	0
X_{25}	0	0	0	0	0	0	0	0	0	0	0	1	0	0	0
X_{34}	0	0	0	0	0	0	0	0	0	0	0	0	1	0	0
X_{35}	0	0	0	0	0	0	0	0	0	0	0	0	0	1	0
X_{45}	0	0	0	0	0	0	0	0	0	0	0	0	0	0	1

terms we want to model, the five main effects and ten two-factor interactions, are independent of each other. This is confirmed by calculating the correlation coefficients between all possible pairs of terms in the model. This is shown in the correlation matrix of model terms in Table 10.3. (The values shown in the table are r values, not r^2, because r^2 values get too small too fast and too many of them would appear as zeros when they really aren't.) All of the off-diagonal correlation coefficients in the matrix are zeros confirming that all terms are independent. In fact, if the correlation matrix were expanded to include all of the higher-order interaction terms, they would also be independent. This is a desirable characteristic, and whatever fraction of the 32 runs we end up keeping in our reduced experiment, it should at least preserve the independence of the main effects and two-factor interactions.

Tables 10.4 and 10.5 show the design matrix and corresponding correlation matrix for a 16-run experiment where the 16 runs were taken randomly from the full 32-run experiment. The correlation matrix shows the consequence of using this method to identify the experimental runs. The off-diagonal terms in the correlation matrix are no longer all zeros. In fact, there are few terms in the model that are completely independent of any others. This indicates that there is substantial confounding of what were supposed to be independent variables. The 16 runs selected here are not unique and other sets of 16 runs will give other confounding patterns, some better and some worse than the one shown here. Of the $\binom{32}{16} = 601,080,390$ possible 16-run subsets, we have to hope that at least some of them behave as we want them to. Thankfully, there is such a solution and we don't have to randomly search through the hundreds of millions of possible subsets to find it.

When we try to build just a fraction of the full 32-run experiment, some correlations between variables apparently are inevitable. Suppose that we try to select the runs to

Table 10.4 Experiment of 16 random runs from the full 32-run experiment.

Run	x_1	x_2	x_3	x_4	x_5	x_{12}	x_{13}	x_{14}	x_{15}	x_{23}	x_{24}	x_{25}	x_{34}	x_{35}	x_{45}
4	−	−	−	+	+	+	+	−	−	+	−	−	−	−	+
5	−	−	+	−	−	+	−	+	+	−	+	+	−	−	+
6	−	−	+	−	+	+	−	+	−	−	+	−	−	+	−
8	−	−	+	+	+	+	−	−	−	−	−	−	+	+	+
9	−	+	−	−	−	−	+	+	+	−	−	−	+	+	+
19	+	−	−	+	−	−	−	+	−	+	−	+	−	+	−
20	+	−	−	+	+	−	−	+	+	+	−	−	−	−	+
21	+	−	+	−	−	−	+	−	−	−	+	+	−	−	+
22	+	−	+	−	+	−	+	−	+	−	+	−	−	+	−
23	+	−	+	+	−	−	+	+	−	−	−	−	+	+	−
25	+	+	−	−	−	+	−	−	−	−	−	−	+	+	+
26	+	+	−	−	+	+	−	−	+	−	−	+	+	−	−
28	+	+	−	+	+	+	−	+	+	−	+	+	−	−	+
30	+	+	+	−	+	+	+	−	+	+	−	+	−	+	−
31	+	+	+	+	−	+	+	+	−	+	+	−	+	−	−
32	+	+	+	+	+	+	+	+	+	+	+	+	+	+	+

Table 10.5 Correlation matrix of experiment of 16 random runs from full 32-run experiment.

	x_1	x_2	x_3	x_4	x_5	x_{12}	x_{13}	x_{14}	x_{15}	x_{23}	x_{24}	x_{25}	x_{34}	x_{35}	x_{45}
x_1	1.00	0.32	−0.05	0.13	−0.05	−0.24	0.13	−0.05	0.13	0.24	0.05	0.40	0.05	−0.13	−0.32
x_2	0.32	1.00	−0.24	−0.13	0.02	0.42	0.13	0.02	0.38	0.10	−0.02	0.13	0.49	0.13	0.02
x_3	−0.05	−0.24	1.00	−0.13	−0.02	0.10	0.38	−0.02	−0.13	−0.10	0.52	0.13	0.02	0.13	−0.27
x_4	0.13	−0.13	−0.13	1.00	0.13	0.00	0.00	0.38	−0.25	0.52	−0.13	0.00	0.13	−0.25	0.13
x_5	−0.05	0.02	−0.02	0.13	1.00	0.36	−0.13	−0.27	0.38	0.16	0.02	−0.13	−0.24	0.13	−0.02
x_{12}	−0.24	0.42	0.10	0.00	0.36	1.00	−0.26	−0.16	0.00	0.07	0.16	0.00	0.16	0.00	0.10
x_{13}	0.13	0.13	0.38	0.00	−0.13	−0.26	1.00	−0.13	0.00	0.26	0.13	0.00	0.13	0.00	−0.13
x_{14}	−0.05	0.02	−0.02	0.38	−0.27	−0.16	−0.13	1.00	0.13	0.16	0.27	0.13	0.02	−0.13	−0.02
x_{15}	0.13	0.38	−0.13	−0.25	0.38	0.00	0.00	0.13	1.00	0.00	0.13	0.25	−0.13	0.00	0.13
x_{23}	0.24	0.10	−0.10	0.52	0.16	0.07	0.26	0.16	0.00	1.00	−0.16	0.00	−0.16	0.00	−0.10
x_{24}	0.05	−0.02	0.52	−0.13	0.02	0.16	0.13	0.27	0.13	−0.16	1.00	0.13	−0.27	−0.13	0.02
x_{25}	0.40	0.13	0.13	0.00	−0.13	0.00	0.00	0.13	0.25	0.00	0.13	1.00	−0.13	−0.25	−0.13
x_{34}	0.05	0.49	0.02	0.13	−0.24	0.16	0.13	0.02	−0.13	−0.16	−0.27	−0.13	1.00	0.13	0.02
x_{35}	−0.13	0.13	0.13	−0.25	0.13	0.00	0.00	−0.13	0.00	0.00	−0.13	−0.25	0.13	1.00	−0.13
x_{45}	−0.32	0.02	−0.27	0.13	−0.02	0.10	−0.13	−0.02	0.13	−0.10	0.02	−0.13	0.02	−0.13	1.00

control the correlations so that they behave in a tolerable manner. Since we don't expect to observe four-factor interactions, and don't even plan on looking for them anyway, let's perfectly correlate or confound x_5 with the four-factor interaction x_{1234} by using only those experimental runs that satisfy the condition:

$$x_5 = x_1 x_2 x_3 x_4 = x_{1234} \tag{10.3}$$

Only 16 of the 32 runs from the full experiment satisfy this condition. This provides a scheme to select 16 of 32 runs from the full experiment with the penalty that x_5 is confounded with x_{1234}, but what other consequences are there? To consider this question, the 16-run experiment is shown in Table 10.6 where only those 16 runs satisfying Equation 10.3 are included. Note that Equation 10.3 is satisfied for each run. The two-factor interactions are also shown in Table 10.6 and the correlation matrix is shown in Table 10.7. The correlation matrix shows that all of the off-diagonal terms are now zeros just as we wanted! How did this happen? This is exactly what we were after—a 16-run experiment that can model main effects and two-factor interactions. But at what price?

To understand the downside of the design in Table 10.6, it's necessary to consider the confounding that occurs between the other potential terms in the model. To check this, try multiplying Equation 10.3 through by x_1. This corresponds to just multiplying the indicated columns together on a row by row basis. This yields:

$$x_1 x_5 = x_1 x_{1234} \tag{10.4}$$

Since $x_1 x_1 = x_1^2 = 1$, this reduces to:

$$x_{15} = x_{234} \tag{10.5}$$

That is, the two-factor interaction x_{15} is perfectly confounded with the three-factor interaction x_{234}. This is an acceptable risk because we don't usually expect to see three-factor interactions in our experiments. All the other two-factor interactions can be generated by multiplying Equation 10.3 through by x_2, x_3, and x_4. When this is done, it's

Table 10.6 Experiment of 16 runs with $x_5 = x_{1234}$ from full 32-run experiment.

Run	x_1	x_2	x_3	x_4	x_5	x_{12}	x_{13}	x_{14}	x_{15}	x_{23}	x_{24}	x_{25}	x_{34}	x_{35}	x_{45}
2	−	−	−	−	+	+	+	+	−	+	+	−	+	−	−
3	−	−	−	+	−	+	+	−	+	+	−	+	−	+	−
5	−	−	+	−	−	+	−	+	+	−	+	+	−	−	+
8	−	−	+	+	+	+	−	−	−	−	−	−	+	+	+
9	−	+	−	−	−	−	+	+	+	−	−	+	+	+	+
12	−	+	−	+	+	−	+	−	−	−	+	+	−	−	+
14	−	+	+	−	+	−	−	+	−	+	−	+	−	+	−
15	−	+	+	+	−	−	−	−	+	+	+	−	+	−	−
17	+	−	−	−	−	−	−	−	+	+	+	+	+	+	+
20	+	−	−	+	+	−	−	+	+	+	−	−	−	−	+
22	+	−	+	−	+	−	+	−	+	−	+	−	−	+	−
23	+	−	+	+	−	−	+	+	−	−	−	+	+	−	−
26	+	+	−	−	+	+	−	−	+	−	−	+	+	−	−
27	+	+	−	+	−	+	−	+	−	−	+	−	−	+	−
29	+	+	+	−	−	+	+	−	−	+	−	−	−	−	+
32	+	+	+	+	+	+	+	+	+	+	+	+	+	+	+

Table 10.7   Correlation matrix for experiment of 16 runs with $x_5 = x_{1234}$ from full 32-run experiment.

	x_1	x_2	x_3	x_4	x_5	x_{12}	x_{13}	x_{14}	x_{15}	x_{23}	x_{24}	x_{25}	x_{34}	x_{35}	x_{45}
x_1	1	0	0	0	0	0	0	0	0	0	0	0	0	0	0
x_2	0	1	0	0	0	0	0	0	0	0	0	0	0	0	0
x_3	0	0	1	0	0	0	0	0	0	0	0	0	0	0	0
x_4	0	0	0	1	0	0	0	0	0	0	0	0	0	0	0
x_5	0	0	0	0	1	0	0	0	0	0	0	0	0	0	0
x_{12}	0	0	0	0	0	1	0	0	0	0	0	0	0	0	0
x_{13}	0	0	0	0	0	0	1	0	0	0	0	0	0	0	0
x_{14}	0	0	0	0	0	0	0	1	0	0	0	0	0	0	0
x_{15}	0	0	0	0	0	0	0	0	1	0	0	0	0	0	0
x_{23}	0	0	0	0	0	0	0	0	0	1	0	0	0	0	0
x_{24}	0	0	0	0	0	0	0	0	0	0	1	0	0	0	0
x_{25}	0	0	0	0	0	0	0	0	0	0	0	1	0	0	0
x_{34}	0	0	0	0	0	0	0	0	0	0	0	0	1	0	0
x_{35}	0	0	0	0	0	0	0	0	0	0	0	0	0	1	0
x_{45}	0	0	0	0	0	0	0	0	0	0	0	0	0	0	1

found that each two-factor interaction is confounded with a particular three-factor interaction. But if we don't expect three-factor interactions to be significant then this compromise is tolerable.

Since the subscripts in the confounding relations such as Equation 10.3 carry all of the information about the confounding between terms, it is common to write the confounding relations as $5 = 1234$ instead of $x_5 = x_{1234}$. All of the confounding relations for the five-variable 16-run experiment implied by Equation 10.3 are shown in the following table:

$1 = 2345$	$12 = 345$	$23 = 145$	$34 = 125$	$45 = 123$
$2 = 1345$	$13 = 245$	$24 = 135$	$35 = 124$	
$3 = 1245$	$14 = 235$	$25 = 134$		
$4 = 1235$	$15 = 234$			
$5 = 1234$				

Although the correlation matrices in Tables 10.3 and 10.7 appear to be identical, they are not. Both tables are incomplete—they don't show the three-, four-, and five-factor interactions—but if they were expanded to show those interactions, the differences would be apparent. Whereas Table 10.3 would be diagonal, with ones on the diagonal and zeros everywhere else, Table 10.7 would have some additional ones in off-diagonal positions because of the confounding between the low-order and high-order terms in the model.

Equation 10.3 is clearly the key to determining how this 16-run experiment is constructed and how it behaves. One way to generate the design of Table 10.6 is to construct a 16-run 2^4 factorial experiment in variables x_1, x_2, x_3, and x_4, and then to determine the required levels for the last variable x_5 using Equation 10.3. Since Equation 10.3 determines the levels of x_5 from the first four variables, it is called the design *generator*. Designs constructed this way are called *fractional factorial* designs. The five-variable design in 16 runs described here is designated a 2^{5-1} design. The –1 in the exponent indicates that only one half of the original $2^5 = 32$ runs of the experiment are used since $2^{-1} = \frac{1}{2}$. For this reason we call this experiment a *half-fractional* factorial. The remaining 16 runs make up the complementary half-fraction and satisfy the generator:

$$5 = -1234 \tag{10.6}$$

The complementary half-fraction experiment is just as useful and valid as the experiment defined by the generator of Equation 10.3; there is no preference between the two. For this reason, generators for fractional factorial designs are usually written with a ± operator to indicate that there are two equivalent choices for the generator, such as:

$$5 = \pm 1234 \tag{10.7}$$

10.3 OTHER FRACTIONAL FACTORIAL DESIGNS

The half-fractional factorial design introduced in the previous section is only one possible fraction that can be defined. Quarter-, eighth-, and higher-order fractional experiments can also be designed. The designations for the half-, quarter-, and eighth-fractional designs are 2^{k-1}, 2^{k-2}, and 2^{k-3}, respectively, where k is the number of variables and the terms –1, –2, and –3 in the exponents indicate the degree of fractionation. (Notice that $2^{-1} = \frac{1}{2}$, $2^{-2} = \frac{1}{4}$, and $2^{-3} = \frac{1}{8}$.) In addition to indicating the degree of fractionation present in a fractional factorial design, the number following the minus sign in the exponent of the design designation indicates the number of generators required for the design, so half-fractional experiments will have one generator, quarter-fractional designs will have two generators, eighth-fractional designs will have three generators, and so on. The generators for the quarter- and higher-order fractional factorial designs are selected on the basis of the same arguments that we used to determine the runs for the half-fractional design but the rules for generators can get quite complicated. It's not worth taking the time to learn how the generators for the higher-order fractional designs are constructed—just refer to an appropriate table of designs and generators to find them. Table 10.8 shows the generators for some of the most common fractional factorial designs.

Fractional factorial designs are commonly used to reduce the number of runs required to build an experiment. They also provide a powerful tool for blocking large experiments. For example, suppose a large 2^k experiment cannot be completed in a single day. Which runs should be made on each day? Your first thought might be to randomly assign the runs of the experiment to days, but we already saw the risk of that choice. If the experiment must be built roughly in quarters, say spread over four days, then a logical choice would be to build a quarter-fraction of the full experiment each

Table 10.8 Fractional factorial designs with number of runs and generators.

k	Design Resolution			Design	Runs	Generators
3	*III*			2^{3-1}_{III}	4	3 = ±12
4		*IV*		2^{4-1}_{IV}	8	4 = ±123
5	*III*			2^{5-2}_{III}	8	4 = ±12, 5 = ±13
			V	2^{5-1}_{V}	16	5 = ±1234
6	*III*			2^{6-3}_{III}	8	4 = ±12, 5 = ±13, 6 = ±23
		IV		2^{6-2}_{IV}	16	5 = ±123, 6 = ±234
			VI	2^{6-1}_{VI}	32	6 = ±12345
7	*III*			2^{7-4}_{III}	8	4 = ±12, 5 = ±13, 6 = ±23, 7 = ±123
	IV			2^{7-3}_{IV}	16	5 = ±123, 6 = ±234, 7 = ±134
	IV			2^{7-2}_{IV}	32	6 = ±1234, 7 = ±1245
			VII	2^{7-1}_{VII}	64	7 = ±123456
8	*IV*			2^{8-4}_{IV}	16	5 = ±234, 6 = ±134, 7 = ±123, 8 = ±124
	IV			2^{8-3}_{IV}	32	6 = ±123, 7 = ±124, 8 = ±2345
		V		2^{8-2}_{V}	64	7 = ±1234, 8 = ±1256
			VIII	2^{8-1}_{VIII}	128	8 = ±1234567

day. Each quarter-fraction of the full experiment, while having some potentially undesirable confounding between variables, can be analyzed by itself. Then, after each day's data become available, the data can be combined and used to analyze the system more completely. If it isn't necessary to build the full experiment and only a half-fraction of the full experiment is required, then two quarter-fractions or four eighth-fractions can be built, yielding the required half-fractional factorial experiment when the data are combined on the last day. This approach also permits you to treat the different days as blocks so that day-to-day differences can be identified and removed.

10.4 DESIGN RESOLUTION

The generators used to construct a fractional factorial design determine the confounding that will be present among the design variables and their various interactions. For the 2^{5-1} design considered earlier, the generator involves five variables: x_1, x_2, x_3. x_4, and x_5, and defines the confounding for a main effect and a four-factor interaction. When the generator is used to determine the confounding for the two-factor interactions, it shows that they are each confounded with a single three-factor interaction. Again this confounding relationship involves five terms—two in the two-factor interaction and three in the three-factor interaction. This observation, that every confounding relation in the 2^{5-1} design involves five terms, is a fundamental characteristic of the design, so the design is referred to as a resolution V design where the roman numeral V for five is used. The design designation 2^{5-1} is enhanced to reflect the design resolution: 2^{5-1}_{V}, where the subscript indicates the resolution. This notation is summarized in Figure 10.1. Table 10.9 summarizes the most common fractional factorial designs by the number of design variables and the design resolution.

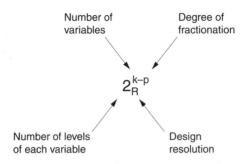

Figure 10.1 Fractional factorial design designation.

Table 10.9 Fractional factorial designs by number of variables and design resolution.

	Design Resolution					
k	*III*	*IV*	*V*	*VI*	*VII*	*VIII*
3	2^{3-1}_{III}					
4		2^{4-1}_{IV}				
5	2^{5-2}_{III}		2^{5-1}_{V}			
6	2^{6-3}_{III}	2^{6-2}_{IV}		2^{6-1}_{VI}		
7	2^{7-4}_{III}	2^{7-3}_{IV}			2^{7-1}_{VII}	
		2^{7-2}_{IV}				
8		2^{8-4}_{IV}	2^{8-2}_{V}			2^{8-1}_{VIII}
		2^{8-3}_{IV}				

Each fractional factorial design has its own inherent design resolution. For example, the 2^{4-1} half-fractional factorial design has a generator given by:

$$4 = 123 \tag{10.8}$$

The generator can be manipulated to show that all main effects are confounded with three-factor interactions and all two-factor interactions are confounded with other two-factor interactions. All of the confounding relations for the 2^{4-1} design are shown in the following table:

$1 = 234$	$12 = 34$
$2 = 134$	$13 = 24$
$3 = 124$	$14 = 23$
$4 = 123$	

In every case there are four variables in each confounding relation, indicating that this is a resolution IV design, so the design is designated 2^{4-1}_{IV}. The design and correlation matrices for the 2^4 and 2^{4-1}_{IV} designs are shown in Tables 10.10, 10.11, 10.12, and 10.13. The correlation matrices nicely summarize the situation but the simple statement that the design is resolution IV provides an even more succinct summary.

Table 10.10 2^4 design in 16 runs.

Run	x_1	x_2	x_3	x_4	x_{12}	x_{13}	x_{14}	x_{23}	x_{24}	x_{34}
1	−	−	−	−	+	+	+	+	+	+
2	−	−	−	+	+	+	−	+	−	−
3	−	−	+	−	+	−	+	−	+	−
4	−	−	+	+	+	−	−	−	−	+
5	−	+	−	−	−	+	+	−	−	+
6	−	+	−	+	−	+	−	−	+	−
7	−	+	+	−	−	−	+	+	−	−
8	−	+	+	+	−	−	−	+	+	+
9	+	−	−	−	−	−	−	+	+	+
10	+	−	−	+	−	−	+	+	−	−
11	+	−	+	−	−	+	−	−	+	−
12	+	−	+	+	−	+	+	−	−	+
13	+	+	−	−	+	−	−	−	−	+
14	+	+	−	+	+	−	+	−	+	−
15	+	+	+	−	+	+	−	+	−	−
16	+	+	+	+	+	+	+	+	+	+

Table 10.11 Correlation matrix for 2^4 full-factorial experiment.

	x_1	x_2	x_3	x_4	x_{12}	x_{13}	x_{14}	x_{23}	x_{24}	x_{34}
x_1	1	0	0	0	0	0	0	0	0	0
x_2	0	1	0	0	0	0	0	0	0	0
x_3	0	0	1	0	0	0	0	0	0	0
x_4	0	0	0	1	0	0	0	0	0	0
x_{12}	0	0	0	0	1	0	0	0	0	0
x_{13}	0	0	0	0	0	1	0	0	0	0
x_{14}	0	0	0	0	0	0	1	0	0	0
x_{23}	0	0	0	0	0	0	0	1	0	0
x_{24}	0	0	0	0	0	0	0	0	1	0
x_{34}	0	0	0	0	0	0	0	0	0	1

Table 10.12 2_{IV}^{4-1} Half-fractional factorial design.

Run	x_1	x_2	x_3	x_4	x_{12}	x_{13}	x_{14}	x_{23}	x_{24}	x_{34}
1	−	−	−	−	+	+	+	+	+	+
2	−	−	+	+	+	−	−	−	−	+
3	−	+	−	+	−	+	−	−	+	−
4	−	+	+	−	−	−	+	+	−	−
5	+	−	−	+	−	−	+	+	−	−
6	+	−	+	−	−	+	−	−	+	−
7	+	+	−	−	+	−	−	−	−	+
8	+	+	+	+	+	+	+	+	+	+

Table 10.13 Correlation matrix for 2_{IV}^{4-1} half-fractional factorial design.

	x_1	x_2	x_3	x_4	x_{12}	x_{13}	x_{14}	x_{23}	x_{24}	x_{34}
x_1	1	0	0	0	0	0	0	0	0	0
x_2	0	1	0	0	0	0	0	0	0	0
x_3	0	0	1	0	0	0	0	0	0	0
x_4	0	0	0	1	0	0	0	0	0	0
x_{12}	0	0	0	0	1	0	0	0	0	1
x_{13}	0	0	0	0	0	1	0	0	1	0
x_{14}	0	0	0	0	0	0	1	1	0	0
x_{23}	0	0	0	0	0	0	1	1	0	0
x_{24}	0	0	0	0	0	1	0	0	1	0
x_{34}	0	0	0	0	1	0	0	0	0	1

The advantage of understanding the design resolution is that if a model has particular requirements then a design of a certain resolution can be specified. If it is desired that a model resolve main effects and two-factor interactions independently, then a resolution V design is needed. If it's acceptable to have main effects confounded with three-factor interactions, and two-factor interactions confounded with other two-factor interactions, then a resolution IV design is appropriate. If main effects and two-factor interactions can be confounded, then a resolution III design is appropriate. Each resolution has its own problems and an associated strategy for managing them.

What if the generator of Equation 10.8 is multiplied through by x_4? Since $x_4^2 = 1$ we will get:

$$1 = x_{1234} \tag{10.9}$$

that is, the four-factor interaction is constant. Try it out. The product of x_1, x_2, x_3, and x_4 for all of the runs in the 2^{4-1} design is one. This means that the four-factor interaction is confounded with the constant of the model. This still follows the rule defined by design resolution IV—that each confounding relation must involve four variables.

When higher fractions than one-half are considered, more generators are required to specify a design. Some designs have generators that contain different numbers of variables. The shortest generator (or confounding relation implied by the generators) determines the design resolution. For example, a 2^{7-4} design requires four generators. From Figure 10.5 they are:

$$x_4 = x_{12}$$
$$x_5 = x_{13}$$
$$x_6 = x_{23}$$
$$x_7 = x_{123}$$

Note that in this case, three of the generators involve three variables and the fourth one involves four. Since the design resolution is determined by the length of the *shortest* generator, which in this case involves three variables, this design is designated 2_{III}^{7-4}.

There is no confounding at all in the 2^k full-factorial experiments; estimates for all main effects, two-factor, three-factor, and higher-order interactions up to the single k-factor interaction can be resolved separately from each other. Confounding only happens in experiments that are fractionated.

10.5 THE CONSEQUENCES OF CONFOUNDING

Every 2^k full-factorial experiment has the desirable quality that all of its main effects, two-factor interactions, and all higher-order interactions up to the single k-factor interaction are independent of each other; consequently, every one of these terms can be included in the model even if they are not expected to be important. In contrast, the 2^{k-p} fractional factorial designs take advantage of the relative rarity of significant higher-order interactions and intentionally confound them with simpler terms like main effects and two-factor interactions that are more likely to be important. Whenever potential model terms are confounded, there are constraints on which terms can be included in the model.

The degree of agreement between two potential terms in a model is measured by the correlation coefficient r introduced in Chapter 8. A convenient way to present the correlation coefficients of the many possible pairs of terms in a model is with a square matrix of correlation coefficients such as were used earlier in this chapter. Those pairs of terms in the matrix with $r = 0$ are independent of each other but in the fractional factorial designs there are frequently cases where $r = \pm 1$, which indicates that the two relevant terms are perfectly correlated. When two terms are perfectly correlated or confounded like this, the columns of their ± 1 values in the design matrix will be exactly the same when $r = 1$, and exactly opposite each other when $r = 1$. That is, the levels of the confounded terms are effectively locked together. Then if one or the other or both terms has a significant effect on the response, it will be impossible to determine which term or terms was the true cause of the effect. The mathematical consequence of this relationship is that only one of the confounded terms can be included in the model and the effect attributed to the included term will actually be a combination of the effects due to both confounded terms. In general, when two or more model terms are confounded with each other, only one of the involved terms can be included in the model but the effect attributed to that term actually will be a combination of the effects of all of the confounded terms.

Example 10.1

Analyze the data from the 2^3 full-factorial experiment with two replicates in Figure 10.2. Then extract and reanalyze those runs that correspond to the one-half fractional factorial design with $x_3 = x_{12}$ and compare the two models.

Row	y	x1	x2	x3	x12	x13	x23
1	77.274	-1	-1	-1	1	1	1
2	78.882	-1	-1	1	1	-1	-1
3	67.014	-1	1	-1	-1	1	-1
4	58.279	-1	1	1	-1	-1	1
5	85.340	1	-1	-1	-1	-1	1
6	130.299	1	-1	1	-1	1	-1
7	63.342	1	1	-1	1	-1	-1
8	112.042	1	1	1	1	1	1
9	70.145	-1	-1	-1	1	1	1
10	80.777	-1	-1	1	1	-1	-1
11	70.425	-1	1	-1	-1	1	-1
12	64.060	-1	1	1	-1	-1	1
13	80.620	1	-1	-1	-1	-1	1
14	131.356	1	-1	1	-1	1	-1
15	67.897	1	1	-1	1	-1	-1
16	108.460	1	1	1	1	1	1

Figure 10.2 Data from a 2^3 full-factorial experiment.

Solution: The experimental data were loaded into a MINITAB worksheet and analyzed. The correlation matrix and the multiple regression analysis output from the full-factorial experiment are shown in Figure 10.3. Figure 10.4 shows the runs and analysis from the indicated 2_{III}^{3-1} design where the generator 3 = 12 was used to select those eight runs to be retained from the original 16-run experiment. The correlation matrix clearly shows the confounding between main effects and two-factor interactions as expected in this resolution III design and the expected pairs of columns are exactly the same in the data table.

Example 10.2

Use the confounding relations to compare the regression coefficients of the models in Figures 10.3 and 10.4.

Solution: Figure 10.3 shows the analysis of the full-factorial design with all of the main effects and two-factor interactions intact. The confounding relations for the 2_{III}^{3-1} experiment extracted from the full-factorial experiment are: 1 = 23, 2 = 13, and 3 = 12. The regression coefficients for x_1 and x_{23} from the full-factorial experiment are $b_1 = 13.28$ and $b_{23} = -2.11$. In the fractional factorial experiment, since x_2 and x_{23} are confounded, only x_1 can be retained in the model but its regression coefficient is a combination of the effects of both terms. That is, b_1 from the fractional factorial experiment equals $b_1 + b_{23}$ from the full-factorial experiment:

$$\left(b_1 + b_{23}\right)_{full} = \left(b_1\right)_{fractional}$$
$$13.28 - 2.11 = 11.17$$

which is in perfect agreement with the coefficient of x_1 reported in Figure 10.4. From the other confounding relations:

```
MTB > corr c2-c7;
SUBC> nopvalues.

Correlations (Pearson)
            x1        x2        x3        x12       x13
x2       0.000
x3       0.000     0.000
x12      0.000     0.000     0.000
x13      0.000     0.000     0.000     0.000
x23      0.000     0.000     0.000     0.000     0.000

MTB > regress c1 6 c2-c7

Regression Analysis
The regression equation is
y = 84.1 + 13.3 x1 - 7.70 x2 + 11.4 x3 - 1.79 x12 + 11.7 x13 - 2.11 x23

Predictor        Coef        StDev         T          P
Constant       84.1381      0.8561       98.28      0.000
x1             13.2813      0.8561       15.51      0.000
x2             -7.6984      0.8561       -8.99      0.000
x3             11.3811      0.8561       13.29      0.000
x12            -1.7858      0.8561       -2.09      0.067
x13            11.7388      0.8561       13.71      0.000
x23            -2.1107      0.8561       -2.47      0.036

S = 3.425        R-Sq = 98.7%       R-Sq(adj) = 97.9%

Analysis of Variance

Source              DF          SS          MS         F          P
Regression          6        8170.1      1361.7     116.11     0.000
Residual Error      9         105.5        11.7
Total              15        8275.6

Source       DF      Seq SS
x1            1      2822.3
x2            1       948.2
x3            1      2072.5
x12           1        51.0
x13           1      2204.8
x23           1        71.3
```

Figure 10.3 Analysis of 2^3 full-factorial experiment.

$$\left(b_2 + b_{13}\right)_{full} = \left(b_2\right)_{fractional}$$
$$-7.70 + 11.74 = 4.04$$

$$\left(b_3 + b_{12}\right)_{full} = \left(b_3\right)_{fractional}$$
$$11.38 - 1.79 = 9.59$$

which are also in perfect agreement with the two figures. The final result of confound-ing in the 2_{III}^{3-1} fractional factorial design is that the model constant is confounded with

```
MTB > print c1-c7
```

Data Display

Row	y	x1	x2	x3	x12	x13	x23
1	78.882	-1	-1	1	1	-1	-1
2	67.014	-1	1	-1	-1	1	-1
3	85.340	1	-1	-1	-1	-1	1
4	112.042	1	1	1	1	1	1
5	80.777	-1	-1	1	1	-1	-1
6	70.425	-1	1	-1	-1	1	-1
7	80.620	1	-1	-1	-1	-1	1
8	108.460	1	1	1	1	1	1

```
MTB > corr c2-c7;
SUBC> nopvalues.
```

Correlations (Pearson)

	x1	x2	x3	x12	x13
x2	0.000				
x3	0.000	0.000			
x12	0.000	0.000	1.000		
x13	0.000	1.000	0.000	0.000	
x23	1.000	0.000	0.000	0.000	0.000

```
MTB > regress c1 6 c2-c7
```

Regression Analysis

```
* x12 is highly correlated with other X variables
* x12 has been removed from the equation

* x13 is highly correlated with other X variables
* x13 has been removed from the equation

* x23 is highly correlated with other X variables
* x23 has been removed from the equation
```

The regression equation is
$$y = 85.4 + 11.2\ x1 + 4.04\ x2 + 9.60\ x3$$

Predictor	Coef	StDev	T	P
Constant	85.4448	0.8869	96.34	0.000
x1	11.1705	0.8869	12.60	0.000
x2	4.0404	0.8869	4.56	0.010
x3	9.5953	0.8869	10.82	0.000

$S = 2.509$ R-Sq = 98.7%   R-Sq(adj) = 97.7%

Analysis of Variance

Source	DF	SS	MS	F	P
Regression	3	1865.41	621.80	98.81	0.000
Residual Error	4	25.17	6.29		
Total	7	1890.58			

Source	DF	Seq SS
x1	1	998.25
x2	1	130.60
x3	1	736.56

Figure 10.4 Analysis of 2_{III}^{3-1} half-fractional factorial experiment.

the three-factor interaction so $(b_0 + b_{123})_{full} = (b_0)_{fractional}$. *Although the three-factor inter-action wasn't reported in Figure 10.2, it must be given by:*

$$\left(b_{123}\right)_{full} = \left(b_0\right)_{fractional} - \left(b_0\right)_{full}$$
$$= 85.44 - 84.14$$
$$= 1.30$$

which could be confirmed by fitting the full model to the full-factorial experiment. This demonstrates, by example, that the consequence of confounding in fractional factorial designs is that the regression coefficients from the full-factorial experiments are literally added together according to the confounding relations and reported as the coefficients of the fractional factorial experiment.

10.6 FRACTIONAL FACTORIAL DESIGNS IN MINITAB

The methods for creating and analyzing fractional factorial designs in MINITAB are substantially the same as those presented in Section 9.7 for the full-factorial designs. The only modifications to those methods address the issues associated with confounding between model terms.

10.6.1 Creating Fractional Factorial Designs in MINITAB

The methods for creating fractional factorial designs in MINITAB are very similar to the methods for creating 2^k full-factorial designs presented in Section 9.7.1, with a few extra steps:

- Copy the design from an existing file.

- Manually enter all of the ±1 values for each column into the worksheet for the base design. Then use the **let** command (or the **Calc> Calculator** menu) and the design generators to create the remaining columns.

- Use the **set** command (or the **Calc> Make Patterned Data> Simple Set of Numbers** menu) to create the necessary pattern of ±1 values for each column of the base design. Then use the design generators and the **let** command to create the remaining columns.

- Use MINITAB's **Stat> DOE> Factorial> Create Factorial Design** menu to specify and create the design.

If you use one of the first three methods, you should make and check the correlation matrix including all of the main effects and two-factor interactions to confirm that the run matrix was created correctly. The correlation matrix should have $r = 1$ on the diagonal and $r = 0$ everywhere for the off-diagonal entries except for certain $r = \pm 1$ values expected from the confounding relations.

Example 10.3

Use MINITAB's **Calc> Make Patterned Data> Simple Set of Numbers** *and* **Calc> Calculator** *dialogs to create the* 2_{IV}^{6-2} *experiment design. Construct the correlation matrix to confirm that the design was created correctly.*

Solution: *The base design of the* 2_{IV}^{6-2} *experiment is a* 2^4 *design with* 16 *runs. The instructions for creating this design manually are given in Example 9.8. The* **Calc> Make Patterned Data> Simple Set of Numbers** *dialog was used to recreate the* 2^4 *base design and then the* **Calc> Calculator** *dialog with the generators taken from Table 10.8 were used to determine* x_5 *and* x_6. *Then the* **Calc> Calculator** *dialog was used again to create all of the two-factor interactions. The MINITAB commands and output are shown in Figure 10.5. If you are mouse-impaired you can type these commands directly at the command prompt instead of using the mouse/menu environment. The correlation matrix was reformatted to fit better in the Session window but the default output by MINITAB is very similar.*

The easiest way to create a fractional factorial design in MINITAB is from the **Stat> DOE Factorial> Create Factorial Design** menu. Designs created in this way have the added advantage that they're automatically recognized by MINITAB when you're ready to analyze the experiment using **Stat> DOE> Factorial> Analyze Factorial**

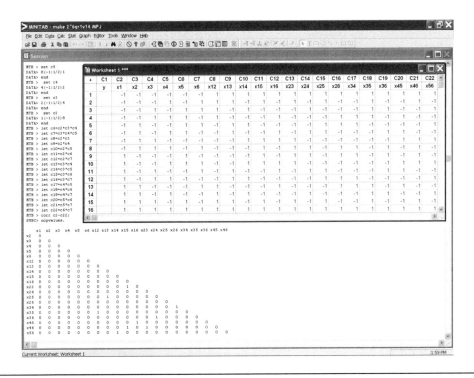

Figure 10.5 MINITAB commands to create the 2_{IV}^{6-2} design and correlation matrix.

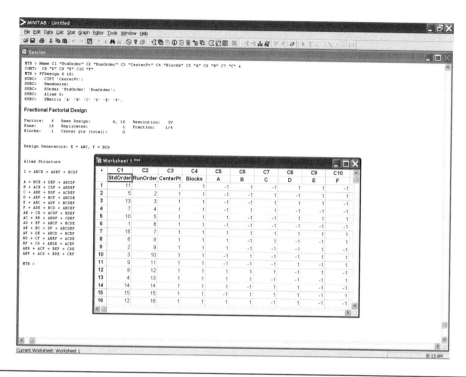

Figure 10.6   Creating the 2_{IV}^{6-2} design using **Stat> DOE> Factorial> Create Factorial Design.**

Design. The steps required to create a fractional factorial design using the **Create Factorial Design** menu are essentially the same as the steps used to create a full-factorial design as described in Section 9.7.1. There are several options available to customize the design but the default settings will be applicable in most cases.

Example 10.4

*Use MINITAB's **Stat> DOE> Factorial> Create Factorial Design** menu to recreate the 2_{IV}^{6-2} experiment design from Example 10.3. Confirm that the design was created correctly.*

Solution: The experiment was created in MINITAB and MINITAB's output is shown in Figure 10.6. The matrix of experimental runs is randomized so it is difficult to compare it to the result from Example 10.3. The runs could be sorted by the standard order and then checked to see if they match, but the output in the Session window indicates that the same design generators were used to create the fifth and sixth variables so we can be confident that the two methods for creating the 2_{IV}^{6-2} designs are equivalent.

10.6.2 Analysis of Fractional Factorial Designs with MINITAB

The analysis methods for full-factorial designs presented in Section 9.7.2 are still applicable for the fractional factorial designs. Those methods were:

- Manual analysis with **Stat> Regression> Regression**.

- Analysis with the custom *mlrk.mac* macros.

- Analysis with **Stat> DOE> Factorial> Analyze Factorial Design**.

For manual analysis, the **Stat> Regression> Regression** method is a bit tedious because you have to create all of the interaction columns and indicator columns for the blocks. But once those steps are complete, the **Stat> Regression> Regression** method is quite flexible and easy to use. The **Stat> ANOVA> General Linear Model** method can also be used to analyze fractional factorial designs, but specify all of the model terms except blocks as covariates to get the regression coefficients in the MINITAB output.

The *mlrk.mac* macros work the same way for fractional factorial designs as they do for full-factorial designs. They use MINITAB's **regress** command instead of the GLM (general linear model) command because the **regress** command automatically retains the first of every confounded set of terms and drops the others from the model. MINITAB prints a warning in the Session window when it must drop a term from the model. For example, if *x*4 is correlated to another term already included in the model, you would see the following statements appear in the Session window:

> * x4 is highly correlated with other x variables
> * x4 has been removed from the equation

The GLM command doesn't have this capability; when confounded terms are included in the model it generates an error and stops.

The **Stat> DOE> Factorial> Analyze Factorial Design** menu works exactly as it did for full-factorial designs. You will still have to specify the response, the terms to be included in the model, and the residuals diagnostic graphs to be constructed. MINITAB automatically includes all of the possible terms that the design allows to be fitted so you shouldn't have to make many changes to the model. MINITAB also reports the confounding relations to assist in the interpretation of the regression coefficients.

Usually with the full-factorial designs, and always when they are replicated, there are enough total degrees of freedom in an experiment to fit an appropriate model and still have degrees of freedom left over to estimate the error. But sometimes, especially when an experiment has very few runs and a large model, the model consumes all available degrees of freedom and there are none left over to estimate the error. Such designs are called *saturated designs*. Unreplicated fractional factorial designs are often saturated designs. When the analysis of these designs is performed in MINITAB, MINITAB completes as much of the analysis as it can before it has to stop. Part of the analysis that it does complete is the calculation of the regression coefficients, but without error degrees of freedom it cannot determine their associated standard errors, *t* values, or *p* values. One method to continue the analysis is to construct the normal probability plot of the regression coefficients and use it to determine which model terms are the weakest. After the weakest terms are dropped from the model they are used to estimate the error and MINITAB can once again complete the rest of the analysis.

One of the most important saturated designs is the 2_V^{5-1} design which has fifteen runs, $df_{model} = 15$, and $df_\varepsilon = 0$. But with so many plotted points in the normal plot of the regression coefficients, it's often quite easy to determine which terms are important and which can safely be dropped from the model. Of course a follow-up experiment should be performed to confirm any conclusions drawn from such a risky design and analysis.

Example 10.5

Perform the analysis of the 2_V^{5-1} design formed from the 16 runs of the 32-run experiment in Example 9.10, using the generator $5 = 1234$. How well does the half-fractional factorial design duplicate the results of the full-factorial experiment?

*Solution: The 16 runs of the original 32-run experiment were copied into a new MINITAB worksheet and the analysis was performed using **Stat> Regression> Regression**. MINITAB's Session window output (after some minor edits) is shown in Figure 10.7. The regression analysis is incomplete because the experiment is saturated—all of the available degrees of freedom are consumed by the model. In order to distinguish significant regression coefficients from insignificant ones, a normal probability plot of*

Data Display

Row	StdOrder	RunOrder	Y	A	B	C	D	E
1	14	2	150	-1	1	1	-1	1
2	15	3	284	-1	1	1	1	-1
3	29	5	287	1	1	1	-1	-1
4	2	6	149	-1	-1	-1	-1	1
5	23	7	53	1	-1	1	1	-1
6	20	11	76	1	-1	-1	1	1
7	22	14	-32	1	-1	1	-1	1
8	3	15	142	-1	-1	-1	1	-1
9	17	16	121	1	-1	-1	-1	-1
10	8	17	-43	-1	-1	1	1	1
11	32	18	200	1	1	1	1	1
12	5	21	1	-1	-1	1	-1	-1
13	26	23	187	1	1	-1	-1	1
14	12	25	233	-1	1	-1	1	1
15	27	29	207	1	1	-1	1	-1
16	9	32	266	-1	1	-1	-1	-1

Correlations: A, B, C, D, E, AB, AC, AD, AE, BC, BD, BE, CD, CE, DE

	A	B	C	D	E	AB	AC	AD	AE	BC	BD	BE	CD	CE
B	0													
C	0	0												
D	0	0	0											
E	0	0	0	0										
AB	0	0	0	0	0									
AC	0	0	0	0	0	0								
AD	0	0	0	0	0	0	0							
AE	0	0	0	0	0	0	0	0						
BC	0	0	0	0	0	0	0	0	0					
BD	0	0	0	0	0	0	0	0	0	0				
BE	0	0	0	0	0	0	0	0	0	0	0			
CD	0	0	0	0	0	0	0	0	0	0	0	0		
CE	0	0	0	0	0	0	0	0	0	0	0	0	0	
DE	0	0	0	0	0	0	0	0	0	0	0	0	0	0

Figure 10.7 Analysis of a 2_V^{5-1} saturated experiment. *Continued*

Continued

```
Regression Analysis: Y versus A, B, ...

The regression equation is
Y = 143 - 5.19 A + 84.2 B - 30.1 C + 1.44 D - 27.6 E - 1.31 AB + 19.7 AC
    - 4.81 AD - 2.06 AE + 33.6 BC + 2.81 BD - 6.69 BE + 9.56 CD - 16.2 CE
    + 0.0625 DE

Predictor        Coef      SE Coef          T        P
Constant      142.563        0.000          *        *
A            -5.18750        0.00000        *        *
B            84.1875         0.0000         *        *
C           -30.0625         0.0000         *        *
D             1.43750        0.00000        *        *
E           -27.5625         0.0000         *        *
AB           -1.31250        0.00000        *        *
AC           19.6875         0.0000         *        *
AD           -4.81250        0.00000        *        *
AE           -2.06250        0.00000        *        *
BC           33.5625         0.0000         *        *
BD            2.81250        0.00000        *        *
BE           -6.68750        0.00000        *        *
CD            9.56250        0.00000        *        *
CE          -16.1875         0.0000         *        *
DE            0.0625000      0.0000000      *        *


S = *

Analysis of Variance

Source           DF           SS          MS          F        P
Regression       15      171667.9     11444.5          *        *
Residual Error    0            *           *
Total            15      171667.9

Source     DF       Seq SS
A           1        430.6
B           1     113400.6
C           1      14460.1
D           1         33.1
E           1      12155.1
AB          1         27.6
AC          1       6201.6
AD          1        370.6
AE          1         68.1
BC          1      18023.1
BD          1        126.6
BE          1        715.6
CD          1       1463.1
CE          1       4192.6
DE          1          0.1
```

the regression coefficients was created. This plot is shown in Figure 10.8. (The plot was created by copying the regression coefficients and their associated terms/labels from the Session window into a MINITAB worksheet. Then the regression coefficients were plotted with the custom **plotnorm** *macro using the* **label** *subcommand.) The plot indicates that there are many terms of near-zero magnitude but that B, C, E, AC, BC, CE, and perhaps CD are outliers that should be retained in the regression model. To preserve model hierarchy, the main effects A and D also need to be retained in the model.*

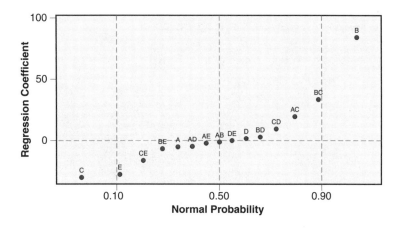

Figure 10.8   Normal plot of the regression coefficients from a saturated experiment.

The refined model is shown in Figure 10.9. The analysis shows that the CD inter-action is barely significant (p = 0.041) so that dropping it and the insignificant D main effect (p = 0.710) might not be a serious compromise. But the AC interaction is highly significant (p = 0.002), so it and the A main effect should be retained in the model. Comparison of this refined model and the refined model determined from the analysis of the full-factorial experiment in Example 9.10 shows that they are substantially the same with comparable regression coefficients. Regression diagnostics for the model in Figure 10.9 (not shown) indicate that the residuals are normally distributed and homoscedastic as required by the analysis method. This example clearly shows that the 16-run 2_V^{5-1} design delivers substantially the same information as the 32-run 2^5 experi-ment even though the 2_V^{5-1} experiment is saturated.

10.7 INTERPRETATION OF FRACTIONAL FACTORIAL DESIGNS

10.7.1 Resolution V Designs

Of the fractional factorial designs, designs of resolution V and higher are the easiest to interpret. Resolution V designs confound main effects with four-factor interactions, and two-factor interactions with three-factor interactions. This means that the model for a resolution V design can contain all of the main effects and two-factor interactions so that the usual methods of Chapter 9 can be used to analyze the data. As long as the assump-tion that three-factor and higher-order interactions are insignificant is true, resolution V designs should provide a safe model. In the absence of hard evidence that three-factor and higher order interactions are insignificant, we rely on Occam to protect us.

In the author's experience, based on many years of building about one experiment a week, I've only ever encountered a handful of experiments where I detected a significant three-factor interaction. In each case, the magnitude of the three-factor interaction was

```
┌─────────────────────────────────────────────────────────────────────────┐
│                                                                           │
│  Regression Analysis: Y versus A, B, C, D, E, AC, BC, CD, CE              │
│                                                                           │
│  The regression equation is                                              │
│  Y = 143 - 5.19 A + 84.2 B - 30.1 C + 1.44 D - 27.6 E + 19.7 AC + 33.6 BC │
│      + 9.56 CD - 16.2 CE                                                  │
│                                                                           │
│  Predictor          Coef     SE Coef          T          P               │
│  Constant        142.563       3.692      38.62      0.000               │
│  A                 -5.187       3.692      -1.41      0.210               │
│  B                 84.187       3.692      22.80      0.000               │
│  C                -30.063       3.692      -8.14      0.000               │
│  D                  1.438       3.692       0.39      0.710               │
│  E                -27.562       3.692      -7.47      0.000               │
│  AC                19.688       3.692       5.33      0.002               │
│  BC                33.563       3.692       9.09      0.000               │
│  CD                 9.563       3.692       2.59      0.041               │
│  CE               -16.188       3.692      -4.38      0.005               │
│                                                                           │
│  S = 14.77       R-Sq = 99.2%      R-Sq(adj) = 98.1%                      │
│                                                                           │
│  Analysis of Variance                                                     │
│                                                                           │
│  Source              DF            SS          MS         F        P      │
│  Regression           9        170360       18929     86.80    0.000      │
│  Residual Error       6          1308         218                         │
│  Total               15        171668                                     │
│                                                                           │
│  Source        DF      Seq SS                                            │
│  A              1         431                                            │
│  B              1      113401                                            │
│  C              1       14460                                            │
│  D              1          33                                            │
│  E              1       12155                                            │
│  AC             1        6202                                            │
│  BC             1       18023                                            │
│  CD             1        1463                                            │
│  CE             1        4193                                            │
│                                                                           │
└─────────────────────────────────────────────────────────────────────────┘
```

Figure 10.9 Refined model from the 2_V^{5-1} saturated experiment.

relatively small so that it wasn't necessary to worry about or bother with it. It was also so hard to imagine a physical mechanism that might cause the three-factor interaction that it was most likely a Type 1 error—an artifact of the particular data set. Furthermore, I never wanted to even attempt to try to explain the significance of a three-factor interaction—especially a weak one—to anyone. The point is that Occam and experience both suggest that three-factor and higher-order interactions are rare so it is generally safe to ignore them.

10.7.2 Resolution IV Designs

Resolution IV designs confound main effects with three-factor interactions, and two-factor interactions with other two-factor interactions. Since three-factor and higher-order interactions should be rare, we can expect to safely recover the main effects; however, the confounding between two-factor interactions can present a problem. A first choice has to be made to decide which two-factor interactions should be included in the model.

In the absence of any prior knowledge of which interactions might be significant, the choice is arbitrary. For each set of confounded interactions, only one of them can be included in the model. When a two-factor interaction is found to be significant, it is up to us to decide which interaction or interactions of each set to attribute the effect to.

Occam's razor and the concept of effect heredity can provide some guidance for deciding which confounded terms should be retained in a model. Generally, if two variables are going to have a significant two-factor interaction then both or at least one of their main effects should be substantial. Consequently, by comparing the list of significant main effects to the pair of two-factor interactions that might be the cause of the effect, its often possible to rule out one of the pair of confounded two-factor interactions.

Despite these difficulties, the good news is that even though only one of each pair of confounded interactions can be included in the model, the effects of both interactions will still be accounted for by that one term. The bad news is that when we can't be certain which of the confounded terms is the real cause of the observed effect, it will be necessary to build a follow-up experiment that resolves the ambiguity.

Example 10.6

An experiment was performed using a 2_{IV}^{4-1} design with generator $4 = 123$. A model including the main effects and three of the six possible two-factor interactions was fitted to the response:

$$y = b_0 + b_1 x_1 + b_2 x_2 + b_3 x_3 + b_{12} x_{12} + b_{13} x_{13} + b_{14} x_{14}$$

The model showed that only coefficients b_2, b_3, and b_{14} were significant. Describe how the model should be refined.

Solution: *It doesn't make sense that variables x_1 and x_4 would be insignificant by themselves but have a significant two-factor interaction. It's more likely that the effect attributed to x_{14} is actually due to x_{23} with which it is confounded. This suggests that the model should actually be:*

$$y = b_0 + b_2 x_2 + b_3 x_3 + b_{23} x_{23}$$

This is significantly simpler and makes much more sense. Of course in any future experiments, it would be a good idea to try to resolve this issue and pin down the true cause of the interaction: x_{14} or x_{23}.

Sometimes there is an opportunity to limit the risks associated with confounding by carefully selecting the terms that are confounded with each other when you design an experiment. If you have prior experience with a system, knowledge of applicable first principles, or just an accurate opinion about which variables are likely to interact with each other, you may be able to structure the confounding so that terms that are expected to be significant are confounded with terms that are not expected to be significant. That way, when a significant interaction term is detected, it should be easier to decide which of the confounded terms is the real cause of the observed effect. Although this trick might appear to be useful, it is relatively rare that sufficient information of the necessary accuracy is available to make it effective.

Example 10.7

An experiment is planned using a 2_{IV}^{6-2} design. The design variables are operator, machine, part design, temperature, lubricant, and assembly torque. Prior experience suggests that there will be interactions between: operator and machine, part design and lubricant, part design and assembly torque, and lubricant and assembly torque. No other interactions are expected. How should the variables be assigned to resolve the expected significant interactions?

Solution: If the 2_{IV}^{6-2} design uses the generators $E = ABC$ and $F = BCD$, then the implied confounding relations between pairs of two-factor interactions are: $AB = CE$, $AC = BE$, $AE = BC = DF$, $BD = CF$, and $BF = CD$. All other two-factor interactions will be confounded with three-factor interactions, which are assumed to be insignificant. If the variables are assigned in the order given in the problem statement, then the operator/machine interaction (AB) will be confounded with the part design/lubricant interaction (CE), which is not acceptable. Under the alternative assignment A: Operator, B: Machine, C: Design, D: Lubricant, E: Temperature, and F: Torque, each suspected significant two-factor interaction (AB, CD, CF, and DF) is paired with one or two insignificant ones.

Example 10.8

When ultrasonic (acoustic) energy causes gas bubbles in a liquid to resonate, the gas bubbles can collapse and form a light-emitting plasma. This process, called sonoluminescence, has applications in the dissolution of materials and possibly in cold fusion. An experiment was performed to identify the most important variables in a device designed to produce sonoluminescence and determine the variable settings that maximize the sonoluminescent light intensity.* Seven variables from a very long list of variables were selected for the study. Due to time and cost limitations the experiment was limited to one replicate of a 2_{IV}^{7-3} design. The seven variables and their levels are shown in Table 10.14. The sixteen runs of the experiment were performed in completely random order. The data are shown in Table 10.15. Analyze the experimental data and try to refine the model. Use the refined model to determine the settings of the variables that maximize the intensity response.

Solution: The experimental design and response data were entered into a MINITAB worksheet. Then the experiment design was specified to MINITAB using **Stat> DOE> Factorial> Define Custom Factorial Design**. To get a preliminary view of the data, main effects and interaction plots were created using **Stat> DOE> Factorial> Factorial Plots**. The main effects plots are shown in Figure 10.10 and the interaction plots are

---

* Eva Wilcox and Ken Inn, NIST Physics Laboratory, 1999, www.itl.nist.gov/div898/handbook/pri/section6/pri621.htm.

Table 10.14 Variables and their levels for the NIST sonoluminescence study.

Variable	−1	+1	Units	Description
x_1 : Molarity	0.10	0.33	mole	Amount of the solute
x_2 : Solute type	Sugar	Glycerol	NA	Type of solute
x_3 : pH	3	11	NA	pH of the solution
x_4 : Gas type	Helium	Air	NA	Type of gas dissolved in the water
x_5 : Water depth	Half	Full	NA	Depth of the water in the flask
x_6 : Horn depth	5	10	mm	Depth of the ultrasonic horn in the solution
x_7 : Flask clamping	Unclamped	Clamped	NA	Method of clamping the flask

Table 10.15 Experimental data from NIST sonoluminescence experiment.

Std	Run	x_1	x_2	x_3	x_4	x_5	x_6	x_7	Y: Intensity
1	15	−	−	−	−	−	−	−	80.6
2	4	+	−	−	−	−	+	+	66.1
3	3	−	+	−	−	+	−	+	59.1
4	10	+	+	−	−	+	+	−	68.9
5	9	−	−	+	−	+	+	+	75.1
6	1	+	−	+	−	+	−	−	373.8
7	14	−	+	+	−	−	+	−	66.8
8	11	+	+	+	−	−	−	+	79.6
9	5	−	−	−	+	+	+	−	114.3
10	8	+	−	−	+	+	−	+	84.1
11	2	−	+	−	+	−	+	+	68.4
12	16	+	+	−	+	−	−	−	88.1
13	12	−	−	+	+	−	−	+	78.1
14	6	+	−	+	+	−	+	−	327.2
15	13	−	+	+	+	+	−	−	77.6
16	7	+	+	+	+	+	+	+	61.9

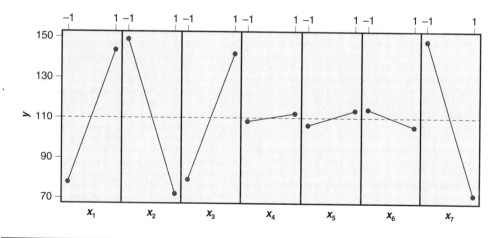

Figure 10.10 Main effects plot from the NIST sonoluminescence experiment.

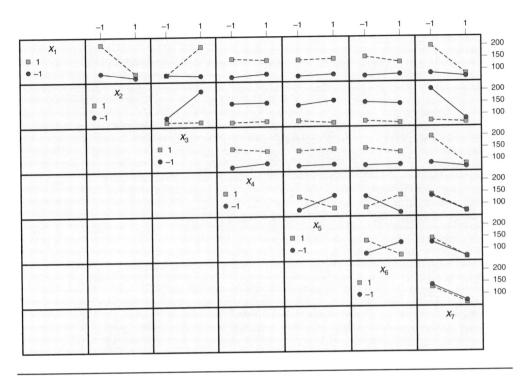

Figure 10.11 Interaction effects plot from the NIST sonoluminescence experiment.

shown in Figure 10.11. The main effects plots suggest that variables x_1, x_2, x_3, and x_7 have much stronger effects than do x_4, x_5, and x_6. The diverging line segments in the interaction plots suggest that there are significant interactions due to x_{12}, x_{13}, x_{17}, x_{23}, x_{27}, x_{37}, x_{45}, x_{46}, and x_{56}; however, since two-factor interactions are confounded with other two-factor interactions, a shorter list of interactions might explain these observations.

*The experiment was analyzed using **Stat> DOE> Factorial> Analyze Factorial Design**. The output from MINITAB is shown in Figure 10.12. All seven of the main effects and the twenty-one two-factor interactions were entered into the model; however, MINITAB recognized that some of the two-factor interactions were confounded with other two-factor interactions and it was only able to retain seven of them in the model. From the confounding relations shown in the MINITAB output we can see that the first terms from each set of three confounded terms were the ones that MINITAB retained in the model.*

Figure 10.12 shows that there are several terms in the model with $p \approx 0.05$ but there is only a single degree of freedom for the error estimate. Some of the surviving interactions are not significant and can be dropped from the model. This simplifies the model and frees up degrees of freedom to improve the error estimate. Three of the interactions, x_{12}, x_{13}, and x_{17}, have nearly significant p values and should be retained in the model, at least until the error estimate is improved. From the confounding relations it can be seen that these three interactions are sufficient to explain all of the interactions that appear to be significant in Figure 10.11. Then it becomes apparent that all of the

```
Alias Information for Terms in the Model.
Totally confounded terms were removed from the analysis.

x1*x2 + x3*x7 + x5*x6
x1*x3 + x2*x7 + x4*x6
x1*x4 + x3*x6 + x5*x7
x1*x5 + x2*x6 + x4*x7
x1*x6 + x2*x5 + x3*x4
x1*x7 + x2*x3 + x4*x5
x2*x4 + x3*x5 + x6*x7
```

Fractional Factorial Fit: Y versus x1, x2, x3, x4, x5, x6, x7

```
Estimated Effects and Coefficients for Y (coded units)

Term         Effect      Coef     SE Coef       T      P
Constant                110.61      2.919    37.90  0.017
x1            66.21      33.11      2.919    11.34  0.056
x2           -78.61     -39.31      2.919   -13.47  0.047
x3            63.81      31.91      2.919    10.93  0.058
x4             3.71       1.86      2.919     0.64  0.639
x5             7.49       3.74      2.919     1.28  0.422
x6            -9.04      -4.52      2.919    -1.55  0.365
x7           -78.11     -39.06      2.919   -13.38  0.047
x1*x2        -59.56     -29.78      2.919   -10.20  0.062
x1*x3         70.01      35.01      2.919    11.99  0.053
x1*x4        -10.49      -5.24      2.919    -1.80  0.323
x1*x5         -0.56      -0.28      2.919    -0.10  0.939
x1*x6        -16.34      -8.17      2.919    -2.80  0.218
x1*x7        -63.46     -31.73      2.919   -10.87  0.058
x2*x4          1.69       0.84      2.919     0.29  0.821

Analysis of Variance for Y (coded units)

Source               DF    Seq SS    Adj SS    Adj MS      F      P
Main Effects          7     83557   83556.6   11936.7  87.57  0.082
2-Way Interactions    7     51428   51428.0    7346.9  53.90  0.105
Residual Error        1       136     136.3     136.3
Total                15    135121
```

Figure 10.12 Analysis of the NIST sonoluminescence data.

main effects and two-factor interactions involving x_4, x_5, and x_6 can be dropped from the model without compromising its quality. That is, a simplified model involving x_1, x_2, x_3, and x_7 and their interactions explains most of the variation accounted for by the model involving all seven variables and their interactions. Remembering Occam, the former model with four predictor variables is preferred.

The refined model, including only x_1, x_2, x_3, x_7, x_{12}, x_{13}, and x_{17}, is shown in Figure 10.13. Residuals diagnostic plots (not shown) indicate that the residuals are normal and homoscedastic with respect to the run order, the fitted values, and the predictors used in the model. All of the terms in the model are highly significant, with p = 0.000.

By inspecting the signs of the model's regression coefficients, the settings (x_1, x_2, x_3, x_7) = (1, −1, 1, −1) should maximize the intensity response. Under these settings, the predicted value of the response is:

```
Fractional Factorial Fit: Y versus x1, x2, x3, x7

Estimated Effects and Coefficients for Y (coded units)

Term          Effect      Coef     SE Coef       T        P
Constant                 110.61      4.204     26.31   0.000
x1             66.21      33.11      4.204      7.87   0.000
x2            -78.61     -39.31      4.204     -9.35   0.000
x3             63.81      31.91      4.204      7.59   0.000
x7            -78.11     -39.06      4.204     -9.29   0.000
x1*x2         -59.56     -29.78      4.204     -7.08   0.000
x1*x3          70.01      35.01      4.204      8.33   0.000
x1*x7         -63.46     -31.73      4.204     -7.55   0.000

Analysis of Variance for Y (coded units)

Source               DF     Seq SS    Adj SS    Adj MS      F       P
Main Effects          4      82950     82950   20737.6   73.32   0.000
2-Way Interactions    3      49908     49908   16635.9   58.82   0.000
Residual Error        8       2263      2263     282.8
  Pure Error          8       2263      2263     282.8
Total                15     135121

Alias Structure

I + x1*x2*x3*x7
x1 + x2*x3*x7
x2 + x1*x3*x7
x3 + x1*x2*x7
x7 + x1*x2*x3
x1*x2 + x3*x7
x1*x3 + x2*x7
x1*x7 + x2*x3
```

Figure 10.13 Refined model for NIST sonoluminescence data.

$$Y(x_1,x_2,x_3,x_7) = 110.6 + 33.1x_1 - 39.3x_2 + 31.9x_3 - 39.1x_7 - 29.8x_{12} + 35.0x_{13} - 31.7x_{17}$$
$$Y(1,-1,1,-1) \ = 110.6 + 33.1\,(1) - 39.3\,(-1) + 31.9\,(1) - 39.1\,(-1) - 29.8\,(1)\,(-1)$$
$$+ 35.0\,(1)\,(1) - 31.7(1)\,(-1)$$
$$= 350.5$$

This predicted value is consistent with the values of the two observations from the data set (373.8, 327.2) that were taken using these settings.

The adjusted coefficient of determination of the refined model is:

$$r^2_{adj} = 1 - \frac{df_{total}SS_{\varepsilon}}{df_{\varepsilon}SS_{total}}$$
$$= 1 - \frac{15 \times 2263}{8 \times 135121}$$
$$= 0.969$$

and the standard error of the model is:

$$s_\varepsilon = \sqrt{MS_\varepsilon} = \sqrt{282.8} = 16.8$$

10.7.3 Resolution III Designs

Resolution III designs are considerably harder to interpret than designs of higher resolution. Consider a model for a 2_{III}^{3-1} design that can only include main effects:

$$y = b_0 + b_1 x_1 + b_2 x_2 + b_3 x_3 \qquad (10.10)$$

The confounding relations are: $1 = 23$, $2 = 13$, and $3 = 12$. Suppose all three main effects are found to be significant. What's really going on here? The true behavior of the system might indeed be as in Equation 10.10 or it could be any one of the following:

$$y = b_0 + b_1 x_1 + b_2 x_2 + b_{12} x_{12} \qquad (10.11)$$

$$y = b_0 + b_1 x_1 + b_3 x_3 + b_{13} x_{13} \qquad (10.12)$$

$$y = b_0 + b_2 x_2 + b_3 x_3 + b_{23} x_{23} \qquad (10.13)$$

Occam's guidance is useless here because it's unclear if the main effects–only model is more likely than one of the two variable models with an interaction. Without any other knowledge about the effects of the variables and their interactions there's no reason to pick one of these models over the others—they are all equally likely. Although all resolution III designs suffer from this ambiguity, they are still used for screening experiments with many variables when only a few of the variables are expected to be significant. If, from the beginning, most of the variables in an experiment are expected to be important then a design of resolution IV or higher should be used.

Many resolution III designs give ambiguous results that have to be clarified with one or more follow-up experiments. The type of follow-up experiment required depends on the results of the original experiment. If only a few variables in the original experiment are found to be significant, then those variables can be used to build a full-factorial or higher-resolution fractional factorial design. If so many of the variables in the original experiment are found to be significant that none of them can be eliminated from consideration, then the follow-up experiment should be another resolution III design that is complementary to the original design. This complementary design, called the *fold-over* design, is created by inverting the signs in all of the columns of the original design. When the results from two resolution III fold-over designs are combined, they always yield a design of resolution IV that provides a better chance of figuring out which variables and interactions are really important. MINITAB will create the fold-over design for a fractional factorial experiment if **Fold on all factors** is selected in the **Create Factorial Design> Options** menu.

Example 10.9

A 2_{III}^{7-4} experiment was performed using generators $4 = 12, 5 = 13, 6 = 23,$ and $7 = 123$. When the experimental data were analyzed, the significant variables were found to be 1, 2, 3, and 5. Identify an appropriate follow-up experiment to resolve the ambiguities from the original experiment.

Solution: Because of the confounding between variables 1, 3, and 5, the following models might explain the experimental results: $y(1, 2, 3, 5), y(1, 2, 3, 13), y(1, 2, 5, 15),$ and $y(2, 3, 5, 35).$ (This assumes that three-factor and higher-order interactions are not significant.) Appropriate follow-up experiments to distinguish between these models are 2^4 and 2_{IV}^{4-1} designs. The 2_{IV}^{4-1} design would be more economical. It is also sufficient to resolve the ambiguity of the original experiment because there is evidence that two of the relevant interactions, 12 and 23, are not significant.

Example 10.10

A 2_{III}^{7-4} experiment was performed using generators $D = AB, E = AC, F = BC,$ and $G = ABC.$ When the experimental data were analyzed, all of the variables were found to be significant. Create the fold-over design and show that when the two designs are combined they yield a resolution IV design.

Solution: The eight-run 2_{III}^{7-4} design was created using **Stat> DOE> Factorial> Create Factorial Design** in MINITAB. This design is shown in the first eight rows in Figure 10.14. Columns A–C contain the base 2^3 design and the remaining four columns were generated using the default generators: $D = AB, E = AC, F = BC,$ and $G = ABC.$ The settings for the fold-over design, shown in rows 9 to 16, were determined by changing all of the signs of A–G from the original design. The 16-run experiment created from the two combined eight-run experiments was analyzed (**Stat> DOE> Factorial> Analyze Factorial Design**) using a simulated response not shown in the figure. The confounding relations from the analysis of the combined designs confirm that the 16-run experiment is a resolution IV design. Notice that although we say that the design is resolution IV, each main effect is confounded with four three-factor interactions and each two-factor interaction is confounded with two other two-factor interactions. The fold-over design also could have been created by specifying the 2_{III}^{7-4} design and then selecting **Fold on all factors** in the **Create Factorial Design> Options** menu.

10.7.4 Designs of Resolution VI and Higher

Because of the rarity of higher-order interactions, designs of resolution VI and higher generally don't present any serious difficulties in analysis. Main effects will be confounded with five-factor or higher-order interactions and two-factor interactions will be confounded with four-factor or higher-order interactions so both types of terms are very safe from confounding issues. For the same reason (the rarity of high-order interactions), designs of resolution VI and higher can be used to study three-factor interactions when such interactions are expected. The resolution V designs are really the threshold

Fractional Factorial Design

```
Factors:   7    Base Design:       7, 8   Resolution:   III
Runs:      8    Replicates:           1   Fraction:     1/16
Blocks:    1    Center pts (total):   0
```

* NOTE * Some main effects are confounded with two-way interactions.

Design Generators: D = AB, E = AC, F = BC, G = ABC

Alias Structure (up to order 3)

```
I + ABD + ACE + AFG + BCF + BEG + CDG + DEF
A + BD + CE + FG + BCG + BEF + CDF + DEG
B + AD + CF + EG + ACG + AEF + CDE + DFG
C + AE + BF + DG + ABG + ADF + BDE + EFG
D + AB + CG + EF + ACF + AEG + BCE + BFG
E + AC + BG + DF + ABF + ADG + BCD + CFG
F + AG + BC + DE + ABE + ACD + BDG + CEG
G + AF + BE + CD + ABC + ADE + BDF + CEF
```

```
MTB > let c12=-c5
MTB > let c13=-c6
MTB > let c14=-c7
MTB > let c15=-c8
MTB > let c16=-c9
MTB > let c17=-c10
MTB > let c18=-c11
MTB > Stack (c1-c11) (c1-c4 c12-c18) (c1-c11).
MTB > print c1-c18
```

Data Display

Row	Std	Run	CP	Blo	A	B	C	D	E	F	G	fA	fB	fC	fD	fE	fF	fG
1	1	1	1	1	-1	-1	-1	1	1	1	-1	1	1	1	-1	-1	-1	1
2	2	2	1	1	1	-1	-1	-1	-1	1	1	-1	1	1	1	1	-1	-1
3	3	3	1	1	-1	1	-1	-1	1	-1	1	1	-1	1	1	-1	1	-1
4	4	4	1	1	1	1	-1	1	-1	-1	-1	-1	-1	1	-1	1	1	1
5	5	5	1	1	-1	-1	1	1	-1	-1	1	1	1	-1	-1	1	1	-1
6	6	6	1	1	1	-1	1	-1	1	-1	-1	-1	1	-1	1	-1	1	1
7	7	7	1	1	-1	1	1	-1	-1	1	-1	1	-1	-1	1	1	-1	1
8	8	8	1	1	1	1	1	1	1	1	1	-1	-1	-1	-1	-1	-1	-1
9	1	1	1	1	1	1	1	-1	-1	-1	1							
10	2	2	1	1	-1	1	1	1	1	-1	-1							
11	3	3	1	1	1	-1	1	1	-1	1	-1							
12	4	4	1	1	-1	-1	1	-1	1	1	1							
13	5	5	1	1	1	1	-1	-1	1	1	-1							
14	6	6	1	1	-1	1	-1	1	-1	1	1							
15	7	7	1	1	1	-1	-1	1	1	-1	1							
16	8	8	1	1	-1	-1	-1	-1	-1	-1	-1							

Alias Structure (up to order 3)

```
A + B*C*G + B*E*F + C*D*F + D*E*G
B + A*C*G + A*E*F + C*D*E + D*F*G
C + A*B*G + A*D*F + B*D*E + E*F*G
D + A*C*F + A*E*G + B*C*E + B*F*G
E + A*B*F + A*D*G + B*C*D + C*F*G
F + A*B*E + A*C*D + B*D*G + C*E*G
G + A*B*C + A*D*E + B*D*F + C*E*F
A*B + C*G + E*F
A*C + B*G + D*F
A*D + C*F + E*G
A*E + B*F + D*G
A*F + B*E + C*D
A*G + B*C + D*E
B*D + C*E + F*G
```

Figure 10.14 Original and fold-over 2^{7-4}_{III} designs and confounding relations when they are combined.

between designs that are difficult to interpret—designs of resolution III and IV—and designs that are very easy to interpret—designs of resolution VI and higher.

10.8 PLACKETT-BURMAN DESIGNS

The Plackett-Burman designs are a special set of highly fractionated two-level factorial designs. They have an integer multiple of four, for example, 8, 12, 16, . . . , for their number of runs and can be used to study one variable fewer than the number of runs. For example, the 12-run Plackett-Burman design can include at most eleven variables. If fewer than the maximum number of variables are used in a Plackett-Burman experiment then the unused variables are not included in the model and their degrees of freedom just contribute to the error estimate.

When all possible $n - 1$ variables are included in an n-run single-replicate Plackett-Burman experiment, the experiment design is saturated. That is, the model consumes all of the available degrees of freedom so there are no remaining degrees of freedom to estimate the error. The usual analysis strategy in this case is to drop from the model the variable with the smallest regression coefficient to begin building an error estimate. Then more weak terms can be dropped from the model one by one until a satisfactory model is reached. A normal probability plot of the regression coefficients from the initial model is often helpful in determining which terms to keep and which to drop.

Plackett-Burman designs are resolution III designs—their main effects are confounded with two-factor interactions. Each main effect is usually confounded with several two-factor interactions. Like other resolution III designs, a Plackett-Burman design can be folded to create a complementary design that, when combined with the original design, gives a resolution IV design. Although the resulting experiment is a resolution IV design, each main effect will be confounded with several three-factor interactions, and several two-factor interactions will be confounded with each other.

Create a Plackett-Burman design using MINITAB from the **Stat> DOE> Factorial> Create Factorial Design** menu using the **Plackett-Burman Design** option. Analyze the design using **Stat> DOE> Factorial> Analyze Factorial Design**. If you want to create the folded Plackett-Burman design, MINITAB will not do it for you so you will have to do it yourself. To create the folded design, copy the original matrix of runs into a new worksheet, invert all of the signs using the **Calc> Calculator** menu or with **let** commands (for example, mtb> let c3=-c3), and then copy and append the new runs onto the original design. You will have to use **Stat> DOE> Factorial> Define Custom Factorial Design** to define the experiment in MINITAB so that it will perform the analysis of the resulting resolution IV design.

10.9 SAMPLE-SIZE CALCULATIONS

The sample-size and power calculations for fractional factorial designs are carried out the same way as they were for the two-level factorial designs as described in Chapter 9.

MINITAB supports calculations for both the fractional factorial designs and the Plackett-Burman designs. Perform sample-size and power calculations for fractional factorial designs in MINITAB from the **Stat> Power and Sample Size> 2 Level Factorial Design** menu. MINITAB anticipates the model that you will probably use so leave the **Design> Number of terms omitted from model** field set to its default zero value. Perform sample-size and power calculations for Plackett-Burman designs from the **Stat> Power and Sample Size> Plackett-Burman Design** menu.

Example 10.11

A screening experiment is to be performed to study five variables in a 2_{III}^{5-2} design. The experiment will have four replicates, which will be built in blocks. The standard error of the model is expected to be $\sigma_\varepsilon = 80$. Use MINITAB to determine the power of the experiment to detect a difference of $\delta = 100$ between the ± 1 levels of the design variables and then confirm the value of the power by direct calculation.

Solution: The experiment design was created in MINITAB using Stat> DOE> Factorial> Create Factorial Design and then Stat> Power and Sample Size> 2 Level Factorial Design was used to perform the power calculation. Figure 10.15 shows MINITAB's output from creating the design and calculating the power, and the windows used to set up the power calculation. MINITAB reports that the power of the experiment to detect an effect of size $\delta = 100$ is $P = 0.9207$.

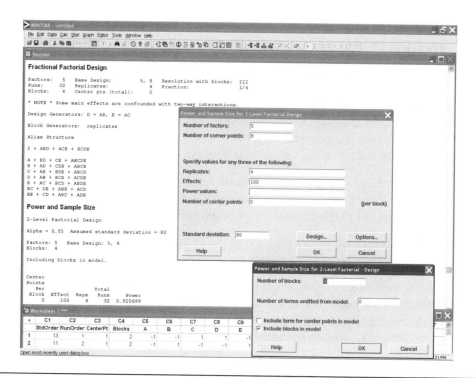

Figure 10.15 Power calculation for 2_{III}^{5-2} design.

In order to confirm the power, we need to know how many error degrees of freedom there will be for the model. MINITAB's output in the Session window indicates the alias structure of the experiment. MINITAB will include a term in the model for each of the main effects, but it will also include terms for the BC and BE interactions and three terms to account for the four blocks. Then the model will have $df_{model} = 5 + 2 + 3 = 10$ degrees of freedom and there will be $df_\varepsilon = 32 - 1 - 10 = 21$ error degrees of freedom. The F distribution noncentrality parameter will be:

$$\lambda = \frac{N}{2a}\left(\frac{\delta}{\sigma_\varepsilon}\right)^2$$
$$= \frac{4(8)}{2(2)}\left(\frac{100}{80}\right)^2$$
$$= 12.5$$

*The power is given by the condition $F_\alpha = F_{P,\lambda}$ where the central and noncentral F distributions have one numerator and $df_\varepsilon = 21$ denominator degrees of freedom. MINITAB's **Calc> Probability Distributions> F** function was used to obtain the solution:*

$$F_{0.05} = 4.3248 = F_{0.9207,12.5}$$

which confirms that the power of the experiment is $P = 0.9207$ for an effect size $\delta = 100$.

10.10 DESIGN CONSIDERATIONS FOR FRACTIONAL FACTORIAL EXPERIMENTS

- Use a fractional factorial design as a screening experiment (step 4 of the 11-step process: preliminary experimentation) before attempting a full-factorial or more complex experiment. This is a low-risk, systematic way of confirming that the levels of all of the variables are safe to use.

- Where possible, use higher-resolution designs rather than designs of low resolution. If necessary, consider removing a variable from an experiment by holding it fixed to increase the design resolution of an experiment.

- Reserve substantial time and resources for follow-up experiments to resolve the ambiguities of a low-resolution design.

- Only use resolution III designs if most of the design variables are likely to be insignificant and if it's safe to assume that two-factor interactions are not significant. Otherwise use a design of higher resolution or plan to do a follow-up experiment to resolve the ambiguities of the resolution III design.

- Combine a resolution III design with its fold-over design to form a design of resolution IV.

- Add a variable to a 2^4 design to create a 2_V^{5-1} design using the same number of runs. The new variable should be chosen to add little risk to the experiment and should have a reasonably high probability of being insignificant.

- Build a full-factorial experiment by combining complementary fractions of fractional factorial designs. Treat the fractional replicates as blocks to test for and control block effects. When possible, analyze the data as the blocks are completed and suspend the test early if the experiment is conclusive to conserve time and resources.

- Be careful which generators you use for a highly fractionated factorial design. Some sets of generators will allow more model terms to be resolved than other sets even though both deliver the same design resolution. Experiment designs that resolve the most model terms are said to be *minimum aberration* designs. MINITAB uses minimum aberration designs.

11

Response-Surface Experiments

11.1 INTRODUCTION

The two-level factorial designs of Chapters 9 and 10 provide a powerful set of experiment designs for studying complex responses; however, our collection of designs is incomplete. Consider the response space shown in Figure 11.1. The horizontal and vertical axes indicate values of independent variables x_1 and x_2, respectively, and the contours correspond to constant values (10, 20, ..., 100) of the response. The five squares in the figure represent five special regions where experiments might be performed. Some of the regions show supplemental contours to clarify the behavior of the response. Regions 1 and 2 are each sensitive to only one variable, x_1 and x_2, respectively. Region 3 is sensitive to both variables but the parallel contours indicate that there is no interaction between x_1 and x_2. The divergence between the response contours in region 4 indicates that, in addition to the main effects of x_1 and x_2, there is a significant interaction between them. The contours in region 5 indicate that with x_2 held constant, the response increases, reaches a maximum value, and then decreases as x_1 increases. The response also shows curvature with respect to x_2 when x_1 is held constant.

Two-level factorial and fractional factorial designs are suitable for studying regions 1–4; however, they are not capable of quantifying or even detecting curvature in the response such as in region 5. The weakness of these designs is due to their use of just two levels of each design variable. As we saw in Chapter 8, a variable must have at least three levels in order to fit a model that can resolve curvature in the response. The purpose of this chapter is to present experiment designs that are capable of resolving curvature in the response associated with each design variable. These designs are called *response-surface designs* or *designs for quadratic models*.

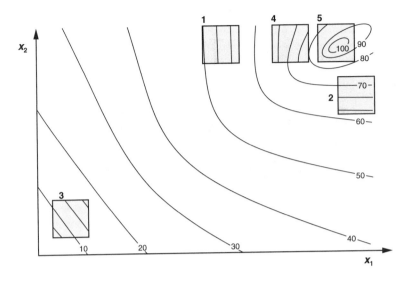

Figure 11.1 Different regions of experimental interest in a response space.

11.2 TERMS IN QUADRATIC MODELS

If we consider an experiment with just one independent quantitative variable x_1, then a model that includes curvature will take the form:

$$y(x_1) = b_0 + b_1 x_1 + b_{11} x_1^2 \tag{11.1}$$

The term x_1^2 may also be written as if it were a two-factor interaction of x_1 and x_1, or $x_1^2 = x_{11}$.

The fits provided by a simple linear model and the quadratic model of Equation 11.1 are shown for data with curvature in Figure 11.2. Notice that the coefficients b_0 and b_1 will be different in the two models. The quadratic model is clearly superior in this case although with just three levels of x_1 the quadratic model must pass exactly through the response means at each level of x_1.

When three levels of each variable are incorporated into an appropriate experiment design such that curvature due to each variable can be quantified, the model has the form:

$$y = b_0 + b_1 x_1 + b_2 x_2 + \cdots + b_{12} x_{12} + \cdots + b_{11} x_1^2 + b_{22} x_2^2 + \cdots \tag{11.2}$$

where three-factor and higher-order interactions have been ignored. This equation defines the response surface, that is, how y depends on $x_1, x_2, \ldots$, which can be represented or thought of as a surface in a multidimensional graph. Designs that can deliver quadratic terms for all of their design variables are called response-surface designs.

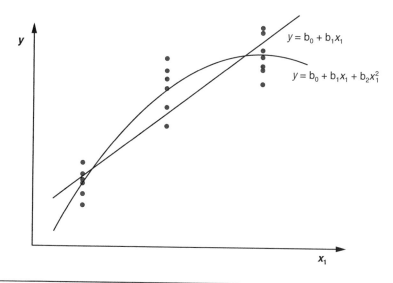

Figure 11.2 Linear and quadratic fits to data with curvature.

Example 11.1

Write out the full model that will be fitted for a four-variable response surface experiment.

Solution: The full model will include main effects, two-factor interactions, and squared terms. For four variables the model will be:

$$
\begin{aligned}
y = b_0 &+ b_1 x_1 + b_2 x_2 + b_3 x_3 + b_4 x_4 \\
&+ b_{12} x_{12} + b_{13} x_{13} + b_{14} x_{14} + b_{23} x_{23} + b_{24} x_{24} + b_{34} x_{34} \\
&+ b_{11} x_1^2 + b_{22} x_2^2 + b_{33} x_3^2 + b_{44} x_4^2
\end{aligned}
$$

The magnitudes of the regression coefficients in Equation 11.2 indicate the strength of the various terms in the model, but the signs of the regression coefficients also play an important role in determining the general shape of the response surface. Figure 11.3 shows surface plots for six different response surfaces where the response Y depends on the variables A and B. (The following analysis still applies to problems that involve more than two design variables but those cannot be easily drawn and are difficult to describe. In such cases, analyze two variables at a time using the method that follows.) In each case the variables A and B are considered over the range from -1.5 to $+1.5$—a meaningful range for coded variables in a designed experiment. Figure 11.3a shows the response surface for $Y(A, B) = 20 - 5A + 8B$, which is just a flat plane. Notice that the various contours for constant A are all parallel to each other as are the contours for constant B. Figure 11.3b shows the response surface for $Y(A, B) = 20 - 5A + 8B + 6AB$. This response surface looks somewhat similar to the previous one except that the plane

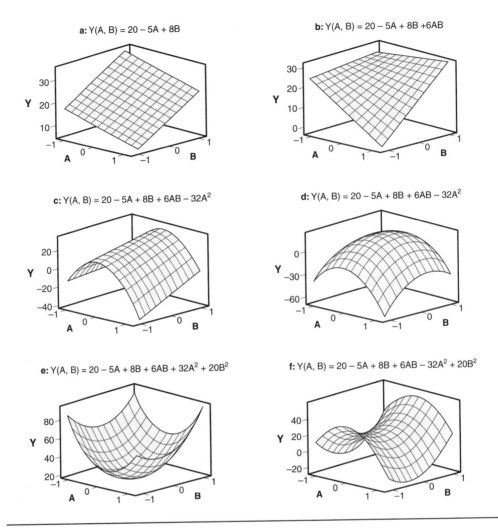

Figure 11.3 Examples of different response surfaces.

is twisted instead of flat. The twisting is caused by the AB interaction term. Notice that even with the twisting of the plane, all of the contours for constant A and B are still straight lines—they just aren't parallel to each other any more. Figure 11.3c shows the response surface for $Y(A, B) = 20 - 5A + 8B + 6AB - 32A^2$. The quadratic term causes the curvature in the response surface for changes made in the A direction, but notice that the B contours are still straight lines because there is no B^2 term in $Y(A, B)$. This surface shows that for a specified value of B there is a unique value of A that maximizes Y. Figure 11.3d shows the response surface for $Y(A, B) = 20 - 5A + 8B + 6AB - 32A^2 - 20B^2$. This response surface has downward curvature in both the A and B directions causing a maximum to occur for Y for a unique choice of A and B. Figure 11.3e shows the response surface for $Y(A, B) = 20 - 5A + 8B + 6AB + 32A^2 + 20B^2$. The equation for Y is very similar to the equation from Figure 11.3d but the signs of the quadratic terms are both positive. This causes the curvature with respect to both A and B to be upward so there is a minimum in Y for a unique choice of A and B. Figure 11.3f shows the response surface for $Y(A, B) = 20 - 5A + 8B + 6AB - 32A^2 + 20B^2$. The signs on the quadratic terms cause this saddle-shaped response surface to be curved downward with respect to A and curved upward with respect to B. For a fixed value of A there is a value of B that minimizes Y and for a fixed value of B there is a value of A that maximizes Y.

Designed experiments to study responses that have surfaces shaped as in Figures 11.3a and b need only two levels of each design variable because there is no curvature in Y due to A or B. Experiments to study responses with surfaces shaped as in Figures 11.3c–f require more elaborate designs with more variable levels to resolve the complex curvature. These are the response-surface designs.

11.3 2^k DESIGNS WITH CENTERS

Center points can be added to the 2^k and 2^{k-p} designs when all k of the design variables are quantitative. If the low and high coded levels of each variable are -1 and $+1$, respectively, then the center points will have coded level zero for each variable. For example, the center points in a 2^3 plus centers experiment will have $(x_1, x_2, x_3) = (0, 0, 0)$. Figure 11.4 shows a three-dimensional drawing of the 2^3 plus centers design.

There are two reasons for adding center points to a 2^k design. First, adding center points to a design increases the number of error degrees of freedom for the analysis without unbalancing the design. The additional error degrees of freedom increase the power of the design to detect small effects, especially when there are few error degrees of freedom before the center cells are added.

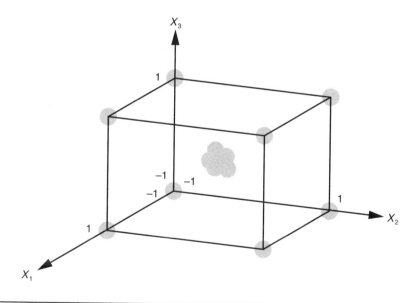

Figure 11.4 2^3 plus centers design.

Table 11.1 Runs of the 2^2 plus centers design.

Run	x_1	x_2	x_{12}	x_1^2	x_2^2
1	–	–	+	+	+
2	–	+	–	+	+
3	+	–	–	+	+
4	+	+	+	+	+
5	0	0	0	0	0

The second and usually more important reason to add center points to a 2^k design is to add a third level of each design variable. Although this provides some information about curvature, unfortunately the information is incomplete. To understand why, consider the matrix of experimental runs for the 2^2 plus centers design in Table 11.1. Notice that the columns for x_1^2 and x_2^2 are identical, that is, $x_1^2 = x_2^2$. This means that the quadratic terms in the model are confounded so it will not be possible to include both of them in the model. The model that can be fitted to the data can have only one generic quadratic term:

$$y = b_0 + b_1 x_1 + b_2 x_2 + b_{12} x_{12} + b_{**} x_*^2 \tag{11.3}$$

where the * is used to indicate the ambiguity of the source of the quadratic effect. The model that we really want to fit is:

$$y = b_0 + b_1 x_1 + b_2 x_2 + b_{12} x_{12} + b_{11} x_1^2 + b_{22} x_2^2 \tag{11.4}$$

which resolves the curvature into its two possible sources. When x_1^2 and x_2^2 are confounded, the b_{**} coefficient will be a combination of the desired b_{11} and b_{22} coefficients, that is:

$$b_{**} = b_{11} + b_{22} \tag{11.5}$$

The statistical significance of b_{**} provides a linear lack of fit test for two-level factorial plus centers designs. If the analysis indicates that b_{**} is not statistically significant then there is a good chance that there is no curvature in the response. (There's only a "good chance" that there's no curvature because there's a small chance that b_{11} and b_{22} are both large and approximately equal in magnitude but opposite in sign so that $b_{**} \simeq 0$.) If, however, b_{**} is statistically significant then one or both terms cause significant curvature in the response but we cannot tell which variable is responsible. This also means that when b_{**} is significant, Equation 11.3 cannot be used to predict the response because the contribution of $b_{**} x_*^2$ to y cannot be determined. (To understand this problem, consider the case $y(x_1, x_2) = y(0, 1)$.)

All of the 2^k and 2^{k-p} plus centers designs suffer from the problem of confounded quadratic effects. This means that these designs are not true response-surface designs. Despite this weakness, the 2^k and 2^{k-p} plus centers designs are still very powerful and popular. They can also be supplemented with additional runs that permit the quadratic model terms to be fully resolved. Typically, these experiments are built in two blocks.

The first block consists of a 2^k or 2^{k-p} plus centers design that is built and checked for linear lack of fit. If there is evidence of lack of fit, then the second block of supplemental runs is built and combined with the first block to fully resolve the quadratic terms. These designs, called central composite designs, are one of several types of very powerful response-surface designs that we will consider in this chapter.

11.4 3^K FACTORIAL DESIGNS

If a factorial experiment is constructed in k quantitative variables with each variable appearing at three evenly spaced levels and all possible combinations of levels are used, then we have a $3 \times 3 \times \ldots \times 3$ or a 3^k factorial experiment. The total number of runs in the experiment, if no replication is performed, is given by 3^k. The 3^k experiments are not used very often because they require so many runs. As k increases, the number of runs 3^k grows much faster than the number of terms in the model. For this reason, other more efficient designs are usually used instead of the 3^k designs.

Example 11.2

Write out the matrix of experimental runs for the 3^3 experiment. Draw the design in three dimensions and describe where the experimental runs fall. Indicate the model that can be fitted with this design and how the degrees of freedom are distributed.

Solution: The 3^3 experiment has three variables, each at three levels, and $3^3 = 27$ total runs in one replicate. The experimental runs are indicated in standard order in Table 11.2. The runs are shown in the three-dimensional drawing in Figure 11.5. There is a run at every corner of the cube, at the center of every edge, at the middle of every cube face, and one run at the center of the cube. The model that can be fitted to this design is the full quadratic model:

$$y = b_0 + b_1 x_1 + b_2 x_2 + b_3 x_3 + b_{12} x_{12} + b_{13} x_{13} + b_{23} x_{23} + b_{11} x_1^2 + b_{22} x_2^2 + b_{33} x_3^2 \quad (11.6)$$

Table 11.2 Table of runs for the 3^3 experiment design.

Std	x_1	x_2	x_3	Std	x_1	x_2	x_3	Std	x_1	x_2	x_3
1	−	−	−	10	0	−	−	19	+	−	−
2	−	−	0	11	0	−	0	20	+	−	0
3	−	−	+	12	0	−	+	21	+	−	+
4	−	0	−	13	0	0	−	22	+	0	−
5	−	0	0	14	0	0	0	23	+	0	0
6	−	0	+	15	0	0	+	24	+	0	+
7	−	+	−	16	0	+	−	25	+	+	−
8	−	+	0	17	0	+	0	26	+	+	0
9	−	+	+	18	0	+	+	27	+	+	+

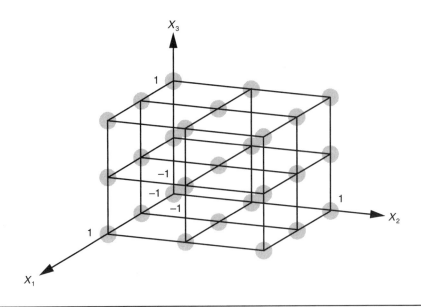

Figure 11.5 3^3 factorial experiment design.

If the experiment has only one replicate then the distribution of the degrees of freedom is $df_{total} = 27 - 1 = 26$, $df_{model} = 9$, and $df_{error} = 26 - 9 = 17$. If some of the model terms are not significant they can be dropped from the model and used to improve the error estimate.

11.5 BOX-BEHNKEN DESIGNS

Although the 3^k designs deliver a full quadratic model, they aren't used very often because there are other designs that are much more efficient. One such family of designs is the Box-Behnken designs. These designs are essentially fractions of the 3^k designs with additional center points to preserve the balance of the design. Table 11.3 shows the matrix of runs for Box-Behnken designs with three to seven variables. The original Box-Behnken paper describes designs for up to twelve variables (Box and Behnken 1960).

Table 11.3 uses a special shorthand notation to simplify the presentation of the experimental runs. In this notation, the matrix of four runs for a 2^2 experiment is written $(\pm 1 \ \pm 1)$, that is:

$$(\pm 1 \ \pm 1) = \begin{array}{|c|c|} \hline x_1 & x_2 \\ \hline - & - \\ \hline - & + \\ \hline + & - \\ \hline + & + \\ \hline \end{array}$$

Table 11.3 Box-Behnken design catalog.

BB(3)

x_1	x_2	x_3	Runs
±1	±1	0	4
±1	0	±1	4
0	±1	±1	4
0	0	0	3
Total Runs			15

BB(4)

Block	x_1	x_2	x_3	x_4	Runs
1	±1	±1	0	0	4
1	0	0	±1	±1	4
1	0	0	0	0	1
2	±1	0	0	±1	4
2	0	±1	±1	0	4
2	0	0	0	0	1
3	±1	0	±1	0	4
3	0	±1	0	±1	4
3	0	0	0	0	1
Total Runs					27

BB(5)

Block	x_1	x_2	x_3	x_4	x_5	Runs
1	±1	±1	0	0	0	4
1	0	0	±1	±1	0	4
1	0	±1	0	0	±1	4
1	±1	0	±1	0	0	4
1	0	0	0	±1	±1	4
1	0	0	0	0	0	3
2	0	±1	±1	0	0	4
2	±1	0	0	±1	0	4
2	0	0	±1	0	±1	4
2	±1	0	0	0	±1	4
2	0	±1	0	±1	0	4
2	0	0	0	0	0	3
Total Runs						46

BB(6)

x_1	x_2	x_3	x_4	x_5	x_6	Runs
±1	±1	0	±1	0	0	8
0	±1	±1	0	±1	0	8
0	0	±1	±1	0	±1	8
±1	0	0	±1	±1	0	8
0	±1	0	0	±1	±1	8
±1	0	±1	0	0	±1	8
0	0	0	0	0	0	6
Total Runs						54

BB(7)

x_1	x_2	x_3	x_4	x_5	x_6	x_7	Runs
0	0	0	±1	±1	±1	0	8
±1	0	0	0	0	±1	±1	8
0	±1	0	0	±1	0	±1	8
±1	±1	0	±1	0	0	0	8
0	0	±1	±1	0	0	±1	8
±1	0	±1	0	±1	0	0	8
0	±1	±1	0	0	±1	0	8
0	0	0	0	0	0	0	6
Total Runs							62

where all permutations of the signs are considered. Similarly, the set of four runs designated by $(0 \pm 1 \pm 1)$ corresponds to:

$$
\left(0 \;\pm 1 \;\pm 1\right) =
\begin{array}{|c|c|c|}
\hline
x_1 & x_2 & x_3 \\
\hline
0 & - & - \\
\hline
0 & - & + \\
\hline
0 & + & - \\
\hline
0 & + & + \\
\hline
\end{array}
$$

Example 11.3
  Write out the matrix of experimental runs for the three-variable Box-Behnken experiment. Plot the design in three dimensions and describe where the observations fall. Write out the model that can be fitted with this design and calculate the degrees of freedom for the model and error.

  Solution: The matrix of experimental runs for the BB(3) design was determined from Table 11.3 and is shown in standard order in Table 11.4. The three-dimensional drawing of the design shown in Figure 11.6 indicates that the experimental runs fall on the edges of the cube and that there are multiple observations at the design center. The model that can be fitted with this experiment is the full quadratic model given in Equation 11.6. The experiment has $df_{total} = 15 - 1 = 14$, $df_{model} = 9$, and $df_{error} = 15 - 9 = 5$. This is a significant savings in runs compared to the 3^3 experiment (15 versus 27). Furthermore, it's likely that when the full model is fitted, some of the model terms will be weak and can be dropped from the model. This simplifies the model and adds degrees of freedom for error estimation.

  Inspection of the Box-Behnken designs in Table 11.3 reveals the rationale used to determine the experimental runs. These designs are expected to resolve main effects, interactions, and quadratic terms in the model. If there are k main effects, then there will be $\binom{k}{2}$ two-factor interactions. These interactions are 12, 13, 14, and so on. Inspection of Table 11.3 shows that for the smaller designs with $k \leq 5$ variables, each noncenter row of each $BB(k)$ design consists of a four-run 2^2 factorial experiment that resolves each two-factor interaction while the remaining $k - 2$ variables are held at their zero levels. Then center cells are added to the experiment to complete the runs required to resolve the quadratic terms. The number of center cells is determined by considerations affecting the estimation of the regression coefficients. This issue is too complex for this book so just use the number of center cells specified in the design catalog. The larger Box-Behnken experiments with $k > 5$ variables use eight-run 2^3 factorial designs involving three variables while the other variables are held at their zero levels.

Example 11.4
  Explain how the 46 runs of the BB(5) design are determined.

Table 11.4 Table of runs for the Box-Behnken three-variable experiment.

	BB(3)					Std	x_1	x_2	x_3
x_1	x_2	x_3	Runs			1	−	−	0
±1	±1	0	4			2	−	+	0
±1	0	±1	4			3	+	−	0
0	±1	±1	4	=		4	+	+	0
0	0	0	3			5	−	0	−
						6	−	0	+
						7	+	0	−
						8	+	0	+
						9	0	−	−
						10	0	−	+
						11	0	+	−
						12	0	+	+
						13	0	0	0
						14	0	0	0
						15	0	0	0

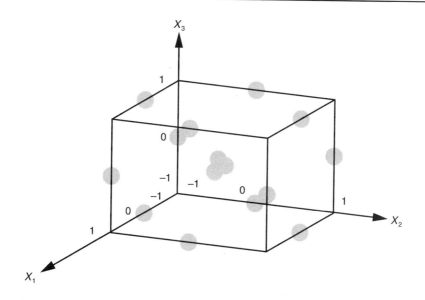

Figure 11.6 Box-Behnken three-variable design: *BB*(3).

Solution: The BB(5) *design is expected to resolve* $\binom{5}{1} = 5$ *main effects,* $\binom{5}{2} = 10$ *two-factor interactions, and five quadratic terms. The 10 two-factor interactions are: AB, AC, AD, AE, BC, BD, BE, CD, CE, DE. A four-run* 2^2 *experiment must be created in each of these pairs of columns while the remaining three variables are held at their zero levels. For example, the runs associated with the AB interaction correspond to the row* $(\pm1, \pm1, 0, 0, 0)$ *of the BB(5) design matrix in Table 11.3, the runs associated with the AC interaction correspond to the row* $(\pm1, 0, \pm1, 0, 0)$, *and the other rows in the matrix are determined in a similar manner. This means that the design will contain* $10 \times 2^2 = 40$ *runs plus some center cells to resolve the quadratic terms. The BB(5) matrix calls for six center runs* $(0, 0, 0, 0, 0)$ *so the design requires a total of* 46 *runs.*

Box-Behnken experiments tend to be large so it is usually necessary to block them.* Blocking plans for the smaller Box-Behnken designs ($k \leq 5$) are shown in Table 11.3. The runs of the larger Box-Behnken designs ($k \geq 6$) can be broken into two blocks by splitting each row of eight runs like (±1 ±1 0 ±1 0 0) into two half-fractions of the implied 2^3 design. The resulting two sets of four runs are then assigned to different blocks. The shorthand notation for the Box-Behnken designs breaks down here—there's no easy way to indicate how the runs behave and the full matrix of runs is too long to display. Details about blocking the Box-Behnken designs are given in Box and Behnken (1960) and MINITAB can create both the unblocked and blocked designs.

11.6 CENTRAL COMPOSITE DESIGNS

Adding center cells to the two-level factorial designs (2^k and 2^{k-p}) is a good attempt to give them the ability to account for curvature, but the fix that they provide is incomplete. Additional runs can be added to these experiments to give them full quadratic modeling capabilities. These designs are the central composite or Box-Wilson designs designated $CC(2^k)$ or $CC(2^{k-p})$ where 2^k and 2^{k-p} indicate the two-level factorial design that is the basis of the central composite design. The runs that must be added to the two-level factorial plus centers designs fall at extreme points outside the usual -1 and $+1$ levels of the two-level factorial part of the design. These points are referred to as star points. The quantity η (eta) is the distance that the star points are located from the center of the design. The value used for η depends on the number of points in the two-level factorial or cube part of the experiment. η is given by:

$$\eta = n_{cube}^{1/4} \qquad (11.7)$$

where n_{cube} is the number of points in a single replicate of the 2^k or 2^{k-p} design. This condition gives the design a special characteristic called *rotatability*. Two star points are added to the original experiment for each variable, one star point at the $-\eta$ level and one at the $+\eta$ level, while all other variables are held constant at their zero level. This gives the central composite designs five levels of each variable: $-\eta, -1, 0, 1, \eta$.

---

* These blocking patterns also provide a way to introduce a qualitative variable into a Box-Behnken experiment. To allow safe conclusions to be drawn about differences between the levels of the qualitative variable, the runs must be randomized over all blocks.

In theory, the number of center points in the central composite designs is determined by:

$$n_0 = 4\sqrt{n_{cube}} - 2k + 4 \tag{11.8}$$

although in practice the exact number used can vary. There are two common conditions used to determine the number of center points. One condition makes the design *orthogonal* and the other condition gives the design a characteristic called *uniform precision*. The uniform precision designs provide equal error variance at the design center and at unit (±1) distance from the design center. The uniform precision designs are the ones that are usually used.

A catalog of central composite designs is shown in Table 11.5. The catalog is not complete—in some cases where there are two designs available for the same number of variables, the smaller of the two designs is shown [for example, $CC(2_{VI}^{6-1})$ is shown but not $CC(2^6)$]. The catalog shows the matrix of runs using the shorthand notation for factorial designs, the number of center points required, the star point coordinates, and the total number of runs.

Example 11.5

Write out the matrix of experimental runs for the three-variable central composite design. Sketch the design in three dimensions and describe where the observations fall. Write out the model that can be fitted with this design and calculate the degrees of freedom for the model and error.

Solution: The matrix of runs for the $CC(2^3)$ design is shown in Table 11.6 and the design is drawn in three dimensions in Figure 11.7. The figure shows that the central composite design has a run at every corner of the cube, there is a star point above each face of the cube, and there are several points at the center of the cube. The star point positions are outside the cube at $(x_1, x_2, x_3) = (-1.682, 0, 0), (+1.682, 0, 0), (0, -1.682, 0), (0, +1.682, 0), (0, 0, -1.682),$ and $(0, 0, +1.682)$. The experiment has twenty observations so $df_{total} = 20 - 1 = 19$. The model that can be fitted to this experiment is the full quadratic model with three main effects, three two-factor interactions, and three quadratic terms so it has $df_{model} = 9$. By subtraction there are $df_{error} = 19 - 9 = 10$ degrees of freedom to estimate the error and more degrees of freedom for error may become available if insignificant terms can be dropped from the model.

Central composite designs can be large and difficult to build but there are excellent plans available for breaking them into blocks of practical size. All of the central composite designs can be broken into two blocks, the first block consisting of the points from the cube plus some center points and the second block consisting of the star points and some center points. The specific number of center points for each block is prescribed and there may be a slight change in the star point position if the total number of center points changes from the original design. If the block of points from the cube is still too large, it may be further broken up into smaller blocks defined by

Table 11.5 Central composite design catalog.

CC (2^2)

x_1	x_2	Runs
±1	±1	4
0	0	5
±1.41	0	2
0	±1.41	2
Total Runs		13

CC (2^{8-2}_V)

x_1	x_2	x_3	x_4	x_5	x_6	x_7	x_8	Runs
±1	±1	±1	±1	±1	±1	1234	1256	64
0	0	0	0	0	0	0	0	10
±2.83	0	0	0	0	0	0	0	2
.	.	.	.	.	.	.	.	.
0	0	0	0	0	0	0	±2.83	2
Total Runs								90

CC (2^3)

x_1	x_2	x_3	Runs
±1	±1	±1	8
0	0	0	6
±1.68	0	0	2
0	±1.68	0	2
0	0	±1.68	2
Total Runs			20

CC (2^{7-1}_{VII})

x_1	x_2	x_3	x_4	x_5	x_6	x_7	Runs
±1	±1	±1	±1	±1	±1	123456	64
0	0	0	0	0	0	0	14
±2.83	0	0	0	0	0	0	2
.	.	.	.	.	.	.	.
0	0	0	0	0	0	±2.83	2
Total Runs							92

CC (2^4)

x_1	x_2	x_3	x_4	Runs
±1	±1	±1	±1	16
0	0	0	0	7
±2	0	0	0	2
.	.	.	.	.
0	0	0	±2	2
Total Runs				31

CC (2^{6-1}_{VI})

x_1	x_2	x_3	x_4	x_5	x_6	Runs
±1	±1	±1	±1	±1	12345	32
0	0	0	0	0	0	9
±2.38	0	0	0	0	0	2
.	.	.	.	.	.	.
0	0	0	0	0	±2.38	2
Total Runs						53

CC (2^5)

x_1	x_2	x_3	x_4	x_5	Runs
±1	±1	±1	±1	±1	32
0	0	0	0	0	10
±2.38	0	0	0	0	2
.	.	.	.	.	.
0	0	0	0	±2.38	2
Total Runs					52

CC (2^{5-1}_V)

x_1	x_2	x_3	x_4	x_5	Runs
±1	±1	±1	±1	1234	16
0	0	0	0	0	6
±2	0	0	0	0	2
.	.	.	.	.	.
0	0	0	0	±2	2
Total Runs					32

Table 11.6 Matrix of experimental runs for the $CC(2^3)$ design.

$CC(2^3)$			
x_1	x_2	x_3	**Runs**
±1	±1	±1	8
0	0	0	6
±1.68	0	0	2
0	±1.68	0	2
0	0	±1.68	2

=

Std	x_1	x_2	x_3
1	−	−	−
2	−	−	+
3	−	+	−
4	−	+	+
5	+	−	−
6	+	−	+
7	+	+	−
8	+	+	+
9	0	0	0
10	0	0	0
11	0	0	0
12	0	0	0
13	0	0	0
14	0	0	0
15	−1.68	0	0
16	+1.68	0	0
17	0	−1.68	0
18	0	+1.68	0
19	0	0	−1.68
20	0	0	+1.68

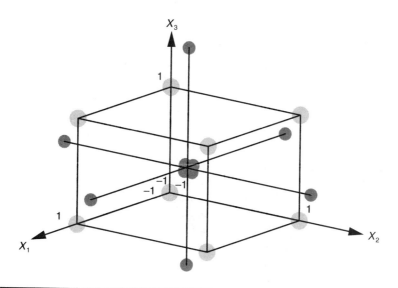

Figure 11.7 Central composite three-variable design: $CC(2^3)$.

complementary fractional factorial designs. As before, some center points are run with each block and the star point position might change a bit if the total number of center points deviates from the original plan. Table 11.7 shows practical blocking plans for some of the central composite designs. In the Definition column, the symbol (*) indicates star points and the symbol (0) indicates center points. Where blocks are fractional factorials, complementary fractions must be used. Different references may show slightly

Table 11.7 Blocking plans for central composite designs.

Design	Number of Blocks	Block	Definition	Runs	Total Runs	η
$CC(2^2)$	1		$2^2 + 4\,(*) + 5\,(0)$		13	1.414
$CC(2^2)$	2	1	$2^2 + 3\,(0)$	7	14	1.414
		2	$4\,(*) + 3\,(0)$	7		
$CC(2^3)$	1		$2^3 + 6\,(*) + 6\,(0)$		20	1.682
$CC(2^3)$	2	1	$2^3 + 4\,(0)$	12	20	1.633
		2	$6\,(*) + 2\,(0)$	8		
$CC(2^3)$	3	1	$2^{3-1} + 2\,(0)$	6	20	1.633
		2	$2^{3-1} + 2\,(0)$	6		
		3	$* + 2\,(0)$	8		
$CC(2^4)$	1		$2^4 + 8\,(*) + 7\,(0)$		31	2.000
$CC(2^4)$	2	1	$2^4 + 4\,(0)$	20	30	2.000
		2	$8\,(*) + 2\,(0)$	10		
$CC(2^4)$	3	1	$2^{4-1} + 2\,(0)$	10	30	2.000
		2	$2^{4-1} + 2\,(0)$	10		
		3	$8\,(*) + 2\,(0)$	10		
$CC(2_V^{5-1})$	1		$2^{5-1} + 10\,(*) + 6\,(0)$		32	2.000
$CC(2_V^{5-1})$	2	1	$2^{5-1} + 6\,(0)$	22	33	2.000
		2	$10\,(*) + 1\,(0)$	11		
$CC(2_{VI}^{6-1})$	1		$2^{6-1} + 12\,(*) + 9\,(0)$		53	2.378
$CC(2_{VI}^{6-1})$	2	1	$2^{6-1} + 8\,(0)$	40	54	2.366
		2	$12\,(*) + 2\,(0)$	14		
$CC(2_{VI}^{6-1})$	3	1	$2^{6-2} + 4\,(0)$	20	54	2.366
		2	$2^{6-2} + 4\,(0)$	20		
		3	$12\,(*) + 2\,(0)$	14		
$CC(2_{VII}^{7-1})$	1		$2^{7-1} + 14\,(*) + 14\,(0)$	72	92	2.828
$CC(2_{VII}^{7-1})$	2	1	$2^{7-1} + 8\,(0)$	72	90	2.828
		2	$14\,(*) + 4\,(0)$	18		
$CC(2_{VII}^{7-1})$	3	1	$2^{7-2} + 4\,(0)$	36	90	2.828
		2	$2^{7-2} + 4\,(0)$	36		
		3	$14\,(*) + 4\,(0)$	18		
$CC(2_{VII}^{7-1})$	5	1	$2^{7-3} + 2\,(0)$	18	90	2.828
		2	$2^{7-3} + 2\,(0)$	18		
		3	$2^{7-3} + 2\,(0)$	18		
		4	$2^{7-3} + 2\,(0)$	18		
		5	$14\,(*) + 4\,(0)$	18		

different preferences for the number of center points used and the values of η, but these differences are generally negligible for practical applications. MINITAB offers several blocking plans for some of the larger designs and recommends the best values for the star point position and the number of center points for each block.

Example 11.6

Describe a blocking plan to build the $CC(2^4)$ experiment in three blocks. Write out the model that can be fitted and describe the distribution of the degrees of freedom if a term for the blocks is included in the model.

Solution: From Table 11.7, the $CC(2^4)$ experiment can be built in three blocks of size 10 each. The three blocks are:

- *Block 1: Eight runs from the 2^{4-1} design with $4 = +123$ plus two center points.*

- *Block 2: Eight runs from the complementary 2^{4-1} design with $4 = -123$ plus two center points.*

- *Block 3: Eight star points with $\eta = 2$ plus two center points.*

The model will be:

$$y = b_0 + b_1 x_1 + b_2 x_2 + b_3 x_3 + b_4 x_4$$
$$+ b_{12} x_{12} + b_{13} x_{13} + b_{14} x_{14} + b_{23} x_{23} + b_{24} x_{24} + b_{34} x_{34}$$
$$+ b_{11} x_1^2 + b_{22} x_2^2 + b_{33} x_3^2 + b_{44} x_4^2$$
$$+ d_2 \left(block = 2 \right) + d_3 \left(block = 3 \right)$$

where terms for the blocks (d_2 and d_3) have been explicitly included in the model. The experiment will have 30 observations so $df_{total} = 29$. The model has four main effects, six two-factor interactions, four quadratic terms, and two terms for the blocks so $df_{model} = 16$. This leaves $df_\varepsilon = 13$ degrees of freedom for the error estimate.

11.7 COMPARISON OF THE RESPONSE-SURFACE DESIGNS

Since all three families of true response-surface designs: 3^k, $BB(k)$, and $CC(2^k)$, deliver models with main effects, two-factor interactions, and quadratic terms, other criteria besides which model can be fitted must be considered in deciding which design to use for a response surface experiment. There are three criteria used to compare the design families:

1. The number of observations in the design and the number of error degrees of freedom.

2. The number of levels required of each design variable.

3. The safety of the highest and lowest variable levels.

As will be seen, these criteria are important enough that different designs tend to be preferred under different circumstances. While one criterion might be more important than the others for a particular design problem, all three criteria must be considered and managed simultaneously.

11.7.1 Number of Observations and Error Degrees of Freedom

As with any other type of experiment design, response-surface designs can be made very sensitive to small effects by building enough replicates of the design. Response-surface designs tend to be large and expensive, however, so they are frequently built using just a single replicate. In this case, the experiment should have enough runs so that the full model can be constructed leaving enough degrees of freedom to provide a good error estimate. Models that have less than about eight error degrees of freedom are often considered to be too risky, and models that have more than about twenty error degrees of freedom are often considered to be wasteful of resources. Frequently, one response-surface design will deliver a model that has error degrees of freedom that fall within this range when the other designs don't.

Table 11.8 shows a comparison of the number of runs (N) and the number of error degrees of freedom provided by all of the response surface designs for two to six variables. Each case in the table considers just one replicate of the experiment design. The table shows that:

- When an experiment has just two variables there are only two designs to choose from: the 3^2 and the $CC(2^2)$ designs. The 3^2 design is very efficient although with a single replicate there are only $df_\varepsilon = 3$ error degrees of freedom. This design should be replicated to have sufficient degrees of freedom for the error estimate or the $CC(2^2)$ design should be used instead. Both of these strategies are frequently used.

- Of the three variable experiments, the 3^3 design with $df_\varepsilon = 17$ is comparatively wasteful of resources. It has too many runs to justify its use over the other two three-variable designs. Compared to the very efficient $BB(3)$ design, even the $CC(2^3)$ experiment seems wasteful. The $BB(3)$ is a bit short on error degrees of freedom, but most of these experiments have several terms that can be dropped from the model to improve the error estimate. Of the three variable experiments, the $BB(3)$ design is probably used most often.

- Of the four variable experiments, the 3^4 is definitely too large compared to the other two designs. The $BB(4)$ and $CC(2^4)$ experiments are comparable in their total number of runs and both have plenty of degrees of freedom for the error estimate. These two designs are probably used with approximately equal frequency.

- Of the five variable experiments, the 3^5 with 243 runs is impractical and the $BB(5)$ design requires 44 percent more runs than the $CC(2_V^{5-1})$. The $CC(2_V^{5-1})$,

Table 11.8 Comparison of the response-surface designs.

k	Design	N	df_{total}	df_{model}	df_ε
2	3^2	9	8	5	3
	$CC(2^3)$	13	12	5	7
3	3^3	27	26	9	17
	$BB(3)$	15	14	9	5
	$CC(2^3)$	20	19	9	10
4	3^4	81	80	14	66
	$BB(4)$	27	26	14	12
	$CC(2^4)$	31	30	14	16
5	3^5	243	242	20	222
	$BB(5)$	46	45	20	25
	$CC(2_V^{5-1})$	32	31	20	11
6	3^6	729	728	27	701
	$BB(6)$	54	53	27	26
	$CC(2_{VI}^{6-1})$	53	52	27	25

which is very efficient, starts out with 11 error degrees of freedom but this number usually grows nicely as terms are dropped from the model. More $CC(2_V^{5-1})$ designs are used than $BB(5)$ experiments. In fact, since a fifth variable can usually be found for most problems that start off with four variables, more $CC(2_V^{5-1})$ designs are built than either the $BB(4)$ or $CC(2^4)$ designs, which are comparable in size. The $CC(2_V^{5-1})$ provides a great opportunity to study a fifth variable in an experiment that starts out with four variables, with little extra time or expense.

- Response-surface designs with six or more variables require so many runs and are so difficult to build and manage that they are rarely built, When they are built, the $CC(2_{VI}^{6-1})$ design is often used because of its convenient blocking. The 2_{VI}^{6-1} plus centers design is usually built, often in two blocks, and analyzed first to see if there is curvature in the design space and if one or more variables can be dropped from further experiments. If there is evidence of curvature and if none of the design variables can be dropped from the experiment, then the block of star points is run and combined with the first block(s). Then the full model with main effects, two-factor interactions, and quadratic terms can be fitted.

11.7.2 Number of Levels of Each Variable

The $BB(k)$ and 3^k experiments have three levels of each variable where the central composite designs have five levels of each variable. In many situations, because of the nature of some of the design variables, getting the necessary five levels for all of the variables for a central composite design is impossible or impractical. This might happen because five levels just aren't available or sometimes the star point positions can't be made with the correct $\pm\eta$ values. In the latter case, if the central composite design is the right design for the problem except that the star point positions can't be achieved exactly, then by all means compromise the η value so that the central composite design can still be used. Incorrect star point positions will degrade the quality of the design, but the compromise is often relatively minor and worth the risk. When there are just too many compromises that have to be made to get the central composite design to work, it might be time to turn to the three-level designs as an alternative.

Of the central composite designs, the $CC(2^4)$ and the $CC(2_V^{5-1})$ deserve some special attention because their five levels $(-\eta, -1, 0, +1, +\eta)$ are all spaced one coded unit apart because they have $\eta = 2$. This might not seem like such a big deal at first, but there are many cases in which a quantitative variable's levels are easiest to achieve if they take on integer values. For example, if the amount of some material is a variable in a central composite design and the material is only available in some quantized form (for example, pill, tablet, and so on) that cannot be easily and accurately subdivided, then the $CC(2^4)$ or the $CC(2_V^{5-1})$ designs might be much easier to build than one of the other designs that has fractional η values. Of course the Box-Behnken designs, with their three evenly spaced levels, also have this advantage and should also be considered.

11.7.3 Uncertainty About the Safety of Variable Levels

There are two forces that affect the choice of the extreme quantitative variable levels for all experiments. The first force is sensitivity—the farther apart the levels of a variable can be spaced, the more sensitive the experiment will be for that variable. The second force is safety—if the levels of a variable are chosen to be too far apart then one or both of the extreme levels may be lost. These issues become more difficult to manage as the number of variables in an experiment increases because there are more opportunities to screw up.

Sometimes enough is known about the safe limits for each variable that there is little to no concern about the choice of levels, but most experiments worth doing have one or more variables that little is known about and there is corresponding uncertainty about the safety of its levels. When safe limits are known for all of the variables in an experiment then the three-level experiments are excellent choices. They also put most of their observations far from the design center so the experiment has high sensitivity. If, however, one or more of the variable levels are chosen inappropriately then a significant fraction of the experimental runs could be lost. So many runs can be lost from one poor choice of variable level that it might be impossible to salvage any model from the runs that survive.

When safe limits are not known, the central composite designs are an excellent choice. Their star points can be placed in questionable territory, leaving the points of the factorial design and center points in complete safety. Even if all of the star points are lost from the experiment, the surviving two-factorial plus centers experiment can still be analyzed for main effects, two-factor interactions, and lack of fit. This strategy is especially good for large experiments where there are just too many (that is, $2k$) opportunities to make a mistake picking a variable level.

Although the 3^k and $BB(k)$ designs both use three levels of each variable, if their ± 1 coded levels have the same physical values then the $BB(k)$ design is somewhat safer than the 3^k design. This is because the $BB(k)$ designs don't use the ± 1 variable levels for all k variables simultaneously like the 3^k designs do. This means that the 3^k experiments have observations that fall farther from the design center than the $BB(k)$ designs. This puts some of the runs of the 3^k designs at greater risk but it also makes the 3^k designs more sensitive to variable effects.

Example 11.7

Compare the sensitivity and safety of the $CC(2^2)$ and 3^2 designs if: 1) safe limits for both design variables are known and 2) safe limits for one or both design variables are not known.

Solution: Figure 11.8 shows the $CC(2^2)$ and 3^2 designs and the surrounding danger zones due to unsafe variable levels. If safe limits for both variables are known with certainty, then the 3^2 experiment would be the preferred design because more of its observations fall farther from the center of the design space than for the $CC(2^2)$ design. This gives the 3^2 design greater sensitivity to x_1 and x_2 effects. If safe limits for one or both variables are not known with certainty, then there is an excellent chance that at least part of the 3^2 design will wander into the dangerous part of the design space so that some if not many of the experimental runs will be lost. Even if just one of four choices of variable levels are picked incorrectly, one third of the runs will be lost and the surviving runs will be difficult to analyze.

By comparison, the $CC(2^2)$ design only puts its star points at risk. If the experiment is placed correctly in the design space, the full model will be obtained, but even if the $CC(2^2)$ wanders off so that some star points are lost, it's likely that the 2^2 plus centers

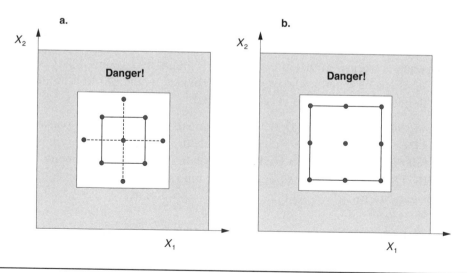

Figure 11.8   Comparison of the risks associated with extreme variable levels for the $CC(2^2)$ and 3^2 designs.

design will survive and can still be analyzed for main effects, two-factor interactions, and lack of fit. Of course the ±1 levels for the 3^2 design could be chosen to fall closer together so that there is less risk of losing observations, but that is all part of the game of picking a design and its variable levels.

Example 11.8
  Compare the risks of the 3^3 and BB(3) designs if safe variable levels are not known and both experiments use the same ±1 and zero variable levels.

  Solution: *Figures 11.5, page 444, and 11.6, page 447, show the 3^3 and BB(3) designs, respectively, plotted in three dimensions. The 3^3 experiment has a run at every corner, on every edge, and at every face of the cube in addition to the single center point. The BB(3) design only has runs on the cube edges and at the center. Since the cube corner points fall farther from the design center than the edge points, the 3^3 design offers greater sensitivity to variable effects but those points are also at greater risk of being lost.*

11.8 RESPONSE-SURFACE DESIGNS IN MINITAB

Response-surface designs can be created and analyzed in MINITAB using methods similar to those described in Section 9.7, with appropriate modifications to account for the quadratic terms. Since the 2^k plus centers designs are not true response-surface designs, use the usual **Stat> DOE> Factorial** tools to create and analyze them.

11.8.1 Creating Response-Surface Designs in MINITAB

A response-surface design can be created in MINITAB by:

1. Manually entering the matrix of experimental runs into a new worksheet.

2. Opening a worksheet that already contains the desired design. Many common designs can be found in the worksheets provided on the CD-ROM included with this book (for example, *cc(2^5h).mtw*).

3. Using MINITAB's **Stat> DOE> Response Surface> Create Response Surface Design** menu to specify and create the design. This menu is very similar to the **Stat> DOE> Factorial> Create Factorial Design** menu. MINITAB provides some options to fine-tune some of the response-surface designs but the default settings are usually appropriate.

11.8.2 Analysis of Response-Surface Designs in MINITAB

Once a response-surface design has been created in MINITAB and the responses have been entered into a column of the worksheet, the data can be analyzed by the same methods described in Section 9.7.2. If the analysis is to be done manually using **Stat>**

Regression> Regression it will be necessary to create columns for the quadratic terms in addition to the columns for the main effects and interactions. If you choose to use **Stat> ANOVA> General Linear Model**, you don't have to create columns for the interactions and quadratic terms in the worksheet but you will have to add them to the **Model** and **Covariates** windows.

The *mlrk.mac* macros automatically create the necessary columns for the quadratic terms and include them in the model. For a 2^k design with centers, MINITAB will only include the first quadratic term in the model and you are responsible for interpreting it as the combined effect of all of the quadratic terms.

MINITAB's **Stat> DOE> Response Surface> Analyze Response Surface Design** menu works just like the **Stat> DOE> Factorial> Analyze Factorial Design** menu. If you didn't use **Stat> DOE> Response Surface> Create Response Surface Design** to create the design, you will have to specify the response-surface design to MINITAB using **Stat> DOE> Response Surface> Define Custom Response Surface Design** first. The **Responses**, **Terms**, and **Graphs** menus all work as before. MINITAB automatically includes all of the possible terms in the model, including the quadratic terms.

Response-surface models often have many insignificant terms. It is your responsibility to use Occam's razor to refine the model. This is especially important when the model has few error degrees of freedom but is not so important for experiments that already have plenty of error degrees of freedom. Sometimes an automated form of Occam called *stepwise regression* can be used to refine the model. Stepwise regression comes in two forms: stepwise backward and stepwise forward. In the backward method, all of the possible model terms are included in the regression model and the model is refined by eliminating the least significant terms one by one. The refining process is stopped when the weakest term is still statistically significant. In stepwise forward, the initial model is small, usually consisting only of main effects, and then terms are added to the model one by one in order of their strength. The addition of terms stops when the next term to be added is not statistically significant. MINITAB's **Stat> Regression> Stepwise** menu supports stepwise forward and backward regression but because of problems with preserving the hierarchy of model terms this method is not recommended.

Many response-surface designs are performed for the purpose of identifying the variable levels that maximize or minimize the response. When none of the variables in a response-surface experiment has a significant quadratic term, the response will be maximized and minimized for specific choices of extreme levels of the important design variables. In contrast, if a response-surface design reveals two or more variables that cause strong curvature in the response, a local maximum or minimum may exist within the range of the experimental variables. Such a maximum or minimum might be found by observation using post-regression diagnostic plots such as the contour and wire-frame plots that MINITAB provides from the **Stat> DOE> Response Surface> Contour/Surface Plots** menu.

For more complicated optimization problems there are analytical and software-based hill-climbing methods to find the design variable conditions that maximize or minimize the response. MINITAB provides such an optimization tool from its **Stat>**

DOE> Response Surface> Response Optimizer menu. The response optimizer can simultaneously solve problems involving several design variables and one or more responses. The response optimizer gets its input from the last run of **Stat> DOE> Response Surface> Analyze Response Surface Design,** so if you've attempted several different models make sure that you run your favorite again before running the optimizer. And sometimes when the response changes very quickly with relatively small changes to the design variables, different models will give substantially different optimized results. The response optimizer also includes an interactive graphic mode which you can use to investigate the local behavior around an optimized solution but this topic, which deserves a whole chapter of its own, is outside the scope of this book. See MINITAB's **Help** menu for assistance with running the response optimizer.

Example 11.9

The basic geometry of a metal halide arctube produced by GE Lighting in Cleveland, Ohio, is shown in Figure 11.9.* The arc chamber is made from quartz tubing blow-molded into an ellipsoidal shape. The length and diameter of the arc chamber are determined by physical calculation of the power input and lumen output requirements of the lamp. A metal halide compound is dosed into the arc chamber, tungsten electrodes are sealed into each end, and a reflective coating or end coat is painted over the arctube's ends. Among others, there are three important factors that affect the lumen output of the finished arctube: the electrode insertion length (EIL), the end coat height (ECH), and the metal halide dose amount measured in milligrams relative to the arc chamber surface area (HAD or metal halide density). The geometry of the EIL and ECH are shown in the figure and the same values are used for both the top and bottom ends of the arctube.

During lamp operation, the metal halide dose melts and covers the coldest areas of the bulb wall. Some of the liquefied metal halide evaporates and enters the arc core

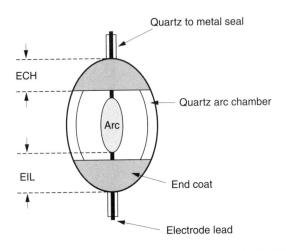

Figure 11.9 Metal halide arctube geometry.

**Source:* Simulation and analysis courtesy of General Electric Company.

where the metal halide molecules dissociate and the metal atoms radiate their characteristic atomic spectra. The combined metal spectra give the lamp its highly efficient light output—about 100 lumens per watt versus about 18 lumens per watt for a standard incandescent light bulb. Generally, the light output from the lamp increases as more of the wall area is covered by liquid metal halide. Since the ends of the arc chamber tend to be cold, EIL and ECH are adjusted to keep them warm and force the liquid metal halide out of the end chambers and onto the bulb wall. The end chambers become warmer as EIL decreases because the arc gets closer to the end chambers, but if the arctube wall gets too hot the lamp will fail prematurely. The end chambers also become warmer as ECH increases because the reflective end coat traps heat there; however, the end coat also prevents some light from escaping from the arctube so the light output falls if the end coat gets too high. The light output tends to increase with the addition of metal halide; however, if too much metal halide is added to the lamp it tends to form puddles that roll down the inner bulb wall and strike the hot electrode shank causing undesirable flares in the light output.

An experiment was performed to determine the appropriate values of EIL, ECH, and HAD for a new arctube design. The experimental variables and results are shown in Table 11.9. The ±1 variable levels were chosen to be near their extreme allowable physical values. The experiment is a BB(3) design with two replicates and the experiment was blocked on replicates. Analyze the experimental data and determine the settings for the three design variables that maximize the light output.

Solution: The experiment design was entered into a MINITAB worksheet and defined using **Stat> DOE> Response Surface> Define Custom Response Surface Design**. The experimental lumen response was entered into a column of the worksheet and then analyzed using **Stat> DOE> Response Surface> Analyze Response Surface Design**. The residuals diagnostic plots shown in Figure 11.10 indicate that the residuals are normally distributed and homoscedastic with respect to the design variables, the run order, and the fitted values as required by the analysis method.

Figure 11.10 also contains a normal probability plot of the regression coefficient t values. The plot shows reference lines at $b_i = 0$ and at $b_i = \pm 2.09$, where the latter correspond to the critical t value that distinguishes significant from insignificant regression coefficients at $\alpha = 0.05$: $t_{\alpha/2, df_\varepsilon} = t_{0.025, 19} = 2.09$. This plot suggests that A, B, AA, and CC are all statistically significant ($p < 0.05$) and that AB, BB, and blocks are marginal ($p \simeq 0.05$).

The results of the MINITAB analysis performed using **Stat> DOE> Response Surface> Analyze Response Surface Design** are shown in Figure 11.11. The model p values confirm that all three design variables have significant main effects and/or quadratic terms, the two-factor interactions are all statistically insignificant or marginal, and the blocks are not significant. The model has enough error degrees of freedom that there's no pressing reason to refine it. The three quadratic terms have mixed signs, which means that the lumen response surface is very complex.

MINITAB's **Stat> DOE> Response Surface> Response Optimizer** was used to determine the A: ECH, B: EIL, and C: HAD settings that maximize the lumens for the

Table 11.9 Variables and design matrices from arc lamp design experiment.

Code	Variable	−1	0	+1	Units	Std	Run	Block	A	B	C	Lumens
A	ECH	1	2	3	mm	1	9	1	−1	−1	0	4010
B	EIL	2.0	2.75	3.5	mm	2	8	1	−1	1	0	5135
C	HAD	1.5	2.75	4.0	mg/cm²	3	10	1	1	−1	0	5879
						4	12	1	1	1	0	6073
						5	3	1	−1	0	−1	3841
						6	15	1	−1	0	1	4933
						7	6	1	1	0	−1	5569
						8	14	1	1	0	1	5239
						9	13	1	0	−1	−1	5017
						10	5	1	0	−1	1	5243
						11	1	1	0	1	−1	6412
						12	11	1	0	1	1	6210
						13	4	1	0	0	0	5805
						14	7	1	0	0	0	5624
						15	2	1	0	0	0	5843
						16	26	2	−1	−1	0	4746
						17	16	2	−1	1	0	6052
						18	27	2	1	−1	0	6105
						19	19	2	1	1	0	6232
						20	23	2	−1	0	−1	4549
						21	30	2	−1	0	1	4080
						22	22	2	1	0	−1	5006
						23	18	2	1	0	1	5438
						24	17	2	0	−1	−1	4903
						25	25	2	0	−1	1	6129
						26	20	2	0	1	−1	6234
						27	29	2	0	1	1	6860
						28	21	2	0	0	0	6794
						29	24	2	0	0	0	5780
						30	28	2	0	0	0	6053

full model in Figure 11.11. The response optimizer's output is shown at the end of that figure. MINITAB found that the optimal settings (A: ECH, B: EIL, C: HAD) = (0.81, 1.0, –0.023) deliver a maximum response of 6435 lumens. The corresponding mechanical settings for the three variables are ECH = 2.8mm, EIL = 3.5mm, and HAD = 2.7mg/cm².

*Contour and response-surface plots were created from the **Stat> DOE> Response Surface> Contour/Surface Plots** menu and are shown in Figure 11.12. Each plot shows the response surface with respect to a pair of design variables while the third variable is held constant at its optimum level. The contour and surface plots of lumens versus A: ECH and C: HAD (the middle pair of plots) clearly show that there is a local maximum in the lumens within the experimental range of these variables. The other*

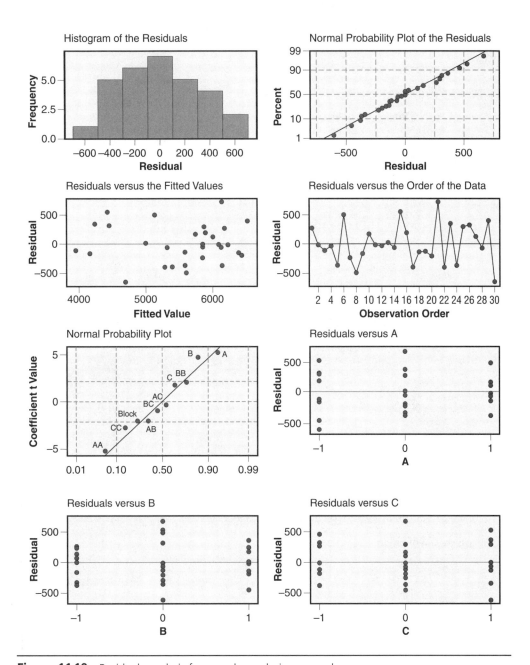

Figure 11.10 Residuals analysis from arc lamp design example.

plots, for lumens versus A: ECH and B: EIL and lumens versus B: EIL and C: HAD, show saddle-type surfaces. Steep slopes in the vicinity of the optimum solution imply that the arctube will demand quite tight manufacturing tolerances to deliver any consistency in lumens.

Response Surface Regression: Lumens versus Block, A, B, C

The analysis was done using coded units.

Estimated Regression Coefficients for Lumens

Term	Coef	SE Coef	T	P
Constant	5983.17	154.95	38.613	0.000
Block	-137.60	69.30	-1.986	0.062
A	512.19	94.89	5.398	0.000
B	448.50	94.89	4.727	0.000
C	162.56	94.89	1.713	0.103
A*A	-749.15	139.67	-5.364	0.000
B*B	294.98	139.67	2.112	0.048
C*C	-402.15	139.67	-2.879	0.010
A*B	-263.75	134.19	-1.965	0.064
A*C	-65.13	134.19	-0.485	0.633
B*C	-128.50	134.19	-0.958	0.350

S = 379.6   R-Sq = 84.8%   R-Sq(adj) = 76.7%

Analysis of Variance for Lumens

Source	DF	Seq SS	Adj SS	Adj MS	F	P
Blocks	1	568013	568013	568013	3.94	0.062
Regression	9	14649728	14649728	1627748	11.30	0.000
Linear	3	7838638	7838638	2612879	18.14	0.000
Square	3	6088550	6088550	2029517	14.09	0.000
Interaction	3	722541	722541	240847	1.67	0.207
Residual Error	19	2737225	2737225	144064		
Lack-of-Fit	15	2159234	2159234	143949	1.00	0.564
Pure Error	4	577991	577991	144498		
Total	29	17954965				

Unusual Observations for Lumens

Obs	StdOrder	Lumens	Fit	SE Fit	Residual	St Resid
21	21	4080.000	4684.975	242.541	-604.975	-2.07 R

R denotes an observation with a large standardized residual.

Response Optimization
Parameters

	Goal	Lower	Target	Upper	Weight	Import
Lumens	Maximum	6000	8000	8000	1	1

Global Solution

A   = 0.81173
B   = 1.00000
C   = -0.02306

Predicted Responses

Lumens   = 6434.92, desirability = 0.21746

Composite Desirability = 0.21746

Figure 11.11 Analysis and optimization of *BB*(3) arc lamp design example.

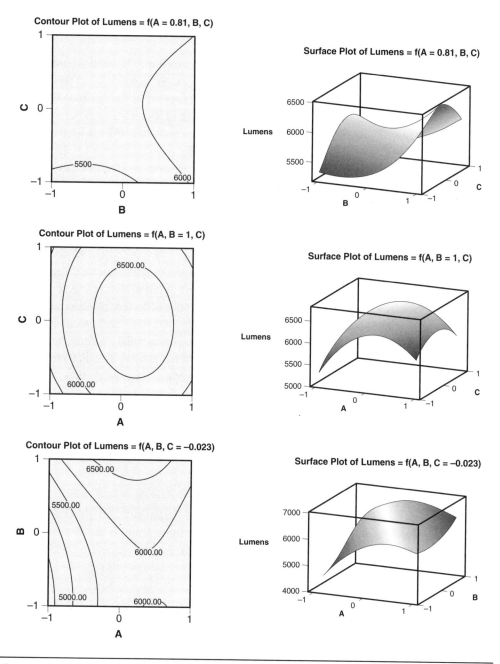

Figure 11.12 Contour and response-surface plots for all pairs of design variables.

11.9 SAMPLE-SIZE CALCULATIONS

Separate sample-size calculations can be considered to determine the model constant, the main effects, and the quadratic terms for the experiment designs considered in this chapter; however, it's most likely that the experimenter will be interested in the sample size necessary to quantify one of the main effects. The development of a condition to determine the required sample size (that is, number of replicates) to determine main effects for the designs in this chapter is similar to the development of the sample-size calculation for the slope of a linear regression problem in Chapter 8. The key difference between the calculations done for linear regression and those necessary here is that the 3^k, $BB(k)$, and $CC(2^k)$ designs have unique forms for their equations for SS_x. All three experiment designs will be considered. Be aware that the calculation of sample size for the 3^k, $BB(k)$, and $CC(2^k)$ designs is not supported in MINITAB so you will have to complete these calculations yourself.

There were two different goals considered in the sample-size calculations of other chapters: we either sought to determine the number of design replicates required to detect a significant effect due to a design variable or we sought to determine the number of design replicates required to quantify the regression coefficient associated with a design variable with specified confidence. Generally, sample-size calculations for response surface designs are done for the latter reason—to quantify a regression coefficient that is already known to be significantly different from zero. This is the approach that will be emphasized for the true response surface designs but be aware that the former goal is still possible.

The goal of the sample-size calculation is to determine the number of replicates (n) of the experiment required to determine the regression coefficient associated with one of the variables to within some specified range of values, as in:

$$P\left(b-\delta<\beta<b+\delta\right)=1-\alpha \tag{11.9}$$

where b is the regression coefficient, β is the true slope parameter, and $1-\alpha$ is the confidence level. Here, and in all of the following calculations, β and b are slopes defined in terms of coded units for x. Since all of the variables use the same ±1 coded levels, the same sample-size calculation applies for all of them.

The value of δ in Equation 11.9 is given by:

$$\delta=t_{\alpha/2}\sigma_b \tag{11.10}$$

where the number of degrees of freedom associated with the t distribution is given by:

$$df_\varepsilon=nN_{design}-1-df_{model} \tag{11.11}$$

where N_{design} is the number of runs in one replicate of the experiment design. The value of σ_b is given by:

$$\sigma_b = \frac{\sigma_\varepsilon}{\sqrt{nSS_x}} \tag{11.12}$$

where

$$SS_x = \sum \left(x_i - \bar{x} \right)^2 \tag{11.13}$$

is the x sum of squares *for one replicate* of the design and n is the number of replicates. The solution of this system of equations for n gives:

$$n \geq \frac{1}{SS_x} \left(\frac{t_{\alpha/2} \sigma_\varepsilon}{\delta} \right)^2 \tag{11.14}$$

The smallest value of n that meets this condition is the minimum number of replicates of the design that will deliver a confidence interval for β that is as narrow or narrower than required. If more replicates are used, the resulting confidence interval will be narrower than necessary and the experiment may become wasteful of resources.

11.9.1 Sample Size for 2^k and 2^{k-p} Plus Centers Designs

The sample-size calculations for 2^k and 2^{k-p} plus centers designs are almost identical to the calculations for these designs without centers, which were presented in Chapters 9 and 10. Although center cells do not make any contribution to SS_x or the noncentrality parameter, they do add error degrees of freedom. When there are very few error degrees of freedom in a 2^k or 2^{k-p} experiment, the addition of a few center cells can improve the power of the design but the benefit diminishes very quickly. The only way to significantly improve the sensitivity of an experiment that already has more than about ten error degrees of freedom is to add replicates.

Sample Size to Detect Significant Effects

The sample-size calculations shown in the next two examples address the goal of detecting significant variable effects, which is the more common goal for the 2^k and 2^{k-p} plus centers designs. These calculations are substantially the same as those described in Section 9.10.1 with the exception that the model consumes an additional degree of freedom to estimate the generic curvature term.

Example 11.10

Calculate the power to detect a difference of $\delta = \sigma_\varepsilon$ between the ±1 levels of one of the variables for one replicate of a 2^3 design with four added center cells. Confirm the answer using MINITAB.

Solution: The noncentrality parameter is:

$$\lambda = \frac{N}{2a}\left(\frac{\delta}{\sigma}\right)^2$$

$$= \frac{8}{2(2)}\left(1\right)^2$$

$$= 2$$

where $N = 2^3 = 8$ is the number of runs in the cube of the experiment. There are twelve runs in the experiment so there will be $df_{total} = 11$ total degrees of freedom. The model will include three main effects, three two-factor interactions, and one generic curvature term for $df_{model} = 7$. By subtraction, the error degrees of freedom will be $df_\varepsilon = 4$. With $\alpha = 0.05$, the power is given by the condition:

$$F_{0.05,1,4} = F_{P,1,4,2}$$

which gives:

$$F_{0.05,1,4} = F_{0.195,1,4,2} = 7.709$$

*The power to detect the effect is $P = 0.195$ or only about 19.5 percent. This answer was confirmed using **Stat> Power and Sample Size> 2-Level Factorial Design**. MINITAB's output is shown in Figure 11.13. Notice that without the additional center cells there would have only been $df_\varepsilon = 7 - 6 = 1$ error degree of freedom and the power would have been much worse.*

```
MTB > Power;
SUBC>    FFDesign 3 8;
SUBC>       Replicates 1;
SUBC>       Effect 1;
SUBC>       CPBlock 4;
SUBC>       Sigma 1;
SUBC>       Omit 1;
SUBC>       FitC;
SUBC>       FitB.
```

Power and Sample Size

2-Level Factorial Design

Alpha = 0.05   Assumed standard deviation = 1

Factors: 3   Base Design: 3, 8
Blocks: none

Number of terms omitted from model: 1
Including a term for center points in model.

Center Points	Effect	Reps	Total Runs	Power
4	1	1	12	0.195232

Figure 11.13 Power calculation for 2^3 plus four centers design.

Example 11.11

Construct a plot of the power versus the total number of runs for 2^3 factorial designs with n = 1, 2, 4, and 8 replicates and additional center cells for up to N = 80 total runs. Include main effects, two-factor interactions, and the lack of fit term in the models. The smallest difference to be detected between ±1 levels is $\delta = \sigma_\varepsilon$. Use $\alpha = 0.05$. When does the use of center cells improve the power of a 2^3 experiment?

Solution: *The power calculations were done from **Stat> Power and Sample Size> 2-Level Factorial Design**. The replicates were not blocked, a term for the center cells was included in the model, and one term corresponding to the three-factor interaction was omitted from the model. The resulting power values are plotted against the total number of experimental runs in Figure 11.14. The circles show the 2^3 designs without center cells. No lack of fit term can be included in their model. The plot shows that when there are relatively few runs in an experiment, such as when there is just one replicate, the addition of center cells can increase the power; however, the main factor that determines the power is the number of replicates. This analysis confirms that the primary reason for adding center cells to 2^k designs is to allow for a test of lack of linear fit.*

Sample Size to Quantify Effects

Sample-size calculations to quantify effects for the 2^k and 2^{k-p} plus centers designs are very similar to those described in Section 9.10.2. A single example is offered here that only differs from the calculations shown in that section in the management of the center cells.

Example 11.12

How many replicates of a 2^4 design with three centers (19 runs total) are required to quantify the slope associated with a design variable to within ±0.01 with 95 percent confidence if the standard error is expected to be $\sigma_\varepsilon = 0.02$?

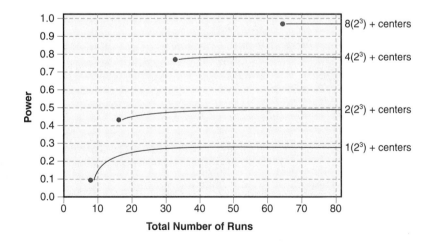

Figure 11.14 Power versus total number of runs for one to eight replicates of the 2^3 plus centers design.

Solution: *Since the center cells don't contribute to SS_x then for a single replicate of the 19-run design:*

$$SS_x = 2^{4-1}(-1)^2 + 3(0)^2 + 2^{4-1}(+1)^2 = 16$$

Then the number of replicates (n) must meet the condition given by Equation 11.14. As a first guess, if there are enough error degrees of freedom that $t_{0.025} \simeq z_{0.025}$, then:

$$n \geq \frac{1}{SS_x}\left(\frac{t_{\alpha/2}\sigma_\varepsilon}{\delta}\right)^2$$
$$\geq \frac{1}{16}\left(\frac{1.96\times0.02}{0.01}\right)^2$$
$$\geq 0.96$$

which of course rounds up to n = 1. The model including main effects, two-factor interactions, and a generic curvature term will require $df_{model} = 4 + 6 + 1 = 11$ degrees of freedom which, with just n = 1 replicate, would only leave $df_\varepsilon = 19 - 1 - 11 = 7$ error degrees of freedom. This is too few degrees of freedom to satisfy $t_{0.025} \simeq z_{0.025}$ so further iterations are required. With n = 2 replicates there will be $df_\varepsilon = 2(19) - 1 - 11 = 26$ error degrees of freedom so $t_{0.025,26} = 2.056$ which gives:

$$n \geq \frac{1}{16}\left(\frac{2.056\times0.02}{0.01}\right)^2$$
$$\geq 1.06$$

Consequently, n = 2 replicates will be sufficient to determine the slope of a design variable to within ± 0.01 with 95 percent confidence.

11.9.2 Sample Size for 3^k Designs

Consider a 3^k experiment where all k of the variables are quantitative with three evenly spaced levels in coded units –1, 0, and +1. One replicate of the experiment will have $N_{design} = 3^k$ runs so the error degrees of freedom for the experiment will be:

$$df_\varepsilon = n3^k - 1 - df_{model} \tag{11.15}$$

Since the design is balanced with –1, 0, and +1 for levels of x, then $\bar{x} = 0$ and the spacing between the levels is $\Delta x = 1$. In one replicate, the number of observations at each level is $(1/3) 3^k = 3^{k-1}$. Then SS_x for one replicate is given by:

$$SS_x = \Sigma(x_i - \bar{x})^2$$
$$= 3^{k-1}(-1)^2 + 3^{k-1}(0)^2 + 3^{k-1}(+1)^2$$
$$= 2\times3^{k-1} \tag{11.16}$$

Then from Equation 11.14:

$$n \geq \frac{1}{2 \times 3^{k-1}} \left(\frac{t_{\alpha/2} \sigma_\varepsilon}{\delta} \right)^2 \qquad (11.17)$$

As in other cases, this expression is transcendental and must be solved by iteration; however, since the 3^k designs involve so many runs and a comparatively small model, the number of error degrees of freedom is usually large enough that $t_{\alpha/2} \simeq z_{\alpha/2}$.

Example 11.13

How many replicates of a 3^3 factorial design are required to determine the slope associated with one of the design variables to within $\delta = \pm 0.05$ if the standard error of the model is expected to be $\sigma_\varepsilon = 0.20$? Use $\alpha = 0.05$.

Solution: The full quadratic model will require $df_{model} = 3 + 3 + 3 = 9$ degrees of freedom and since one replicate of the design will contain $3^3 = 27$ runs, the number of error degrees of freedom should be large enough that $t_{0.025} \simeq z_{0.025}$. Then the number of replicates is given by:

$$\begin{aligned}
n &\geq \frac{1}{2 \times 3^{k-1}} \left(\frac{t_{\alpha/2} \sigma_\varepsilon}{\delta} \right)^2 \\
&\geq \frac{1}{2 \times 3^2} \left(\frac{1.96 \times 0.20}{0.05} \right)^2 \\
&\geq 3.4
\end{aligned}$$

This indicates that $n = 4$ replicates will be required to determine the slope to within the specified range of values. The total number of runs in the experiment will be $4 \times 27 = 108$.

11.9.3 Sample Size for Box-Behnken Designs

The total number of runs in one replicate of a k variable Box-Behnken design where $3 \leq k \leq 5$ is given by:

$$N_{design} = 4 \binom{k}{2} + n_0 \qquad (11.18)$$

where n_0 is the number of center points. One third of the non–center points will be run at each of the three levels of x. Then SS_x for one replicate is given by:

$$\begin{aligned}
SS_x &= \Sigma \left(x_i - \bar{x} \right)^2 \\
&= \frac{4}{3} \binom{k}{2} (-1)^2 + \left(\frac{4}{3} \binom{k}{2} + n_0 \right) (0)^2 + \frac{4}{3} \binom{k}{2} (+1)^2 \\
&= \frac{8}{3} \binom{k}{2}
\end{aligned} \qquad (11.19)$$

The number of replicates is given by:

$$n \geq \frac{1}{\frac{8}{3}\binom{k}{2}}\left(\frac{t_{\alpha/2}\sigma_{\varepsilon}}{\delta}\right)^2 \tag{11.20}$$

where the number of degrees of freedom for the t distribution is:

$$df_{\varepsilon} = n\left(4\binom{k}{2} + n_0\right) - 1 - df_{model} \tag{11.21}$$

The sample-size condition is transcendental but when the number of error degrees of freedom is large enough it is safe to take $t_{\alpha/2} \simeq z_{\alpha/2}$.

When a Box-Behnken design with six or more variables is used, Equation 11.18 no longer gives the total number of runs in the design and unique calculations for SS_x and df_{ε} must be done.

Example 11.14

Find the number of replicates required if a Box-Behnken design is used for the situation presented in Example 11.13.

Solution: One replicate of the BB(3) design requires only 15 runs, but if three or more replicates are required there will be enough error degrees of freedom that it is safe to take $t_{0.025} \simeq z_{0.025} = 1.96$. Then the number of replicates is given by:

$$n \geq \frac{1}{\frac{8}{3}\binom{k}{2}}\left(\frac{t_{\alpha/2\sigma_{\varepsilon}}}{\delta}\right)^2$$

$$\geq \frac{1}{\frac{8}{3}\binom{3}{2}}\left(\frac{1.96 \times 0.20}{0.05}\right)^2$$

$$\geq 7.7$$

This indicates that the experiment will require $n = 8$ replicates. The total number of runs in the experiment will be $8 \times 15 = 120$.

Example 11.15

How many replicates of a BB(6) design are required to determine the slope associated with one of the design variables to within $\delta = 4$ if the standard error of the model is expected to be $\sigma_{\varepsilon} = 6$? Use $\alpha = 0.05$.

Solution: From the design matrix for the BB(6) design in Table 11.3, page 445, there are 24 runs with each design variable at its −1 level, 24 runs with each design *variable at its +1 level, and 32 runs with each design variable at its zero level. [Each row like (+1 +1 0 +1 0 0) consists of eight runs and there are eight center cells.] SS_x for one replicate is given by:*

$$SS_x = 24(-1)^2 + 32(0)^2 + 24(1)^2 = 48$$

The number of replicates must meet the condition:

$$n \geq \frac{1}{48} \left(\frac{t_{\alpha/2} \sigma_\varepsilon}{\delta} \right)^2$$

With $t_{0.025} \simeq z_{0.025}$ the sample size is:

$$n \geq \frac{1}{48} \left(\frac{1.96 \times 6}{4} \right)^2 = 0.18$$

which of course rounds up to n = 1. The model will consume 6 + 15 + 6 = 27 degrees of freedom so with n = 1 replicate there will be $df_\varepsilon = 80 - 1 - 27 = 52$ error degrees of freedom. This means the $t_{0.025} \simeq z_{0.025}$ condition is satisfied and the sample-size calculation is valid.

11.9.4 Sample Size for Central Composite Designs

The number of runs in one replicate of a central composite design is given by:

$$N_{design} = n_{cube} + n_0 + n_{star} \tag{11.22}$$

With respect to one design variable, there will be one star point at its $-\eta$ level, one star point at its $+\eta$ level, $n_0 + n_{star} - 2$ points at its center (0) level, $n_{cube}/2$ points at its -1 level, and $n_{cube}/2$ points at its $+1$ level. Then SS_x for one replicate of a central composite design is given by:

$$
\begin{aligned}
SS_x &= \Sigma(x_i - \bar{x})^2 \\
&= (-\eta)^2 + \tfrac{1}{2} n_{cube}(-1)^2 + (n_0 + n_{star} - 2)(0)^2 + \tfrac{1}{2} n_{cube}(+1)^2 + (+\eta)^2 \\
&= 2\eta^2 + n_{cube}
\end{aligned}
\tag{11.23}
$$

and the sample size must meet the condition:

$$n \geq \frac{1}{2\eta^2 + n_{cube}} \left(\frac{t_{\alpha/2} \sigma_\varepsilon}{\delta} \right)^2 \tag{11.24}$$

This condition is transcendental and n must be rounded up to the nearest integer. When the experiment design is large enough and the error degrees of freedom is large it is safe to take $t_{\alpha/2} \simeq z_{\alpha/2}$.

Example 11.16

Find the number of replicates required if a central composite design is used for the situation presented in Example 11.13.

Solution: *The CC(2^3) design requires $n_{cube} = 8$, $n_{star} = 6$, and $n_0 = 6$ for a total of $N_{design} = 20$ runs in one replicate. The star point position is given by $\eta = 1.682$. If the number of replicates is large enough then it is safe to take $t_{0.025} \simeq 1.96$ so that the number of replicates must meet the condition:*

$$n \geq \frac{1}{2\eta^2 + n_{cube}} \left(\frac{t_{\alpha/2}\sigma_\varepsilon}{\delta} \right)^2$$

$$\geq \frac{1}{2(1.682)^2 + 8} \left(\frac{1.96 \times 0.20}{0.05} \right)^2$$

$$\geq 4.5$$

This indicates that the experiment will require $n = 5$ replicates. The total number of runs in the experiment will be $5 \times 20 = 100$ and there will be $df_\varepsilon = 100 - 1 - 9 = 90$ error degrees of freedom. Notice that where the 3^3 and BB(3) designs had their extreme levels at $x = \pm 1$, the central composite design has its cube points at $x = \pm 1$ but its star points lie further outside the cube at $x = \pm \eta$. If these extreme levels are too far away from the design center, it may be necessary to redefine the actual physical levels corresponding to the coded levels of x. This will have an affect on the ability of the experiment to determine the slopes associated with the different variables.

11.10 DESIGN CONSIDERATIONS FOR RESPONSE-SURFACE EXPERIMENTS

- An experiment should have enough error degrees of freedom to provide a good error estimate but not so many that it is wasteful of resources. Often a single replicate of the appropriate design is sufficient.

- If it is difficult to obtain the required five levels for a central composite design then one of the three-level designs (3^k or BB(k)) might be easier to build.

- If your experiment has three variables, a Box-Behnken design (15 runs) is more economical than a central composite design (20 runs).

- If your experiment has five variables, a central composite design (32 runs) is more economical than a Box-Behnken design (43 runs).

- If you don't know safe upper and lower limits for all of the design variables, use a central composite design instead of a Box-Behnken design. Position the cube points inside the known safe region of the design space and let the star points fall in questionable territory. If any or all of the star points of the central composite design are lost, the remaining factorial or fractional factorial design with centers can be still be analyzed for main effects, two-factor interactions, and lack of fit.

- If you know the safe upper and lower limits for all of the design variables, use a Box-Behnken design instead of a central composite design. The Box-Behnken design puts points further from the center of the design space so the power of the design to detect small effects is greater than the power provided by the central composite design.

- Build a central composite design in blocks. If you are uncertain about the safety of the extreme levels of the design variables, build the star points first to demonstrate that they are all safe. If you don't know that a quadratic model is really necessary, build the factorial plus centers block first, test it for lack of linear fit (that is, curvature), and then decide whether it's necessary to build the block of star points. Get commitment from management to build the full experiment at the beginning of the project but build it in blocks anyway. If you have to build the full experiment then it's planned and budgeted for. If you don't have to build the block of star points, you can declare victory sooner and at a lower cost.

- Use blocks to introduce a qualitative variable into a Box-Behnken design, but randomize over all runs so that it is safe to make claims about differences between the levels of the variable.

Appendix A

Statistical Tables

Table A.1 Greek characters.

Name	Lower Case	Upper Case	Arabic
alpha	α	A	a
beta	β	B	b
gamma	γ	Γ	g
delta	δ	Δ	d
epsilon	ϵ or ε	E	e
zeta	ζ	Z	z
eta	η	H	h
theta	θ	Θ	y
iota	ι	I	i
kappa	κ	K	k
lambda	λ	Λ	l
mu	μ	M	m
nu	ν	N	n
xi	ξ	Ξ	x
pi	π	Π	p
rho	ρ	P	r
sigma	σ	Σ	s
tau	τ	T	t
upsilon	υ	Υ	u
phi	ϕ or φ	Φ	f
chi	χ	X	q
psi	ψ	Ψ	c
omega	ω	Ω	w

Table A.2 Normal Distribution: Values of $p = \Phi$ ($-\infty < z < z_p$).

	0.00	0.01	0.02	0.03	0.04	0.05	0.06	0.07	0.08	0.09
−3.00	0.0013	0.0013	0.0013	0.0012	0.0012	0.0011	0.0011	0.0011	0.0010	0.0010
−2.90	0.0019	0.0018	0.0018	0.0017	0.0016	0.0016	0.0015	0.0015	0.0014	0.0014
−2.80	0.0026	0.0025	0.0024	0.0023	0.0023	0.0022	0.0021	0.0021	0.0020	0.0019
−2.70	0.0035	0.0034	0.0033	0.0032	0.0031	0.0030	0.0029	0.0028	0.0027	0.0026
−2.60	0.0047	0.0045	0.0044	0.0043	0.0041	0.0040	0.0039	0.0038	0.0037	0.0036
−2.50	0.0062	0.0060	0.0059	0.0057	0.0055	0.0054	0.0052	0.0051	0.0049	0.0048
−2.40	0.0082	0.0080	0.0078	0.0075	0.0073	0.0071	0.0069	0.0068	0.0066	0.0064
−2.30	0.0107	0.0104	0.0102	0.0099	0.0096	0.0094	0.0091	0.0089	0.0087	0.0084
−2.20	0.0139	0.0136	0.0132	0.0129	0.0125	0.0122	0.0119	0.0116	0.0113	0.0110
−2.10	0.0179	0.0174	0.0170	0.0166	0.0162	0.0158	0.0154	0.0150	0.0146	0.0143
−2.00	0.0228	0.0222	0.0217	0.0212	0.0207	0.0202	0.0197	0.0192	0.0188	0.0183
−1.90	0.0287	0.0281	0.0274	0.0268	0.0262	0.0256	0.0250	0.0244	0.0239	0.0233
−1.80	0.0359	0.0351	0.0344	0.0336	0.0329	0.0322	0.0314	0.0307	0.0301	0.0294
−1.70	0.0446	0.0436	0.0427	0.0418	0.0409	0.0401	0.0392	0.0384	0.0375	0.0367
−1.60	0.0548	0.0537	0.0526	0.0516	0.0505	0.0495	0.0485	0.0475	0.0465	0.0455
−1.50	0.0668	0.0655	0.0643	0.0630	0.0618	0.0606	0.0594	0.0582	0.0571	0.0559
−1.40	0.0808	0.0793	0.0778	0.0764	0.0749	0.0735	0.0721	0.0708	0.0694	0.0681
−1.30	0.0968	0.0951	0.0934	0.0918	0.0901	0.0885	0.0869	0.0853	0.0838	0.0823
−1.20	0.1151	0.1131	0.1112	0.1093	0.1075	0.1056	0.1038	0.1020	0.1003	0.0985
−1.10	0.1357	0.1335	0.1314	0.1292	0.1271	0.1251	0.1230	0.1210	0.1190	0.1170
−1.00	0.1587	0.1562	0.1539	0.1515	0.1492	0.1469	0.1446	0.1423	0.1401	0.1379
−0.90	0.1841	0.1814	0.1788	0.1762	0.1736	0.1711	0.1685	0.1660	0.1635	0.1611
−0.80	0.2119	0.2090	0.2061	0.2033	0.2005	0.1977	0.1949	0.1922	0.1894	0.1867
−0.70	0.2420	0.2389	0.2358	0.2327	0.2296	0.2266	0.2236	0.2206	0.2177	0.2148
−0.60	0.2743	0.2709	0.2676	0.2643	0.2611	0.2578	0.2546	0.2514	0.2483	0.2451
−0.50	0.3085	0.3050	0.3015	0.2981	0.2946	0.2912	0.2877	0.2843	0.2810	0.2776
−0.40	0.3446	0.3409	0.3372	0.3336	0.3300	0.3264	0.3228	0.3192	0.3156	0.3121
−0.30	0.3821	0.3783	0.3745	0.3707	0.3669	0.3632	0.3594	0.3557	0.3520	0.3483
−0.20	0.4207	0.4168	0.4129	0.4090	0.4052	0.4013	0.3974	0.3936	0.3897	0.3859
−0.10	0.4602	0.4562	0.4522	0.4483	0.4443	0.4404	0.4364	0.4325	0.4286	0.4247
−0.00	0.5000	0.4960	0.4920	0.4880	0.4840	0.4801	0.4761	0.4721	0.4681	0.4641

Continued

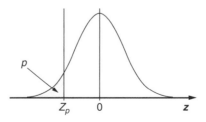

Continued

	0.00	0.01	0.02	0.03	0.04	0.05	0.06	0.07	0.08	0.09
0.00	0.5000	0.5040	0.5080	0.5120	0.5160	0.5199	0.5239	0.5279	0.5319	0.5359
0.10	0.5398	0.5438	0.5478	0.5517	0.5557	0.5596	0.5636	0.5675	0.5714	0.5753
0.20	0.5793	0.5832	0.5871	0.5910	0.5948	0.5987	0.6026	0.6064	0.6103	0.6141
0.30	0.6179	0.6217	0.6255	0.6293	0.6331	0.6368	0.6406	0.6443	0.6480	0.6517
0.40	0.6554	0.6591	0.6628	0.6664	0.6700	0.6736	0.6772	0.6808	0.6844	0.6879
0.50	0.6915	0.6950	0.6985	0.7019	0.7054	0.7088	0.7123	0.7157	0.7190	0.7224
0.60	0.7257	0.7291	0.7324	0.7357	0.7389	0.7422	0.7454	0.7486	0.7517	0.7549
0.70	0.7580	0.7611	0.7642	0.7673	0.7704	0.7734	0.7764	0.7794	0.7823	0.7852
0.80	0.7881	0.7910	0.7939	0.7967	0.7995	0.8023	0.8051	0.8078	0.8106	0.8133
0.90	0.8159	0.8186	0.8212	0.8238	0.8264	0.8289	0.8315	0.8340	0.8365	0.8389
1.00	0.8413	0.8438	0.8461	0.8485	0.8508	0.8531	0.8554	0.8577	0.8599	0.8621
1.10	0.8643	0.8665	0.8686	0.8708	0.8729	0.8749	0.8770	0.8790	0.8810	0.8830
1.20	0.8849	0.8869	0.8888	0.8907	0.8925	0.8944	0.8962	0.8980	0.8997	0.9015
1.30	0.9032	0.9049	0.9066	0.9082	0.9099	0.9115	0.9131	0.9147	0.9162	0.9177
1.40	0.9192	0.9207	0.9222	0.9236	0.9251	0.9265	0.9279	0.9292	0.9306	0.9319
1.50	0.9332	0.9345	0.9357	0.9370	0.9382	0.9394	0.9406	0.9418	0.9429	0.9441
1.60	0.9452	0.9463	0.9474	0.9484	0.9495	0.9505	0.9515	0.9525	0.9535	0.9545
1.70	0.9554	0.9564	0.9573	0.9582	0.9591	0.9599	0.9608	0.9616	0.9625	0.9633
1.80	0.9641	0.9649	0.9656	0.9664	0.9671	0.9678	0.9686	0.9693	0.9699	0.9706
1.90	0.9713	0.9719	0.9726	0.9732	0.9738	0.9744	0.9750	0.9756	0.9761	0.9767
2.00	0.9772	0.9778	0.9783	0.9788	0.9793	0.9798	0.9803	0.9808	0.9812	0.9817
2.10	0.9821	0.9826	0.9830	0.9834	0.9838	0.9842	0.9846	0.9850	0.9854	0.9857
2.20	0.9861	0.9864	0.9868	0.9871	0.9875	0.9878	0.9881	0.9884	0.9887	0.9890
2.30	0.9893	0.9896	0.9898	0.9901	0.9904	0.9906	0.9909	0.9911	0.9913	0.9916
2.40	0.9918	0.9920	0.9922	0.9925	0.9927	0.9929	0.9931	0.9932	0.9934	0.9936
2.50	0.9938	0.9940	0.9941	0.9943	0.9945	0.9946	0.9948	0.9949	0.9951	0.9952
2.60	0.9953	0.9955	0.9956	0.9957	0.9959	0.9960	0.9961	0.9962	0.9963	0.9964
2.70	0.9965	0.9966	0.9967	0.9968	0.9969	0.9970	0.9971	0.9972	0.9973	0.9974
2.80	0.9974	0.9975	0.9976	0.9977	0.9977	0.9978	0.9979	0.9979	0.9980	0.9981
2.90	0.9981	0.9982	0.9982	0.9983	0.9984	0.9984	0.9985	0.9985	0.9986	0.9986
3.00	0.9987	0.9987	0.9987	0.9988	0.9988	0.9989	0.9989	0.9989	0.9990	0.9990

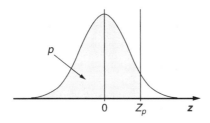

p	0.001	0.0025	0.005	0.01	0.025	0.05	0.10
Z_p	3.09	2.81	2.575	2.33	1.96	1.645	1.28

Table A.3 Student's *t* Distribution: Values of t_p where $P(t_p < t < \infty) = p$.

ν	0.001	0.0025	0.005	0.01	0.025	0.05	0.10
				p			
1	318.289	127.321	63.656	31.821	12.706	6.314	3.078
2	22.328	14.089	9.925	6.965	4.303	2.920	1.886
3	10.214	7.453	5.841	4.541	3.182	2.353	1.638
4	7.173	5.598	4.604	3.747	2.776	2.132	1.533
5	5.894	4.773	4.032	3.365	2.571	2.015	1.476
6	5.208	4.317	3.707	3.143	2.447	1.943	1.440
7	4.785	4.029	3.499	2.998	2.365	1.895	1.415
8	4.501	3.833	3.355	2.896	2.306	1.860	1.397
9	4.297	3.690	3.250	2.821	2.262	1.833	1.383
10	4.144	3.581	3.169	2.764	2.228	1.812	1.372
11	4.025	3.497	3.106	2.718	2.201	1.796	1.363
12	3.930	3.428	3.055	2.681	2.179	1.782	1.356
13	3.852	3.372	3.012	2.650	2.160	1.771	1.350
14	3.787	3.326	2.977	2.624	2.145	1.761	1.345
15	3.733	3.286	2.947	2.602	2.131	1.753	1.341
16	3.686	3.252	2.921	2.583	2.120	1.746	1.337
17	3.646	3.222	2.898	2.567	2.110	1.740	1.333
18	3.610	3.197	2.878	2.552	2.101	1.734	1.330
19	3.579	3.174	2.861	2.539	2.093	1.729	1.328
20	3.552	3.153	2.845	2.528	2.086	1.725	1.325
21	3.527	3.135	2.831	2.518	2.080	1.721	1.323
22	3.505	3.119	2.819	2.508	2.074	1.717	1.321
23	3.485	3.104	2.807	2.500	2.069	1.714	1.319
24	3.467	3.091	2.797	2.492	2.064	1.711	1.318
25	3.450	3.078	2.787	2.485	2.060	1.708	1.316
26	3.435	3.067	2.779	2.479	2.056	1.706	1.315
27	3.421	3.057	2.771	2.473	2.052	1.703	1.314
28	3.408	3.047	2.763	2.467	2.048	1.701	1.313
29	3.396	3.038	2.756	2.462	2.045	1.699	1.311
30	3.385	3.030	2.750	2.457	2.042	1.697	1.310
40	3.307	2.971	2.704	2.423	2.021	1.684	1.303
50	3.261	2.937	2.678	2.403	2.009	1.676	1.299
60	3.232	2.915	2.660	2.390	2.000	1.671	1.296
80	3.195	2.887	2.639	2.374	1.990	1.664	1.292
100	3.174	2.871	2.626	2.364	1.984	1.660	1.290
∞	3.090	2.807	2.576	2.326	1.960	1.645	1.282

Table A.4 χ^2 Distribution: Values of χ^2_p where $P(0 < \chi^2 < \chi^2_p)$.

						p					
v	0.005	0.01	0.025	0.05	0.1	0.9	0.95	0.975	0.99	0.995
1	0.00	0.00	0.00	0.00	0.02	2.71	3.84	5.02	6.63	7.88
2	0.01	0.02	0.05	0.10	0.21	4.61	5.99	7.38	9.21	10.60
3	0.07	0.11	0.22	0.35	0.58	6.25	7.81	9.35	11.34	12.84
4	0.21	0.30	0.48	0.71	1.06	7.78	9.49	11.14	13.28	14.86
5	0.41	0.55	0.83	1.15	1.61	9.24	11.07	12.83	15.09	16.75
6	0.68	0.87	1.24	1.64	2.20	10.64	12.59	14.45	16.81	18.55
7	0.99	1.24	1.69	2.17	2.83	12.02	14.07	16.01	18.48	20.28
8	1.34	1.65	2.18	2.73	3.49	13.36	15.51	17.53	20.09	21.95
9	1.73	2.09	2.70	3.33	4.17	14.68	16.92	19.02	21.67	23.59
10	2.16	2.56	3.25	3.94	4.87	15.99	18.31	20.48	23.21	25.19
11	2.60	3.05	3.82	4.57	5.58	17.28	19.68	21.92	24.73	26.76
12	3.07	3.57	4.40	5.23	6.30	18.55	21.03	23.34	26.22	28.30
13	3.57	4.11	5.01	5.89	7.04	19.81	22.36	24.74	27.69	29.82
14	4.07	4.66	5.63	6.57	7.79	21.06	23.68	26.12	29.14	31.32
15	4.60	5.23	6.26	7.26	8.55	22.31	25.00	27.49	30.58	32.80
16	5.14	5.81	6.91	7.96	9.31	23.54	26.30	28.85	32.00	34.27
17	5.70	6.41	7.56	8.67	10.09	24.77	27.59	30.19	33.41	35.72
18	6.26	7.01	8.23	9.39	10.86	25.99	28.87	31.53	34.81	37.16
19	6.84	7.63	8.91	10.12	11.65	27.20	30.14	32.85	36.19	38.58
20	7.43	8.26	9.59	10.85	12.44	28.41	31.41	34.17	37.57	40.00
21	8.03	8.90	10.28	11.59	13.24	29.62	32.67	35.48	38.93	41.40
22	8.64	9.54	10.98	12.34	14.04	30.81	33.92	36.78	40.29	42.80
23	9.26	10.20	11.69	13.09	14.85	32.01	35.17	38.08	41.64	44.18
24	9.89	10.86	12.40	13.85	15.66	33.20	36.42	39.36	42.98	45.56
25	10.52	11.52	13.12	14.61	16.47	34.38	37.65	40.65	44.31	46.93
26	11.16	12.20	13.84	15.38	17.29	35.56	38.89	41.92	45.64	48.29
27	11.81	12.88	14.57	16.15	18.11	36.74	40.11	43.19	46.96	49.65
28	12.46	13.56	15.31	16.93	18.94	37.92	41.34	44.46	48.28	50.99
29	13.12	14.26	16.05	17.71	19.77	39.09	42.56	45.72	49.59	52.34
30	13.79	14.95	16.79	18.49	20.60	40.26	43.77	46.98	50.89	53.67
35	17.19	18.51	20.57	22.47	24.80	46.06	49.80	53.20	57.34	60.27
40	20.71	22.16	24.43	26.51	29.05	51.81	55.76	59.34	63.69	66.77
45	24.31	25.90	28.37	30.61	33.35	57.51	61.66	65.41	69.96	73.17
50	27.99	29.71	32.36	34.76	37.69	63.17	67.50	71.42	76.15	79.49
55	31.73	33.57	36.40	38.96	42.06	68.80	73.31	77.38	82.29	85.75
60	35.53	37.48	40.48	43.19	46.46	74.40	79.08	83.30	88.38	91.95
70	43.28	45.44	48.76	51.74	55.33	85.53	90.53	95.02	100.43	104.21
80	51.17	53.54	57.15	60.39	64.28	96.58	101.88	106.63	112.33	116.32
90	59.20	61.75	65.65	69.13	73.29	107.57	113.15	118.14	124.12	128.30
100	67.33	70.06	74.22	77.93	82.36	118.50	124.34	129.56	135.81	140.17

Table A.5 *F* Distribution: Values of F_p where $P(F_p < F < \infty) = p$ and $F = s_1^2/s_2^2$.

F Distribution: Values of $F_{0.05}$

ν_2	ν_1 1	2	3	4	5	6	7	8	9	10	12	15	20	24	30	40	60	120	∞
1	161.4	199.5	215.7	224.6	230.2	234.0	236.8	238.9	240.5	241.9	243.9	245.9	248.0	249.1	250.1	251.1	252.2	253.3	254.3
2	18.51	19.00	19.16	19.25	19.30	19.33	19.35	19.37	19.38	19.40	19.41	19.43	19.45	19.45	19.46	19.47	19.48	19.49	19.50
3	10.13	9.55	9.28	9.12	9.01	8.94	8.89	8.85	8.81	8.79	8.74	8.70	8.66	8.64	8.62	8.59	8.57	8.55	8.53
4	7.71	6.94	6.59	6.39	6.26	6.16	6.09	6.04	6.00	5.96	5.91	5.86	5.80	5.77	5.75	5.72	5.69	5.66	5.63
5	6.61	5.79	5.41	5.19	5.05	4.95	4.88	4.82	4.77	4.74	4.68	4.62	4.56	4.53	4.50	4.46	4.43	4.40	4.36
6	5.99	5.14	4.76	4.53	4.39	4.28	4.21	4.15	4.10	4.06	4.00	3.94	3.87	3.84	3.81	3.77	3.74	3.70	3.67
7	5.59	4.74	4.35	4.12	3.97	3.87	3.79	3.73	3.68	3.64	3.57	3.51	3.44	3.41	3.38	3.34	3.30	3.27	3.23
8	5.32	4.46	4.07	3.84	3.69	3.58	3.50	3.44	3.39	3.35	3.28	3.22	3.15	3.12	3.08	3.04	3.01	2.97	2.93
9	5.12	4.26	3.86	3.63	3.48	3.37	3.29	3.23	3.18	3.14	3.07	3.01	2.94	2.90	2.86	2.83	2.79	2.75	2.71
10	4.96	4.10	3.71	3.48	3.33	3.22	3.14	3.07	3.02	2.98	2.91	2.85	2.77	2.74	2.70	2.66	2.62	2.58	2.54
11	4.84	3.98	3.59	3.36	3.20	3.09	3.01	2.95	2.90	2.85	2.79	2.72	2.65	2.61	2.57	2.53	2.49	2.45	2.40
12	4.75	3.89	3.49	3.26	3.11	3.00	2.91	2.85	2.80	2.75	2.69	2.62	2.54	2.51	2.47	2.43	2.38	2.34	2.30
13	4.67	3.81	3.41	3.18	3.03	2.92	2.83	2.77	2.71	2.67	2.60	2.53	2.46	2.42	2.38	2.34	2.30	2.25	2.21
14	4.60	3.74	3.34	3.11	2.96	2.85	2.76	2.70	2.65	2.60	2.53	2.46	2.39	2.35	2.31	2.27	2.22	2.18	2.13
15	4.54	3.68	3.29	3.06	2.90	2.79	2.71	2.64	2.59	2.54	2.48	2.40	2.33	2.29	2.25	2.20	2.16	2.11	2.07
20	4.35	3.49	3.10	2.87	2.71	2.60	2.51	2.45	2.39	2.35	2.28	2.20	2.12	2.08	2.04	1.99	1.95	1.90	1.84
25	4.24	3.39	2.99	2.76	2.60	2.49	2.40	2.34	2.28	2.24	2.16	2.09	2.01	1.96	1.92	1.87	1.82	1.77	1.71
30	4.17	3.32	2.92	2.69	2.53	2.42	2.33	2.27	2.21	2.16	2.09	2.01	1.93	1.89	1.84	1.79	1.74	1.68	1.62
40	4.08	3.23	2.84	2.61	2.45	2.34	2.25	2.18	2.12	2.08	2.00	1.92	1.84	1.79	1.74	1.69	1.64	1.58	1.51
60	4.00	3.15	2.76	2.53	2.37	2.25	2.17	2.10	2.04	1.99	1.92	1.84	1.75	1.70	1.65	1.59	1.53	1.47	1.39
120	3.92	3.07	2.68	2.45	2.29	2.18	2.09	2.02	1.96	1.91	1.83	1.75	1.66	1.61	1.55	1.50	1.43	1.35	1.25
∞	3.84	3.00	2.60	2.37	2.21	2.10	2.01	1.94	1.88	1.83	1.75	1.67	1.57	1.52	1.46	1.39	1.32	1.22	1.00

Continued

Continued

F Distribution: Values of $F_{0.01}$

v_2 \ v_1	1	2	3	4	5	6	7	8	9	10	12	15	20	24	30	40	60	120	∞
1	4052	4999	5404	5624	5764	5859	5928	5981	6022	6056	6107	6157	6209	6234	6260	6286	6313	6340	6366
2	98.50	99.00	99.16	99.25	99.30	99.33	99.36	99.38	99.39	99.40	99.42	99.43	99.45	99.46	99.47	99.48	99.48	99.49	99.50
3	34.12	30.82	29.46	28.71	28.24	27.91	27.67	27.49	27.34	27.23	27.05	26.87	26.69	26.60	26.50	26.41	26.32	26.22	26.13
4	21.20	18.00	16.69	15.98	15.52	15.21	14.98	14.80	14.66	14.55	14.37	14.20	14.02	13.93	13.84	13.75	13.65	13.56	13.46
5	16.26	13.27	12.06	11.39	10.97	10.67	10.46	10.29	10.16	10.05	9.89	9.72	9.55	9.47	9.38	9.29	9.20	9.11	9.02
6	13.75	10.92	9.78	9.15	8.75	8.47	8.26	8.10	7.98	7.87	7.72	7.56	7.40	7.31	7.23	7.14	7.06	6.97	6.88
7	12.25	9.55	8.45	7.85	7.46	7.19	6.99	6.84	6.72	6.62	6.47	6.31	6.16	6.07	5.99	5.91	5.82	5.74	5.65
8	11.26	8.65	7.59	7.01	6.63	6.37	6.18	6.03	5.91	5.81	5.67	5.52	5.36	5.28	5.20	5.12	5.03	4.95	4.86
9	10.56	8.02	6.99	6.42	6.06	5.80	5.61	5.47	5.35	5.26	5.11	4.96	4.81	4.73	4.65	4.57	4.48	4.40	4.31
10	10.04	7.56	6.55	5.99	5.64	5.39	5.20	5.06	4.94	4.85	4.71	4.56	4.41	4.33	4.25	4.17	4.08	4.00	3.91
11	9.65	7.21	6.22	5.67	5.32	5.07	4.89	4.74	4.63	4.54	4.40	4.25	4.10	4.02	3.94	3.86	3.78	3.69	3.60
12	9.33	6.93	5.95	5.41	5.06	4.82	4.64	4.50	4.39	4.30	4.16	4.01	3.86	3.78	3.70	3.62	3.54	3.45	3.36
13	9.07	6.70	5.74	5.21	4.86	4.62	4.44	4.30	4.19	4.10	3.96	3.82	3.66	3.59	3.51	3.43	3.34	3.25	3.17
14	8.86	6.51	5.56	5.04	4.69	4.46	4.28	4.14	4.03	3.94	3.80	3.66	3.51	3.43	3.35	3.27	3.18	3.09	3.00
15	8.68	6.36	5.42	4.89	4.56	4.32	4.14	4.00	3.89	3.80	3.67	3.52	3.37	3.29	3.21	3.13	3.05	2.96	2.87
20	8.10	5.85	4.94	4.43	4.10	3.87	3.70	3.56	3.46	3.37	3.23	3.09	2.94	2.86	2.78	2.69	2.61	2.52	2.42
25	7.77	5.57	4.68	4.18	3.85	3.63	3.46	3.32	3.22	3.13	2.99	2.85	2.70	2.62	2.54	2.45	2.36	2.27	2.17
30	7.56	5.39	4.51	4.02	3.70	3.47	3.30	3.17	3.07	2.98	2.84	2.70	2.55	2.47	2.39	2.30	2.21	2.11	2.01
40	7.31	5.18	4.31	3.83	3.51	3.29	3.12	2.99	2.89	2.80	2.66	2.52	2.37	2.29	2.20	2.11	2.02	1.92	1.80
60	7.08	4.98	4.13	3.65	3.34	3.12	2.95	2.82	2.72	2.63	2.50	2.35	2.20	2.12	2.03	1.94	1.84	1.73	1.60
120	6.85	4.79	3.95	3.48	3.17	2.96	2.79	2.66	2.56	2.47	2.34	2.19	2.03	1.95	1.86	1.76	1.66	1.53	1.38
∞	6.63	4.61	3.78	3.32	3.02	2.80	2.64	2.51	2.41	2.32	2.18	2.04	1.88	1.79	1.70	1.59	1.47	1.32	1

Table A.6 Critical Values for Duncan's Multiple Range Test ($r_{0.05,p,df_\varepsilon}$).

df_ε	Number of Means (p)								
	2	**3**	**4**	**5**	**6**	**7**	**8**	**9**	**10**
1	17.97								
2	6.09	6.09							
3	4.50	4.52	4.52						
4	3.93	4.01	4.03	4.03					
5	3.64	3.75	3.80	3.81	3.81				
6	6.46	3.59	3.65	3.68	3.69	3.70			
7	3.34	3.48	3.55	3.59	3.61	3.62	3.63		
8	3.26	3.40	3.48	3.52	3.55	3.57	3.57	3.58	
9	3.20	3.34	3.42	3.47	3.50	3.52	3.54	3.54	3.55
10	3.15	3.29	3.38	3.43	3.47	3.49	3.51	3.52	3.52
11	3.11	3.26	3.34	3.40	3.44	3.46	3.48	3.49	3.50
12	3.08	3.23	3.31	3.37	3.41	3.44	3.46	3.47	3.48
13	3.06	3.20	3.29	3.35	3.39	3.42	3.46	3.46	3.47
14	3.03	3.18	3.27	3.33	3.37	3.40	3.43	3.44	3.46
15	3.01	3.16	3.25	3.31	3.36	3.39	3.41	3.43	3.45
16	3.00	3.14	3.23	3.30	3.34	3.38	3.40	3.42	3.44
17	2.98	3.13	3.22	3.28	3.33	3.37	3.39	3.41	3.43
18	2.97	3.12	3.21	3.27	3.32	3.36	3.38	3.40	3.42
19	2.96	3.11	3.20	3.26	3.31	3.35	3.38	3.40	3.41
20	2.95	3.10	3.19	3.25	3.30	3.34	3.37	3.39	3.41
24	2.92	3.07	3.16	3.23	3.28	3.31	3.35	3.37	3.39
30	2.89	3.03	3.13	3.20	3.25	3.29	3.32	3.35	3.37
40	2.86	3.01	3.10	3.17	3.22	3.27	3.30	3.33	3.35
60	2.83	2.98	3.07	3.14	3.20	3.24	3.28	3.31	3.33
120	2.80	2.95	3.04	3.12	3.17	3.22	3.25	3.29	3.31
∞	2.77	2.92	3.02	3.09	3.15	3.19	3.23	3.27	3.29

Source: Reproduced from H. L. Harter, "Critical Values for Duncan's Multiple Range Test." This table contains some corrected values to those given by D. B. Duncan, "Multiple Range and Multiple F Tests," *Biometrics* 1, no. 1 (1955): 1–42.

Table A.7 Critical Values of the Studentized Range Distribution ($Q_{0.05}$ (k)).

df_ε	Number of Means (k)								
	2	**3**	**4**	**5**	**6**	**7**	**8**	**9**	**10**
1	17.970	26.980	32.820	37.080	40.410	43.120	45.400	47.360	49.070
2	6.085	8.331	9.798	10.880	11.740	12.440	13.030	13.540	13.990
3	4.501	5.910	6.825	7.502	8.037	8.478	8.853	9.177	9.462
4	3.927	5.040	5.757	6.287	6.707	7.053	7.347	7.602	7.826
5	3.635	4.602	5.218	5.673	6.033	6.330	6.582	6.802	6.995
6	3.461	4.339	4.896	5.305	5.628	5.895	6.122	6.319	6.493
7	3.344	4.165	4.681	5.060	5.359	5.606	5.815	5.998	6.158
8	3.261	4.041	4.529	4.886	5.167	5.399	5.597	5.767	5.918
9	3.199	3.949	4.415	4.756	5.024	5.244	5.432	5.595	5.739
10	3.151	3.877	4.327	4.654	4.912	5.124	5.305	5.461	5.599
11	3.113	3.820	4.256	4.574	4.823	5.028	5.202	5.353	5.487
12	3.082	3.773	4.199	4.508	4.751	4.950	5.119	5.265	5.395
13	3.055	3.735	4.151	4.453	4.690	4.885	5.049	5.192	5.318
14	3.033	3.702	4.111	4.407	4.639	4.829	4.990	5.131	5.254
15	3.014	3.674	4.076	4.367	4.595	4.782	4.940	5.077	5.198
16	2.998	3.649	4.046	4.333	4.557	4.741	4.897	5.031	5.150
17	2.984	3.628	4.020	4.303	4.524	4.705	4.858	4.991	5.108
18	2.971	3.609	3.997	4.277	4.495	4.673	4.824	4.956	5.071
19	2.960	3.593	3.977	4.253	4.469	4.645	4.794	4.924	5.038
20	2.950	3.578	3.958	4.232	4.445	4.620	4.768	4.896	5.008
24	2.919	3.532	3.901	4.166	4.373	4.541	4.684	4.807	4.915
30	2.888	3.486	3.845	4.102	4.302	4.464	4.602	4.720	4.824
40	2.858	3.442	3.791	4.039	4.232	4.389	4.521	4.635	4.735
60	2.829	3.399	3.737	3.977	4.163	4.314	4.441	4.550	4.646
120	2.800	3.356	3.685	3.917	4.096	4.241	4.363	4.468	4.560
∞	2.772	3.314	3.633	3.858	4.030	4.170	4.286	4.387	4.474

Source: Adapted from H. L. Harter. *Order Statistics and Their Use in Testing and Estimation, Volume 1: Tests Based on Range and Studentized Range of Samples from a Normal Population.* Washington, DC: U.S. Government Printing Office, 1969.

Table A.8   Critical Values for the One-Way Analysis of Means ($h_{0.05,k,df_\varepsilon}$).

df_ε	Number of Treatments (k)							
	3	**4**	**5**	**6**	**7**	**8**	**9**	**10**
3	4.18							
4	3.56	3.89						
5	3.25	3.53	3.72					
6	3.07	3.31	3.49	3.62				
7	2.94	3.17	3.33	3.45	3.56			
8	2.86	3.07	3.21	3.33	3.43	3.51		
9	2.79	2.99	3.13	3.24	3.33	3.41	3.48	
10	2.74	2.93	3.07	3.17	3.26	3.33	3.40	3.45
11	2.70	2.88	3.01	3.12	3.20	3.27	3.33	3.39
12	2.67	2.85	2.97	3.07	3.15	3.22	3.28	3.33
13	2.64	2.81	2.94	3.03	3.11	3.18	3.24	3.29
14	2.62	2.79	2.91	3.00	3.08	3.14	3.20	3.25
15	2.60	2.76	2.88	2.97	3.05	3.11	3.17	3.22
16	2.58	2.74	2.86	2.95	3.02	3.09	3.14	3.19
17	2.57	2.73	2.84	2.93	3.00	3.06	3.12	3.16
18	2.55	2.71	2.82	2.91	2.98	3.04	3.10	3.14
19	2.54	2.70	2.81	2.89	2.96	3.02	3.08	3.12
20	2.53	2.68	2.79	2.88	2.95	3.01	3.06	3.11
24	2.50	2.65	2.75	2.83	2.90	2.96	3.01	3.05
30	2.47	2.61	2.71	2.79	2.85	2.91	2.96	3.00
40	2.43	2.57	2.67	2.75	2.81	2.86	2.91	2.95
60	2.40	2.54	2.63	2.70	2.76	2.81	2.86	2.90
120	2.37	2.50	2.59	2.66	2.72	2.77	2.81	2.84
∞	2.34	2.47	2.56	2.62	2.68	2.72	2.76	2.80

Source: Nelson. "Exact Critical Values for Use with the Analysis of Means." *Journal of Quality Technology* 15, no. 1 (January 1983): 40–44. Used with permission.

Table A.9 Fisher's Z Transformation: values of $Z = \frac{1}{2} ln\left(\frac{1+r}{1-r}\right)$.

r	0.000	0.005	0.010	0.015	0.020	0.025	0.030	0.035	0.040	0.045	0.050	0.055	0.060	0.065	0.070	0.075	0.080	0.085	0.090	0.095
0	0.000	0.005	0.010	0.015	0.020	0.025	0.030	0.035	0.040	0.045	0.050	0.055	0.060	0.065	0.070	0.075	0.080	0.085	0.090	0.095
0.1	0.100	0.105	0.110	0.116	0.121	0.126	0.131	0.136	0.141	0.146	0.151	0.156	0.161	0.167	0.172	0.177	0.182	0.187	0.192	0.198
0.2	0.203	0.208	0.213	0.218	0.224	0.229	0.234	0.239	0.245	0.250	0.255	0.261	0.266	0.271	0.277	0.282	0.288	0.293	0.299	0.304
0.3	0.310	0.315	0.321	0.326	0.332	0.337	0.343	0.348	0.354	0.360	0.365	0.371	0.377	0.383	0.388	0.394	0.400	0.406	0.412	0.418
0.4	0.424	0.430	0.436	0.442	0.448	0.454	0.460	0.466	0.472	0.478	0.485	0.491	0.497	0.504	0.510	0.517	0.523	0.530	0.536	0.543
0.5	0.549	0.556	0.563	0.570	0.576	0.583	0.590	0.597	0.604	0.611	0.618	0.626	0.633	0.640	0.648	0.655	0.662	0.670	0.678	0.685
0.6	0.693	0.701	0.709	0.717	0.725	0.733	0.741	0.750	0.758	0.767	0.775	0.784	0.793	0.802	0.811	0.820	0.829	0.838	0.848	0.858
0.7	0.867	0.877	0.887	0.897	0.908	0.918	0.929	0.940	0.950	0.962	0.973	0.984	0.996	1.008	1.020	1.033	1.045	1.058	1.071	1.085
0.8	1.099	1.113	1.127	1.142	1.157	1.172	1.188	1.204	1.221	1.238	1.256	1.274	1.293	1.313	1.333	1.354	1.376	1.398	1.422	1.447
0.9	1.472	1.499	1.528	1.557	1.589	1.623	1.658	1.697	1.738	1.783	1.832	1.886	1.946	2.014	2.092	2.185	2.298	2.443	2.647	2.994

r	0.001	0.002	0.003	0.004	0.005	0.006	0.007	0.008	0.009
0.80	1.101	1.104	1.107	1.110	1.113	1.116	1.118	1.121	1.124
0.81	1.130	1.133	1.136	1.139	1.142	1.145	1.148	1.151	1.154
0.82	1.160	1.163	1.166	1.169	1.172	1.175	1.179	1.182	1.185
0.83	1.191	1.195	1.198	1.201	1.204	1.208	1.211	1.214	1.218
0.84	1.225	1.228	1.231	1.235	1.238	1.242	1.245	1.249	1.253
0.85	1.260	1.263	1.267	1.271	1.274	1.278	1.282	1.286	1.290
0.86	1.297	1.301	1.305	1.309	1.313	1.317	1.321	1.325	1.329
0.87	1.337	1.341	1.346	1.350	1.354	1.358	1.363	1.367	1.371
0.88	1.380	1.385	1.389	1.394	1.398	1.403	1.408	1.412	1.417
0.89	1.427	1.432	1.437	1.442	1.447	1.452	1.457	1.462	1.467
0.90	1.478	1.483	1.488	1.494	1.499	1.505	1.510	1.516	1.522
0.91	1.533	1.539	1.545	1.551	1.557	1.564	1.570	1.576	1.583
0.92	1.596	1.602	1.609	1.616	1.623	1.630	1.637	1.644	1.651
0.93	1.666	1.673	1.681	1.689	1.697	1.705	1.713	1.721	1.730
0.94	1.747	1.756	1.764	1.774	1.783	1.792	1.802	1.812	1.822
0.95	1.842	1.853	1.863	1.874	1.886	1.897	1.909	1.921	1.933
0.96	1.959	1.972	1.986	2.000	2.014	2.029	2.044	2.060	2.076
0.97	2.110	2.127	2.146	2.165	2.185	2.205	2.227	2.249	2.273
0.98	2.323	2.351	2.380	2.410	2.443	2.477	2.515	2.555	2.599
0.99	2.700	2.759	2.826	2.903	2.994	3.106	3.250	3.453	3.800

Bibliography

Agresti, A. 2002. *Categorical Data Analysis.* 2nd ed. Hoboken, NJ: John Wiley & Sons.

AIAG. 2002. *Measurement Systems Analysis.* 3rd ed. Automotive Industry Action Group.

Bhote, K., and A. Bhote. 2000. *World Class Quality: Using Design of Experiments to Make It Happen.* 2nd ed. New York: AMACOM.

Box, G. E. P., and D. W. Behnken. 1960. Some New Three Level Designs for the Study of Quantitative Variables. *Technometrics* 2, no. 4: 455–475.

Box, G. E. P., W. G. Hunter, and J. S. Hunter. 1978. *Statistics for Experimenters: An Introduction to Design, Data Analysis, and Model Building.* New York: John Wiley & Sons.

Christensen, R. 1997. *Log-Linear Models and Logistic Regression.* New York: Springer-Verlag.

Davies, O. 1963. *The Design and Analysis of Industrial Experiments,* 2nd ed. New York: Hafner.

Freund, J. E., and R. E. Walpole. 1980. *Mathematical Statistics.* 3rd ed. New Jersey: Prentice-Hall.

Hicks, C. R. 1993. *Fundamental Concepts in the Design of Experiments.* 4th ed. New York: Saunders College Publishing.

Hoaglin, D. C., F. Mosteller, and J. W. Tukey. 1991. *Fundamentals of Exploratory Analysis of Variance.* New York: John Wiley & Sons.

Kevles, D. J. 1998. *The Baltimore Case.* New York: W. W. Norton and Company.

Montgomery, D. C. 1991. *Design and Analysis of Experiments.* 3rd ed. New York: John Wiley & Sons.

———. 1997. *Introduction to Statistical Quality Control.* 3rd ed. New York: John Wiley & Sons.

Neter, J., M. H. Kutner, C. J. Nachtsheim, and W. Wasserman. 1996. *Applied Linear Statistical Models.* 4th ed. Boston: McGraw-Hill.

Ostle, B., K. Turner, C. Hicks, and G. McElrath. 1996. *Engineering Statistics: The Industrial Experience.* Belmont, CA: Duxbury Press.

Ross, P. J. 1988. *Taguchi Techniques for Quality Engineering*. New York: McGraw-Hill.

Sagan, C. 1996. *A Demon-Haunted World: Science as a Candle in the Dark*. New York: Random House.

Sokal, R. R., and F. J. Rohlf. 1995. *Biometry: The Principles and Practice of Statistics in Biological Research*. 3rd ed. New York: W. H. Freeman and Co.

Tufte, E. 1983. *The Visual Display of Quantitative Information*. Cheshire, CT: Graphics Press.

Weaver et al. 1986. Altered Repertoire of Endogenous Immunoglobulin Gene Expression in Transgenic Mice Containing a Rearranged Mu Heavy Chain Gene. *Cell* 45: 247–59.

Index